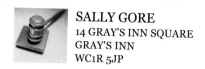

SALLY GORE
14 GRAY'S INN SQUARE
GRAY'S INN
WC1R 5JP

MENTAL HEALTH LAW

CW00840971

MENTAL HEALTH LAW

MENTAL HEALTH LAW

by

BRENDA HALE
Rt Hon the Baroness Hale of Richmond,
DBE, FBA, Hon FRCPsych
A Justice of the Supreme Court of the United Kingdom
Visiting Professor, King's College London
Chancellor, University of Bristol

SWEET & MAXWELL

 THOMSON REUTERS

First Edition 1976
Second Edition 1984
Third Edition 1990
Fourth Edition 1996
Fifth Edition 2010

Published in 2010 by Thomson Reuters (Legal) Limited (Registered in England & Wales, Company No 1679046. Registered Office and address for service:
100 Avenue Road, Swiss Cottage, London NW3 3PF)
trading as Sweet & Maxwell

For further information on our products and services, visit
www.sweetandmaxwell.co.uk

Computerset by Interactive Sciences, Gloucester
Printed in Great Britain by Ashford Colour Press, Gosport, Hants

No natural forests were destroyed to make this product; only farmed timber was used and replanted

ISBN: 9780414041691

A CIP catalogue record for this book is available from the British Library

FOREWORD

Genevra Richardson, CBE, FBA, Hon FRCPsych
Professor of Law, King's College London

Much has changed since 1976 when the first edition of this book was published. Certainly our attitudes to mental disorder have shifted significantly over the intervening years. The legislative landscape similarly has experienced major upheavals. The Mental Health Act itself has evolved from its 1959 beginnings, through its original 1983 form to its present, much amended, post 2007 incarnation. But the Mental Health Act does not operate in a legislative vacuum. The Children Act 1989, the National Health Service and Community Care Act 1990, the Human Rights Act 1998 and the Mental Capacity Act 2005, for example, have all effected major changes in the way the law provides for people with mental disabilities of all sorts. At the same time the case law, both domestic and European, has expanded beyond all recognition.

In 1976 *Mental Health* was ground-breaking. It provided a clear explanation of the law for the benefit of the many professionals involved in the provision of care for those with mental disabilities. Now in 2010 and four editions later the author employs her unique experience to guide us through the new and infinitely more complicated legal landscape. Baroness Hale is not only one of the UK's most senior judges, having sat in the Family Division of the High Court, the Court of Appeal and now the Supreme Court, she was also the Law Commissioner most directly involved in the work leading up to the Children Act and the Mental Capacity Act. This rich experience is used throughout to explain the law in the context of the decisions which regularly confront those working in the field. With clarity of expression which belies her subject matter Brenda Hale presents an account of the law that is keenly analytical, of course, but also practical and accessible. Mental health law in its various guises has to be applied daily by health and social care professionals across the country. But in its raw form this law is all but inaccessible to busy professionals. In *Mental Health Law* Brenda Hale provides the answer. Bringing all her unrivalled experience to bear she achieves clarity against formidable odds and manages to distil the essentials from the mass of statutory detail and related case law, presenting them in a form that is readily understandable.

While the law relating to mental disability has expanded vastly in scope and complexity since the 1970s, the last decade has been an exceptionally intense period of legislative activity. Writing in 1996, in his foreword to the fourth edition of this book, Sir Louis Blom-Cooper expressed the widely held view that the Mental Health Act 1983 was out of date and out of step with the times. He went on to recommend a process for its review. In 1998 a review was finally initiated but unfortunately the path from that review to the eventual amendment of the 1983 Act in 2007 was long, tortuous and at times unedifying. Much heat was generated and much ink spent, many new alliances were forged and many arguments, both old and new, were aired. In *Mental Health Law* Brenda Hale does not neglect these underlying debates. They are fully recognised and explained so that the reader may understand the context from which the law has emerged in its present form, but they are never allowed to confuse the description of the law.

v

In her introduction Brenda Hale leads us elegantly through the untidy history of recent reforms, describing the essential dilemmas. In particular she explains how we have arrived at our current position, two separate legislative schemes, one for mental health and one for mental capacity, each with their attendant Codes of Practice. In the chapters which follow she deals with the practical consequences of all this legislative activity and presents an extraordinarily clear account of the law as it must be applied on behalf of people with mental disorder. All the hard analytical work is done below the surface so that the reader is required simply to reap the benefit. When, for example, she grapples with the consequences which flow from the existence of two parallel statutory frameworks and describes the intricacies of the Deprivation of Liberty Safeguards (DoLs), the underlying tensions are explained but the law is presented in a lucid and practical fashion. In other chapters, particularly in the context of moving out of hospital and of community care, Brenda Hale brings together a complex array of case law and statute from many different sources and somehow manages to explain how they relate one to the other. For the legal reader this is fascinating and revelatory, for the non-lawyer it must be close to miraculous.

The fifth edition of *Mental Health Law* is a formidable achievement. It is essential reading for lawyers. But, more than that, it provides an unmatched source of clarity and wisdom for all the health and social care professionals who are concerned with the welfare of those with mental disabilities.

PREFACE

This book has at long last reached its fifth edition. It started life in 1975 when I was a lecturer in the University of Manchester, teaching law to social workers and psychiatrists. We all needed a textbook to help us understand a field of law from which the lawyers had mostly retreated. The second edition came in 1984, after the changes which became the Mental Health Act 1983, when the lawyers were beginning to get more interested in the subject. The third edition was published in 1990 when I was a Law Commissioner, and just embarking on a review of the law relating to mental incapacity. The fourth edition arrived in 1996 after I had become a full time judge. Since then the law seems to have been under almost constant review. Only last year did it reach a point where we might all draw breath and reflect upon the position which had been reached. It was time for a fifth edition.

This is meant to be a textbook for people who need to learn the law, a companion to Richard Jones' invaluable practitioners' Manuals. It started life as an easy read. I doubt if it is so now. In 1975 it was not difficult to get all the law of England, Wales and Scotland into 236 pages. Now it is no longer possible even to cover all the law of England and Wales in 345. But the references to Welsh law are there for those who need to follow them up. The aim is still to give a plain but critical account of all the law, bringing together both mental health and mental capacity, with food for thought and ideas for discussion in the commentary sections which end most chapters.

A new edition would not have been possible without the help of three very special people: Tia Sedley (who also helped with the third edition), Elizabeth Prochaska (now of Matrix Chambers), and Sophie Farthing (now with Liberty). I am enormously grateful to them for all their hard work, finding new material, checking the old, chasing references, proofing the whole, and above all putting up with me. I also owe a huge debt to Richard Jones for reading the draft and saving me from error and to Genevra Richardson for contributing the flattering Foreword. But no-one else is to blame for any remaining mistakes or deficiencies, which are entirely my own. Nor are they to blame for any of the views expressed. These are, of course, entirely the views of an author aiming to stimulate debate and not of a judge deciding a case. The judge's views may end up entirely differently in the real world of a real case where she has heard both sides.

Most mental health professionals are women, so I have made them female in the text. Most mental health patients are men, so I have made them male. It helps to distinguish the two. But no disrespect to either sex is intended. I have tried to state the law as it was on 26 February 2010 when the memory stick was delivered to the publishers, who have been most helpful and efficient in turning it into print.

Brenda Hale
22 April 2010

CONTENTS

TABLE OF CASES

xiii

TABLE OF STATUTES

TABLE OF STATUTORY INSTRUMENTS

TABLE OF CIRCULARS

TABLE OF EUROPEAN AND INTERNATIONAL MATERIAL

TABLE OF ABBREVIATIONS

The following abbreviations are in general used throughout the Work:

AMHP	=	approved mental health professional
AC	=	approved clinician
ASW	=	approved social worker
CA	=	Children Act 1989
CJA	=	Criminal Justice Act 2003
CLRC	=	Criminal Law Revision Committee
CPA 2004	=	Civil Partnership Act 2004
CPA	=	care programme approach
CPD	=	continuing professional development
CPR 1998	=	Civil Procedure Rules 1998
CPR 2007	=	Court of Protection Rules 2007
CPS	=	Crown Prosecution Service
CQC	=	Care Quality Commission
CSA	=	Care Standards Act 2000
CSA Regs	=	Children (Secure Accommodation) Regulations 1991
CSDPA	=	Chronically Sick and Disabled Persons Act 1970
CTO	=	community treatment order
DDA	=	Disability Discrimination Act 1995
DoL Regs	=	Mental Capacity (Deprivation of Liberty: Standard Authorisations, Assessments and Ordinary Residence) Regulations 2008
DoLS	=	deprivation of liberty safeguards
DoLS Code	=	Deprivation of Liberty Code of Practice
DoLS Monitoring Regs	=	Mental Capacity (Deprivation of Liberty: Monitoring and Reporting; and Assessments—Amendment) Regulations 2009
DSM-IV	=	American Psychiatric Association's Diagnostic and Statistical Manual of Mental Disorders
DVCVA	=	Domestic Violence, Crimes and Victims Act 2004
ECHR	=	European Convention on Human Rights
ECT	=	electro-convulsive therapy
EPA	=	enduring power of attorney
HASSASSA Act	=	Health and Social Services and Social Security Adjudications Act 1983
HRA	=	Human Rights Act 1998
HSPHA	=	Health Services and Public Health Act 1968
ICD-10	=	World Health Organisation's International Classification of Diseases
IMCA	=	independent mental capacity advocate
IMCA General Regs	=	Mental Capacity Act 2005 (Independent Mental Capacity Advocates) (General) Regulations 2006
IMHA	=	Independent Mental Health Advocates
IMHA Regs	=	Mental Health Act 1983 (Independent Mental Health Advocates) (England) Regulations 2008

IPPC	=	Independent Police Complaints Commission
LCSA	=	local children's services authority
LEA	=	Local Education Authority
LHB	=	local health board
LPA	=	lasting power of attorney
LPA etc Regs	=	Lasting Powers of Attorney, Enduring Powers of Attorney and Public Guardian Regulations 2007
LSSA	=	local social services authority
MA	=	managing authority
MCA	=	Mental Capacity Act 2005
MHA	=	Mental Health Act 1983
MHAC	=	Mental Health Act Commission
MHHGT Regs	=	Mental Health (Hospital, Guardianship and Treatment) Regulations 2008
MIND	=	National Association for Mental Health
MRCPsych	=	membership of the Royal College of Psychiatrists
NAA	=	National Assistance Act 1948
NHSA	=	National Health Service Act 2006
NHSCCA	=	National Health Service and Community Care Act 1990
PACE	=	Police and Criminal Evidence Act 1984
PCT	=	primary care trust
PTO	=	Public Trust Office
PVS	=	persistent vegetative state
RC	=	responsible clinician
RCPsych	=	Royal College of Psychiatrists
RMO	=	responsible medical officer
RPA	=	Representation of the People Act 1983
SB	=	supervisory body
SCT	=	supervised community treatment
SHA	=	strategic health authority
SHSA	=	Special Hospitals Service Authority
SOA	=	Sexual Offences Act 2003
SOAD	=	second opinion appointed doctor
UNCRPD	=	United Nations Convention on the Rights of Persons with Disabilities 2006
YJCEA	=	Youth Justice and Criminal Evidence Act 1999

INTRODUCTION
THE STORY SO FAR

Mental health law serves a shifting mass of conflicting interests and ideologies. Principally, of course, it should serve the interests of people with mental disorders and disabilities. But their carers, whether private or professional, also deserve consideration. And the law-makers are often most concerned about the interests of the public. The public's views can be contradictory. Most agree that "people with mental illness are far less of a danger than most people suppose"; but most disagree that "less emphasis should be placed on protecting the public from people with mental illness" (TNS, 2009). The public are understandably pre-occupied with offending and anti-social behaviour. They may be suspicious that mental disorder is too readily used as an excuse for bad behaviour. They may not know that for the offender (at least since the abolition of the death penalty) the consequences of being found mentally disordered may be just as severe as the consequences of being found guilty and sometimes more so. One reason for this is the public outcry which greets any mistaken decision to set a mentally disordered offender free. We can all perceive the benefits in keeping mental patients of all kinds in institutions out of harm's way, especially if this holds out some comforting hope of eventual improvement or cure. Most people disagree that "mental hospitals are an outdated means of treating people with mental illness" (TNS, 2009). The Victorians were prepared to spend more public money on keeping patients in asylums than on keeping paupers in the workhouse. But they wanted watertight guarantees against confinement of the wrong people. The fit pauper did not deserve it and the sane person did not want it.

Given such public attitudes, the Mental Health Act 1959 was little short of revolutionary. There had been such advances in psychiatric treatment that the medical profession were able to persuade the law-makers that both they and their patients should be set free from legal constraints. Mental patients should be treated no differently from any others. They should be admitted to hospital without special formalities and looked after in the community if they did not need to be in hospital. It should still be possible to compel them to accept hospital treatment if they refused to accept their doctors' advice, but this should be done with the minimum of formality and only when strictly necessary. Mentally disordered offenders should be able to be admitted to hospital for treatment in the same circumstances as other mental patients and treated in the same way when they were there, unless they were so dangerous that special safeguards were needed to protect the public. That apart, the length of time patients would spend in hospital, and the treatment they would receive while there, could safely be left to the medical profession. The patients undoubtedly benefited from the new psychiatry. But the new law was just as liberating for the psychiatrists as it was for their patients. Freed from their duty to guard society's misfits and rejects in isolated barracks in the countryside, they could concentrate on their new-found power to cure the sick. This was an almost wholly medical and therapeutic approach to patient treatment and care.

In the 20 years which followed the 1959 Act, it became clear that many of the patients formerly given asylum did not fit the new medical model. The elegant new scheme applied to both mentally ill and mentally disabled people, but was mental disability a medical problem at all? What was to happen to the chronic or psycho-geriatric patients who took up so many psychiatric beds? Above all, should hospitals have to take offenders with aggressive, inadequate, or irresponsible personalities whom society did not want but whom the courts might want to send to hospital rather than to prison? As the regime in ordinary psychiatric hospitals and units became more and more open, the high security special hospitals filled up with patients who in the past would have easily been managed in an asylum, until eventually there was nowhere prepared to have them (apart from the prisons, which had no choice).

The medical model was also challenged by the "anti-psychiatrists" within the profession itself. They argued that mental illness was not an objective fact, but a label applied to behaviour which the psychiatrist regards as abnormal because of his own ideas about what is appropriate in any given situation. The mythical label, it was said, places the patient in complete subjection to the doctor, ruling out effective communication between them. Instead of helping the patient, it manipulates him for its own ends. More practical challenges came from other professions, who claimed also to have a role in understanding and helping people with mental disorders. These added to the distrust of institutional solutions and stressed the importance of social factors in the causation and identification of mental illness.

Lawyers in this country played little part in all this ferment until the 1980s. Human rights had not yet arrived on the legal scene and lawyers were not involved in the compulsory procedures except in the criminal courts. Lawmakers were still mainly concerned with protecting society from mentally abnormal offenders, the subject of the Butler Report of 1975. But a series of scandals in mental hospitals also revealed that many patients were not dangerous at all, rather a chronically underprivileged group who were particularly vulnerable to exploitation both in and out of hospital.

The National Association for Mental Health (MIND) began to subject the comfortable assumptions in the 1959 Act to an increasingly uncomfortable scrutiny. Their legal officer, Larry Gostin, produced two influential studies of the Act in practice, with suggestions for reform in line with principles then being developed in the United States (Gostin, 1975 and 1977). DHSS reviews (DHSS, 1976 and DHSS et al, 1978) attempted to reconcile the irreconcilable views of all the different professions and interests involved. The result was the Mental Health Act 1983, which improved the procedural safeguards and introduced some independent control over what went on in hospitals. But it changed the underlying substance and purpose very little. The focus was still on hospital treatment. The purpose was still to ensure that people suffering from mental disorder of almost any description could be given the hospital treatment and care which their doctors thought they needed. If there was nothing the doctors could do for them, they could not be detained.

Since 1983, the lawyers have become more and more involved. Legal aid brought them into mental health review tribunals and into judicial review in the High Court. Awareness of the human rights dimension rapidly grew, although the various United Nations instruments concerned with mentally disabled and disordered people do not form part of United Kingdom law. The United Nations adopted a Declaration on the Rights of Mentally Retarded Persons in 1971, a Declaration on the Rights of Disabled Persons in 1975, and Principles for the Protection of Persons with Mental Illness and for the Improvement of Mental Health Care in 1991. But the first binding instrument is the Convention on the

Rights of People with Disabilities 2006, ratified by the United Kingdom in 2009, with its optional protocol allowing individuals to bring complaints before the UN Committee on the Rights of Persons with Disabilities. Persons with disabilities include:

"those who have long term physical, mental, intellectual or sensory impairments which in interaction with various barriers may hinder their full and effective participation in society on an equal basis with others" (art 1).

Key principles include "respect for inherent dignity, individual autonomy including the freedom to make one's own choices, and independence of persons" (art 3(a)), "full and effective participation and inclusion in society" (art 3(c)), and "respect for difference and acceptance of persons with disabilities as part of human diversity and humanity" (art 3(d)), as well as non-discrimination and equality, and "respect for the evolving capacities of children with disabilities" (art 3(h)).

These instruments are not part of our law. But the Human Rights Act 1998 has turned the rights set out in the European Convention on Human Rights into rights enforceable in the United Kingdom. Four of these are key: the right in article 3 not to be subjected to torture or to inhuman or degrading treatment or punishment; the right in article 5 not to be deprived of liberty except on defined grounds, which include "unsoundness of mind", and to be able to go to court and be released if detention is not justified; the right in article 6 to a fair and public hearing within a reasonable time before an independent and impartial court or tribunal in the determination of both civil rights and obligations and of any criminal charge; and the right in article 8 to respect for private and family life, home and correspondence, unless the interference can be justified as a proportionate response to a legitimate aim.

The Government which introduced the Human Rights Act also launched a thorough-going review of the Mental Health Act. In part this was a response to the new legal culture; in part it was a response to "modern patterns of clinical and social care" and the shift of professional attention away from detention and treatment in hospital towards multi-disciplinary community-based treatment and care; but in part it was a response to continued concern about mentally disordered people who committed horrendous crimes. In October 1998, Michael Stone was convicted (for the first time) of a vicious and unprovoked attack upon a mother and her two daughters which left two of them dead and one severely injured. His complex mental problems included a severe anti-social personality disorder. He had a long criminal record but also many contacts with the mental health services. There developed an intense media-led concern that, because his personality disorder was not amenable to treatment, he could not be detained in hospital. The Government determined to remedy this, alongside providing a new legal framework for "the vast majority of patients with mental illness [who] pose no threat to other people and in many cases are among the most vulnerable in our society" (Department of Health and Home Office, Cm 5016, 2000, p 5).

They first sought advice from an expert committee, chaired by Professor Genevra Richardson (Richardson, 1999). They published this together with a green paper consulting on somewhat different proposals for reform (Department of Health, Cm 4480, 1999). They followed this with a white paper (Cm 5016, 2000, above). Next came a draft Mental Health Bill for consultation

3

(Department of Health, Cm 2002, 5538), followed by a further draft Bill, presented to Parliament for pre-legislative scrutiny (Department of Health, Cm 6305, 2004a; Joint Committee on the Mental Health Bill, 2004–05, HL 79, HC 95). All of these proposed the complete replacement of the 1983 Act. Key features were that all compulsory care and treatment for more than 28 days would have to be sanctioned by an independent tribunal (or in the case of offenders, a court), which could approve a plan for treatment either in hospital or in the community. The treatment would have to be available, but not necessarily able to do any good. Offenders who posed a serious risk of harm to the public could be detained indefinitely.

This approach was attacked by professionals, lawyers and client groups alike, because it was seen as allowing the long term detention of people who had committed no crime and who would gain no benefit from treatment. It would also have required a new and costly tribunal structure, absorbing resources which many might think better devoted to patient care. The possibility of forcible treatment in the community remained controversial. Eventually, the Government decided only to make essential changes to the 1983 Act, which remains in force as amended by the Mental Health Act 2007. It continues to cater for the psychiatric care and treatment of people suffering from mental disorder.

But that is not the only legal problem posed by mental disorder and disability. Increasing numbers of mentally disabled people are living in the community but lack the ability to take some or all of the necessary decisions about such things as where they are to live, how they are to be looked after, what treatment for physical as well as mental disorders they should have, or how their finances should be managed. This might not matter when most lived in institutions where everything was taken care of for them. But in the community families and carers needed to know where they stood. The Law Commission began to study the problem in 1989. Its report was published in 1995. This proposed to clarify the test of when someone could or could not take a decision for himself; the circumstances in which others could do so for him; the principle that such decisions must always be in the best interests of the person concerned; and to provide new machinery for resolving doubts and disputes in court. After further consultation (LCD, 1997, 1999), and pre-legislative scrutiny (Cm 5859; Joint Committee on the draft Mental Incapacity Bill, 2002–03, HL 189, HC 1083), most of these proposals became law in the Mental Capacity Act 2005.

There was still a gap. The comfortable assumption of the 1959 and 1983 Acts, that people could be admitted to hospital for mental treatment without formality, provided that they did not object, was dealt a serious blow by the European Court of Human Rights in Strasbourg (*HL v United Kingdom* (2005) 40 EHRR 761). If the reality was that a person was being deprived of his liberty within the meaning of article 5, there had to be some safeguards to protect him against arbitrary action, even if this was meant for his own good. Indeed, safeguards against unjustified deprivation of liberty were needed, whether the reason for it was mental or physical disorder or simply to keep him safe. The result was the Deprivation of Liberty Safeguards (universally known as the DoLS), inserted into the Mental Capacity Act 2005 Act by the Mental Health Act 2007.

So now, instead of the simple, elegant and coherent scheme of the 1959 Act, we have two separate legislative schemes, each with its own set of English and Welsh Regulations, English and Welsh Codes of Practice under the Mental Health Act and two Codes of Practice under the Mental Capacity Act. There is also a mass of case law, with its own specialist law reports to ensure that nothing is missed. The problems that the two schemes address are different, but they may both apply to the same person. A mentally ill person may be living in the community and unable to decide upon treatment for a physical disorder: the Mental Capacity Act will apply, including the DoLS if he has to be detained for his own good. A mentally disabled person may need hospital treatment for mental disorder: the Mental Capacity Act will apply if he does not object. But if he does object, the Mental Health Act will apply. The lives of patients and professionals of all kinds have become a great deal more complicated. Part of the object of this book is to bring the two schemes together and discuss how each will operate in any given situation.

But there is a surprising degree of agreement about the values which should underpin the law and practice in both schemes. They could be put in this way:

- The starting point is non-discrimination: people with mental disorders and disabilities should have the same rights (and duties) as anyone else, unless and until a good reason is shown to treat them differently (but views differ as to what constitutes a good reason).
- They should be treated in such a way as to promote and enhance their own self-determination and personal responsibility; they should be presumed to have the capacity to decide things for themselves until the contrary is shown; even if they are unable to decide for themselves, or matters have to be taken out of their hands for their own sake or that of others, they should be consulted and their views given proper weight.
- Care and treatment in the community is to be preferred to care and treatment in institutions; informal or consensual care is to be preferred to compulsory care; any kind of compulsory care should be provided under conditions of no greater control, segregation or security than is necessary and proportionate.
- There should be a comprehensive multi-disciplinary approach to assessing and providing care and treatment in hospital or the community; this should include the views, not only of the professionals, but also of family, friends and carers.
- People should be looked on as individuals, having proper regard to their sex, race, social and cultural background and other characteristics but without discrimination and stereotyping.
- Legal procedures should be available to protect people who are unable to protect themselves from ill-treatment, neglect or exploitation; whenever compulsion is used, there should be safeguards at least as good as those required by the European Convention on Human Rights.
- The use of compulsion brings with it a reciprocal obligation to provide the care and treatment which the person needs.

Many of these values have been made explicit in the Mental Capacity Act 2005:

- A person must be assumed to have the capacity to decide for himself unless it is established that he does not (s 1(2)).
- A person is not to be treated as unable to make a decision unless all practicable steps to help him to do so have been taken (s 1(3)); even then,

he must, so far as practicable be allowed and encouraged to participate as fully as possible in the decision (s 4(4)).

- A person is not to be treated as unable to make a decision merely because he makes an unwise decision (s 1(4)).
- Anything done and any decision made for someone who lacks capacity must be done or made in his best interests (s 1(5)); this includes taking account of his past and present wishes and feelings, his beliefs and values, and the other factors which he would be likely to consider if able to do so (s 4(6)); people must not leap to conclusions because of his age or appearance or a condition he has or some aspect of his behaviour which might lead people to make assumptions about what might be best for him (s 4(5)).
- Before doing anything or taking a decision, regard must be had to whether the purpose could be as effectively achieved in a way which is less restrictive of his rights and freedom of action (s 1(6)).

The Mental Health Act has no such statement of principle, but the Code of Practice (Department of Health, 2008a) begins with five guiding principles:

- The purpose principle: decisions under the Act must be taken with a view to minimising the undesirable effects of mental disorder, by maximising the safety and wellbeing (mental and physical) of patients, promoting their recovery and protecting other people from harm (para 1.2).
- The least restriction principle: people taking action without a patient's consent must attempt to keep to a minimum the restrictions they impose on the patient's liberty, having regard to the purpose for which the restrictions are imposed (para 1.3).
- The respect principle: people taking decisions under the Act must recognise and respect the diverse needs, values and circumstances of each patient, including their race, religion, culture, gender, age, sexual orientation and any disability. They must consider the patient's wishes and feelings (whether expressed at the time or in advance), so far as they are reasonably ascertainable, and follow those wishes wherever practicable and consistent with the purpose of the decision. There must be no unlawful discrimination (para 1.4).
- The participation principle: patients must be given the opportunity to be involved, as far as is practicable in the circumstances, in planning, developing and reviewing their own treatment and care to help ensure that it is delivered in a way that is as appropriate and effective for them as possible. The involvement of carers, family members and other people who have an interest in the patient's welfare should be encouraged (unless there are particular reasons to the contrary) and their views taken seriously (para 1.5).
- The effectiveness, efficiency and equity principle: people taking decisions under the Act must seek to use the resources available to them and to patients in the most effective, efficient and equitable way, to meet the needs of patients, and achieve the purpose for which the decision was taken (para 1.6).

It is apparent, therefore, that the purpose of a decision under the 1983 Act may be to protect other people from harm, rather than to promote the safety, wellbeing and recovery of the patient. This colours and qualifies all the other principles. On the other hand, a decision under the 2005 Act, including a decision to deprive the person of his liberty, must always be taken in his best interests.

What follows is a textbook designed for everyone who has an interest in helping mentally disabled or disordered people whether they are in or out of hospital; for social workers, nurses and other carers who look after them in the community but who may have to invoke compulsory powers; for doctors, nurses and other healthcare professionals who offer them medical treatment and therapy, but sometimes have to recommend detention; and for lawyers, advocates and advice workers who try to protect their legal rights. It tries to explain the law, the history and the policy arguments which led up to where we are now. But it is not a work of philosophy committed to any particular point of view, except to the proper recognition of the status and needs of all concerned.

1 INFORMALITY AND INTERVENTION: THE BASICS

There are now two pieces of legislation concerned with the lives of people with mental disorders or disabilities. Roughly speaking, the Mental Health Act 1983 (the MHA) caters for the psychiatric care and treatment of people suffering from mental disorder, while the Mental Capacity Act 2005 (the MCA) caters for all kinds of decision making on behalf of people who, because of mental disorder or disability, are unable to take the decision for themselves. The MHA is mainly concerned with people who have mental illnesses or personality disorders, while the MCA is mainly concerned with people who have mental disabilities. But the same person may be covered by both.

Underlying both the MHA and the MCA was the common law principle of necessity, although this may not have been appreciated when the Mental Health Act 1959 was passed. This holds that people who lack the mental capacity to decide about their own care and treatment may be looked after by professionals and other carers in their own best interests without any particular legal formalities (*Re F (Mental Patient: Sterilisation)* [1990] 2 AC 1). But extra safeguards are needed before people can be deprived of their liberty, in order to protect them against violations of the right to liberty contained in article 5 of the European Convention on Human Rights (ECHR).

Before we look at the present law, however, it is worth taking a brief look at the law as it was before the 1959 Act, to appreciate what a revolutionary break it was with the traditions of the past. Some may fear that safeguards and formalities now required risk putting the clock back to the olden days.

1. OUT OF MIND AND OUT OF SIGHT

In the early days, the only forms of mental disorder recognised in law were "lunacy" or "madness" and "idiocy". The common law allowed the confinement of the dangerously insane, those who seemed disposed to do mischief to themselves or others (Lanham, 1974; see also chapter 4), but not the harmlessly eccentric or weak-witted. The insane might be kept in conditions which we now think appalling, and often subject to individual "mechanical restraint" (a euphemism for shackles, manacles, cages and the like). By the turn of the eighteenth and nineteenth centuries, a growing body of opinion was inspired by the more humane system of "moral treatment" pioneered in places such as the Retreat, the Quaker institution in York. Reformers pressed for the licensing and supervision of private madhouses run for profit (beginning with the Act for regulating Madhouses of 1774) and later for supervision of charitable hospitals funded by public subscription. They also persuaded the county authorities to set up rate-funded asylums (first permitted in the County Asylums Act of 1808), mainly for pauper and criminal lunatics, but soon allowed also to take in paying patients. The culmination of these efforts came in 1845, when the Lunatic Asylums Act obliged all county and borough authorities to set up asylums, and the Lunatics Act established the Lunacy Commissioners. They were an independent body with power to supervise standards and protect patients in all the hospitals, asylums and licensed houses in the country (the oldest charitable hospital of them all, Bethlem, escaped control until 1854). The Commissioners were reconstituted as the Board of Control in 1913 and continued in being until the 1959 Act.

The nineteenth century reformers thought that the answer to the bad institutions of the past lay in the good institutions of the future. They still assumed that mental patients were to be segregated and detained, whether or not they could be treated or made better. Demand for places in asylums grew and grew, as workhouses and families recognised the opportunity of providing more humane surroundings for people who did not fit into the harsh deterrent principles underlying the "new" Poor Law of 1834, not only the conventionally insane but also the aged mentally infirm. In 1807, there were only 2,248 people (or 2.26 per 10,000 of the population) officially recognised as insane, both in and out of institutions. By 1890, there were 86,167 (or 29.26 per 10,000). Ninety per cent of these were paupers and all but a small proportion, particularly in the county and borough asylums, were acknowledged to be incurable (Scull, 1979). Not surprisingly, considerations of economy had turned these huge and isolated "warehouses for the insane" into very different places from the humane sanctuaries which the early reformers had envisaged.

The other concern of the legislators (often bitterly opposed by the pioneers of reform, such as Lord Shaftesbury) was with the procedures for putting people into these institutions. Ordinary members of the public could perceive the benefit in removing mentally disordered people from society but only if there was no risk that they themselves might be confined. Well-publicised mistakes (or worse) fuelled the demand for more elaborate safeguards, particularly for private patients. These culminated in the Lunacy Act of 1890, which required formal certification by a judicial order, following a petition by relatives or Poor Law officials and supported by medical evidence. The same approach was adopted when publicly-financed institutions for mentally disabled people were established under the Mental Deficiency Act of 1913, following the Report of the Royal Commission on the Care and Control of the Feeble-minded of 1908 (Radnor, 1908). The most severely handicapped "idiots" had previously been included in the definition of "lunatics", but the 1913 Act extended the concept of segregation to a much wider class of socially inadequate or inconvenient, as well as intellectually disabled, people.

These developments had two results which were unpopular with medical opinion from at least the end of the nineteenth century. First, because of the original desire to improve standards in institutions, patients who were certified under the Acts could only be admitted to the specialised institutions controlled under them. Mentally ill patients could only be committed to asylums, mental hospitals and madhouses, although these became known as "designated" public mental hospitals, "registered" hospitals, or "licensed" private nursing homes. Mental "defectives" could only be committed to "directed" public institutions or "certified" private ones. A mental "defective" could not be admitted to a mental illness hospital, although the personality disorders which were included as "defects" are now treated (if at all) as part of psychiatry rather than the care of people with learning disabilities. Nor could a mentally ill patient be admitted to a mental handicap institution. A growing number of other hospitals were prepared to treat patients outside the ambit of the Acts altogether (some of them in "de-designated" parts of mental hospitals), but these could only take patients informally and could never use the compulsory procedures.

Secondly, although private nursing homes were allowed to take "voluntary boarders" who could afford to pay, the public asylums and institutions were only permitted to take certified patients. The poor, who were the great majority, could not be treated in hospital on a voluntary basis. Formal certification involved a stigma which many doctors shrank from imposing upon their patients until, it was said, it was too late for treatment to have any chance of success. At the same time, the medical profession was identifying forms of mental disorder falling far short of obvious "madness" or "lunacy" and for which formal certification and confinement were thought neither necessary nor appropriate. The "shell shock" cases of the First World War increased public awareness of these. The first step towards freely available treatment without certification was taken when the Maudsley Hospital was founded in 1915, with a special statutory dispensation to admit voluntary non-paying patients.

For most mentally ill patients, however, the major change came with the Mental Treatment Act 1930, following the Royal Commission on Lunacy and Mental Disorders of 1924 to 1926 (MacMillan, 1926). This began the break away from the procedural formality and institutional dominance of the late nineteenth century, towards the informality and integration with general medicine which were the hallmarks of the mid-twentieth century (Unsworth, 1987). "Asylums" were renamed "mental hospitals" and "lunatics" became "persons of unsound mind". A "voluntary" status was introduced for patients who were able to make a written application to be treated in hospital and a "temporary" status was introduced for non-volitional patients who required treatment for no more than a year. Until the 1959 Act, then, patients in mental illness hospitals might be voluntary or temporary patients under the 1930 Act or certified patients under the 1890 Act.

For mental "defectives" there was a totally different, if rather less complex, set of procedures under the Mental Deficiency Acts of 1913 and 1927. These did not include a voluntary status, but the institutions were not expressly prohibited from taking patients without formality. Looking after people who lacked the capacity to look after themselves was permitted by the common law doctrine of necessity, although this may not have been generally recognised at the time. After 1952, this was officially encouraged for short stays, and in 1957 the Royal Commission on the Law relating to Mental Illness and Mental Deficiency of 1954 to 1957 (the Percy Commission) recommended that it could be extended to long-stay patients without waiting for legislation.

Two developments lay behind much of the Percy Commission's thinking. First was the creation of the National Health Service in 1948. Most hospitals, including the former county asylums and the charitable hospitals, were now vested in the Ministry of Health. The Commission believed that NHS hospitals did not need the strict legal supervision which earlier institutions had done. Also, as improvements depend upon the availability of resources, full responsibility should rest with the government department which controlled the allocation of resources within the health service as a whole. The Board of Control could safely be abolished and with it the legal segregation of mental hospitals from the mainstream.

Second was the optimism about the advances in medical treatment for the major mental illnesses, through psycho-surgery, electro-convulsive therapy and above all the new breed of psycho-tropic drugs, the major tranquillisers. These made it possible for increasing numbers of seriously disordered patients to be discharged into the community or treated on open wards in ordinary hospital conditions. It no longer seemed necessary for the law to assume that these patients were inevitably different from physically sick or injured patients. For the most part, they could be admitted to hospital in the same way. Compulsory procedures should be kept only for those for whom they were absolutely necessary. Once in hospital, their treatment and care could be left in the hands of the medical profession. As many as possible would be discharged back into the community just like other patients, although compulsory treatment would only be possible in a hospital.

Thus the Percy Report and the 1959 Act were all about breaking down boundaries, between different kinds of hospital, between hospital admissions for mental and for physical disorders, and between the compulsory procedures for admitting people with mental illness and people with mental disability. Removing the legal controls over mental patients was inextricably linked with removing the legal controls over their doctors. The 1983 Act was mainly concerned to reintroduce some control over the doctors and the 2007 Act with broadening the scope of possible control over their patients.

2. INFORMAL ADMISSION TO HOSPITAL

The basic principle introduced by the 1959 Act is now contained in section 131(1) of the 1983 Act:

> "Nothing in this Act shall be construed as preventing a patient who requires treatment for mental disorder from being admitted to any hospital or registered establishment in pursuance of arrangements made in that behalf and without any application, order or direction rendering him liable to be detained under this Act, or from remaining in any hospital or registered establishment in pursuance of such arrangements after he has ceased to be so liable to be detained."

This means that patients may enter hospital for treatment for mental disorder in just the same way that they may enter hospital for a physical disorder, without any special formalities making them liable to be detained or compelled. Things have changed a great deal since 1959. In 1955, only 27 per cent of admissions to mental illness hospitals were compulsory; but 70 per cent of the patients in hospital at any one time were certified, because the voluntary patients tended to stay only for a short time, while compulsion was still used for the long stay chronically ill. By 1986, the proportion of compulsory admissions to mental illness hospitals had fallen to 8.1 per cent and to mental handicap hospitals to less than one per cent. Fewer than five per cent of the patients in NHS mental illness or mental handicap hospitals were detained.

Nowadays, the mental health services have changed so much that the figures are not broken down in this way (Health and Social Care Information Centre, 2008a and 2008b). In 2006–2007, more than a million people consulted the specialist NHS psychiatric services in hospital or in the community; about 100,000 of these spent some time as an inpatient in a mental hospital; and about one in four of these spent some time compulsorily detained under the 1983 Act. The actual numbers of compulsory admissions to hospital rose from around 16,300 in 1987/1988 to around 25,400 in 1997/1998. Since then the rise has been rather less steep. In 2007/2008, there were around 28,000 compulsory admissions to NHS and independent hospitals in England alone; and on top of that some 19,500 patients were made subject to compulsory powers after they had been informally admitted to hospital, making a total of 47,600 formal detentions in the course of that year. These are not insignificant numbers.

Theoretically, at least, informal patients enjoy two legal rights which detained patients do not. They may leave hospital whenever they like (cf chapter 7) and they may refuse to accept any form of treatment which they do not want (see chapter 6). Their mail is not censored in any way, they may be registered to vote, and they have unimpeded access to the courts to complain about their treatment. In practice, however, there are several different types of informal patient. Only those who appreciate the need to be in hospital and are generally content to accept their doctors' advice can be classed as completely "voluntary". There are three other categories to whom that description cannot be applied and for whom the benefits of having "informal" rather than "compulsory" status are harder to assess.

First, there are those who are reluctant to accept their doctors' advice and wish either to leave the hospital or to refuse a suggested course of treatment. They may however be persuaded to stay and accept treatment, because they know or believe that they could otherwise be forced to do so, by being "sectioned" under sections 2 or 3 of the 1983 Act (see section 6, below). To prevent their leaving the hospital before this can be done, they may be detained for a short period under section 5 (see section 5, below). As we now know, a very considerable number of patients who came into hospital informally later become subject to detention: in 2007/2008, some 8,500 in-patients were detained under section 5, and 3,000 for assessment under section 2, and 5,200 for treatment under section 3.

Secondly, there are some children who are "volunteered" for admission by their parents or others, including local children's services authorities, who have parental responsibility for them. Growing numbers of children are admitted to psychiatric facilities or to other units where they may be given treatment which they do not want, because of their emotional or behavioural problems. Children who have reached 16, and have the capacity to consent to their own admission, are in the same position as any adult with that capacity: they may agree to enter hospital informally even if there is someone with parental responsibility for them who does not want this; and if they do not agree, they cannot be admitted to hospital on the basis of the consent of a person with parental responsibility (MHA, s 131(2), (3) and (4)). The position of children of any age who lack the capacity to decide for themselves, or of children under 16 who do have that capacity, is discussed in chapter 3. They constitute another group who may be informally admitted without being genuine volunteers.

Finally, there is a large group of people who cannot give an informed consent to admission and treatment, perhaps because of brain damage or dementia, but who do not actively object to entering or remaining in hospital. A major conclusion of the Percy Commission was that such patients need no longer automatically be subjected to compulsory powers. The non-objecting could be equated with the consenting rather than with the dissenting: hence the expression "informal" rather than "voluntary" admission. That did not mean that the hospitals could detain, restrain or treat these patients as they saw fit. But there was a great deal of uncertainty about what they could do. No doubt most acted with the best of intentions in what they saw as the best interests of their patients, avoiding what is still seen as the stigma of the compulsion. But those compulsory procedures also bring safeguards, which these patients were denied, although in practice their situation amounted to detention. This became known as the "Bournewood gap", after a case challenging an informal admission to Bournewood hospital. The legislation has now tried to bridge that gap, at the price of even more complexity than is involved in the MHA compulsory procedures.

13

3. COMMON LAW NECESSITY AND THE BOURNEWOOD GAP

The problem was brought to light by two important decisions of the House of Lords. In *Re F (Mental Patient: Sterilisation)* [1990] 2 AC 1, the issue was whether a profoundly mentally disabled young woman should have a hysterectomy, not because of any physical disorder but to prevent her becoming pregnant and having a child. Before the 1959 Act, there was power to decide such issues under the ancient prerogative jurisdiction of the monarch, as *parens patriae*, to look after children and adults who lacked the capacity to look after themselves. The powers over children remain, and are usually exercised by making them wards of court. But the royal warrant delegating the Queen's powers over adults was revoked when the 1959 Act came into force. It was thought that such powers were only needed in relation to property matters; powers over personal matters had scarcely ever been used and could safely be left to the common law or to guardianship under the 1959 Act. However, the High Court does have jurisdiction to declare whether something is lawful. In *Re F*, therefore, it was held that treatment or care, which might otherwise be an assault upon a person who lacked the capacity to agree to it, was lawful under the common law doctrine of necessity, provided that it was in the best interests of the person concerned. Furthermore, the court could declare in advance that something would be lawful under that principle. In cases of doubt or difficulty, in particular non-therapeutic sterilisations, such a declaration should be sought.

But how far does that go? *Re F* involved a major abdominal operation with irreversible effects upon the fundamental human right to bear children. Might the same doctrine of necessity be applied to justify the detention and treatment of mental patients who lacked the capacity to decide for themselves? This question arose in *R v Bournewood Community and Mental Health NHS Trust, ex p L* [1999] 1 AC 458. Mr L was in his forties, autistic, profoundly mentally disabled, and unable to consent to medical treatment. He had lived in a hospital for many years, but three years earlier he had left the hospital to live with paid carers. On 22 July 1997, he became agitated at his day centre, a doctor and social worker were called, and he was sedated and taken to A & E. A psychiatrist assessed him as needing in-patient treatment but by then it was not thought necessary to "section" him, as he appeared to be fully compliant and unresisting. So he was admitted informally. His carers were very suspicious of the hospital's intentions and proceedings were started in L's name to challenge his admission. The Court of Appeal held that he had been detained and that his detention was unlawful. The MHA was a complete statutory code leaving no room for the operation of the common law doctrine of necessity. Section 131(1) applied only to people who consented, not to people who did not dissent. It was troubling that textbooks (Hoggett, *Mental Health Law*, 4th edn 1996, p 9 and Jones, *Mental Health Act Manual*, 5th edn 1996, p 340) supported the contrary view. On the day of this decision, Mr L was detained under section 5(2) of the MHA and then for treatment under section 3. He was released to his carers five weeks later and formally discharged a week after that. Meanwhile the hospital appealed to the House of Lords.

The House of Lords were given a much fuller account of the legislative background which had led to section 131(1). They were also introduced to the old case law which had applied the doctrine of necessity to the detention of mental patients (see *R v Coate* (1772) Lofft 73; *Scott v Wakem* (1862) 3 F & F 328; *Symm v Fraser* (1863) 3 F & F 859, pp 111–113 later). They were told that the Court of Appeal's judgment would lead to vastly more people being detained under the Act—an additional 22,000 patients on any one day and an additional 48,000 admissions per year. There was widespread professional concern about the implications, especially for nursing homes looking after elderly people, although the Mental Health Act Commission was also concerned about the lack of safeguards for incapable informal patients. All the Law Lords held that section 131(1) applied both to capable consenting and to incapable non-dissenting patients. All held that it was the intention of section 131(1) that informal patients be given such treatment and care as was in their best interests. Mr L's removal to hospital, treatment and care in hospital were therefore lawful under the common law doctrine of necessity confirmed in *Re F.*

Three of the five Law Lords also held that he had not actually been detained: he had stayed on an unlocked ward and made no attempt to leave. But two considered that he had been detained: he was sedated both to get him to the hospital and while he was there; he would have been sectioned if he had tried to leave; his carers were at first prohibited from visiting in case he wanted to leave with them; the hospital was not prepared to release him back into the care of his carers until it thought him ready. Lord Steyn described the suggestion that he was free to leave as "a fairy tale" (p 495). The detention had been justified under the doctrine of necessity, but Lord Steyn regarded the lack of protection for someone in Mr L's position as "an indefensible gap in our mental health law" (p 493). Lord Steyn also pointed out that the doctrine of necessity might even on occasions justify the detention of non-compliant patients (as in the earlier cases on the necessity to detain mental patients).

Mr L's case then went the European Court of Human Rights in Strasbourg, complaining of breach of article 5(1) and (4) of the ECHR:

"(1) Everyone has the right to liberty and security of person. No-one shall be deprived of his liberty save in the following cases and in accordance with a procedure prescribed by law: . . .

(e) the lawful detention . . . of persons of unsound mind, . . .

(4) Everyone who is deprived of his liberty by arrest or detention shall be entitled to take proceedings by which the lawfulness of his detention shall be decided speedily by a court and his release ordered if the detention is not lawful."

In *HL v United Kingdom* (2005) 40 EHRR 761, the Court agreed with Lord Steyn that Mr L had indeed been "deprived of his liberty" within the meaning of article 5(1) of the ECHR. The health care professionals treating and managing him exercised complete and effective control over his care and movements from the moment he presented problems on 22 July 1997 until he was compulsorily detained in October. The reality was that he was not free to leave. The hospital would have prevented him from doing so had he tried. The Court accepted that he had been "of unsound mind" for the purpose of article 5(1)(e). However, his detention had not been "lawful". It was not enough that the detention was lawful under English law. It had also to meet the Convention standard of lawfulness. This requires the law to be sufficiently precise to allow the citizen to foresee the consequences of any given action. It also means that any detention has to comply with the essential objective of article 5(1), "which is to prevent individuals being deprived of their liberty in an arbitrary fashion". There were no procedural rules for the admission and detention of compliant incapacitated people, no grounds, no statement of purpose, no limits of time or treatment, and no requirement of continuing clinical assessment. This lack of safeguards meant that patients were not protected against being arbitrarily deprived of their liberty on the purported ground of necessity. It was thus in breach of article 5(1). The lack of a speedy judicial review of the merits of his detention was also in breach of article 5(4).

Under section 6(1) of the Human Rights Act 1998, it is now unlawful for a public authority to act in a way which is incompatible with the Convention rights. The law of England and Wales had therefore to provide a way in which people who lacked the capacity to consent could be deprived of their liberty without breaching their article 5 rights. Simply requiring that the compulsory procedures in the MHA were used for compliant as well as for non-compliant mental hospital patients would not have been enough. People who lack capacity may be deprived of their liberty in other settings, for example when in hospital for the treatment of a physical condition, or when living in a care or nursing home. A broader solution was found through amendment of the MCA 2005.

4. THE DEPRIVATION OF LIBERTY SAFEGUARDS (DoLS)

In its original form, the MCA gave all kinds of carers a general authority to act in the best interests of an incapacitated person, but that general authority did not extend to depriving him of his liberty. As amended by the 2007 Act, the MCA does not authorise anyone to deprive another person of his liberty, except in three circumstances: first, where the Court of Protection has authorised this; second, where it is authorised under the DoLS scheme set out in Schedule A1 to the Act, which provides for the circumstances in which people may be deprived of their liberty in hospitals and care homes by means of "standard authorisations" given by the relevant supervisory body or "urgent authorisations" given by the managing authority of the hospital or home; and third, as an interim measure pending the decision of the court upon an issue about whether the deprivation is authorised, but only for the purpose of giving the person life-sustaining treatment or doing something reasonably believed to be necessary to prevent a serious deterioration in the person's condition: MCA, sections 4A and 4B.

(a) What is a deprivation of liberty?

The DoLS scheme authorises *detention* for all kinds of purposes, whether for general care or for treatment for physical or mental disorder. But it does not cover *all kinds of decision* about people who lack the capacity to decide whether or not they should be in a hospital or care home. The general principle still is that they can be looked after in their own best interests without any legal formalities (s 5; see p 30, below; also p 191, later). The scheme only deals with detaining them in circumstances which amount to a "deprivation of liberty" within the meaning of article 5 of the ECHR. This is not always easy to spot. Liberty means the physical liberty of the person, not simply the freedom to live one's life as one chooses. Deprivation is more than mere restriction, but it can cover more than being locked up in a prison cell. The Strasbourg Court has said that:

> "the difference between deprivation of and restriction upon liberty is . . .
> merely one of degree or intensity, not one of nature or substance . . . some

borderline cases are a matter of pure opinion" (*Guzzardi v Italy* [1980] 3 EHRR 33, para 93).

The starting point has to be the actual situation of the person concerned and account must be taken of a whole range of factors, "such as the type, duration, effects and manner of implementation of the measure in question" (para 92). In that case exiling a person to a small area of an island where his movements were strictly controlled was held to deprive him of his liberty. It may also be that measures designed for the benefit of the person concerned are less likely to constitute a deprivation of liberty than measures designed to protect other people: see *HM v Switzerland* (2004) 38 EHRR 314. In that case placing an elderly lady in ordinary nursing home conditions in order to provide her with satisfactory living conditions and necessary medical care was held not to deprive her of her liberty.

Two English cases decided before the DoLS illustrate the dividing line. In *LLBC v TG* [2007] EWHC 2640 (Fam), a 78-year-old man with dementia and cognitive impairment was *not* deprived of his liberty by being placed in an ordinary care home, with only the ordinary restrictions on liberty which that entailed, with relatively unrestricted visits and outings, and where he said that he was happy (but note that at all times his placement was authorised by the court, so why would there be a breach of article 5?). In *JE v Surrey CC* [2007] EWHC 3459 (Fam), on the other hand, a 76-year-old man, who was blind and suffered from dementia, but was often able to express his wishes forcefully, *was* deprived of his liberty when he was placed in an ordinary care home and prevented from leaving when both he and his wife wished him to return to live with her.

The Code of Practice on the *Deprivation of Liberty Safeguards* (the DoLS Code) (Ministry of Justice and Public Guardian, 2008) suggests that the following factors may be relevant to deciding whether a case has crossed the line from restriction to deprivation (para 2.5):

- Restraint is used, including sedation, to admit a person to an institution where that person is resisting admission.
- Staff exercise complete and effective control over the care and movement of a person for a significant period.
- Staff exercise complete control over assessments, treatment, contacts and residence.
- A decision has been taken by the institution that the person will not be released into the care of others, or permitted to live elsewhere, unless the staff in the institution consider it appropriate.
- A request by carers for a person to be discharged to their care is refused.
- A person is unable to maintain social contacts because of restrictions placed on their access to other people.
- A person loses autonomy because they are under continuous supervision and control.

On the other hand, preventing someone leaving the home unaccompanied because there is a risk that they might cross the road in a dangerous way, or locking a door to guard against immediate harm, or transporting them from home to hospital is thought unlikely to amount to a deprivation of liberty (paras 2.10, 2.14), any more than the ordinary precaution of locking external doors overnight would be.

(b) The criteria for authorisation

The DoLS Code is more than 100 pages long, which is some indication of the complexity of the scheme. Deprivation of liberty may only be authorised under the DoLS where the person concerned meets the six qualifying criteria (MCA, Schedule A1, paras 12 to 20):

(a) he is aged *18 or over* (paras 12(1)(a), 13);

(b) he suffers from *mental disorder* within the meaning of the 1983 Act (disregarding any exclusions from that Act of people with learning disabilities) (see chapter 2 for the definition of mental disorder) (paras 12(1)(b), 14);

(c) he *lacks the capacity* to decide whether or not he should be accommodated in the relevant hospital or care home for the purpose of being given the relevant care or treatment (see chapter 2 for the definition of lack of capacity) (paras 12(1)(c), 15);

(d) he meets the *"best interests" requirement*, in that the detention is in his best interests (see chapter 2 for the approach to deciding on a person's best interests); additionally, the detention must be necessary in order to prevent his suffering harm, and a proportionate response both to the likelihood and to the seriousness of that harm (paras 12(1)(d), 16);

(e) he is *not ineligible* because he falls within a Mental Health Act regime (see below) (paras 12(1)(e), 17, Sch 1A); and

(f) there is *no valid and conflicting refusal* of some or all of the relevant care or treatment, either by an advance decision which he has made himself, or by the donee of a lasting power of attorney to whom he has given that power, or by a deputy to whom the court has given that power (paras 12(1)(f), 18, 19, 20).

The Code contemplates that a large number of people covered by the scheme will have significant learning disability, or be older people with dementia or some similar disability, but they may have other neurological conditions, for example as a result of brain injury (para 1.7). The qualifications of the assessors are dealt with in chapter 3 and the procedure for authorisations in chapter 4.

(c) The eligibility requirement

The eligibility requirement, defined in Schedule 1A to the MCA, is there to exclude people who are, or could be, subject to the compulsory powers in the Mental Health Act 1983. The aim is to ensure that where a patient is to be deprived of his liberty in a hospital for the purpose of receiving medical treatment for mental disorder to which he objects, he is sectioned under the MHA and not detained under the DoLS. But the DoLS can be used for that purpose if he does not object: that was what the *Bournewood* case was all about. The Schedule applies, not only to authorisations under the DoLS scheme, but also to deprivations of liberty authorised by the Court of Protection under its general welfare jurisdiction (MCA, s 16A) (Sch 1A, para 1). The concepts are simple but the drafting is not. The Schedule divides people into five different Cases (para 2).

(i) Case A

This covers someone who is "subject to the hospital treatment regime" and actually detained in a hospital under that regime (para 2). A person is "subject to the hospital treatment regime" if he is subject to an application, order or direction making him liable to be detained under the MHA; this includes an emergency application under section 4, but not the in-patient holding powers under section 5 or the place of safety powers under sections 135 and 136. Also covered are people detained under some other statutory provision to the same effect as the MHA powers, principally the Criminal Procedure (Insanity) Act 1964 (para 8). These people are automatically ineligible for the DoLS (para 2)

(ii) Case B

This covers someone who is subject to the hospital treatment regime but not actually detained in hospital at the moment (para 2). Patients subject to the community treatment regime (see Case C below) are regarded for the time being as not subject to the hospital treatment regime (para 8(2)). So Case B will mainly cover MHA patients on leave of absence. These people are ineligible for the DoLS if the purpose of their detention consists wholly or partly of medical treatment for mental disorder in a hospital (para 4). They are also ineligible if the purpose is inconsistent with a requirement of their MHA regime (para 3). So, for example, the DoLS cannot be used to make them live somewhere other than where they are required to live as a condition of their leave of absence. But the DoLS could be used to support their MHA regime, by keeping them where they are supposed to live, or for some other purpose, such as treatment for physical disorder.

(iii) Case C

This covers someone who is subject to the "community treatment regime" (para 2). This means a community treatment order (CTO) under the MHA but also a statutory obligation to the same effect as a CTO (para 9). This is presumably meant to include the conditional discharge of a restricted patient, which is very similar to, although not the same as, a CTO. People covered by Case C are in the same position as people covered by Case B. So all these people can only be returned to hospital for treatment for mental disorder under the terms of the MHA.

(iv) Case D

This covers people subject to guardianship orders or applications under the MHA or to obligations under another statute which has the same effect (para 10). They, like people covered by Cases B and C, are ineligible if the purpose of the DoLS is to require them to do something inconsistent with a requirement of their MHA regime (para 3). They are also ineligible in the same circumstances as a person covered by Case E is ineligible (para 2).

(v) Case E

This covers people who are "within the scope of the Mental Health Act" but not currently subject to any compulsory powers (or their equivalents) (para 2). A person is "within the scope" of the MHA if he *could* be detained under section 2 or section 3 were an application to be made (para 12). (If the grounds are met, it is to be assumed that the necessary medical recommendations have been given; and in deciding whether the grounds for section 3 are met, it is to be assumed that the necessary treatment cannot be provided under the MCA: these are drafting devices to get round technical objections.) These people are ineligible for the DoLS if the purpose is to authorise them to be accommodated in a hospital for treatment for mental disorder *and* they object either to admission to hospital or to some or all of that treatment (paras 5 and 16). They are also ineligible if a donee or deputy has given a valid consent to everything to which they object (para 5(5)).

In other words, the DoLS scheme is not to be used for an actively objecting patient who could be sectioned under the MHA. The DoLS Code points out that the issue here is simply whether or not the person is objecting, not whether the objection is reasonable (para 4.47); and where there is reason to think that a person would object if he were able to do so, he should be taken to be objecting (para 4.46). The MCA requires the eligibility assessor or court to have regard to all the reasonably ascertainable circumstances including the person's behaviour, his wishes and feelings and his views, beliefs and values (Sch 1A, para 5(7)).

The early case law has been pre-occupied with the eligibility criteria. The exclusion only covers people who are or are to be given treatment for their mental disorder in a hospital. Thus the DoLS (or the Court) can authorise treatment for mental disorder in a care home. In *W PCT v TB, V, S MBC, C & W Partnership NHS Foundation Trust, W MBC* [2009] EWHC 1737 (Fam), the Court authorised the patient's detention in a care home for intensive neuro-psychological and neuro-behavioural therapy to treat her chronic delusional disorder.

But if a person is to be treated in a hospital, what amounts to treatment for his mental disorder? Treatment for mental disorder can include treatment for the physical consequences of mental disorder, such as self-injury and self-poisoning, but not treatment for unrelated physical conditions where the treatment will not impact upon the mental disorder. In *GJ v Foundation Trust, PCT, SS for Health* [2009] EWHC 2972, Charles J pointed out that the scheme did not allow professionals to choose between the MHA and the MCA. The scheme gives primacy to the MHA where it applies. Whether the patient "could" be sectioned under the MHA should be judged by the person doing the eligibility assessment—did she think that the grounds for sectioning were made out? And when asking whether the patient was to be accommodated in a hospital for treatment for mental disorder, a "but for" test should be applied: "but for" the need for treatment for a physical disorder (in that case diabetes) which was unconnected with his mental disorder (in that case vascular dementia, Korsakoff's syndrome and Amnestic Disease due to alcohol) would the patient have to be detained at all? In that case, the reason for depriving the patient of his liberty was the need to treat his uncontrolled diabetes, and not his mental disorders, so this could be authorised under the MCA.

(d) MHA or MCA?

As we have just seen, if the patient is ineligible, the MHA must be used: the professionals cannot choose which scheme is best for the patient. But sometimes it may be preferable to use the MHA even if the patient is not ineligible under the MCA. The MHA Code of Practice (Department of Health, 2008a) advises that if admission to hospital for assessment or treatment for mental disorder is necessary for a patient who lacks the capacity to consent to it, the MHA procedures should be used in two situations. The first is because providing the necessary care or treatment will unavoidably involve depriving the patient of his liberty and the MCA deprivation of liberty safeguards cannot be used (para 4.16). This will arise if the patient is under 18, or has validly refused treatment in an advance decision, or using the MCA scheme would conflict with a decision of the Court of Protection or the patient's attorney or deputy, or most commonly where he objects to being admitted to or remaining in hospital (unless his attorney or deputy consents) (para 4.18). The second is where "for any other reason, the assessment or treatment of the patient [sic] needs cannot be safely or effectively delivered by relying on the MCA alone" (para 4.16). For example: where the patient's lack of capacity to consent is fluctuating or temporary and he is not expected to consent if he regains capacity; or a degree of restraint is required which is justified by the risk to other people but not allowed under the MCA because it is not proportionate to the risk to the patient; or there is some other specific identifiable risk that the patient might not get the treatment needed and either the patient or others might suffer harm as a result (para 4.21). These are the kinds of case in which MHA compulsion might have been used against an apparently compliant incapable patient in the past, but the MCA has brought them more sharply into focus by cutting down the scope of what could be done under the common law doctrine of necessity.

Even if the MCA scheme could be used, because the patient does not object, there may be advantages for everyone in using the MHA instead. The detailed procedures and effects under each scheme will be discussed in later chapters. In summary, however, the MCA scheme requires there to be an assessment of whether each of conditions (a) to (f) (p 18 above) is met. The managing authority of a hospital or care home must request an authorisation from their supervisory body where all six requirements are likely to be met and the person concerned either is already, or is likely within 28 days to become, a detained resident in that hospital or care home. If those six requirements are met, the supervisory body must give the authorisation requested. They can decide how long it should last, which must not be more than the best interests assessment suggests, and in any event no longer than a year. The person concerned, his representative or the hospital or home can request a review. And the whole scheme is subject to the power of the Court of Protection to decide whether the six requirements are met, and upon the period, purpose and conditions of any authorisation: 2005 Act, section 21A. The scheme also provides for an independent mental capacity advocate to be appointed for a person who is subject to the scheme and has no-one, other than a professional or paid carer, whom it would be appropriate to consult about what would be in his best interests.

It remains to be seen whether these procedures will safeguard the interests of patients detained in hospital for treatment for mental disorder as effectively as the MHA procedures are meant to do. They are of course the only procedures which authorise detention in an ordinary care home or in hospital for treatment for physical disorders. The MHA procedures can be seen as a protection of, rather than a threat to, the patient's integrity. They are designed to ensure that active and precise attention is given to the patient's case by medical staff. The case must periodically be reconsidered at consultant level. The time limits are shorter and there is speedy access to a tribunal rather than to the Court (compare the length and complexity of the proceedings in *W PCT v TB, V, S MBC, C & W Partnership NHS Foundation Trust, W MBC* [2009] EWHC 1737 (Fam) and *GJ v Foundation Trust, PCT, SS for Health* [2009] EWHC 2972 with tribunal proceedings). The patient can conduct his own case before the tribunal whereas before the Court he has to be represented by a litigation friend. The MHA covers what care and treatment may be given to detained patients. The

MCA deprivation of liberty scheme does not deal with this, but leaves it to the general principles in the Act: see below and chapter 6.

5. IN-PATIENTS' DETENTION UNDER SECTION 5 OF THE MENTAL HEALTH ACT

Section 5(1) of the MHA makes it clear that an application for compulsory "admission" to hospital for treatment for mental disorder may be made in respect of a patient who has already been informally admitted to hospital. Indeed, we have already seen that a substantial number of applications relate to patients in hospital, most of them informal. If the authorities are not immediately able to complete an application, perhaps because a relative or approved mental health professional is not available, section 5 provides two procedures for keeping an informal patient in the hospital for a short time. Neither can be used to prolong the detention of a patient whose "section" is about to expire (s 5(6)) and neither gives any statutory power to impose treatment without consent (s 56(3)(b)).

Both powers apply only to someone who is already an "in-patient," a term which is not defined. In ordinary language, it is usual to distinguish between an out-patient, who attends for an appointment with a specialist or for emergency treatment in casualty, and an in-patient, who has been allocated a bed in a ward. The MHA Code confirms that it refers to patients admitted for treatment for physical or mental disorder, including those who are subject to the MCA DoLS, but not to those already subject to compulsory admission or community treatment under the MHA, or to outpatients (paras 12.6, 12.7). Thus these powers should not be used as a way of preventing a would-be suicide from leaving casualty when he comes round after having been "washed out", or to convert a day patient into an in-patient.

(a) The clinician's power

Under section 5(2), the doctor or approved clinician (for definition see p 102, later) in charge of an in-patient's treatment may furnish the hospital managers with a report which authorises the patient's detention in the hospital for 72 hours from the time when the report is "furnished". The Code suggests (para 12.5) that this is when it is put into the hospital's internal mail system, no doubt because the Mental Health (Hospital, Guardianship and Treatment) Regulations 2008 (SI 2008/1184) (the MHHGT Regs), reg 3(7), provides that where a document is delivered using an internal mail system "service" takes place then; but the prescribed form requires the hospital managers to record the time of receipt which suggests that it is only "furnished" to them when received (reg 4(1)(g), Form H1). The section is not specific about who may do the detaining (compare s 6(2), p 120, later). For example, could the doctor authorise the staff to detain the patient even though the hospital managers wished to release him? The doctor or approved clinician "in charge" is thought to mean the consultant (or other) on whose list the patient is; but she may nominate *one* other doctor or approved clinician, whether or not on the staff of the same hospital, to act for her in her absence (s 5(3), (3A); that delegate cannot herself delegate to another, for "*delegatus non potest delegare*"). Some doubt whether allowing an approved clinician who is not a doctor to authorise detention is compatible with article 5 of the ECHR, which requires that "unsoundness of mind" be established on the basis of "objective medical expertise", but this may be possible for a short period in an emergency (*Winterwerp v The Netherlands* (1979) 2 EHRR 387).

The criterion for making these reports is simply that "it appears to" the doctor concerned "that an application ought to be made" for compulsory admission under the Act. This is not as wide as at first it appears. The words do not suggest that a purely speculative detention of a patient who *might* be liable to compulsion is allowed, still less of a patient whom the doctor does not genuinely believe to be "sectionable". The prescribed form requires her to explain the reasons for her opinion, including why informal treatment is not or is no longer appropriate. Nevertheless, the power does apply to *any* doctor or approved clinician in charge of *any* patient in *any* hospital for *any* reason. It allows, for example, an obstetrician to detain a woman whom she believes has become "sectionable" after childbirth; but the Code advises that she should contact a psychiatrist immediately (para 12.10) and if a patient is under the care of both a psychiatrist and a non-psychiatrist, the former should be preferred for this purpose (para 12.4).

(b) The nurse's power

Section 5(4) permits even swifter action by a nurse registered in sub-parts 1 or 2 of the register kept by the Nursing and Midwifery Council whose entry indicates that her field of practice is mental health or learning disabilities nursing (see the Mental Health (Nurses) Order 2008, art 2). The in-patient must already be "receiving treatment for mental disorder". The nurse must believe:

"(a) that the patient is suffering from mental disorder to such a degree that it is necessary for his health or safety or for the protection of others for him to be immediately restrained from leaving the hospital; and (b) that it is not practicable to secure the immediate attendance"

of the doctor or clinician who could act under section 5(2). The power is clearly aimed at patients who are threatening to leave the hospital at any minute. It should not be used to restrain or seclude patients during an episode of disturbed behaviour.

The nurse must record her belief on the prescribed form (reg 4(1)(h), Form H2). The *form* does not require reasons, but the Code (para 12.31) states that these should be recorded in the patient's notes; and that before acting the nurse should assess: the likely arrival time of the doctor as against the likely intention of the patient to leave; and the harm to the patient or others if he did leave before the doctor arrived (para 12.27); in balancing these, nurses should consider the patient's expressed intentions, the likelihood of his harming himself or others or behaving violently, any evidence of disordered thinking, his current behaviour and, in particular, any changes in his usual behaviour, any recent messages from relatives or friends, whether the date is one of special significance for the patient, any recent disturbance on the ward, any relevant involvement of other patients, and history of unpredictability or impulsiveness, any formal risk assessments undertaken (specifically looking at previous behaviour) and "any other relevant information from other members of the interdisciplinary team" (para 12.28).

There is then *immediate* authority to detain the patient in the hospital for six hours or until the earlier arrival of the doctor. Accurate recording of the time when the report is made is obviously essential. The initial record must be delivered to the managers, either by the nurse or someone authorised by her, as soon as possible after it is made. Once again, it is not clear what would happen if the managers disagreed. The Code advises that the doctor or approved clinician should treat it as an emergency and not wait until the six hours are nearly up before arriving (para 12.32). If no-one arrives within the six hours, this should be treated as a "serious failing" (para 12.34). When the doctor or clinician arrives, she may invoke the power under section 5(2), although in theory the patient might disappear while she is doing so; the 72 hours are then calculated from the time when the nurse made the record (s 5(5)). If the doctor does nothing, however, the section 5(4) detention lapses and the patient is free to go.

(c) Use and effect

Both powers envisage a decision by a doctor, clinician or nurse who is on the spot (see, for example, the reference to the "attendance" of the doctor in section 5(4)). It is clearly unlawful to leave blank forms ready signed to be used by other staff as and when needed (see Code, para 12.17). The Act does not specify (as it does elsewhere) that the doctor must have examined the patient, but the Code does require this (para 12.9) and it is probably unlawful for her to rely on information given over the telephone. There have been allegations of such tactics (Miller, 1975) and, more seriously, of using the power as a handy substitute for the full compulsory procedures, for example by persuading a patient to enter hospital informally and making a report the same day (Bean, 1980), or as a periodic means of persuading long-stay patients to co-operate in their treatment. More worrying still would be the use of this power to facilitate the transfer of a difficult patient from one hospital to another. However, as the Code (para 12.40) points out, it is not possible for patients detained under section 5 to be transferred to another hospital under section 19 (see p 239, later). So they may only lawfully be transferred with their consent or perhaps under the common law doctrine of necessity, where urgent treatment is essential and the patient is unable to decide for himself; but transferring an acutely disturbed patient can be dangerous, disruptive and frightening for him.

Detaining a patient under section 5(2) or 5(4) gives no power under the MHA to treat the patient without his consent. In this respect they are in the same position as an informal patient (see further in chapter 6). The detention cannot be renewed (although it can be invoked periodically from time to time). If not replaced by an admission for assessment under section 2 or for treatment under section 3, or an authority to detain under the MCA DoLS, therefore, the patient is free to go and must be told so immediately (Code, para 12.20). The time of lapse should be recorded, preferably using a standardised system established by the hospital managers, along with the reason why the patient is no longer detained and what has happened to him (Code, para 12.35).

Official figures used to imply that section 5 was very rarely used; indeed, if only status on admission was recorded, they should have shown that it was not used at all. Now that changes in legal status are recorded, the figures confirm the Mental Health Act Commission's experience that "considerable use" is made of it in some hospitals: in England in 2007–2008, 7,171 informal patients were detained under section 5(2) and 1,365 under section 5(4); 986 detentions under section 5(4) were converted into detentions under section 5(2). 2,430 detentions under section 5(2) were converted into admissions for assessment under section 2, and 2,721 into admissions for treatment under section 3. Only 82 detentions under section 5(4) led immediately to admissions under section 2 or 3 (Health and Social Care Information Centre, 2008a). No doubt doctors and nurses are reluctant to jeopardise their relationships with informal patients by holding this sort of threat over them, although the patient who knows that the power exists may not appreciate this. The existence of compulsory powers casts an inevitable shadow over all hospital admissions for mental disorder, even if most informal patients are less affected by it than might be supposed (Cavadino, 1988).

6. AN OUTLINE OF THE OTHER MENTAL HEALTH ACT POWERS

Although most patients are admitted informally, the use of compulsion is a comparatively common event. Before the details are examined in later chapters, it may be helpful to summarise all the various MHA powers to admit "patients" to hospital, or persons to a place of safety, or to place patients under guardianship or compulsory treatment in the community. A "patient" is "a person suffering or appearing to be suffering from mental disorder" (s 145(1)). Also mentioned will be some analogous powers under other legislation.

(a) Hospital admission under Part 2 of the MHA

Most compulsory patients are admitted to hospital by means of a formal application, made by the patient's nearest relative or an approved mental health professional (AMHP) with medical support, to a particular hospital. If accepted by that hospital, it is sufficient authority to detain and usually to treat the patient against his will. There are three types of application for admission to hospital, colloquially known as "sections". All are subject to review by an independent tribunal.

(i) Under section 2, an application for *admission for assessment* authorises the patient's detention for up to 28 days. Most forms of treatment for his mental disorder may be given without his consent during that time. The application may be made either by the patient's nearest relative or by an AMHP and must be supported by recommendations from two doctors, one an approved specialist in mental disorder, to the effect that:

(a) the patient "is suffering from mental disorder of a nature or degree which warrants the detention of the patient in a hospital for assessment (or for assessment followed by medical treatment) for at least a limited period; and

(b) he ought to be so detained in the interests of his own health or safety or with a view to the protection of other persons."

(ii) Under section 4, an application for *admission for assessment* may be made *in an emergency* by the nearest relative or by an AMHP with the support of only one medical recommendation. The doctor need not be an approved specialist, although she should, if possible, be previously acquainted with the patient (for example, his GP). The grounds are the same as for a section 2 admission, but both the applicant and the doctor must also state that "it is of urgent necessity for the patient to be admitted and detained under section 2" and that "compliance with the provisions . . . relating to applications under that section would involve undesirable delay". The application authorises detention for up to 72 hours, but the admission may be converted into an ordinary section 2 admission by the provision of a second medical recommendation within that time. Unless and until that is given, however, there is no statutory power to impose treatment without consent.

(iii) Under section 3, an application for *admission for treatment* may again be made either by the nearest relative or by an AMHP. However, if the nearest relative objects to the admission, the AMHP must seek authority from a county court. An admission under section 2 is extended while this is being decided. If admitted under section 3, a patient may be detained in the first instance for up to six months. Then the detention may be renewed, on the advice of the responsible clinician (RC), for a second six months and thereafter for a year at a time. Most forms of treatment for the patient's mental disorder may be given without his consent. The initial application must be supported by recommendations from two doctors, one an approved specialist, to the effect that:

   (a) the patient "is suffering from mental disorder of a nature or degree which makes it appropriate for him to receive medical treatment in a hospital; and ...

   (c) it is necessary for the health or safety of the patient or for the protection of other persons that he should receive such treatment and it cannot be provided unless he is detained under this section; and

   (d) appropriate medical treatment is available for him."

(b) Community treatment and guardianship under Part 2 of the MHA

(i) Under section 17A, introduced by the 2007 Act, the responsible clinician (RC) (for definition, see p 102, later) may discharge a patient detained for treatment subject to his being liable to recall to hospital. This is known in the Act as a *community treatment order* (CTO) but in the MHA Code as supervised community treatment (SCT). An AMHP must agree that the criteria are met and that the order is appropriate. The criteria are that:

   (a) the patient is suffering from mental disorder of a nature or degree which makes it appropriate for him to receive medical treatment;

   (b) it is necessary for his health or safety or for the protection of other persons that he should receive such treatment;

   (c) subject to his being liable to recall, such treatment can be provided without his continuing to be detained in hospital;

   (d) it is necessary that the responsible clinician should be able to recall him to hospital; and

   (e) appropriate medical treatment is available for him.

The order must contain conditions, necessary or appropriate to ensure that the patient receives treatment, to prevent risk of harm to the patient, or to protect other people. However, a patient with capacity cannot be given treatment without his consent and a patient without capacity cannot be given treatment which he resists, so there is no power to impose forcible treatment while the patient is in the community. The admission for treatment continues but the power to detain under it is suspended. The patient may be recalled to hospital if the RC thinks that he needs hospital treatment for his disorder and that there would a risk of harm to the patient or others if he were not recalled.

(ii) Under section 7, an application for the reception of a patient aged 16 or over into the *guardianship* of a local social services authority or private individual may be made in the same way as an application for admission for hospital treatment but to the local authority rather than the hospital. The grounds are:

(a) that the patient "is suffering from mental disorder of a nature or degree which warrants his reception into guardianship under this section"; and

(b) that "it is necessary in the interests of the welfare of the patient or for the protection of other persons that the patient should be so received."

The guardian can dictate where the patient is to live, how he is to spend his time and who must be allowed to see him, but cannot insist that he accepts treatment for his disorder.

(c) Powers over criminal offenders under Part 3 of the MHA

A much smaller number of patients are admitted as a result of the orders of a court or the directions of the Justice Secretary, after they have been accused or found guilty of criminal offences. All are conditional on a bed actually being available within a limited time.

(i) Before an accused is tried or a convicted person sentenced, section 35 of the 1983 Act allows both a magistrates' court and the Crown Court to *remand him to hospital for a report* on his mental condition. The court must have evidence from one specialist doctor that "there is reason to suspect that the accused person is suffering from mental disorder" and be of the opinion that it would be impracticable to make such a report if he were remanded on bail. Remands are for up to 28 days at a time and only 12 weeks in total.

(ii) Under section 36, the Crown Court may *remand an accused person to hospital for treatment* where there is evidence from two doctors, one an approved specialist, that he is suffering from mental disorder of a nature or degree which makes it appropriate for him to be detained in hospital for treatment and appropriate treatment is available.

(iii) Under section 38, all courts may make an *interim hospital order*, for up to six months in all, over a convicted offender, if they have evidence from two doctors, one approved, that he is suffering from mental disorder and that there is reason to suppose that the disorder is such that a hospital order may be appropriate.

(iv) Under section 37, all courts may make an ordinary *hospital order* over certain criminal offenders, provided that a suitable hospital bed is available. The effect is almost identical to that of an admission for treatment under section 3 of the 1983 Act, so that the patient's fate is controlled by the medical authorities or a tribunal rather than the court or the Ministry of Justice. The grounds are that:

"(a) the court is satisfied, on the written or oral evidence of two registered medical practitioners, that the offender is suffering from mental disorder and that ... the mental disorder from which the offender is suffering is of a nature or degree which makes it appropriate for him to be detained in a hospital for medical treatment ... and

(b) the court is of the opinion, having regard to all the circumstances including the nature of the offence and the character and antecedents of the offender, and to the other available methods of dealing with him, that the most suitable method of disposing of the case is by means of an order under this section."

There is no express requirement, as there is in all the other long term powers, that appropriate medical treatment actually be available.

(v) Under section 41, the Crown Court may make a *restriction order* if, in addition to the grounds for making an ordinary hospital order,

> "it appears to the court having regard to the nature of the offence, the antecedents of the offender and the risk of his committing further offences if set at large, that it is necessary for the protection of the public from serious harm so to do ... ".

A restriction order removes the usual power of the RC or hospital to decide whether a patient may move or leave. Moving hospitals is the exclusive province of the Justice Secretary and discharge is decided either by the Justice Secretary or by a tribunal. Discharge may be absolute or conditional, but a conditionally discharged patient remains liable to be recalled to hospital by the Justice Secretary. Under section 43, a magistrates' court which has the evidence required for a hospital order may commit an offender to the Crown Court with a view to a restriction order being made; under section 44, the committal may be to hospital if a bed is available.

(vi) Under section 48, the Justice Secretary may direct the *transfer to hospital* of remand and civil prisoners and people detained under the Immigration Act 1971, if he has reports that they are suffering from mental disorder of the appropriate nature or degree, in urgent need of medical treatment, and appropriate medical treatment is available. Remand prisoners must also be made subject to restrictions, but civil prisoners or immigration detainees may be restricted or unrestricted.

(vii) Under section 47, the Justice Secretary may direct the *transfer to hospital* of people serving prison and other custodial sentences, if he has reports that they are suffering from mental disorder of a nature or degree which makes it appropriate for them to be detained in hospital for medical treatment and appropriate treatment is available. Transfers may be with or without restrictions. Any restrictions must end when the imprisonment would have ended, but a patient who was transferred during a prison sentence may remain subject to an ordinary hospital order. Patients transferred with restrictions may be returned to the prison system if the transfer is no longer warranted on medical grounds.

(viii) Under section 45A, the Crown Court which imposes a prison sentence may make a "*hybrid order*" also directing the prisoner's admission to hospital. The criteria and effects are the same as when the Justice Secretary directs the transfer of a sentenced prisoner, but there must also be a limitation direction, which has the same effect as a transfer with restrictions.

(ix) Under section 37 of the MCA, the courts also have power to make a *guardianship order* placing an offender aged 16 or older under the guardianship of a local social services authority or a private individual. The patient must be suffering from mental disorder of a nature or degree which warrants his reception into guardianship and, as with a hospital order, the court must consider this the most suitable method of disposing of the case.

(d) Other powers in criminal cases

(i) The Crown Court may decide that an accused person is *unfit to plead* because of mental disorder but did the deed charged against him or is *not guilty by reason of insanity* of what would otherwise be a crime. Under the Criminal Procedure

(Insanity) Act 1964, section 5(2), the court must choose between a hospital order, with or without restrictions, a supervision order (which may contain a requirement for mental health treatment), or an absolute discharge. People found unfit to plead who are placed under restrictions may have to return to face trial if they become fit to do so.

(ii) Under the Criminal Justice Act 2003, sections 177(1)(h) and 190(1)(h), all courts which impose a community order or a suspended prison sentence upon a convicted offender may include a *mental health treatment requirement* in the order. This means that he must submit to treatment for his mental condition by or under the direction of a doctor or chartered psychologist. There must be evidence from one specialist doctor that the offender's mental condition requires and may be susceptible to treatment but does not warrant a hospital or guardianship order. The court must be satisfied that the necessary arrangements have been or can be made and that the offender consents. If the patient is admitted to hospital, however, he is an informal patient unless other compulsory powers are taken and thus there is no statutory power to impose treatment without his consent, although his failure to co-operate may sometimes be a breach of the order.

(e) Detention in a "place of safety" under the MHA

There are two provisions of the MHA under which a person may be taken to and detained for up to 72 hours in a "place of safety". This includes (among other places) both a hospital and a police station. These give no authority to treat the patient without his consent.

(i) Under section 136, if a police officer finds in a place to which the public have access "a person who appears to him to be suffering from mental disorder and to be in immediate need of care or control", he may, if he thinks it necessary in the interests of that person or for the protection of other persons, remove the person to a place of safety.

(ii) Under section 135(1), an AMHP may apply to a magistrate for a warrant which will permit a police officer to enter premises, by force if need be. The AMHP must swear that:

> "there is reasonable cause to suspect that a person believed to be suffering from mental disorder (a) has been, or is being, ill-treated, neglected or kept otherwise than under proper control, or (b) being unable to care for himself, is living alone".

The police officer must be accompanied by an AMHP and a doctor, and once entry has been gained, the person may, if thought fit, be removed to a place of safety without being formally "sectioned".

(f) Similar powers under other legislation

Some people who are suffering from mental disorder may find themselves detained in hospital, or elsewhere, under quite different legislation. The two major examples relate to the young and the old respectively.

(i) Under the *Children Act 1989*, children who are being looked after by local authorities, whether under a care order or other compulsory powers or by arrangement with their parents, may be placed for treatment or assessment in psychiatric facilities. Provided that certain conditions and procedures are fulfilled, these may include secure facilities.

(ii) Under section 47 of the *National Assistance Act 1948*, a local authority may apply to a magistrates' court for the removal to hospital "or other suitable place" of a person who, according to the certificate of the community physician: (a) is suffering from grave chronic disease *or* being aged, infirm or physically incapacitated, is living in insanitary conditions; *and* (b) is unable to devote to himself, and is not receiving from other persons, proper care and attention. The initial order is for up to three months, but it may be renewed for further periods of up to three months at a time. If the evidence of two doctors is available, there is an emergency procedure under the National Assistance (Amendment) Act 1951 for applying to a single magistrate without giving notice to the person concerned.

7. AN OUTLINE OF THE MENTAL CAPACITY ACT POWERS

The MCA is intended to cover the ground covered by the common law doctrine of necessity and the inherent jurisdiction of the High Court to declare whether acts or proposed acts relating the people who lack capacity are lawful (which still remain), and the former MHA jurisdiction of the Court of Protection over the property and affairs of people found incapable of managing these for themselves (which is replaced). It authorises certain people to take particular decisions on behalf of a person who lacks the capacity to take that decision (for the test see chapter 2). It does not authorise anyone to deprive a person of his liberty, except in the three circumstances already explained (see above). All decisions must be taken in the best interests of the person concerned and for no other reason.

(i) Section 5(1), (2) authorises a person (D) to *act in connection with the care or treatment* of another person (P) if:

"(a) before doing the act, D takes reasonable steps to establish whether P lacks capacity in relation to the matter in question, and
(b) when doing the act D reasonably believes—

(i) that P lacks capacity in relation to the matter, and
(ii) that it will be in P's best interests for the act to be done."

This does not allow acts intended to restrain P, unless D reasonably believes that the act is necessary in order to prevent harm to P and the act is a proportionate response both to the likelihood and the seriousness of the harm (s 6(1), (2), (3)). Restraint means using or threatening force to secure the doing of an act which P resists or restricting P's liberty of movement whether or not he resists (s 6(4)).

(ii) Section 9(1) allows a person (P) to make a *lasting power of attorney* (LPA) giving another person or persons power to make decisions about his personal welfare (after he becomes incapable of acting for himself) or his property and affairs (whether or not he becomes incapable). The donee can only act within the scope of the authority that P has given him. Additionally, he cannot restrain P unless the conditions in (i) above apply: reasonable belief that P lacks capacity and that it is necessary to prevent harm to P and proportionality to both the likelihood and the seriousness of the harm (s 11(1), (2), (3), (4)). Nor can the donee give or refuse consent to life-sustaining treatment unless expressly authorised in the LPA to do so (s 11(8)).

(iii) Section 16(2)(c) allows the Court of Protection to *appoint a deputy* to take decisions on P's behalf in relation to specified matters. Unlike a donee, a deputy cannot take any decision which P has capacity to take for himself (s 20(1)), nor can he refuse consent to life sustaining treatment (s 20(5)). He cannot be authorised to take any decision which is inconsistent with the decision of a donee (within the donee's authority) (s 20(4)). He too cannot restrain P unless acting within the scope of his authority from the court and the other three conditions are also satisfied (s 20(7), (8), (9), (10), (11)).

(iv) The Court of Protection can *make decisions* about the personal welfare or property and affairs of a person who lacks the capacity to make that decision (s 16(1), (2)(a)). This is to be preferred to appointing a deputy (s 16(4)(a)). The Court can order almost anything which is in the best interests of P, including deprivation of liberty (s 4A(3), (4)) unless P is ineligible because the MHA takes precedence (s 16A). It can also make declarations about whether a person does or does not lack capacity to take a particular decision (s 15(1)(a)) or decisions about particular matters (s 15(1)(b)) or about whether an act done or to be done is lawful or unlawful (s 15(1)(c)). It has a supervisory jurisdiction over the DoLS scheme (s 21A) and over the validity and operation of lasting powers of attorney (ss 22, 23).

8. HOSPITALS, HOMES AND MANAGERS

The distinction between a hospital and somewhere else is important, because the MHA only provides for patients to be detained and forcibly treated if they have been admitted to a hospital. But it is not as important as it was, for two reasons. First, patients who lack capacity may be detained in either a hospital or a care home under the MCA scheme. Secondly, the MCA makes it clear that patients who lack capacity may be given treatment without their consent (though not forcibly except in certain emergencies) wherever they are.

(a) Definitions

(i) A hospital under the MHA

The main definition of a "hospital" in the MHA is in section 145(1), which lists the various sorts of NHS hospital:

"(a) any health service hospital within the meaning of the National Health Service Act 2006 or the National Health Service (Wales) Act 2006; and

(b) any accommodation provided by a local authority and used as a hospital by or on behalf of the Secretary of State under the National Health Service Act 2006, or of the Welsh Ministers under the National Health Service (Wales) Act 2006; and

(c) any hospital as defined by section 206 of the National Health Service (Wales) Act 2006 which is vested in a Local Health Board."

The definition does not include prison hospitals, because these are provided by the Secretary of State for Justice under prison legislation, although they are now serviced by local NHS staff. The definition does include Broadmoor, Ashworth and Rampton, the three high security psychiatric hospitals. These used to be known as special hospitals and managed separately from the ordinary NHS facilities but have now been transferred to their local specialist mental health NHS trusts. It also includes hospitals where both high security psychiatric services and other services are provided. If so, the high security unit is treated as a separate hospital from the rest of the hospital for the purpose of the MHA (s 145(1AA)). This means that a patient admitted or ordered to be detained in that unit can only be detained there.

The definition above does not include independent hospitals. But they are brought into the MHA by another route. A "hospital within the meaning of Part 2 of this Act" has the meaning given in section 34 (s 145(1)). Section 34(2) provides that Part 2 applies to a "registered establishment" as it applies to a hospital. Section 34(1) in effect defines a "registered establishment" as one:

"in respect of which a person is registered under Part 2 of the Care Standards Act 2000 as an independent hospital in which treatment or nursing (or both) are provided for persons liable to be detained under this Act".

Under section 2(2) of the Care Standards Act 2000 a hospital which is not a health service hospital is an independent hospital and under section 2(3) a hospital is:

"(a) an establishment

(i) the main purpose of which is to provide medical or psychiatric treatment for illness or mental disorder or palliative care; or
(ii) in which (whether or not other services are also provided) any of the listed services are provided;

(b) any other establishment in which treatment or nursing (or both) are provided for persons liable to be detained under the Mental Health Act 1983."

The listed services referred to in section 2(3)(a)(ii) are medical treatment under anaesthesia or sedation, dental treatment under general anaesthesia, obstetric services and medical services in connection with childbirth, termination of pregnancies, cosmetic surgery, and treatment using prescribed techniques or prescribed technology. The definition therefore covers a wide variety of hospitals and other clinics. But if their main purpose is to provide medical or psychiatric treatment for mental disorder, or if they provide treatment or nursing or both for patients liable to be detained under the MHA, they have to have additional policies and procedures about safety, the management of disturbed behaviour and visitors (see Private and Voluntary Health Care (England) Regulations 2001, SI 2001/3968, Pt 3; for Wales, see SI 2002/325).

Patients can be admitted under the MHA to any hospital (within the above definitions) which is willing to admit them. Hospitals are free to accept or reject any patient they choose. They cannot be obliged to accept anyone even in an emergency. A maternity hospital, for example, could not be made to admit a violently psychotic man. Unfortunately, however, hospitals are equally free to refuse patients for whom their facilities are quite suitable. There are some prospective patients, particularly those who have appeared before the courts, for whom it can be extremely difficult to find any facilities at all. Courts cannot send anyone to hospital unless they have evidence that a bed will be available within seven days, in the case of a remand, or within 28 days, in the case of a hospital order or direction.

(ii) The hospital managers under the MHA

The decision to accept or reject any patient is technically one for the hospital "managers", who also have a number of other important functions under the MHA. In section 145(1) of the MHA, "the managers" are defined as:

"(a)   in relation to a hospital vested in the Secretary of State for the purposes of his functions under the National Health Service Act 2006, or in the Welsh Ministers for the purposes of their functions under the National Health Service (Wales) Act 2006, and in relation to any accommodation provided by a local authority and used as a hospital by or on behalf of the Secretary of State ... or the Welsh Ministers ... [under those Acts], the Primary Care Trust, Strategic Health Authority, Local Health Board or Special Health Authority responsible for the administration of the hospital;

(bb) in relation to a hospital vested in a Primary Care Trust or a National Health Service trust, the trust;

(bc) in relation to a hospital vested in an NHS foundation trust, the trust;

(bd) in relation to a hospital vested in a Local Health Board, the Board;

(c)   in relation to a registered establishment, the person or persons registered in respect of the establishment".

(iii) A hospital under the MCA

For the purpose of the MCA scheme authorising the detention of a person in a hospital or care home, para 175(1) of Schedule A1 defines a "hospital" as either an NHS hospital or an independent hospital. An NHS hospital is defined in the same way as in MHA section 145(1)(a) and (c), above, but not (b). An "independent hospital" means a hospital as defined by section 2(3) of the Care Standards Act 2000.

(iv) A care home under the MCA

Paragraph 178 of Schedule A1 to the MCA gives "care home" the same meaning as in section 3 of the Care Standards Act 2000:

"(1) ... an establishment is a care home if it provides accommodation, together with nursing or personal care, for any of the following persons.

(2)   They are (a) persons who are or have been ill; (b) persons who have or have had a mental disorder; (c) persons who are disabled or infirm; (d) persons who are or have been dependent on alcohol or drugs.

(3)   But an establishment is not a care home if it is (a) a hospital, (b) an independent clinic, or (c) a children's home ... ".

(v) The managing authority under the MCA

Paragraph 176 of Schedule A1 to the MCA defines the "managing authority" in relation to an NHS hospital to the same effect as does section 145(1) of the MHA above (all that differs is the sub-paragraph lettering). In relation to an independent hospital or a care home, the managing authority is the person registered *or required to be* registered under Part 2 of the Care Standards Act 2000 (paras 177, 179). This suggests that these powers may be exercised even though the person is not in fact registered under the Act.

(b) Hospital facilities

Within these wide definitions, what are the facilities in fact available for the care and treatment of people with mental disorders and disabilities? In particular, can the law make any contribution towards ensuring that patients are cared for in the settings most appropriate for them and "under conditions of no greater security than is justified by the degree of danger they present to themselves or others" (Reed, 1992, para 3.3)?

In 2008, there were 255 providers of mental health in-patient care in England and Wales, 98 of them in the NHS and 157 in the independent sector. The NHS still provides the great majority of beds, some 26,700 or 86.2 per cent in 2008; but the independent sector now provides around 4,300 or 13.8 per cent, up from 3,260 or less than 10 per cent, in 2005 (Healthcare Commission, 2008). This increase in independent sector provision is one of the more striking developments over the half century since the 1959 Act was passed on the assumption that the NHS would provide for everyone. The other development is the dramatic reduction in the number of in-patient beds available and the changing nature of the services they provide.

In 1955, there were around 149,000 mental illness beds available in the NHS. But when the 2008 national in-patient census was taken, there were only 31,020 such patients (Healthcare Commission, 2008). For many years the plan was to run down and eventually close the old mental illness hospitals, the former asylums, and replace them with smaller community hospitals and psychiatric units in district general hospitals. In 1979, the Royal Commission on the National Health Service (Merrison, 1979) pointed out that standards in those old hospitals had not been helped, either by the expectation that they would eventually be closed, or by the then widely-held view (founded on the work of sociologists such as Erving Goffman) that such places are inevitably harmful to their patients. The Audit Commission (1994, para 17) reported that:

> "people receiving community care, however inadequate, hardly ever wish to return to hospital. Psychiatric hospital care seems to be strongly disliked by most of the people who have experienced it . . . ".

The Commission also described a vicious circle where most of the money was still tied up in hospital beds; this could not be released until suitable alternative facilities were in place, which in turn needed money; thus sending patients back into hospital unnecessarily and increasing pressure on hospital beds. The division of responsibility for community services, principally between the health and social services authorities, also caused difficulties. Added to this was public resistance based upon the perception of mentally ill people as dangerous to themselves and others. But mental health was identified as one of the five key areas in improving *The Health of the Nation* (Department of Health, 1992). A great deal of effort has since been put into developing a comprehensive range of hospital and community services, especially since targets were set by the *National Service Framework for Mental Health* in 1999. The specialist psychiatric services target their efforts on severely mentally ill people, both in and out of hospital, leaving the primary care services to cater for the less severely ill.

But alongside the reduction in hospital beds has been an increase in the proportion of patients who are detained under the MHA when first admitted to hospital. This was 45 per cent of the patients counted in the 2008 census, an increase from 40 per cent in 2005. This should not surprise us. If the great majority of people with mental health problems can now be treated outside hospital, those who are admitted are likely to have more complex needs which may require at least sometimes to be met within the compulsory framework. This is so irrespective of the type of hospital or unit to which they are admitted. But there are now many different types of unit available.

An aim of the 1959 Act was to enable psychiatric patients to be treated on open wards in just the same way as other patients. But ordinary hospitals found it more and more difficult to manage the more challenging patients on open wards within the usual staffing levels. In the decade after the 1959 Act, this led to a considerable rise in the numbers of patients transferred from ordinary mental illness hospitals to the high security special hospitals which were not then part of the NHS (Parker and Tennent, 1979). Mr Ashingdane (p 37, below) was an example. It also led to an increasing reluctance to admit offender patients, particularly on restriction orders, to ordinary hospitals, whether directly or when they were thought ready to leave the special hospitals.

The obstacles to transferring patients out of special hospitals were enormous (Dell, 1980; Dell and Robertson, 1988). Many patients would be unable to cope if they were released directly into the community from the highly structured environment of a special hospital (see Boynton, 1980; Cohen, 1981; Blom-Cooper, 1992 for descriptions). The public outcry should they offend again would be much louder than any concern at their continued imprisonment. Transfer to an ordinary hospital might encounter opposition from both the staff and the local community (Gunn, 1979). The Mental Health Act Commission regularly highlighted the problem of transfer delays. It attributed these to a combination of lack of alternative facilities, slow decision-making by medical and Home Office authorities and the "tendency of some patients to be unobtrusive" (1989, para 10.1).

The problem then was that there was no half way house. The Butler Committee on Mentally Abnormal Offenders were so horrified by what they found at Broadmoor that they rushed out an interim report (1974) recommending the setting up of secure units in each NHS region as a matter of urgency. Progress was slow at first, not least because some regional health authorities found other more pressing (and popular?) uses for the money. By 1989, however, the Mental Health Act Commission reported that "the most fashionable forensic area is suddenly the Regional Secure Unit" (1989, para 11.9). In the 2006 patient Census, more than half (55 per cent) of detained patients were in general mental health wards, 20 per cent were in low secure wards, another 20 per cent in medium secure wards, and only about 5 per cent were in the three high security hospitals (Healthcare Commission, 2007b).

The high security hospitals have now been integrated into the NHS. But for many years they were managed completely separately from the mainstream services. Broadmoor was opened in 1863 in response to pressure from the Lunacy Commissioners and others to make special provision for dangerous criminal lunatics; Rampton and Moss Side were opened respectively in 1910 and 1919, originally to cater for difficult mental "defectives", whether or not offenders; Park Lane was opened next door to Moss Side in 1974, to reduce overcrowding at Broadmoor; Moss Side and Park Lane together became Ashworth Hospital in 1990. Until 1948, Broadmoor was managed by a Council of Supervision appointed by the Home Secretary, and Rampton and Moss Side were managed by the Board of Control. In 1948 they were transferred to the Ministry of Health, but until 1959 all three were managed by the Board of Control. With the demise of the Board of Control, the Ministry of Health took over. Major policy and resource decisions were taken by central government officials but day to day management was left to the local management team.

"This situation combined notional central control with actual neglect ... The end result was a management vacuum at local level which the Prison Officers' Association in particular was happy to fill." (Fallon, 1999, para 1.18.10).

Dissatisfaction with this led to the creation of the Special Hospitals Service Authority (SHSA) in 1989, with the aims of improving the services offered by the hospitals and developing closer working relationships with the local and regional NHS services. The SHSA in turn was abolished and replaced by three separate health authorities in 1996. Finally, in 2001 these too were abolished and management transferred to the local Trusts.

Not surprisingly, there were many criticisms of the special hospitals, and many critical reports (Boynton, 1980; Health Advisory Service, 1988; Blom-Cooper, 1992). These focussed mainly on their geographical and professional isolation, problems in recruiting staff, and emphasis on containment rather than cure. It was argued that:

"the continuation of these large and unwieldy institutions into the 1990s, when most large mental hospitals have closed, perpetuates anachronistic attitudes and makes the altruistic aim of transforming them into 'centres of excellence' difficult, if not impossible" (Bluglass, 1992).

But then, attempts to make them more like hospitals and less like prisons soon led to concerns that they were now unable to balance security and therapy properly. There were further inquiries into allegations of security lapses at Broadmoor (Broadmoor Management Review, 1997) and Ashworth (Fallon, 1999). One of the problems identified was the treatment of patients with personality disorders on the same wards as those with psychotic illnesses. When more relaxed regimes were introduced, the "psychotic patients appreciated the improvements, whereas the personality disordered patients took advantage of them" (Fallon, 1999, para 1.20.16). One consequence has been a severe reduction in the numbers of patients treated at each of the three hospitals (now less than 1,000 in all). Another has been the development of specialist units within Broadmoor and Rampton treating patients with "dangerous and severe personality disorder", a diagnosis which is by no means universally accepted by psychiatrists.

(c) Getting the right bed

There undoubtedly were some inappropriate admissions to special hospitals in the past. Perhaps the best known example is Nigel Smith (referred to by Scarman LJ in *R v McFarlane* (1975) 60 Cr App R 320 at 324). He was admitted to Broadmoor on a restriction order after committing a relatively minor series of frauds. He had no prior history of violence or mental illness, but he did make the mistake of confessing violent feelings towards his mother during an interview in prison with a Broadmoor psychiatrist. Scarman LJ remarked that "one wonders how the criteria indicated" for such admissions "could have been said to have been met". But because there was no other suitable place for him to go, "inevitably he goes to the sort of hospital which should not be cluttered up with cases of his sort". This is much less likely today, but there are still many offenders who ought to be in hospital but have to be sent to prison because there is no hospital bed available.

Two sections of the MHA are aimed at meeting the difficulties in securing an appropriate hospital bed. First, section 140 obliges every Primary Care Trust (PCT) and Local Health Board (LHB) to notify all the local social services authorities in their area of the hospitals run by or available to them in which there are arrangements to receive patients in cases of "special urgency". As amended by the 2007 Act, section 140 also requires the PCT or LHB to notify social services of hospitals where there are arrangements to provide accommodation or facilities "designed so as to be specially suitable" for patients under the age of 18. This was to meet the obvious concern that children were being treated on unsuitable adult wards. There is as yet no statutory provision designed to meet the equally obvious concern that vulnerable women patients are being treated on unsuitable mixed-sex wards.

Before the 1983 Act, there was a strong call for a legal obligation actually to supply a bed, at least for mentally ill offenders. MIND (see Gostin, 1977) reported many cases where judges had felt forced to send disordered offenders to prison simply because no suitable bed could be found. However much the judges may say that the prisons should not be used to fill the gaps in the hospital and social services, they often have little option because prison is the only default disposal. Section 39(1) of the MCA allows any court which is thinking of making a hospital order or interim hospital order to request from the PCT or LHB for the area where the patient lives or last lived, or from the Welsh National Assembly or any other PCT or LHB which it thinks appropriate, such information as they have or can reasonably obtain about hospitals in their area or elsewhere which might be prepared to take the patient. For prospective patients under 18, this power also applies to courts minded to remand the child to hospital for reports or treatment, and the court may request information about facilities or accommodation specially designed for them (s 39(1A), (1B). The Trust, Board or Assembly must comply with the request for information, but is still at liberty to say that there is nothing available.

Is there any legal remedy available to a patient who requires treatment but has been refused a bed, or has been kept in a secure hospital or unit longer than necessary because a more suitable bed has not been provided, or been sent to prison because no hospital will have him? The short answer is "not likely". In *Ashingdane v Department of Health and Social Security* [1981] CLY 175u, CA, 18 February 1980, a Broadmoor patient was deemed ready to transfer back into his local hospital but was refused a bed because the nurses' trade union operated a ban on taking restriction order patients. He launched actions against the union branch secretaries, the Secretary of State and the area health authority. He claimed that the Secretary of State was in breach of the duty under the (then) National Health Service Act 1977 Act section 3(1)(a), to supply "hospital accommodation to the extent that he considers necessary to meet all reasonable requirements". He also claimed that it was unlawful for both the Secretary of State and the health authority to take any account of the union ban in reaching their decisions. The actions against the Secretary of State and the health authority were stayed, for at that time the 1959 Act gave them virtual immunity from action (see the discussion of what is now section 139 of the 1983 Act in chapter 10). The action against the nurses was allowed to proceed, because it was not their business to decide upon admissions under the Mental Health Act and so they were not covered by the immunity; it was eventually discontinued when Mr Ashingdane was transferred. (There was a suggestion by Lawton LJ, in *R v*

Harding (Bernard) (1983) 5 Cr App Rep (S) 197, that it might be contempt of court to frustrate a court order in such a way.)

A duty placed by statute upon a public authority to provide certain services does not give rise to a right to sue for damages (or some other remedy to enforce it directly) unless the statute expressly or impliedly intends this (*Cocks v Thanet DC* [1983] 2 AC 286). Many duties to provide services are only "target" or "framework" duties owed to the client population at large rather than to the particular individual (*R (G) v Barnet LBC* [2003] UKHL 57, [2004] 2 AC 208). This is certainly true of the duty to provide NHS services (compare some community care duties in chapter 9).

Nevertheless a person may sometimes be able to bring judicial review proceedings to challenge a decision to deny him a service, not on the ground that the decision was wrong, but on the ground that it was illegal, irrational or procedurally unfair. The courts have not been afraid to use judicial review to challenge the individual decisions of doctors, tribunals and the Home Secretary under the MHA procedures. But that is a very different matter from saying that individuals have a right to be provided with a particular service or to have the court devise the authorities' policies and priorities in relation to the level of service provided. In *R v Cambridge District Health Authority, ex p B* [1995] 1 WLR 898, for example, the Court of Appeal would not interfere with the authority's decision to refuse to fund further treatment for a child suffering from leukaemia; the Master of the Rolls held that it was not for courts to make the agonising judgments about how best to allocate a limited budget for the maximum advantage of the maximum number of patients. Even so, an allocation policy, or a decision to refuse a particular patient a bed might be challenged if it were reached on obviously irrational or unfair grounds: see, eg, *R v North West Lancashire Health Authority, ex p A* [2000] 1 WLR 977, where the authority's policy of treating gender dysphoria only by psychiatric reassurance was struck down. The problem is that judicial review can only oblige the NHS body to think again. And any bed, however unsuitable, might be better than no bed at all.

Has the Human Rights Act 1998 made any difference? Mr Ashingdane took his case to the European Court of Human Rights in Strasbourg: see *Ashingdane v United Kingdom* (1985) 7 EHRR 528. Among other things, he complained that his detention in Broadmoor was not covered by "the lawful detention of persons of unsound mind" in article 5(1)(e) because he did not need to be there. The Strasbourg Court accepted that there had to be a relationship between the ground for detention and the place and conditions of detention. In principle it would only be lawful to detain someone on the ground of mental disorder in a hospital, clinic or other place appropriate for that purpose. But different though the regimes at Broadmoor and the local hospital were, and important though this was for the patient's quality of life, they were both psychiatric hospitals. Keeping him in Broadmoor longer than was strictly necessary did not change the character of his detention or make it unlawful.

In other cases, it has been argued that the conditions in hospital, especially the high security hospitals, fall foul of the absolute prohibition of torture or inhuman or degrading treatment or punishment in article 3 of the ECHR. In *B v United Kingdom*, App no 6870/75, a patient complained that his detention in a special hospital constituted "inhuman or degrading treatment or punishment". This was based partly on the conditions in Broadmoor and partly on the deleterious effects of being confined in a place which was inappropriate both to his offences and to his needs. The European Commission on Human Rights investigated the facts, but decided by eight votes to five that there had been no violation of article 3. Nevertheless, it is not at all impossible that the effect upon the patient of being detained in wholly unsuitable surroundings which are actually damaging rather than beneficial to his health might bring a case within article 3. In *R v Drew* [2003] UKHL 25, [2003] 1 WLR 1213, at para 18, Lord Bingham agreed that:

> "to subject a defendant [qualifying for an automatic life sentence] to unnecessary suffering, humiliation, distress and deterioration of his mental condition could properly be regarded as inhuman or degrading treatment or punishment".

If this applies to a mentally ill offender who is kept in prison when he should be in hospital, it might also apply to a compulsory patient who is kept in a hospital environment which is seriously damaging his health when he should be elsewhere.

9. THE CODES OF PRACTICE

(a) The MHA Codes

Section 118 of the MHA requires the Secretary of State for Health to draw up a Code of Practice in consultation with other concerned bodies (s 118(1), (3)) and to revise it from time to time. The Care Quality Commission may make proposals to him about what the English Code should contain (s 118(7)). The code must be laid before Parliament, which can reject it by passing a resolution within 40 days (s 118(4), (5)). The Code has two purposes: (a) to give guidance to doctors, approved clinicians, managers and staff of hospitals, including independent hospitals and care homes, and to AMHPs, in relation to the admission of patients to hospital, including registered establishments, and to guardianship and community patients under the Act; and (b) to give guidance to doctors and other professionals about the medical treatment of patients suffering from mental disorder (s 118(1)). The former could cover guidelines for distinguishing between informal and compulsory cases. The latter is not limited to hospital patients but only covers medical treatment. In particular, the Code is expected to identify treatments which give rise to such concern that they "should not be given" without both informed consent and a second opinion, even though this has not been made a legal requirement (s 118(2)).

In *R (Munjaz) v Mersey Care NHS Trust* [2005] UKHL 58, [2006] 2 AC 148, the House of Lords gave a wide meaning to "admission", so that the Code could cover nursing and caring for a patient in seclusion even though seclusion could not properly form part of a treatment programme. However, the Law Lords also held that the Code was guidance, not instruction. Any hospital should consider it with great care and only depart from it for "cogent reasons". But it could do so as a matter of general policy and not just in individual cases. The stance taken by the various parties in *Munjaz* also reflects some of the differences of opinion between the Secretary of State and the Mental Health Act Commission (MHAC) over the years.

Section 118 dates back to the 1983 Act. The MHAC prepared a draft Code of Practice in 1985. This was apparently found helpful by some practitioners but did not find favour with the Secretary of State. He arranged for an independent working group to draft a Code which was laid before Parliament in December 1989 and revised in 1993. A further Code, in which the MHAC played a considerable part, was promulgated in 1999 with the coming into force of the Human Rights Act 1998 very clearly in mind. But in *Munjaz*, the Secretary of State sided with the hospital in arguing that his own Code did not have to be observed, while the MHAC and MIND sided with the patient in arguing that it did. The outcome of the particular dispute is that the new Code leaves considerable freedom to hospitals to segregate particularly dangerous patients (see chapter 6). However, the Act does now make it explicit that the persons mentioned in (a) and (b) above must have regard to the Code when performing their functions under the MHA (s 118(2D)).

Further, although the MHA itself does not contain a statement of principles, the Code must now do so (s 118(2A)). This must address respect for the patient's past and present wishes and feelings, respect for diversity generally, minimising restrictions on liberty, the involvement of patients in planning, developing and delivering care and treatment, the avoidance of discrimination the effectiveness of treatment, the views of carers and other interested parties, patient well-being and safety, and public safety (s 118(2B)). But the Secretary of State must also have regard to the efficient use of resources and the equitable distribution of services (s 118(2C)). Most of these are reflected in the five guiding principles which form chapter 1 of the 2008 Code (see p 6, earlier).

Since devolution, the Welsh Ministers have taken over responsibility for health and social services in Wales. The Minister for Health and Social Services has therefore issued a separate Code of Practice for Wales, in both Welsh and English, which differs in structure and sometimes in content from the English Code. Unfortunately, there is not space in this book to cover them both.

(b) The MCA Codes

Section 42 of the MCA requires the Lord Chancellor to issue one or more Codes of Practice for the guidance of carers, donees of lasting powers of attorney, deputies appointed by the Court of Protection, researchers, independent mental capacity advocates, people operating the DoLS, representatives of people subject to the DoLS, and with respect to advance decisions. Donees, deputies, researchers, advocates, representatives and people operating the DoLS all have a duty to "have regard" to any relevant code when taking action about a person who lacks capacity, as do others who are acting in a professional capacity or are paid (s 42(4)). So unpaid carers do not have to follow the Code (although they may find it very useful) while unpaid donees, deputies and representatives do; so do doctors, nurses, care-workers, social workers, ambulance personnel, police and others whose work brings them in contact with people who lack capacity to make their own decisions. Courts and tribunals have to take account of the Code and a failure to comply with it, if this is relevant in any civil or criminal proceedings they are conducting (s 42(5)). The main MCA Code explains that this does not mean that these people have to "comply" with it, but that if they do not, they will be expected to have good reasons for departing from it.

The main MCA Code was published in 2007 when the Act came into force and is nearly 300 pages long. But it is written in clear, accessible language with many helpful examples of how the Act may work in practice—although it is quick to say that these should not be used as templates for what to do in similar situations. Another Code was published in 2009 when the Deprivation of Liberty Safeguards came into force. Both MCA Codes apply in Wales as well as in England.

2. MENTAL DISORDER, MENTAL CAPACITY AND THE GROUNDS FOR INTERVENTION

1. PSYCHIATRY IS A PROBLEM

Defining mental disorder is not a simple matter, either for lawyers or for doctors. Lawyers realise that "psychiatry is not an exact science. Diagnosis is not easy or clear-cut": *R (B) v Ashworth Hospital Authority* [2005] UKHL 20, [2005] 2 AC 278, para 31. Doctors have been observing, defining and categorising mental disorders since medieval times. Yet they, too, acknowledge that there are special difficulties which mean that defining and diagnosing mental disorder is not as straightforward as defining and diagnosing physical disorder. And for both lawyers and doctors, the underlying problem is to identify just what it is about a mental disorder which justifies different legal consequences from the consequences of a physical disorder.

A disorder of the "mind" is not the same as a disorder of the "brain", although the former may be caused by the latter. The Oxford English Dictionary definition of "mind" includes "the seat of consciousness, thoughts, volitions and feelings". But how are we to know when these functions have become so abnormal as to warrant the term "disorder or disability"? It is often said (in psychiatric textbooks) that with a physical disease or disability, a doctor can presuppose a state of perfect or "normal" bodily health (however unusual that may be in practice) and then point to the ways in which the patient's condition falls short of this. A state of perfect mental health is probably unattainable and certainly cannot be defined. The doctor has instead to presuppose some average standard of mental functioning; and it is not enough that the patient deviates from this, for some deviations are in the better-than-average direction. Even if the patient's mental state is below the average, the doctor still has to decide how far below is sufficiently abnormal, among the vast range of possible variations, to be labelled a "disorder or disability".

If this be so, it casts doubt upon the *validity* of many diagnoses of mental disorder, for they cannot have the same objectivity as a finding of physical disorder. However, in practice, the distinction between them is nothing like as clear cut. A very similar relativity is involved in determining whether an impairment of bodily functioning is thought bad enough to be called a disorder. The patient's evaluation, and to some extent the doctor's, will be influenced by social and cultural norms. The diagnosis will at first be a hypothesis, which will act as a guide to treatment and may give some indication of the future course of the disorder, but may well have to be modified as more is learnt about its underlying causes, either in the particular case or in general.

Some disorders of the mind are the result of bodily defects (such as syphilis or arterio-sclerosis) and can be approached in much the same way: by alleviating the painful or distressing symptoms while recognising the connection between them and the underlying defect, which may (or more often may not) be capable of remedy. There is a school of psychiatric thought which believes that all mental disorders worthy of the name will eventually be traced to physical or organic causes and can thus be fitted into this conventional disease model. On this view, where the cause is not yet known, psychiatry is simply at the same stage as medicine has been (and still is) with many physical disorders: the stage of minute observation and recognition of distinct clusters of symptoms, categorising them into discrete syndromes, alleviating the pain and distress which they cause to the patient and attempting to predict the future course from similar cases, while at the same time searching for clues to the underlying cause.

The advantage of this model of mental disorder from the legal point of view is that it is capable of limiting the scope of psychiatric intervention and competence—it lays no claim to solving all the ills that mind and spirit as well as flesh are heir to. The disadvantage is that it enables physical treatments, some with potentially serious side-effects, to be employed for disorders which have not yet been shown to have a physical cause. This is all very well if the patient understands the position and agrees. It is not so obvious that the hypothesis of a physical cause should justify the imposition of physical treatments against the patient's will.

Then there are other schools of psychiatric thought which, in varying degrees and varying combinations, reject the notions of organic causes, of discrete disease entities, and of the more radical physical treatments. They seek other causes and other solutions. Their various therapies may be aimed at the patient's individual psyche or at its interaction with family or societal pressures. The disadvantage of these psychotherapeutic models from the legal point of view is that they can carry the province of psychiatry far beyond the normal concerns of the medical profession, in an attempt to explain and cure the wider ills of the individual, his family and society. This is not medicine in the conventional sense nor are its practitioners always or even usually medically qualified. From the patient's point of view, however, the advantage is that their methods of treatment can usually only succeed with his co-operation.

There is a third school of thought, which concentrates, not on the causes of the disorder, but on attacking its behavioural manifestations. This school has developed systems of behaviour modification which rely upon the consistent reinforcement of desired behaviour and the equally consistent discouragement of the undesired, whether it be addictions, compulsions, criminality or whatever. Lawyers may find it particularly curious that offenders are removed from the penal system, which claims very similar methods and objectives, for this purpose. But in theory the treatment is much more intensive and aimed at the particular problems of the particular patient. It can claim to do wonders for just those patients whom many more conventional psychiatrists now admit that they cannot treat, those whose disorders are manifested mainly by their anti-social or compulsive behaviour. Unless it is allied to a clear distinction between the normal and the abnormal, therefore, it is an obvious recipe for enabling offenders to escape their just deserts while subjecting some relatively harmless non-offenders to civil compulsion.

These various models offered ample scope to the critics of psychiatry within the profession itself, let alone to outsiders. The organically-minded were accused, for example, of failing to enter into the patient's own view of his life and to grasp the underlying rationality of what he says and does (found particularly in the work of Laing); or of perverting the concept of disease or illness to justify the imposition of treatment upon socially inconvenient people, both for their own and for society's ends (found particularly in the work of Szasz). Those attacked, on the other hand, tended to accuse the anti-psychiatrists of ignoring the problems of the really ill and concentrating on the much pleasanter (and in America at least more profitable) task of ministering to the neuroses of the middle classes. Clare (1980), for example, pointed out that the countries in which the practice of psychiatry was most controversial are also those (the USA and the former Soviet Union) in which the widest definitions of the most serious illnesses were employed.

Clare argued that the majority of doctors in the NHS would claim to do their best to incorporate the good features of every approach into their clinical practice. The so-called "medical model" is not synonymous with the organic theory of mental disease, for it can encompass a sympathetic understanding of the patient's experience, a broad-minded evaluation of the complex of possible causal factors, and a cautious approach to treatment. But its prime claim is to apply the ordinary scientific methods to the identification of a disorder, so that, for example, no-one is labelled a schizophrenic without exhibiting the precise symptoms which have been agreed to indicate this particular diagnostic category. Once criteria have been laid down and practitioners properly trained in their use, psychiatric diagnosis can indeed become very *reliable*. In other words, the chances of two or more psychiatrists coming up with the same label for the same patient become as good as, if not better than, those in any other branch of medicine.

Unfortunately, however, this does not answer the question of its *validity*. A high degree of reliability in the identification of witches was achieved by the witch-hunters of the seventeenth century using similar methods. But the "cure" for witchcraft was to kill the witches, whereas the "cure" for mental disorder is to improve people's lives. Hence the key question has become, not which model, but "what works" to make things better? In recent years, the focus has been on *recovery*, a concept introduced by service users themselves:

"Recovery is not just about what services do to or for people. Rather, recovery is what people *experience themselves* as they become *empowered to manage their lives* in a manner that allows them to achieve a fulfilling, meaningful life and a contributing positive sense of belonging in their communities".

The vision involves

"a process of changing one's orientation and behaviour from a negative focus on a troubling event, condition or circumstances to the positive restoration, rebuilding, reclaiming or taking control of one's life" (NIMHE, 2005).

This changes the focus from the professionals to the people they are trying to help, emphasises the role which service users have in planning their own recovery, and understands them as individuals within their own families, cultures and communities. It integrates a variety of professional perspectives and approaches, accentuating their strengths rather than their weaknesses, and aiming to recover mental well-being and functioning rather than to "cure" in the conventional sense. This approach has influenced NHS policy and development in the decade between the *National Service Framework for Mental Health* (Department of Health, 1999) and *New Horizons, A shared vision for mental health* (Department of Health, 2009b), which widens the focus to prevention as well as cure.

It has both mirrored and influenced the development of legal policy, with a much greater emphasis on patient autonomy and involvement, dignity and equality (as shown in the common values outlined in the Introduction). But despite the acknowledgement that people with mental health problems should be seen in the same way as people with physical health problems, it is still possible to intervene in their lives without their consent. These various accounts of the nature and causes of mental affliction do not provide a justification for allowing professionals to detain or treat people whether those people like it or not. We do not permit surgeons to remove appendices simply because they are better at identifying when an appendix is diseased and at performing a successful operation. This is not to argue that justifications for intervention do not exist, merely that they do not lie in the expertise of the professionals alone. But before considering what those justifications might be, we must consider the legal grounds for intervention under both the Mental Health Act 1983 (MHA) and the Mental Capacity Act 2005 (MCA).

2. CLASSIFYING THE MENTAL DISORDERS

Before the 2007 amendments, mental health law had always tried to categorise mental disorders into those which did, and those which did not, justify particular forms of legal intervention. Since medieval times it had distinguished between "lunatics", who might have lucid intervals or even be cured, and "idiots", whose condition could never be cured. Until the Mental Health Act 1959, people with mental illnesses were dealt with under separate legislation from people with mental disabilities. The 1959 Act unified the procedures but still drew important distinctions between the generic term "mental disorder" and the four specific forms of disorder which it defined, and between the more and the less serious of those specific disorders.

Short term interventions might be justified if the patient were simply suffering from a "mental disorder" but longer term interventions required a more specific finding of mental illness, mental subnormality, or psychopathic disorder. And this was not all. Long term intervention was only justified if an adult patient suffered from the most serious categories of mental disorder, mental illness and severe mental subnormality, unless he had committed a criminal offence. The less serious categories, non-severe mental subnormality and psychopathic disorder, only justified long term intervention before the age of 21 (although the patient might sometimes be kept after that age) or after the commission of a criminal offence.

This scheme had the great attraction of reserving the most serious forms of legal intervention for what were then thought to be the most serious forms of disorder, disorders in which the capacity to make reasoned decisions was most likely to be seriously impaired. But it soon ran into all sorts of difficulties.

(a) No definition of "mental illness"

First was the lack of a definition of "mental illness". The Percy Commission, whose 1957 report led to the 1959 Act, probably thought that it corresponded roughly with the conditions which had previously been labelled "madness" or "lunacy" and had by then become known as psychoses, but not with neuroses or personality disorders. However, in *W v L* [1974] QB 711, the patient, a young man of 23, had put a cat in a gas oven; had made a cat inhale ammonia and then cut its throat with a cup; had hanged a puppy in the garage; had strangled a terrier with wire; had threatened his wife with a knife; and last had threatened to push her downstairs as a means of disposing of the baby she was expecting. The psychiatrists disagreed on their diagnosis. Lawton LJ took what he no doubt saw as a "common sense" view of "mental illness" (p 719B–D):

"The words are ordinary words of the English language. They have no particular medical significance. They have no particular legal significance . . . ordinary words of the English language should be construed in the way that ordinary sensible people would construe them . . . I ask myself, what would the ordinary sensible person have said about the patient's condition in this case if he had been informed of his behaviour to the dogs, the cat and his wife? In my judgment such a person would have said 'well, the fellow is obviously mentally ill'."

It is impossible not to think of this as "the man-must-be-mad test". It did nothing to confine the concept to the major mental illnesses which had previously been thought of as lunacy or to distinguish between illness and personality disorder. It focussed upon what the "ordinary sensible person" would think of the patient's behaviour, rather than upon what the skilled professional would think of his mental state. As Cavadino (1991a) pointed out, lay people's understanding of mental illness is notoriously limited or faulty. It would have made more sense to focus on the commonly accepted medical meaning of the phrase (as the other judges, Lord Denning MR and Orr LJ seem to have done).

The Butler Report on Mentally Disordered Offenders (1975) did distinguish between mental illness and innate conditions, defining illness as a "disorder which has not always existed in the patient but has developed as a condition overlying the sufferer's usual personality". The Committee also proposed a detailed definition of "severe mental illness" for the purpose of their proposed verdict of "not guilty by reason of mental disorder" (to replace the verdict of "not guilty by reason of insanity"). When the 1959 Act was reviewed during the 1970s, the Government (DHSS, 1976) canvassed the idea of a definition of mental illness based upon the Butler Committee's proposals. This would have required one or more of the following characteristics: (i) more than temporary impairment of intellectual functions shown by a failure of memory, orientation, comprehension and learning capacity; (ii) more than temporary alteration of mood of such a degree as to give rise to the patient having a delusional appraisal of his situation, his past or his future, or that of others or to the lack of any appraisal; (iii) delusional beliefs, persecutory, jealous or grandiose; (iv) abnormal perceptions associated with delusional misinterpretation of events; (v) thinking so disordered as to prevent the patient making a reasonable appraisal of his situation or having reasonable communication with others.

Unfortunately perhaps, this helpful idea was abandoned, ostensibly because the lack of a definition was not thought to have caused any difficulties in practice (DHSS et al, 1978). Of its very nature, lack of precise definition will not cause problems to the professionals who operate the law; indeed, it may make their task easier; but it may very well cause problems for their patients. The point of the proposed definition was to focus attention upon those symptoms which might be thought to invalidate the patient's own decision-making, rather than upon his need for treatment. The two ideas were combined in the definition suggested by the Northern Ireland Review Committee on Mental Health Legislation (MacDermott, 1981):

" . . . a state of mind of a permanent or temporary (but not merely transient) nature in which the individual exhibits such disordered thinking, perceiving or emotion *as impairs his judgment of his situation* to the extent that he requires care, treatment or training in his own interests or in the interests of other persons."

45

In the Mental Health (Northern Ireland) Order 1986, article 3(1), this was subtly altered to "a state of mind which affects a person's thinking, perceiving, emotion or judgement to the extent that he requires care or medical treatment ... ". But the notion that the patient's mental disorder should significantly impair his decision-making ability has since been adopted in the Mental Health (Care and Treatment) (Scotland) Act 2003 (eg s 36(4)) and in the proposed new mental health and mental capacity legislation in Northern Ireland (Bamford, 2007; Northern Ireland Executive, 2009).

Meanwhile, In England and Wales, "mental illness" remained completely undefined in the legislation. This had the advantage that it could be adapted to fit with developments in psychiatric classification, which was increasingly abandoning the distinction between psychoses and neuroses in favour of grouping disorders according to common themes or descriptive likenesses. The International Classification of Diseases, for example, abandoned it in the ICD-10 (WHO, 1992) although it had been evident in the ICD-9 (1977).

(b) Learning disability confused with mental illness

Before the 1959 Act, the Mental Deficiency Acts 1913 and 1927 catered for people with mental disabilities. The Percy Commission's attempt to integrate mental illness and mental disability into a single elegant scheme was never wholly accepted by the professionals or by the families and carers of people with learning disabilities. The terminology had, of course, changed, but there was much more to the objection than that. To have a learning disability did not necessarily mean that a person was handicapped in his or her interaction with others:

> "The term 'disability' summarizes a great number of different functional limitations ... People may be disabled by physical, intellectual or sensory impairment, medical conditions or mental illness ... The term 'handicap' means loss or limitation of opportunities to take part in the life of the community on an equal level with others. It describes the encounter between the person with a disability and the environment ... " (United Nations, 1994, p 9).

Associating all people with learning disabilities with people who were mentally ill could suggest that the former were always disturbed in their thinking, feelings or behaviour, when this is very far from true.

Hence, before the 1983 Act, there was a vigorous campaign to take people with learning disabilities out of the Act altogether. The campaigners argued that, if there was a need for compulsory intervention at all, it stemmed not from the disability as such, but from some additional psychiatric illness or behaviour disorder (which might even be the result of how supposedly normal people had reacted to the disability). Furthermore, learning disabilities cannot be "cured" in the way that some mental illnesses can be cured, although a person's level of functioning may be significantly improved. If patients were committed to hospital, therefore, they might find it much harder to obtain their release. This was a particular problem with people who were sent to hospital after committing criminal offences. The hospital may be a pleasanter place than prison, but they might have to stay there for a great deal longer than was commensurate with the seriousness of the offences they had committed.

On the other hand, the Butler Committee (1975) did not want to deny disabled offenders the possibility of a more humane disposal than prison, but recommended that the court should have evidence from a specialist in mental handicap. The Government (DHSS et al, 1978) decided that it might also be necessary compulsorily to admit non-offenders in order to protect them from exploitation. MIND (1978) commented that "it is a curious society which, in order to prevent abuse of its vulnerable citizens, suggests confinement for the abused, while allowing freedom for those who exploit." However, vulnerable people do sometimes have to be removed from abusive situations and compulsion might have meant guardianship in the community rather than confinement in a hospital, just as it does with children who have to be protected from abuse.

In the result, the 1983 Act was a compromise. It replaced "severe subnormality" and "subnormality" with "severe mental impairment" and "mental impairment". This required severe or significant impairment, not only of intelligence but also of social functioning, thus focussing on the handicap rather than the disability; it also required that the impairment be associated with "abnormally aggressive or seriously irresponsible conduct". This may not have made much difference in criminal cases, for arguably all offending which is serious enough to require some form of custodial disposal is seriously irresponsible, even if it is not abnormally aggressive. The main problem for the criminal courts was not the legal definition but the lack of suitable hospital places. But the change also restricted the eligibility of mentally disabled people for guardianship in the community. This was little used while people with learning disabilities were still cared for in large mental handicap hospitals, but once they were cared for in smaller units closer to home, it was arguably the most suitable form of long term intervention for them.

(c) Did psychopathic disorder exist?

The third difficulty with the categories in the 1959 Act lay with "psychopathic disorder", which it defined as:

> "a persistent disorder or disability of mind (whether or not including significant impairment of intelligence) which results in abnormally aggressive or seriously irresponsible conduct on the part of the person concerned".

The origins of this concept are complicated and disputed. In the nineteenth century, the term "moral insanity" was coined to describe people who did not exhibit the obvious symptoms, such as delusions or hallucinations, associated with lunacy. It originally meant:

> "madness, consisting in a morbid perversion of the natural feelings, affections, inclinations, temper, habits, moral dispositions, and natural impulses, without any remarkable disorder or defect of the interest or knowing and reasoning faculties . . . " (Prichard, 1835).

"Moral" in those days meant "emotional" or "psychological" rather than the reverse of "immoral". In Germany, the term "psychopathy" or "constitutional psychopathic inferiority" was used for a whole range of conditions where the patient's personality deviated from some supposed biological norm.

The idea of a specific personality disorder closely associated with antisocial behaviour seems to have stemmed from the observation that there were people

47

whose persistent and apparently incorrigible misbehaviour began at a very early age. In England, these were termed "moral imbeciles", with the obvious risk of confusion with the originally wider concept of moral insanity and the quite different condition of intellectual imbecility. The Mental Deficiency Acts of 1913 and 1927 covered "idiots", defined as those who were unable to guard themselves against common physical dangers such as fire, water or traffic; "imbeciles" who could do this but were incapable of managing themselves or their affairs; "feeble-minded" who required care, supervision or control for their own protection or that of others; and "moral imbeciles", who from an early age displayed some permanent mental defect coupled with strong vicious or criminal propensities on which punishment had little or no effect.

By the time of the Percy Commission, efforts to categorise and define specific personalities which might be called pathological had concentrated on predominantly "aggressive" or predominantly "inadequate" characteristics. From this it was a short step to the Percy Commission's conclusion that there was a mental *disorder* called psychopathy, which could be defined largely in terms of the adequacy of the person's social functioning and included people with mild to moderate learning difficulties. Hence they suggested three categories of mental disorder: mental illness, severe mental subnormality, and "psychopathic disorder". "Severe mental subnormality" would more or less correspond with "idiocy" and "imbecility". "Psychopathic disorder" would cover "any type of aggressive or inadequate personality which does not render the patient severely subnormal but which is recognised medically as a pathological condition." If it included "marked limitation of intelligence" the term "feebleminded psychopath" was proposed.

This classification was criticised for failing to distinguish sufficiently between personality disorder and mental handicap. Hence the 1959 Act provided separate categories of "mental subnormality" and of psychopathic disorder, defining the latter in terms which emphasised the connection with serious antisocial behaviour. It is questionable, therefore, how far the concept had come from the former idea of "moral imbecility" (Anderson, 1962). Yet psychiatrists were by no means agreed on the existence of a specific clinical entity corresponding to the statutory definition. Nor could some commentators (see particularly Wootton, 1959) understand why, if it did exist, a constitutional propensity to anti-social behaviour should justify confining an offender in a hospital rather than in a prison. The criminal law expects people to control their natural inclinations, however hard they may find this.

As long ago as 1994, therefore, it was recommended that the disputed category of "psychopathic disorder" be replaced by the more generally understood and less stigmatising term "personality disorder" (Reed, 1994b). More recently, the Government has encouraged the development of proper services for the treatment of personality disorder within both the general and the forensic mental health settings: no longer should it be a "diagnosis of exclusion" (NIMHE, 2003). At the same time, however, it has promoted special units for the treatment of "dangerous and severe personality disorder", although this is by no means a universally recognised diagnosis.

(d) Age limits or "treatability"?

The Percy Commission took the view that long term civil compulsory powers should be reserved for the two most serious disorders. People with what they called psychopathic disorder were not suffering from the gross distortions of perception, thinking or mood which were involved in a diagnosis of serious mental illness; nor were their capacities so impaired that they were no more capable of looking after themselves than a small child. Social misfits, such as unmarried mothers, should not be detained at all. People with psychopathic disorders, and people with mild to moderate learning disabilities, might properly be subject to compulsion while they were still growing up or if they had committed criminal offences, but once they reached the age of majority (then 21) they were entitled to the same presumption of innocence as everyone else.

But in the years that followed, this important principle was forgotten. Some saw the age limits as an arbitrary restriction upon the power to provide treatment where it might do good. Others may have wanted a form of preventive detention for people who were not mentally ill but whose doctors thought them dangerous. This seems to have been the view of the Court of Appeal in *W v L* [1974] QB 711 (p 44, above). The patient clearly fell within the definition of psychopathic disorder; but as he was over the age of 21, he could not be obliged to remain in hospital for longer than 28 days unless he was convicted of a criminal offence or could be termed "mentally ill". The Court of Appeal decided that he was both psychopathic and mentally ill. This was convenient if unprincipled.

Doctors, on the other hand, did not want to be expected simply to provide preventive detention, even if the person had committed a crime (*particularly* if the person had committed a crime). Many in the forensic psychiatry service were sceptical of their ability to treat psychopathic disorder. In practice, therefore, the label "psychopath" was likely to do an offender more harm than good, resulting not in a hospital admission but in a prison sentence at the top end of the applicable range. The Butler Report (1975) considered that responsibility for psychopaths should lie principally with the prison rather than the hospital services. The Government (DHSS, 1976; DHSS et al, 1978) recognised that "psychopath" had become a damaging label involving much stigma, but wanted to keep the possibility of treatment from those who might benefit from it.

Hence in 1983 the age limits were abolished and replaced by a "treatability" requirement: that non-severe mental impairment or psychopathic disorder be such that hospital treatment is "likely to alleviate or prevent a deterioration of his condition". This concept, of making the patient better or at least preventing his getting worse, is difficult to apply where the condition is not susceptible to conventional psychiatric treatment, although it may be susceptible to cognitive behavioural therapy or psychotherapeutic treatment. These require some co-operation from the patient, but his refusal to undergo them did not mean that his condition was untreatable (*R v Cannons Park Mental Health Review Tribunal, ex p A* [1995] QB 60, CA; overruled on another point in *Reid v Secretary of State for Scotland* [1999] 2 AC 512). In effect, therefore, the "treatability" test protected the hospitals from having to take patients they did not want, but provided no protection for the patient who did not want to be in hospital (Gunn, 1979).

3. "MENTAL DISORDER" AFTER THE 2007 ACT

It is not surprising that, once the original rationale for the different categories of mental disorder had been eroded or forgotten, the 2007 amendments should abolish them and replace them with a single all-purpose concept of "mental disorder" which is subject to a few exceptions and qualifications. But there are still some mental health professionals who regret this (see Forrester, Ozdural, Muthukumaraswamy and Carroll, 2008).

Although the definition of a "patient" in the MHA covers a "person suffering or appearing to be suffering from mental disorder" (s 145(1)), most of the compulsory powers in the Act require that the patient is *currently suffering* from mental disorder. For an admission to hospital for assessment (including an emergency admission) (s 2(2)(a)) or for treatment (s 3(2)(a)), or reception into guardianship (s 7(2)(a)), or a hospital or guardianship order (including a restriction order) (s 37((2)(a)) or an interim hospital order (s 38(1)(a)), a hybrid order (s 45A(2)(a)), a transfer from prison to hospital (ss 47(1)(a), 48(1)), or a remand to hospital for treatment (s 36(1)), the patient must actually be suffering from "mental disorder". The same is required when any of the long term powers is renewed (s 20(4)(a)) or a tribunal are considering whether the patient should be discharged (s 72(1)(a)(i), (b)(i)).

For a remand to hospital for reports (s 35(3)(a)) and for a warrant to gain entry and remove a person to a place of safety (s 135(1)), there must be "reason to suspect" that he is so suffering; and he must so "appear" to a police officer taking a person found in a place to which the public has access to a place of safety (s 136(1)).

So what does "is suffering" mean? Some mental disorders are permanent. Others come and go. In some of these, the symptoms may be controlled by medication but are likely to return if medication is discontinued. In *Devon CC v Hawkins* [1967] 2 QB 26, it was held, in relation to a person whose epilepsy was controlled by drugs, that "so long as drugs are necessary to prevent the manifestation of disease, the disease . . . remains". Such a person, then, is still suffering (see Blom-Cooper, Hally and Murphy, 1995; also Disability Discrimination Act 1995, p 324, later). If the patient does not have symptoms which currently require medication, then it is difficult to say that he "is suffering" from the disorder, even if his psychiatrist believes that it is likely to recur in due course. The psychiatrist might regard him as a sick person whose illness is in remission, while the patient might see himself as a well person whose illness may return.

"Mental disorder" is now defined in section 1(2) of the MHA 1983 as "any disorder or disability of mind". As ordinary words of the English language, these are wide enough to cover any mental condition which deviates sufficiently from the supposed norm to be thought abnormal and sufficiently deleterious (unlike, for example, abnormally high intelligence) to be termed a disorder or a disability. They cover both an illness, which overlays the patient's usual personality and may be temporary or fluctuating, and a personality disorder or disability, which is permanent, although it need not have been there from birth. In practice, it means any condition of mind which has been recognised and described by psychiatrists in one or both of the internationally accepted classifications of mental disorders, the World Health Organisation's International Classification of Diseases (currently the ICD-10, 1992) or the American Psychiatric Association's Diagnostic and Statistical Manual of Mental Disorders (currently the DSM-IV, 1994; see also DSM-IV-TR, 2000). Although these deal separately with disorders of the mind and injuries to the brain, the concept would cover an impairment or disturbance of mental functioning which was caused by an injury to the brain.

This is the view of the MHA Code of Practice, which advises that:

"relevant professionals should determine whether a patient has a disorder or disability of the mind in accordance with good clinical practice and accepted standards of what constitutes such a disorder or disability" (para 3.2).

A non-exhaustive list of conditions is given: affective disorders, such as depression and bipolar disorder; schizophrenia and delusional disorders; neurotic, stress-related and somatoform disorders, such as anxiety, phobic disorders, obsessive compulsive disorders, post-traumatic stress disorder and hypochondriacal disorders; organic mental disorders such as dementia and delirium (however caused); personality and behavioural changes caused by brain injury or damage (however acquired); personality disorders; mental and behavioural disorders caused by psychoactive substance use; eating disorders, non-organic sleep disorders and non-organic sexual disorders; learning disabilities; autistic spectrum disorders (including Asperger's syndrome); and behavioural and emotional disorders of children and adolescents (para 3.3).

The Code makes an important point (para 3.6):

"Difference should not be confused with disorder. No-one may be considered to be mentally disordered solely because of their political, religious or cultural beliefs, values or opinions, unless there are proper clinical grounds to believe that they are the symptoms or manifestations of a disability or disorder of the mind. The same is true of a person's involvement, or likely involvement, in illegal, anti-social or 'immoral' behaviour. Beliefs, behaviours or actions which do not result from a disorder or disability of the mind are not a basis for compulsory measures under the Act, even if they appear unusual or cause other people alarm, distress or danger."

Hence the Code also warns that (para 3.5):

"Care must be taken to avoid diagnosing, or failing to diagnose, mental disorder on the basis of preconceptions about people or failure to appreciate cultural or social differences. What may be indicative of mental disorder in one person, given their background and individual circumstances, may be nothing of the sort in another person."

This is all very well, but it gives no guidance at all on *how* to distinguish between oddity and disorder. That has to be left to good clinical practice. Still less does it distinguish between those disorders or disabilities which so distort the patient's capacity to make decisions for himself as to justify compulsory measures against the patient's will and those which do not.

As the Code points out, the MHA no longer distinguishes between different forms of mental disorder. Hence it applies to personality disorders of all types in exactly the same way as it applies to mental illness and other mental disorders (para 3.18). This was, of course, always true of the shorter term powers. It may be a relief to those professionals who doubted the existence of a recognisable disorder falling within the old definition of psychopathic disorder. So too may be the Code's assertion that only "a very small subgroup of people with personality disorders may be anti-social and dangerous" (para 35.2). Nevertheless, this further emphasises how greatly the potential scope of the Act has been expanded by the 2007 amendments.

4. THE EXCLUSIONS FROM "MENTAL DISORDER" IN THE MHA

The Act as amended in 2007 makes special provision on two matters which are dealt with in the ICD-10 and DSM-IV and would otherwise fall within the definition of mental disorder.

(a) Learning disability

Section 1(2A) preserves the 1983 Act's position on learning disability:

"But a person with learning disability shall not be considered by reason of that disability to be—
  (a) suffering from mental disorder for the purposes of the provisions mentioned in subsection 2B below; or
  (b) requiring treatment in hospital for the purposes of the sections 17E and 50 to 53 below,
unless that disability is associated with abnormally aggressive or seriously irresponsible conduct on his part."

"Learning disability" is a term new to the Act but defined by section 1(4) consistently with the old law:

"In subsection 2A above, 'learning disability' means a state of arrested or incomplete development of mind which includes significant impairment of intelligence and social functioning."

Only a person who falls within this definition will be covered by the exclusion. The Code is of the opinion that:

"an adult with arrested or incomplete development of mind is one who has experienced a significant impairment of the normal process of maturation of intellectual and social development that occurs during childhood and adolescence ... [It] does not include people whose intellectual disorder derives from accident, injury or illness occurring after they completed normal maturation" (para 34.4).

If this is so, it is difficult to see why child accident victims are excluded from much of the MHA but adult victims are not. Significant impairment of intelligence "is not defined rigidly by the application of an arbitrary cut-off point such as an IQ of 70" (para 34.4). Significant impairment of social functioning refers to "the nature and extent of social competence", for which reliable and recent observation "from a number of sources who have experience of interacting with the person in social situations" will be helpful (para 34.4). It is important to assess the person as a whole (para 34.5).

However, the Code takes a firm position that autistic spectrum disorders are not learning disabilities within this definition and thus do not fall within the exclusion (para 3.16). Yet the Code describes these disorders as "disorders occurring from early stages in development in which the person shows marked difficulties with social communication, social interaction and social imagination" (para 34.19) and as "developmental in nature and ... not mental illnesses in themselves" (para 34.20). If, therefore, a person with an autistic spectrum disorder also has significantly impaired intelligence, he would appear to fall squarely within the definition of a person with learning disability.

The exclusion does not apply if the learning disability is associated with *abnormally* aggressive behaviour or *seriously* irresponsible conduct. The Code points out that assessing whether conduct meets this threshold will depend not only on the nature of the behaviour and the circumstances in which it occurs but also upon the risk caused to the patient or to others (para 34.7). In assessing whether behaviour is "abnormally aggressive", the Code advises taking account of how persistent and severe it has been, whether there was a specific trigger or it seemed disproportionate to whatever trigger there was, whether and to what extent it resulted in harm or distress to others or actual damage to property, how likely it is to recur, and how common similar behaviour is in the population generally (para 34.8). In assessing whether conduct is "seriously irresponsible", relevant factors may include whether it suggests disregard for its serious or dangerous consequences, how recently or persistently it has been observed, how seriously detrimental to the patient or to others the conduct might have been, whether it has actually resulted in harm, and if not recent, how likely it is to recur (para 34.9).

The exclusion applies to the provisions listed in section 1(2B)(a). These are all those provisions which used to be limited to some or all of the four specific forms of mental disorder under the Act as it used to be: admission for treatment (s 3); reception into guardianship (s 7); making a community treatment order (s 17A); renewing hospital admission, guardianship or community treatment (ss 20 and 20A); remanding to hospital and making a hospital order in criminal proceedings (ss 35 to 38); making a hybrid order in criminal proceedings (s 45A); transferring prisoners to hospital (ss 47, 48 and 51); and a tribunal's decision to discharge (s 72(1)(b) and (c) and (4)). Section 17E deals with the recall of community patients who now require treatment in hospital; sections 50 to 53 deal with the return of transferred prisoners who no longer require treatment in hospital.

By this roundabout route the position under the 1983 Act is preserved. Learning disability alone is sufficient for all the short term civil powers, including removal to a place of safety and admission to hospital for assessment, but not for any of the longer term civil powers or for the powers available to the criminal justice system. This means that MHA guardianship is still not available for people with learning disabilities. The MCA 2005 may fill the gap in civil powers. However, given that the Code takes the view that it is rarely, if ever, appropriate to use the Mental Health Act for people with a learning disability or autistic spectrum disorder unless they also have some other mental disorder (paras 3.16, 34.3 and 34.18), it might have been simpler to exclude them altogether.

(b) Dependence on alcohol or drugs

Section 1(3) provides another exclusion from the definition of "mental disorder":

> "Dependence on alcohol or drugs is not considered to be a disorder or disability of the mind for the purposes of subsection (2) above."

The 1959 and 1983 Acts went further, and provided that no-one could be dealt with as suffering from mental disorder of any kind "by reason only of promiscuity or other immoral conduct, sexual deviancy or dependence on alcohol or drugs" (old s 1(3)). No doubt the exclusion of promiscuity and other immoral conduct was to deal with specific injustices which had been known to happen under the pre-1959 Act law but are thought unlikely to happen again these days. On the other hand, the previous exclusion of sexual deviancy may have been thought to go too far (see, for example, the problems in interpreting the provisions in the Act associated with treating abnormalities of sex drive in *R v Mental Health Act Commission, ex p X* (1988) 9 BMLR 77, pp 202–203, later). The ICD-10 and DSM-IV list a number of disorders associated with sexuality, including disorders of sexual preference such as paedophilia. Homosexuality used to be included but the ICD-10 now firmly states that "sexual orientation alone is not to be regarded as a disorder". The Code is equally clear that "A person's sexual orientation towards people of the same gender (or both the same and the other gender) is not a mental disorder for any purpose" (para 3.7).

As to the continuing exclusion of dependence on alcohol and drugs, the Code points out that this may be accompanied by or associated with a mental disorder which does fall within the Act (para 3.10). It may also be the cause of mental disorders such as "withdrawal state with delirium or associated psychotic disorder, acute intoxication and organic mental disorders associated with prolonged abuse of drugs or alcohol" (para 3.11). And if addressing the alcohol or drug dependence is an appropriate part of treating the mental disorder, then it counts as medical treatment under the Act (para 3.12). Once again, we have an exclusion which is designed more to separate out the appropriate treatment facilities, distinguishing between psychiatric treatment and drug or alcohol detoxification and rehabilitation, rather than upon a principled approach to what is and is not a disorder of the mind.

5. THE ADDITIONAL CRITERIA FOR COMPULSION UNDER THE MHA

Given that the definition of "mental disorder" is now so broad, it becomes even more important to see whether the additional criteria, especially for civil commitment, are an effective way of separating the "sheep", who should not be subject to compulsion, from the "goats", who could be. Many people might wish to take a narrower view of the grounds for forcibly detaining and treating a non-offender than of the circumstances justifying a court in sending an offender to hospital rather than to prison. Others might take the opposite view, that a non-offender should always be enabled to receive the care and treatment he needs, while an offender should normally be expected to serve the punishment which his offending deserves. The Act still draws remarkably little distinction between the two.

In 1957, the Percy Commission (para 317) set out the principles which they believed would justify the use of civil compulsion. First and foremost, there had to be a pathological mental disorder for which the patient required hospital or community care. Secondly, this care could not be provided without compulsion because the patient or his family would not accept it. Thirdly, if the patient would not accept treatment, there should be "at least a strong likelihood that his unwillingness is due to a lack of appreciation of his own condition deriving from the mental disorder itself". Finally, there should be one of two advantages to be gained: *either* a,

"good prospect of benefit to the patient from the treatment proposed—an expectation that it will either cure or alleviate his mental disorder or strengthen his ability to regulate his social behaviour in spite of the underlying disorder, or bring him substantial benefit in the form of protection from neglect or exploitation by others"

or a "strong need to protect others from anti-social behaviour by the patient".

However, the Commission did not suggest that all these principles should be expressed in legislation. Instead, as we have seen, they recommended a scheme

54

which distinguished between the various types of disorder in a way which they believed would translate their views into action. Their third principle would be achieved by restricting long term treatment to the more serious forms of disorder. Their fourth principle was to be achieved by the additional criteria in the grounds for commitment. As modified in the 1983 Act, there are now *three* matters of which the recommending doctors must be satisfied, in addition to the diagnosis of mental disorder discussed above. These are: (a) the "nature or degree" requirement, (b) the necessity requirement and (c) the appropriate treatment requirement.

(a) The "nature or degree" requirement

For civil admission for *assessment,* the patient's disorder must be:

"of a nature or degree which warrants the detention of the patient in a hospital for assessment (or for assessment followed by medical treatment) for at least a limited period" (s 2(2)(a)).

For civil admission for *treatment,* the patient's disorder must be "of a nature or degree which makes it appropriate for him to receive medical treatment in a hospital" (s 3(2)(a)). For the *remand* of an accused person to hospital for treatment and for a *hospital order* or *hybrid order* in criminal proceedings, and for the *transfer of prisoners* to hospital, the disorder must be "of a nature or degree which makes it appropriate for him to be detained in a hospital for medical treatment" (ss 36(1)(a), 37(2)(a)(i), 45A(2)(b), 47(1)(b), 48(1)(b)).

The Code rightly points out that:

"the fact that someone has a mental disorder is never sufficient grounds for any compulsory measure to be taken under the Act. Compulsory measures are permitted only where specific criteria about the potential consequences of a person's mental disorder are met" (para 3.4).

However, this additional criterion focuses, not on the consequences as such, but on the disorder itself. It ought to exclude the mild, the trivial or the transient. But "nature or degree" must be construed disjunctively, so that a disorder may still be of a *nature* making hospital treatment appropriate even if it is currently not of a *degree* to do so: see *R v Mental Health Review Tribunal for the South Thames Region, ex p Smith* (1999) 47 BMLR 104; also *R (Secretary of State for the Home Department) v Mental Health Review Tribunal and CH* [2005] EWHC 746 (Admin).

The Code (para 4.3) repeats from the *Smith* case:

"Nature refers to the particular mental disorder from which the patient is suffering, its chronicity, its prognosis, and the patient's previous response to receiving treatment for the disorder. Degree refers to the current manifestation of the patient's disorder".

However, a simpler reading might be that "nature" refers to the *type* of disorder from which the patient is suffering, while "degree" refers to its current *severity.*

At the very least, this requirement ought to mean that the patient's disorder is currently such that he ought to be in hospital. Considerable progress was made after 1999 in developing alternatives to hospital care for people in crisis (see Appleby, 2004). This requirement does go some way towards insisting that patients are cared for in the "least restrictive environment" possible. The Code advises that "consideration must be given to whether there are alternative means of providing the care and treatment which the patient requires", including whether there are other effective forms of care which the patient might accept and whether guardianship would be appropriate (para 4.4). In all cases, consideration should be given to the patient's wishes and views of their needs; the patient's age and physical health; any past wishes or feelings expressed by the patient; the patient's cultural background; his social and family circumstances; the impact of future deterioration or lack of improvement on his children, family or carers, especially those living with the patient; and the effect upon the patient and those close to him of a decision to admit or not to admit under the Act (para 4.5).

In practice, of course, doctors in NHS hospitals will insist that they do not admit any patient who does not need to be in hospital, because the pressure on their beds is so great. But we should not forget that compulsory powers are also available to admit paying customers to private establishments. And what about people who could survive quite well in the community as long as they have their regular injections of the long-acting drugs which keep their symptoms under control? Is it "appropriate" for them to receive medical treatment in a hospital? In *R v Hallstrom, ex p W; R v Gardiner, ex p L* [1986] QB 1090 McCullough J held that this was only so if the patient's condition required *in*-patient treatment. There was, as the judge acknowledged (p 1104F), a case for giving doctors the power to impose treatment outside hospital:

> "There is, however, no canon of construction which presumes that Parliament intended that people should, against their will, be subjected to treatment which others, however professionally competent, perceive, however sincerely and however correctly, to be in their best interests. What there is is a canon of construction that Parliament is presumed not to enact legislation which interferes with the liberty of the subject without making it clear that this was its intention."

However, a more relaxed view was taken by the Court of Appeal in *B v Barking, Havering and Brentwood Community Healthcare NHS Trust* [1999] 1 FLR 106, where it was held sufficient if there needed to be "an in-patient element to the treatment" (p 113) even if the patient was out on leave for most of the time. Later cases have tended to assimilate treatment "in" a hospital to treatment "at" a hospital (see p 232, later), which would reduce the protection given by this requirement almost to vanishing point.

But might this "nature or degree" requirement go further than requiring that the patient's condition is bad enough for him to be treated in hospital? If it must be bad enough to "*warrant his detention*" is this also asking for a *moral* judgment about whether it is bad enough to *force* him to go? An illustration is the case of Mrs X, who was a socially isolated 65-year-old Viennese refugee Jewess. Her GP reported to the mental welfare team that she was again becoming paranoid. The team agreed (with some reservations because of cultural factors). Paranoia is undoubtedly a mental disorder. Mrs X would probably have been better off in hospital for her own sake. Nevertheless, the team thought themselves unable to compel her to go, because "she was sufficiently in contact with reality" (Beebe, Ellis and Evans, 1973). Clearly they were making both a clinical and a moral judgment about whether her disorder was such as to justify compelling her to be in hospital. And they saw that justification in terms of her capacity to appreciate her situation and make reasoned decisions about it.

Taken seriously, the requirement that the disorder be such as to "warrant" admission could come close to the Percy Commission's third principle: that the patient's unwillingness to enter hospital should result from a failure to appreciate his need for treatment, a failure caused by the mental disorder itself (and not, for example, by ordinary independence of mind, dislike of hospitals, or distrust of doctors).The Scottish and the proposed Northern Irish legislation (Bamford, 2007) require that patient's ability to make decisions about his treatment be significantly impaired because of his disorder (Mental Health (Care and Treatment) (Scotland) Act 2003, ss 36(4), 44(4), 57(3)(d)). But the MHA does not. An attempt by the House of Lords to insert such a requirement was defeated by the House of Commons. And the wording is not the same for an admission for treatment. This simply insists that the patient's condition is of a nature or degree "which makes it appropriate for him to receive medical treatment in a hospital". There is no mention of its being appropriate to *compel* him to go. There seems to be no moral or capacity judgment involved here other than the patient's need for treatment.

The Richardson Committee's version of the "nature or degree" requirement was more precise. It required the presence of mental disorder of such seriousness that the patient required care and treatment under the supervision of specialist mental health services and that the care and treatment proposed was the least restrictive and invasive alternative available consistent with safe and effective care (Richardson, 1999, para 5.95). The Committee also drew a principled distinction, in their proposed necessity requirement (below), between people who lacked the capacity to consent to care and treatment for their mental disorders and people who did not.

(b) The necessity requirement

For civil admission for *assessment*, the MHA requires that the patient "ought to be so detained in the interests of his own health or safety or with a view to the protection of other persons" (s 2(2)(b)). The equivalent in an admission for *treatment* is that:

> "it is necessary for the health or safety of the patient or for the protection of other persons that he should receive such treatment and it cannot be provided unless he is detained under this section" (s 3(2)(c)).

There is no such requirement in criminal cases. The criminal charge or conviction, coupled with the discretion of the court or the Justice Secretary, is thought to meet this necessity test.

The necessity requirement is meant to add something to the mental disorder requirement. There must be an element of risk to the patient or others if the patient is not detained (in the case of an admission for assessment) or admitted (in the case of an admission for treatment). But how great must the risk be? In practice, psychiatrists commonly believe that it means that the patient must be dangerous to himself or others (see even Clare, 1980). Bean (1980), for example, found that, while a high rating for psychiatric disorder was needed before the patient would be admitted to hospital at all, whether he was admitted informally or compulsorily depended mainly on his "dangerousness" rating.

These psychiatrists are to be commended for their caution, although they may be using the term dangerousness in a very loose sense. But in fact, dangerousness is *not* what the law requires. The Act uses the criterion that the patient is likely to "act in a manner dangerous to other persons or to himself" for the quite different purpose of preventing his nearest relative from discharging him (s 25(1); p 242, later). The criteria for the initial admission to hospital were meant to be broader than those for keeping him there against the wishes of his family.

The difference between the two phrases is clear. A patient is only dangerous *to himself* if he is likely to kill or injure himself, either deliberately or through extreme self-neglect. But a patient may need hospital treatment "in the interests of his own health or safety" whenever this is the best way of providing him with the appropriate care or treatment, or of safeguarding him against the risks, temptations or other stresses to which he might be subjected elsewhere. Although "necessary" is a strong word, it would appear to follow that once the doctor has reached the conclusion that the patient's disorder is bad enough to make it appropriate for him to receive treatment in a hospital, and this cannot be done unless he is detained, it follows that his detention will be necessary for his own health, if not his safety.

The MHA Code also takes a broad approach to "health or safety". It advises that the following factors should be taken into account in deciding whether patients should be detained for their own health or safety: evidence suggesting that they are at risk of suicide, self-harm, self-neglect or being unable to look after their own health or safety, jeopardising their own health or safety accidentally, recklessly or unintentionally, or that their mental disorder is otherwise putting their health or safety at risk; evidence suggesting that their mental health will deteriorate if they do not receive treatment; the reliability of such evidence, including what is known of the history of the patient's disorder; the views of the patient and of any carers, relatives or close friends, especially those living with the patient, about the likely course of the disorder and the possibility of its improving; the patient's own skills and experience in managing the condition; the potential benefits of treatment, weighed against any adverse effects that being detained might have on the patient's wellbeing; and whether other methods of managing the risk are available (para 4.6).

There are also some patients whose condition does not warrant hospital admission for their own sake but is thought to warrant it for the sake of other people. If the law required such patients to be *dangerous*, there would have to be a risk that they would attack and harm someone else. But the Act simply requires that it be necessary to "protect other persons". This leaves it to practitioners to decide who those other persons might be and what they are entitled to be protected from. A good illustration (from personal experience) is Mrs Y. She displayed none of the first rank symptoms of schizophrenia (thought control, auditory hallucinations or delusions) but was described by her psychiatrist as "bats". She was a very bad house-keeper, was loud, argumentative and often irrelevant in conversation, and made a thorough nuisance of herself by pestering and arguing with her neighbours. Her own psychiatrist remarked that it had been a mistake to give her a "good" council house with house- and garden-proud neighbours. Most of the usual drugs had been tried and he did not suggest that keeping her in hospital was likely to do her any good at all.

So how far was he entitled to go in trying to protect other people from her? Does the Act simply intend that they should be protected from physical harm? Or can it at least be extended to protecting families from the enormous physical and mental strain which caring for a disordered relative can impose? Or spouses and partners from the emotional and sometimes financial suffering caused by living with someone who is clearly going out of his mind? Or children from the developmental damage when their parents cannot cater adequately for their intellectual and emotional needs? Or neighbours from the irritation and nuisance suffered by living near someone like Mrs Y? The general consensus might well stop at around the third point on this scale but it is not clear that the law insists that the psychiatrist does.

The MHA Code advises that when considering whether detention is necessary for the protection of others, the factors to consider are the nature of the risk to other people arising from the patient's mental disorder, the likelihood that harm will result, and the severity of any potential harm, taking into account that it is not always possible to differentiate risk of harm to the patient from the risk of harm to others; the reliability of the available evidence, including any relevant details of the patient's clinical history and past behaviour, such as contact with other agencies and (where relevant) criminal convictions and cautions; the willingness and ability of those who live with the patient and provide care and support for him to cope with and manage the risk; and whether other methods of managing the risk are available (para 4.7). The Code also states that harm to other people includes psychological as well as physical harm (para 4.8) This tends to support the view that the law stops around the third point in the scale above. But the only confident statement is that the protection of property alone is not enough.

The Richardson Committee (1999) recommended different necessity requirements for patients who did, and patients who did not, have the capacity to decide upon their own care and treatment. For a patient without capacity, it would have to be necessary for the health and safety of the patient, or for the protection of others from *serious harm*, or for the protection of the patient from *serious exploitation*, that he be subject to the proposed care and treatment, and that this could not be implemented unless he was compelled to have it (para 5.95iv). For a patient who had capacity, there would have to be a "substantial risk of serious harm to the health or safety of the patient or to the safety of other persons" if he remained untreated and that there were positive measures in the care plan which were likely to prevent deterioration or secure an improvement in his mental condition (para 5.95v). Indeed, the Committee pointed out that, consistently with their philosophy of non-discrimination between people with mental and physical disorders, the only principled justifications for treatment without consent were lack of capacity and the risk of serious harm to the safety of other people. But they included the risk of serious harm to a patient with capacity for pragmatic reasons. In any event, these recommendations were not adopted. The Mental Health Act Commission (2006, 2008, 2009a) had reservations about a capacity-based threshold for compulsion, because its experience of monitoring treatment given without consent under Part 4 of the MHA suggested that this could lead to more stringent tests of capacity in order to legitimate what the doctors thought best (see p 204, later).

But what about the patient who does need to be in hospital, but who does not need to be detained, either because he is willing to go or because he is in no state to object? The Code states that informal admission is usually appropriate when a patient who has the capacity to do so consents to admission (para 4.9), but that this is not an absolute rule "especially if the reason for considering admission is that the patient presents a clear danger to themselves or others because of their mental disorder" (para 4.10).

There must be some cases in which the detention of an apparently willing patient is in fact necessary. The Code (para 4.11) advises that:

"Compulsory admission should, in particular, be considered where a patient's current mental state, together with reliable evidence of past experience, indicates a strong likelihood that they will have a change of mind about informal admission, either before or after they are admitted, with the resulting risk to their health or safety or to the safety of other people."

Examples are the schizophrenic woman who asked for the security of the hospital but warned that her voices might tell her to leave, or the alcoholic who had frequently left before and was plagued by intrusive thoughts that he should kill his wife and child (Beebe, Ellis and Evans, 1973). The patient may be willing to stay in hospital but unwilling to accept the medical treatment which his doctor thinks necessary.

But what if the psychiatrist concentrates on discovering symptoms of mental disorder and whether the patient is "dangerous" without exploring his willingness to seek treatment? Despite all the Code's emphasis on discovering the patient's own wishes and feelings, it is still possible that these things may happen. And what if an informal admission is only inappropriate for administrative reasons? There have been tales of hospitals that would not admit patients out of normal hours, or without a prior interview with the hospital psychiatrist, or during industrial action, unless there was the clear mark of urgency which a compulsory admission is thought to provide. Is detention lawful then?

Section 2 (admission for assessment) requires that the patient's condition warrant his *detention* and that he ought to be so *detained*. If the only reason that detention is thought warranted is that the hospital has administrative objections to an informal admission or no-one has bothered to consult the patient, these conditions have not been fulfilled. Section 3 (admission for treatment), however, merely requires that the appropriate hospital treatment "cannot be provided unless he is detained under this section" (s 3(2)(c)). Although this is meant to limit the section to cases in which the compulsion as well as the treatment is necessary, it could be read to cover a case in which it was the hospital rather than the patient who was unwilling to agree to an informal admission.

(c) The appropriate treatment requirement

In all *admissions for treatment*, both *civil and criminal*, it is now required that "appropriate medical treatment is available for him" (ss 3(2)(d); 36(1)(b); 37(2)(a)(i); 45A(2)(c); 47(1)(c); 48(1)(c)). This does not apply to admissions for assessment (s 2), remands to hospital for reports (s 35) or to interim hospital orders (s 38), where the purpose may be to determine what treatment, if any, is appropriate. "Appropriate medical treatment" means "medical treatment which is appropriate in his case, taking into account the nature and degree of the mental disorder and all the circumstances of his case" (s 3(4); applied throughout by s 145(1AB)).

This is a new and welcome requirement introduced by the 2007 amendments. The Percy Commission put "treatability" forward as a condition for the commitment of *all* patients, apart from those whose detention was necessary to protect other people from antisocial behaviour. This did not find its way into the 1959 Act, but the 1983 Act required that in some circumstances the patient's disorder be such that treatment was likely to alleviate or prevent a deterioration in his condition (this applied to psychopathic and non-severely impaired patients on admission and renewal and to mentally ill and severely impaired patients on renewal, unless they were unlikely to be able to care for themselves, or to obtain the care they needed or to guard themselves against serious exploitation). The new requirement is different from the old in two respects. First, it applies whatever the nature of the patient's mental disorder, and not only on admission but also on renewal or on review by a tribunal. Secondly, it is linked to the treatment which is *actually* available for the patient, not to whether the patient's condition is theoretically amenable to it.

There is an equivalent requirement in the Scottish legislation (Mental Health (Care and Treatment) (Scotland) Act 2003, s 57(3)(b)). It reflects a fundamental belief in reciprocity. How can it be justifiable to detain someone in a hospital, at least in his own interests, if there is nothing constructive which can be done to help him? But it also applies to people who are being detained as much for the protection of other people as in their own interests. In *Keenan v United Kingdom* (2001) 33 EHRR 38 at para 110, and in many other cases, the European Court of Human Rights has stated that "the authorities are under an obligation to protect the health of persons deprived of liberty". They must not only have systems in place for providing them with appropriate health care but must actually provide it. The House of Lords have said that principles which apply to prisoners apply a fortiori to patients detained under the Mental Health Act (*Savage v South East Essex Partnership NHS Foundation Trust (MIND intervening)* [2008] UKHL 74, [2009] 1 AC 681).

But what is "appropriate medical treatment" in this context? In section 145(1) of the MHA, medical treatment is widely defined to include "nursing, psychological intervention and specialist mental health habilitation, rehabilitation and care". In *R v Mersey Mental Health Review Tribunal, ex p D, The Times*, 13 April 1987, it was held appropriate to continue to detain a patient in a special hospital even though there was nothing other than nursing care which could be given to him. However, this definition is now subject to section 145(4):

"Any reference in this Act to medical treatment, in relation to mental disorder, shall be construed as a reference to medical treatment the purpose of which is to alleviate, or prevent a worsening of, the disorder or one or more of its symptoms or manifestations."

This suggests that the available medical treatment must be something which positively improves the patient's condition or at least prevents its getting worse. Could this possibly apply to purely preventive detention in a hospital? Nursing care might inhibit the manifestations of the patient's disorder but is that the same as alleviating or preventing them from getting worse? It will be interesting to see what the tribunal and the courts decide. They have not so far taken the view that is enough that the doctors *think* that the criteria are met, but it could be difficult to disprove a doctor's assertion that he does indeed intend to provide the appropriate treatment.

6. THE CONCEPTS IN THE MENTAL CAPACITY ACT

The Mental Capacity Act 2005 covers a much wider range of decisions than the Mental Health Act. It lays down two essential criteria: that the person concerned lacks the capacity to take the decision for himself and that the decision is taken in the best interests of that person. There is no power under the MCA to take action for the protection of other persons. The principles are the same whether the decision being taken is what to have for breakfast or whether to have major surgery. The law only requires elaborate formal assessments when operating the deprivation of liberty safeguards (DoLS); but of course evidence will be required if a case gets to court and everyone has to be in a position to justify their decisions if need be. It would be a shame, however, if an Act, which was meant to reassure and support carers who are doing their best, made life more rather then less difficult for them and the people they are looking after.

(a) Capacity

(i) The presumption of capacity

A person must be presumed to have capacity unless it is established that he does not (MCA, s 1(2)). As the MCA Code puts it, "anyone who believes that a person lacks capacity should be able to prove their case" (para 2.5). Capacity is not an all-or-nothing thing. It is specific to the particular decision being taken and to the time when it is being taken. A person may be quite capable of taking some decisions but not others. A person may also be quite capable of taking a decision at some times but not at others. Of course, a particular individual may be permanently unable to take some or all decisions, but that is not to be assumed. The Law Commission (1995) rejected the so-called "status" test, according to which certain categories of people, such as patients detained under the MHA or people with a particular level of intelligence, are automatically deemed incapable of making decisions; it was "out of tune with the policy aim of enabling and encouraging people to take for themselves any decision which they have the capacity to take" (para 3.3).

The presumption of capacity affects people who may be tempted to take a decision on behalf of another person in slightly different ways, but the effect is to protect someone who reasonably believes that person to lack capacity. Hence, a carer doing an act in connection with the care or treatment of another (P), must first take reasonable steps to establish whether P lacks capacity (s 5(1)(a)). But having done so, she will be protected if she reasonably believes that P does lack capacity in relation to the matter in question (s 5(1)(b)(i)). The donee of a lasting power of attorney may act in relation to the donor's property and affairs even though the donor still has the capacity to act for himself; but she may not make decisions about the donor's personal welfare unless P lacks, or the donee reasonably believes that he lacks, capacity to take the decision for himself (s 11(7)(a)). And a deputy appointed by the Court of Protection cannot make any kind of decision on P's behalf if she knows or has reasonable grounds for believing that P has capacity in relation to the matter (s 20(1)). The Court of Protection, however, can only take a decision or appoint a deputy if it concludes that P actually does lack capacity in relation to the matter in question (s 16(1)).

The Act also insists that "a person is not to be treated as unable to make a decision unless all practicable steps have been taken to help him to do so without success" (s 1(3)). This means helping the person to make his own decision, not pressurising him to make the decision the helper wants (Code, para 2.8). The help must be tailored to the individual's needs and abilities as well as to the particular decision being made (paras 3.3, 3.8). Obviously, some decisions require more careful handling than others: moving house is different from having lunch. So the Code advises helpers to check whether the person has all the relevant information, including information about any alternative choices available; whether the information could be presented in a way which is easier to understand; whether different methods of communication could be used (such as pictures, tapes, sign language) or whether anyone else could help with communication (including a professional interpreter); whether there are times of day or places where the person feels more at ease; whether the decision could be put off to a better time for him; and whether anyone else could give him support (chapter 3).

Section 2(3) of the MCA insists that a lack of capacity cannot be established merely by reference to a person's age, appearance, condition or behaviour. "Appearance" covers not only skin colour, dress, piercings or the like, but also the physical features linked to Down's syndrome or the spasms caused by cerebral palsy (Code, para 4.8). "Condition" includes physical or mental disabilities or inebriation. "Behaviour" could be shouting or gesticulating or talking to oneself (Code, para 4.9). The point is that everyone is to be judged equally: assumptions are not to be made on the basis of matters which may prove completely irrelevant to the legal test of capacity.

(ii) Lack of capacity

Section 2(1) of the MCA defines a lack of capacity in this way:

> "For the purposes of this Act, a person lacks capacity in relation to a matter if at the material time he is unable to make a decision for himself in relation to the matter because of an impairment of, or a disturbance in the functioning of, the mind or brain."

There are therefore two components: (a) an impairment of, or a disturbance in the functioning of, the mind or brain; and (b) a resulting inability to make the decision.

Impairment or disturbance in the functioning of mind or brain is wider than mental disorder in both the conventional and the legal sense. It may be permanent or temporary (s 2(2)). The mind or brain of a person who is knocked out for a time by an accident or an assault, or who has been permanently deprived of all powers of communication by trauma or a stroke, or who is suffering the effects of alcohol or drug use or abuse, will be impaired or disturbed even though that person does not have a mental disorder within the meaning of the MHA. But it is difficult to think of a conventional mental disorder which is not covered. The obvious examples which are covered are significant learning disabilities, dementia and the long term effects of brain damage. But the essential characteristic of mental disorder is a disturbance in the functioning of the mind, so many mental illnesses could potentially lead to an inability to take decisions. Most of them, of course, will not.

(iii) Inability to decide

Section 3(1) of the MCA defines what is meant by an inability to make a decision. Each element must be the result of the impairment or disturbance:

> "For the purposes of section 2, a person is unable to make a decision for himself if he is unable—
>
> (a) to understand the information relevant to the decision;
> (b) to retain that information;

63

> (c) to use or weigh that information as part of the process of making the decision; or
>
> (d) to communicate his decision (whether by talking, using sign language or any other means)."

This test involves the ability both to understand the information needed to make the decision and to use that information to make a choice. It expands upon, rather than contradicts, the existing common law tests (Law Commission, 1995, para 3.23). Indeed it mirrors closely the test adopted in relation to healthcare decisions before the Act. The leading case is *Re MB (Adult: Medical Treatment)* [1997] 2 FLR 426, CA, which largely adopted *Re C (Adult: Refusal of Medical Treatment)* [1994] 1 WLR 290. In *Re C* a Broadmoor patient with delusions of medical grandeur was nevertheless held capable of deciding whether or not to have a below-knee amputation for gangrene. The judge in that case included an extra requirement, that the patient believe the relevant information, but that cannot be necessary because the information given could be wrong. The important thing is that the patient is capable of weighing it up; and of course he may not be able to do that if his impairment or disturbance prevents him from believing it: see *R (B) v S (Responsible Medical Officer Broadmoor)* [2005] EWHC 1936 (Admin), [2005] MHLR 347.

In relation to section 3(1)(a), the understanding part of the test, what information does the person have to be able to understand? Section 3(4) provides that it includes information about the reasonably foreseeable consequences of deciding one way or another or of not deciding at all: putting off a decision may be just as momentous as making it. But the MCA goes no further in explaining the level of information required. How much detail and how subtle? The common law expects an explanation in "broad terms and simple language". The MCA Code (para 3.9) suggests that in some cases a simple broad explanation will be enough, but it must not miss out important information. The risks and benefits should be explained, and the effects on the person concerned and those close to them. Sometimes access to advice from elsewhere, such as a doctor or financial adviser, or family or friend, may be important (para 3.9). The Code points out that if a decision could have serious or grave consequences, it is even more important that a person understands the relevant information (para 4.19). But the MCA does not say that the more important the decision, the more detailed the information has to be, perhaps because some important decisions are very simple and some less important ones very complicated.

The MCA does insist that:

> "a person is not to be regarded as unable to understand the information relevant to a decision if he is able to understand an explanation given to him in a way which is appropriate to his circumstances (using simple language, visual aids or any other means)" (s 3(2)).

This reinforces the duty to help him to take the decision for himself and may suggest that the ability to understand a "broad terms and simple language" explanation is all that is required (but why then was the Law Commission's proposal to this effect not adopted: cf 1995, para 3.18?). It would be in keeping with the general aim of promoting autonomy and participation, setting the bar as low as is consistent with a real decision being made.

The retention test in section 3(1)(b) is also rather puzzling. Section 3(3) provides that the fact that a person is able to retain the relevant information for only a short period does not prevent him from being regarded as able to make the decision. The point must be that he should be able to remember it for long enough to use it to make the particular decision. The Code gives the example of an elderly man with dementia who can recognise each of his great-grandchildren but not remember their names (para 4.20), which it considers enough for him to be able to decide to divide his money between them. As with the belief test, it is difficult to see what the retention test adds to the understanding and ability to use tests.

The MCA has nothing more to say about the "ability to use" test in section 3(1)(c), but this adds an important dimension to the understanding test. A person may be quite capable of understanding all the relevant information but quite incapable of making use of that information in coming to a decision. The examples given by the Law Commission (1995, para 3.17; see also MCA Code, para 4.22) were an anorexic who always decides not to eat or a mentally disabled person who was not able to exert his will against a stronger person. But a mentally ill person whose delusions caused him to reject information might also be covered: see *R v Collins and Ashworth Hospital Authority, ex p Brady* [2000] Lloyd's Rep Med 355, [2000] MHLR 17.

Finally, the communication test in section 3(1)(d) recognises that there are a few people who are or may be capable of making their own choices but incapable of communicating these, no matter how much help they are given. The obvious examples are people who are unconscious or in a coma, people with the rare Guillain-Barre or "locked in" syndrome, or people suffering the effects of a massive stroke (Law Commission, 1995, para 3.13; MCA Code, para 4.23). But there are people who can communicate by blinking an eye or squeezing a hand or with other specialist help (Code, paras 4.34, 4.25).

Thus the MCA takes what is known as the "functional" approach to the assessment of capacity. It was adopted by the Law Commission (1995) and the MCA in preference, not only to the "status" test but also to the "outcome" test, which focuses on the final content of a person's decision. The cynical might fear that professionals and judges are much more likely to think that a person has the capacity to agree with their advice than they are to think that he has the capacity to disagree. But capacity should not depend upon whether the assessor agrees with the decision, for this penalises individuality and demands conformity at the expense of personal autonomy (Law Commission 1995, para 3.4). Section 1(4) of the MCA reinforces this: a person is not to be treated as unable to make a decision merely because he makes an unwise decision.

(b) The best interests test

Section 1(5) of the MCA is adamant:

> "An act done, or decision made, under this Act on behalf of a person who lacks capacity must be done, or made, in his best interests".

Thus the MCA specifically provides that the authority conferred by a lasting power of attorney, the authority conferred upon a deputy appointed by the Court of Protection, and powers of the Court to make decisions or to appoint deputies to make decisions about a person's personal welfare or property and affairs are subject to the principles in section 1 and the best interests requirements in section 4 (ss 9(4)(a)), 20(6), and 16(3)). Section 5 provides that a person doing an act in connection with the care and treatment of another person (P) is protected if she reasonably believes that it will be in P's best interests for the act to be done (s 5(1)(b)(ii), (2)). For most day to day decisions, this will be the person actually looking after the person concerned; but for medical treatment, it will be the doctor responsible for carrying it out; and for nursing or other health care, it will be the professional providing the care (see MCA Code, para 5.8).

Furthermore, among the qualifying requirements for depriving a person of his liberty under the DoLS is that it is in the best interests of that person for him to be a detained resident (Sch A1, paras 12(1)(d), 16(3)). On top of that it must be necessary for him to be detained in order to prevent harm *to him*, and detaining him must be a proportionate response to the likelihood and seriousness of the harm feared (Sch A1, paras 16(4), 16(5)). There is no question here of detaining a person for the sake of other people and there is a specific requirement of proportionality which is quite absent from the criteria for detention under the MHA.

There are some limited exceptions to the best interests rule. First, decision-makers cannot override a valid and applicable advance refusal of treatment made by the person himself. In this respect, his expressed wishes while he has capacity outweigh what others may think to be in his best interests when he does not (ss 5(4), 11(7)(b)). Secondly, people without capacity to consent may in certain circumstances be involved in research even if this is not in their own best interests (both exceptions are discussed in chapter 6).

The Law Commission chose the "best interests" test, where the decision-maker does what she thinks best, in preference to the so-called "substituted judgment" test, where the decision-maker does what she thinks the person concerned would have done. The substituted judgment test is generally thought preferable in theory:

> "Thinking oneself into the shoes of the person concerned and recognising the value we all place on personal preferences (not all decisions are, or should be, taken on reasonable grounds) is a mark of respect for human individuality..." (Law Commission 1991, para 4.23).

But it is difficult to apply in practice, especially where someone has never had the capacity to make serious decisions. The Commission concluded that the two need not be mutually exclusive. "The best interests test should be modified by a requirement that the substitute decision-maker first goes through an exercise in substituted judgment" (Law Commission 1993a, para 2.14).

The MCA prescribes the process. Any decision-maker must take the following steps before making the decision (MCA, s 4(2), 4(8)). She must first consider whether it is likely that the person concerned will at some time have capacity to decide the matter in question, and if so, when that is likely to be (s 4(3)). Once and for all decisions, in particular, should not be taken before they need to be, if the person concerned is likely to regain capacity in time. Some people are much more likely to recover capacity than others—even the common law recognised that people with major mental illnesses might have "lucid intervals"—and others who have hitherto lacked capacity may learn new skills (see Code, para 5.28).

Next, the decision-maker must, so far as reasonably practicable, permit and encourage the person concerned to take part, or improve his ability to take part, in acts or decisions affecting him (MCA, s 4(4)). In any event, she must consider, so far as reasonably ascertainable: (a) that person's past and present wishes and feelings (in particular, any relevant written statement made when he had capacity), (b) the beliefs and values which would be likely to influence his decision if he had capacity, and (c) the other factors he would be likely to consider if he could (s 4(6)). How can it be in a person's best interests to give him food which he hates or which was contrary to the religious beliefs in which he was brought up? On the other hand, it may well be in his best interests to give him a tetanus jab after cutting his leg, even if he is scared of needles (see Code, para 5.38). And actions which benefit other people can also benefit him: see *Re Y (Mental Patient: Bone Marrow Donation)* [1997] Fam 110; *Re A (Male Sterilisation)* [2000] 1 FLR 549.

On top of this exercise in working out what the person concerned might have done, the decision-maker must take into account, if it is practicable and appropriate to consult them, the views of: (a) anyone named by that person as someone to be consulted about matters of the kind in question, (b) anyone caring for him or interested in his welfare, (c) any donee of an LPA, and (d) any deputy appointed by the court. Those views should cover the views, values and beliefs of the person concerned, as well as what would be in his best interests (MCA, s 4(7)).

Having done all that, the decision-maker has to consider "all the relevant circumstances" (s 4(2)). This means all the circumstances of which she is aware and which it would be reasonable to regard as relevant (s 4(11)). As with the assessment of capacity (see above), she must not leap to conclusions based upon a person's age, appearance, condition or behaviour (s 4(1)). If the decision relates to life-sustaining treatment (that is, treatment which the person providing healthcare for the person concerned considers necessary to sustain life), she must not be motivated by a desire to bring about his death (s 4(5), (10)). But the Code suggests that this:

"cannot be interpreted to mean that doctors are under an obligation to provide, or to continue to provide, life-sustaining treatment where that treatment is not in the best interests of the person concerned, even if death is foreseen" (para 5.33).

Decision-makers are also bound by the general principles in section 1 (see pp 5–6, earlier), which include having regard to whether the purpose for which the act or decision is needed can be as effectively achieved in a way which is less restrictive of the rights and freedom of action of the person concerned (s 1(6)).

Provided that the decision-maker has gone through all the hoops erected by section 4(1) to (7), it is enough that she reasonably believes that what she does or decides is in the best interests of the person concerned (s 4(9)). This is to protect carers, donees and deputies who are doing their best. It may be reasonable for a doctor to give an accident victim a blood transfusion to save his life, but once she knows that he is a Jehovah's Witness, she will have to take those views, and those of his family, into account in deciding what to do for the best (see Code, para 5.61). Reasonable belief is not enough for the Court of Protection but of course the Court will be doing what it thinks best and if it is wrong the appeal court can put it right.

The checklist in section 4 is very different from the checklist of factors relevant to deciding what is in the best interests of a child (see Children Act 1989, s 1(3)). It is mostly concerned with process rather than what to take into account. The Code (para 5.19) points out that a doctor making a decision about major medical treatment would have to consider the patient's clinical needs, and the benefits and burdens on his health and life expectancy: see *A Hospital NHS Trust v S* [2003] EWHC 365 (Fam), [2003] Lloyd's Rep Med 137. But life expectancy would not be relevant to deciding whether to give an aspirin for a headache or put a plaster on a cut. "These kinds of issues can only be worked out on a case by case basis" (Code, para 5.20).

7. COMMENTARY

The MHA is now much more transparent than it used to be. In effect it allows the professionals to use compulsion whenever *they* need to do so in order to give the patient the hospital treatment for his mental disorder which *they* think he needs. Ought there to be more to it than that? We must start from the assumption that mentally distressed or disabled people are people like anyone else and entitled to the same rights as others, including the right to liberty and self-determination, and then ask what entitles us to take away those rights.

The MHA suggests two different justifications for civil commitment. The first is the person's own health or safety. One problem with this is whether it is ever justifiable to take away a person's freedom solely for his own sake. Mill (1859) argued that self-protection was the only object for which mankind was justified in interfering with another's freedom. A man must be allowed to go to the devil if he wishes, provided that he does not infringe the equal rights of other people in the process. The argument is familiar in the seat-belt and smoking controversies of yesterday. The usual answer is that these particular examples of self-neglect also have adverse effects upon other people, not least because they result in a disproportionate claim on the resources of the NHS, to the detriment of other patients or taxpayers. But in the case of people with mental disorders, the result of failing to intervene to protect them will probably be a smaller rather than a greater claim on public expenditure. Indeed, Sedgwick (1982) pointed out that some of the implications of anti-psychiatry, although it has been enthusiastically espoused by many on the left, are extremely attractive to those on the right who wish to limit the provision of public facilities for mentally disordered people.

The easy answer is that Mill's argument was never intended to apply to people who are incapable of participating in the system of rights and duties implied by the concept of equal freedom. A child must be brought up and educated to a point where he is capable of participating in society, whether he or his parents like it or not. We must want for him the very minimum that he would want for himself, whatever else he might want (Freeman, 1980). Can we apply the same idea to mentally disordered people? One difficulty is that childhood can be defined by reference to an objective and easily proved criterion. A second difficulty is that the purpose of the intervention is to enable the child eventually to take his place as a fully responsible member of society, whereas this may never be possible for some mentally disordered people.

To expand upon the second difficulty, some anti-psychiatrists have argued that compulsory psychiatric intervention is of no help to the patient. If mental illness is defined by reference to the psychiatrist's own standards of normality, by definition she takes no account of the standpoint of the very person she is supposed to be helping. The patient's conduct appears irrational or inappropriate because the doctor cannot put herself in the patient's place. For these reasons, she can do little to help. In fact, she can only make matters worse. The label "mentally ill" places the patient too low, and indeed may imprison him in an institution which can only do him damage (Goffman, 1961), while the label "psychiatrist" places the doctor so high, that effective communication between them is ruled out (Laing, 1959; Laing and Esterson, 1971). This must be doubly so where the normal relationship of trust between doctor and patient is destroyed by the imposition of compulsory powers.

It is indeed curious that two centuries of laws have been designed on the assumption that psychiatrists can cure their involuntary patients. Yet in the nineteenth century the percentage of cures was extremely low, particularly among pauper patients (Scull, 1979). Even today, numerically the most important problems are the incurable diseases of old age and the major functional psychoses, where the symptoms may be treated but not the cause. However, there are many patients whom the doctors can help and in some cases, particularly depression, they can be tolerably confident that they will be able to produce such an improvement that the patient will be glad that his wishes were overborne. The same can apply to people with learning disabilities. They can benefit from patient and skilled education for participation in society, although this is not usually a task for the medical profession.

But is the fact that the doctor can bring about such an improvement that the patient will thank him in the end enough? Of course it is not. I may be glad when the dentist has taken my teeth out, but he cannot do so by force. There still must be something about the patient which disqualifies him from the right to make that choice. The law has hitherto paid far too little attention to the precise mental qualities which add up to a disqualification. It has assumed that a diagnosis of mental illness or mental disorder is enough and that once such a diagnosis has been made, we can take it for granted that the refusal to accept help is the result of that diagnosis, rather than of ordinary stubbornness, political or religious conviction, or a different approach to the calculation of the odds. But how should we approach the question of capacity to make the choice?

There are several possibilities. We could look at the common law's criterion for enjoying ordinary legal rights. This depends upon understanding in broad terms what is involved in making the decision and the effects of making it. Eccentricity, caprice, forgetfulness, the inability to make choices which others regard as sensible or wise or good, these do not disqualify. The minimum requirement is to know what one is about. This is a very useful criterion when it comes to the status of people with learning disabilities, because their disorder consists mainly in a deficiency in just this quality. Once they have reached a certain point, there is no reason to believe that the disability alone will distort their capacity to participate in the system of rights and duties of which we speak.

The same test might also be applied to mental illness. But the patient's consciousness may be unimpaired and his understanding distorted in a rather different way. He knows where he is and what he is about. He can understand what he is told. But the way in which he thinks about things may be quite different from other people. It is not, or should not be, that he has different moral, political or religious views. It is, or should be, that the kinds of perception and the kinds of thinking which lead him to make decisions based upon what he knows are not the same as other people's (this is reflected in the Butler Report's attempted definition of severe mental illness on p 45, above).

69

The test of incapacity now laid down in sections 2 and 3 of the Mental Capacity Act 2005 (see above) encompasses both of these ideas. As we have seen, it covers both understanding the relevant information and using that information to arrive at a decision. It does not cover someone simply because he makes an unwise decision. The MCA covers all kinds of decisions about personal welfare, physical health care and financial matters, but not the matters which are or could be dealt with under the Mental Health Act. But is there any reason in principle or practice why those principles should not apply just as much to the decision to enter hospital for psychiatric treatment or to accept a particular type of treatment as they do to treatment for physical disorders? The Richardson Committee recommended different criteria for the compulsory treatment of people who lacked capacity and people who did not (see p 59, above). The Scottish and proposed Northern Irish laws require at least a significant impairment of decision-making capacity (see p 46, above). In Northern Ireland it is proposed to go even further, and have a single piece of legislation covering all the ground covered by the MHA and the MCA here. Yet in England and Wales, the 1983 Act contains no trace of an incapacity test as a precondition of compelling a person to accept admission and treatment for mental disorder.

But suppose that we have found that the patient lacks capacity on some test or other. Many would argue that this is a minimum requirement for compulsion for the sake of his own health, even if we know that we can do him some good. Equally, however, even if we know that we cannot do him any good, he still lacks capacity. Is there any reason why we should not treat him like a perpetual child? The justification for helping the child to reach maturity is not there, but neither is the qualification for participation in legal rights and duties. We would obviously still owe him the duties of humanity, to provide him with the necessities which might promote the development of his physical, mental and emotional health as best we can. We should try to take decisions in his best interests rather than those of anyone else, as the 2005 Act requires us to do. There is no reason to do this in a particularly restrictive environment, out of touch with everyday life. We ought never to give up hope that one day he might improve or progress and this can best be promoted by as much contact with ordinary life as is possible.

What about the other possible justification for compulsion, the protection of other persons? For people who reject the arguments based on impaired capacity this may be the only possible reason for intervention. For others, including the Richardson Committee, it may be an alternative justification. But what are other people entitled to be protected against? They are certainly entitled to some protection against conduct which the law defines as criminal. There is a need for society to admit that in some cases it can protect itself against this, even though it cannot demonstrate the offender's blameworthiness in the usual way (Kittrie, 1971). But how far beyond the confines of the criminal law is the civil law entitled to go? At present, it goes far beyond being "dangerous" and indeed there are other things against which people may legitimately claim protection. But we ought to know what they are.

The other question is whether the machinery of civil commitment should be used for the purpose of protecting the public. It has, as we shall see, enormous advantages over the criminal process, both for the professionals and for the person concerned. But the risks involved are also manifest. If in effect we are creating a special sort of crime called "antisocial mental disorder", should we not admit it? There are some who fear that the 2007 amendments, by broadening the categories of people who may be compelled under the MHA, have introduced the possibility of preventive detention for just such an offence. But it still has to be shown that there is treatment available which will do some good.

However, we might also bear in mind Carson's (1989a) stricture that:

> "Legalistic approaches are not well known for being successful in ensuring that more resources are obtained for patients or that higher standards are consistently enforced but other approaches are not either."

Even if psychiatry is a problem, law is a problem too. The law is a tool of intervention as well as a protection against it. Legal interventions deserve just as much scrutiny as do medical.

3 PROFESSIONALS AND FAMILIES

This chapter is about the respective roles of the various professionals and the patient's family in making decisions under both the Mental Health Act 1983 (MHA) and Mental Capacity Act 2005 (MCA). There used to be only two kinds of professional who had a formal role to play under the MHA. Approved social workers employed by the local social services authority were responsible for making applications for compulsory admission to hospital and guardianship. Doctors, usually approved psychiatrists, were responsible for providing the recommendations and evidence upon which the compulsory powers were based. Doctors were also responsible for what happened to the patient in hospital and played a large part in the decisions about how long he would stay. The only other professional role was the nurses' holding power under section 5. Among the most important changes introduced by the 2007 amendments is the recognition of the contribution which other professions can make to the assessment, care and treatment of people with mental disorders and disabilities. The approved social worker's role has been taken over by a range of approved mental health professionals who need no longer be local authority employees. The responsible medical officer's role has been taken over by a range of approved clinicians, one of whom will take overall charge as responsible clinician. The MCA deprivation of liberty process also depends upon a series of professional assessments, most of which can be conducted by the same range of professionals as can operate the procedures in the MHA.

The only roles which remain the exclusive preserve of the medical profession are the provision of medical recommendations and evidence to support compulsory admission to hospital or guardianship under the MHA and making the mental health assessment to support a deprivation of liberty authorisation under the MCA (perhaps because of the decision in *Winterwerp v The Netherlands* (1979–80) 2 EHRR 387, p 98, below). The MHA process of civil commitment has two curious features. The first is that the doctor never has the final word. She may recommend but she cannot decide. The second is that the decision to apply can be made either by a detached professional or by a lay person who is closely involved with the patient. The parallel roles of approved mental health professional (AMHP) and nearest relative are a hangover from the old procedures for admitting private and pauper patients under the Lunacy Acts, which depended on who was going to pay for the patient's incarceration.

1. PATIENTS AND PAUPERS

The common law allowed anyone to restrain a dangerous lunatic. Any relative, friend or neighbour who was prepared to foot the bill could arrange for him to be confined in a private madhouse or public hospital, without going to the trouble and expense of invoking the Crown's ancient jurisdiction over the person and property of those found lunatic by inquisition. Libertarian lawyers such as Lord Mansfield (see *Coate's Case* (1772) Lofft 73) were clearly troubled by this and the first Act for regulating Madhouses (1774) made it unlawful for them to take patients without the written and sealed order of a physician, surgeon or apothecary. In 1828, the Act to regulate the Care and Treatment of Insane Persons in England extended this idea to the public subscription hospitals (but not yet to the oldest charitable hospital of all, Bethlem or Bedlam as it was popularly known) and laid down a procedure which was remarkably like that of today. An order was made by the person who would see that the bill was paid, and supported by two medical certificates (except for a short term emergency confinement, where one was enough). This pattern continued, with refinements, until 1890. Then for the first time, it was laid down that the initial petition should, if possible, be made by the husband or wife or a relative of the patient and, except in an emergency, the order of a judicial authority was required. At first the doctors had been seen as a protection against unscrupulous families and madhouse keepers. By the end of the nineteenth century, the patient was thought to need protection against unscrupulous doctors as well.

For pauper or vagrant lunatics, however, the position was quite different. The earliest Acts expressly dealing with the confinement of lunatics were the Vagrancy Acts of 1713 and 1744, which were designed to prevent a variety of social misfits wandering about and becoming a charge on parishes other than their places of origin. Two justices were allowed to confine "persons who by lunacy or otherwise are furiously mad or so disordered in their senses that they may be dangerous to be permitted to go abroad" even if they were not chargeable to the parish as paupers. Those who were chargeable to the parish might in any event be disposed of as the parish officials thought fit. Increasingly, this meant confinement, usually in the poorhouse or workhouse, although some were sent to charitable hospitals and more and more to the private madhouses. There, the condition of pauper lunatics was so terrible that the reform movement campaigned to set up county asylums where they might be better cared for (see chapter 1). The next step was to devise procedures which would oblige the poor law officials to identify suitable candidates and send them there. These generally involved the parish overseers, and later the poor law relieving officers, in bringing pauper or vagrant lunatics before the justices, who could then direct them into an asylum. The early nineteenth century reports and statutes chronicle the battle between the reformers' ambition to secure proper care and treatment (as they saw it) in an asylum or hospital and the more economically-minded poor law authorities. As early as 1811, however, the justices had to call for medical assistance before issuing a warrant to take the patient to an asylum. The patient's family had nothing to do with it, unless they were prepared to assume financial responsibility, in which case they were allowed to discharge him if he was not actually dangerous. The Lunacy Act 1890 brought together all the procedures for both paying and non-paying patients, but the differences between them remained until the National Health Service Act 1946.

The procedures under the Mental Deficiency Act 1913 allowed parents to commit their young or severely handicapped children without any judicial order, provided that there were two medical certificates. More commonly, "defectives" were committed by judicial order on the petition of a relative, friend or relieving officer, again with two medical certificates. It was this Act which introduced the idea that one of the doctors should be specially approved for the purpose. But it also allowed a policeman or relieving officer to take an abandoned, neglected or ill-treated "defective" to a place of safety without any medical certificate at all.

With the dismantling of the old poor law administration following the Local Government Act 1929, relieving officers became local authority public assistance officers, but they continued to be "duly authorised" under both the lunacy and mental deficiency legislation to operate the admission procedures for non-paying patients. Under the Mental Treatment Act 1930, "pauper lunatics" became "rate-aided persons of unsound mind" but it also became possible to admit them direct to certain hospitals for a short period without any medical certificate at all.

The 1930 Act made cautious moves in the direction of community care, authorising local authorities to establish psychiatric outpatient clinics and to arrange after-care. Already, with the setting up of the first training course for psychiatric social workers at the London School of Economics in 1929, there was an idea that social workers might have a professional role to play in the care of people with mental disorders. When the NHS was set up in 1948, the responsibilities of local health authorities to provide services for the care and after-care of many types of patient were expanded. The particular function of arranging the compulsory admission of mental patients was given to them, and shorn of its connection with the relief of poverty, which was transferred to central government. Many of the former public assistance officers stayed as mental welfare officers, duly authorised as before. But the authorities were also recruiting an entirely different type of social worker to undertake case work as part of their care and after-care functions. Their training, skills and outlook were radically different from those of the former public assistance officers. In some places their roles were not fully integrated until after the 1959 Act.

The 1959 Act did away with the need for judicial involvement in compulsory admission (unless it was necessary to gain entry to private property by force). The Percy Commission (1957, para 390) thought that the best protection against unjustified admissions was:

"that the working of the new procedures should be in the hands of people who have the sort of knowledge and experience needed to form a sound judgment on the questions at issue."

The Commission had no doubt that these people were doctors. Stronger safeguards would be provided by requiring more than one medical opinion, by insisting that one of the doctors was specially qualified to give it, and by removing the power to detain patients without medical advice.

The Report gave little attention to why, in that case, it was necessary for the relative or mental welfare officer to be involved at all, although there is discussion of the methods of overcoming the relative's objections. It was assumed that the age old practice of an application by a relative or local official should continue. Much emphasis was given to improving services for patients in the community. But it does not seem to have occurred to the Commission that trained and experienced social workers might not be content to see themselves as errand boys and girls for the family or the doctors. Nevertheless, although "no responsible relative or mental welfare officer would lightly disregard or dissent from [the doctors'] advice", (para 404) the Report conceded that in the last resort both must be free to do so. The more professional the officials involved have become, the more questionable becomes the role of the relative, whose only qualification is proximity to the patient. Not only may this "distort detached perception", but he "may himself be an integral part of the patient's mental disorder" (Gostin, 1975). Indeed, it is not always clear who should be labelled the "patient" and who the "relative".

2. APPROVED MENTAL HEALTH PROFESSIONALS

(a) Definition and qualifications

Under the 1959 Act, local health authorities had a duty to appoint sufficient mental welfare officers to carry out the role in their area. Some appointed all their field social workers. Some appointed only those with a special interest in the work, who might include former untrained duly authorised officers as well as trained psychiatric or hospital social workers. After these functions were transferred to the new all-purpose social services departments under the Local Authority Social Services Act 1970, specialist training courses gave way to generic social work training and field-workers might no longer be able to concentrate on the client groups for whom they had special skills or experience. For a while, less specialism might mean less expertise and less independence.

The 1983 Act tried to shift the emphasis towards a fully independent and specialist professional role. Mental welfare officers were replaced by approved social workers (ASWs). The 2007 amendments have carried this process further, by expanding the range of professionals who may become approved mental health professionals (AMHPs). They have also broken the link with local government, in that AMHPs do not have to be employed by a local authority at all. They do, however, have to be approved by a local social services authority (LSSA) and authorised to act on behalf of that or another LSSA. Although they may only be approved by one authority they may be authorised to act for more than one. Self-employed fee-paid practice has become possible.

Technically, an AMHP is a person approved by an LSSA to act as an AMHP for the purposes of the MHA (MHA, s 114(1) and (10)). The LSSA must be satisfied that she "has appropriate competence in dealing with persons who are suffering from mental disorder" (s 114(3); Mental Health (Approved Mental Health Professionals) (Approval) (England) Regulations 2008, SI 2008/1206, reg 3(1)). In deciding this, the LSSA must take into account (a) that the person fulfils at least one of the "professional requirements" listed in Schedule 1 and (b) the other matters listed in Schedule 2 (reg 3(2)). Four professions are listed in Schedule 1: social workers registered with the General Social Care Council, first level nurses whose entry in the Nursing and Midwifery register indicates that their field of practice is mental health or learning disabilities nursing, occupational therapists registered under the Health Professions Order, and chartered psychologists listed with the British Psychological Society and holding a practising certificate from the Society. The Act expressly excludes registered medical practitioners from approval as AMHPs (s 114(2)).

Schedule 2 lists five key competence areas to be taken into account. These begin with the application of key values to the AMHP role: the ability to identify, challenge and, where possible, redress discrimination and inequality in relation to AMHP practice; an understanding of and respect for individuals' qualities, abilities and diverse backgrounds, and the ability to identify and counter any decision which may be based upon unlawful discrimination; the ability to promote the rights, dignity and self determination of patients consistent with their own needs and wishes, to enable them to contribute to the decisions made affecting their quality of life and liberty; and a sensitivity to individuals' needs for personal respect, confidentiality, choice, dignity and privacy. These values are obviously closely linked to the guiding principles of respect and autonomy in the MHA Code of Practice (see p 6, earlier).

The other four "competencies" put particular stress on the social perspective on mental disorder. In summary they cover: *knowledge and understanding of the legal and policy framework*, including the particular needs of children and young people and a sensitivity to race and culture in the application of the legislation; *a critical understanding of models of mental disorder*, the social perspective on disorder and mental health needs, the implications of mental disorder for parents, relatives and carers, and the implications of a range of treatments and interventions for patients, relatives and carers; *the ability to articulate the social perspective*, to work in partnership with patients, relatives, carers and other professionals and agencies, to recognise, assess and manage risk, to manage anxiety, risk and conflict, to plan, negotiate and manage compulsory admissions and community treatment orders, and the relevant legal and practical processes, and to balance the competing demands of confidentiality and effective information sharing; and finally *the ability to "make properly informed independent decisions"*, to analyse and share appropriate information "having due regard to confidentiality", to fill in the necessary forms, provide clear and reasoned oral and written reports, and present a case at a legal hearing, and to evaluate outcomes and communicate decisions.

The Welsh Regulations (Mental Health (Approval of Persons to be Approved Mental Health Professionals) (Wales) Regulations 2008, SI 2008/2436) are drafted differently but to similar effect; they include knowledge of Welsh language legislation and policy and consideration for people for whom Welsh is the language of choice (Sch 2, paras 2.2, 1.6).

This is a tall order indeed and it is unusual to see the knowledge and skills required for any job set out in this detail in Regulations, which are not as easy to change in the light of experience as is Departmental guidance. Whatever their professional background, new AMHPs cannot be approved unless they have completed within the past five years a training course approved by the General Social Care Council or the Care Council for Wales (reg 3(3)). These will be at the higher specialist post qualification level, which is a step up from the old ASW training (General Social Care Council, 2007).

Approval may be for a period of five years (reg 4). It must be on condition that the AMHP does at least 18 hours agreed post qualification training each year (reg 5(a)). AMHPs must also undertake to inform the LSSA if they agree to act for another LSSA (reg 5(b)), or if they are suspended from their professional register or listing (reg 5(c)), or are no longer registered or listed (reg 5(d)). Approval is suspended if the AMHP's professional registration is suspended, but if the suspension is lifted the approval must be restored for the remainder of the term, unless the LSSA are not satisfied that the AMHP has appropriate competence (reg 6). Approval can end prematurely if the AMHP resigns, no longer meets the professional requirements, is in breach of the conditions, or the LSSA are no longer satisfied that the AMHP has appropriate competence (reg 7). Despite its serious consequences for the practitioner, no mechanism is laid down for challenging the LSSA's decision to "disapprove" an AMHP. It would, of course, be susceptible to challenge in the Administrative Court on normal judicial review principles (illegality, irrationality or unfairness). It is, perhaps, unlikely that the right to practise as an AMHP is an aspect of the right to respect for private life protected by article 8 of the ECHR (but compare the situation of care workers prevented from doing any sort of care work under the former system for black-listing people working with children and vulnerable adults: *R (Wright) v Secretary of State for Health* [2009] UKHL 3, [2009] 1 AC 739).

The guidance for approving authorities (NIMHE, 2008) emphasises that the Act now distinguishes between being approved as an AMHP, which can only be done by one LSSA at a time, and being authorised to act on behalf a particular LSSA. An AMHP may be authorised to act on behalf of other authorities too. If so, she must notify the approving LSSA in writing as soon as reasonably practicable (reg 5(b)). It is also possible that one LSSA may approve a person who has already been approved by another LSSA. If they do so knowingly, they must notify the former LSSA (reg 7(5)). The earlier approval ends automatically on approval by another authority (reg 7(2)(iii)).

When professional approval was first introduced in 1983 there was quite a battle, reflecting the same ambiguities about the social worker's role as there had been before. Some criticised the original training scheme, not only for restricting the numbers who might enter, but also for concentrating too heavily on legal and psychiatric knowledge, rather than on the social factors and social work strategies involved, both in assessment and in finding alternatives to hospital admission and detention (Barnes, Bowl and Fisher, 1990; Prior, 1992). Under the new scheme, the competencies stress the social aspects of mental disorder and meeting mental health needs, but the pool has been widened to include professionals who are usually more closely associated with the clinical rather than the social perspective on these issues.

(b) Role in compulsory procedures

The tasks of an AMHP fall into three broad categories. They begin with the rarely needed powers under sections 115 and 135 of the MHA to gain access to mentally disordered people living in the community who may need her help (see chapter 4). Next, and much the most important, is her role in the process of arranging compulsory admission to hospital. This is discussed in detail here. She has a similar but much less frequently invoked role in arranging reception into guardianship, and if a social worker she may also be involved in carrying out the responsibilities of a guardian on behalf of the LSSA or in supervising the work of a private guardian (see chapter 9). Lastly, an AMHP is amongst those who are entitled to recapture absconding or escaping compulsory patients. She also has a formal role in arranging community treatment orders (see chapter 7).

Under section 11(1) of the MHA, applications for compulsory admission to hospital either for assessment or for treatment may be made either by an AMHP or by the patient's nearest relative. Even if the professional opinion of the AMHP is that the application should not be made, she cannot prevent the relative from making it (even, in the case of an emergency application, on the recommendation of the family doctor or of a locum with no previous knowledge of the family at all). In practice, of course, the AMHP carries the necessary forms and knows about the admission policies of the local hospitals. She may therefore be tempted to deny the relative access to these. This would be most improper, for the Act gives the relative the right to apply whatever the AMHP may think. However, as the MHA Code points out, an:

"AMHP is usually a more appropriate applicant than a patient's nearest relative, given an AMHP's professional training and knowledge of the legislation and local resources, together with the potential adverse effect than an application by the nearest relative might have on their relationship with the patient" (para 4.28).

Wherever a patient is compulsorily admitted on the application of his nearest relative (except on an emergency application), section 14 of the MHA requires the managers to notify the LSSA, for the place where the patient lives, as soon as practicable. The authority must then arrange as soon as practicable for an AMHP to interview the patient and provide the hospital with a report on his social circumstances. The hospital doctors need as much information as possible about the context in which the incident or behaviour which triggered the admission took place, and also about other methods of handling the problem, and this is what an AMHP is trained to assess. It was obviously intended that this duty should apply to all compulsory admissions except those which only last for 72 hours. Unfortunately, it is not entirely clear whether it applies when an emergency admission is converted into an ordinary admission for assessment. Ideally, the hospital should have an objective social assessment as soon as possible after any admission in which this was not available beforehand (or if available was ignored).

Equally, the nearest relative cannot prevent an AMHP from making an application for admission for assessment. But the Act clearly contemplates that the AMHP will involve the nearest relative. Before or within a reasonable time after making such an application (which includes an emergency application: see *Re GM* [2000] MHLR 41), the AMHP must "take such steps as are practicable" to inform the person (if any) who appears to be the patient's nearest relative that the application is to be or has been made and of the relative's right to discharge the patient (s 11(3)). As an admission for assessment only lasts for 28 days, or 72 hours if in an emergency, "within a reasonable time" must mean as soon as possible. But when telling the relative of his power to discharge, it would be wise also to tell him that the patient's doctor may prevent this if the patient "would be likely to act in a manner dangerous to other persons or to himself" (s 25(1)).

However, an AMHP may not make an application for the patient's long term admission to hospital for treatment (or, for that matter, reception into guardianship), without first consulting the person (if any) who appears to her to be the nearest relative (s 11(4)(b)). The Act does not impose a duty to make inquiries about who is the nearest relative and the AMHP's conclusion about whom to consult can only be attacked on traditional judicial review grounds (*Re D (Mental Patient: Habeas Corpus)* [2000] 2 FLR 848). The consultation can be done before or after the AMHP interviews the patient (see p 82, below) (*Re Whitbread (Habeas Corpus: Compulsory Admission)* [1997] EWCA Civ 1944; (1998) 39 BMLR 94, CA) and it may be proper to use an intermediary, for example because the nearest relative does not speak English (*B v Cygnet Healthcare* [2008] EWHC 1259 (Admin), [2008] 1 MHLR 106). But it means a "genuine invitation to give advice and genuine consideration of that advice"; merely informing the nearest relative will not do (*Re Briscoe* [1998] EWHC 771 (Admin)); nor will "doing no more than nod" in the direction of such a dialogue, by leaving it as late as possible to consult the nearest relative, thus seriously inhibiting his chances of having an effective input (*GD v Edgware Community Hospital and Barnet LBC* [2008] 1 MHLR 282).

The only exceptions are where this is "not reasonably practicable" or would involve "unreasonable delay" (s 11(4)(b)). The Code advises that the nearest relative need not be consulted when it is not practicable to establish who he is or where he is, or "where to do so would involve an excessive amount of investigation involving unreasonable delay" or where consultation is not possible because of the nearest relative's own health or mental incapacity (para 4.59). In theory, an admission for assessment ought to give ample time to trace and consult the relative. The old Code (para 2.13) used to advise that "practicability" referred only to the *availability* of the nearest relative and not to how appropriate it was to inform or consult him. However, in *R (E) v Bristol City Council* [2005] EWHC 74 (Admin), Bennett J questioned this:

"Is the approved social worker really bound to inform/consult the nearest relative of a patient who may intensely dislike a patient and/or who would, or might, not act in the patient's best interest? The answer, in my judgment, is, of course not and particularly so where the patient, as here, is competent and has strongly expressed her wish that her nearest relative [her sister, Mrs S] is not informed or consulted" (para 28).

The answer, in his view, was that the AMHP had to balance two competing interests. On the one hand, it was clearly intended that the nearest relative should have a significant role in protecting the patient and this should not be lightly removed by invoking impracticability. On the other hand, the patient had a right to respect for her private life, of which her medical and psychiatric treatment and care is undoubtedly an important aspect. The Code now advises the AMHP to consider the detrimental impact upon the patient's article 8 rights:

"Detrimental impact may include cases where patients are likely to suffer emotional distress, deterioration in the mental health, physical harm, or financial or other exploitation as a result of consultation" (para 4.60).

Decisions not to consult should not be taken lightly, and AMHPs should consider the benefit to the patient from involving the nearest relative, the patient's wishes and capacity, any detrimental effect, and whether there is reason to think that the patient's objection may be intended to prevent relevant information being discovered (para 4.61).

Wise advice though this is, it should also be borne in mind that the procedure for replacing the nearest relative now covers cases where the patient or the AMHP considers him unsuitable to act (see p 86, below). Invoking this procedure may be preferable to failing to involve the nearest relative at all. His right to be consulted could only be outweighed by clear evidence of detriment to the patient if the nearest relative were to be informed of the situation. The Code rightly points out that "consultation must not be avoided purely because it is thought that the nearest relative might object to the application" (para 4.63). That might even be an unjustified interference with the relative's article 8 rights.

Whether or not he has been consulted, the nearest relative has the right to prevent an admission for treatment (or a reception into guardianship). An AMHP may not make the application if the nearest relative has notified that AMHP, or the LSSA on whose behalf the AMHP is acting, that he objects (s 11(4)(a)). The Act does not insist that the AMHP obtain the relative's positive consent. But she must record in the application whether or not she has consulted the relative, if not why not, and if she has, that the relative does not object (see Mental Health (Hospital, Guardianship and Treatment) (England) Regulations 2008, SI 2008/1184, (the MHHGT Regs), Form A6; for Wales, see Mental Health (Hospital, Guardianship, Community Treatment and Consent to Treatment) (Wales) Regulations 2008, SI 2008/2439). An application which states that the wrong person has been consulted as nearest relative is not "duly completed" (*R v South Western Hospital Managers, ex p M* [1993] QB 683). If the

AMHP makes the application without consulting the person she should have consulted or if that person objects, the patient's detention will be unlawful (*Re S-C (Mental Patient: Habeas Corpus)* [1996] QB 599, see also pp 128 and 281, later; *Re Briscoe* [1998] EWHC 771 (Admin)). She may, however, apply to a county court for the relative to be replaced, on the ground that the objection is unreasonable (see later).

More commonly, however, the patient's relatives are anxious for him to be admitted, but would like the AMHP to take the responsibility. This is natural enough, although some social workers may feel that if the family want the admission so much, they should be prepared to face the facts and take the responsibility themselves. But it is not surprising that the Code advises otherwise. The AMHP's professional training should enable her to withstand and overcome any antagonism from the patient. If this proves impossible, it is far more important for the patient's own future health and well-being that he should retain a good relationship (if he has one) with his family than with the mental health professional.

AMHPs can come under a great deal of pressure to act, not only from families but also from GPs and others. The MHA insists that they do at least consider the case. If the nearest relative of a patient living in their area "requires" this, the LSSA *must* make arrangements for an AMHP to consider the patient's case on their behalf with a view to making an application for his admission to hospital (s 13(4)). There is no discretion to refuse, however unreasonable the demand. This caused a great deal of worry initially, but apparently formal requests are very rare (Barnes, Bowl and Fisher, 1990). The duty only applies to a "patient", who is defined (in s 145(1)) as a "person suffering or appearing to be suffering from mental disorder". If the AMHP decides not to make an application, she must give the relative a written explanation (s 13(4)). The Code rather unhelpfully suggests that this "should contain, as far as possible, sufficient details to enable the nearest relative to understand the decision while at the same time preserving the patient's right to confidentiality" (para 4.80).

Referrals can, of course, come from many other sources. If an LSSA "have reason to think" that an application for hospital admission or guardianship may need to be made in respect of a patient in their area, they *must* make arrangements for an AMHP to consider the case on their behalf (s 13(1)). This means that they must have enough AMHPs available round the clock to do this for them. The duty applies to all patients within their area, not simply to those who are ordinarily resident there. This is as it should be: as with looking after children in need, the imperative is to get on with the job, not to waste time working out who should pay. If the patient is admitted for assessment to a hospital which is not within their area, and the LSSA "have reason to think" that an application for admission for treatment may need to be made, they remain under the duty to make the necessary arrangements (s 13(1B), (1C)).

Unless different arrangements have been agreed locally, the AMHP should have overall responsibility for co-ordinating the assessment (Code, para 4.40). This means trying to get the right professionals together to consider the case and the alternatives. Whether at the end of the day an application is made is, of course, entirely a matter for the AMHP. "Although AMHPs act on behalf of a LSSA they cannot be told by the LSSA or anyone else whether or not to make an application" (Code, para 4.51). Section 13(1A) now makes it clear that the AMHP *must* make an application if (a) she is satisfied that it ought to be made in respect of the patient, and (b) she is "of the opinion, having regard to any wishes expressed by relatives of the patient or any other relevant circumstances,

81

that it is necessary or proper" for the application to be made *by her*. She has no duty to act in any case which she does not herself judge to merit it, whatever the family or the doctors may say; but if the case does merit it, there is a clear indication that she should be ready to do the job herself if this is what the family wants.

However, before an AMHP makes any application for admission to hospital, she *must* "interview the patient in a suitable manner" and satisfy herself that "detention in a hospital is in all the circumstances of the case the most appropriate way of providing the care and medical treatment of which the patient stands in need" (s 13(2)). This can present difficulties, both legal and practical. What is meant by an "interview" and how can it be done?

We tend to think of a two-way oral exchange, such as happens on television or radio or when we apply for a job. The AMHP should try to establish whether the patient has particular communication needs and take steps to meet them, for example by arranging a signer or professional interpreter or providing a hearing aid for a deaf patient who does not have one. Communication difficulties can also add to the problems of making an accurate assessment of people from certain ethnic minorities, for example some Asian women. But what if the patient cannot communicate at all or (perhaps understandably) refuses to do so? The Oxford English Dictionary contains old definitions which involve only a personal meeting, or getting a "view, glance or glimpse". Could that be enough to be "suitable" in such cases? The problem with this is that the Act also requires that any applicant has "personally seen" the patient, either within the 14 days which end on the date of the application (s 11(5)) or, in an emergency application, within the past 24 hours (s 4(5)). An "interview" suggests something more than just seeing the patient, although perhaps not more than making the best attempt possible to establish two-way communication with him. If the AMHP has done her best, but the patient refuses to co-operate, that should be enough: see *M v South West London and St George's Mental Health NHS Trust* [2008] EWCA Civ 1112, [2008] MHLR 306.

The Code advises that it is not desirable for patients to be interviewed through a closed door or window, which should only be considered where other people are at serious risk. Unless there is an immediate risk of physical danger to the patient or others, AMHPs should consider applying for a warrant to enable the police to gain access (para 4.54). Similarly, if interviewing is difficult because of the short term effects of alcohol or drugs, AMHPs should wait until the effects have worn off. If this is not realistic, because the patient's behaviour is disturbed and action is urgent, she should do her best on the basis of whatever information she can obtain from reliable sources (para 4.55). Patients should be given an opportunity of seeing the AMHP alone, unless the AMHP has reason to fear physical harm (para 4.53); but unless the case is urgent, patients should also be helped to have someone else, such as a friend or mental health advocate, present if they want (para 4.52).

As well as seeing the patient and consulting the nearest relative, the AMHP will also want to consider consulting other significant people, such as the parents of a patient under 18, other relatives, carers and friends (Code, paras 4.66, 4.67). She will obviously want to consider how the patient feels about this, whether there is any evidence of hostility, abuse or exploitation, and what sort of a relationship they have with the patient (para 4.68). Other agencies which have been involved in the patient's care, not only in the mental health services but in other services, for example for older people or substance misusers, should also be consulted where possible (para 4.69).

Whatever decision the AMHP makes, she should explain this to the patient, and "subject to normal considerations of patient confidentiality" to the nearest relative, the doctors involved, the GP, and the patient's care co-ordinator if he has one (para 4.78). If the decision is not to apply, the AMHP should also advise the nearest relative of his right to do so instead, and suggest that he consult the doctors involved if he wishes to pursue this (para 4.79). The mechanics of making the actual application are discussed in chapter 4.

Once an AMHP has been involved in compelling a patient to go into hospital, the oddity is that she has little formal role to play in what happens after that. She has no legal voice in the treatment of the patient while he is in hospital or in whether the patient is ready to be discharged. Unlike the nearest relative, she has no power to discharge the patient. An AMHP may be asked to supply a social circumstances report for the hospital or for a tribunal (see chapter 8) or to arrange the after-care for which her LSSA are responsible when the time comes for the patient to be discharged (see chapters 7 and 9), but these tasks may also be given to other professionals. On the other hand, she may remain part of the multi-disciplinary team concerned with the patient and she has a formal role in the arrangements for community treatment orders, which is similar but not identical to her role in arranging reception into guardianship (see chapters 7 and 9).

3. THE PATIENT'S FAMILY

(a) Definitions of "relative" and "nearest relative"

The patient's "nearest relative" is normally determined by taking whoever comes first on the MHA's list of relatives (s 26(1) and (3)). If there is more than one in the same category, the elder is preferred regardless of sex, and full-blood relationships are preferred over half-blood (s 26(3)). But any relative who is caring for the patient or with whom the patient ordinarily resides (or, if now an in-patient, last lived with or was cared for by) is promoted to the top of the list (s 26(4)). This is particularly likely to affect people looking after their elderly kin, who might otherwise yield to an older or closer relative. It does not, however, promote those relatives who give the most devoted care while the patient is in hospital unless they also did so before he went in. It could also lead to difficult conflicts between those with whom the patient lives and those who claim to be caring for him. Fortunately, for the purpose of section 11(4)(b), p 79, above, the AMHP need only consult the person who "appears" to be the nearest relative and the court will only hold that she has consulted the wrong person if she has applied the wrong legal test or reached a conclusion which no reasonable AMHP could have reached (*Re D (Mental Patient: Habeas Corpus)* [2000] 2 FLR 848; see also *R (WC) v South London and Maudsley NHS Trust* [2001] MHLR 187).

People whose parents were not married to one another are regarded as related only to their mother's side of the family and not to their father unless he "has" parental responsibility for them (s 26(2)). Parental responsibility comes to an end when the child reaches 18, so does this mean that the relationship also comes to an end for this purpose? This is an outdated exception to the general rule (in the Family Law Reform Act 1987, s 1(1)) that relationships are to be traced without regard to whether or not a person's parents were married to one another. It is surprising that the opportunity was not taken to correct it in the 2007 amendments.

Anyone who does not "ordinarily reside" in the United Kingdom, Channel Islands or Isle of Man must be ignored if the patient does reside here (s 26(5)(a)). A person under the age of 18 must be ignored unless he is the patient's spouse, civil partner (or recognised cohabitant, see below) or parent (but who now would "section" a tiny child?) (s 26(5)(c)). Curiously, a relative who is himself a mental patient (informal or compulsory) is not automatically ignored, although he may be replaced by a county court (see later).

The list of relatives is as follows:

(i) *Husband, wife or civil partner.* A spouse or civil partner comes first even if aged under 18, but must be ignored if the couple are permanently separated, either by agreement or under the order of a court, or if one of them has deserted the other "for a period which has not come to an end" (s 26(5)(b)). These are not exactly easy questions for an AMHP or hospital to determine, especially at short notice. They use technical terms dating back to family law as it was before the 1959 Act. Desertion means the intentional withdrawal from cohabitation, without the other's consent or a good excuse. Technically, to be separated by agreement or court order would require a formal agreement or order relieving the parties of their duty to live together. These are rarely made these days. So perhaps an informal agreement to separate or a court order keeping one party away from the other would be sufficient. However, being separated is not the same as living in different places. Spouses and civil partners who live in different places (perhaps because one has been in hospital) but still regard themselves as a couple and intend to resume cohabitation when they are able to do so would not be excluded.

If the patient is not married or in a civil partnership, or if his spouse or civil partner must be disregarded because of permanent separation (under s 26(5)(b)), then a person who has been living with the patient "as the patient's husband or wife or as if they were civil partners" for at least six months and is still doing so (or was until the patient went into hospital) must be treated as a spouse (s 26(6)). Perhaps wisely, a cohabitant does not become nearest relative simply because the patient's spouse is not ordinarily resident in the United Kingdom (so must be disregarded under s 26(5)(a)). Such a situation is by no means far-fetched in these days of international migration. Instead, an adult relative resident here would become nearest relative in preference to the cohabitant. This result may be sensible, but it certainly adds to the difficulty of the AMHP trying to make such sensitive judgments on the ground.

(ii) *Son or daughter.* This includes adopted children, but not stepchildren or the children of an unmarried father without parental responsibility (see s 26(2) above). If there are several, the eldest is preferred regardless of sex (s 26(3)), subject now to the preference given to the "caring" relative.

(iii) *Father or mother.* The 1983 Act places father and mother on an equal footing, so the elder or carer will take priority (s 26(3)), but unmarried fathers do not count unless they have parental responsibility and possibly not at all once the patient has grown up (see s 26(2) above). Children under 18 are not often subject to compulsory powers but the nearest relative is usually the older parent. However, a guardian appointed by a court or by a deceased parent, a person with whom a child is to live under a residence order (s 28), or a local authority having parental

84

responsibility under a care order, is nearest relative (except where the child has a spouse or civil partner: s 27).

(iv) *Brother or sister. Grandparent. Grandchild. Uncle or aunt. Nephew or niece.* Within each of these categories, the principles applicable to sons or daughters also apply. The eldest in any category comes first, regardless of sex, relatives of the whole blood are preferred to those of the half-blood; and children of unmarried parents are treated as if they were the marital children of their mothers, but unrelated to fathers who do not have parental responsibility for them (s 26(2) and (3)); and the caring relative is promoted (s 26(4)).

(v) *Non-related caretakers.* The list of "relatives" ends with any person who is not a relative within any of the above categories, but with whom the patient ordinarily resides (or did so before he was last admitted to hospital) and has done so continuously for at least five years (s 26(7)). Such people come last in the list but may gain promotion because of the rule relating to carers in section 26(4). They can never be treated as the nearest relative of a patient with a spouse or civil partner unless the spouse or partner can be ignored because of permanent separation or desertion.

(vi) *Wards of court.* If a child is a ward of court, no application for compulsory admission to hospital can be made without the court's leave and the functions of nearest relative can only be exercised by or with leave of the court (s 33(1),(2)); reception or transfer into MHA guardianship is not allowed at all (s 33(3)), presumably because the child is already in the guardianship of the court; and community treatment orders are subject to any direction of the court (s 33(4)).

(b) Authorising another to act as nearest relative

Under regulation 24 of the MHHGT Regulations, the nearest relative can authorise someone else to act on his behalf (apart from applying to a tribunal if the patient is subject to a hospital order). He cannot authorise the patient, or someone who must be ignored under section 26(5), or someone who has been replaced under section 29 (see below). The authorisation must be in writing and given to the person authorised. The nearest relative must immediately notify the patient, the hospital managers if the patient is already detained in that hospital, the LSSA if the patient is in the authority's guardianship, both the LSSA and the guardian if the patient is in private guardianship, and the managers of the responsible hospital if the patient is subject to a community treatment order. The authorisation can be revoked at any time in the same way.

This is obviously a sensible provision for the nearest relative who has little contact with the patient or who for any other reason does not wish to perform the role. It is also a less formal alternative to a court order when the patient would prefer someone else to act and the nearest relative agrees to this. Contrary to the view taken by the local authority in *R (E) v Bristol City Council* [2005] EWHC 74 (Admin), this can mean that the person authorised has the right to receive information about the patient and thus avoids the distress which some patients may feel at their estranged relatives knowing all about them. There is no requirement to notify the LSSA of the authorisation before any question of compulsion arises, but it would obviously be sensible to do so. Otherwise, an AMHP may only find out about it when she contacts the nearest relative, which rather defeats the object of the exercise.

(c) Appointment of acting nearest relative by a county court

Under section 29 of the MHA, a county court may appoint an acting nearest relative, either as a way either of supplying a functioning nearest relative for a patient who has none, or more commonly of overriding the wishes of the relative he does have or, now, of replacing a relative whom the court thinks unsuitable. These proceedings are not very common but they do tend to take a very long time, while the need to act may be very urgent. The MHA does not provide for interim orders, but the courts have sensibly decided that the general power to make interim orders under section 38(2) of the County Courts Act 1984 applies (*R v Central London County Court, ex p AX London* [1999] EWCA Civ 988, [1999] QB 1260). Indeed, if the matter is urgent, the order may be made without notice to the nearest relative (see also *R v Uxbridge County Court, ex p B* [2000] 1 MHLR 179; *R (Holloway) v Oxfordshire CC and others* [2007] EWHC 776 (Admin)). The effect, however, is that the professionals can then get on with doing what they think best before the relative has had a chance of having his objections properly heard. If it later turns out that the relative's objections are or were reasonable, then it may be arguable that the patient's detention is unlawful (see *R v Central London County Court, ex p AX London*, above, para 22). But the nearest relative would in any event be in a position to discharge the patient, unless he were now dangerous (in which case it is, perhaps, unlikely that the relative's objections would be reasonable: it all depends at what time the question has to be judged).

(i) Applications

Applications to the court may be made by the patient himself, by any relative, by any other person with whom the patient is living or was living just before going into hospital, or by an AMHP (s 29(2)). The addition of the patient to the list puts right a long-standing injustice. In *JT v United Kingdom* [2000] MHLR 254, [2000] 1 FLR 909, the UK Government conceded that the patient's inability to object to his nearest relative was an unjustified interference with the right to respect for his private life, contrary to article 8 of the ECHR. Legislation was promised but postponed because the whole MHA was under review. Then the Human Rights Act 1998 came into force and in *R (M) v Secretary of State for Health* [2003] EWHC 1094 (Admin), [2003] MHLR 348 Maurice Kay J made a declaration that the law was incompatible with the patient's convention rights. This was a particularly striking case. The patient was a deeply disturbed young woman who self-harmed at the age of 11 and ran away from home at the age of 14. She alleged that her adoptive father had sexually abused her. He denied this but her clinicians believed it to be true. She was extremely distressed to know that, as her nearest relative, he had access to confidential information about her and the legal standing to interfere in her life. Her doctor confirmed that this "caused her anguish and could also adversely affect her mental state". But there was no power for her or for anyone else to have him replaced, however unsuitable he was for the role. This has now been put right.

(ii) Grounds

The 2007 amendments have both added the patient to the list of applicants and unsuitability to the list of grounds. There are now five possible grounds (s 29(3)):

(a) that the patient has no nearest relative or that it is not reasonably practicable to discover whether he has one or who it is; or

(b) that the nearest relative is incapable of acting because of mental disorder or other illness; or

(c) that the nearest relative unreasonably objects to the making of an application for admission for treatment or a guardianship application; or

(d) that the nearest relative has exercised, or is likely to exercise, the power to discharge the patient without due regard to the patient's welfare or the interests of the public; or

(e) that the nearest relative is otherwise not a suitable person to act as such.

Ground (c) is the one which has featured most often in the courts, because it enables an AMHP to proceed despite the nearest relative's objections. But when is a relative being unreasonable? And when should one judge that this is so?

In *W v L* [1974] QB 711 (see also p 44, earlier) the patient, had committed a variety of sadistic acts against pet animals and had also threatened his wife and the baby she was expecting. His 28 day admission was about to run out and the baby had been born. His wife objected to an admission for treatment. She was confident that she could keep him under control with the drugs prescribed. No doubt she did not wish to break up the family and jeopardise her husband's employment just at the birth of their first child. The Court of Appeal decided that the test was not what she subjectively considered reasonable, but what an objectively reasonable relative would do in the particular circumstances of the case. In this case, a reasonable person would regard it as too great a risk, particularly to the baby, to have the husband home until he had been cured. The wife was therefore replaced as nearest relative so that the application could be made.

Sometimes, there are two reasonable views open to such a person, and the court must not interfere simply because it would have chosen the other one (see *Re W (An Infant)* [1971] AC 682). But will it ever be reasonable for the relative to disagree with the professional opinions? In *B (A) v B (L) (Mental Health Patient)* [1980] 1 WLR 116, the law report does not explain why both the doctors and the social worker considered an application necessary. Two doctors had recommended it, but as their examinations had been more than seven days apart, their recommendations were not technically sufficient to found an application. The patient's mother objected and the county court judge thought her objection unreasonable. On appeal, the mother complained that she had not seen the medical recommendations and that she could not be unreasonable if these were not sufficient. The Court of Appeal held that it was enough that her solicitor had seen them and that the applicant did not have to "get his tackle in order" for the admission application before going to the county court. That may be done after the court has ruled on whether the objection is unreasonable.

The second point is fair enough, for the evidence on which an AMHP takes the case to court ought to be much fuller than the formal medical recommendations required for admission to hospital and will probably be out of date before she comes to make the application for admission. Unfortunately, the judgment in this case is couched in such a way as to suggest that the mother *must* have been unreasonable, simply because the two doctors had recommended admission. This cannot be right. The Act's scheme relies upon the independent concurrence of the applicant and doctors as an effective protection for the patient. It was never intended that the decision should be left solely to the doctors. As the Act gives the relative a veto unless the court decides otherwise, it clearly contemplates that the court should evaluate the reasonableness of the relative's attitude in the light of all the available evidence, and not simply rubber-stamp the original doctors' views.

In *S v G* [1981] JSWL 174, a county court judge took as his starting point the merits of the doctors' case for detention, stating that "it is vitally important that matters about which doctors have to be satisfied should be clearly proved". The doctors disagreed about the precise diagnosis, but they had no doubt that the patient was mentally ill. Equally, however, his detention was no longer necessary in the interests of his own health or safety. The question was whether it was necessary for the protection of other persons. The judge concluded from the evidence that it was not. Hence the father's objection could not be unreasonable. The judge did not have to consider whether there might be two reasonable views. His approach is the logical one and seems to have been adopted in later cases: to consider first whether there is a case for the admission for treatment (or reception into guardianship) and then to decide whether the relative's attitude to it is reasonable.

But this raises the question of when these conditions have to be fulfilled—at the date when the section 29 application was made or at the date of the hearing? In *Lewis v Gibson and MH* [2005] EWCA 587, Thorpe LJ and Wall LJ expressed the view that it had to be both. At the date of the application, in order for the court to have jurisdiction, the patient had to qualify for admission for treatment or guardianship, as the case might be, and the relative's objection had to be unreasonable then. But the court has a discretion whether or not to make the order, and it would be difficult to defend a decision to displace the nearest relative when the grounds no longer existed. That might create a difficult dilemma if the grounds undoubtedly existed at the date of the hearing, but it was difficult to show that they had existed at the date of the application: a swift new application might have to be made.

(iii) Procedure

The procedure is governed by the County Court Rules 1981, SI 1981/1687, Part 49, rule 12. Rule 12(3)(a) requires that the nearest relative be made a respondent to the application, unless it is made on ground (a) above "or the court otherwise orders". The Code (para 8.20) suggests that this may be appropriate where the patient has concerns that telling the nearest relative why the patient thinks him unsuitable may have implications for the patient's safety. But the court would be very slow to deprive the nearest relative of this basic component of the right to a fair trial, guaranteed by article 6(1) of the ECHR, especially as his article 8 right to respect for family life may also be engaged.

It was for just this reason that rule 12(3)(b) was amended in 2005, so that the patient is no longer excluded from the court's power to make "any other person" a respondent. In *Lewis v Gibson and MH*, above, at para 40, the Court of Appeal said that the patient should always be notified of the proceedings and his "right to be joined" and a litigation friend should be appointed for a patient who lacked the capacity to take part. Thorpe LJ found it "difficult to conceive of circumstances in which a patient could lawfully be deprived of any opportunity to participate in proceedings". However, in *R (Holloway) v Oxfordshire CC and others* [2007] EWHR 776 (Admin), Beatson J said that this did not cast doubt on the validity of an urgent interim order where this had not been done.

If the patient is not already detained in hospital and the matter is urgent, it may be justifiable to make an interim order, perhaps without even notifying the nearest relative. But if the patient is currently detained for assessment, and an application for the replacement of the nearest relative on ground (c) or (d) (but not (e)) is made before the 28 days run out, section 29(4) provides that the patient may still be detained for assessment (which includes treatment) until the application has been finally disposed of. This includes the time limited for appealing from the county court to the Court of Appeal and the time taken for any such appeal to be heard or withdrawn. If, at the end of all that, the nearest relative is replaced, the patient may be detained for a further seven days to enable the formalities of an admission for treatment to be completed. In *R v Central London County Court, ex p AX London* [1999] EWCA Civ 988, [1999] QB 1260, para 21, the Court of Appeal suggested that it was undesirable to use the interim order procedure if section 29(4) applied, because the matter was no longer urgent. But in *R (M) v Homerton University Hospital* [2008] EWCA Civ 197, [2008] 1 MHLR 92, the Court of Appeal confirmed that it was possible to admit the patient under section 3, following an interim replacement order, even though the section 2 admission was automatically extended under section 29(4).

The argument against relying on the automatic extension of the admission for assessment under section 29(4) is that the patient has no immediate right to apply to a tribunal; so he might have been better off if his relative had agreed to the admission after all, for then he could apply straightaway. *R (H) v Secretary of State for Health* [2005] UKHL 60, [2006] 1 AC 441 concerned the same severely mentally disabled young woman who was the subject of the section 29 application in *Lewis v Gibson and MH*, above. Her mother had found it difficult to look after her and her behaviour had become more and more aggressive. She was admitted for assessment in January 2003. Her mother tried unsuccessfully to discharge her and objected to a proposed guardianship application. An application was made to replace the mother and the court made an interim order. This meant that the patient could go into a suitable residential placement. But the section 29 proceedings were not concluded until May 2005, so in theory MH could have been detained in hospital for assessment all that time without recourse to a tribunal. The Court of Appeal made a declaration that section 29(4) was incompatible with the right of a detained person to speedy access to a court under article 5(4) of the ECHR. The House of Lords overturned the declaration of incompatibility, but only because the Secretary of State can and should refer such cases to a tribunal to avoid a violation of the patient's rights. There is now a duty to do so once six months have passed since the patient was admitted to hospital (see p 258, later).

(iv) Effects

The court may appoint the person nominated in the application to act as the patient's nearest relative, provided that that person is suitable and willing to do so; otherwise the court must specify some other suitable and willing person (s 29(1A)). All the statutory functions of a nearest relative (including the right to apply to a tribunal if the patient is subject to a hospital order) are transferred to the person appointed (s 29(1)). If an LSSA are given the powers of a nearest relative, they must arrange for the patient to be visited in any hospital or care home to which he is admitted for any reason and do whatever else would be expected of the patient's parents (s 116). This obviously involves far more than the legal functions of a nearest relative.

If the nearest relative was displaced on ground (c) or (d), he cannot apply to the county court for the order to be discharged (see s 30(1)(b)). However, the object of replacement on these grounds is to overcome his objections to a *particular* admission or reception into guardianship. So if the patient was liable to be detained or subject to guardianship when the order was made, or became so within three months, or was a community patient when the order was made, the order will come to an end when the patient is discharged or the particular admission ceases for some other reason to have effect (s 30(4)(a)). Otherwise, it lapses automatically within three months of the order (s 30(4)(a)). (This applies to all kinds of detention under the Act, apart from remands to hospital and interim hospital orders in criminal cases, s 30(4A).) So the displacement is only likely to be long lasting if the admission or guardianship is likely to be long lasting, as guardianship may well be.

If the order was made on ground (a), (b) or (e), the object is to provide a long term substitute for a missing, incapable or unsuitable relative. The court itself may specify a maximum duration (s 29(5)) and the displaced relative can apply for it to be discharged (s 30(1)(b)). However, a person replaced under ground (e) because he was unsuitable can only apply for discharge with the leave of the court (s 30(1A)). It is hard to see why a similar approach was not taken to relatives displaced under grounds (c) and (d). However, if the patient is still in hospital, the displaced nearest relative can apply for the patient's case to be reviewed by a tribunal once in every 12 month period after the order (s 66(1)(h) and (2)(g)). In practice, this will cover relatives displaced under grounds (c), (d) and (e).

The patient and the person appointed to take the place of the nearest relative can always apply for the order to be discharged (s 30(1)(a)). So may a person who becomes nearest relative when the person displaced ceases to be the nearest relative, for example because he has died or the patient has divorced him (s 30(1)(b)). The patient and the person appointed to take the place of the nearest relative may also apply for the order to be varied to appoint someone else instead (s 30(2)). Oddly, an AMHP may apply to vary the order but not for its discharge (s 30(2)). If the person appointed in place of the nearest relative dies, then any relative can apply for the discharge or variation of the order (s 30(4)).

The assumptions underlying all of this are curious, to say the least. The admission procedures assume that the patient is an irrational being whose liberty may properly be removed by extra-judicial process, subject only to later review by a tribunal if the patient asks. His nearest relative, on the other hand, is assumed to be a rational individual, with a significant role to play in the patient's care which may only be removed after a judicial hearing in the courts. In some families, it can be difficult to decide who should be labelled the "patient" and who the "relative", but the consequences of that initial allocation are crucial for all concerned.

(d) Role

The nearest relative has a role which is parallel to that of an AMHP in arranging the patient's compulsory admission to hospital or reception into guardianship, but unlike the AMHP he has a right to be consulted before an admission for treatment or to guardianship and to object (see above). Unlike the AMHP, he also has power to discharge a civil patient from detention or guardianship, although discharge from hospital may be prevented if the patient would be likely to act dangerously were he to be released. He has no right to object to a community treatment order, but must be consulted and informed unless the patient has requested otherwise. Nor, of course, does he have the right to discharge a patient from a hospital admission or guardianship ordered by a court or directed by the Justice Secretary (see chapter 7). However, whenever he cannot himself discharge a patient who is liable to be detained or subject to guardianship, he may apply to a tribunal (see chapter 8).

In the debates leading up to the 1982 amendments, many suggested that the powers of the nearest relative should be removed. An independent social assessment was certainly needed in addition to the medical opinions, but the relative could not supply it. He had no professional knowledge, either of mental disorder or of the facilities available for treatment. He might be too closely involved with the patient to judge the situation dispassionately and could easily assume that the only response to a crisis was immediate admission to hospital. Alternatively, he might be so committed to the patient's care that he could not see that there might be better alternatives which the patient might also prefer. Yet it was for just these reasons that the Government argued that the relative should retain his powers:

" . . . some relatives may prefer to feel that they are in control of the situation, and they will be in the best position to judge when they are unable to cope any longer with the patient" (DHSS et al, 1978, para 3.16).

With the increased emphasis on the need for expert social as well as medical assessment, with the importance of being able to look for and arrange community alternatives to hospital admission, and with the developing professionalism of the AMHP role, it is difficult indeed to justify the continuing legal functions of the patient's relatives. They do, of course, have a very important part to play in the assessment process and in the provision of support for the patient, but that is very different from having a formal legal role in the process of compulsion.

4. CHILD PATIENTS, THEIR PARENTS AND LOCAL AUTHORITIES

The MHA compulsory procedures can be used for children of any age, whereas the MCA deprivation of liberty scheme applies only to people who have reached 18 (MCA, Sch A1, para 13). The MHA Code rightly says that "the legal framework governing the admission to hospital and treatment of children is complex" (para 36.3) but the Code does not cover the whole field. This is because there are several ways of overcoming any opposition, either from the child or from his family, to the care or treatment which the professionals think most appropriate to the child's needs. The choice between them is not straightforward, but there seems to be some reluctance to use the MHA, although there is much to be said for this from the child's point of view. There are, in any event, extra safeguards before any child under 18 can be given ECT (electro-convulsive therapy), whether or not he is detained under the MHA (see pp 201–202, later).

(a) Parental responsibility, competent and incompetent children

The general rule is that married parents share parental responsibility for their children (Children Act 1989, s 3(1)). If the parents are not married to one another, the mother always has parental responsibility (s 3(2)). The father can acquire it by a court order or a formal agreement with the mother or by being registered as the father after 1 December 2003 (s 4). Step-parents may also share parental responsibility by a formal agreement with the parent or parents who have parental responsibility or by court order (s 4A). Other people in whose favour a residence or special guardianship order has been made, and a local children's services authority (LCSA) in whose favour a care order has been made, also have parental responsibility for as long as the order is in force (ss 12(2), 14C, and 33(3)).

The general principle is that anyone with parental responsibility can give a valid consent to a child's medical treatment and admission to hospital for that purpose (s 2(7)). This means that parents may "volunteer" their children for treatment for both physical and mental disorders and disabilities. But this general proposition is subject to a number of qualifications.

First, not all people with parental responsibility are in the same position. If there is an order that the child is to live with one of the parents, the other cannot agree to anything which is inconsistent with that order (s 2(8)); but the courts have also said that the parent with whom the child lives should consult the other about big decisions in the child's life. So it may be unwise to take that parent's word for it in particularly serious or contentious situations (see the MHA Code, para 36.13). On the other hand, if the child is in care, the LCSA can limit the parents' exercise of parental responsibility (s 33(3)). Special guardians can exercise it to the exclusion of anyone else (s 14C(1)(b)).

Secondly, there may be some procedures which are so serious or controversial that they do not fall within the scope of parental responsibility at all. Sterilisation for non-therapeutic reasons is the only procedure which definitely falls within this category (see *Re B (A Minor) (Wardship: Sterilisation)* [1988] AC 199, 205; *Re W (A Minor) (Medical Treatment)* [1993] Fam 64; and *Re E (A Minor) (Medical Treatment)* [1991] 2 FLR 585). The Code suggests that there may be other treatments falling outside what it calls the "zone of parental control", for example, ECT which could be considered particularly invasive or controversial (para 36.14). There is no UK case law to support this. The Code says that the "zone of parental control" is derived from the case law of the European Court of Human Rights, but refers only to *Neilsen v Denmark* (1988) 11 EHRR 175. This case, far from limiting parental authority, recognised that it extended to allowing a 12-year-old child to be locked up for several months in a closed psychiatric ward (see p 95 below).

Thirdly, some children have a say in their own treatment and care. Section 8(2) of the Family Law Reform Act 1969 provides that the consent of a child aged 16 or 17 is as good as if he were of full age. This only applies where the child has capacity to make the decision. Furthermore, in *Gillick v West Norfolk and Wisbech Area Health Authority* [1986] AC 112, the House of Lords decided that even below the age of 16 a child might be able to consent to his own medical treatment. If the child can and does consent to the treatment, the parents cannot prevent it and indeed the child can ask that the treatment be kept confidential. A mother's complaint that this was an unjustified interference with her right to respect for her family life failed in *R (Axon) v Secretary of State for Health* [2006] EWHC 37 (Admin), [2006] 2 FLR 206. It is customary to refer to these children as "*Gillick* competent". Whether the test of "competence" in a child is, or should be, any different from the test of "capacity" for an adult (see chapter 2) is controversial. There are passages in *Gillick* which suggest that more understanding is expected of a competent child than the MCA expects of an adult. An adult, as we have seen, is not to be taken to lack capacity simply because he makes an unwise decision. But should we expect a child to have reached a certain degree of wisdom and maturity, as well as understanding and free will, before we respect his decisions?

It might have been thought that, if the child is competent to give consent to his own treatment, he also has the capacity to refuse it. But Lord Donaldson MR has twice said that anyone with parental authority may give an alternative consent which can override the child's objections: see *Re R (A Minor) (Wardship: Consent to Medical Treatment)* [1992] Fam 11, which concerned a 15-year-old girl with fluctuating psychotic behaviour and suicidal tendencies, where the other two judges did not support him; and *Re W*, above, which concerned a 15-year-old girl with anorexia nervosa, where one judge did but the other did not. There is also at least one High Court case stating that a local authority do not need to apply to the court for an order authorising treatment against the child's wishes if they have parental responsibility for the child: see *Re K, W and H (Minors) (Consent to Treatment)* [1993] 1 FLR 854. This assumes that any person with parental responsibility can authorise treatment against the child's wishes. It is, to say the least, an unattractive thought that a parent, or even a local authority, may authorise the forcible treatment of a competent adolescent without any of the safeguards attached either to court proceedings or to admission under the MHA. The reality is, as the Code points out, that these cases were decided before the Human Rights Act. The right to respect for private life protected by article 8 of the ECHR includes protection of physical and psychological integrity against compulsory medical intervention unless it can be justified under article 8(2): see eg *YF v Turkey* (2004) 39 EHRR 34. In relation to 16 and 17-year-olds, the Code advises that "it is not wise to rely on the consent of a person with parental responsibility in these circumstances" (para 36.33).

The MHA puts beyond doubt the position of a 16 and 17-year-old who does have capacity in relation to informal admission to hospital for treatment for mental disorder. Section 131(3) provides that if he consents, he may be admitted irrespective of the views of anyone with parental responsibility. Section 131(4) provides that if he does not consent, he may not be admitted even with the consent of a person with parental responsibility. Of course, he may have the capacity to consent to hospital admission but not to every element in his treatment and care. However, the Act does not also deal with the position of *Gillick* competent children under 16 (cf the Children Act 1989, below). But again the Code advises that:

> "the trend in recent cases is to reflect greater autonomy for competent under 18s, so it may be unwise to rely on the consent of a person with parental responsibility" (para 36.43).

It is unfortunate that the 2007 amendments did not also put this matter beyond doubt. Competence is a more rational and defensible dividing line than chronological age, however hard it may be to determine in practice.

If the child is not competent, or expresses no view, then it will generally be possible to rely on parental consent, subject to the limitations already discussed. The Code makes the interesting point that a child may have the intellectual capacity to make the decision but in fact be unable to do so, because he is so overwhelmed by the situation (paras 36.28, 36.37). However, some would argue that all children, whether competent or not, have liberty interests which should be protected against the well-meaning but potentially arbitrary decisions of their parents. With the best will in the world, parents of mentally disturbed or disabled children will find it hard to recognise their children's best interests all of the time. Equally, the children's welfare may be damaged even further if they are forced into confrontation. Hence Gostin (1975) argued that parents should not be able to "volunteer" their children for admission to mental hospitals at all, without some additional check, such as an automatic tribunal review.

(b) Orders in the family courts

A fourth limitation on parental responsibility is that a court may always override the decision of parent or child. Thus the court can prohibit a treatment proposal even though it is supported both by the parents and by the doctors. In *Re D (A Minor) (Wardship: Sterilisation)* [1976] Fam 185, for example, an educational psychologist made an 11-year-old girl with Sotos' syndrome a ward of court in order to prevent the sterilisation proposed by her mother with the support of her paediatrician and an obstetrician. This case established the important principle that a girl should only be deprived of her human right to bear children if this was indeed necessary in her own best interests. On the other hand, the court may allow treatment which the parents oppose. In *Re B (A Minor) (Wardship: Medical Treatment)* [1981] 1 WLR 1421, for example, the Court of Appeal sanctioned an operation to save the life of a Down's syndrome baby after the parents had decided that it would be kinder to allow her to die.

There are several procedures available for seeking a decision from the court. One possibility is to invoke the inherent (non-statutory) jurisdiction of the High Court to protect the welfare of all children, usually by making the child a ward of court. Under the Children Act 1989, however, disputes about any particular aspect of parental responsibility can be resolved by a "specific issue order" (s 8(1)), so the inherent jurisdiction should rarely be necessary for this type of "single issue" case (*Re HG (Specific Issue Order: Sterilisation)* [1993] 1 FLR 589; *Re R (A Minor) (Blood Transfusion)* [1993] 2 FLR 757; cf *Re O (A Minor) (Medical Treatment)* [1993] 2 FLR 148). A non-parent, including a local authority, usually needs the court's permission to apply for a specific issue order (see s 10(1), (2), (9)), but this should not be an obstacle to an LCSA or NHS trust, or to a professional such as the educational psychologist in *Re D* (above), who is or appears to be acting in the best interests of her patient or client. An LCSA are not supposed to use the inherent jurisdiction to obtain a result which they could obtain by an order under the 1989 Act (1989 Act, s 100(5)), so a specific issue order should be their preferred route: see *Re R (A Minor) (Blood Transfusion)*, above, though the point seems to have been missed in *Re S (A Minor) (Medical Treatment)* [1993] 1 FLR 376 and *Re O (A Minor) (Medical Treatment)*, above. A specific issue order cannot be made if a child is in care under a care order (1989 Act, s 9(1)), but this is because the local authority have parental responsibility and can usually make the decision for themselves. If the local authority cannot make the decision, because it is not within the scope of parental responsibility (or "zone of parental control"), they may have to seek leave to invoke the inherent jurisdiction.

Although that jurisdiction is theoretically based upon the status of the Crown as *parens patriae*, it is thought that the court's powers are wider than those of the parents and do include the power to override the wishes of even a competent child. The decided cases go beyond saving the child's life (*Re W (A Minor) (Medical Treatment: Court's Jurisdiction)* [1993] Fam 64; *Re R (A Minor) (Wardship: Consent to Medical Treatment)* [1992] Fam 11) and have authorised more conventional psychiatric treatment irrespective of the child's competence (*Re K,*

W and H (Minors) (Medical Treatment) [1993] 1 FLR 854; *South Glamorgan CC v W and B* [1993] 1 FLR 574; *Re C (Detention: Medical Treatment)* [1997] 2 FLR 180). This is controversial: why should a competent child be in any different position from a competent adult (Huxtable, 2000)? There is, however, all the difference in the world between a parent (or local authority) being allowed to override the refusal of a competent child without any resort to "due process" and a court being allowed to do so after a fair hearing in which all sides of the argument are allowed to put their case and the best interests of the child are the paramount consideration (1989 Act, s 1(1)). The court, like any other public authority, is also bound to respect the child's Convention rights.

The inherent jurisdiction of the High Court could cover depriving the child of his liberty within the meaning of article 5 of the ECHR, provided that the circumstances fell within those permitted by article 5(1), which include the lawful detention of persons of unsound mind. The extent to which this falls within the scope of parental responsibility is more controversial. In *Nielsen v Denmark* (1988) 11 EHRR 175, the European Court of Human Rights held that it was not a breach of the article 5 rights of a 12-year-old boy for his mother to arrange for him to be admitted to a psychiatric hospital, apparently for no better reason than that he wanted to go and live with his father. This was held not to be a deprivation of liberty within the meaning of article 5 but the exercise of her parental responsibilities:

> "The care and upbringing of children normally and necessarily require that the parents or only parent decide where the child must reside and also impose, or authorise others to impose, various restrictions on a child's liberty. Thus, the children in a school or other educational or recreational institution must abide by certain rules which limit their freedom of movement and their liberty in other respects" (para 61).

It is noteworthy that this case sanctioned the use of parental responsibility to deprive a child of his liberty in controversial circumstances where many might think that either the court processes or the MHA procedures ought to have been invoked.

If a child under 17 has long term needs which are unlikely to be properly met unless the local authority take parental responsibility for him, the proper course would be for the LCSA to bring care proceedings under the 1989 Act. They must first prove: (a) that the child is suffering or is likely to suffer significant harm (including harm to his mental health or development); and (b) that the harm or likely harm is attributable to the care or likely care given to the child not being what it would be reasonable to expect a parent to give to him (or to his being beyond control) (s 31(2)). The order must also be consistent with the paramount consideration of the child's welfare and better for the child than any other order the court might make under the Act or making no order at all (s 1(1), (3), (5)).

A care order confers parental responsibility upon the local authority until the child reaches 18 (s 91(12)). The authority become the child's nearest relative (MHA, s 27) and so could apply for his compulsory admission to hospital; but they have a wide discretion to decide where the child is to be placed (1989 Act, s 23) and this includes the same power as a parent to arrange for the child's informal admission to hospital (*R v Kirklees Metropolitan DC, ex p C (A Minor)* [1993] 2 FLR 187, CA). A care order brings with it a great many other responsibilities towards the child, but the MHA also provides that the local authority must arrange for a child in their care to be visited in any hospital or care home to which he is admitted (whether for treatment for mental disorder or otherwise) and do whatever else would be expected of his parents (MHA, s 116).

If the criteria for making a care order are met, but the child can be properly safeguarded and looked after in his own home, a supervision order under the 1989 Act may be an alternative. The court can include requirements for psychiatric examination and/or treatment (1989 Act, ss 31(1), 35, Sch 3, paras 4, 5). Psychiatric examinations of the child can also be directed as part of the process of assessment in care or emergency protection proceedings or even before any other proceedings are begun (1989 Act, ss 44(6)(b), 38(6), 43). However, a child who has sufficient understanding to make an informed decision may refuse to consent to such a requirement in a supervision order (1989 Act, Sch 3, paras 4(4)(a), 5(5)(a)) or to submit to an examination directed by the court (1989 Act, ss 44(7), 38(6), 43(8)). In *South Glamorgan CC v W and B* [1993] 1 FLR 574, it was held that these statutory rights of refusal might be overridden in the inherent jurisdiction of the High Court, but this must be controversial.

LCSAs also have welfare responsibilities towards children who are being cared for in health service accommodation, hospitals or care homes. They must be notified if any child is, or is intended to be, accommodated by a local health board, special health authority, primary care trust, NHS trust, NHS Foundation trust, local education authority, or in a care home or independent hospital, for more than three months. The children's authority must then consider whether the child's welfare is adequately safeguarded and promoted and whether they should exercise any of their Children Act functions in relation to him (1989 Act, ss 85, 86).

(c) Keeping a child in secure accommodation

The Children Act 1989 also contains restrictions on the circumstances in which both competent and incompetent children who are looked after away from home may be kept in "accommodation provided for the purpose of restricting liberty" (s 25(1)). These restrictions date back to the early 1980s, and were obviously introduced with article 5 of the ECHR in mind, but before there was so much focus on the difference between deprivation of liberty, which can only be done in the circumstances allowed by article 5, and restrictions upon liberty, which are permitted as long as they do not fall foul of some other article, such as the right to respect for private life in article 8 (see chapter 1). They were aimed at the "secure accommodation" where troublesome children being looked after by local authorities might be locked up. But they apply to all kinds of accommodation provided for the purpose of restricting children's liberty. This includes locked wards in mental hospitals, regional secure units and other secure facilities (*R v Northampton Juvenile Court, ex p Hammersmith and Fulham LBC* [1985] FLR 192). It has also been held to include a maternity ward controlled by a key or pass where the nursing staff were instructed not to let the patient leave (*A Metropolitan BC v DB* [1997] 1 FLR 767), but not a clinic providing treatment for eating disorders where there were no devices restricting entry or exit (*Re C (Medical Treatment)* [1998] 1 FLR 384). Hence the restrictions can cover children being looked after by a local authority (whether compulsorily under a care order or by arrangement with their parents); or accommodated by NHS bodies or local education authorities, in which case applications to the court should be made by the accommodating body; or in independent hospitals and care homes, in which case applications should be made by the person carrying on the home or hospital unless the child is accommodated there by a LCSA (see Children (Secure Accommodation) Regulations 1991, SI 1991/1505 (the CSA Regs), reg 7; Children (Secure Accommodation) (No 2) Regulations 1991, SI 1991/2034, reg 2).

Children cannot be kept in secure accommodation unless they are likely either: (a) to abscond from other accommodation and to suffer significant harm if they do, or (b) to injure themselves or others if kept anywhere else (1989 Act, s 25(1); different criteria apply to children remanded to local authority care in criminal proceedings). No child can be kept in secure accommodation for more than 72 hours in any 28 days without a court order (CSA Regs, reg 10(1)). The court can authorise up to three months more (reg 11) and then further periods of up to six months at a time (reg 12). The child must be given an opportunity of legal representation (1989 Act, s 25(6)) and a CAFCASS officer will be appointed for him unless the court thinks this unnecessary. Admission to secure accommodation, including a youth treatment centre, does not automatically bring with it the power to impose treatment without consent. This is governed by the general principles outlined above.

(d) Secure accommodation or the MHA?

The secure accommodation regime does not apply to children who are detained under the MHA (CSA Regs, reg 5(1)). Nor does it cover all the situations in which mentally disordered children may have to be deprived of their liberty. It may therefore be necessary to invoke the assistance of the court or to use the MHA procedures. Despite the courts' reluctance to expose children to the stigma of MHA compulsion, this is in many ways preferable. The secure accommodation provisions, which many associate with bad behaviour, may not provide the most appropriate safeguards for children whose behaviour is the result of mental disorder or disability. The speed and comparative informality of the MHA safeguards may be preferable to the long drawn out court room drama. The MHA Code advises that the choice between using the MHA compulsory procedures and authorising the use of secure accommodation under the 1989 Act depends upon whether the primary purpose is to provide medical treatment for mental disorder (para 36.17). If the child is seriously mentally ill, he may require MHA admission. But if he is behaviourally disturbed and there is no need for him to be hospitalised, secure accommodation may be more appropriate. Professionals:

"should attempt to select the option that reflects the predominant needs of the child . . . whether that is to provide specific mental healthcare and treatment or to achieve a measure of safety and protection. In any event, the least restrictive option consistent with the care and treatment objectives for the child . . . should be adopted" (para 36.18).

If children are admitted to hospital for treatment of their mental disorder, the environment should be suitable to their age (subject to their needs) (MHA, s 131A). The Code advises that this means that they should have appropriate physical facilities, staff with the right training, skills and knowledge, a routine which allows their personal social and educational development to continue as normally as possible, and equal access to educational opportunities if they can make use of them (para 36.68). Where possible, everyone involved in the treatment and care of children should be child specialists (para 36.70). In any event there should be consultation with Child and Adolescent Mental Health Service specialists (paras 36.69, 36.75). The children should have the same access to education as their peers (paras 36.4, 36.77). Fine words, but we still await the day when children are no longer accommodated on adult wards which are completely unsuited to their needs and 72 per cent of children who urgently need specialist psychiatric care are not turned away by adolescent in-patient units (see Mental Health Act Commission, 2004; Children's Commissioner, 2007, 2008).

5. DOCTORS AND APPROVED CLINICIANS UNDER THE MHA

In *Winterwerp v The Netherlands* (1979–80) 2 EHRR 387, at para 39, the leading case about the detention of "persons of unsound mind" under article 5 of the ECHR, the European Court of Human Rights stressed that:

"... except in emergency cases, the individual concerned should not be deprived of his liberty unless he has reliably been shown to be of 'unsound mind'. The very nature of what has to be established before the competent national authority calls for objective medical expertise. Further, the mental disorder must be of a mature or degree warranting compulsory confinement. What is more, the validity of the continued confinement depends upon the persistence of such a disorder."

(a) The recommending doctors

Doctors therefore retain an exclusive role in the initial assessment of whether the grounds for compulsory admission or guardianship under the MHA exist. Applications for admission to hospital under section 2 (for assessment) or section 3 (for treatment), or for reception into guardianship under section 7, must be supported by the recommendations of two doctors (ss 2(3), 3(3) and 7(3)). Remands to hospital for treatment, hospital orders and directions, and transfers to hospital from prison all require the evidence of two doctors (ss 36(1), 37(2)(a), 38(1), 45A(1), 47(1) and 48(1)). Emergency admissions for assessment under section 4 and remands to hospital for reports require the support of only one (ss 4(3) and 35(3)). A warrant under section 135(1) to gain entry to private premises and remove the patient to a place of safety can only be executed if a doctor is present (s 135(4)), although the patient can be taken to hospital without any formal recommendation. The only compulsory MHA procedure in which the support, or at least the presence, of a doctor is not required is the police power to remove a person from a public place to a place of safety under section 136 (see chapter 5).

Whenever the MHA requires the recommendations of two doctors, one of them must be on the list of those approved by the Secretary of State under section 12(2) "as having special experience in the diagnosis or treatment of mental disorder". Approval is delegated to the Strategic Health Authorities (SHAs), who may band together in consortia for this purpose but may not delegate approval to Primary Care Trusts (Department of Health, 2007). The Code requires SHAs to take active steps to encourage sufficient doctors to apply for approval; to ensure that there are arrangements for 24 hour on-call rotas of enough doctors to cover each area for which they are responsible; and to ensure that there are up to date lists of approved doctors, giving contact numbers and hours of availability, and that these are available to all who may need them (para 4.103).

"Special experience" is a necessary but not always sufficient qualification for approval (*R v Trent Regional Health Authority, ex p Somaratne, The Times,* 10 December 1993). There is no hard and fast definition of "special experience". Like the Percy Commission (1957), the Department does not expect approval to be limited to qualified psychiatrists, let alone to consultants. Others, such as GPs, prison medical officers, and police doctors, should be encouraged to apply. But before being accepted for training, GPs should have at least three years' full time experience as a principal and at least six months experience of psychiatric work involving use of the MHA during their post graduate training. They would normally be expected to have Membership of the Royal College of General Practitioners. Psychiatrists should have Membership of the Royal College of Psychiatrists (MRCPsych) or equivalent, and be up to date with their Continuing Professional Development (CPD). Other qualifications or "special experience" may also be considered.

Before approval, suitably qualified doctors must attend a training course accredited by the Royal College of Psychiatrists or the Royal College of General Practitioners. Running such courses is one of the responsibilities of the panels of expert doctors set up by the SHAs to do the actual approval, although they may delegate this to local universities. A course may be offered to trainee psychiatrists as part of their MRCPsych training. Approval is usually for a period of five years at a time, although it may be shorter. CPD evidence may be required for re-approval. Any doctor who is an "approved clinician" for the purposes of the Act (see below) is automatically treated as approved for the purpose of section 12(2) (s 12(2A)). (So it is odd that approval of doctors under s 12 cannot be delegated to PCTs whereas approval of clinicians can.)

It may come as a surprise that all approved doctors are not at least qualified psychiatrists. The problem is that these are still in short supply. The Royal College of Psychiatrists only came into being in 1971 and had then to bring post-graduate training into line with that of other medical specialisms. The content of the section 12 approval courses is not as closely prescribed as is the content of the AMHP courses. Thus, while the section 12 doctor should know more about the diagnosis of mental disorder than the AMHP knows, it is still possible that the AMHP will know more about the law and the other relevant factors than the section 12 doctor knows. Even in the field of diagnosis, there is the problem that learning disabilities are very different from psychiatric illnesses and child psychiatry is very different from adult. It would be sensible if doctors whose only special experience is with one did not make recommendations about another. However this cannot be made a condition of approval.

In all applications, one of the doctors must, if practicable, have "previous acquaintance" with the patient (s 12(2)). The Code suggests that "preferably this should be a doctor who has personally treated the patient. But it is sufficient for the doctor to have had some previous knowledge of the patient's case" (para 4.73). If it has not been possible to use such a doctor, the applicant must explain why (MHHGT Regs, Forms A1, A2, A5, A6, A9, G1 and G2). This is thought particularly important in an emergency application, where the solitary doctor need not be an approved specialist, although previous acquaintance is still only required if practicable (s 4(3)). Sometimes the approved doctor will know the patient beforehand, for example because of previous treatment in hospital, at an out-patients clinic or on a domiciliary visit. But it was originally expected that the patient's GP would supply the second recommendation. The Code suggests that if a doctor does not have previous acquaintance with the patient, it is preferable for her to be section 12 approved (para 4.74). There is, of course, nothing wrong with both doctors knowing the patient beforehand and/or both being section 12 approved (subject to the conflict of interest regulations; see below).

The Department of Health (2001) also takes the view that:

"GPs play a vital role in caring for the mental health needs of their patients. Arranging or undertaking assessments of their patients for possible compulsory admission to hospital . . . is an important part of that task. GPs can bring detailed knowledge of the patient, including relevant information about their medical history, and sometimes about their personal situation, that may be important for a proper understanding of the person's circumstances and assessing whether compulsory powers should be used".

Whether the GP is much of a safeguard for the patient may be doubted. She may not have much knowledge of psychiatry or experience of mental disorder. She is under much more pressure than the specialist psychiatrist to consider the welfare of her other patients in the family or the neighbourhood. Psychiatrists often claim that they spend more time resisting the pressure to admit patients than forcing them in (see, for example, Bean, 1980). Once the specialist has decided to admit the patient, the GP is unlikely to disagree. Whatever her experience, qualifications or private views, the structure of relationships between specialists and GPs is not such as to encourage this.

There will be some emergency admissions where the patient has the protection neither of a specialist nor of a doctor who knows him. Many psychiatric emergencies arise in inner cities with floating populations, at times when one doctor is deputising for another, or where there is no psychiatric emergency team to make domiciliary visits at all hours. But these admissions may not always be lawful (see the report of the Divisional Court's decision in *R v D'Souza* [1992] Crim LR 119, a House of Lords case discussed on p 114, later). It could well be "practicable" for the proposed applicant to chase up a doctor who does know the patient, even though that doctor is not on duty or does not usually make domiciliary visits. Administrative arrangements are not the sole criterion for what is practicable in the eyes of the law.

The Code states that, unless otherwise agreed locally, it is the job of the recommending doctors to find the patient a bed (para 4.75). In practice, of course, it is often extremely difficult to obtain a hospital bed unless a doctor from that hospital has already seen the patient. The law, however, does not insist that one of the doctors must be on the hospital staff. Indeed, because of the spectre of collusion which dominated the procedures for paying patients in the past, it used to start from the presumption that both of them should be independent of it. Now the matter is dealt with in the Mental Health (Conflicts of Interest) (England) Regulations 2008 (see below).

Although it is possible for the nearest relative with the necessary recommendations to apply without involving an AMHP at all, the Code warns doctors who are approached by a nearest relative to advise that it is preferable for an AMHP to consider the case and that the relative has a right to require this under section 13(4) (p 81, above). Doctors should never advise a nearest relative to make an application in order to avoid involving an AMHP in an assessment (para 4.30).

(b) The medical recommendations

Each doctor must have "personally examined" the patient (s 12(1)). The Act does not define an examination, which presents much the same difficulty as the social worker's interview (see p 82, above). An interview might exceptionally include holding a conversation through a locked door, but an examination implies that the doctor must at least see the patient. If access cannot be negotiated, consideration must be given to requesting an AMHP to obtain a warrant under section 135 (Code, para 4.72) (see chapter 4). On the other hand, while it is difficult to hold an interview with someone who cannot or will not speak, it may be possible to examine him. The Code states that it is the job of the AMHP to anticipate communication difficulties and arrange professional interpreters or communication aids where needed (para 4.41). The Code also states that a medical examination must involve direct personal examination of the patient and his mental state and consideration of all the available relevant clinical information, including information held by others, both professional and non-professional (para 4.71). As with an AMHP's interview, however, if the doctors have done their best and the patient refuses to co-operate with the assessment, this should be enough: see *M v South West London and St George's Mental Health NHS Trust* [2008] EWCA Civ 1112, [2008] MHLR 306.

If there are two doctors, their examinations may be joint. But if they examine separately, not more than five days may elapse between the days on which their examinations took place (s 12(1)). The Code advises that, unless there are good reasons for making separate assessments, patients should be seen by the AMHP and at least one of the recommending doctors together (Code, para 4.44). If the doctors do not see the patient together, both should discuss the case with the proposed applicant (Code, para 4.45).

The MHA does not specify that the recommendation must be signed at the same time as the medical examination. But it is important to state both dates accurately on the forms, for two reasons. First, the recommendations must be *signed* on or before the date of the application itself (s 12(1)). In principle, the applicant should not make an application and then go looking for the evidence to support it. Secondly, the application only remains valid for 14 days beginning with the *date* of the last medical *examination*, or in an emergency admission, for 24 hours beginning with the *time* when the examination actually took place or the application if earlier (s 6(1)). If the patient does not arrive at hospital within these time limits, it is unlawful either to take him or to detain him there. The only exception to this timetable is where a second medical recommendation is provided after an emergency admission to convert it into an ordinary admission for assessment (s 4(4)). This can obviously happen after the application has been signed, but in all other respects it must comply with the Act's requirements.

Medical recommendations may also be single or joint but must be in the forms prescribed by the MHHGT Regulations. Recommendations on forms required for one section cannot be used for another, which may be important to an AMHP choosing between an ordinary and an emergency admission for assessment. In an admission for assessment, both ordinary and emergency, the Act only requires the doctors to confirm that the statutory grounds are made out (ss 2(3), 4(3)). But the prescribed forms require them to give reasons why each element in the grounds is made out and, as part of this, to describe the patient's symptoms and behaviour and explain how these lead to that opinion; and to explain why the patient ought to be admitted to hospital and why informal

101

admission is not appropriate (see Form A3 for joint and Form A4 for separate recommendations). In an emergency application, the recommendation also has to explain how long it would take to obtain a second medical recommendation and what risk this would pose to the patient or to other people (see Form A11). In an admission for treatment, or reception into guardianship, the Act itself requires the doctors to give reasons for their opinions (ss 3(3) and 7(3)). The forms require, not only an explanation of the patient's symptoms and behaviour, but also whether other methods of treatment or care (such as outpatient treatment or social services) are available and, if so, why they are not appropriate and why informal admission is not appropriate. They must also state that, taking everything into account, appropriate medical treatment is available at one or more named hospitals (or part of a hospital). Preferably, therefore, they should know in advance the name of the hospital to which the patient is to be admitted (Code, para 4.77) Guardianship recommendations must explain why the grounds are made out, including why the patient cannot appropriately be cared for without powers of guardianship (Forms G3 and G4).

(c) Approved and responsible clinicians

Once the compulsory powers have been invoked, the old law gave important legal functions to the patient's responsible medical officer (RMO), the doctor in overall charge of the patient's treatment. Under the 2007 amendments, that role has been separated into those elements which can be performed by an approved clinician (AC) and those elements which can only be performed by the patient's responsible clinician (RC). The details of their roles will be discussed in later chapters. Generally speaking, there must be an *approved clinician* in charge of the particular treatment which the patient is being given under the powers in Parts 4 and 4A of the MHA and it is that clinician who decides whether or not that treatment is given.

The *responsible clinician*, on the other hand, is the person in overall charge. He is defined: (a) in relation to a patient liable to be detained by virtue of an application for admission for assessment or for treatment (which includes all patients admitted from the criminal justice system except for those remanded to hospital for reports) or a community patient, as "the approved clinician with overall responsibility for the patient's care"; or (b) in relation to a patient under guardianship, as "the approved clinician authorised by the responsible local social services authority to act (either generally or in any particular case or for any particular purposes) as the responsible clinician" (MHA, s 34(1)). The responsible clinician may very well be the approved clinician in charge of some aspects of the patient's treatment, but his formal role relates to the patient's legal status. The RC has to review the case for continued compulsion, may grant leave of absence from hospital, and (if another professional agrees) decide whether or not the detention should be renewed. The RC decides whether or not to make a community treatment order (if an AMHP agrees), what the conditions should be, and whether to recall a community patient to hospital. The RC also decides whether or not a hospital or community patient should be discharged and whether to block discharge by the nearest relative.

Both roles have been opened up to professions other than medicine: chartered psychologists, first level nurses whose field of practice is mental health or learning disabilities, registered occupational therapists, and registered social workers may become ACs and even RCs as well as doctors. But they can only carry out the AC role in relation to a treatment which they are qualified to give:

102

so an AC who was not qualified to prescribe drugs would not be able to direct that a patient be given medication without consent. An individual patient may therefore have several ACs but only one RC. And while an RC must be an AC, an AC will not necessarily ever be an RC. This will depend upon who is in overall charge of the particular patient. *New Roles* (NIMHE, 2008) advises that an individual patient's RC should be "the available AC with the most appropriate expertise to meet the patient's main treatment needs" (para 2.6). These, and thus the RC, may change over time, especially if there is a community treatment order. But it could well be that the clinician who decides whether to recommend the renewal of a long term patient's detention is not a qualified doctor. Views differ on whether this is sufficient to comply with the *Winterwerp* principles (see p 98, above).

The process of approving ACs is laid down in the Mental Health Act 1983 Approved Clinician (General) Directions, made under the National Health Service Act 2006. It is very similar to the process of approving AMHPs (see above), but carried out by SHAs who may delegate it to PCTs. The arrangements may be built upon the panels for approving doctors under section 12, but reflecting the new multi-disciplinary approach. There should be someone on the panel from the same profession as the applicant, as well as user and carer representation (NIMHE, 2008). The duration, conditions, suspension and termination provisions are essentially the same as those for AMHPs. There is mutual recognition of approval between England and Wales if the patient is in one country and the relevant hospital in the other (see Mental Health (Mutual Recognition) Regulations 2008, reg 3).

The person approved must fulfil at least one of the professional requirements in Schedule 1 to the Directions, possess the relevant competencies in Schedule 2, and have completed the initial training course within the previous two years (there are transitional provisions for doctors who are approved or treated as approved because they have recently been carrying out the functions of an RMO under the previous law, or been in overall charge of medical treatment for mental disorder, or been appointed to a consultant psychiatrist post). The professional requirements are the same as those for AMHPs except that they also include doctors. The relevant competencies are the clinical equivalents of those required for AMHPs. In addition to applied knowledge of mental health law, the codes of practice, national and local policy and guidance, other relevant legislation, practice and policy, and NICE guidance, these cover: diagnosis, clinical risk assessment, and the "demonstrated ability to undertake mental health assessments incorporating biological, psychological, cultural and social perspectives"; treatment, including different treatment approaches and their applicability to different patients, and a "high level of skill in determining whether a patient has capacity to consent to treatment"; care planning, developing care plans which combine health, social services and other resources; leadership and multi-disciplinary working. This last is, of course, what the changes are all about. The competencies also cover equality, diversity and non-discrimination issues and communication skills, again on very similar lines to those for AMHPs.

6. CONFLICTS OF INTEREST UNDER THE MHA

It is important that both AMHPs and doctors should be free from conflicts of interest which might cast doubt upon their ability to form a truly independent judgment. Opening up the range of professionals who may be involved in compulsory admissions to hospital or guardianship obviously increases the risk that conflicts of interest might arise. The Mental Health (Conflicts of Interest) (England) Regulations 2008, SI 2008/1205 (made pursuant to MHA, s 12A; for the Welsh equivalent, see the Mental Health (Conflicts of Interest) (Wales) Regulations 2008, SI 2008/2440) lay down the circumstances in which there is a potential conflict of interest, such that an AMHP must not make an application for admission to hospital or for guardianship or a doctor make the required medical recommendation. The AMHP and doctor are collectively referred to as "assessors" for this purpose. These are of four kinds of potential conflict—financial, business, professional and personal.

A *financial conflict* arises if an assessor has a financial interest in the outcome of the decision to apply (reg 4(1)). This would usually arise if the assessor stood to gain from an admission, either by a fee for arranging the admission or from the fees paid to the establishment after the patient was admitted. It would not arise if a fee were paid for an assessment or examination, as long as it was payable regardless of the outcome.

A *business conflict* arises if both the assessor and the patient or another assessor are closely involved in the same business venture (reg 5(1)). Business is not necessarily limited to private enterprise. In the Department's view, it includes being on the Board of a particular hospital (NIMHE, 2008, Annex F).

A *professional conflict* arises where an assessor directs the work of, or employs, the patient or one of the other assessors involved in the case (reg 6(1)), or is a member of a team "organised to work together for clinical purposes on a routine basis" and the patient or the other two assessors are members of the same team (reg 6(2)). This does not exclude the possibility that two of the three professionals involved in an assessment are members of the same team. Nor does the team conflict apply if it is of urgent necessity for an application to be made and delay would involve serious risk to the health and safety of the patient or others (reg 6(3)).

A *personal conflict* arises if an assessor is closely related to another assessor, to the patient, or, if the nearest relative is making the application, to the nearest relative. The relationships are: parent, sister, brother, son or daughter, including step-relationships; uncle, aunt, grandparent, grandchild, first cousin, nephew, niece, parent-in-law, grandparent-in-law, grandchild-in-law, sister-in-law, brother-in-law, son-in-law or daughter-in-law, including step-relationships; half-sister and half-brother; spouse, ex-spouse, civil partner or ex-civil partner; and living with the other assessor, patient or nearest relative as if they were a spouse or partner (reg 7). "In-law" relationships include those based on civil partnership as well as marriage but not the equivalent relationships with people who are only living together.

There are some extra rules for assessors who are doctors. Thus if the patient is to be admitted to a hospital which is a registered establishment, there is a financial conflict if both are on its staff (reg 4(2)), but not if only one of them is. If the nearest relative is making the application, the doctor will have a business conflict if both she and the relative are closely involved in the same business venture (reg 5(2)). Similarly, the doctor will have a conflict for professional reasons if she directs the work of or employs the nearest relative or vice versa (reg 6(2)). Thus, while both doctors may be on the staff of the same NHS hospital, provided that the AMHP is not a member of the same clinical team, they may not both be members of staff of an independent hospital to which the patient is to be admitted.

The new regulations are much clearer than the old, but their object is still confusing. They prevent a doctor recommending the admission of someone who is to be her private patient at a private hospital where she is on the staff or has a financial interest, but they do not prevent a consultant getting together with one of her junior doctors or even another full time consultant in an NHS hospital. If the aim is to provide two genuinely informed opinions, these might be more satisfactory than the consultant and GP. If, on the other hand, the aim is to reassure the patient, he may not regard them as truly independent of one another or of the hospital. The rules do, however, prevent a surgeon on the staff of the admitting hospital from applying for the admission of his wife with the support of two of his psychiatric colleagues (an example drawn from experience).

An AMHP, as the person making the final decision whether or not to apply, should obviously be aware, not only of her own potential conflicts of interest, but also of those of the recommending doctors.

7. MENTAL CAPACITY ACT ASSESSORS

No less than six assessments are required before a person may be deprived of his liberty under the MCA 2005 (see chapter 1). This sounds complicated, but one person can carry out more than one assessment. The people eligible to do the various assessments are laid down in the Mental Capacity (Deprivation of Liberty: Standard Authorisations, Assessments and Ordinary Residence) Regulations 2008, SI 2008/1858 (the DoL Regs) (for the Welsh equivalent see SI 2009/783). Assessors are chosen by the relevant supervisory bodies, the LSSA for a person in a care home, and the PCT for a person in hospital. The supervisory body must be satisfied, not only that the assessor is has the required qualifications to do the job, but also that she is suitable for the particular case (reg 3(3)).

The Deprivation of Liberty Code of Practice (the DoLS Code) therefore suggests that, when choosing assessors, the supervisory body should consider the reason for the proposed deprivation of liberty, the potential assessor's experience of working with the user group in question (eg older people, people with learning disabilities, people with autism or people with brain injury), her experience of working with people with the cultural background in question, and any other specific needs, such as communication difficulties, of the person being assessed (para 4.14). The decisions are those of the assessor alone, and no-one should try to influence her (para 4.16). Assessors must therefore be covered by appropriate professional indemnity insurance or indemnity arrangements (DoL Regs, reg 3).

The *mental health assessment,* that is the diagnosis of mental disorder, can only be carried out by a doctor who is either approved under MHA section 12 or has at least three years post registration experience in the diagnosis or treatment of mental disorder. The doctor must also have completed the training programme provided by the Royal College of Psychiatrists (reg 4). This is to comply with the *Winterwerp* principles (see p 98, above) for proving that the person concerned is "of unsound mind" within the meaning of article 5(1) of the ECHR, so that he may lawfully be deprived of his liberty (DoLS Code, para 4.34). It may therefore be helpful if the doctor knows the person concerned. The doctor must also report to the best interests assessor on how being deprived of his liberty is likely to affect the mental health of person being assessed (Code, paras 4.38, 4.39).

The *"best interests", age and "no refusals" assessments* can only be carried out by a best interests assessor (DoL Regs, regs 5, 8 and 9), though not necessarily by the same one. This may be an AMHP, a registered social worker, a registered first level nurse, a registered occupational therapist, or a listed chartered psychologist with a practising certificate. The assessor must also have at least two years' post qualification experience, have completed the training programme approved by the Secretary of State, and have "the skills necessary to obtain, evaluate and analyse complex evidence and differing views and to weigh them appropriately in decision making" (reg 5(3)(e)). The best interests assessment is the key to the whole process.

The *mental capacity assessment* may be carried out by someone who is qualified to do *either* the mental health assessment *or* the best interests assessment (DoL Regs, reg 6). The DoLS Code points out that this assessor should have an "understanding and practical experience of the nature of the person's condition and its impact on decision-making" (para 4.31). A person who already knows the person concerned may be best placed to make this assessment, which may also reduce any distress it could cause (para 4.31). These factors would point against the mental capacity and best interests assessments being done by the same person, as the best interests assessor cannot be someone involved in the individual case.

The *eligibility assessment* (designed to avoid conflict with the MHA powers) may be carried out *either* by a section 12 doctor who is eligible to do the mental health assessment *or* by an AMHP who is eligible to do a best interests assessment (reg 7). The eligibility assessor is not there to assess the person's best interests. However, she might well form the view that the person concerned is not eligible for the MCA procedure but should be assessed for admission or recall under the MHA. If so, steps should be taken to arrange this (DoL Code, para 4.56, 4.57). As we have already seen in chapter 1, the MCA does not contemplate choosing between the MHA and the DoLS: if the MHA could be used to authorise the patient's detention, the DoLS cannot be.

The upshot of all of this is that every assessment will require at least two professionals, one a doctor to do the mental health assessment and the other from a different profession to do the best interests assessment. Every assessment will also require either a section 12 doctor or an AMHP to do the eligibility assessment. So if the doctor doing the mental health assessment is not section 12 approved, it would make sense to use an AMHP to do the best interests assessment. It may be that PCTs will find it convenient for section 12 doctors, with another best interests assessor, to assess people in hospital and that LSSAs will find it convenient for AMHPs, with a qualified doctor, to assess people in care homes. But many other permutations are possible. The mental health and best interests assessments cannot be carried out by the same person.

However, although the best interests assessor may (with one exception) be an employee of either the supervisory body or the managing authority of the hospital or home concerned, she cannot be someone who is involved in the care, or making decisions about the care, of the person concerned (DoL Regs, reg 12(1)). This means that she cannot be the person assessing the client's community care needs (see chapter 9), even though the need for accommodation, and the type of accommodation needed, may be inextricably linked with whether the client may be deprived of his liberty. If the managing authority is also the supervisory body, as where the client is resident in a local authority's home, the best interests assessor must not be their employee or someone supplying them with services (apart, it must be assumed, from

106

assessment services (reg 12(2)).This is the main guarantee of independent assessment in the whole process, so the role will be an extremely important one.

There are other rules about conflict of interest. No assessor may be a relative of the person concerned or of someone who has a financial interest in the care of the person concerned (DoL Regs, reg 10(1)). The prohibited relationships cover the same ground as the relationships prohibited in the Mental Health (Conflicts of Interest) (England) Regulations 2008 (see above) although they are differently expressed (DoL Regs, reg 10(2)). No assessor may have a financial interest in the case (reg 11(1)). A financial interest means being a partner, director, other office-holder or major share-holder in the managing authority of the care home or independent hospital which is asking for the authorisation (reg 11(2)). This is fair enough as far as it goes, but may well not cover all the situations in which the assessor could have something to gain from keeping the person concerned in the hospital or care home concerned. The DoLS Code advises that supervisory bodies should try to avoid appointing assessors with any other possible conflicts of interest that might call in question the objectivity of their assessment (para 4.13).

The best interests assessment is governed by the general principles in section 4 of the MCA which apply to making all kinds of decisions on behalf of people who are unable to make them for themselves (see chapter 2). These entail consulting, so far as practicable and appropriate, anyone named by the person concerned as someone he would like consulted on such matters, anyone engaged in caring for him or interested in his welfare, and any donee of a lasting power of attorney or deputy appointed by the court (MCA, s 4(7)). They also entail considering the person's own wishes and feelings, beliefs and values, and other factors which would be likely to influence his decision (MCA, s 4(6)). So the best interests assessor should involve the person concerned in the assessment process as much as possible and help him to take part (DoLS Code, para 4.69). She should also be best placed to recommend someone to be appointed as the person's representative if the authorisation is given (DoLS Code, para 4.76; see chapter 4). In many respects, therefore, the MCA has put into legislative form the principles which ought to guide all mental health assessment.

8. COMMENTARY: A MULTI-DISCIPLINARY ASSESSMENT?

The MCA begins with a statement of guiding principles which has no equivalent in the MHA, although the MHA Code of Practice begins with a statement which is in some ways very similar and in some ways rather different (see pp 5–6, earlier). But both place some emphasis upon respect for the patient's individuality and autonomy, on finding the solution which is least restrictive of his freedom of action, and upon promoting his best interests. The MCA scheme for depriving people of their liberty also spells out much more clearly the content of the different types of assessment than does the MHA. But in both schemes, if any one of the assessments is "negative", the detention cannot be authorised.

The theory underlying both procedures is plain. Professional assessment is better than legal adjudication. And "two (or more) professional heads are better than one". In this perfect world, as Peay (2003, p 16) puts it:

"all parties would bring to the decision their own expertise within their discipline, an adequate knowledge and understanding of the law and an ability to apply that expertise to the particular factual situation posed by the patient".

So the psychiatrist would bring her expertise in diagnosing mental disorder, understanding the prognosis, and assessing the treatment which would best suit the particular patient. The GP would have had longer and more frequent contact with the patient, and would thus be able to compare his current presentation with his usual mental state (GPs are supposed to know their patients well as well as unwell). The AMHP would bring an understanding of the social factors influencing the presentation of mental disorder, knowledge of and access to the facilities available to look after the patient in the community and support for him and his family. The reality can be very far from perfect, but then who is to say that adjudication would be any better?

The MHA Code emphases that doctors and AMHPs making assessments have to apply professional judgment and reach decisions independently of one another "but in a framework of co-operation and mutual support" (para 4.43). Support may be particularly important where there is a risk of the patient causing physical harm (para 4.46). But it is one thing to say that the AMHP has the right to act independently and another thing to put this into practice. At best, the doctors may see her as a junior member of a professional team which is devoted to securing the best possible care and treatment for the patient. At worst, they will see her as little more than a messenger to supply the forms, arrange transport to hospital, and smooth over any difficulties with the patient and his family (see Bean, 1980). This tendency could become worse as clinical professionals move into the AMHP role.

In the early days of the 1959 Act, the psychiatric social workers who became mental welfare officers experienced some conflict between their professional training and their statutory role. It was not only that:

"to be able to impose a course of action by physical force if necessary upon another human being is such a violation of the rights of personality that in normal conditions the social worker's integrity no less than the patient's would suffer emotional damage" (Le Mesurier, 1949).

Their training was based on principles drawn from psycho-therapy. These included a non-authoritarian or "non-judgmental" attitude towards the client and a respect for his right to "self-determination". Compulsion could be seen as a failure of casework technique which would jeopardise the building of a successful relationship with the client in future. The clinicians who may now be approved as AMHPs are likely to experience these conflicts just as strongly as did the psychiatric social workers in the past. They too are committing the client to a situation which is outside their control, yet they may also have a continuing therapeutic relationship with the patient which they do not wish to put in jeopardy. On the other hand, as clinicians, they may put the interests of the patient's health and safety (or the safety of others) above the values of autonomy and capacity.

Casework principles no longer figure so prominently in social work training, but any modern course is bound to include sociology, in which the views of the "anti-psychiatrists" (diverse though these are) may be aired. Students will also learn about the triggers within the client's family and social setting which bring about the perceived need for hospitalisation. They will be aware of class, gender and ethnic biases in the recognition and treatment of mental disorder (eg Showalter, 1987; Littlewood and Lipsedge, 1993; Audini and Lelliott, 2002; Healthcare Commission, 2007b). Most of them will have come into the profession with a commitment to redressing the more glaring inequalities in society. Indeed, the AMHP competencies (see above) require them to have a critical understanding of these issues.

Nevertheless, if an AHMP believes that all mental illness is a myth invented by psychiatrists as part of the structure of social control over the disenfranchised classes, the job is not for her. Part of the task is to reconcile her assessment of the patient's needs with her respect for the patient's rights and integrity and to impose a solution if need be. The other part of the AMHP's task is to reconcile the different pressures from the patient, his family, the doctors and her own assessment of the situation. This in the end comes down to identifying a proper sphere of professional competence within which the AMHP may disagree with the doctors, for of her right to disagree with both patient and family there can be no doubt.

The statutory forms expect the doctors to certify that the grounds for admission exist and to explain why informal admission or other solutions are not appropriate. Section 13(2) expects the AMHP to satisfy herself that detention in hospital is the most appropriate way of providing the care and medical treatment which the patient needs. It stops short of requiring her to satisfy herself about what that care and treatment is or why it is needed. Yet practitioners have to confront the issue of what is properly a medical problem and what is properly a social problem or a mixture of the two. Places where this has been done by co-operation between the health and social services seem most successful in finding alternatives to compulsory admission (Barnes, Bowl and Fisher, 1990).

In fact, each of the components in the grounds for admission could contain both a medical and a social element. The first is a diagnosis of mental disorder. This is a clinical matter, but it is necessary to set the patient's behaviour into its social, familial and cultural context in order to make a proper assessment of its meaning. An AMHP ought to be able to recognise behavioural symptoms of mental disorder and mental disability, and to appreciate the impact of the cultural and ethnic background of clients. The next component is that the disorder is bad enough to warrant (or make appropriate) the patient's treatment in hospital. Much will depend upon the medical treatment which is needed and whether the patient is willing to accept it. The doctors' assessment is bound to be coloured by the fact that a patient can only be obliged to accept treatment in hospital. The AMHP may be able to suggest and arrange for other types of care to be given and in different settings. However, it has been suggested that social work assessment is more successful in reducing the use of compulsory admission than in identifying alternative sources of care and treatment in the community (Barnes, Bowl and Fisher, 1990). This may now have changed, with the greater availability of specialist care in the community.

Even if the AMHP is not able to disagree with the opinion that hospital treatment is necessary for the patient's own health, she should be able to ascertain whether it is necessary to use compulsory admission in order to secure it. Sometimes it may be possible to do so in less restrictive conditions. Sometimes it may be possible to explore whether the patient is prepared to accept treatment voluntarily. Bean (1980) suggested that this was not always adequately covered by the doctors, who concentrated upon finding symptoms of mental illness and assessing "dangerousness". In practice, he found, it was the dangerousness rating which determined whether an admission was informal or compulsory. Peay (2003) too discerned that the doctors were more consistently focussed on the patients' clinical needs than on his rights and autonomy.

In general "psychiatrists have not shown themselves to be particularly skilled at predicting dangerousness" (Clare, 1980). According to Clare, the reason for the popular belief that they have some special skill lies in the equally erroneous belief that most psychiatric patients are actually or potentially violent. They are not, although there may be an association between acute psychotic conditions and violence to self or others (see Crichton, 1995). Few psychiatrists have gone as far as Clare in attempting to dispel this faith in their omni-competence, but there is a great deal of American research casting doubt upon it (see, for example, Steadman, 1979). It is equally doubtful whether social scientists have any sufficiently precise knowledge of the causes of dangerous behaviour to enable them to make valid predictions (compare Prins, 1975, with Webb, 1976). But if these are possible at all, they must be based upon the interaction between the patient and his social circumstances (see, for example, Hepworth, 1982).

Barnes, Bowl and Fisher (1990, p 150) argued that for an approved social worker's

"assessment to be truly independent it should not be based on borrowings from psychiatry, but derive from the skills of social workers in understanding how social pressures can affect individual behaviour, and how the relationship between the individual and the social world can be changed by practical assistance, therapeutic relationships, and temporary or more permanent removal from the source of stress".

All of this suggests that, despite their different roles in the process, there is scope for disagreement between the professionals. The MHA Code points out that there is nothing wrong with disagreements. Properly handled, they offer an opportunity to safeguard the interests of patients by widening the discussion of the best way of meeting their needs. Doctors and AMHPs should be prepared to consult other professionals (especially care co-ordinators and other involved in the patient's present care) (para 4.100). If there is an unresolved dispute about the use of compulsion, it is essential that the professionals do not abandon the patient. They should agree upon an alternative plan, including a risk assessment and arrangements for managing the risk (para 4.101).

Peay (2003) found that few of the professional interactions she studied involved overt conflict, but it was surprising how little reference was made to the Act or the Code of Practice. The psychiatrists relied upon the social workers for this, and discussions about the law were "often ill-informed and based upon an intuitive understanding which was not necessarily correct" (p 29). This should not surprise us, but it may have been one reason why the Richardson Committee (1999) recommended that all long term compulsory treatment would have to be approved by a tribunal. They also recommended that the patient's nearest relative should no longer have a legal role in compulsory admission. If the point of lay involvement is to counter-balance the over-mighty power of the professionals who know what's best for us, the relatives are the last people to supply the detached and confident judgment which is required. But then would the lawyers be any better?

4 THE MACHINERY FOR DETAINING PEOPLE

The grounds upon which people may be compulsorily detained in hospital under the Mental Health Act 1983 (MHA), or deprived of their liberty under the Mental Capacity Act 2005 (MCA), and the role of professionals and families in doing this, have already been covered in earlier chapters, but there are many procedural details still to be mentioned. Under the MHA these include the process of making an application, getting a patient to hospital, the duration and possible renewal of his detention there, and the monitoring of the admission documents. Under the MCA, they include the standard and urgent procedures for authorising detention in a hospital or care home. There are also procedures for removing some people, particularly the elderly, to hospitals or care homes under the National Assistance Act 1948. But before anything can be done, there may be a problem of gaining access to the person causing concern. And all of these statutory processes were built upon the underlying common law, so we must first consider what, if anything, is left of it.

1. WHAT IS LEFT OF THE COMMON LAW?

The common law undoubtedly permitted that a:

> "private person may, without an express warrant, confine a person disordered in his mind, who seems disposed to do mischief to himself or to any other person" (*Bacon's Abridgement*, Vol IX, p 469).

In *Black v Forsey* 1988 SLT 572, the House of Lords held that such a power was part of the common law of Scotland. It was this, and not any statutory authority, which justified the admission of non-pauper patients to private madhouses and charitable hospitals in the olden days. It could easily be taken too far—hence Lord Mansfield's strictures in *R v Coate (Keeper of a Madhouse)* (1772) Lofft 73, 98 ER 539, that keepers of madhouses should be taught "that the circumstances of the case alone could support their action", that "everything must appear strictly, with all diligence and due advice, to be done for the best" and that "all unnecessary severity, all confinement other than for the best purpose of the unhappy person's recovery" would be subject to censure; but he had no doubt that such a power existed.

When the Act for regulating Madhouses was passed in 1774, it was designed to provide additional procedural protection, but left the common law grounds for confinement untouched (see s 31). Lord Campbell CJ applied the same approach to the Lunacy Act of 1845, which gave statutory protection to people acting under the certificates and orders which it prescribed, but not to the people actually making the orders. There are several cases which deal with the effect of failure to comply with the 1845 Act's procedures and take contradictory views. But both Lord Denman CJ in *Shuttleworth's Case* (1846) 9 QB 651 and Coleridge J in *R v Pinder, Re Greenwood* (1855) 24 LJQB 148, stated that the common law would permit them to refuse to release an insane person who was dangerous either to the public or to himself. And in *Scott v Wakem* (1862)

3 F & F 328, 176 ER 147, Bramwell B directed the jury that if the defendant (who was a surgeon):

> "had made out that the plaintiff was, at the time of the original restraint, a dangerous lunatic, in such a state that it was likely that he might do mischief to any one, the defendant would be justified in putting a restraint upon him, not merely at the moment of the original danger, but until there was reasonable ground to believe that the danger was over"

(indeed he went further than this, and suggested that if the plaintiff's wife had called the defendant in to cure her husband of delirium tremens, or if the plaintiff himself had afterwards approved of what was done, the defendant would have been justified, providing that he did no more than was necessary and proper in the circumstances). Finally, in *Symm v Fraser* (1863) 3 F & F 859, 176 ER 391, Coleridge CJ directed the jury that the defendant doctors might have succeeded in a plea of justification (they had in fact pleaded that they were not responsible for what was done by attendants whom they had sent after being called in by the plaintiff herself), because what they had done had resulted in the preservation of her life and health, and the prevention of serious mischief to herself or others, while she was suffering from delirium tremens.

However, it would appear that a reasonable belief in insanity was not enough. Thus in *Fletcher v Fletcher* (1859) 1 El & El 420, 120 ER 967, Lord Campbell found for a plaintiff against an uncle, who had committed his nephew in the reasonable belief that the nephew was insane but who did not allege that there was actual insanity at the time: "By the common law of England no person can be imprisoned as a lunatic unless he is actually insane at the time." And as the common law tended to contrast the dangerous lunatic with the harmless eccentric it may be that a reasonable belief in dangerousness is also not enough. In *Sinclair v Broughton* (1882) 47 LT 170, the Judicial Committee of the Privy Council stated that there was no law permitting a magistrate or police officer (in India) to confine a person:

> "in consequence of a bona fide belief that a person is dangerous by reason of actual lunacy; . . . a fortiori, this cannot be done in the case of a bona fide belief of danger from impending lunacy."

But these remarks could be understood in several ways. In any event, it is clear that the powers are limited to doing what is necessary and proper for as long as the danger lasts.

The MHA does not expressly abrogate the common law power. In *Black v Forsey* 1988 SLT 572 the House of Lords held that the Mental Health (Scotland) Act 1984 contained a comprehensive code which impliedly removed any common law powers of the hospital authorities. But in *R v Bournewood Community and Mental Health NHS Trust, ex p L* [1999] AC 458, the House of Lords considered the old cases of *R v Coate*, *Scott v Wakem*, and *Symm v Fraser* (above) and held that the common law doctrine of necessity legitimated the informal admission and treatment of patients in hospital. Indeed, Lord Steyn pointed out that it would justify detention too. *Black v Forsey* was not relevant because it was concerned with a lacuna in the compulsory powers.

The MCA does not expressly abrogate the common law doctrine either. But under the Human Rights Act 1998 (HRA), it is clear that people can only be deprived of their liberty in circumstances which meet both the grounds and the procedures required by article 5 of the ECHR. The MCA provides that the general authority it gives to act in the best interests of incapacitated people does not allow anyone to deprive a person of his liberty, except by order of the court or by an authorisation under the MCA deprivation of liberty scheme or in the limited emergency situations laid down in the Act (MCA, ss 4A and 4B). As the common law doctrine of necessity only applies to people who lack the capacity to make decisions for themselves, it looks as if any common law power to detain the insane has virtually disappeared. The only room for its operation would be in situations which amounted to detention under the common law but not to the deprivation of liberty under the ECHR. There may, of course, be other powers to restrain people from doing immediate harm to themselves or others, but that is another matter (discussed at p 205, later).

2. GAINING ACCESS

(a) The problem

The three "sections" in Part 2 of the MHA will not always give the authorities everything they need to deal with a psychiatric crisis. There is no power to apprehend or detain a person until an application has been "duly completed" (s 6(1)). This cannot be done unless the applicant has personally seen the patient (s 11(5)) and an approved mental health professional (AMHP) applicant must also interview him (s 13(2)). Any application must be "founded on" the requisite medical recommendations (ss 2(3), 3(3), and 4(3)). To give these the doctors must have personally examined the patient (s 12(1)). For this, they will need to gain access to him. The difficulty is illustrated by the salutary example of *Townley v Rushworth* (1963) 62 LGR 95.

The defendant's wife had signed an application form for his emergency admission but the doctor had not yet made the medical recommendation. When the doctor went to the house with another relative and two police officers, the defendant told them to leave. The doctor replied that the defendant must go to hospital whether he wanted to or not and began to prepare an injection. One of the officers restrained the defendant from leaving the room. Seeing a scuffle, the other officer came up and the defendant punched him on the nose. The doctor then injected the defendant and summoned an ambulance. Only after that did the doctor sign the medical recommendation. Subsequently, the defendant was convicted of assault occasioning actual bodily harm to the police officer. His appeal to the Divisional Court, however, was allowed. As the application form had not been "duly completed" by the addition of the medical recommendation, the four people in the house had no power to restrain the defendant, and indeed were trespassers. As they were trespassers, the defendant was entitled to use reasonable force to resist them. So,

"unless it is to be said that a householder is to sit down and submit, not only to his liberty being infringed in his own house, but also to assault by injection, and to his liberty being removed in hospital, I cannot say that to hit out with the fist is an unreasonable use of force" (Lord Parker of Waddington CJ, at p 98).

Lanham (1974) has argued that the decision is wrong and that the Act itself authorised the doctor to do what he did. He suggests that because the recommendation can be signed after the application form (provided that both are on the same day) a signed application is enough to authorise the doctor to enter the premises and make his examination. This cannot be right. An application does not authorise anything until it is duly completed and the provisions quoted above indicate that this cannot happen until the recommendation has been made. Indeed, the court itself went too far, because Lord Parker assumed that all would have been well if the doctor had signed the recommendation beforehand. This he was not entitled to do unless he had examined the defendant very recently. In any event, under section 6(1) a duly completed application merely authorises the taking and conveying to hospital of the patient. There is no reference to entering premises without consent, which is provided for elsewhere by the procedure for getting a magistrate's warrant if entry is refused (see (c) below). Practitioners should not assume that completing the forms, even if it can lawfully be done without seeing the patient immediately, is sufficient to justify entry to private premises, with or without force.

However, the court in *Townley v Rushworth* (1963) 62 LGR 95 did not consider whether the common law might have provided a lawful justification for what was done. It was not clear whether the common law power to "arrest the insane" gave a right of entry to private premises. Lanham (1974) argued that "where a person has a power to arrest the insane and dangerous he can also enter the latter's premises to make the arrest". He based this on the analogy of the common law power to break into premises to prevent a felony and arrest the offender or to follow a felon into his house in order to arrest him. But a power of arrest does not invariably carry with it the right to enter premises by force and there is no case acknowledging this right in relation to the insane. Indeed, in *Anderdon v Burrows* (1830) 4 C & P 210, Lord Tenterden CJ implied the contrary. But if the HRA and the MCA have between them removed the common law power to detain the insane, any power to enter premises in order to do so must also have gone. It could not possibly justify the interference with the right to respect for the home and private life which is protected by article 8.

Of course, there may be some other occupier of the premises who is entitled to grant entry. If the defendant in *Townley v Rushworth* (1963) 62 LGR 95 had owned his house jointly with his wife, she could at least have prevented the doctor and policeman being trespassers, although there might still have been an assault before the forms were signed. Indeed, it ought to be the case that a wife's rights to occupy the matrimonial home also give her the right to license visitors whether her husband likes it or not (and this was held to be so, at least in the case of domestic violence against her, in *R v Thornley* (1980) 72 Cr App R 302). Similarly, a patient living in a flat or bed-sitter may not always have exclusive rights of occupation, so that the landlord may be entitled to authorise entry.

All the common law rules allowing police officers to enter premises without a warrant authorising entry, apart from those to deal with or prevent a breach of the peace, were abolished by the Police and Criminal Evidence Act 1984 (PACE), section 17(5) and (6), and replaced with specific statutory powers. Under section 17 of PACE, a police officer may enter premises without a warrant for a number of specified purposes. As well as arresting a person for any indictable offence and for a number of other offences listed (s 17(1)(a) to (cb), an officer can enter for the purpose "of recapturing any person whatever who is unlawfully at large and whom he is pursuing" (s 17(1)(d)). In *D'Souza v DPP* [1992] 1 WLR 1073, a patient detained under section 2 of the MHA arrived back home at 15:55 The police turned up at 19:00 and used reasonable force to gain entry after the patient's daughter refused them. The House of Lords held that a compulsory patient who is absent without leave from hospital is "unlawfully at large" but "pursuing" connotes an act of pursuit or chase; it was not enough simply to turn up at the premises where they believed the person to be; so the police were not "in the execution of their duty". The final specified purpose is "of saving life or limb or preventing serious damage to property" (s 17(1)(e)). This can cover a person who has gone berserk or is about to commit suicide. In *Baker v Crown Prosecution Service* [2009] EWHC 299 (Admin), (2009) JP 215, the Divisional Court held that the words "saving life or limb" are wide enough to cover saving a person from seriously harming himself, as well as from seriously harming third parties.

The police still have a common law power of entry where a serious breach of the peace is being committed, but the essence of a breach of the peace is putting other people in fear for themselves and the disturbed behaviour of a patient alone in a locked room can scarcely do this.

The MHA Code of Practice advises AMHPs to consider applying for a warrant under section 135 (see below) in two situations where direct access to the patient is not possible. The first is where the AMHP cannot interview the patient face to face and there is no immediate danger to the patient or to anyone else which might justify interviewing him through a closed door or window (para 4.54). The second is where it is not desirable to postpone the medical examination in order to negotiate access for the doctor (para 4.72). Although these appear inconsistent, the Act's requirements for interviews and medical examinations are different, and it is always possible that the patient is willing to allow one professional in but not the other.

(b) Entry under section 115

Section 115(1) empowers an AMHP to enter and inspect any premises (other than a hospital) in which a "mentally disordered patient" is living, if she has reasonable cause to believe that the patient is not under proper care. She must, if asked to do so, produce some duly authenticated document (for which no statutory form is laid down) showing that she is an AMHP (s 115(2)). Section 145(1) defines a "patient" as a person who is suffering or appears to be suffering from mental disorder: but the addition of the words "mentally disordered" in section 115 could limit this power to those who are in fact disordered.

The power is undoubtedly useful, but it is aimed at discovering and protecting patients who for some reason may not be receiving proper care, and not at producing a situation in which the patient may lawfully be "sectioned". Thus, it relates only to an AMHP, although once there she may be able to persuade the occupier to allow entry to a doctor as well. Secondly, it is only exercisable "at all reasonable times" and it is debatable whether this includes the middle of the night, even if a serious psychiatric emergency threatens, although in that case it probably does. Finally, while it might grant a defence to an AMHP who entered without permission or stayed when asked to leave, it certainly does not permit her to gain entry by force. If she is acting within her powers, however, it is an offence for anyone to obstruct her without reasonable cause (s 129).

As part of their comprehensive scheme for the protection of vulnerable people, the Law Commission (1995) proposed replacing this power with a wider one to enter and inspect premises and interview the person in private. This was not taken up in the MCA, but the Law Commission seems reluctant to return to the subject (see chapter 9).

(c) Warrants under section 135(1)

Under section 135(1), an AMHP (and only an AMHP) may lay an information on oath before a magistrate, at any time or any place. It must appear to the magistrate:

> "that there is reasonable cause to suspect that a person believed to be suffering from mental disorder—
>
> (a) has been, or is being, ill-treated, neglected or kept otherwise than under proper control, in any place within the jurisdiction of the justice, or
> (b) being unable to care for himself, is living alone in any such place."

The magistrate may then issue a warrant, which need not name the patient (s 135(5)) but must specify the premises to which it relates. It is addressed to any police officer (who need not be named) and not to the AMHP, but in executing it the police officer must take with him an AMHP (not necessarily the informant) and a doctor (s 134(4)). It may be helpful if the doctor is section 12 approved (MHA Code, para 10.3). The warrant authorises the police officer to enter, by force if need be, the specified premises in which the person is believed to be, and, if thought fit (it is not clear by whom), to remove him to a place of safety, with a view to making an application for compulsory admission or guardianship under the MHA or other arrangements for his treatment or care (s 135(1)). It would be unwise, therefore, for the police officer to remove a person whom the doctor or the AMHP did not think to be in need of treatment or care.

A "place of safety" is defined for this purpose as "residential accommodation provided by a local social services authority under Part 3 of the National Assistance Act 1948" (see chapter 9), a hospital as defined by the MHA (see chapter 1), a police station, an independent hospital or care home for mentally disordered persons, or "any other suitable place the occupier of which is willing temporarily to receive the patient" (s 135(6)). The MHA Code (paras 10.21, 10.22) advises that it is preferable for a person thought to be suffering from mental disorder to be detained in a hospital or other healthcare setting. A police station should not be the automatic second choice. A care home or the home of a relative or friend should be considered. A police station should only be used on an exceptional basis, perhaps because the person's behaviour would pose an unmanageable risk in any other place. Otherwise the person concerned may be caused distress and anxiety by the impression that he is suspected of committing a crime and this may affect his co-operation with the assessment (para 10.24).

A police officer, AMHP or someone authorised by either may take the person from one place of safety to another (s 135(3A)). So if a police station is used at first, health and social care agencies should work with the police to transfer the person to a more suitable setting (para 10.23).

A patient who is taken to a place of safety may be detained there, or in another such place to which he is moved, for up to 72 hours from when he first arrived at a place of safety (s 135(3), (3B)). There is therefore no need to "section" the patient once entry has been gained to the premises, even if he is reluctant to come to hospital. The purpose, however, is to arrange an assessment, and this should be done as soon as possible after arrival and if possible by the doctor and AMHP together (Code, para 10.28). If the doctor is not section 12 approved, the reasons should be recorded (para 10.27). If the person concerned appears to have learning disabilities or be under or around the age of 18, it is desirable for either the doctor or the AMHP to have relevant knowledge and experience (paras 10.29, 10.30).

The maximum period of detention is 72 hours, but as the removal is "with a view to making" an application or other arrangements for him, the Code takes the view that the person detained must be released as soon as it is concluded either that he is not suffering from mental disorder or that no application or arrangements need to be made (para 10.31). But if the doctor concludes that the person concerned does have a mental disorder, she should still involve an AMHP even if she thinks that no arrangements need be made (para 10.33). If compulsory admission is indicated, the AMHP should arrange a second doctor. It is thought unlikely that an emergency application for admission would be justified, as the patient can be transferred to hospital under section 135 (paras 10.51, 10.52).

Neither section 135 nor an emergency admission under section 4 gives any statutory power to treat the patient without his consent (s 56(3)(a) and (b)). There is therefore much to be said for delaying the potentially stigmatising process of "sectioning" until the situation has cooled down somewhat.

Section 135(1) is the obvious answer to the problem of gaining entry. The Code emphasises the importance of locally agreed policies about providing places of safety, providing prompt assessments, arranging transport, and dealing with people who are also under the effects of alcohol or drugs or behaving violently (paras 10.16 to 10.19). But getting a warrant is bound to cause some delay, which could be dangerous if the patient is suicidal or destructive. Carson (1982a) has also pointed out that the grounds are not apt to cover every case in which a compulsory admission might be appropriate. A seriously ill, depressed or suicidal person may be able to care for himself and may not be ill-treated or neglected by anyone else. Nor is he necessarily "being kept otherwise than under proper control".

Health Service statistics suggest that only a few people each year are taken to hospital under section 135, although the numbers are rising: from 246 in 1997–1998 to 503 in 2007–2008 (Health and Social Care Information Centre, 2008a). But statistics are not kept on people taken to police stations and other places of safety. The Law Commission (1995) recommended replacing this power with a simpler power to obtain entry by warrant, which might if necessary be coupled with or followed by an order for assessment or for temporary removal to protective accommodation. This has not been implemented and the Commission's review of adult social care may not include it (see chapter 9).

(d) Warrants under section 135(2)

Section 135(2) deals with the problem of entry once a patient has become liable to compulsion under the MHA (or under the equivalent Scottish legislation). Information may be laid before a magistrate by any constable or other person who is authorised under the MHA to take a patient to any place, or to take into custody or retake a patient who is liable to be so taken or retaken. It must appear to the magistrate:

(a) that there is reasonable cause to believe that the patient is to be found on premises within the magistrate's jurisdiction, and
(b) that admission to the premises has been refused or a refusal is apprehended.

Once again, the warrant authorises any police officer to enter the premises, by force if need be, and remove the patient. The police officer may be accompanied by a doctor and by any person authorised to take or retake the patient, but it is not essential (s 135(4)). It is good practice, however, to take someone from the hospital (or LSSA) who is authorised to take the patient back to where he ought to be (Code, para 10.6). Now that the House of Lords have decided (in *D'Souza v DPP* [1992] 1 WLR 1073; p 114, above) that the power of entry under section 17(1)(d) of PACE is limited to the actual pursuit of absconders, there may be more need to seek such warrants. The legal effects are the same as for section 135(1), but the purpose is different.

3. ADMISSION FOR ASSESSMENT UNDER THE MHA

(a) Ordinary admission under section 2

An ordinary application for admission for assessment must be made by an AMHP on Form A2, prescribed by the Mental Health (Hospital Guardianship and Treatment) Regulations 2008, SI 2008/1184 (the MHHGT Regs), reg 4(1) and Sch 1 (for Wales see Mental Health (Hospital, Guardianship, Community Treatment and Consent to Treatment) (Wales) Regulations 2008, SI 2008/2439), or by the patient's nearest relative or someone authorised by him or by a county court to exercise his functions, in which case the authorisation must be attached, on Form A1 (s 11(1)). The forms require the applicant to state when she last saw the patient, which must be within the 14 days ending on the date of the application (s 11(5)). Form A2 also requires an AMHP to identify the nearest relative if she can and to state whether or not she has yet told him about the application and his power of discharge. She must also state that she has interviewed the patient and is satisfied that detention in hospital is the most appropriate way of providing the care and medical treatment he needs (s 13(2)).

The application must state that it is "founded on" either a joint medical recommendation, which must be in Form A3, or two separate medical recommendations, each in Form A4, and complying with the requirements of section 12 (see p 101, earlier). Each must state the date on which they examined the patient, because if they examined him separately not more than five days must have elapsed between the two examinations (s 12(1)). The reasons why they are of the opinion that the grounds are made out must be explained. The application forms no longer state that they are accompanied by the medical recommendations, but it is hard to see how an application can be "founded on" something that has not yet been done.

The application is made to the managers of the particular hospital and must be personally delivered to an officer whom they have authorised to receive it (reg 3(2)). So there should be such a person on duty at all times when the hospital may admit patients (MHA Code, para 13.7). The application cannot simply be addressed to an NHS Trust and if there are separate units under different management on the same site it can only be addressed to one of those units (paras 4.90, 4.91). The Code says that it is the doctors' responsibility to arrange the hospital bed (para 4.75). But as the applicant has the job of getting the patient there, sometimes against his will, the patient should not be moved unless it is clear that the hospital addressed is willing to have him (para 4.92). The applicant should confirm in advance that the hospital is expecting the patient, give them the likely time of arrival, and if possible get the name of the officer to whom the papers should be given (para 11.24).

The documents give no authority to take the patient anywhere other than the named hospital. This has caused problems where physical treatment (for example after an attempted suicide) is urgently needed, but it is known that the general hospital will not admit compulsory patients. Should the application be made to that hospital, so that the patient can be taken there for life-saving treatment in casualty, and then a fresh application made so that he can be taken to the psychiatric hospital which will admit him? Or should the application be made to the psychiatric hospital, with the intention of taking a detour to the general hospital en route? The latter may be acceptable if there is no intention to admit the patient to an in-patient bed at the general hospital. If there is, the former is more in keeping with the letter of the law. But the administrators should not allow the problem to arise.

An application "duly completed in accordance with the provisions of this Part of this Act" is sufficient authority for the applicant, or any person authorised by the applicant, to take the patient and convey him to hospital at any time within the 14 days beginning with the date of the last medical examination (s 6(1)). This means that unless the case requires prompt action (as most do) the applicant does have a breathing space to see whether the patient's condition changes or other arrangements can be made (MHA Code, para 4.87). An AMHP applicant should also ensure that arrangements have been made to look after any children, dependent relatives, pets and property while the patient is away (para 4.89).

Getting the patient to hospital is the applicant's task. If the applicant is the nearest relative, any AMHP and other professionals involved in the assessment should give him help and advice, but they should not assist in the patient's detention unless they believe it to be justified and lawful (para 11.15). If the applicant is an AMHP, it is her responsibility to make the transport arrangements, choosing which method to use in consultation with the other professionals involved, the patient and (as appropriate) his carer, family or other supporters (para 11.16).

"Patients should always be conveyed in a manner which is most likely to preserve their dignity and privacy consistent with managing any risk to their health and safety or to other people" (para 11.2).

There should be clear arrangements with the various services locally so that people needing help to transport patients can get it without delay. Usually, an ambulance will be best. Sometimes, however, the patient may be violent or dangerous, in which case the police should be asked to help. Even then, an ambulance should normally be used. If the risk is such that it is necessary to use a police vehicle, then a qualified member of the ambulance crew should go with the patient and the ambulance follow directly behind (paras 11.18, 11.20). A car should only be used if it will not put the patient or others at risk of harm and there should be someone to escort the patient as well as a driver (para 11.21). Patients may have someone else to go with them, provided that this will not increase the risk of harm to the patient or others (para 11.23). If the applicant authorises others to take the patient, it is advisable to do so in writing. The authorisation gives them the legal power to transport patients against their will. No more force may be used than is reasonably necessary to effect the purpose (see eg *Allen v Metropolitan Police Commissioner* [1980] Crim LR 441) but the applicant should not be held responsible for the excesses of delegates whom it was reasonable to call in and who should have known better. If the applicant is not travelling in the same vehicle as the patient, the application form and medical recommendations should be given to the authorised delegate for presentation to the hospital (Code, para 11.25).

If the patient escapes, either before he can be apprehended or on the way to hospital, he may be recaptured by the person who had his custody immediately before the escape, or by any police officer or by any AMHP (s 138(1)(a) and s 137(1)). But this only applies during the period of 14 days beginning with the date of the second medical examination. If the patient does not arrive at the hospital within that period, there is no power to take him there, or to admit him if he gets there (s 6(1) and (2)). A proposed patient who learns of the application before he is "taken", therefore, might be well advised to disappear for a fortnight. Provided that he does arrive in time, however, the "duly completed" application is sufficient authority for the managers to detain him there in accordance with the MHA (s 6(2)).

The hospital is also protected by section 6(3), which provides that any application:

"which appears to be duly made and founded on the necessary medical recommendations may be acted on without further proof of the signature or qualification of the person by whom the application or any such medical recommendation is made or given or of any matter of fact or opinion stated in it".

However, although this protects the people involved from civil liability towards the patient, it cannot turn an unlawful detention into a lawful one. If the proper requirements have not in fact been fulfilled, the application is not "duly completed" for the purpose of section 6(1) and (2) (see *R v South Western Hospital Managers, ex p M* [1993] QB 683); and section 6(3) does not mean that the detention can continue simply because the documents *look* correct (see *Re S-C (Mental Patient: Habeas Corpus)* [1996] QB 599, p 81, earlier and p 281, later).

If the patient is formally admitted, or an in-patient is formally detained, the managers must make a record of this, including the date and the time, in Part 1 of Form H3 and attach it to the application (MHHGT Regs, reg 4(4)).

Once admitted to hospital, the patient may be detained there for up to 28 days, beginning with the day on which he was admitted (s 2(4)). But he may be discharged before then, either by the responsible clinician (RC), or by the hospital managers, or (unless prevented by the RC) by his nearest relative (see chapter 7) or by a tribunal (see chapter 8). If he wishes to apply to a tribunal, he must do so within 14 days. Once the 28 days have elapsed, the patient may remain in hospital informally (s 131(1)) but he cannot be further detained unless other compulsory powers are taken *before* the admission for assessment runs out (s 2(4)). There is no power to renew an admission for assessment and it is clear from section 5(1) and (6) that an admission for assessment cannot be replaced with a second admission for assessment or with a "holding power" under section 5(2) or (4) (see chapter 1). Thus, unless the patient becomes subject to a court order or Justice Secretary's direction, any further detention must be by an application for admission for treatment, the criteria for which are a little stricter. The only situation in which the admission for assessment can itself extend beyond 28 days is where before that date an application has been made to a county court for the replacement of the nearest relative (see chapter 3). If an admission for assessment runs out before anything else is done, there is no power to detain the patient, either under the MHA (*R v Wilson, ex p Williamson* [1996] COD 42) or at common law (*Black v Forsey* 1988 SLT 572).

The MHA does not specify what period must elapse before a patient whose detention under section 2 has lapsed can be sectioned again. A series of separate admissions for assessment, interspersed with periods in the community or as an informal patient, might avoid the slightly stricter criteria of admission for treatment. Nor does the Act prohibit an application for admission for treatment being made even though a tribunal has ordered that a section 2 patient be discharged. In *R (Von Brandenburg) (aka Hanley) v East London and the City Mental Health NHS Trust* [2003] UKHL 58, [2004] 2 AC 280, the patient was admitted under section 4 on 15 March 2000, converted to section 2 that same day. On 31 March, he was discharged by a tribunal, but discharge was deferred for seven days so that accommodation could be found and a care plan devised. On 6 April, the day before he was due to leave hospital, an application was made to admit him under section 3. This was supported by his responsible medical officer, who had opposed his discharge before the tribunal, and by another doctor, who had supported the section 2 admission. The patient argued that it was unlawful for the hospital to admit him in those circumstances unless there had been a relevant change since the tribunal's decision.

In the House of Lords, Lord Bingham tried to reconcile principle with practicality. Article 5(4) of the ECHR gives detained patients the right to take proceedings to obtain their release if their detention is not lawful within the meaning of article 5(1)(e). Further (para 8),

> "the rule of law requires that effect should be loyally given to the decisions of legally constituted tribunals in accordance with what is decided . . . It follows that no one may lawfully act in a way which has the object of nullifying or setting at nought the decision of such a tribunal . . . It is not therefore open to the nearest relative of a patient or [an AMHP] to apply for admission of the patient, even with the support of the required medical recommendations, simply because he or she or they disagree with a tribunal's decision to discharge. That would make a mockery of the decision."

However (para 9), psychiatric assessment "is not an exact science" and there is room for bona fide differences of opinion; the patient's mental state may not be static, so a tribunal's decision may not remain sound; indeed the tribunal are assessing the case for detention at the time they make their decision and are not called upon to make an assessment which will remain valid indefinitely; crucially,

> "A conscientious doctor whose opinion has not been accepted by the tribunal will doubtless ask himself whether the tribunals' view is to be preferred and whether his own opinion should be revised. But if, having done so, he adheres to his original opinion he cannot be obliged to suppress or alter it. His professional duty to his patient, and his wider duty to the public, require him to form, and if called upon express, the best professional judgment he can, whether or not that coincides with the judgment of the tribunal."

Finally, the AMHP was under a statutory duty (s 13(1)) to make an application if satisfied that it ought to be made.

So how could those professional and statutory duties be reconciled with the rule of law? The principle Lord Bingham adopted, supported by all the other judges, was that (para 10):

"an [AMHP] may not lawfully apply for the admission of a patient whose discharge has been ordered by the decision of [a tribunal] of which the [AMHP] is aware unless the [AMHP] has formed the reasonable and bona fide opinion that he has information not known to the tribunal which puts a significantly different complexion on the case compared with that which was before the tribunal".

For example, the AMHP may since have learned of previous suicide attempts, or the patient may have refused to take the medication which he had promised the tribunal that he would take (which was the allegation in this case), or there may have been a significant deterioration in his mental condition. The AMHP ought to explain (so far as possible) why the earlier tribunal decision was not thought to govern the case.

So there is no need for a change in circumstances as long as there is fresh information, not before the tribunal, which puts a "different complexion" on things. No question here, it seems, of the normal rule requiring litigants to put all the relevant evidence they reasonably can before the court and take the consequences if they do not.

Section 2 is the most commonly used of the three "sections". The statistics for admission to NHS hospitals in England suggest that there were 23,000 uses of section 2 in 2007–2008, some 15,000 direct from the community and the remainder through changes in the status of existing in-patients. Statistics also suggest that, while a significant proportion of patients admitted under section 2 are then detained for treatment under section 3 (over 5,000 in 2007–2008), the majority become informal (well over 16,000 in 2007–2008); and some, no doubt, are simply discharged into the community (Heath and Social Care Information Centre, 2008a).

(b) The choice between admission for assessment and admission for treatment

Once in hospital under section 2, the treatment which can be given to the patient is the same as that which may be given to long term compulsory patients admitted for treatment. For this reason, it has been argued that admission for assessment should have been abolished. It allows a serious intervention in the patient's life, but the grounds are more appropriate to a short period of observation alone. On the other hand, a short term intervention is more consistent with the "least restrictive" principle. Somewhat obviously, the Code advises that section 2 should be used if "the full extent of the nature and degree of a patient's condition is unclear"; or

"an initial in-patient assessment is necessary to formulate a treatment plan or decide whether the patient will accept treatment on a voluntary basis; or a new in-patient assessment is necessary" (para 4.26).

Section 3 should be used if the patient is already detained under section 2 or the patient's disorder, treatment plan and (un)likelihood of accepting treatment voluntarily are known (para 4.27).

(c) Emergency admission under section 4

This is simply a shortcut version of an ordinary admission for assessment. By itself, it lasts for no more than 72 hours, and gives no power to impose treatment without consent (s 56(3)(a)). But it may easily be converted into an ordinary 28-day admission, with power to treat, once the patient is in hospital.

The application must be made by the nearest relative on Form A9 or an AMHP on Form A10. The applicant must have seen the patient within the previous 24 hours (ss 11(5) and 4(4)). Only one medical recommendation is required, on Form A11. The doctor need not be section 12 approved, but he must "if practicable" know the patient beforehand (s 4(3)). If he does not, the applicant must explain why it was not practicable to use a doctor who did. Both the applicant and the doctor must state that in their opinion it is of urgent necessity for the patient to be admitted and detained under section 2 *and* that compliance with the Act's requirements for that section would involve "undesirable" delay. This can only refer to the need to obtain two recommendations, one from an approved specialist. Thus it is clear that section 4 should only be used where the need for admission is so urgent that a second or approved doctor cannot be found in time. The doctor must explain how long it would take to obtain the second recommendation and what risk this would pose to the patient or other people. It would not therefore be appropriate to use an emergency application following the detention of an in-patient under section 5(2). It would also be wrong to use section 4 simply because it would be more convenient for the second doctor to examine the patient in hospital (Code, para 6.4).

The procedure for removing the patient and admitting him to hospital is the same as for an ordinary section 2 admission. But the patient must arrive at the hospital within the period of 24 hours beginning at the time of the medical examination or at the time of the application, whichever is the earlier (s 6(1)(b) and (2)). The application may be signed before the recommendation, provided that they are signed on the same day (s 12(1)).

An emergency application ceases to have effect once 72 hours have elapsed from the time of the patient's admission to hospital, *unless* a second medical recommendation is given and received by the managers within that time, and the two medical recommendations together comply with all the usual requirements of section 12 (apart, of course, from the requirement that both must be signed on or before the date of the application) (s 4(4)). Once that recommendation is given and received, therefore, the admission is *automatically* converted into an ordinary section 2 admission. The hospital must record the date and time when the second recommendation was received in Part 2 of Form H3, which will have recorded the patient's initial emergency admission to hospital. The authority to detain is extended to 28 days, beginning on the day on which the patient was originally admitted under section 4; and the patient may then be treated in the same way as an ordinary section 2 patient. There is no need to bring in the nearest relative or an AMHP to make a fresh application. Indeed, as the patient has already been admitted for assessment, the effect of section 5(1) and (6) is that this cannot be done without allowing the emergency admission to lapse. There is nothing to prevent the patient applying to a tribunal the moment he is admitted under section 4. If the second medical recommendation is not forthcoming, of course, the application will be otiose. But if the recommendation is given, valuable time may be saved.

(d) The choice between sections 2 and 4

Emergency admission is the most controversial of the three "sections". From having been the most commonly used under the 1959 Act, it has now become the least commonly used and is still reducing. From nearly 1,600 in 1997–1998, admissions have fallen to under 850 in 2007–2008. Well over half are converted into section 2 admissions, and some are superseded by a section 3 admission (which does require a fresh application and two fresh medical recommendations). The Code says that an:

> "emergency may arise where the patient's mental state or behaviour presents problems which those involved cannot reasonably be expected to manage while waiting for a second doctor".

So the applicant and doctor should have evidence of an immediate and significant risk of mental or physical harm to the patient or others, a danger of serious harm to property, or a need for physical restraint of the patient (para 5.6). Emergency applications should never be used for administrative convenience, for example because it is more convenient for the second doctor to examine the patient in hospital (para 5.5).

There are considerable regional variations, not only in the use of any form of compulsion, but also in the relative use of the various sections. Not surprisingly, London has much the highest rate of compulsory admissions. Some of this is because certain London hospitals treat patients from outside their area. Some of it is because of differences in the age, gender and ethnicity of the local populations. But historically at least it has also been due to the different arrangements made for handling these cases, in particular the provision of specialist community services (Barnes, Bowl and Fisher, 1990). No longer are the psychiatrists confined to their hospitals along with their patients. It is all part of the same pattern of radical change in the nature of psychiatric services, particularly following the 1999 National Service Framework for Mental Health, which contributed to the 2007 amendments.

4. ADMISSION FOR TREATMENT UNDER THE MHA

Historically, admission for assessment under section 2 was more often used than admission for treatment under section 3, but for the last decade very similar numbers of uses have been made of each. In 1997–1998, there were 19,000 uses of section 2 and 20,700 uses of section 3 in NHS hospitals in England; in 2007–2008, there were 23,000 uses of section 2 and 22,400 uses of section 3. Some of the section 3 uses were changes from section 2. At any one time, of course, the greater proportion of patients detained under the MHA will be there under the longer term powers (Healthcare Commission, 2008).

(a) Application and admission

The application must be made by the patient's nearest relative, or by someone authorised by that relative or a county court to act as such, on Form A5, or by an AMHP on Form A6. The contents are the same as for a section 2 admission, except that the AMHP must record one of two things: either that she has consulted a named nearest relative (or person authorised to act as such) and that person has not notified either her or the LSSA on whose behalf she is acting that he or she objects to the application being made; or that she cannot find out who the nearest relative is, or that the patient has no nearest relative, or that she understands that a named person is the nearest relative but it is not reasonably practicable or would involve unreasonable delay to consult that person. Reasons for the last must be given (and see p 79, earlier, for what may be covered by "not reasonably practicable").

As with a section 2 admission, the applicant must have seen the patient within the 14 days ending on the date of the application (s 11(5)) and an AMHP applicant must also have interviewed the patient (s 13(2)). A joint medical recommendation in Form A7, or two recommendations on Form A8, are necessary. As with a section 2 admission, these must give reasons for their opinion that the grounds are made out. Unlike section 2, the grounds include the requirement that appropriate medical treatment is available for the patient at a particular hospital or at one of a number of named hospitals. If appropriate treatment is only available in a particular part of the hospital, for example, if the patient is a child, they must say which part. Clearly, therefore, the doctors must have taken steps to ascertain that treatment will be available in the place or places named.

The procedure for taking the patient to hospital, if he is not already there, for recapturing him if he absconds before getting there, and for admitting him to the hospital when he arrives is the same as in an ordinary admission for assessment. The patient must therefore reach the hospital within the period of 14 days, beginning on the date of the second medical examination (s 6(1)(a)).

(b) Duration and renewal

The rules governing what may happen to the patient in hospital are the same as those for an ordinary admission for assessment (see s 56(3) and chapter 6). The differences between them lie in the grounds for admission and in the potential duration of the patient's detention. Once admitted to hospital for treatment, the patient may initially be detained for six months beginning with the day on which he was admitted (s 20(1)) but he may be discharged before then, either by the responsible clinician (RC), or by the hospital managers, or (unless prevented by the RC) by his nearest relative (see chapter 7), or by a tribunal (see chapter 8). He may apply to a tribunal at any one time during those first six months. He may remain in hospital informally after the authority for his detention has lapsed or he has been discharged from detention (s 131(1)).

At the end of the first six months, the authority for his detention can be renewed for a further period of six months and thereafter for periods of one year at a time (s 20(2)). The RC must examine a patient who is liable to be detained for treatment within the period of two months ending on the day on which the authority to detain would expire. If the RC considers that the requisite conditions are fulfilled, she must make a report to the managers on Parts 1 and 3 of Form H5 (s 20(3) and reg 13(1)). But before making the report, she must consult one or more people who have been professionally concerned with the patient's medical treatment. These may be other doctors, nurses, psychologists or other therapists (s 20(5)). Further, she cannot make the report at all unless another professional concerned in the patient's treatment, who belongs to a different profession from the RC, has agreed in writing that the conditions for renewal are satisfied (s 20(5A). She does this by completing Part 2 of Form H5 (reg 13(2)). The second professional does not have to give reasons for her opinion but the RC does.

The criteria for renewing the patient's detention mirror the grounds for admission, that is: (a) that the patient is suffering from mental disorder of a nature or degree which makes it appropriate for him to receive medical treatment in a hospital; (b) that it is necessary for the health or safety of the patient or for the protection of other persons that he should receive such treatment and it cannot be provided unless he continues to be detained; and (c) that appropriate medical treatment is available for him (s 20(4)). These conditions cannot be fulfilled unless at least some hospital treatment is appropriate, but not necessarily as an in-patient, and a patient on leave of absence need not actually be receiving hospital treatment at the point of renewal (*B v Barking, Havering and Brentwood Community Healthcare NHS Trust* [1999] 1 FLR 106, p 232, later).

If the report is made to the managers, the authority for the patient's detention is renewed automatically for the appropriate period from the expiration of the current period (s 20(2) and (8)), *unless* the managers decide to discharge the patient under section 23 despite the RC's advice (s 20(3)). The managers should consider the patient's case and not simply rubber stamp the RC's recommendation. If the detention is renewed, the patient must be informed and a new right to apply to a tribunal arises. The managers must record on Part 4 of Form H5 that the report was either furnished through the hospital's internal mail system or received on the date recorded.

(c) Patients detained before the 1959, 1983 or 2007 Acts came into force

It is now 50 years since the 1959 Act was passed, but there may still be a handful of patients who have been detained since before it came into force. Some were transferred from the penal system and are now treated as though they were subject to a transfer direction, with restrictions, under sections 47 or 48 with 49, as appropriate (MHA, Sch 5, para 37; see also paras 38 and 39). Some of these "mental defectives" might remain subject to civil compulsion after their court orders ceased, and are like ordinary hospital order patients today, in that their nearest relatives have no power to discharge them (para 34(4)). In other respects, however, both they and the patients originally admitted under the civil powers in the Lunacy and Mental Deficiency Acts are to be treated as if they had been admitted for treatment under Part 2 of the MHA (para 34(1)). The only difference between them and patients admitted since the 1959 Act is that the authority for their detention may still be renewed for periods of two years at a time (paras 34(2) and 33(1), (2) and (4)). However, the procedure for renewal is the same, and this includes the criteria laid down in section 20(4) (para 34(3)).

Patients admitted under the 1959 Act before the 1983 Act came into force became subject to the new regime at their next renewal. Thus if they were originally admitted for treatment for psychopathic disorder or non-severe mental impairment, they lost the benefit of the repealed age limit of 25 but gained the benefit of the new "treatability" test. The same principle applies to patients admitted under the 1983 Act before the 2007 amendments came into force. The new law applies from their next renewal, or tribunal determination, or consideration of discharge. They lose any benefit from the different classifications of mental disorder but gain the benefit of the new "appropriate treatment" test (see MHA 2007, Sch 6, para 2).

126

(d) Patients transferred from guardianship

Section 19(1)(b) provides that a patient under guardianship may be transferred to hospital in the circumstances and conditions prescribed by the MHHGT Regulations. The transfer is effected by the responsible LSSA in Part 1 of Form G8, but only where the procedure for an ordinary admission for treatment has been carried out. Thus there must be an application by an AMHP on the usual form (Form A6) and the usual rules about consulting the nearest relative and the duties of the AMHP apply (MHHGT Regs, reg 8(2)(a), (3)). The application must be founded on two medical recommendations on the usual forms (Form A7 or A8), so the usual grounds apply (reg 8(2)(b)). The local authority must be satisfied that a bed will be available within 14 days beginning with the date on which the patient was last examined by a doctor for this purpose (reg 8(2)(c)). The transfer has to take place within that time; otherwise the patient remains under guardianship (reg 8(5)). When the transfer takes place, the hospital managers have to record the date and time of the admission in Part 2 of Form G8.

All of this suggests that the patient will then be regarded as an ordinary admission for treatment on the date when he is admitted to hospital. He certainly has the usual right to apply to a tribunal within six months. But section 19(2)(d) provides that Part 2 of the Act is to apply to him as if the original guardianship application were an application for admission for treatment and he had been admitted to hospital at the time when the guardianship application was accepted. Strictly speaking, therefore, the renewal dates should be calculated from when the guardianship began rather than from when he was admitted to hospital. In practice, no one in the hospital will know when that was, unless the guardianship forms are also transmitted with the transfer. Once the patient no longer needs hospital treatment, the same options, for discharge, community treatment or transfer back into guardianship will be available as they are for any other patient admitted under section 3 (see chapter 7).

5. SCRUTINY AND RECTIFICATION OF MHA DOCUMENTS

There are a few circumstances in which minor mistakes in applications or medical recommendations can be rectified, under section 15(1), or a fresh medical recommendation substituted for one which is insufficient, under section 15(2) or (3). (These do not apply to orders made by a court, which may on occasions be just as defective and can sometimes be corrected by the court under the "slip rule".) Scrutiny for this purpose should be more thorough than the quick check which the officer receiving the admission documents should do to ensure that the application appears to be "duly completed". It should be delegated to a limited number of officers who may include clinical staff (MHA Code, para 13.7). If the receiving officer is not also authorised to scrutinise, it should be done as soon as possible and no later than the next working day (para 13.11). Documents should be checked for accuracy and completeness and to see that they do not reveal any failure to comply with the procedural requirements of the MHA. Medical recommendations should be checked by an appropriate clinician to see that the reasons appear sufficient to support the conclusions (para 13.12).

The MHA Code does not give any guidance on what defects may be corrected. Section 15(1) permits any application or recommendation "which is found to be in any respect incorrect or defective" to be amended by the person who signed it, provided that the hospital managers consent. This may be done within 14 days of the patient's admission (although of course an emergency admission can never last longer than 72 hours unless it is converted into an ordinary admission for assessment).

"Incorrect" probably means "inaccurate" in the sense of mis-stating names, dates, places or other details which had they been correctly stated would have justified the admission. It does not mean that a document which accurately reflects the facts can be rectified if those facts do not fall within the legal requirements. For example, a frequent fault is that the medical recommendations are undated or dated later than the application (see s 12(1)). If in fact they were signed on or before the date of the application, the mistake can be rectified. But if they were signed later, then the application is invalid and the detention illegal.

"Defective" probably means "incomplete" in the sense that all the information required in the forms has not been given. It cannot mean that forms which are complete and accurate statements of the facts can be falsified in order to provide legal justification for detention where none exists. Thus a form may be amended if a vital date or qualification is omitted: but not if the date which is accurately stated contravenes the MHA's time limits or if the person signing the document is not qualified to do so or if it wrongly states that the nearest relative has been consulted (*R v South Western Hospital Managers, ex p M* [1993] QB 683). According to Sir Thomas Bingham MR in *Re S-C (Mental Patient: Habeas Corpus)* [1996] QB 599 (see also pp 81, 120, 281), there is "nothing in that section which enables a fundamentally defective application to be retrospectively validated". Further, an unsigned form cannot be regarded as an application or recommendation at all.

In one respect, however, section 15 does permit the remedying of a genuine deficiency which might otherwise invalidate the admission. If one of the two medical recommendations required for an ordinary admission for assessment or for admission for treatment is "insufficient to warrant the detention of the patient", the matter can be cured by obtaining a fresh recommendation which is sufficient. The hospital managers should notify the applicant (not the person who signed the document as under section 15(1)) and if a fresh medical recommendation is received within 14 days of the patient's admission, the application is treated as if it had been valid from the outset (s 15(2)).

This procedure may be used where one of the recommendations does not disclose adequate grounds for the admission. If it fails to convince the scrutinising officer, the recommendation may be "insufficient" but could be remedied by a fresh one, provided of course that the facts warrant it. The new recommendation could be provided by the same or a different doctor.

The same procedure can be used where the two recommendations are good in themselves but taken together do not fulfil the Act's procedural requirements (s 15(3)). The obvious example is where neither doctor is an approved specialist, but the section may also apply where the dates of their examinations were too far apart. A fresh recommendation may cure this, and need not comply with the requirements about the interval between the examinations or about signing the recommendation on or before the date of the application (s 15(2)(a)). But together the new recommendation and the old must comply with every other requirement in the Act (s 15(2)(b)).

This procedure cannot apply where it is the recommendation in itself, rather than in its relationship with the other one, which is bad: for example, where one of the doctors is not qualified at all or where he is disqualified from making the recommendation under the conflict of interest rules. It could certainly not be used to render lawful the detention of a patient who had arrived at hospital more than 14 days after the date of the second medical examination, for it is not then the recommendation which is insufficient. Thus the mistakes which can be put right under section 15 are very limited.

6. DEPRIVATION OF LIBERTY UNDER THE MCA

As it is no longer lawful (if it ever was) to deprive an incapacitated person of his liberty under the common law doctrine of necessity, managers of hospitals or care homes who think that they may need to do this must now obtain authorisation either from the Court of Protection under section 16(2)(a) or from the authorities under the deprivation of liberty scheme (the DoLS) in Schedule A1 to the MCA (see MCA, s 4A). The legislation takes up a lot of space: principally the MCA, sections 4A, 4B, 16A, 39A to 39E, Schedule A1, consisting of 187 paragraphs, and Schedule 1A, consisting of 17 paragraphs, and the Mental Capacity (Deprivation of Liberty: Standard Authorisations, Assessments and Ordinary Residence) Regulations 2008, SI 2008/1858 (the DoL Regs); for Wales, see the Mental Capacity (Deprivation of Liberty: Assessments, Standard Authorisations and Disputes about Residence) (Wales) Regulations 2009, SI 2009/783. This is mainly because the draftsman has tried to set out the procedures rather like an algorithm or flow chart, so that they ought to be easy to follow. The Code of Practice on the *Deprivation of Liberty Safeguards* (the DoLS Code) (Ministry of Justice and Public Guardian, 2008) also runs to some 121 pages. Unlike the MHA, the same Code applies in both England and Wales. Most of it simply paraphrases the statutory provisions, but there are also some nuggets of practical advice and guidance.

Fortunately, the processes and concepts are much simpler and clearer than all these words might suggest. Administrative authorisations under Schedule A1 are of two kinds: a standard authorisation given by the supervisory body (SB) and an urgent authorisation given by the managing authority (MA) of the hospital or home where the person is or is to be detained. The managing authority is defined on p 33, earlier. For a hospital, the supervisory body is the Primary Care Trust (PCT) which commissioned the relevant care or treatment, and otherwise the PCT for the area where the hospital (or most of it) is (Sch 1A, para 180). For a care home, the supervisory body is the local social services authority for the area where the person concerned is ordinarily resident, and otherwise for the area where the care home is (Sch 1A, para 182). So the SB could change while an authorisation is in force, for example because the person concerned moved house. This makes no difference: the new SB takes over without affecting the validity of, or liability for, what was done by the old (see Sch 1A, Pt 7).

Standard forms for the requests and notifications required are available but not prescribed by law. It is important to bear in mind that these are only authorisations: the resident does not have to be deprived of his liberty unless this is necessary in his own best interests. The authorisations merely make it lawful if it is. It is also important to bear in mind that only the deprivation of liberty is authorised. Anything else, such as taking the person concerned to hospital or giving him medical treatment, will have to be justified under the normal MCA principles. As with compulsory admission under the MHA, an authorisation under Schedule A1 may be challenged after the event, but in the Court of Protection rather than in a tribunal (MCA, s 21A). As we shall see in chapter 8, a tribunal has many advantages over the Court, at least for the person detained.

(a) Standard authorisations: the initial process

Standard authorisation is normally granted by the supervisory body (SB) at the request of the managing authority (MA) of the hospital or care home where the person is or is to be detained. If a health or social care professional thinks that an authorisation is needed, perhaps as a result of a care review or needs assessment, she should inform the MA (DoLS Code, para 3.2). The MA must request a standard authorisation in three situations (Sch A1, para 24):

- where the person concerned is not yet accommodated by them, but is likely to become a detained resident within the next 28 days; or
- where the person is already accommodated by them and is likely to be detained at some time in the next 28 days; or
- where the person is already detained by them.

In each case, it must appear to the MA that the person concerned will meet all six of the qualifying requirements (discussed in chapter 1 earlier) when admitted, or when detained, or is likely to do so within the next 28 days.

Obviously, the MA should try to identify the correct SB to which to send the request (see earlier), in order to cut down delays. But if it is sent to the wrong one, it can be passed on to the right one without a new request being needed (DoLS Code, para 3.13). The regulations require the MA to supply the following basic information: name, gender and, if known, age of the person concerned (if not known, a statement that the MA reasonably believe him to be 18 or over); address and telephone number of his current location; name, address and telephone number of the MA with the name of the person dealing with the request; the purpose for which the authorisation is requested; the date from which it is sought; and whether the MA has given an urgent authorisation.

The MA must include further information if available or reasonably obtainable: relevant information about the person's health; the diagnosis of the mental disorder that he is suffering from; any relevant care plans or needs assessments; his racial, ethnic or national origins; whether he has any special communication needs; details of the proposed restrictions on his liberty; whether the duty to instruct an independent mental capacity advocate (IMCA) under section 39A applies (see chapter 6); whether, if the purpose is to provide treatment, the person concerned has made what may be a valid advance decision applicable to some or all of that treatment; whether he is subject to the hospital, guardianship or community treatment regimes under the MHA; and the name, address and telephone numbers of anyone he has nominated to be consulted about his welfare, of anyone engaged in caring for him or interested in his welfare, of any donee of a lasting power of attorney, of any deputy appointed by the court, and of any IMCA appointed for him (Sch A1, para 31 and DoL Regs, reg 16(1)(a) to (g), 16(2) (a) to (j)).

The MA should tell the person's family, friends and carers and any IMCA already involved that they have made the request, unless this is impossible, impracticable or undesirable in the interests of the person's health or safety (DoLS Code, para 3.15). Certain people have the right to be consulted during the assessment of the person's best interests (see p 67 earlier). The views of the person concerned about who should be informed and consulted should also be taken into account.

The Code (para 3.17) suggests that the SB has a discretion about whether to pursue any request for deprivation of liberty to be authorised, but the MCA appears to give them no choice. The SB has to organise assessments of the six qualifying requirements (see chapter 1) from assessors who are eligible to carry them out (see chapter 3) (Sch A1, paras 33 to 48). A minimum of two assessors, one of them a doctor to supply the mental health assessment, is required. The most important assessments, however, are those of the person's mental capacity and his best interests. These may be carried out by the same "best interests" assessor, who may well be an AMHP. If the doctor is not section 12 approved, an AMHP will in any event be required to do the eligibility assessment. The best interests assessment must be done by someone who is not involved in the care, or in making decisions about the care, of the person concerned. And if the MA and SB are the same body (for example in a local authority care home) the best interests assessor must not be an employee of, or someone who is providing services to, the SB (other than, of course, the assessment itself) (DoL Regs, reg 12(1) and (2)). All these assessments have to be done within 21 days of receiving the request (reg 13(1)).

But the SB do not have to arrange a new assessment if they already have on file an assessment complying with all the requirements in the Schedule which (except for an age assessment) was done in the last 12 months for any purpose and there is no reason to think may no longer be accurate (taking into account any information or submissions from the person's representative or an IMCA) (Sch 1A, para 49). They must also call a halt to the assessment process the moment any one of them turns up "negative" (para 133).

The statutory scheme makes elaborate and rather confusing provision for appointing someone to speak up for the person concerned during and after the assessment process. The expectation is that if the authorisation is given, there will be a family member, friend or carer to look after his interests. However, if there is no such person suitable, a professional representative may be appointed. And before this happens, if the MA are satisfied that there is no-one other than professional or paid carers whom it would be appropriate to consult in deciding what would be in the best interests of the person concerned, the SB must appoint an IMCA for him under section 39A of the MCA (see chapter 6).

If all the assessments are "positive" (a strange word for meeting the various qualifications for being deprived of one's liberty without a court order) and the SB have them in writing, the SB must grant the authorisation (Sch 1A, para 50). The SB decide how long this should last, but it cannot be longer than the maximum period stated in the best interests assessment (para 51). This is as long as the assessor thinks it appropriate for the person to be detained, up to a maximum of one year (para 42(1), (2); there is power to prescribe a shorter maximum period in regulations but this has not been done). The DoLS Code advises that the deprivation of liberty should be for as short a time as possible, so the authorisation could be for quite a short period; for example where the usual care arrangements have temporarily broken down or a brain injured patient is in rehabilitation and his mental condition may soon change (para 5.9). The authorisation may come into force after it is actually given (Sch A1, para 52); but this should be no later than when the person concerned is to be detained, for otherwise the detention will be unlawful. Unlike the MHA, however, there is no maximum period between the authorisation and when the detention may begin, but the authorisation must state when it begins and could add a condition stating that the detention must have begun before a particular date.

The SB can decide what, if any, conditions to impose, having regard to any recommendations made by the best interests assessor (para 53). These might be around contact, cultural issues or other matters directly relevant to the deprivation of liberty—they are not a substitute for a care plan (DoLS Code, paras 4.74, 4.75). If the SB decide not to impose conditions which the best interests assessor recommends, they should discuss this with her, as it might affect her other conclusions (para 5.5).

The authorisation itself must be in writing. A standard form is available, but not prescribed by law. It must name the person concerned, the hospital or care home where he may be detained, when it begins and when it ends, the purpose for which authorisation is given, any conditions to which it is subject, and the reason why each qualifying requirement is met; for the eligibility requirement, this means saying which of cases B, C, D or E in paragraph 2 of Schedule 1A applies (Sch A1, para 54) (see p 19, earlier). Copies of the authorisation must be given to the person concerned, his representative, the MA, any section 39A IMCA involved, and every interested person consulted by the best interests assessor (para 57(2)). The MA must then do what they can to ensure that the person concerned understands what the authorisation means, his right to challenge the authorisation in court (see chapter 8 later), his right to request a review (see below), and his right to have an IMCA instructed and how to go about this. Any written information must also be given to the person's representative (para 59).

If the SB cannot give the authorisation, because any or all of the assessments are negative, they must notify the person concerned, the MA, any IMCA and every interested person consulted by the best interests assessor as soon as practicable after it becomes apparent to them that they cannot give it (by definition there will be no representative, because they are only appointed after an authorisation has been given) (para 58). This would mean as soon as any of the assessments turns out negative. The MA will then have to review the care arrangements to ensure that the person concerned is not in fact deprived of his liberty (DoLS Code, para 5.20). The options will depend upon the reasons why the request was turned down (para 5.22). The MA cannot make a fresh request unless it appears to them that there has been a change in the case which makes it likely that an authorisation will be given this time (para 28).

As we have seen (chapter 1), the eligibility requirement is there to avoid overlap with situations in which the MHA powers are, or should be, used. So if the person concerned becomes subject to an MHA regime which makes him ineligible for the MCA regime, the MA must give notice to the SB and the authorisation is suspended from the time that notice is given. The SB must notify the person concerned, his representative and the MA of the suspension (Sch A1, paras 91 to 93). The suspension is lifted if the MA notify the SB that the person concerned has become eligible once more. The same people, plus any IMCA must be notified of this (paras 94, 95). However, the suspension can only last for up to 28 days. If it is not lifted by then, the authorisation comes to an end and a new request will be required if the person becomes eligible once more (para 96). Whilst an authorisation is suspended, no review may be requested and no steps may be taken under any current review (para 122).

Whenever a standard authorisation comes to an end, the SB must give notice of this to the person concerned, his representative, the MA and any interested person consulted by the best interests assessor. This is to be done as soon as practicable after the authorisation ends, whereas one might have thought it a better safeguard to notify this in advance.

(b) Representatives

The SB have a duty to appoint a representative for the person concerned as soon as practicable after a standard authorisation is given (Sch A1, para 139(1)). But the process of appointing a representative must begin as soon as the best interests assessor is chosen (Mental Capacity (Deprivation of Liberty: Appointment of Relevant Person's Representative) Regulations 2008, SI 2008/1315 (the Appointment Regs), reg 10; for Wales see the Mental Capacity (Deprivation of Liberty: Appointment of Relevant Person's Representative) (Wales) Regulations 2009, SI 2009/266). The best interests assessor must decide whether the person concerned has the capacity to choose his own representative (reg 4). If he does, he may, if he wishes, choose a family member, friend or carer (reg 5). If he does not have that capacity, but he does have an attorney or deputy who has authority to do so, the attorney or deputy may, if he wishes, choose the representative and that could be himself (reg 6). The best interests assessor must confirm whether or not the person chosen is eligible (reg 7). Failing either of these, the best interests assessor may choose a family member, friend or carer as representative, unless the person concerned or an attorney or deputy objects to her choice (reg 8). Failing this, the SB may select a professional representative who is not a family member, friend or carer for the person concerned (reg 9).

Any representative has to be someone who will keep in touch with the person concerned and represent and support him in matters connected with depriving him of his liberty under the Schedule (Sch A1, para 140). He cannot have a financial interest in the MA or be related to anyone who has; if the authorisation is sought by a care home, he must not be employed by or provide services to the MA; if it is sought by a hospital, he must not be employed by the MA in a role which might be related to the case; nor can he be employed by the SB in a role which might be related to the case (reg 3). Once a representative is appointed, the powers and duties of the section 39A IMCA no longer apply (except that, like anyone else, he can apply to the court to challenge the authorisation, taking into account the representative's views) (para 161).

(c) Variations, renewals and reviews

Unlike the MHA, Schedule A1 does not provide for transfers of the power to detain from one hospital or care home to another (there are also specific provisions about changes of residence in sections 38 and 39 of the MCA; see chapter 9). Instead, paragraph 25 provides that if there is a standard authorisation in place and the person concerned ceases or will cease to be detained in one hospital or care home and becomes or will become detained in another, the MA of the new hospital or care home must request a new authorisation. If granted, the old authorisation ends when the new one begins; if refused it does not affect the existing authorisation (para 62). Unlike ordinary requests under paragraph 24, paragraph 25 does not give a time-scale, but it would obviously be wise to make the request before the person concerned is moved because the new hospital or home will have no power to detain him unless they can give themselves an urgent authorisation (DoLS Code, paras 5.14, 5.15).

Similarly, Schedule A1 does not provide for the renewal of an existing authorisation. Instead, the MA must apply for a new one. However, they can make the request for a new authorisation to follow on immediately after the existing one expires whenever they want, if they think that it would be unreasonable to delay making the request until nearer the expiry date (para 29). The same applies where the MA request a new authorisation to take effect after an authorisation given by the court is due to expire (para 27). Thus there is no statutory limit on how far in advance of expiry a new authorisation may be requested, but if the SB think that it has been made too soon, they should raise the matter with the MA in the hope that the request may be withdrawn (see DoLS Code, para 3.20).

On these new requests, all the usual assessments have to be done, unless there is one on file which was done within the last 12 months and there is no reason to think that it no longer applies (para 49, see above). An age assessment does not have to be done again unless there is reason to think that the one filed may have been wrong. But it should not usually be necessary to instruct an IMCA because the person concerned will already have a representative.

The SB may review an authorisation at any time and must do so if asked by the person concerned, his representative or the MA (para 102). The MA should be monitoring the situation carefully, because they must ask for a review if they think that any of the qualifying requirements are reviewable (para 103). The SB must notify the person concerned, his representative and the MA if they are to conduct a review, if practicable before this begins (para 108).

There are three possible grounds for review (para 104). The first is the "non-qualification ground": that the person concerned does not meet one or more of the six qualifying requirements (para 105). But the eligibility requirement is only reviewable on the ground that the person concerned is ineligible because he objects to mental health treatment (see Sch 1A, para 5). In any other situation where he becomes ineligible because of the MHA regime, the authorisation is automatically suspended (see above). This will be readily discoverable from the MHA documentation. Objection to treatment, on the other hand, is a matter for judgment. No doubt the professionals will debate whether he "could" be sectioned under the MHA.

The second ground for review is the "change of reason ground": that the reason why the person meets a requirement is not the reason stated in the authorisation (para 106). Obviously, this does not apply to the age requirement as there can only be one reason why this is not met.

The third ground for review is the "variation of conditions ground". This only applies to the best interests requirement. It can be reviewed if there has been a change in the case which makes it appropriate to vary any of the conditions to which the authorisation is subject (para 107). The Schedule does not expressly state that this includes inserting conditions where there were none before, but this would make sense. The DoLS Code gives the example of a young woman with severe brain damage who was making good progress but the best interests assessor needed the advice of her rehabilitation team before concluding that the authorisation was no longer in her best interests. So she recommended conditions that rehabilitation specialists assess the detained person's progress and that a full case review be held within the month (para 8.16).

The SB must decide which of the qualifying requirements is reviewable and arrange a review assessment of any that are. However, there does not have to be a review assessment for a variation of conditions if the change in the person's case is not significant (paras 109, 110, 111). In that case the SB may simply vary the conditions as they think appropriate (para 114).

If any review assessment concludes that the relevant qualifying requirement is not met, the authorisation must be ended immediately (para 117). Otherwise, the SB must decide whether any of the assessed qualifying requirements is reviewable on the change of reasons ground and if so vary the authorisation to state the current reason (para 115(2)(a) and (3) for the best interests qualification and para 116(4), (5) for the others). Also, if the best interests qualification is reviewable on the variation of conditions ground, the SB must vary the conditions if they think the change is significant, and may do so if it is not (para 115(2)(a) and (b), (4) and (5)). If the SB conclude that no change of conditions or variation of reasons is required, they do not have to do anything (para 115(6), 116(6)). Indeed they have no power to do anything.

Once the review is complete, the SB must notify the person concerned, his representative, the MA and any IMCA of the outcome and any variation which has been made to the authorisation as a result.

However, to avoid duplication of effort, if a request for a new standard authorisation is under consideration, no review may be requested and no steps may be taken under any current review until that request has been disposed of (para 123). Furthermore, where a review has been requested or is underway, paragraph 30 provides that the MA may if they wish request a new standard authorisation to take effect on or before the expiry of the current one, even though they would not otherwise be in a position to make a new request under paragraph 24 (because they could wait until nearer the expiry of the current one). If they do this, no steps can be taken in the review until the request has been disposed of (para 124). The outcome of the new request will in most cases also determine the outcome of the review.

(d) Urgent authorisations

The hope is that good planning will avoid the need for urgent authorisations of detention, bearing in mind that there is also the possibility of going to the court (see s 4A(3), (4) and 16(2)(a)) and that pending an application to the court, section 4B allows deprivations of liberty which are necessary in order to give a person life saving treatment or do any act which the person doing it reasonably believes necessary to prevent a serious deterioration in his condition. Also, restraint falling short of deprivation of liberty is permitted under section 6, if it is a proportionate response to the need to protect the person from harm (see p 30, earlier; also p 191, later); an example might be where gentle restraint is used to calm down a disturbed patient who needs treatment in Accident and Emergency for a physical injury (see DoLS Code, para 6.19).

The Code also advises that urgent authorisations should not be used for situations which are likely to resolve themselves very quickly so that a standard authorisation will not be needed (DoLS Code, paras 6.3, 6.4). But it is not clear what the legal basis is for this: if what is proposed amounts to a deprivation of liberty, this will be unlawful and a violation of the Convention rights, unless authorised by the Court or under the DoLS. Perhaps the Code is getting at the elusive distinction between detention and deprivation of liberty (see chapter 1).

The MA are able to give themselves an urgent authorisation without any independent assessment of whether or not the qualifying requirements for a standard authorisation are met. Hence the Code emphasises that this should be done at a senior level and after consulting carers (who are likely to know how the person will react to being deprived of his liberty), family and friends (DoLS Code, paras 6.11 to 6.13). The Code is also cautious about using an urgent authorisation to move a person from home to hospital, because such a move could have a detrimental effect upon his mental health and distort the assessment process. It might be better to leave him where he is while that is going on. His GP, community mental health team or social services (if already involved) should be consulted (paras 6.14, 6.15). The problems raised are likely to be the same as those raised by removal from home under the National Assistance Act (see below). On the other hand, fears have been expressed (Clements, 2009) that care homes will feel obliged to give themselves urgent authorisations if under pressure to accept residents who are about to be discharged from hospital because there may be sanctions if discharges are unnecessarily delayed (see chapter 9). Standard authorisations can take at least 21 days (see above).

The grounds for an urgent authorisation are that the MA are required to request a standard authorisation under paragraph 24 or 25 (above) or have already done so (Sch A1, para 76(2), (3)). This means that they must believe that all the qualifying requirements are met. It also means that, in theory at least, they cannot lawfully give themselves an urgent authorisation without also requesting a standard authorisation from the SB. They must also believe that "the need for the relevant person to be a detained resident is so urgent that it is appropriate for the detention to begin" before the request to the SB is made or disposed of as the case may be (para 76(2)(b), (3)(b)).

The urgent authorisation comes into force the moment it is given (Sch A1, para 88) and can last for no longer than seven days (para 78). It must be in writing, stating the name of the person concerned and of the hospital or care home, when it begins and when it ends, and its purpose (paras 79, 80). The MA must do what they can to ensure that the person concerned understands the effect of the authorisation and his right to apply to the court. This must be done both orally and in writing as soon as practicable after the authorisation is given (para 83).

The MA cannot give themselves another urgent authorisation. Instead they can make one request to the SB for an extension (Sch A1, para 77). The SB may grant the extension if the MA have made the required request for a standard authorisation and "there are exceptional reasons why it has not yet been possible for that request to be disposed of" and "it is essential for the existing detention to continue" until then (para 84(4)). The Code advises that staff shortages are not a good reason, but the need to contact a particular person in order to make a proper best interests assessment might be (DoLS Code, paras 6.23, 6.24). The extension can last for no more than seven days (Sch A1, para 85(2), (3)). The SB must notify the MA, who must alter the authorisation to show the new expiry date. They must also give a copy to the person concerned and any IMCA instructed, and do their best to explain matters once more to the person concerned (para 85(4), (5), (6)). If the SB decide not to extend the authorisation, they must notify the MA of the decision and their reasons, and the MA must give a copy to the person concerned and any IMCA (para 86).

Once there has been an urgent authorisation, the assessments required for the standard authorisation requested must be completed while the urgent authorisation is still in force (DoL Regs, reg 13(2)), which does not give them much time. If the SB give the requested standard authorisation, the urgent authorisation ends when the standard one comes into force (Sch A1, para

89(3)). If the SB refuse it, the urgent authorisation ends when the MA are notified of the refusal (para 89(4)). The SB must notify the person concerned and any IMCA that the urgent authorisation has ended as soon as practicable after it has done so (para 90).

The upshot is that a person might be deprived of his liberty under an urgent authorisation for up to 14 days without any professional assessment that he suffers from mental disorder, that he lacks the capacity to decide whether to be in the hospital or care for the purpose of being given the relevant treatment, and that it is in his best interests for him to be detained. Doubts have been expressed about whether this is too long to wait before the person has "reliably been shown to be of 'unsound mind'" on the basis of "objective medical expertise" for the purpose of article 5 (see *Winterwerp v The Netherlands* (1979–80) 2 EHRR 387, para 39).

(e) Unauthorised detention suspected

As we have seen in chapter 1, there is no clear cut dividing line between deprivation of liberty, which is only lawful if authorised under the MCA, and mere restriction of liberty, which is lawful if it falls within the general permission given by the Act. It is a matter of fact and degree rather than a difference in kind. So there is a formal procedure for people to ask the SB to decide whether or not there is an unauthorised deprivation of liberty. Anyone other than the MA of the hospital or care home where the person is resident can do this. Though termed a "third party" in the Act, this includes the person himself, any relative, friend, carer or other person (Sch A1, para 68). The third party must first notify the MA that it appears to him that there is an unauthorised deprivation of liberty and ask the MA to request a standard authorisation for that detention if they wish it to continue (or to stop the claimed deprivation of liberty). A standard letter is available for doing this. It may be that the MA can resolve matters informally by making some adjustments to the care regime (DoLS Code, para 9.2). Otherwise, if the MA do not make a request for a standard authorisation within a reasonable time (the Code, para 9.1, suggests that this would normally mean 24 hours) the third party can ask the SB to decide whether there is an unlawful deprivation of liberty (Sch A1, para 68).

The SB do not have to act on this request if they think it "frivolous or vexatious" or if the question of unauthorised detention has already been decided and nothing seems to have changed since then (para 69(3), (4), (5)). Otherwise, they must appoint someone to carry out an assessment of whether or not the person concerned is detained (para 69(2)). This must be done by someone who is suitable and eligible to undertake a best interests assessment (para 69(6)). The SB must notify the third party, the resident concerned, the MA and any IMCA of the request, whether they have appointed someone to make the assessment, and if so, who that person is (para 69(7), (8)).

The SB and the assessor have to act quickly, because the assessment must be carried out within seven days of receiving the request from the third party (para 70(1) and DoL Regs, reg 14). The assessor will obviously have to speak to the hospital or care home, to the person who raised the concern, and if possible to family and friends. If there is no-one appropriate to consult among the family and friends, the assessor should get the SB to instruct an IMCA (DoLS Code, para 9.9). If the assessor concludes that the resident is not detained, or that the detention is authorised, all the SB have to do is to notify the same people to that effect (paras 72, 73). If the third party does not like the outcome, he can of course take the matter to the Court of Protection. But if the assessor concludes that the resident is detained and the detention is not authorised, the case has to be treated as if the MA had applied for a standard authorisation, and the SB have to notify the same people to that effect (para 71). The whole Schedule applies, so the MA could give themselves an urgent authorisation while the standard assessment process is completed (para 71(2); DoLS Code, para 9.13).

Unauthorised detention is, of course, a serious matter. A person unlawfully detained ought in any event to be able to secure his release through habeas corpus and to gain damages for breach of his article 5 rights under the Human Rights Act 1998 (see chapter 8). Some might think it unfortunate, to say the least, that the very body who are doing the unauthorised detaining are able to give themselves even temporary authority to continue, and without the benefit of any independent assessment. It would be difficult for them to do this if the best interests assessor had also reported that in her view it was not in the resident's best interests for him to be detained, but that is not what this assessment is about.

(f) Records and monitoring

MAs have to keep written records of each request they make for a standard authorisation and their reasons (Sch A1, para 32(1)); of why they have given an urgent authorisation (para 82(2)); and of why they have asked for any extension (para 84(2)). They should also, of course, keep case files on each of their residents or patients, in which copies of all the relevant information, assessments and notices should be kept.

SBs must keep written records of each request for a standard authorisation (Sch A1, para 32(2)), of the details of each such authorisation given, and of requests refused (para 60), of each request for a review, its outcome, each review, its outcome, and any variations resulting (para 121), of each request to extend an urgent authorisation, any extension, and any refusal (paras 84(5), 85(7), and 86(4)). They should also record their reasons for not acting on a request to consider whether there is an unauthorised detention (DoLS Code, para 9.5). They too will be sent copies of all the assessments.

Assessors have to make a record of each assessment (Sch A1, para 134) as well as sending copies to the SB, who will then copy them to the MA, the person concerned, his representative and any IMCA (para 135).

The operation of these procedures will be monitored in England by the Care Quality Commission, which has taken over the functions of the Commission for Social Care Inspection, the Healthcare Commission and the Mental Health Act Commission, and in Wales by Health Inspectorate Wales (see further in chapter 6) (Mental Capacity (Deprivation of Liberty: Monitoring and Reporting; and Assessments—Amendment) Regulations 2009, SI 2009/827). They can visit hospitals and care homes, visit and interview the people accommodated there, inspect the records of people who are subject to Schedule A1 authorisations or whom they think ought to have been or should be so subject (reg 4). They must report on the operation of the Schedule to the Secretary of State or Welsh Ministers (reg 3) as requested (which will be annually) and may at any time offer advice and information about it (reg 5). This is not meant to be an extra review or appeal in individual cases, as opposed to seeing how the safeguards are working in practice, but if the inspectors come across a case where they think that there may be unauthorised deprivation of liberty, they should tell the SB, just as any other "third party" may do (DoLS Code, para 11.6).

7. THE NATIONAL ASSISTANCE ACT PROCEDURES

People may also be compulsorily admitted to hospital or other types of residential care under section 47 of the National Assistance Act 1948 (NAA) and its emergency version in the National Assistance (Amendment) Act 1951. It is not known how many orders are made each year. But it does seem clear that they almost always relate to elderly or aged people who are living alone and are no longer looking after either themselves or their homes as well as the people around them would wish. Grey (1979) traces the origin back to the Webbs' Minority Report of the Poor Law Commission of 1909, which referred to the need,

> "for some power of compulsory removal of infirm old men or women who refuse to accept an order for admission to the workhouse, and who linger on, alone and uncared for, in the most shocking conditions of filth and insanitation."

But they saw this, not as an aspect of poor relief, but of public health. And it was in that guise that forerunners of the present provision appeared in local Acts for Bradford and London (and perhaps other places) during the 1920s.

There is obviously a delicate borderline between the physical and the mental infirmities of old age, and there are many cases in which the National Assistance Act, Mental Health Act and Mental Capacity Act procedures might all have to be considered. However, the idea is that each fulfils its own particular purpose and they do not overlap. Hence the 1948 Act has been amended so that it cannot be used in two situations in which the MCA is or may be invoked. The first is where there is an order of the Court of Protection authorising a hospital or care home to provide the person concerned with proper care and attention. In that case, there is no need for any other court order. The second is where an authorisation to deprive the person of his liberty under Schedule A1 to the MCA is already in force, or where the managing authority of a hospital or care home are under a duty to apply for a standard authorisation under paragraph 24 (NAA, s 47(1A)). The 1948 Act is therefore only likely to be used where physical illness or mental infirmity short of incapacity is the problem. As the procedures require that the managers of the place to which the person concerned is to be taken is aware of what is going on, the duty to apply under the MCA for DoLS authorisation should arise in all cases where the proposed resident is thought to lack capacity.

(a) The grounds

The grounds for proceeding under the 1948 Act have three components: (i) that the person is suffering from grave chronic disease *or*, being aged, infirm or physically incapacitated, is living in insanitary conditions; *and* (ii) that the person is unable to devote to himself, and is not receiving from other persons, proper care and attention; *and* (iii) that his removal from home is necessary, either in his own interests or for preventing injury to the health of, or serious nuisance to, other persons (s 47(1) and (2)).

It is important to remember that the person must either be suffering from "grave chronic disease" or living in "insanitary" conditions. Harvey (1979) gives as a typical example of the use of the power an old lady called Agnes. She was apparently quite fit, but caused concern to neighbours and her doctor by her occasional reluctance to turn off the gas. Yet she had a home help and was apparently very critical of the quality of the help's work. Where was the evidence, either of grave chronic disease or of her living in insanitary conditions? At its widest, insanitary may mean "injurious to health", but it is normally associated with the spread of infection or lack of proper sanitation.

It is also necessary that the person be unable to look after himself *and* not be receiving proper care from other people. This raises even more explicitly than the MHA the question of whether the person could cope at home if only the right sort of community services were available: "the definition of need is a function not only of the person's disability but of the level of services available in the community" (Grey, 1979). Although the Act refers only to what is, or is not, being provided, it would be as well to consider also what *could* be provided before taking such a drastic step.

It is also well known (see Norman, 1980) that removing elderly people from their own homes, particularly when they are reluctant to accept this, is likely to lead to a swifter deterioration than leaving them at home would have done. It may therefore be difficult to say that removal is necessary in their own interests, and conditions would have to be very bad indeed before they constituted a risk to the health of other people, or even a serious nuisance to them. A nuisance in law is something which causes either physical damage to the neighbours' property or a substantial interference with its use and enjoyment. None of this, therefore, suggests that section 47 is simply a way of overcoming the reluctance of an old lady who might be safer or more comfortable in an old people's home.

(b) The full procedure

The full procedure under the 1948 Act is initiated by the community physician, who is employed by the health service and not by the local authority. He certifies in writing to the district or unitary local authority that the grounds exist. But in the non-unitary authorities the district local authority is not the LSSA which is responsible for arranging residential accommodation and providing social services to people in their own homes. The district or unitary authority make the application to the local magistrates' court, but the social workers who may have been helping the old person will not necessarily be involved.

Seven clear days' notice of the hearing must be given to the person concerned "or to some person in charge of him" (s 47(4)(a)). This last is a curious idea, as by definition the proposed patient is not being properly looked after by those around him, so that it seems most unjust to deprive him of his right to notice by giving it to them instead. These days, it would be difficult to justify proceeding against a person who has the capacity to make his own decisions about where he should be living, without giving him the fair hearing required by article 6 of the ECHR. Seven clear days' notice must also be given to the "person managing" the place to which it is proposed to remove the patient, unless that person is heard in the proceedings (s 47(3)). It seems likely that "person managing" would be construed to mean the same as the "managing authority" of a hospital or care home; that is the body in overall control rather than the individual in actual charge of the premises. But even though they must be given a hearing, the section does not expressly state that they must agree to accept the resident.

The court must hear oral evidence of the allegations in the certificate. If satisfied of these, and that it is "expedient" to do so, the court may order the removal of the patient to a "suitable hospital or other place" and also "his detention and maintenance therein" (s 47(3)). The actual removal is the task of an officer of the applicant local authority, who must be specified in the order (s 47(3)). The court fixes the duration of the order, up to a maximum of three months (s 47(4)). But the court may extend this for further periods of up to three months, provided once again that the patient or some person in charge of him (who could presumably be the officer in charge of the home) is given seven clear days' notice (s 47(4) and (7)). On the other hand, once six weeks have gone by since the original order or any extension, the patient (or someone acting on his behalf) may apply to the court for the order to be revoked (s 47(6)). This time, seven clear days' notice must be given to the community physician (s 47(7)). In practice, however, the chances of rehabilitating an old person who has been removed from home in this way are extremely slim. He will probably remain where he is whether or not the order continues in force. There is no right of appeal on the merits, only on a point of law to the High Court.

The magistrates' court may vary the place at which the person is to be kept, provided once again that the manager is either heard or given notice (s 47(5)). If the person is kept in an NHS hospital, the accommodation is free. If he is in a care home where accommodation is provided by or by arrangement with an LSSA under Part 3 of the 1948 Act (see chapter 9), the LSSA foots the bill, but the usual procedure for levying charges from the resident applies. If it is anywhere else, the district or unitary authority pays, but may recover the costs from the resident in the same way as for Part 3 accommodation (s 47(8) and (9); see chapter 9). This is controversial enough where people volunteer, however reluctantly, for residential care; where they are forced to accept it, it must feel like adding injury to insult.

(c) The emergency procedure

However controversial and deficient the full section 47 procedure may be, it does at least provide one form of judicial hearing, usually with notice to the person whose life is to be disrupted. There is, however, an emergency version in the National Assistance (Amendment) Act 1951, which is probably more frequently used. The district community physician and a second doctor (usually, but not necessarily the GP) must both certify that in their opinion the person fulfils conditions (i) and (ii) for the full procedure and that it is necessary in his own interests to remove him without delay (1951 Act, s 1(1)). This then permits several modifications to the basic procedure.

First, the application may be made either by the local authority or by the district community physician, provided that the local authority have given her general authorisation to do so (s 1(3)). Secondly, it may be to a single justice, rather than to a full magistrates' court (s 1(3)). The requirement of seven clear days' notice to the person concerned or the person in charge of him does not apply (s 1(1)) and the order can be made *ex parte* (s 1(3)), that is without any notice at all. The requirement of notice to the manager of the hospital or home is also waived, provided that it is shown that he has agreed to have the person (s 1(2)). The magistrate must still have oral evidence of the grounds. Any order made under the emergency procedure can only last for up to three weeks (s 1(4)) and the right to apply for revocation after six weeks is therefore inapplicable. An application to the full court, with the appropriate notice, is necessary to obtain a further order. But this may very well not be necessary once the initial break with home has been achieved.

(d) What does an order allow?

The Acts are by no means clear about what may be done with the person once he has been removed. Section 47(1) of the 1948 Act declares that the purpose is to secure "the necessary care and attention" for the person concerned; and section 47(3) provides that the court may order his removal to the hospital or home, and his "detention and maintenance therein". It would be difficult, therefore, to argue that it did not authorise the deprivation of liberty within the meaning of article 5 of the ECHR (even though not all removals to care homes in fact amount to this: see p 17, earlier). It seems that the 1951 Act was expressly passed because a doctor had been unable to persuade a person with a broken leg to go to hospital for treatment. Yet the Acts say nothing about imposing medical treatment, as opposed to care, attention and maintenance, without the patient's consent. In this they are very like the Mental Health Act 1959, which assumed that getting the patient to hospital and keeping him in was the only problem. What happened once he was there could safely be left to the clinical judgment of the doctors. Nowadays, however, we are much less inclined to read such powers into statutes which do not expressly contain them (see Jacob, 1976). Any treatment to which the patient did not consent would have to be justified under the MCA principles or the common law doctrine of necessity. Both, of course, depend upon the patient lacking the capacity to decide for himself and the treatment being in his best interests.

The 1948 Act procedures deprive a person, who by definition now does have the capacity to decide for himself, of his liberty in circumstances which have not yet been tested under the Human Rights Act. Under what limb of article 5(1) do they fall? How can the merits of an ex parte order under the 1951 Act be speedily challenged as required by article 5(4)? How can proceeding without notice to the person concerned, and without provision for a speedy return to court, give him a fair hearing in the determination of his civil rights as required by article 6? In 1995, the Law Commission proposed replacing these powers, along with those in sections 115 and 135(1) of the MHA, with a comprehensive scheme for the protection of vulnerable people living in the community which sought to answer these questions, but this was not taken up. The Commission (2010) have now proposed the repeal of these powers while leaving it to others to decide what, if anything, should replace them.

8. COMMENTARY

Which would you rather be? Admitted to a hospital or care home by court order under the National Assistance Act, deprived of your liberty by administrative act under the Mental Capacity Act, or "sectioned" under the Mental Health Act? The National Assistance Act conforms much more closely to the model of due process, because it involves a judicial decision by "an independent and impartial tribunal established by law" (in the words of article 6(1) of the ECHR). In practice, however, the person most nearly affected is not usually given notice of the proceedings and no adversarial process takes place. The Percy Commission (1957) thought that the intervention of a judicial authority in such circumstances was little more than a rubber stamp and they were probably right. It would be different if the person concerned were given notice, the right to representation, and a full-dress hearing before his liberty was infringed. But apart from the procedure for finding lunatics by inquisition, that has never been on offer to mental patients, even during the so-called triumph of legalism under the Lunacy Act 1890.

The biggest objection to the MHA procedures is that a person's rights are so crucially affected by the initial decision that he is a "patient". This defines whether he or his nearest relative is to be regarded as a rational human being. This defines whether he can be taken to hospital, detained, and given treatment without anything at all in the nature of due process ever having taken place. And the label "patient", as we all know, is extremely sticky. On the other hand, the MHA procedure does have enormous attractions. It is quick. It is private. It was naive of the Percy Commission to believe that it would do away altogether with the stigma of certification, for there is certainly a stigma in being "sectioned". But this may be less than that involved in any of the earlier procedures, if only because the consequences are now so much less drastic. It is meant to protect the patient's liberty and his needs better than a trial would do, by involving just those people who might be expected to assess them both properly. It does assume that all the participants will be able to act independently of one another. But as we have seen in chapter 3, this is by no means guaranteed. The only entirely free agent is likely to be whoever controls access to the hospital beds. The doctors do have to examine the patient and the AMHP has to interview him, but that is the limit of the patient's involvement. However, he does have the right to go to a tribunal straightaway.

And what of the new Mental Capacity Act DoLS? They are designed to provide people who are in fact deprived of their liberty with safeguards equivalent to those of mental patients who have to be compelled to receive the care and treatment they need. Is it possible, therefore, to justify the differences between them? That under the MCA a resident may be detained for up to 14 days without any medical evidence of mental disorder at all? That the very body which does the detaining can authorise this without any independent advice? That in the public sector the same body may be both the detaining managers and the supervising authorisers? That the standard authorisation can last for a year at a time? That the patient's nearest relative has so much less to do with the process than he does under the MHA? That any challenge lies to a court where the procedures are much slower and more cumbersome than in a tribunal and where the presumption of capacity is ignored? These are just some of the questions which may arise when the courts come to scrutinise the DoLS through the lens of the Human Rights Act.

5 MENTALLY DISORDERED OFFENDERS

The fact that a person who is alleged to have committed a criminal offence may be mentally disordered can affect the normal processes of the criminal justice system at several points. The police may decide to take the matter no further or deal with it in other ways. The Crown Prosecution Service may decide not to prosecute. If a prosecution is launched, the accused may be remanded or transferred to hospital before coming to trial or he may be found unfit to stand trial. At the trial, mental disorder may occasionally provide a defence to the charge. More commonly, it allows the court to choose a therapeutic rather than a penal disposal or (since 1997) both at once. Even if a prison sentence is chosen, the Justice Secretary may later transfer the prisoner to hospital.

Since 1990, the official policy has been to divert as many mentally disordered offenders as possible away from the criminal justice system (Home Office Circular No 66/90). In a perfect world, according to the Review of Health and Social Services for Mental Disordered Offenders (Reed, 1992), they should be cared for as far as possible in the community rather than in institutions, under conditions of no greater security than are justified by the degree of danger they present, so as to maximise their rehabilitation and chances of sustaining an independent life, and as close as possible to their own homes and families. In practice, reality "often falls a long way short of what is desirable" (para 3.1). Progress since then has been patchy and slow. This is partly because of a competing reality, the fear of crimes committed by people with personality disorders who are amenable neither to conventional psychiatric treatment nor to conventional deterrence. But it is also because of a chronic shortage of suitable treatment facilities for offenders with treatable mental disorders.

Over the same period, penal policies have led to a rapidly increasing prison population. The old dichotomy between an open-ended therapeutic disposal and a determinate punitive one has been eroded. The result is an alarmingly high incidence of mental health problems in the prison population, especially among the women (Chief Inspector of Prisons, 2007). Lord Bradley's Review of people with mental health problems or learning disabilities in the criminal justice system (Bradley, 2009) stressed the need to raise awareness of mental health issues throughout the system and to establish local Criminal Justice Mental Health teams everywhere; but he also devoted a good deal of attention to improving the treatment available for mentally disordered and disabled people in prison. Diversion is no longer seen as the only answer.

But which would you rather be? Sentenced to a fixed term in a prison where there could be a stimulating range of educational and other opportunities available, smoking is allowed and forcible medical treatment can hardly ever be imposed? Or sentenced to an indeterminate term in a medium or high security psychiatric hospital, where the facilities are less varied, smoking is not allowed, but forcible medical treatment is?

1. POLICE AND PROSECUTION

(a) Detention under section 136 of the Mental Health Act

A police officer may remove to a place of safety any person whom he finds in a "place to which the public have access" and who appears to him to be suffering from mental disorder and in immediate need of care or control, provided that the officer thinks the removal is necessary in the interests of the person concerned or for the protection of other persons (MHA, s 136(1)). The officer need not suspect that a criminal offence has been committed. No magistrate's warrant, written application or medical evidence is required, as it normally would be if the person were on private premises.

A "place to which the public have access" covers more than public highways and open spaces where all are free to come and go as they please. It includes places like railway platforms and football grounds and car parks, to which members of the public are admitted on payment, or shops and public houses, which are only open at certain times of the day. These are not included at other times, but while they are open the concept may cover parts of the premises to which general access is denied. Even if some members of the public are not allowed in, a place may qualify if others are admitted qua public, for example to a hospital accident and emergency department. A place would not qualify if people are only admitted as lawful visitors to private premises, for example, on hospital wards or in private homes and gardens. Whether lifts, landings and staircases serving a block of flats qualify will depend upon whether and how access is controlled. A communal balcony was assumed to be public in *Carter v Metropolitan Police Commissioner* [1975] 1 WLR 507 and open walkways linking dwellings on a housing estate were so found in *Knox v Anderton* (1983) 76 Cr App R 156.

Officers have been known to "entice" a person out of private premises in order to be able to detain him outside (Independent Police Complaints Commission (IPPC), 2008, p 18). In *Seal v Chief Constable of South Wales* [2007] UKHL 31, [2007] 1 WLR 1910, the would-be claimant had first been arrested in his mother's home, which would not qualify under section 136. But if the first arrest had been for a breach of the peace and the officer had detained him under section 136 after they got outside, the position is more doubtful. Could the officer be said to "find" the claimant outside when it was the police officer who had taken him there (see para 60)? It may be that it would be wrong for an officer to arrest a person on some other pretext, with a view to detaining him under section 136 the moment they got outside; but that it would be permissible for an officer, who had arrested or taken a person outside for a bona fide reason, to decide that the section 136 criteria were met and detain him then (and see *McMillan v Crown Prosecution Service* [2008] EWHC 1457 (Admin)).

The definition of a place of safety is the same as that in section 135 (s 135(6); see p 116, earlier). This includes both a hospital and a police station. The available evidence suggests that nearly twice as many people detained under section 136 are held in police cells as are held in health care settings (Independent Police Complaints Commission (IPPC), 2008). But hospital accident and emergency departments are also not ideal. The Royal College of Psychiatrists' Standards on the use of section 136 (RCPsych, 2008) advocated the setting up of specialist psychiatric units, properly staffed for 24 hours a day, to which people detained under section 136 could be taken for assessment. They stressed, as does the MHA Code, that a police station should be used "only on an exceptional basis" (Code, para 10.21); nor should a police station be assumed to be the automatic second choice if the first choice is not available (para 10.22). Where there are available alternatives and good multi-agency co-operation, the police also seem better able to avoid using section 136 altogether (IPPC, 2008).

A police station is a frightening place (RCPsych, 2008). A person taken to a police station under section 136 is likely to be processed in the same way as any other arrested person (see Mental Health Act Commission (MHAC), "24 hours in a police cell", 2009a, para 2.134). This will give him the impression that he is suspected of having committed a crime and may affect his co-operation with the assessment (MHA Code, para 10.24). Section 136 is technically a power of arrest for the purpose of the Police and Criminal Evidence Act 1984 (PACE). The person arrested is entitled to have someone else informed (PACE, s 56); and if held in a police station, to have access to legal advice (PACE, s 58). The PACE Codes of Practice, especially Code C, (Home Office, 2008) apply. The police have the same powers of search as they have under PACE (see MHA Code, para 10.45). So people detained in a police station are likely to be given an explanation of their rights under PACE but are much less likely to be told their position under the MHA. None of this is likely to improve their mental health.

Detention under section 136 must be:

"for the purpose of enabling him to be examined by a registered medical practitioner and to be interviewed by an approved mental health professional (AMHP) and of making any necessary arrangements for his treatment or care" (s 136(2)).

No-one can be detained in a police station if the custody officer concludes that detention is no longer appropriate (MHA Code, para 10.32), so an unknown number of detainees may be released without being assessed. But the MHAC (2009, para 2.136) doubted whether a police officer could properly reach that conclusion without suitable professional advice. Whenever possible, the doctor should be "approved" (MHA Code, para 10.28) but few police surgeons are. Preferably the doctor and the AMHP should do the assessment together (para 10.28). The patient should also be seen by an AMHP (para 10.33). Releasing a person before all this is done might cast doubt upon whether it was the real purpose of the detention and would clearly be inappropriate if there were still grounds for thinking that the person was mentally disordered and in need of care. There is now power to transfer a person detained under section 136 from one place of safety to another. This can be done by a police officer, an AMHP or someone authorised by either (s 136(3)). It can be done before, during or after the assessment, but the benefits of any move need to be weighed against the delay and distress it may cause (MHA Code, para 10.37).

Once the person has been assessed and any necessary arrangements made, the authority for his detention lapses (see, eg, PACE Code C, para 3.16). If the doctor arrives first and concludes that there is no mental disorder, the detainee should be released immediately (MHA Code, para 10.31). If the doctor concludes that there is mental disorder, the detainee should still be seen by an AMHP even if the doctor does not think that compulsory admission is necessary, because other arrangements may be needed (para 10.33). The maximum period of detention is 72 hours from when the patient reached the first place of safety (s 136(4)). Section 136 detention is not an admission to hospital under the MHA and gives no power to impose medical treatment without consent (MHA s 56(2), (3)(b)).

147

The MHA Code stresses the need for health, social services and police to have clear local policies for the operation of section 136, including collecting statistics and monitoring its use (paras 10.16 to 10.19; see also RCPsych 2008; Bradley, 2009). Unlike all other MHA detentions, there is no need for any court order or statutory form. Some people may be detained under section 136 and released without seeing any professionals. Hospital admissions are centrally recorded, but detentions in other places are not. Reliable data are hard to obtain. But in 2005–2006 there were about 5,900 detentions in hospital and 11,500 in police stations (IPPC, 2008). These are very significant numbers for such an informal and unregulated procedure.

It may be that people whom the police take straight to hospital show high rates of chronic mental illness, or are at least as disturbed as those admitted under sections 2 or 4, and even more socially isolated and out of touch with the community services (see Fahy, 1989; Dunn and Fahy, 1990, Bean et al, 1991; Mokhtar and Hogbin, 1993). Other studies in the 1990s found that most people detained under section 136 had a past psychiatric history and had previously been compulsorily detained (Pipe et al, 1991; Turner et al, 1992). These and later studies found that a high proportion of those detained were then admitted to hospital (Simmons and Hoar, 2001; Bather, 2006). But there are persistent concerns that black and minority ethnic groups are grossly over-represented (IPCC, 2008; MHAC, 2005, 2009a). Given its broad terms and the lack of any medical opinion before the person is detained, section 136 is clearly open to misuse if not abuse. Professionals called to assess the person detained, especially at a police station, may also feel themselves under pressure to "section him or we prosecute".

It is still not clear what section 136 is for. In *Carter v Metropolitan Police Commissioner* [1975] 1 WLR 507, it was a convenient but possibly discriminatory way of diffusing the situation when bizarre behaviour was causing a disturbance: an African-Caribbean woman with no history of mental disorder was taken to hospital by police officers who said that they found her on the communal landing, shouting abuse and with excrement on her hands following a dispute with her neighbours. As one officer put it more recently (IPPC, 2008, p 17): " . . . it's the man walking round the railway line with no clothes on and acting daft that will get the actual dead obvious 136". If so, is it acceptable that the police should be able to detain someone as "of unsound mind" without any medical or other professional advice? In other cases, it gives the police another way of dealing with an obvious offender who seems equally obviously disordered. But if so, why not insist that there should always be grounds for arresting the person instead (Percy, 1957)? The reality is, however, that the police will almost always have the option of arresting for breach of the peace, if not for some more serious offence. Some forces see section 136 as more troublesome to process than an arrest (IPPC, 2008), so perhaps there is as great a risk of under-use as of over-use.

(b) Diversion, interrogation and prosecution

Apart from section 136, there are several other options open to the police when they encounter a possible offender who may be mentally disordered. If he is an absconding compulsory patient, they may simply detain and return him to hospital under sections 18 or 138; if he is on leave of absence, they may contact the hospital to recall him, so that section 18 will apply (see chapter 7). If he is not already a compulsory patient, they may be able to refer him to the specialist mental health services with a view to their taking responsibility for him. All of this depends upon the police officers' ability to recognise that an offender may be mentally disordered or disabled and to establish contact with the appropriate services: hence the need for awareness training, especially for custody officers, and for generally available liaison and diversion services (Bradley, 2009).

In principle, an arrested person is entitled to be told at the time under which power he is being detained (*Christie v Leachinsky* [1947] AC 573; see also European Convention on Human Rights, article 5(2)). In practice, the police may avoid putting a label on the detention until the decision between arrest and diversion has been made (Bean et al, 1991). Part of the process of deciding will be to interview the suspect. Special procedures for questioning mentally disordered and otherwise mentally vulnerable people are laid down in the PACE Code C, on the Detention, Treatment and Questioning of Persons by Police Officers, helpfully summarised at Annex E (Home Office, 2008). These apply where an officer has any suspicion or is told in good faith that a person of any age may be mentally disordered or otherwise mentally vulnerable or mentally incapable of understanding the significance of questions or their replies (PACE Code C, para 1.4).

If a mentally disordered or mentally vulnerable person is detained, an "appropriate adult" must be informed and asked to come to the police station. An appropriate adult is a relative, guardian or other person responsible for his care or custody; or someone (other than a police officer or employee) who has experience of dealing with mentally disordered or handicapped people; or failing these, some other similarly independent responsible adult (PACE Code C, para 1.7). An AMHP is an obvious candidate, but should not be asked both to make an assessment under section 136 and to act as an appropriate adult, because the roles may conflict (Home Office, 1995). A trained or experienced person may be more appropriate than an unqualified relative, but the detained person's own wishes should if practicable be respected. The adult should be there when the detained person is "read his rights" (eg to tell someone that he is detained, to consult a lawyer and to consult the Codes: Code C, paras 3.1 to 3.5). If this has been done before the adult arrives it must be done again (Code C, paras 3.15 to 3.17). He can request access to legal advice on the detained person's behalf (Code C, para 3.19). The object is said to be to protect a person who does not understand the significance of what is said (Code C, Annex E, para E1).

A suspect may be questioned (within limits) before or after arrest or detention. The PACE Code recognises that although mentally disordered or vulnerable people "are often capable of providing reliable evidence, they may, without knowing or wanting to do so, be particularly prone in certain circumstances to provide information which is unreliable, misleading or self-incriminating"; special care and, if possible, corroboration of any admissions, are therefore required (Code C, Annex E, para E2). It is all too easy for a police officer to extract admissions from a vulnerable or pliant person and then thankfully regard the case as closed without checking the story further. The best known example is Colin Lattimore, who was convicted almost entirely on his own admission of taking part in the killing of Maxwell Confait, although this had taken place at a time when he could not possibly have been there. The risk of unreliable admissions may be increased, now that (under the Criminal Justice and Public Order Act 1994, ss 34 to 36) a suspect must be warned that his failure to explain clues or his presence at the scene of the crime, or to put forward an explanation which he later uses in his defence, may be held against him in court.

Hence, if a mentally disordered or handicapped person has been cautioned before the appropriate adult arrives, this must be repeated when he arrives (Code C, para 10.12). A mentally disordered or vulnerable person must not be interviewed or asked to provide or sign a written statement without an appropriate adult present, unless a superintendent or above considers that the delay would lead to interference with or harm either to evidence or to other people, or would alert other suspects who have not yet been arrested, or would hinder the recovery of property. Once the risk is averted, the questioning must stop (Code C, paras 11.1, 11.15, and 11.18 to 11.20). The adult must be told that he is not there just to observe, but to advise the person being interviewed, to observe whether or not the interview is being conducted properly and fairly, and to facilitate communication with him (Code C, para 11.17). All this is, of course, in addition to the normal rules and directions about questioning.

A breach of the PACE Code does not necessarily make a statement inadmissible in evidence. But a confession must be excluded unless the prosecution can prove that it was not obtained "(a) by oppression of the person who made it; or (b) in consequence of anything said or done which was likely, in the circumstances existing at the time, to render unreliable" any confession which might be made by him as a result (PACE, s 76(2)). Breaches of the Code may combine with other circumstances to amount to oppression, which "excites hopes (such as the hope of release) or fears, or so affects the mind of the subject that his will crumbles and he speaks when otherwise he would have remained silent" (Lord MacDermott, adopted in *R v Prager* (1971) 56 Cr App R 151). An example is *R v Westlake* [1979] Crim LR 652: the accused had a mental age of 11 or 12 and was kept in custody for 24 hours before his interrogation. He was then questioned repeatedly over the next five days. No attempt was made to have his father present, although this was practicable.

Even if there is no inducement or oppression, the judge still has a discretion to exclude prosecution evidence if in all the circumstances, including those in which the evidence was obtained, admitting it "would have such an adverse effect on the fairness of the proceedings that the court ought not to admit it" (1984 Act, s 78(1)). In *R v Aspinall* [1999] 2 Cr App R 115, the police interviewed a man, whom they knew to be a schizophrenic on regular medication, without an appropriate adult present because they thought him lucid and fit to be interviewed. The Court of Appeal pointed out that this was not the test: the test was whether the absence of an appropriate adult, with all the safeguards which that was designed to bring, had had such an adverse effect upon the fairness of the interview that it should be excluded. One aspect of this was that the defendant might appear normal to a lay person or to the jury when an appropriate adult would have known that he was not (but cf *R v Gill and others* [2004] EWCA Crim 3245, where the judge was entitled to conclude that an appropriate adult would have made no difference).

If the evidence is admitted, section 77 of PACE requires the judge, in a case which relies wholly or mainly on the confession of a mentally handicapped person made without the presence of an independent person, to warn the jury "that there is a special need for caution" before convicting him in reliance on it. However, in *R v Moss* (1990) 91 Cr App R 371, giving this warning was not enough to make safe the conviction of a man who was just above mental handicap level, which relied solely on confessions made after he had been in custody for nine days, interviewed nine times, and without a solicitor present. The courts, at least, have become increasingly alive to the dangers.

Early studies of police diversion (principally Rollin, 1969; Walker and McCabe,

1973) suggested that the two most important factors were the nature of the offence and the police knowledge of the offender's history. The police were more likely to prosecute for crimes against property, which they probably thought more blameworthy, involving a higher degree of thought and planning, than the public order offences which were common amongst the unprosecuted group and often involved outstandingly abnormal behaviour. The unprosecuted offenders were more likely to be seriously ill (or soon discovered to be so) and also less likely to have a serious criminal record. There was also evidence that chance played a large part in these decisions. Whitehead and Ahmad (1970) were concerned that so many of their hospital order patients appeared to have committed minor public order offences directly related to their disorder (such as shouting at their "voices"). Walker and McCabe (1973), on the other hand, discovered several unprosecuted offenders whose crimes were very serious. The Government view is that, while people should not be drawn into the criminal justice system unnecessarily and certainly not in the hope that they will receive appropriate treatment in prison, if their behaviour appears to put others at risk, it is preferable to prosecute, so that the court can consider whether a therapeutic disposal is required for the protection of the public as well as enabling their health and care needs to be met (Home Office, 1995).

If the police consider that a person should be prosecuted, the case is referred to the Crown Prosecution Service (CPS). The legal guidance offered by the CPS is that:

"There is no presumption either in favour of or against prosecution of a mentally disordered offender. Each case must be considered on its merits, taking into account all available information about any disorder, and its relevance to the offence, in addition to the principles set out in the Code for Crown Prosecutors" (Crown Prosecution Service, 2010b).

The Code prescribes two stages in the decision. There must first be enough evidence to provide a realistic prospect of conviction, so the admissibility and reliability of any confession will be considered at this stage. Only then will the prosecutor decide whether a prosecution is needed in the public interest. Among the factors making this less likely is that:

"the subject is, or was at the time of the offence, suffering from significant mental or physical ill health unless the offence is serious or there is a real possibility that it may be repeated. Prosecutors apply Home Office guidelines about how to deal with mentally disordered offenders and must balance a suspect's mental or physical ill health with the need to safeguard the public or those providing care services to such persons" (Code for Crown Prosecutors, 2010a, para. 4.17(j)).

As with the police, the CPS can only do this if they are alive to the issue (which depends upon their being told that there is one) and have access to appropriate liaison and diversion schemes locally. Presumably, a crucial factor is whether there should be the option of a custodial penalty or a hospital order with restrictions, for other forms of diversion can be achieved without going to court at all. But there are reasons quite apart from public protection for being sceptical about diversion. Even the most disturbed patient may feel a sense of grave injustice at prolonged detention in hospital without trial. Many professionals now believe that people with learning disabilities should be prosecuted and held responsible where responsibility exists (see Carson, 1989b). This is an essential element in recognition as a human being. It is also important to establish the truth about an incident, especially in an institution. There is a popular conception that mentally disordered or disabled people are more likely than others to commit crimes. Mostly they are not. There is evidence that active psychotic symptoms are associated with an increased risk of violence, but the accurate assessment of risk is acknowledged to be a difficult and inexact science (Hodgins, 1993; Crichton, 1995). While diversion out of the criminal justice system is of real benefit to some, we should not forget the advantages of a proper investigation of the evidence and of the alternative disposals. Nor should psychiatrists be asked to make judgments which are more appropriate to the forensic process (Carson, 1992).

2. PROCEDURE BEFORE TRIAL

(a) Obtaining the medical evidence

A court must always have medical evidence of the grounds for any compulsory psychiatric diversion or disposal. Sometimes one medical report is required and sometimes two, but the evidence of an approved doctor (see p 98, earlier) is always needed. But none of the rules in the civil procedures about the timing of medical recommendations, or avoiding conflicts of interest between the doctors, apply in criminal proceedings. The medical reports could be quite old and the doctors from the same hospital. The court must also have evidence, from the hospital managers or the proposed responsible clinician (RC), that the offender can be admitted to a particular hospital within the prescribed deadline or that community arrangements can be made. If the court is contemplating a restriction order or a hybrid order (see below), one of the doctors must give oral evidence (MHA, ss 41(2), 45A(4)). The court will want to know what the hospital thinks about taking the patient with restrictions, although the decision is always a matter for the court (*R v Blackwood* (1973) 59 Cr App R 170; *R v Royse* [1981] Crim LR 426).

Otherwise, the medical evidence may be given in writing, although the court may always insist on the doctor's attendance if it wishes (s 54(2A)). Written reports from the hospital managers or a doctor can be given in evidence without formal proof of the signature or qualifications (s 54(2)). Reports which are not presented on behalf of the defendant must be disclosed to his legal representative. If he has none, the substance must be disclosed to him personally, or to his parent if he is a young offender. The defence is entitled to insist that the doctor gives oral evidence, so that he may be cross-examined, and to call evidence to rebut what he says (s 52(3)), except where the evidence relates solely to the availability of a bed.

Reports may be obtained either by the prosecution, or by the defence, or at the request of the court. It used to be routine for the court to obtain a report in homicide cases. But the Court of Appeal has now said that this is not necessary. There should be no difficulty in the defence obtaining a report, usually at public expense, if they wish to raise an issue. If the issue is pursued, the prosecution can obtain its own report (*R v Reid* [2001] EWCA Crim 1806, (2002) 1 Cr App R 21). However, defence lawyers should also be prepared to subject "favourable" reports to critical scrutiny and be on their guard against the assumption that a hospital order is always a soft option or what the client wants. Once the possibility is raised, the judge may well consider the unwelcome addition of a restriction order (see Gostin, 1977). Furthermore, the risks to the public can override the duty of confidentiality, so that a psychiatrist instructed on behalf of the defence may make his report available to the court, which can act upon it whether the defendant likes it or not (*R v Crozier* (1990) 12 Cr App R (S) 206).

Some (eg Kenny, 1983) argue that expert evidence is not suitable for adversarial combat and should be called to assist the court rather than by the parties. This assumes that the court's expert is right and anyone else is wrong, which in a field like psychiatry is manifestly absurd. Judges themselves seem to veer from an exaggerated contempt to an equally exaggerated respect (eg King, 1981). The Butler Report on Mentally Disordered Offenders (1975) comforted itself that the unedifying "battle of the experts" had diminished, since the abolition of the death penalty and the shift of most decisions to the sentencing stage. The doctors are much more comfortable discussing possible disposals with a professional judge than giving evidence to a jury about the effect of mental disorder on criminal responsibility.

The prior problem is getting someone to recognise that there may be mental disorder or disability which would benefit from a specialist disposal and commissioning the necessary assessments and reports. Without both awareness of the issue and access to the appropriate services, many offenders with mental health needs will slip through the net. The MHA Code valiantly declares that people who are subject to criminal proceedings have the same rights to psychiatric treatment and assessment as anyone else. Anyone who is in police or prison custody or before the courts on a criminal charge and who is in need of medical treatment for mental disorder should be considered for admission to hospital (para 33.2). Their needs should be considered at the earliest possible opportunity (para 33.3). Primary Care Trusts should ensure the prompt medical assessment of defendants so as to assist the speedy completion of the trial process and the most suitable disposal of the offender (para 33.6). But implementing Lord Bradley's recommendation (2009) for liaison and diversion schemes everywhere would be necessary to make this a reality.

The MHA Code also gives advice about the content of medical reports. Doctors should bear in mind that the court wants their help in deciding what order to make and not a general report on the patient's condition (para 33.8). One of the two doctors "should have access to a bed" or, if they do recommend admission, take responsibility for referring the case to someone who does have access (para 33.10). They should request sight of other relevant pre-sentence reports, psychiatric reports, information about the alleged offence, information about the previous history, and consult the multi-disciplinary team if hospital admission is likely to be recommended (paras 33.9, 33.11, 33.12). The report should not speculate about guilt or innocence, but should make recommendations for the disposal of the case (paras 33.16, 33.18). Like any expert's report, it should set out the material on which it is based, how that material relates to the opinion given, the factors relating to the presence of mental disorder which may affect the risk which the person presents to himself or other, and what (if any) special treatment or security is recommended if the patient is admitted to hospital (para 33.16). All of this is designed to enhance the report's credibility with the court, especially if it has been commissioned on behalf of the defence, as will often be the case.

(b) Remands for reports

All courts have a specific power to remand offenders for reports after conviction. Magistrates may do so (for three weeks at a time in custody and four on bail)

153

without convicting, if they are satisfied that the defendant did the act or made the omission charged (Magistrates' Courts Act 1980, s 30). The usual presumption in favour of bail applies to all these remands (Bail Act 1976, s 4(4)).

If an accused is remanded in custody, it may be easy to obtain a report, but prison is scarcely the most favourable environment in which to make a psychiatric assessment. If the accused is remanded on bail, the court may make whatever condition appears necessary to ensure that he makes himself available, so that a report may be made to assist the court in dealing with him for the offence (1976 Act, s 3(6)(d)). Where a person charged with murder is granted bail, the court must make it a condition that he is examined by two doctors, one of them approved, unless satisfactory reports have already been obtained (1976 Act, s 3(6A)). Bail can include a condition of residence in hospital, but unless the accused is separately "sectioned" he is an informal patient whom the hospital cannot detain.

Following a recommendation in the Butler Report, section 35 of the 1983 Act introduced a power to remand to hospital for reports before conviction. This applies to anyone awaiting trial or sentence in the Crown Court for any offence punishable with imprisonment (including those charged with, but not yet convicted of, murder). Magistrates may only remand after convicting the accused of an imprisonable offence, or finding that he did the act or made the omission charged, or with his consent (s 35(2)). These remands can only be made where it would be impracticable for a report on his mental condition to be made if he were on bail, so prison would almost always be the alternative. Nevertheless, it was thought that a normal offender might resent being sent to hospital, so the court must have written or oral evidence from one approved doctor that there is reason to suspect that the accused is suffering from mental disorder (s 35(3)). There must be the usual evidence that a bed will be available, for this purpose within seven days, beginning with the date of the remand (s 35(4)).

The accused may be kept in a "place of safety" before he is taken to hospital. For this and other orders under Part 3 of the Act, a "place of safety" is a police station, prison or remand centre, or another hospital which is willing to have him for the time being (s 55(1)). Once in hospital, he must be detained (s 35(9)) and if he escapes he may be arrested without warrant and must then be brought back to court (s 35(10)). The Act expressly allows him to obtain his own medical report at his own expense, so that he can ask for the remand to be ended (s 35(8)). A remand under this section cannot last for more than 28 days at a time (s 35(7)), but the accused may be remanded again and again if the doctor states that this is necessary (s 35(5)). He need not be brought back to court for the purpose, provided that he has a legal representative who is given an opportunity of being heard (s 35(6)). But the total period cannot be longer than 12 weeks in all and the court can always end it earlier (s 35(7)).

These remands are an excellent idea in theory. Official figures suggest there were only 269 in 1998–1999 and 145 in 2007–2008, although there may be many more (Gunn and Joseph, 1993). But the psychiatric services would be swamped if everyone remanded in custody for reports were remanded to hospital instead (Fennell, 1991a). Those who do go to hospital cannot be treated without their consent (1983 Act, s 56(2), (3)(b)) unless they are "sectioned" under civil powers as well. In *R v North West London Mental Health Trust, ex p Stewart* [1997] 4 All ER 871 it was held that a person who was subject to compulsory powers under Part 3 of the MHA (in that case a conditionally discharged restricted patient) could also be "sectioned" under Part 2. This must be very confusing for a patient remanded for reports, who would not know when the authority for his detention came to an end or who was in charge.

(c) Hospital care while awaiting trial or sentence

If a person awaiting trial or sentence is remanded or committed in custody, the Justice Secretary may direct his transfer to hospital under section 48 (s 48(2)(a) and (b); this section also applies to people imprisoned for debt or detained under the Immigration Act 1971; s 48(2)(c) and (d)). The Justice Secretary must have reports from at least two doctors, one approved, that the prisoner is suffering from mental disorder, of a nature or degree which makes it appropriate for him to be detained in hospital for medical treatment, that he is in urgent need of this treatment and that appropriate medical treatment is available for him (s 48(1)). The direction is of no effect unless the patient arrives in the specified hospital within 14 days (s 47(2)).

All transfers from prison to hospital have the same effect as a hospital order (s 47(3)). The patient may be treated without his consent; but he may also apply to a tribunal, even during his first six months in hospital. However, the transfer of a remand prisoner must take effect as a restriction order (s 49(1) and (2)). This means that the tribunal do not have power to discharge him into the community (see p 274, later).

The precise consequences of a transfer depend upon the court in which the patient is waiting to appear. If he is waiting to appear in a magistrates' court, the transfer lasts as long as the remand, unless the court remands him again (which it may do in his absence if he has appeared before the court within the last six months) or commits him for trial in the Crown Court (which again it may do in his absence if the RC reports that he is unfit to take part). But the magistrates themselves may end the transfer, even if the remand has not expired or the patient has been committed to the Crown Court, if the RC reports to them that the patient no longer needs treatment for mental disorder, or that no effective treatment can be given in that hospital (s 52). If and when the magistrates finally deal with a transferred patient, they may be able to make a hospital order, sometimes without convicting him, but they cannot do so in his absence (see s 37(3), p 160, below).

If the patient is waiting to appear in the Crown Court, the transfer lasts until the Court disposes of the case. However, the Justice Secretary always has power to transfer the patient back to prison, if notified by the RC, any other approved clinician or a tribunal that he no longer needs treatment or that no effective treatment can be given in the hospital to which he has been transferred (s 51(3)). And the court having jurisdiction to try or dispose of the offender may itself end the transfer if notified to the same effect by the RC. But the court may choose to release him on bail rather than transfer him back to custody whereas the Justice Secretary cannot (s 51(4)).

If the patient is still in hospital when he comes up for trial or sentence, the Crown Court may make a hospital order in his absence and without convicting him, provided that three conditions are fulfilled. First, it must be "impracticable or inappropriate" to bring him before the court. Secondly, there must be written or oral evidence from at least two doctors, one approved, that he is suffering from mental disorder of a nature or degree which makes it appropriate for him to be detained in hospital for medical treatment. Lastly, the court must think that this is proper, after considering the depositions and any other documents sent to court (s 51(5) and (6)). The hospital order may be with or without restrictions.

The effect of this is that both a magistrates' court and the Crown Court may make a hospital order over a transferred remand prisoner without ever trying him. The Crown Court does not even have to be satisfied that he did the act or made the omission charged. This amounts to indefinite detention without trial. Indeed, the transfer alone may have this result, for the court may be persuaded to go on remanding the patient, or to refrain from listing his case, until he recovers enough to be tried (see Gostin, 1977). In *R (Kenneally) v Snaresbrook Crown Court* [2001] EWHC Admin 968, [2002] QB 1169, the Divisional Court emphasised that to pass sentence without first convicting the defendant was a step which could only be taken in exceptional circumstances: the fear that a schizophrenic defendant might behave in a disruptive manner while being tried for indecent assault was not enough to make it "inappropriate" to try him. The Court did not deal with the obvious argument that this might also be contrary to his right under article 6(1) of the European Convention on Human Rights to a fair trial "in the determination of any criminal charge against him".

Magistrates' courts have no power to make restriction orders, but they may commit a person over 14 to the Crown Court with a view to a restriction order being made (s 43(1)). The magistrates must already have convicted the offender and received the evidence necessary for a hospital order. They may commit the defendant direct to hospital if they have evidence from the approved clinician who would be in charge, or some other representative of the hospital managers, that a bed is available, and in this case there is no time limit on when he must be admitted (s 44). Once again, the committal has the same effect as a restriction order, which is scarcely an inducement to bring the case quickly before the Crown Court. Once there, the Crown Court can either make a hospital order, with or without restrictions, or deal with him in any way in which the magistrates might have done (s 43(2)).

Following another recommendation of the Butler Report (1975), concerned that mentally disordered people might be languishing in prison awaiting trial when they ought to be receiving treatment in hospital, section 36 of the 1983 Act gives the Crown Court (but not magistrates) power to remand direct to hospital for treatment people who are awaiting trial or sentence for any offence punishable with imprisonment, except for murder. This is illogical: once a person is convicted of murder, the court has no option but to sentence him to life imprisonment, but a person awaiting trial for murder may never be convicted, or may be convicted of a lesser offence, and in the meantime might be receiving the treatment he needs.

The evidence of mental condition is the same as that required for a transfer from prison, except that treatment need not be urgently needed (s 36(1)). There must be the usual evidence from the hospital that a bed will be available within seven days. As the object is to secure treatment for the patient's disorder, the usual provisions about medical treatment of detained patients apply (see chapter 6). Apart from that, however, the effects of the order, its duration and renewal up to a maximum of 12 weeks, are the same as in a remand to hospital for reports (see above).

As three months is by no means a long time to be waiting to appear in the Crown Court, these patients may well have to be returned to prison, unless the Justice Secretary can be persuaded to make a transfer direction. It is ironic that an admission which is ordered by the Crown Court should be so much less drastic in its effects than one which is directed by the Justice Secretary. It scarcely indicates a consistent view about whether it is worse to languish in prison without treatment or to languish in hospital without trial. But transfer from prison may well be quicker and can operate as a substitute for trial in some cases. Transfers with restrictions under section 48 were between 300 and 400 for most of the decade from 1997–1998 to 2007–2008, while section 35 remands fell from 25 to 17.

(d) Fitness to plead

Occasionally a person appearing before the Crown Court may be so disabled that he is unfit to stand trial. This has nothing to do with his state of mind at the time of the alleged offence. The question is whether he has "sufficient intellect" to be able to plead to the indictment and understand the proceedings sufficiently to be able to challenge jurors, take in the evidence, and make a proper defence: *R v Pritchard* (1836) 7 C & P 303. An illiterate deaf-mute, or someone who is incapable of communicating with the court or his legal advisers, may not be fit (*R v Sharp* (1957) 41 Cr App R 196). Someone suffering from amnesia about the relevant events, but who can understand the trial, is fit (*R v Podola* [1960] 1 QB 325). This is controversial. If genuine, amnesia can obviously make it impossible for the accused to defend himself and is quite different from mere forgetfulness (Walker, 1981). But the fact that the accused is highly abnormal and cannot act in his own best interests does not necessarily mean that he cannot understand the trial (*R v Robertson* (1968) 62 Cr App R 690).

The enactment of the Mental Capacity Act 2005 (MCA) has highlighted a serious criticism of the *Pritchard* test: its concentration on the ability to understand rather than on the ability to make a real decision about how to conduct the case. Why should not the test of capacity be the same as the test for conducting any other sort of legal proceedings (see Scott Moncrieff and Vassall-Adam, 2006; also Grubin, 1993)? Then, as well as understanding the basic information, the defendant would have to be able to use or weigh that information as part of the process of making decisions about the trial (MCA, s 3(2)(c)). Another difficulty with the present law is its all or nothing attitude. The accused may be able to understand a trial on a simple charge, but not on a more complicated matter.

The question of fitness to plead is usually raised before the trial begins. Normally it must be decided as soon as it arises (Criminal Procedure (Insanity) Act 1964, s 4(4)). However, the judge may postpone this until any time before the opening of the defence case, if having regard to the nature of the supposed disability, it is expedient and in the interests of the accused to do so (1964 Act, s 4(2)); and if in the meantime the jury acquit him on all counts, it will never be decided at all (1964 Act, s 4(3)). The question of fitness to plead is now to be determined by a judge, as recommended both by the Butler Report (1975) and the Auld Review of the Criminal Courts of England and Wales (2001) (1964 Act, s 4(5)). To make a finding of unfitness, the judge must have the written or oral evidence of two or more doctors, one of them approved (1964 Act, s 4(6)). He does not need that evidence to make a finding that the accused is fit to plead (*R v Ghulam (Habib)* [2009] EWCA Crim 2285, [2010] 1 Cr App R 12).

If the accused is found fit, then the trial will proceed in the normal way. If he is found unfit, then a jury must still decide whether or not they are satisfied that he did the act or made the omission charged; and if they are not so satisfied he must be acquitted in the normal way (1964 Act, s 4A). This requirement, to hold as good a trial of the facts as is possible in the circumstances, was introduced to meet the criticism that the accused might have a perfectly good defence to the charge. Grubin (1991) found that the evidence linking the accused to the

157

offence "seemed good" in more than 80 per cent of cases. The issue is whether the accused did the deed, not what his mental condition was at the time, and so he cannot plead diminished responsibility as well (*R v Antoine* [2000] UKHL 20, [2001] 1 AC 340). The issue can be tried at the same time as the full trial of a co-accused, provided that this is fair (*R v B* [2008] EWCA Crim 1997, [2009] 1 WLR 1545). So an accused who was not unfit might plead diminished responsibility at the same trial in which an accused who was unfit could not. In *R v H* [2003] UKHL 1, [2003] 1 WLR 411, the House of Lords held that this "trial of the facts" is not the determination of a criminal charge for the purpose of article 6(1) of the European Convention on Human Rights, because none of the orders in which it might result was a punishment (see *Engel v The Netherlands (No 1)* (1976) 1 EHRR 647, para 82). It would be odd indeed if a procedure introduced to protect the accused were held incompatible with the Convention.

Before the Criminal Procedure (Insanity and Unfitness to Plead) Act 1991, the inevitable result of a finding of disability (as it is technically called) was indefinite detention as a restriction order patient, with the prospect of eventually being returned to stand trial when fit to do so. Not surprisingly, very few people claimed to be unfit. This remains the compulsory disposal where the charge is murder ("an offence the sentence for which sentence is fixed by law"). In such a case, section 5(3) of the 1964 Act provides that the court must add a restriction order to a hospital order even if it would not otherwise have power to do so (but it does now insist that there is the evidence required for a hospital order: see below). Since 1991 there has been a wider choice of disposals for other offences. The court *must* make one of the following orders (s 5(2)). Before doing so, it has the same powers to remand to hospital for reports or treatment or to make an interim hospital order as it has over an accused person (1964 Act, s 5A(2)).

(i) An *absolute discharge* (1964 Act, s 5(2)(c)).

(ii) A *supervision order* (1964 Act, s 5(2)(b) and Sch 1A). This places the person under the supervision of a social worker from the local social services authority or a probation officer for the area where he lives or will live, who must be willing to undertake the supervision (paras 2(2)(a), 3(1)), for a specified period of not more than two years (para 1(1)). The basic requirement is to keep in touch (para 3(5)), but the order may also include a residence condition (para 8). If the supervised person moves to another area, a magistrates' court may amend the order accordingly (para 10).

More importantly, provided that the arrangements have been made (para 2(2)(b)), the order may include one or both of two requirements for medical treatment for the whole or part of the time (para 1(2)). If the court has the written or oral evidence of two or more doctors (at least one approved) that his mental condition requires and may be susceptible to treatment but is not such as to warrant a hospital order, it may require him to submit to treatment by or under the direction of a doctor with a view to the improvement of his mental condition. This must be either as a non-resident patient at a specified place or institution or otherwise by or under the direction of a specified doctor (para 4). If the court has the written or oral evidence of two or more doctors that "because of his medical condition, other than his mental condition, the supervised person is likely to pose a risk to himself or others" and "the condition may be susceptible to treatment", it can include the same requirements but with a view to the improvement of the medical condition in question (para 5). This could, perhaps, be a way of dealing with alcohol or drug abuse, or physical conditions such as diabetes, which are not regarded as mental disorders but could lead to a finding of disability. In either case, the doctor directing the treatment may, with his consent, make arrangements for him to be treated at a different place, and this could be as a resident patient (para 6).

The residence and treatment conditions can be varied, cancelled or inserted by a magistrates' court, on the application of either the supervisor or the supervised person (para 11). If the doctor in charge thinks that the treatment is no longer needed, or should be extended beyond the permitted period, or should be varied, or if he is no longer willing to continue, he must report to the supervisor so that the supervisor can apply for a variation (para 12).

A magistrates' court may also revoke the order, on the application of either the supervisor or the supervised person, if having regard to circumstances which have arisen since it was made, this would be in the interests of the health or welfare of the supervised person (para 9(1)). The court which made the order may of its own motion revoke it if the circumstances have changed and it is no longer appropriate (para 9(2)). There is, however, no sanction for breach of the order or any of its conditions. They "simply provide a framework for treatment" (Domestic Violence, Crimes and Victims Act 2004, Explanatory Notes).

Oddly enough, the Domestic Violence, Crime and Victims Act 2004, when replacing the powers introduced in 1991, removed the power to make a guardianship order, which might have been thought the most suitable long term disposal for a person found unfit to plead because of severe learning disability.

(iii) *A hospital order, with or without a restriction order* (1964 Act, s 5(2)(a)). These have the same meaning as that given in sections 37 and 41 of the MHA respectively (1964 Act, s 5(4)). It is clear from the explanatory notes that the intention was to incorporate the conditions for making a hospital order set out in section 37(2) (see p 167, below). If so, this means that the court may be precluded from making a hospital order if no appropriate treatment is available even though the deed which the unfit (or insane) person had done was extremely dangerous; instead it would have to grant an absolute discharge or make a supervision order, because it must do one of the three (s 5(2)).

The offence does not have to be punishable with imprisonment (1964 Act, s 5A(1)(b)); the court does not have to have evidence that a bed will be available within 28 days; and the managers of the specified hospital will have to admit the patient (1964 Act, s 5A(1)(c)). Given that detention cannot be justified under article 5(1)(a) of the European Convention on Human Rights, "after conviction by a competent court", but only under article 5(1)(e), as a "person of unsound mind", the patient will have to be got to hospital without delay (*Morcarska v Poland* [2008] 1 MHLR 228, App no 26917/05, 6 November 2007; *Pankiewicz v Poland*, App no 34151/04, 22 January 2008).

If a person found unfit to plead is detained under a restriction order, and the restrictions have not been lifted, the Justice Secretary can send him back for trial, either straight from hospital to the court or via a prison, if he is satisfied after consultation with the RC that the patient can properly be tried (1964 Act, s 5A(4)). This brings the hospital and restriction order to an end. As the person found unfit must already have had as good a trial of the facts as possible in the circumstances, the main object will be to impose punishment. A quarter of those found unfit from 1976 to 1988 were returned for trial of whom six per cent were acquitted (Grubin, 1991). The risk of return is now much diminished, as any other order made by the court is the end of the matter. Furthermore, the Justice Secretary has no power to send the accused back to be tried if he has been discharged from hospital by a tribunal.

The 1991 changes certainly increased the attractions for the accused of raising the issue of fitness to plead. He might be acquitted altogether or made subject to a wholly therapeutic disposal which put his fate in the hands of the medical authorities. Even if he were subject to a restriction order, which the court might still be inclined to choose if the offence was serious, he might be discharged by a tribunal and avoid the risk of return to the court for a full trial. There are still at least two serious criticisms: the outdated test of incapacity to stand trial and the limited scope of the trial of the facts. The accused cannot run other defences based on his mental condition at the time of the offence at the same time as claiming that he is unfit to plead; and it is not clear whether he can raise defences such as accident, mistake or self-defence. The Law Commission has embarked upon a project which will attempt to identify better and more up to date legal tests and rules (Law Commission, 2008b).

Findings of disability are not available in magistrates' courts, but they have a different way of achieving a similar result (White, 1991). They have power to make an ordinary hospital order without convicting, provided that they are satisfied that the accused did the act or made the omission charged (1983 Act, s 37(3)). In *R v Lincoln (Kesteven) Magistrates' Court, ex p O'Connor* [1983] 1 WLR 335, the accused was so severely handicapped that he was unable to understand what it meant to consent to summary trial on a charge which would usually give him the option of jury trial. The Divisional Court held that the magistrates could have made a hospital order without trying him, although it was stressed that the circumstances in which this would be appropriate were very rare and would usually require the consent of his lawyers. In *R v Ramsgate Justices, ex p Kasmarek* (1984) 80 Cr App R 366, it was held that magistrates could do this even though the defendant had chosen trial by jury; but the offence must not be one which can only be tried in the Crown Court (*R v Chippenham Magistrates' Court, ex p Thompson* [1996] 160 JP 207, [1996] BMLR 69).

3. MENTAL DISORDER AS A DEFENCE

(a) Insanity

Until the Criminal Procedure (Insanity and Unfitness to Plead) Act 1991, there was also little incentive for a defendant to plead that because of his mental state at the time of the offence he was not responsible for actions which offended against the criminal law. Any defendant who was found "not guilty by reason of insanity" (the "special verdict" laid down by the Trial of Lunatics Act 1883, s 2(1)) had, like one found unfit to plead, to be detained indefinitely as if he were a restriction order patient. Even in a murder case, where the sentence has to be life imprisonment, the defence of diminished responsibility provided a wider and more flexible alternative. The perception, that a special verdict had a draconian effect to be avoided if possible, was not necessarily borne out in practice. Mackay (1990) showed that although rare, the defence was raised in cases other than murder; that most patients were not sent to special hospitals; and that most of those were discharged within a relatively short time. Even so, it was not unknown for the prosecution to allege insanity while the defence put forward diminished responsibility or some other defence. If the judge ruled that the defence amounted to one of insanity, it might be rapidly withdrawn and a plea of guilty substituted. But after the 1991 Act there is now the same range of disposals on a "special verdict" as on a finding of disability (1964 Act, ss 5, 5A, Sch A1, above). This means, it appears, that a hospital order can only be made if the grounds for doing so exist.

The present definition of the defence of insanity was laid down by the judges in response to questions from the House of Lords when debating the case of Daniel M'Naghten, who was found not guilty on the ground of insanity of murdering Sir Robert Peel's secretary (see *M'Naghten's Case* (1843) 10 Cl & Fin 200): that at the time of his act he was:

"labouring under such defect of reason from disease of the mind as not to know the nature and quality of the act he was doing, or, if he did know it, that he did not know it was wrong".

This may be proved by the defence on the balance of probabilities or by the prosecution (to counter his claim of diminished responsibility or automatism) beyond reasonable doubt.

The so-called M'Naghten Rules have two different limbs. Both depend upon "a defect of reason from disease of the mind", thus raising all sorts of questions. Why just a "defect of reason" rather than disorders of personality or mood? Is "disease" to be equated with "illness" and if so must there be a physical cause? And when is a disease of the brain which can have a temporary impact upon mental capacities, such as epilepsy or diabetes, included? In the first limb, the defect must lead to his not knowing what he is doing: the obvious example is assaulting someone with an axe believing him to be a block of wood. The disorder has negated the existence of the guilty mind, the element of intention or recklessness which, depending upon the offence charged, would normally be required for a conviction. In the second limb, the defect must lead to his not knowing that what he did was wrong: an example is killing someone in the belief that one is God and thus entitled to do it. To that extent, a person with a diseased mind is relieved from the presumption that we all know and understand the law and its relationship to our actions.

Neither limb will excuse a man who knows what he is doing and knows it to be against the law, even though he is acting on the orders of his "voices", or under the delusion that his victim is persecuting him, or in the belief that he has a divine mission to "put down" the Roman Catholic Church. Some Commonwealth countries have therefore extended the Rules to include cases where the accused did the act "under the influence of a delusion of such a nature as to render him ... an unfit subject for punishment of any kind in respect of such act": see *Phillip v The Queen* [2007] UKPC 31. Nor do the Rules apply to a man whose perception, knowing and reasoning faculties are unaffected, but whose capacity to resist his impulses or to conform his behaviour to the law is substantially impaired by his disorder. Attempts to refine the defence in the United States (see, eg, Morris, 1978) tend to concentrate on whether these sorts of case should be included.

Most of the English case law, however, is concerned with the distinction between the person who does not know what he is doing because of "disease of the mind" and the person who is not in control of his bodily functions for some other reason (such as a fit of sneezing or sleep-walking) and is entitled to an ordinary acquittal because of "non-insane automatism". What does the law mean by a "disease of the mind"? It is not limited to mental illnesses in the psychiatric sense, which was certainly what the judges were dealing with in *M'Naghten's Case*, but can include physical and neurological conditions which impair mental functioning, either temporarily or permanently. The judges have approached this question in the light of what they see as the purpose of the special verdict, which is not to excuse the defendant but to protect society.

In *R v Kemp* [1957] 1 QB 399, Devlin J defined "mind" in its ordinary sense of the mental faculties of reason, memory and understanding. Insanity could therefore include a malfunctioning of these faculties brought on by arteriosclerosis. This definition was adopted by Lord Diplock in the unanimous but controversial House of Lords decision in *R v Sullivan* [1984] AC 156 (following *Bratty v AG for Northern Ireland* [1963] AC 383), which concerned the unconscious violence of an epileptic in the post-ictal stage of grand mal. The defence argued that the M'Naghten Rules did not apply at all to unconscious movements, as opposed to those carried out in a deluded state of consciousness. But the House of Lords held that "not to know the nature and quality of the act" did include not knowing what he was doing at all. The defence also argued that the loss of consciousness was not caused by mental disease, for this could not include a loss of faculties which lasted for such a short time. But the Law Lords decided (with Lord Diplock, at p 172) that:

"If the effect of a disease was to impair these faculties so severely as to have either of the consequences referred to in the latter part of the rules, it matters not whether the aetiology of the impairment is organic, as in epilepsy, or functional, or whether the impairment is permanent or is transient and intermittent, provided that it subsisted at the time of the commission of the act. The purpose of the legislation relating to the defence of insanity, ever since its origin in 1800, has been to protect society against recurrence of the dangerous conduct."

However, they did not rule out the possibility of non-insane automatism if a temporary impairment resulted from some external factor, such as a blow on the head or the therapeutic administration of drugs. Such a transitory malfunctioning was held *not* to be disease of the mind in *R v Quick* [1973] QB 910, which concerned *hypo*glycaemia brought on by a combination of insulin, alcohol and lack of food. However, a diabetic who knows that this might make him aggressive or uncontrolled could be sufficiently reckless to justify a conviction for a crime which does not require any specific intent (*R v Bailey* [1983] 1 WLR 760). Further, it was held in *R v Hennessey* [1989] 1 WLR 287 that malfunctioning brought on by *hyper*glycaemia, caused by a diabetic *not* taking his insulin, was a disease of the mind. The test is, therefore, not the nature of the underlying disability, but whether it is the disability or some external factor which has caused the loss of control. Hence a poorly controlled diabetic is sometimes covered and sometimes not, though his level of culpability is identical. Sleep-walking is caused by an internal factor which can amount to a disease of the mind, especially if it results in violence and may recur (*R v Burgess* (1991) 93 Cr App R 41).

The so-called hysterical dissociated states also cause difficulty, not least to those judges who find it hard to believe that the accused was indeed unconscious of what he was doing. If a man, for example, is driving purposefully and therefore partially in control, "hysterical fugue" is no defence to a charge of reckless driving (see *R v Isitt* (1977) 67 Cr App R 44; see also *AG's Reference (No 2 of 1992), The Times*, 31 May 1992). However, the list of "external factors" is not closed. Perhaps surprisingly, a judge in the Crown Court ruled that post traumatic stress disorder, resulting from rape, was not a disease of the mind, so that if it led to complete rather than partial loss of control, the defence of non-insane automatism could be raised (*R v T* [1990] Crim LR 256).

Transitory malfunctionings which are unrelated to any underlying disability should still lead to an acquittal. So should failure to use one's mental faculties, for example when walking out of a shop without paying in a fit of absence of mind, even if this is exacerbated by depression (*R v Clarke* [1972] 1 All ER 209). But what if someone suggests that the element of dishonesty, required in many offences against property, is not present, for example because as a result of post traumatic stress disorder he did not realise that he should not have been claiming means-tested benefits while working? Despite *R v T*, this would appear to fall squarely within the second limb of the Rules.

The Butler Report (1975) proposed revising the special verdict to cover two situations. The first was where evidence of any type of disorder is put forward to negative the existence of the state of mind required for the particular offence. This would have brought in all cases of non-insane automatism, apart from transitory states produced by the use or non-use of drugs or alcohol, or by physical injury. The second was where the accused was suffering from "severe mental illness" or severe mental handicap, even if there were no causal connection between the disorder and the offence, for lack of any real blameworthiness could be assumed. One difficulty with these ideas is that they would have brought into the special verdict many cases where the accused is at present entitled to an acquittal (Law Commission, 1989).

This may not matter now that the range of disposals is so much wider. But the issue of over-inclusion is just as important as the issue of under-inclusion. How do we distinguish between people who have committed crimes for which they should be liable to punishment (even if the court chooses a therapeutic disposal instead); people who have committed what would otherwise be a crime and do not deserve to be liable to punishment at all but should be subject to compulsory care and control for their own or other people's protection; and people who should not be liable either to punishment or to care and control? It is tempting to suggest that the middle category should logically be dealt with through civil rather than criminal powers, but such is the understandable public concern over the horrific crimes sometimes committed by seriously disordered people (such as setting on fire the priest and the congregation in *Phillip v The Queen*, above) that this is unlikely to be acceptable. The Law Commission has firmly grasped the nettle in its new project encompassing both insanity and unfitness to plead (Law Commission, 2008b).

(b) Infanticide

This offence was created in 1922 to avoid the so-called "black cap farce" in which mothers convicted of murdering their babies had to be sentenced to death although they were almost invariably reprieved. Under the Infanticide Act 1938, section 1(1), it now applies where a woman kills her child aged under 12 months, in circumstances which would otherwise amount to murder or (once s 57 of the Coroners and Justice Act 2009 comes into force) manslaughter, but at the time "the balance of her mind was disturbed by reason of not having fully recovered from the effect of giving birth to the child or by reason of the effect of lactation consequent on the birth" at the time. The court can then impose any penalty it thinks fit and imprisonment is now rare (see Mackay, 2006). Infanticide can be charged as an offence in its own right or raised as a defence to murder or (once s 57 comes into force) manslaughter (s 1(2)). In practice, if raised by the defence, the prosecution often agree to charge infanticide and drop the murder charge (Mackay, 2006).

When this offence was created, the partial defence of diminished responsibility (see below) did not exist. Now that it does, should infanticide be abolished? The Butler Report (1975) thought that it could be, but the Criminal Law Revision Committee (CLRC) (1980) disagreed. It does have the advantage that it can be charged by the prosecution, upon whom the burden of disproving the defence also lies. Also, it does not require any causal connection between the killing and the mother's "disturbance" of mind. In theory, however, it is restricted to mental disorders which arise because of the effects of childbirth or lactation upon the gestational mother. It does not cover disorders resulting from social or environmental factors or difficulties in bonding with the new baby. The CLRC proposed that stresses caused by "circumstances consequent on the birth" should be included, but why then should the defence not apply to non-gestational mothers, to fathers or to other carers driven to distraction by similar stresses? The Law Commission, after very thorough consideration (Law Commission, 2005, 2006), has concluded that, although no (or perhaps one) diagnosis is specific to childbirth, there is evidence that giving birth, and even lactation, makes some women more vulnerable to mental disorder, thus justifying special treatment, so the law should stay as it is.

The other problem, raised by the Court of Appeal in *R v Kai-Whitewind* [2005] EWCA Crim 1092, [2005] 2 Cr App R 31, is what to do about the mother whose "disturbance of mind" leads her to deny having killed her baby and to reject the medical examination which might provide her with an infanticide defence? The Law Commission (2006) proposed that the trial judge should be able to order a medical examination after a conviction and then "fast track" an appeal if there was evidence to support an infanticide defence.

(c) Diminished responsibility

The defence of diminished responsibility was introduced by section 2 of the Homicide Act 1957, to mitigate the mandatory sentences of death or life imprisonment for murder. It results in a conviction for manslaughter, for which the sentence may range from an absolute discharge to life imprisonment. The charge is still murder, but the judge may accept a plea of guilty to manslaughter without a trial if the evidence warrants it. The burden of proof, however, lies on the defence (1957 Act, s 2(2)). The plea was accepted in over three quarters of the cases in Mackay's study of most (but not all) the cases from 1997 to 2001 in which the defence was raised (Mackay, 2004). The overall failure rate was 13.4 per cent (compared with less than 10 per cent found by Dell, 1982). A successful plea resulted in a hospital order (the great majority with restriction orders) in roughly half the cases, but there were also substantial sentences of imprisonment, as well as probation or supervision. Infanticide is treated more leniently than diminished responsibility manslaughter, which covers a much wider range of people and behaviour.

The original definition required that the accused be:

"suffering from such abnormality of mind (whether arising from a condition of arrested or retarded development of mind or any inherent cause or induced by disease or injury) as substantially impaired his mental responsibility for his acts or omissions in doing or being a party to the killing" (1957 Act, s 2(1)).

This had two elements, one mental and one moral. A generous view was taken, both of what might constitute an "abnormality of mind" and of the required causes (see *R v Byrne* [1960] 2 QB 396). It might cover, for example, transient abnormalities of the sort which may result in mercy killings or battered babies and the "slow burn" in which domestic abuse leads to the "battered woman's syndrome". Even more of a problem was the moral element, the substantial impairment of responsibility, a question on which doctors have no particular expertise, and would probably prefer not to express an opinion, although they are often asked to do so. Does responsibility mean responsibility in the legal sense? If so, can someone who knows what he is doing, knows it to be wrong, and could have prevented himself if he chose, be regarded as having impaired responsibility? And how is it possible to have degrees of such responsibility? What the defence was really getting at is degrees of culpability or moral turpitude, which is a rather different matter. The Butler Report (1975) suggested that the disorder should be "such as to be an extenuating circumstance which ought to reduce the offence". The CLRC, however, thought this too lax and suggested "a substantial enough reason to reduce this offence to manslaughter" (1980), which is not much better.

Under the Coroners and Justice Act 2009, the test is to be replaced with one which broadly corresponds to that recommended by the Law Commission (2006). It is much more closely related to legal concepts of responsibility than previously. The accused must have been suffering from an abnormality of mental functioning which arose from a recognised mental condition (s 2(1)(a)). The Law Commission would also have included an abnormality resulting from developmental immaturity in a defendant under 18, but unfortunately this has not been taken up. The abnormality must substantially impair the ability of the accused to understand the nature of his conduct, to form a rational judgment and/or to exercise self-control (s 2(1)(b), (1A)). And this must have caused, or have been a significant contributory factor in causing, the defendant to act as he did (s 2(1)(c), (1B)).

Many serious commentators (eg Butler Report, 1975; Walker, 1981; Dell, 1982, Prison Reform Trust, 1993) would have preferred to solve the whole problem by abolishing both the mandatory life sentence for murder and the defence of diminished responsibility, leaving sentencing in all these cases to the discretion of the judge. The psychiatrists would then be spared the unwelcome task of giving evidence relevant to innocence or guilt and could enter into a more comfortable dialogue with the judge about the most promising ways of dealing with the offender. However, some think that abolition of the mandatory life sentence does not necessarily mean that diminished responsibility should go. Juries might shrink from convicting at all if this less stigmatising verdict were not available; and judges prefer to have the benefit of the jury's view in a disputed case. The House of Lords Select Committee on Murder and Life Imprisonment (1989) favoured both abolition of the mandatory penalty and retention of both diminished responsibility and infanticide.

The Law Commission's solution to the homicide problem was to propose a three-fold division into first degree murder (for which the sentence would remain life imprisonment) and second degree murder and manslaughter (for which it would be at large) (Law Commission, 2006). A successful plea of diminished responsibility would result in a conviction for second degree murder, mainly so that it could march hand in hand with provocation, as they are often alternatives in contested cases. But this would return to branding, for example, women with battered wife syndrome as murderers and has not been adopted. Even so, the new definition raises the question of why a person whose capacities are "substantially impaired" in this way should be convicted and potentially face a punitive disposal, while a person who falls within the M'Naghten Rules should be acquitted and face only a therapeutic disposal. In retrospect, it might have been better to consider the insanity defence first.

4. SENTENCING

While the criminal justice system has so far stuck to a very strict view of criminal responsibility, it has now been provided with a wide range of therapeutic methods of disposal after conviction. In the olden days, there was perceived to be a simple dichotomy: either the offender was "bad" and should receive the penalty appropriate to the gravity of his offence and his previous record, or he was "mad" and should be committed to the medical authorities for as long as was necessary to "cure" him. This simplicity was always blurred in some cases: an offender who fell into the "mad" category might be detained in hospital for as long as he was thought a danger to the public even if the hospital thought that he was no longer mentally ill or there was nothing more they could do for him. But now the simplicity itself has gone: an offender may be both "bad" enough to warrant a penal disposal but "mad" enough to warrant a therapeutic order at the same time. So the menu of orders which may be imposed on grounds of mental disorder includes three exclusively non-penal disposals (hospital, restriction and guardianship orders); and two disposals which combine or may combine elements of treatment and punishment (prison with a hospital direction and community orders with a condition of treatment); there is also the possibility that an offender who is sentenced to imprisonment may later be transferred to hospital because of his mental disorder. The structure of the Act makes it simpler to deal with hospital and restriction orders and transfers from prison before turning to hybrid orders and the two community disposals.

(a) Hospital orders

Before the 1959 Act, the courts had power to send "mental defectives" (who included the people later labelled psychopaths) to hospital rather than to prison. The 1959 Act extended this power to people with mental illness, as well as psychopathic disorder and mental impairment. The 1983 Act excluded people with mental impairment, unless this was associated with abnormally aggressive or seriously irresponsible behaviour on their part. It also introduced a "treatability" test for people with psychopathic disorder or "significant" (as opposed to severe) mental impairment, that medical treatment was likely to do some good. The 2007 amendments have broadened the range of disorders and replaced "treatability" with the availability of treatment for all.

A hospital order can be made for any offence for which the trial court could have sentenced the offender to imprisonment or some other form of custody, apart from murder for which the sentence of life imprisonment is fixed by law (MHA, s 37(1)). Other offences attracting mandatory penalties are not excluded (MHA, s 37(1A), (1B)). The Crown Court must first convict the offender, except where he has already been transferred from prison to hospital before trial or committed to hospital by the magistrates with a view to a restriction order being made (sentence without trial is controversial; see p 155, above). Magistrates, however, may make a hospital order without recording a conviction, provided that they are satisfied that the defendant did the act or made the omission charged (s 37(3); see p 160, above).

(i) The medical criteria

Two doctors, one of them approved, must state that the offender is suffering from mental disorder "of a nature or degree which makes it appropriate for him to be detained in a hospital for medical treatment" (s 37(2)(a)(i)). The concept of mental disorder is now broad enough to cover all kinds of mental illness and personality disorder but learning disability is still only covered if it is associated with "abnormally aggressive or seriously irresponsible conduct" on the part of the offender (s 1(2A), (2B)(b)). Dependence on alcohol or drugs is not considered to be a mental disorder for MHA purposes (s 1(3)). Subject to these two exclusions, the doctors no longer have to force their diagnosis into the formal categories which used to apply. But the courts may find the limited application to people with learning disabilities frustrating: it is just these inadequate and inconvenient offenders who reveal the greatest gap between the expectations of the courts and the policies of the healthcare providers. The courts do not like sending mentally disabled people to prison but there is little hospital provision for them because they are not usually susceptible to "cure" by conventional psychiatric treatment. If they are sent to hospital they may have to stay for a very long time before anyone can be satisfied that they are unlikely to offend again. The place for able-bodied people with learning disabilities is in the community under guardianship but the courts may feel that this is not an adequate response to their offending.

The doctors have also to report that appropriate medical treatment is available for the defendant (s 37(2)(a)(ii)). "Appropriate medical treatment" means treatment which is appropriate to the individual patient, taking into account the nature and degree of his mental disorder and all the other circumstances of his case (ss 3(4), 145(1AA)). This replaces the old "treatability" test, which used to apply only to offenders with psychopathic disorder or significant mental impairment. It is welcome in that it focuses on the individual patient and ought to ensure that no-one is compulsorily hospitalised (except for a limited time) unless suitable treatment is actually available (as opposed to the possibility of benefit from treatment which may not in reality be available). On the other hand, it increases still further the power of the healthcare providers to decide what treatment they will offer and therefore which patients they will take. Debate still rages over whether there is such a thing as dangerous and severe personality disorder and if so whether the prisons or the hospitals should take responsibility for dealing with it. Having once been quite anxious to claim that they could alter aberrant personalities, the medical profession now accept that there may be little they can do and do not want a purely custodial role.

In practice, the requirement that a bed in a named hospital be available within 28 days of the order (s 37(4)) means that the doctors have always been able to pick and choose. The decision to offer a bed is that of the hospital managers, but they act on the advice of the clinical team. Consultant psychiatrists these days recognise that other professions, particularly the nursing staff who will have day-to-day contact with the patient, must have a voice in deciding who can be accepted on to their wards. But in effect the decision is theirs. The difficulties in finding a suitable bed, and the courts' powers to put pressure upon the authorities to do so, have already been mentioned in chapter 1.

(ii) The judicial criteria

Once the court has the required medical evidence, it must decide whether the order is the "most suitable" way of disposing of the case, having regard to all the circumstances including the nature of the offence, the character and antecedents of the offender, and to the other available methods of dealing with him (s 37(2)(b)). The court cannot impose a fine, custodial sentence, community order, referral order, supervision order or parental recognisances order as well as a hospital order, although it can make other ancillary orders, for example for compensation or confiscation (s 37(8)).

The court is entitled to take the need to protect the public into account. In *R v Gunnell* (1966) 50 Cr App R 242, it was held that an offender who deserved punishment could be sent to prison, even though he qualified for a hospital order and a suitable bed was available. In *R v Birch* (1989) 11 Cr App R (S) 202, 215, the Court of Appeal pointed out that prison might be chosen instead of hospital either because the offender was dangerous and no suitable hospital bed could be found or because there was an element of culpability in the offence which merited punishment, for example where there was no connection between the mental disorder and the offence. In *R v Drew* [2003] UKHL 25, [2003] 1 WLR 1213, the House of Lords held that the automatic life sentence for second time serious violent or sex offenders (under the Powers of Criminal Courts (Sentences) Act 2000, s 109) was not incompatible with a mentally disordered offender's right under article 3 of the ECHR not to be subjected to inhuman or degrading treatment or punishment. To subject such a defendant to "unnecessary suffering, humiliation, distress and deterioration in his mental condition" by denying him the medical treatment he needed, could properly be regarded as inhuman or degrading; but this could be avoided by the Justice Secretary transferring him to prison under section 47 (see below).

An ordinary hospital order has several drawbacks from the point of view of protecting the public (see, eg, *R v Gardiner* [1967] 1 WLR 464). The hospital may discharge the patient at any time and is quite likely to do so within a year. It may make little attempt to recapture him if he absconds. His detention cannot be renewed beyond the initial six months unless the medical criteria, including the availability of appropriate treatment, still exist. These days, the availability of community treatment orders may increase the likelihood that the offender will be discharged from hospital within a relatively short time. Whether or not the patient is restricted, unless a bed is found in a suitably secure hospital or unit the court will be concerned about the practical problem of security. Hence the deciding factor for the court is often, not whether a bed is available, but whether a bed which the court thinks sufficiently secure is available (see *R v Morris* [1961] 2 QB 237; *R v Cox* (1967) 52 Cr App R 130; *R v McFarlane* (1975) 60 Cr App R 320; *R v Harding (Bernard), The Times*, 15 June 1983).

On the other hand, if such a bed can be found, the courts seem quite happy to accede to the medical recommendations. In *R v Jonathan Paul Simpson* [2007] EWCA Crim 2666, [2007] 1 MHLR 320, for example, the Court of Appeal pointed out that, as the source of the danger posed by the schizophrenic offender was his complex delusional belief system, treating him in secure conditions in hospital gave a better chance of minimising future danger than would imprisonment. Indeed, the courts were as vociferous as any in pressing for more secure accommodation in the NHS. In *R v Harding (Bernard), The Times*, 15 June 1983, Lawton LJ remarked that it was a form of cruelty to keep a mentally sick person in prison. Of course, a hospital order may be equally severe in some cases. Some offenders are likely to remain in hospital for longer than they would have stayed in prison and some might have avoided prison altogether. The utilitarian answer (Walker and McCabe, 1973) is that, however it may seem to the patient, it is not unjust to make the commission of an offence the "occasion" for sending to hospital a patient who ought to be there and who could just as easily have been "sectioned" under civil powers. This is a little too neat. The patient might never have been considered a suitable case for compulsory hospitalisation had it not been for the offence. The offence will undoubtedly colour the views of both the hospital and any tribunal about whether or not he should be discharged (see Peay, 1989).

The law is a little inconsistent about the proportionality of imposing a hospital order. The offence must be punishable with imprisonment. But the courts do not seem to take the triviality of the offence into account. By definition, there is no necessary element of proportionality between the duration and conditions of a patient's detention under a hospital order and the seriousness of the offence. The Court of Appeal has refused to regard a hospital order, even an unlimited restriction order, as "more severe" than a prison sentence (*R v Bennett* [1968] 1 WLR 988; *R v Sodhi* [1978] Crim LR 565). This means that it can be substituted for a custodial sentence on appeal. The Butler Report (1975) recommended that a hospital order should not be imposed on appeal without the offender's consent, which suggests some ambivalence about the justice of indeterminate therapeutic disposals. Gostin (1977) suggested that a hospital order should never be made without consent. This is not as radical as it seems. Hospitals much prefer their patients to be receptive to the idea of treatment. The notion that an offender should not be allowed to choose his punishment ought not to be applied to an order which is not supposed to be a punishment at all. Other kinds of therapeutic disposal do require consent. The question is, rather, whether a person whom we are prepared to call an offender should be entitled to the benefit of the normal principle of proportionality in sentencing, unless both he and the court are prepared to waive it.

(iii) The legal effect

Ordinary hospital orders are almost indistinguishable from admissions for treatment under section 3. All the rules relating to the duration and renewal of detention, leave of absence, absconding, community treatment orders and discharge by the authorities are the same (MHA, s 40(4) and Sch 1, Pt 1). There are only two important differences. First, the patient's nearest relative cannot discharge him, but can instead apply for the case to be reviewed by a tribunal within the same periods that the patient himself can apply (s 69(1)(a)). Secondly, the offender does not have the right of a patient admitted under section 3 to apply to a tribunal within the first six months of his admission. This was taken away from ordinary hospital order patients when restriction order patients were given rights of application (as a result of the decision of the European Court of Human Rights in *X v United Kingdom* (1981) 4 EHRR 188, see p 173, below). Understandably, the Government did not see why restriction order patients should be allowed to go to a tribunal within six months of a court's decision that they were a serious risk to the public. But the right to a review is one of those "set forth in the Convention" and under article 14 these must be enjoyed by all "without discrimination on any ground such as sex, race, colour, language, religion, political or other opinion, national or social origin, association with a national minority, property, birth or other status". It was feared that restricted patients might complain of discrimination if ordinary hospital order patients could apply when they could not. Hence a right which had existed since the 1959 Act, had never been known to cause difficulties, but might benefit a few patients (of whom Michael Fagan, the Queen's intruder, was one) was taken away.

The hospital order is authority for a police officer, an AMHP or any other person directed to do so by the court, to take the patient to the hospital named in the order within 28 days, and for the hospital to detain him (s 40(1)). Once he is admitted, any previous compulsory admission or hospital order ceases to have effect, unless the new order is quashed on appeal (s 40(5)). The court may direct that, until his admission to hospital, he is taken to and kept in a place of safety, usually the prison where he was held on remand (s 37(4); for the definition, p 154, above). If within the 28 days the Justice Secretary finds that, because of an emergency or some other special circumstances, it is not possible to admit the patient to the named hospital, he may arrange admission to another one (s 37(5)). If the patient is not admitted to hospital within the 28 days, the order will expire and it will be unlawful to detain or treat the patient under it (*R (DB) v Nottinghamshire Healthcare NHS Trust* [2008] EWCA (Civ) 1354, [2009] 2 All ER 792). The Justice Secretary has power by Order in Council to reduce, but not to increase, the 28 day period but has not done so (s 54A).

(b) Interim hospital orders

The stark choice between treating an offender as mad or bad was thought, by the Butler Committee and others, to present another difficulty. Unlike a community order, a hospital order gives no means of returning to court for a more suitable disposal if it turns out that a mistake has been made. It may not matter if an offender is discharged from hospital in a very short time because his illness has been cured or brought under control. It does matter if there has been a mistaken diagnosis (perhaps brought about by his own deception), or if there is no appropriate treatment, or if he has refused to co-operate with any sort of treatment. The power to remand to hospital for reports or for treatment (see above) may help to avoid these mistakes, but the 1983 Act also allows the courts to have a "second bite at the cherry" by first making an interim hospital order under section 38. The court must have convicted the defendant of an offence which would qualify for a full hospital order. There must be evidence from two doctors, one of them approved, and at least one of them employed at the hospital which is named in the order (s 38(3)). They must state that the offender is suffering from mental disorder and that "there is reason to suppose that the mental disorder from which the offender is suffering is such that it may be appropriate for a hospital order to be made in his case" (s 38(1)). There must be the usual evidence from the approved clinician who would have overall responsibility for his case or from the hospital managers that a bed will be available within 28 days (s 38(4)). The court then has a complete discretion to try out an interim order before finally deciding how to deal with the offender.

As with an ordinary hospital order, the court may direct that the offender be taken to and kept in a place of safety before his admission (s 38(4)). He must be taken to hospital by a police officer or other person directed by the court and the hospital must then admit and detain him (s 40(3)). The usual provisions about the medical treatment of detained patients apply (s 56(2), (3)). Otherwise, however, the order is not like an ordinary hospital order. Neither the patient nor his nearest relative may apply to a tribunal. No one has any right to discharge the patient or even to grant him leave of absence. If he absconds, a police officer may arrest him without warrant and must then bring him as soon as practicable back to the court which made the order (s 38(7)). The order lasts in the first instance for whatever period the court specifies, up to a maximum of

12 weeks; but the court may renew it for further periods of not more than 28 days at a time, up to a maximum of twelve months in all, if the RC reports that this is warranted (s 38(5)). The patient does not have to be in court for the renewal, provided that he has a legal representative who is given an opportunity of being heard (s 38(6)). The court may even replace the interim order with a full hospital order without the patient being there, but with the same proviso (s 38(2)). But if the RC reports against renewing the interim order or making a full order, or if the court wishes to do something different, he must be brought back to court for the decision about what to do instead.

Once an interim order is at an end, the court has a completely free choice among the disposals available for the offence in question. If the evidence is there, it may make a full hospital order. This means that the patient will have to spend another six months in hospital before his case can be reviewed by a tribunal. On the other hand, the court could choose to impose a penalty instead. This may be all very well if the offender turns out not to have been mentally disordered after all or to be unsuitable for medical treatment. Even then, it seems undesirable to impose a further custodial sentence if only a short period in custody would have been appropriate. But it would seem quite wrong to impose an alternative penalty if the hospital order turns out to have been such a wise choice that the offender has already been cured. The court may be tempted to make a community order with a condition of some form of psychiatric after-care in such a case. But it could not have done this had it made a full hospital order in the first place. Interim hospital orders are counted along with committals under section 44 (see p 156, above), totalling 180 in 1997–1998 and 134 in 2007–2008 (Health and Social Care Information Centre, 2008).

(c) Restriction orders

Restriction orders were originally an attempt to combine the therapeutic advantages of a hospital order with the preventive advantages of indefinite detention coupled with a power of recall after release. The decision of the European Court of Human Rights in *X v United Kingdom* (1981) 4 EHRR 188, forced a reconsideration of this. Restrictions are still, however, imposed because of the risk which the offender is thought to present.

(i) The court's powers

A restriction order can only be made in the Crown Court (s 41(1)). If a magistrates' court has convicted an offender aged 14 or more, and has the evidence required for a hospital order, it may commit him to the Crown Court with a view to a restriction order being made (s 43(1); for the power to commit to hospital rather than prison, see p 156, above). If the Crown Court disagrees with the magistrates' court, it may only impose an order or penalty which they could have imposed, unless the magistrates have also committed him with a view to a greater penalty than they can give. The Crown Court can remand to hospital for reports or treatment, or make an interim order, as if it had itself convicted the offender (s 43(2), (4) and (3)).

Technically, a restriction order has no independent existence. The Crown Court must first make a hospital order (s 41(1)). At least one of the doctors who gave the evidence required for the hospital order must attend court to give evidence in person (s 41(2)). This does not have to be the doctor who would be in charge of the patient, although the court must have the usual evidence that a bed will be available. It is obviously important to have the hospital's views about whether a restriction order is appropriate, but in the end the choice between an ordinary hospital order or a restriction order is one for the judge (*R v Blackwood* (1974) 59 Cr App R. 246; *R v Royse* [1981] Crim LR 426).

The court must consider the restriction order necessary "for the protection of the public from serious harm", having regard to the nature of the offence, the antecedents of the offender, and the risk of his committing further offences if set at large (s 41(1)). There was no reference to serious harm in the 1959 Act and orders were made in cases where their severity was not appropriate (Butler Report, 1975; Gostin, 1977). Amongst the most obvious was Nigel Smith (see *R v McFarlane* (1975) 60 Cr App R 320). He was a "petty fraudster" with no history of violence or even mental illness, who found himself not only in Broadmoor, but also under a restriction order of unlimited duration. It is difficult to say what effect the tightened criteria have had. Hospital orders of either kind are not common and there may be many reasons for the fluctuations in the numbers and proportion of restriction orders. However, once there, restriction order patients stay longer—on average, apparently, for nine years (Ashworth, 2010). Thus they form a much higher proportion of resident hospital order patients, especially in the high security hospitals.

"Serious" qualifies the harm rather than the "risk". In *R v Courtney* [1988] Crim LR 730, the Court of Appeal quashed a restriction order upon a man of good character, who had killed his wife while undergoing treatment for depression, because there was no medical evidence that he was a danger to the public at large. In *R v Czarnota* [2002] EWCA Crim 785, [2002] MHLR 144, a restriction order imposed upon a mentally impaired man for breaking a restraining order under the Protection from Harassment Act 1997 was quashed because the judge had not addressed the question of whether it was necessary to protect the public from serious harm rather than from serious nuisance. In the leading case of *R v Birch* (1989) 90 Cr App R 78, it was pointed out that the question was *not* the seriousness of the risk of re-offending but the seriousness of the harm which the public would suffer if he did so. A high probability of repeating minor offences was *not* enough. However, if there was a risk of serious harm, there was no requirement of proportionality: the index offence need not itself be serious (see *R v Kean* (1987) 9 Cr App R(S) 455). Nevertheless, the 1983 Act had not affected the decision in *R v Gardiner* [1967] 1 WLR 464: there the Court of Appeal had said that there should be compelling reasons for not imposing restrictions in crimes of violence or the more serious sex offences, particularly if the offender has a similar record or a history of mental disorder involving violent behaviour. *Birch* itself concerned a wife who had shot and killed her husband; a low risk of repeating such a serious offence could justify a restriction order; but in that case there was no material on which to conclude that the order was necessary. As in *Courtney* and *Czarnota*, the restriction order was quashed, leaving the defendant subject to an ordinary hospital order. However, the seriousness of the harm is not necessarily determined by the seriousness of the harm done in the past. In *R v Golding* [2006] EWCA Crim 1965, [2007] 1 Cr App R (S) 79 (approving a similar approach in *R (Jones) v Isleworth Crown Court* [2005] EWHC 662, [2005] MHLR 93), the Court of Appeal held that the judge had been entitled to conclude that a persistent burglar suffering from paranoid schizophrenia might react violently if confronted by a householder whose house he was burgling even though he had never done so in the past. If they do not have to evaluate the degree of risk that something *will* happen, the courts may find it easier to imagine that something serious *could* happen, perhaps particularly when dealing with a drug or alcohol abusing paranoid schizophrenic.

(ii) The legal effects

The restrictions now last indefinitely (s 41(1)). The old power to impose them for a limited period has been abolished. Unlike a prison sentence, the purpose is not to reflect the gravity of the offence in the length of the restriction order but to ensure that the patient is not discharged until he is ready. As there is usually no means of knowing when this will be, the Court of Appeal stated in *R v Gardiner* [1967] 1 WLR 464 (and approved in *R v Birch* (1989) 90 Cr App R 78) that unlimited orders should be made unless the doctors could confidently predict recovery within a limited period.

The court has no power to lift the restrictions once they are imposed. But the Justice Secretary can lift them at any time, if he is satisfied that they are no longer necessary to protect the public from serious harm (s 42(1)). If the patient is still in hospital when the restrictions end, he is treated as if he had been admitted under an ordinary hospital order on the day the restriction order ended (ss 41(5) and 42(1)), but he will be able to apply to a tribunal during the first six months. If, however, the patient has been conditionally discharged from hospital before the restrictions end, he will achieve an automatic absolute discharge on that date (s 42(5)).

While the restrictions last, they are severe. The patient cannot be discharged, transferred to another hospital, or even given leave of absence, without the Justice Secretary's consent (s 41(3)(c)). Either the Justice Secretary or the RC may recall him from leave, and the former can do so at any time (s 41(3)(d)). Absconders can be recaptured however long they have been at large (s 41(3)(d)). The RC cannot make a community treatment order (s 41(3)(aa)).The Justice Secretary has an independent power to discharge the patient, which is more commonly used because the discharge may be absolute or conditional (s 42(2)). A conditionally discharged patient is subject to compulsory supervision (although not medical treatment) and may be recalled to hospital at any time (s 42(3)). All of these are dealt with further in chapter 7. Clearly, they present a substantial obstacle to the hospital's usual efforts to rehabilitate the patient back into the community.

The other crucial difference between an ordinary hospital order and a restriction order is that the latter continues indefinitely. For as long as the restrictions last and the patient has not been absolutely discharged, there is no need for his detention to be renewed periodically under section 20 (s 41(3)(a)). This means that no-one is under any statutory obligation to consider whether the criteria for detaining him still apply. It also used to mean that the Justice Secretary did not feel under an obligation to agree to a discharge simply because there were no longer any medical grounds for keeping the patient in hospital. He might require to be satisfied, not only that the patient was sane, but also that he was safe. For that reason, Gostin (1977) argued that a restriction order was a penal rather than a therapeutic disposal and ought to be governed by the same principle of proportionality to the heinousness of the crime committed.

In the event, the decision of the European Court of Human Rights in *X v United Kingdom* (1981) 4 EHRR 188, put a different complexion on the matter. Having been convicted of a serious attack upon a workmate, X spent two-and-a-half years in Broadmoor before his conditional discharge in 1971. After three apparently blameless years in the community, he was recalled in April 1974. It later turned out that this was because of the alarming things which his wife said to his supervisor when announcing her intention of leaving him. Habeas corpus proceedings were unsuccessful. Under the 1959 Act, he could not ask for a reference to a tribunal until six months after his recall. Even then the tribunal's role was purely advisory.

His main complaint, which succeeded, was the lack of a speedy judicial review of the merits of his detention, as required by article 5(4) of the ECHR. This was remedied in the 1983 Act. But the patient also complained that his second period of detention in Broadmoor was in breach of article 5(1) of the Convention. This states, among other things, that:

"No person shall be deprived of his liberty save in the following cases . . . (a) the lawful detention of a person after conviction by a competent court; . . . (e) the lawful detention . . . of persons of unsound mind . . . ".

In *Winterwerp v The Netherlands* (1979) 2 EHRR 387, the court had laid down three minimum conditions for detention under article 5(1)(e): except in an emergency, the person must be reliably shown to be of unsound mind, that is, a true mental disorder must be established on the basis of objective medical expertise; the mental disorder must be of a kind or degree warranting compulsory confinement; and the validity of the continued confinement will depend upon the persistence of such a disorder. The Government argued that these did not apply because X's detention fell within article 5(1)(a). The court agreed that the detention before his conditional discharge fell within both (a) and (e); but that his detention after his recall would have to meet the article 5(1)(e) requirements. On the facts, however, they found no reason to disagree with the Broadmoor doctor's judgment that the *Winterwerp* requirements did exist when X was recalled to hospital. The court's approach in *X* was consistent with their later approach to indefinite sentences which contain both a punitive and a protective element: once the punitive "tariff" has been served, the risk factors justifying continued detention may change over time (as does a person's mental condition), and thus there must be the possibility of judicial review of the justification for the detention.

The message of *X* was plain. If the patient is no longer suffering from mental disorder of a nature or degree which makes his detention in hospital appropriate, he should no longer be detained there, no matter how dangerous he might be. The MHA provides that the RC must examine the patient and report to the Justice Secretary at such intervals as the latter may require, but not exceeding a year (s 41(6)). There is still no formal renewal procedure and the MHA does not require the Justice Secretary to agree to a discharge if the patient no longer meets the criteria. Nevertheless, he should clearly do so (see chapter 7). A tribunal is now bound to discharge the patient if the hospital cannot show that the criteria for detention persist (see chapter 8).

If the patient has committed one of the sexual or violent offences listed for the purpose of Chapter 2 to Part 3 of the Domestic Violence, Crimes and Victims Act 2004, the victim has the right to say whether she wants to make representations about whether he should be subject to conditions if discharged from hospital and to be told about those conditions if he is discharged. This applies to all restricted patients: those subject to a restriction order following conviction or a finding of disability or of insanity, those subject to a hybrid order, and those transferred from prison. This means that the Justice Secretary or the tribunal will have to tell the local probation service if he is contemplating lifting the restrictions or they are considering discharging the patient, so that representations can be sought and information given (see further in chapter 7).

But both the Justice Secretary and the tribunal are obliged to discharge the patient if he no longer meets the criteria, no matter how serious the offence or how dangerous he is still considered to be (see Peay, 1988; Home Office, 1996). The old style restriction order was a remarkably effective method of protecting the public. After the 1983 Act, it was believed that something else was needed.

(d) Transfer from prison

The incidence of mental disorders and disabilities in the prison population is alarmingly high. Even if a prisoner is ill enough to be placed in the hospital wing of a prison where the medical officer has psychiatric experience, he cannot expect to receive the treatment which he would get in a hospital. According to the Prison Reform Trust (2009), "There is a huge gap between what happens to a severely mentally ill person in prison and one who falls ill in the community". The MHA powers to impose treatment without consent do not apply. However, if a prisoner lacks the capacity to make treatment decisions for himself, the MCA confirms the power of all carers, including prison medical officers, to make decisions in his best interests (MCA, s 5; see p 191, later). This only allows the use of restraint where it is reasonably believed necessary to prevent harm to the prisoner and the restraint is a proportionate response to the seriousness of the harm and the likelihood of the prisoner suffering it (MCA, s 6(1), (2), (3)). Restraint for this purpose means the use or threat of force to secure the doing of an act which the prisoner resists; or restricting his liberty of movement, whether or not he resists (MCA, s 6(4)). So forcible treatment is only possible to prevent harm to a prisoner who lacks the capacity to make the decision for himself.

Depriving a mentally disordered prisoner of the treatment he needs could amount to inhuman or degrading treatment or punishment contrary to article 3 of the ECHR (*R v Drew* [2003] UKHL 25, [2003] I WLR 1213; a view confirmed by the finding of the European Court of Human Rights in *Riviere v France*, App no 33834/03, 11 July 2006, that confining a seriously psychotic man in prison without adequate medical care was a breach of article 3) or to an interference with his mental or physical integrity contrary to article 8 (*R (D) v Secretary of State for the Home Department* [2004] EWHC 2857 (Admin), [2005] MHLR 17). Such is the vulnerability of mentally disordered prisoners that failing to do all that could reasonably be done to prevent a psychotic prisoner who was a known suicide risk from committing suicide was a breach of his right to life protected by article 2 (*Renolde v France* (2009) 48 EHRR 42). Putting him in a punishment cell for 45 days was also a breach of article 3 (see also *Keenan v United Kingdom* (2001) 33 EHRR 38).

Under section 47 of the MHA, the Justice Secretary has power to direct that offenders serving prison sentences be transferred to hospital, provided that he has the necessary medical reports and is of the opinion, having regard to the public interest and all the circumstances that it is "expedient" to do so (s 47(1)). This also applies to offenders sentenced to other types of detention (such as young offenders) or imprisoned for non-payment of fines and other sums payable on conviction or committed to custody for refusing to be bound over to keep the peace or be of good behaviour (s 47(5)). Once the Prison Service have

175

reasonable grounds to believe that a prisoner requires treatment in a mental hospital, the Justice Secretary is under a duty to take reasonable steps to obtain medical advice and arrange a transfer if so advised (*R (D)*, above).

There must be reports from two doctors, one of them approved, that the prisoner is suffering from mental disorder of a nature or degree which makes it appropriate for him to be detained in hospital for medical treatment and that appropriate medical treatment is available for him (s 47(1)). The patient must arrive at the hospital within 14 days of the direction (s 47(2)), so the Justice Secretary must have secured a bed for him beforehand. However, there is no limit on the time that can elapse between the medical reports and the direction. Long delays are not at all unknown, with an obvious risk of injustice to a prisoner whose condition may not warrant detention in hospital when transferred (Grounds, 1990).

Convicted prisoners may be transferred either with or without restrictions (s 49(1)). Restrictions are "almost always" imposed, except where the prisoner is very close to his earliest release date (Ministry of Justice, 2008c). The restrictions cease automatically on the patient's "release date" (s 50(2)). This means the date on which he would be entitled to be released (whether unconditionally or on licence) from the place where he might have been detained had he not be transferred to hospital; but disregarding any powers of the Parole Board to release or recommend his earlier release and any practice of the Justice Secretary in relation to his discretionary powers of early release (s 50(3)), and adding on any period during which he was absent without leave from the hospital (s 50(4)).

For as long as the restrictions last, the transfer has the same effect as a restriction order (s 49(2); see above). The RC must make regular examinations and reports to the Justice Secretary at the intervals which the Justice Secretary requires but not less than once a year (s 49(3)). If the Justice Secretary is notified by the RC, any other approved clinician or a tribunal that the patient no longer requires treatment in hospital for mental disorder or that no effective treatment for his disorder can be given in the hospital to which he has been transferred, the Justice Secretary has the power to direct that the patient be transferred back to prison to serve the rest of his sentence as if he had never been transferred, but he does not have to do so. He may alternatively exercise any power of releasing the patient on licence or discharging him under supervision which could have been exercised if the patient had been sent back to prison (s 50(1)).

The patient can apply to a tribunal within the first six months and then at the usual intervals, and the case may also be referred to a tribunal in the usual ways (see chapter 8).The tribunal must then notify the Justice Secretary whether, if he were a restriction order patient, he would be entitled to an absolute or conditional discharge (s 74(1)). If he is, and the Justice Secretary agrees to a discharge within 90 days, the tribunal must discharge the patient accordingly (s 74(2)). If he does not agree, the hospital must transfer the patient back to prison, unless the tribunal recommended that a patient who would be entitled to a conditional discharge should be allowed to stay in hospital if not discharged (s 74(3), 74(1)(b)). The Justice Secretary may accept this recommendation. But this is without prejudice to the Justice Secretary's powers (under s 50(1)) to send him back to prison or to release him on licence as if he had been sent back to prison. These powers often depend upon a decision or recommendation of the Parole Board, so if the patient is entitled to be discharged from hospital it has to be possible to get his case before the Parole Board. Otherwise (especially if a prisoner serving a life or indefinite sentence has served his tariff) his detention might no longer be justified either under article 5(1)(a) of the European Convention on Human Rights, as a convicted offender, or under article 5(1)(e), as a "person of unsound mind" (see *R (D) v Secretary of State for the Home Department* [2002] EWHC 2805 (Admin), [2003] 1 WLR 1315). Hence if the tribunal do this, the fact that there is still a restriction or limitation direction in force does not prevent an application or reference to the Parole Board. If the Parole Board decide that the patient would be entitled to be released from prison, whether unconditionally on licence, then the restriction or limitation direction will end when he would have been entitled to release from prison (s 74(5A)).

Therefore, if the criteria for detention in hospital no longer apply, the Justice Secretary can choose to transfer the patient back to prison or to exercise his powers to release on licence or under supervision. If notified by the RC or another AC to this effect, or if recommended by a tribunal under section 74(1)(b), the Justice Secretary could alternatively do nothing, thus leaving the patient detained in hospital. But if the patient would prefer to be in prison, this might be vulnerable to attack under article 5(1) of the ECHR, because the place of detention must be related to the grounds for the detention, which would be the prison sentence rather than the continued need for treatment in hospital. Either way, if the Justice Secretary elects to leave a transferred prisoner in hospital, the hospital may have to detain a patient who does not qualify to be there. Transferred "lifers" are likely to be released, if at all, on a life licence, rather than by conditional discharge under the 1983 Act (see *R v Secretary of State for the Home Department, ex p Stroud* [1993] COD 75). If the patient is still in hospital when the restrictions cease, he remains liable to be detained under an ordinary hospital order (s 41(5)).

A transfer without restrictions has the same effect as an ordinary hospital order (s 47(2)). It is normally chosen if the prisoner is coming to the end of his sentence when transferred, but it can mean that he will remain legally liable to be detained in hospital beyond the time when he would have been released from prison. The Butler Committee did not think this unjust, because he could in any event have been compulsorily admitted under the civil powers, but the MHAC has been expressing concern about these transfers for a very long time (MHAC, 1989, 2005, 2009a). Orville Blackwood's perception that his detention was unjust may well have been a contributing factor in the events which led to his death while secluded in Broadmoor (Prins, 1993). A prisoner such as TF (see *R (TF) v Secretary of State for Justice* [2008] EWCA Civ 1457) is bound to feel a very considerable sense of injustice. On the day that he was due to be released from a young offenders institution, he was handed his release plan, which told him that he would be under the supervision of a probation officer or social worker for three months. When he reached the reception area in his civilian clothes, expecting to be released, he was served with a transfer direction and taken to a medium secure psychiatric hospital.

The Court of Appeal emphasised that TF could only be transferred on the grounds of his medical condition and its treatability (under the old law), and not because he was thought a danger to the public. The material on which the decision was based must be reliable (citing *R v Secretary of State for the Home Department, ex p Gilkes* [1999] 1 MHLR 6). A report may be unreliable because it is out of date or does not address the statutory criteria to which the decision-maker in the Ministry must also address her mind. "Treatability" had not been properly considered and so the transfer and detention were unlawful. The Mental Health Unit at the Ministry of Justice has taken this to heart. They point out that a late transfer is likely to be counter-productive for public safety, as a person transferred when expecting release in unlikely to co-operate with treatment and may become more disturbed and dangerous. Hence requests for transfers late in sentence will be turned down unless there is good evidence that hospital treatment will benefit the prisoner and reasons why a transfer could not have been achieved earlier (Ministry of Justice, 2009d).

The number of prison transfers is rising but remains very low when compared with the rapidly rising prison population. In the mid 1990s there were 17 patients transferred with restrictions for every 1,000 prisoners, but in 2006 there were only 11 (MHAC, 2009a, para 4.27). Yet the Government has estimated the rates of psychotic illness among prisoners at 11 per cent for men and 15 per cent for women (Home Office, 2005), and there are many more with personality disorders or learning disabilities who might benefit from more appropriate care and treatment. Although the incidence of mental health problems is higher amongst women prisoners, they seem to have benefited less than the men from the increasing rate of transfer (MHAC, 2009a, para 4.29).

The problems of finding suitable hospital places for prisoners with serious mental disorders remain huge. The high security hospitals take many fewer patients than they used to take. High security places are available only to the most severely disturbed and dangerous. Regional secure units were originally designed as halfway houses between the high security hospitals and mainstream provision, rather than for a long term semi-custodial role. Ordinary NHS hospitals are part of a network which includes hostels, centres, group homes and other facilities. It takes a considerable effort of imagination on the part of some to see this as an appropriate setting for people sentenced to imprisonment.

(e) Hybrid orders

The 1983 Act substantially reduced the preventive effect of a restriction order; transfers from prison were difficult and slow. Meanwhile, the Reed Report (1992) recommended that further work was needed on psychopathic disorder and the uncertainties about whether it could be successfully treated in hospital: if it turned out to be untreatable but a restriction order had been made the patient would have to be released no matter how dangerous he was thought to be. The solution recommended as a result (Reed, 1994b) was a "hybrid order" combining a hospital order with a prison sentence. This was taken up by the Home Office (1996), which found a rather different rationale: that there were cases where both treatment and a fixed period of detention were required, perhaps because the offender bore "some significant degree of responsibility for the offence" or because the link between the offending behaviour and the disorder was not clear at the time of sentencing (1996, para 8.14). The Crime (Sentences) Act 1997 introduced such an order for offenders with psychopathic disorder, now extended to all forms of mental disorder by the 2007 amendments. The 1997 Act also introduced mandatory life sentences for repeat serious violent or sex offenders and this was a way of combining such a sentence with hospital treatment (cf *R v Drew*, above).

Under section 45A of the MHA 1983, the Crown Court may make a "hospital and limitation direction" at the same time as imposing a prison sentence upon an offender convicted of any offence apart from murder (s 45A(1)). It must first have considered making a hospital order (s 45A(1)(b)), so must presumably have concluded that a hospital or restriction order will not do, unless the case is one in which a life sentence is mandatory. The court must have the written or oral evidence of two doctors that the offender is suffering from mental disorder of a nature or degree which makes it appropriate for him to be detained in a hospital for medical treatment and that appropriate medical treatment is available for him (s 45A(2)). One of the doctors must give oral evidence in court (s 45A(4)). There must also be evidence, either from the approved clinician who would be in overall charge of his treatment or the hospital managers, that arrangements have been made for his admission to their hospital within 28 days beginning with the date of the order (s 45A(5)). The court also has power to ask the local PCT or Health Board for information about possible hospitals in their area or elsewhere (ss 45A(8) and 39(1)) and, if there is evidence to support it, to make an interim hospital order first (ss 45A(8) and 38(1) and (5)).

The hospital and limitation direction has two elements. The first is a "hospital direction": that, instead of being taken to prison, the offender is to be taken to the specified hospital (s 45A(3)(a)). As with a hospital order, the court may give directions for him to be taken to and detained in a "place of safety" in the meantime (s 45A(5)) and the Justice Secretary can change the specified hospital if an emergency or other special circumstances arise during the 28 days (s 45A(6)). The direction authorises a constable or anyone else directed by the court to take the patient to the specified hospital within 28 days and the hospital to admit him within that period (s 45B(1)). The second element is a "limitation direction": that the offender be subject to the same restrictions as in a restriction order (s 45A(3)(b)). These elements operate alongside the "relevant sentence" of imprisonment imposed for the offence in question (s 45A(1)(b)) and also any other sentence of imprisonment imposed on the same or an earlier occasion (s 45A(9)).

The effect is exactly the same as a transfer from prison with restrictions directed by the Justice Secretary (s 45B(2)). The responsible clinician must make the same regular reports (s 45B(3)). The Justice Secretary's options, if the RC or a tribunal conclude that the criteria for keeping the patient in hospital no longer exist, are exactly the same—return him to prison, release him on licence if there is power to do so, agree to an absolute or conditional discharge by the tribunal, or (unless a tribunal has said that he is entitled to an absolute discharge) leave him in hospital (see pp 176–177, above).

From the beginning there was disquiet about the combination of "tariff" punishment with hospital treatment (eg Eastman, 1996; Eastman and Peay, 1998). The MHAC, 2005 expressed concern that this notion that criminal responsibility is "not to go unpunished" rests upon the outdated concept of criminal responsibility established under the M'Naghten Rules (p 161, above). As it happens, very few orders have been made, perhaps because the courts still find restriction orders adequate except where their hands are tied. The MHAC, 2005 argued that:

"public policy should continue to emphasise diversion from punitive sanctions and a health care model for the treatment of mentally disordered offenders that provides a socially human response to their needs while recognising the needs of public safety" (para 5.97).

The prospect of punishment may undermine treatment, reluctance to send a patient off to prison may increase hospital stays beyond what is clinically necessary, tribunals may be deterred from recommending transfer or community treatment. Preventive detention, thought the MHAC, should be pursued through the criminal justice system rather than mental health law (para 5.98).

Despite all this, the 2007 amendments have broadened the scope of these hybrid orders, although it remains to be seen whether they will prove any more popular with the courts.

It could be said, of course, that most of these concerns apply with equal force to transfers from prison by the Justice Secretary. But it may well be that the populations addressed are different: transferred prisoners having serious psychotic illnesses where hospital treatment is more obviously needed and hybrid order patients having personality disorders whose role in their offending and suitability for hospital treatment is much harder to determine.

(f) Treatment conditions in community orders

Community orders have been around for over 100 years. Probation orders were introduced in 1907 and became community rehabilitation orders in 2001. The original intention was to treat, to address offending behaviour, and not to punish. Community service orders were introduced in 1972 and became community punishment orders in 2001. Their original intention was as a more constructive alternative to prison. Combining probation and community service first became possible in 1991. Drug treatment and testing orders were introduced in 2000. Under the Criminal Justice Act 2003 (CJA), all adult community sentences have been replaced by the community order. This can only be imposed for an offence which the court could have punished with imprisonment (s 150A) or where the offender has been fined on three previous occasions (ss 150A, 151) and the court must consider the offence or offences serious enough to warrant it (s 148(1)). They cannot be imposed where the law prescribes a mandatory penalty (s 150).

Community orders offer the sentencer a menu of 12 requirements which may be imposed upon an offender who has reached the age of 16 (s 177(1)(a) to (l)). The idea is both to tailor the requirements to the needs of the individual case (s 148(2)) and to increase public confidence in community sentences. Unlike orders under the MHA, sentencers are expected to have regard to the five purposes of sentencing when imposing them: these are punishment, crime reduction, reform and rehabilitation, public protection and reparation (s 142(1), (2)(d)).

They count, therefore, as another kind of "hybrid order", in which the purpose may be wholly or mainly therapeutic and rehabilitative, or wholly or mainly punitive and protective, or a mixture of the two. Thus (Seymour and Rutherford, 2008) a requirement to perform unpaid work for between 40 and 300 hours is meant as punishment, but also reparation and rehabilitation; a requirement not to take part in a prohibited activity (such as attending football matches), or to keep out of certain areas, or to abide by a curfew is meant both to punish and to protect the public; a requirement (for under 25-year-olds) to spend time at an attendance centre is meant as a punishment; a requirement to live at a particular place is meant both to rehabilitate and to protect the public; a requirement to take part in a specified activity is mainly rehabilitative but could involve reparation to the victim; and a requirement to attend appointments with a supervisor, or an accredited programme designed to change thinking and behaviour, or a drug rehabilitation programme, or an alcohol treatment programme, is intended to be wholly rehabilitative.

Also in this last category is the mental health treatment requirement (s 177(1)(h)). These have a longer history than most of the other requirements (apart from supervision). With the growth of psychiatric out-patient clinics and voluntary hospital treatment in the 1930s, some enterprising magistrates began to use probation as an unofficial means of persuading disordered offenders to seek treatment. The position was regularised in 1948, when courts were given express power to insert such conditions. At one time they were the most common form of psychiatric disposal, but their use declined and they were phased out after 2001, only to be reinstated under the 2003 Act (which came into force in 2005).

The court must have evidence from one MHA approved doctor that the offender's mental condition is such as requires and may be susceptible to treatment but is not such as to warrant the making of a hospital or guardianship order under the MHA 1983 (2003 Act, s 207(3)(a)). Strictly, then, the court cannot choose between these disposals as the medical requirements are mutually exclusive. The offender must have "expressed his willingness" to comply with the requirement (s 207(3)(c)). If satisfied that arrangements for the intended treatment have been or can be made (s 207(3)(b)), the court can then impose one of three requirements: treatment as a resident patient in an NHS or independent hospital (but not a high security hospital) or care home, treatment as a non-resident patient at a specified institution or place, or treatment by or under the direction of a specified doctor or registered psychologist (s 207(2)).

Further than this, the court is not allowed to be precise: it is for the doctor or psychologist or the clinicians at the hospital, home or other institution to decide what sorts of treatment the patient should have. The doctor or psychologist directing the treatment may arrange for the patient to be treated at another place, provided that it is by or under the direction of a doctor or psychologist and the patient consents (s 208(1)). This could involve the patient receiving all or part of his treatment as a resident patient at a place which could not have been specified in the original order (s 208(2)). The doctor or psychologist must notify the patient's responsible officer and the patient is required to submit to the new arrangements (s 208(3)). However, he cannot be detained or compulsorily treated even if he is required to be a resident patient in a hospital.

The requirement can last for any period up to three years (s 177(5)) and can be combined with any of the other possible requirements provided that they do not conflict with one another (s 177(6)). All people subject to community orders must keep in touch with their responsible officer and let him know any changes of address (s 220). But even if there is a supervision requirement, the supervisor is precluded from active supervision while the offender is being treated as a resident patient. Failures of communication between the medical and probation services, when the patient leaves hospital or fails to co-operate with treatment, are not unknown (Lewis, 1980).

The doctor or psychologist can also report to the responsible officer if for any reason he is no longer willing to be responsible for the patient; or if he thinks that the treatment should continue beyond the period specified, or that the patient needs a different one of the three kinds of treatment, or that he is not susceptible to or no longer requires treatment. The supervisor must then apply to the court for the condition to be varied or cancelled accordingly. The Act does not insist that the court does so, but usually it will have little choice (Sch 8, para 18).

So what is to happen if, having given his consent in court (which many might do to avoid a worse fate), the patient later changes his mind and refuses to co-operate with treatment? Variation or cancellation negates the court's object. The clinician can only report to the responsible officer, who must first give the offender a warning, and may then take proceedings for breach if the offender again fails to comply, unless in each case he has a reasonable excuse (paras 5 and 6). The possible sanctions are imposing more onerous requirements in the order, sentencing the offender afresh for the original offence, or if the failure is wilful and persistent, imposing a sentence of up to six months' imprisonment (paras 9 and 10). But an offender cannot be treated as having failed to comply with a mental health treatment requirement when all he has done is to refuse to undergo any surgical, electrical or other treatment, if the court decides that the refusal is reasonable in all the circumstances (para 11).

These requirements can also be imposed as part of a suspended sentence of imprisonment. A court which passes a prison sentence of at least 14 days but not more than six months (in a magistrates' court) or 12 months (in the Crown Court) can impose one or more of the same 12 requirements, lasting for a "supervision period" of between six months and two years, and suspend the sentence, for an "operational period" of between six months and two years. The supervision period cannot be longer than the operational period. The prison sentence will only take effect if the offender fails to comply with the requirement(s) during the supervision period or commits another offence during the operational period (2003 Act, s 189). So, if the offence merits it, an offender could be required to undergo mental health treatment with the threat of a prison sentence hanging over him if he fails to comply.

It will be seen that the essentials of a mental health treatment requirement in either a community order or a suspended sentence are the equivalent of those in a supervision order which may be imposed upon a person found unfit to plead or not guilty by reason of insanity (see p 158, above). The same requirement may be included in a supervision order made under the Powers of Criminal Courts (Sentencing) Act 2000 over an offender aged under 18 (2000 Act, Pt 4, Ch 5 and Sch 6, para 6; see also Sch 7, para 6 for reports by the doctor or psychologist in charge). The consent of a young person of 14 or over is required and the condition cannot last after the offender reaches 18 (Sch 6, para 6(3)). Apart from dealing with the offender again for the original offence, the sanctions available for breach are a fine, curfew or attendance centre order (Sch 7, para 2).

In the first two years of their introduction, more than 1,300 community orders with a mental health treatment requirement were issued. This is a tiny proportion of those sentenced to community orders who have mental health problems. Most were combined with a supervision requirement (thus reflecting the old law) but not with any other requirement on the menu. Drug treatment requirements, in contrast, numbered more than 13,000 each year. Possible legal obstacles are the mental condition criteria (which in theory do not offer the court a choice between a community and a hospital order); the need to have the arrangements in place or nearly in place; and the need for consent (Seymour and Rutherford, 2008). There is undoubtedly a dearth of mental health provision for offenders in the community (Home Office and Department of Health, 2005). It may be difficult to obtain the necessary psychiatric assessment, preferably from a clinician who has access to local mental health services, even if the possibility has been identified by the offender's lawyers or the court. And despite the flexibility of the legal provision, services on the ground are in short supply for offenders with complex needs.

(g) Guardianship orders

Guardianship could be a very useful order, but in practice it is hardly ever used. It may be made for the same offences as a hospital order, provided that the offender has reached 16. There must be written or oral evidence from two doctors, one of them approved, that the offender is suffering from mental disorder "of a nature or degree which warrants his reception into guardianship under this Act" (s 37(2)(a)(ii)). Mental disability is again limited to mental impairment which is associated with abnormally aggressive or seriously irresponsible conduct. The court must again consider the order the most suitable method of disposing of the case (s 37(2)(b)).

The duration and procedure for renewal are basically the same as in an ordinary hospital order, which means that an order can last for a very long time if the criteria still exist; so are the rights of application to a tribunal, save that guardianship order patients can apply during their first six months. The effect of the order, however, is quite different. The patient is placed under the guardianship either of the local social services authority (LSSA) or of some other individual approved by them (s 37(1)). The order cannot be made unless the proposed guardian agrees (s 37(6)). The LSSA is entitled to disagree with the judge, if they think that a guardianship order is not appropriate because the risks posed cannot be managed within the limited powers that a guardian has (*R (Buckowicki) v Northamptonshire CC* [2007] EWHC 310 (Admin), [2007] 1 MHLR 121). A court which is minded to make a guardianship order may require the LSSA for the area where the offender lives or last lived, or any other LSSA, to inform the court whether they, or any person approved by them, is willing to receive the offender into guardianship and if they are, how they could be expected to exercise their powers (s 39A).

A guardianship order gives the guardian the same powers as a civil guardianship application (s 40(2); see further in chapter 9): he may decide where the patient should live, and when and where the patient should go for treatment, occupation, education or training, and he may insist that any named doctor, social worker or other person sees the patient at home (s 8(1)). He cannot insist that the patient accepts any medical or other treatment on offer, although if that becomes necessary and the medical recommendations are available, he may transfer the patient to hospital. The patient may be recaptured and returned if he absconds from the place where he is required to live. Otherwise, however, there are no sanctions against a patient who refuses to co-operate (although other people might be guilty of harbouring him or obstructing the authorities). The order is therefore quite different from a community order with a condition of psychiatric treatment, and of course it is operated by the social services rather than the probation or health care services.

This is no doubt why it has been so little used. The order requires liaison between the doctors, who will have to give evidence, the LSSA, which will have to take at least some of the responsibility, and the courts, who will not usually have a representative of that authority on hand to consult. The Butler Report recommended closer co-operation with a view to using guardianship more frequently. It is also hard to see why it is possible to make an interim hospital order but not an interim guardianship order (Mental Health Act Commission, 1993).

(h) Alternatives

Before imposing a custodial sentence upon an offender who is or appears to be mentally disordered, the court must obtain a report from an approved doctor unless the court considers this unnecessary in the circumstances (CJA 2003, s 157(1), (2), (6)). Even if there is no such report (which is likely), the court is supposed to consider any information it has about the offender's mental condition, the likely effect of a custodial sentence on that condition and the available treatment (s 157(3)). Given the high incidence of mental disorder among offenders sentenced to imprisonment, especially amongst women, and the small numbers of psychiatric disposals when compared with the size of the prison population, this exhortation would appear to have had little effect.

If an offender cannot be sent to a hospital which the court considers sufficiently secure, a mentally disturbed offender who commits very serious offences is undoubtedly at greater risk of a sentence of life imprisonment than are other offenders, because of the perceived likelihood that he will not be deterred from committing further offences in future. The Criminal Justice Act 2003 has also introduced the indefinite sentence for public protection, a penal form of preventive detention which was recommended by the Butler Report nearly 30 years earlier. Mental instability has also been taken into account in justifying determinate sentences at the top end of the "tariff" for violent offenders.

At the other end of the scale, the courts have often expressed their frustration at the lack of suitable community facilities for the "socially inconvenient". In *R v Clarke* (1975) 61 Cr App R 320, at p 323, Lawton LJ memorably observed that:

"Her Majesty's Courts are not dustbins into which the social services can sweep difficult members of the public. Still less should Her Majesty's judges use their sentencing powers to dispose of those who are socially inconvenient. If the Courts became disposers of those who are socially inconvenient the road ahead would lead to the destruction of liberty. It should be clearly understood that Her Majesty's judges stand on that road barring the way. The courts exist to punish according to law those convicted of offences. Sentences should fit crimes."

A £2.00 fine was substituted for a sentence of 18 months' imprisonment upon a former Rampton patient who was admittedly very difficult to handle but had only been convicted of breaking a flower pot.

No matter how many secure units are built, they will not solve the problem of people like Dawn Clarke, who was repeatedly discharged from Rampton by a tribunal. There are many people who are not dangerous in any sensible meaning of the term, but who are difficult and a nuisance to all and sundry, and for whom there is precious little that hospitals as such can do. Hospitals are not dustbins any more than prisons are. The alternative of good facilities in the community simply does not exist in many places. The courts, and the rest of us, may have to accept that there are some troublesome people whom we must try to tolerate as best we can.

5. COMMENTARY

The MHA Code of Practice proudly proclaims that:

"People who are subject to criminal proceedings have the same rights to psychiatric assessment and treatment as anyone else. Any person who is in police or prison custody or before the courts charged with a criminal offence and who is in need of medical treatment for mental disorder should be considered for admission to hospital" (para 33.2).

However, we all know that this does not always happen. Diversion at all stages of the criminal justice process happens far less frequently than it might. The disorder may not be recognised or the facilities for treating it may not exist. But that is not a legal problem.

At the legal level, the old dichotomy between the "mad", who should be committed to the medical authorities to be looked after until they are cured, and the "bad", who should be punished in proportion to their crimes, has never been fully accepted and is now largely abandoned. We still cling to an outdated concept of criminal responsibility which fails to recognise that mental disorder may prevent a person from making the right choices as well as from understanding what the choices are. But if we were to reform the defence of insanity, perhaps along similar lines to the reformed defence of diminished responsibility (requiring that the accused have no, rather than an impaired, ability to understand the nature of his conduct, to form a rational judgment, and/or to exercise self-control), would we be entirely happy with the result?

When an offender is sent to hospital rather than to prison, we do not look for when he is "cured" but simply for when the hospital can do no more for him. However broad our definitions of medical treatment and the benefits it may bring, there may come a time when a patient who has committed a very serious crime and is still thought dangerously unpredictable will have to be released. Not surprisingly, perhaps, the courts and the public do not always think that this is enough. They would prefer the offender to be treated as both "mad" and "bad": either by sending him to prison with the possibility of transfer to hospital or by sending him to hospital with the possibility of transfer to prison. Neither possibility is much used, with the result that many offenders who might benefit from hospital treatment remain in prison.

This is coming to seem acceptable. The Bradley Report (2009) commends the improvements in prison mental health care which have resulted from the NHS taking over responsibility and makes proposals for further improvement. The MHA Code suggests two situations in which transfer to hospital should be considered. The first is where the prisoner requires treatment in hospital which he cannot get in prison, perhaps because he is unwilling to consent to it: such prisoners should be transferred within a time frame equivalent to that of patients admitted from the community (para 33.31). The second is where a prisoner has a severe and enduring mental disorder and has consented to treatment in prison but the prison environment is contributing to his disorder: then the assessment should consider whether the prison healthcare centre is capable of providing for his care if he is too unwell to return to the residential wings (para 33.32). On this basis, many prisoners with serious mental health problems might still have to stay in prison.

It is of course possible that some offenders would prefer a determinate time in prison to an indeterminate time in hospital where they can be treated against their will and some of the rules may be less congenial than those in prison. An offender may be prepared to accept the loss of the right to a proportionate sentence, in the hope that a therapeutic disposal will do him some good, or at least be more pleasant than the alternative. But if he has the capacity to make the choice, perhaps he should be allowed to decide whether or not to do so.

However, the traditional link between the seriousness of the crime and the length of the sentence is being eroded, partly by the introduction of mandatory life sentences in some circumstances and partly by the introduction of indefinite sentences for public protection. More and more prisoners are serving a sentence which comprises both a "tariff" period commensurate with the sentence they would otherwise have received and a preventive period during which they can be held until it is thought safe to release them. Their status after the tariff has been served is not unlike the status of a restricted patient before the 1983 Act. So the "bad" may be seen as a little "mad" as well.

Perhaps that does not matter. Perhaps the true moral distinction is not between those who are suffering from mental illness and those who are not, but between those who are considered a long term danger to others and those who are not. There are plenty of sane people who are dangerous, just as there are plenty of insane people who are not. But that is not how we have traditionally looked at the criminal law: as Lawton LJ put it "sentences should fit crimes". And how do we know who is dangerous and who is not? And where should the burden of proof lie? If we are going to deprive people of either proportionality or the normal principles of guilt and innocence in order to protect society against serious risk, we should be concentrating on the accurate identification and discovery of that risk rather than on anything else.

6 TREATMENT AND CARE

This chapter is about the treatment, management and care of all patients with mental disorders and disabilities, compulsory or informal, in or out of hospital. It used to be assumed that any patient who was liable to be detained under the Mental Health Act 1959 was automatically unable to decide for himself what medical treatment he should have for his disorder. It was also assumed that such patients needed no special protection against what might be done with them while they were in hospital. Nowadays it is realised that neither assumption is necessarily correct. The development of the law has also been influenced by articles 3 and 8 of the European Convention on Human Rights (ECHR).

Article 3 requires that "no-one shall be subjected to torture or to inhuman or degrading treatment or punishment". This is an absolute right. There is no question of justification. Hence for treatment to be prohibited by the article it or its effects must be very severe. The leading Strasbourg case about treatment in psychiatric hospitals is *Herczegfalvy v Austria* (1992) 15 EHRR 437. The patient had been force-fed, forcibly given psychotropic drugs and kept for more than two weeks in handcuffs tied to a security bed. He complained that this was degrading treatment contrary to article 3. The Court accepted that "the position of inferiority and powerlessness which is typical of patients confined in psychiatric hospitals calls for increased vigilance in reviewing whether the Convention has been complied with". But "as a general rule, a measure which is a psychiatric necessity cannot be regarded as inhuman and degrading". Necessity should be judged according to the "recognised rules of medical science" or "the established principles of medicine" (para 82). The patient had failed to show that his treatment had not been justified by medical necessity according to the standards prevailing at the time.

Article 8 protects the right to respect for private and family life, home and correspondence. The scope of "private life" is very broad. In *Storck v Germany* (2006) 43 EHRR 6, at para 143, it was said to cover even a minor interference with the physical integrity of an individual if carried out without consent. The patient had been placed in a locked ward of a private psychiatric clinic and forcibly medicated against her will. The state had a positive obligation to protect her against such invasions of her article 8 (as well as her article 5) rights. However, this is a qualified right, so the state's interference may be justified if it is in accordance with the law and,

"necessary in a democratic society in the interests of national security, public safety or the economic well-being of the country, for the prevention of disorder or crime, for the protection of health or morals or for the protection of the rights and freedom of others."

Once again, therefore, medical necessity will mean that there is no breach.

Nevertheless, articles 3 and 8 have provided some protection to detained patients in respect of their contacts with the outside world, the use of seclusion, and the imposition of forcible treatment. They may also have prompted some changes in the legislation and Codes of Practice. The MHA 1983, while allowing much treatment to be given to detained patients without their consent, did introduce regulation of some treatments. The 2007 amendments have tightened this and extended it to community patients. The Mental Capacity Act 2005 (MCA) governs the treatment of patients who lack the capacity to decide for themselves what treatment they should have, both for mental and for physical disorder. It also puts on a statutory basis the common law principles governing "advance refusals", which allow people who have capacity to decide what treatment they may be given if and when they lose it. But these are all subject to the MHA's rules about treatment for mental disorder.

These developments are part of the wider move towards increased respect for individual autonomy and preferences. But professionals do not always find it easy to reconcile these constraints with their duty to provide proper care and treatment for their patients or with the need to control the violent or challenging behaviour of a few of these.

1. TREATMENT OUTSIDE THE MENTAL HEALTH ACT

The common law normally respects the right of any person to decide what shall be done with his own body. Thus any action which involves the use or the threat of force, however slight, upon his person will amount to a tort (and often also a crime) unless there is consent or some legal justification for acting without consent. There are, of course, psychological treatments and other activities which involve no such force and usually depend upon the co-operation of the patient. Even here, however, the deliberate infliction of psychological harm is a tort, and some patients may well experience group or individual psychotherapy as coercive and distressing. Behaviour modification programmes run an even greater risk of interfering with the patients' basic rights. Other measures commonly employed would undoubtedly be tortious. These include conventional medical treatments, such as injections with drugs, operations, and electro-convulsive therapy (ECT). They also include the various forms of restraint or confinement used, ranging from the bodily restraint of one person by another, through periods of enforced "seclusion" in a locked room, to confinement in a locked ward, or eventually in a high security psychiatric hospital. In this section we shall look at the legal justifications for treatment apart from the provisions of the MHA 1983.

(a) Consent

The patient may give his express consent to the invasion of his normal legal rights. The general view is that this constitutes a defence which the defendant must prove (rather than that lack of consent is an essential ingredient of the tort which the claimant must prove). It is only a defence where what has been done is what the patient agreed could be done, so it is important to make this clear at the outset: for example, that the patient has agreed to all the elements of a behaviour modification programme, which may involve deprivation of ordinary legal rights through a "token economy" or periods of "time out". However, the fact that the patient has given his consent does not mean that the doctor or clinician is obliged to provide treatment against her better judgment: *Re J (A Minor) (Child in Care: Medical Treatment)* [1993] Fam 15, CA.

Consent has to be "real". It may therefore be invalid if induced by force or fraud. Clerk & Lindsell (19th edn, para 15–102) suggest that "a claimant cannot give a real consent unless he has in fact the freedom to choose whether or not

188

he should do so". An informal patient who gives his consent under the threat that he will be sectioned might complain that he has been deprived of his freedom to choose. So might a hospital order patient complain, like the prisoner in *Freeman v Home Office (No 2)* [1984] QB 524, CA, that the coercive nature of the institution, and the power of the responsible clinician to decide whether he should be released, prevent his consent being freely given. A conditionally discharged or community patient might, like the patient in *R (H) v Mental Health Review Tribunal* [2007] EWHC 884, say the same of the condition that he "shall comply" with his doctor's instructions on pain of possible recall to hospital and forcible medication there. It was decided in *Freeman* that this was a question of fact in each case: the patient's will may have been overborne by such circumstances or it may not. But an abuse of authority could vitiate consent even if there was no use or threat of force.

Although common law requires that the patient's consent be "real", it does not require that it be fully "informed" upon all the arguments for or against a particular treatment. In *Sidaway v Board of Governors of the Bethlem Royal Hospital and the Maudsley Hospital* [1985] AC 871, the House of Lords held that the duty to warn patients of the risks of treatment was governed by the law of negligence. Lord Bridge, in the majority, considered that the decision on what risks should be disclosed was primarily a matter of clinical judgment. However, if there was a substantial risk of grave adverse consequences, disclosure might be so obviously necessary to the patient's choice that no reasonably prudent doctor would fail to make it. This approach coincides with the general approach to questions of medical negligence, laid down in *Bolam v Friern Hospital Management Committee* [1957] 1 WLR 582. The patient had agreed to ECT and was badly injured when it was given without a muscle relaxant. The judge took the view that it was not negligent to do this if a responsible body of medical opinion would have done the same, even if another body of opinion would not. Further, the evidence suggested that even if the patient had been fully informed of the risk, he would have agreed in any event, so that it was not the doctor's failure to warn him which had caused the injury. Indeed, even if the patient would not have had the treatment had he been warned, it could be said—indeed was said by the House of Lords in *Chester v Afshar* [2004] UKHL 41, [2005] 1 AC 134—that it is not the failure to warn which causes the risk to materialise. However, the House also held that the point of the duty to warn was not only to reduce the risk but also to enable the patient to make a proper choice. A failure to warn violated that right and so could be treated as having caused the damage if the risk materialised. It is fair to say that professional views of the risks which ought to be disclosed to the patient have evolved over the years, in line with the general move towards patient autonomy. *Bolam* might not be decided in the same way today.

For consent to be valid, the patient must have the mental capacity to give it. Both at common law and under the MCA 2005 he is presumed to have that capacity until the contrary is shown. Before the MCA came into force, the courts had developed a test of capacity to consent to medical treatment which is very like the test in the 2005 Act and indeed drew upon the deliberations of the Law Commission which led up to that Act. In *Re C (Refusal of Medical Treatment)* [1994] 1 FLR 31, a schizophrenic Broadmoor patient, with grandiose delusions about his own medical qualifications and experience, refused to undergo a below knee amputation for gangrene although advised that he stood an 85 per cent chance of imminent death. The judge found helpful a forensic psychiatrist's analysis of the decision-making process into three stages: first, comprehending and retaining treatment information, secondly believing it, and thirdly, weighing it in the balance to arrive at a choice. The judge decided that the patient did understand the relevant information, that there was no direct link between his refusal and his persecutory delusions, and that he had arrived at a clear choice. As it happened, the patient was right, because conservative treatment succeeded.

In *Re MB (Medical Treatment)* [1997] 2 FLR 426, at 437, the Court of Appeal laid down a test which has been adopted ever since:

"A person lacks capacity if some impairment or disturbance of mental functioning renders the person unable to make a decision whether to consent to or refuse treatment. That inability to make a decision will occur when:

(a) the patient is unable to comprehend and retain the information which is material to the decision, especially as to the likely consequences of having or not having the treatment in question;

(b) the patient is unable to use the information and weigh it in the balance as part of the process of arriving at the decision . . . ".

Lack of belief in what the doctors were saying, or panic induced by fear, might not indicate a lack of capacity, because they could be perfectly rational; but a patient's disorder might "stifle belief" and fear might "paralyse the will", thus destroying the capacity to make a decision. In that case, a pregnant woman had agreed to a Caesarean but panicked at the last moment because of a phobia of needles. It was held that she was temporarily unable to make a decision.

On the other hand, if a pregnant woman (or any other patient) does have the capacity to decide according to this test, the fact that she is putting her own life, and that of her unborn child, at risk by refusing treatment does not entitle anyone to force it upon her: see *St George's Healthcare NHS Trust v S; R v Collins, ex p S* [1999] Fam 26. In practice, however, both professionals and the courts will find it easier to accept that a patient has the capacity to say "yes" to treatment than to say "no", especially in life-threatening situations: see, for example, the earlier case of *Re T (Consent to Medical Treatment) (Adult Patient)* [1993] Fam 95. The Court of Appeal held that the doctors were justified in giving the patient a blood transfusion after an emergency Caesarean section, despite her express written refusal; at the time she signed the form, they held, she was unable to make a genuine decision, because of the combined effect of her medical condition and pressure from her mother who was a convinced Jehovah's Witness.

These cases are still good law, but they have largely been overtaken by the MCA 2005, which gives an express authority to treat incapacitated patients without consent in certain circumstances and lays down the test of capacity for that purpose (see (b) below). The MCA also makes it possible for donees of a lasting power of attorney and deputies appointed by the Court of Protection to give a valid consent to treatment on behalf of a patient who lacks the capacity to consent for himself (see further in chapter 10).

Finally, even if a valid consent has been given, it may be withdrawn. A patient could agree to a course of drug treatment or ECT but withdraw his consent before it has been completed. He may agree to the hospital's practice of locking the ward door at night, or to a programme of behaviour modification involving periods of time out, but change his mind and ask to be released. In principle, consent can be revoked at any time, unless the patient is contractually bound not to do so (like a passenger on a ferry or a miner down the mine: see *Robinson v Balmain New Ferry Co* [1910] AC 295; *Herd v Weardale Steel, Coal and Coke Co Ltd* [1915] AC 67). An NHS patient would not make such a contract and it is perhaps unlikely that a private patient would do so either.

(b) The best interests of patients without capacity: the common law and the Mental Capacity Act 2005

Until the decision of the House of Lords in *Re F (Mental Patient: Sterilisation)* [1990] 2 AC 1 there was great uncertainty about what could be done for a patient who was incapable of giving a real consent. The Law Lords accepted that there was no individual authorised by law to give that consent on behalf of an incapable patient; the High Court had no jurisdiction to do so; and that there might be no statutory power to treat under the MHA or any other legislation. However, where a patient was incapable of giving consent, it was lawful at common law to give him such treatment as was necessary to preserve his life or health. The obvious example is an unconscious road accident victim. A less obvious example is a patient who has consented to one operation, during which it is discovered that further treatment is urgently required. In both cases, the doctor can carry on with treatment which it would be unreasonable, as opposed to merely inconvenient, to postpone: the Canadian cases of *Marshall v Curry* (1933) 3 DLR 260 and *Murray v McMurchy* (1949) 2 DLR 442 were approved in *Re F*. Where the patient is more permanently incapacitated, it was lawful to give any treatment which was in his best interests. What was in the patient's best interests could be judged by the same test as in *Bolam v Friern Hospital Management Committee* [1957] 1 WLR 582: whether the treatment proposed would be accepted as proper by a responsible body of medical opinion, even if there is another body of opinion which would not do so. Although the High Court could not give consent, it could make a declaration that the proposed treatment would, or would not, be lawful under this doctrine. The House strongly advised that this should be done for especially sensitive treatments, of which sterilisation was the most obvious example.

The decision in *Re F* was warmly welcomed by doctors, professionals and other carers, but the requirement to take some decisions to court soon proved inconvenient. The High Court later decided that declarations need not be sought for so-called "therapeutic" sterilisations, not only those to treat an existing disease or condition of the reproductive organs but also those to control excessive menstruation (*Re GF (Mental Patient: Medical Treatment)* [1992] 1 FLR 293; *Re E (A Minor) (Medical Treatment)* [1991] 2 FLR 585), or for abortions (*Re SG (Adult Mental Patient: Abortion)* [1991] 2 FLR 329). The Court has recognised that costly and elaborate legal proceedings are not necessarily the best way to check upon professional practice unless there is a real dispute to be resolved. In *Re H (Mental Patient)* [1993] 1 FLR 29, the deputy judge (who is now Wilson LJ) refused to grant a declaration that a CT scan was in the best interests of a schizophrenic woman with a suspected brain tumour, even though it was. The same principles applied to both diagnostic and therapeutic procedures, but he did not want to send a signal that they should be delayed pending an application to the court.

The MCA 2005 has not replaced the common law principles, but it has clarified and refined them so that doctors, nurses and others looking after people who may be without capacity to make decisions for themselves can now rely on the Act rather than the common law. Section 5 of the MCA applies where anyone (D) does an act in connection with the care or treatment of another person (P), provided that:

(a) before doing the act D takes reasonable steps to establish whether P lacks the capacity to make his own decision about it; and
(b) when doing the act, D reasonably believes both that P does lack that capacity and that it will be in P's best interests for the act to be done (s 5(1)).

D is then in the same position as if P did have capacity and had consented to the act (s 5(2); see above). This does not, of course, excuse D if he acts negligently (s 5(3)).

We have already seen (in chapter 2) how the MCA defines the capacity to take a decision. In summary, the patient must be assumed to have capacity until the contrary is shown (s 1(2)). He will lack capacity if he is unable to make the particular decision for himself because of an impairment of or disturbance in the functioning of his mind or brain, whether temporary or permanent (s 2(1), (2)). But he is not to be taken to be unable to make a decision for himself unless all practicable steps have been taken to help him to do so without success (s 1(3)). A patient is unable to make a decision for himself if he cannot:

(a) understand the relevant information (including information about the reasonably foreseeable consequences of deciding one way or another or not deciding at all);
(b) retain that information for long enough to make the decision;
(c) use or weigh the information as part of the process of making a decision; or
(d) communicate the decision he has made in any way.

He is not to be regarded as unable to understand the relevant information if he can understand an explanation given in a way which is appropriate for him (using simple language, visual aids or the like) (s 3(2)). This largely repeats the common law test, but it does emphasise the need to try and help the patient to understand and to make his own decision. It does not expect any great sophistication in the content of the explanation given or in the patient's understanding of it.

It has been pointed out that the transatlantic concept of fully informed consent places more emphasis on what the patient can understand than on what he wants (Goldstein, 1975). It may encourage the authorities to deprive people who cannot fully understand all the ramifications of a particular treatment of their right to choose what they want. But if the "relevant information" is sensibly interpreted to mean a reasonably simple explanation of the pros and cons of a particular course of treatment, then many patients should be capable of understanding it and giving—or refusing—their consent.

We have also seen in chapter 2 the MCA's approach to deciding what will be in the best interests of a patient who, despite everything that is done to help him to decide, is still unable to do so. There are also three important limits to the authority given by section 5 to impose treatment without consent. There are no statutory safeguards for especially controversial treatments, such as non-therapeutic sterilisation, although the Law Commission recommended these (see Law Commission, 1993b, 1995). However, the MCA Code of Practice (para 6.18) says that applications "must" be made to the Court of Protection in respect of those treatments which had previously required the approval of the High Court.

First, section 5 does not allow any act intended to restrain the patient, unless the person doing it reasonably believes that it is necessary in order to prevent harm to the patient (not to anyone else) *and* the act done is in fact a proportionate response to the likelihood of the harm feared and its seriousness (s 6(1), (2), (3)). Restraining the patient means using or threatening force to secure the doing of an act which the patient resists or restricting his movement whether or not he resists (s 6(4)). It is the restraining act which must be proportionate to the harm, rather than the act which the restraint is designed to get done. But that act will only be lawful if it is reasonably believed to be in the best interests of the patient. Of course, if there are doubts or disputes they can be taken to the Court of Protection, which can either make a declaration about what will be lawful, or decide the matter for itself, or appoint a deputy to do so.

Secondly, section 5 does not affect the operation of an advance decision to refuse treatment (see (c) below). Nor does it authorise treatment which conflicts with a decision taken by the donee of a lasting power of attorney or a deputy appointed by the court if it is within the scope of his authority (s 6(6)). So a donee or deputy can refuse as well as consent to treatment. But this does not stop anyone providing life-sustaining treatment or doing something he believes necessary to prevent a serious deterioration in the patient's condition, while a decision is sought from the Court (s 6(7)).

Thirdly, section 5 does not allow anyone to deprive a person of his liberty (whatever that may mean: see chapter 1). So if it is not practicable to provide the patient with the treatment which he needs for a physical disorder or disability without depriving him of his liberty, authorisation will have to be sought either through the MCA deprivation of liberty scheme (the DoLS) or from the Court of Protection. The DoLS scheme simply allows the deprivation of liberty—any medical treatment must be covered by section 5 or authorised by the Court.

Where the patient requires treatment for mental disorder, the position is more complicated. It may be possible to treat him under section 5, subject to the limitations in section 6 (above). But there are two further limitations. First, nothing in the MCA authorises anyone to give, or give consent to, the particular forms of treatment which are regulated under Part 4 of the MHA (s 28(1); giving ECT to a patient under 18 who is not subject to MHA compulsion is an exception, see section 2, below). That has to be done under the MHA. Second, the patient cannot be deprived of his liberty either under the DoLS or by order of the Court if he is "ineligible" within the meaning of Schedule 1A to the 2005 Act. As we have seen in chapter 1, this is designed to ensure that, if a patient has to be deprived of his liberty for the purpose of receiving treatment for mental disorder in a hospital (but not in a care home) to which he objects, he is sectioned under the MHA rather than made subject to the DoLS. It does not prevent a compliant informal patient being subject to the DoLS—indeed that was the whole point of the *Bournewood* saga. But if the patient is "within the scope of the Mental Health Act" and he objects to being in hospital or to being given some or all of his treatment for mental disorder, then he is ineligible for the DoLS and should be sectioned instead (MCA, Sch A1, paras 2, Case E, and 5) . He is "within the scope of the Mental Health Act" if he could be detained under section 2 or 3 were an application made and the required medical recommendations given (para 12). The position of patients who are already subject some form of compulsion under the MHA is dealt with in chapter 1.

Giving treatment is not always the issue. What about withholding or withdrawing it? In *Airedale NHS Trust v Bland* [1993] AC 789, the House of Lords had to consider the legality of withdrawing artificial nutrition and hydration from a patient in a persistent vegetative state (PVS). No doctor can be obliged to provide medical treatment which he does not consider to be medically indicated (*Re J (A Minor) (Child in Care: Medical Treatment)* [1993] Fam 15), although of course he must live up to the usual standard of care in reaching that decision. But someone who has assumed the responsibility of caring for a helpless person is not allowed to neglect his basic needs (*R v Stone* [1977] QB 354). In *Bland*, the Law Lords decided that it was lawful to withdraw artificial sustenance from a PVS patient but that each case should be brought to court so that there could be a full investigation and independent evidence obtained (for examples, see *Swindon and Marlborough NHS Trust v S, The Guardian*, 10 December 1994, *Frenchay Healthcare NHS Trust v S* [1994] 1 WLR 601). The courts have purported to apply the "best interests" criterion laid down in *Re F* (above) to these cases. But it is difficult to disagree with Lord Mustill that "the distressing truth which must not be shirked is the proposed conduct is not in the best interests of Anthony Bland, for he has no best interests of any kind" (*Bland*, above, p 897). Some (if not all) of these cases will be covered by section 5 and once again the MCA does not lay down any special safeguards—save to insist that, when deciding upon life-sustaining treatment, the decision-maker must not be motivated by a desire to bring about death (s 4(5)).

(c) Advance decisions

It was clear that at common law the refusal of future treatment by a patient who had the capacity to do so had to be respected, even after he lost capacity, provided that it was "clearly established and applicable in the circumstances": see principally *Re T (Consent to Medical Treatment) (Adult Patient)* [1993] Fam 95; and *Bland*, above. One possible exception, on grounds of public policy, was for "basic care", such as oral feeding and fundamental hygiene. It was also held in *Home Secretary v Robb* [1995] 1 FLR 412 (cf *Leigh v Gladstone* (1909) 26 TLR 139) that the prison authorities could lawfully refrain from force-feeding a prisoner on hunger strike.

The MCA 2005 provides that if a patient with capacity has made a *valid* advance decision which is *applicable* to a particular treatment, it has the same effect as it would have if he were making it at the time when the carrying out or continuing of the treatment has to be decided (s 26(1)). But an advance decision is not applicable if the patient still has capacity at that time (s 25(3)).

An "advance decision" means a decision, taken at a time when a patient (aged 18 or more) has capacity to make it, to the effect that if at some later time and in specified circumstances a specified treatment is proposed and he then lacks the capacity to consent to it, the specified treatment is not to be carried out or continued (s 24(1)). It does not matter that the circumstances or the treatment are described in layman's terms ("do not resuscitate me if I have stopped breathing for more than ten minutes"). An advance decision does not have to be in writing unless the treatment involved is "life-sustaining": that is treatment which the patient's health care provider considers necessary to sustain life. Then the decision must be verified by a statement by the patient that it is to apply to that treatment even though life is at risk. Both the decision and the statement must be in writing, signed by the patient or by another person in the patient's presence and at his direction; the signature must be made or acknowledged by the patient in the presence of a witness; and the witness must also sign, or acknowledge his signature, in the patient's presence (s 25(5) and (6)).

An advance decision can be withdrawn at any time when the patient has capacity to do so and this need not be in writing even if the decision itself was in writing (s 24(3) and (4)). An advance decision can also be altered at any time when the patient has capacity. This too does not need to be in writing unless the alteration refers to life-sustaining treatment, in which case the same formalities are required (s 24(4) and (5)).

Obviously, an advance decision is *not valid* if it has been withdrawn (s 25(2)(a)). It is also not valid if the patient has, since making the decision, granted a lasting power of attorney which gives the donee power to give or refuse consent to the treatment in question—in other words if the patient has since ceded the power of decision-making to someone else (s 25(2)(b)). Any other power of attorney does not affect the validity of the decision (s 25(7)). This is reasonably easy for a professional to decide, but the Act also provides that a decision is not valid if the patient "has done anything else clearly inconsistent with the advance decision remaining his fixed decision" (s 25(2)(c)). This leaves more room for argument.

An advance decision is *not applicable* to the treatment proposed if this is not the treatment specified in the decision (s 25(4)(a)) or if the circumstances specified in the decision are absent (s 25(3)(b)). This again is relatively straightforward, but the Act also provides that a decision is not applicable if "there are reasonable grounds for believing that circumstances exist which [the patient] did not anticipate at the time of the advance decision and which would have affected his decision had he anticipated them" (s 25(4)(c)). This will leave a great deal of room for argument.

The general effect of an advance refusal is, of course, that it is not lawful to carry out or continue the specified treatment and the doctors cannot be blamed for failing to do so. The Act provides that a person is not liable for withholding or withdrawing treatment if, at the time, he reasonably believes that a valid and applicable advance decision is in existence (s 26(3)). However, the Act also provides that a person is not liable for carrying out or continuing the treatment unless, at the time, he is "satisfied" that there is a valid and applicable advance decision in existence (s 26(2)). This places quite a burden on the patient, or those who are anxious to ensure that the patient's wishes are respected, to make sure that the advance refusal is drawn to the doctors' attention and recorded in the hospital notes.

If there is any doubt or dispute about whether there is an advance decision, which is both valid and applicable to the treatment in question, the matter can be referred to the Court of Protection, which can make a declaration about it (s 26(4)). Pending the court's decision, the advance decision does not stop anyone providing life sustaining treatment or doing anything he reasonable believes necessary to prevent a serious deterioration in the patient's condition (s 26(5)).

But does the MCA replace the common law? What if an advance refusal is not "applicable" to life-sustaining treatment under the Act, because it has not been signed and witnessed as the Act requires, but is nevertheless plainly genuine and crystal clear in its meaning?

Advance decisions can apply to any sort of treatment, whether for a physical illness, injury or disability, or for a mental disorder or disability. So an advance refusal by an informal hospital patient should be respected in the same way as any other. But there is statutory power to treat compulsory hospital patients for their mental disorder without their consent, so the MHA Code of Practice points out that an advance refusal of treatment may be a reason to "section" a patient (para 17.6). However, the Code also points out that even if there is power to treat the patient compulsorily, clinicians should try to comply with the patient's wishes expressed in an advance decision (para 17.8). They must, of course, comply with a valid and applicable advance refusal of treatment which is not for mental disorder, whether or not the patient is detained (para 17.9). But even in the case of mental disorder, the patient may have a better understanding than the clinicians of what treatment will make the best contribution to his recovery.

2. TREATMENT UNDER THE MENTAL HEALTH ACT

The 1959 Act had nothing to say about the treatment and care of hospital patients, whether informal or detained. The official view was that this could safely be left to the clinical judgment of the doctors in charge and that detained patients could lawfully be given any recognised form of treatment for their disorder, whether or not they consented (although a more cautious view was later adopted towards patients detained "for observation"). Others (notably Jacob, 1976, and Gostin, 1979; see also Butler Report, 1975) pointed out that the 1959 Act gave no express power to impose such treatment and that the common law might still apply. In other words, patients could only be treated without consent if they lacked the capacity to decide for themselves. These doubts increased the attractions of legislating to permit compulsory treatment while introducing safeguards over the use of the more controversial treatments, principally psychosurgery and ECT. The safeguards introduced by the 1983 Act have been extended by the 2007 amendments, which also cover community patients.

The Human Rights Act 1998 has also brought the courts into these decisions. Hospitals and doctors might always be liable in damages if they treated a patient unlawfully or negligently (subject to MHA, s 139(1); p 342, later). But treatment without consent is an interference with the right to respect for private life under article 8 of the ECHR unless justified in the interests of the patient's health or to protect the rights of others; and forcible treatment which is not shown to be a medical or therapeutic necessity might reach the level of severity to amount to inhuman or degrading treatment contrary to article 3. So the court may have to inquire into the merits of a decision of the responsible clinician or the doctor giving a second opinion under the Act (the Second Opinion Appointed Doctor, or SOAD) on its merits, in order to see whether medical necessity is indeed established: see *R (Wilkinson) v Broadmoor Special Hospital Authority* [2001] EWCA Civ 1545, [2002] 1 WLR 419; *R (JB) v Haddock (Responsible Medical Officer)* [2006] EWCA Civ 961, [2006] HRLR 40. But the courts are not anxious to hold full-blown trials on the issue: if the MHA requirements are properly complied with, they say, it will not often be necessary to hear oral evidence from the doctors: *R (N) v M* [2002] EWCA Civ 1789, [2003] 1 WLR 562; *R (B) v Dr SS (RMO)* [2006] EWCA Civ 28, [2006] 1 WLR 810.

(a) Hospital patients—the general rule

Section 63 of the MHA 1983 provides:

"The consent of a patient shall not be required for any medical treatment given to him for the mental disorder from which he is suffering, not being a form of treatment to which sections 57, 58 or 58A above applies, if the treatment is given by or under the direction of the approved clinician in charge of the treatment".

By section 56(2) this applies only to patients falling within section 56(3) or (4). Section 56(3) covers all patients liable to be detained under the Act, apart from: (a) those admitted for assessment in an emergency under section 4 where the second medical recommendation converting it into a full admission for assessment under section 2 has not yet been given and received; (b) hospital in-patients detained under either of the short term holding powers in section 5; patients held in a "place of safety" under sections 135, 136 or pending admission to hospital under a hospital order or direction; patients remanded to hospital for reports under section 35; and (c) conditionally discharged restricted patients who have not been recalled to hospital. Section 56(4) covers community patients who have been recalled to hospital under section 17E.

This statutory power to impose treatment without consent upon the great majority of compulsory patients is subject to several important limitations. The first is that it must be "medical treatment". This includes "nursing, psychological intervention, and specialist mental health habilitation, rehabilitation and care" (s 145(1)). However, it must have the purpose "to alleviate, or prevent a worsening of, the disorder or one or more of its symptoms or manifestations" (s 145(4)). It is not always easy to distinguish milieu therapy in a maximum or medium secure hospital from a system of detention and discipline for its own sake. Expecting patients to conform to very high or artificial norms of behaviour, to fit into the system for the system's sake rather than their own, or to be punished for their misdeeds prior to their admission to hospital (all of which were reported by the Rampton review team; see Boynton, 1980) can scarcely qualify as medical treatment even under the widest definition. But a carefully designed programme of behaviour modification, or a therapeutic community, which will meet the needs of the particular group of patients for whom it is designed, could qualify. The wide variety of therapeutic approaches available is one reason why professionals other than doctors can now be the approved clinicians in charge of the treatment in question. It is also possible for one clinician to be in charge of one element in the treatment and another clinician in charge of another.

The second important limitation is that the medical treatment must be given for the *mental disorder* from which this particular patient is suffering. The MHA gives no power to impose treatment for physical disorders which are unrelated to any mental disorder within the meaning of the Act. This is not an easy distinction. Some physical disorders can be either the cause or a consequence of a mental disorder: in that case, treating the cause or the consequence is treating the mental disorder. In *R v Mental Health Act Commission, ex p X* (1988) 9 BMLR 77, it was said that where the patient was mentally disordered and sexually deviant, the two might be inextricably linked, so that treatment for one could be treatment for the other. Artificial feeding is a treatment "for" anorexia nervosa (*Re KB (Adult) (Mental Patient: Medical Treatment)* (1994) 9 BMLR 144; see also *Riverside Mental Health NHS Trust v Fox* [1994] 1 FLR 614) and for a personality disorder leading to a compulsion to self harm (*B v Croydon Health Authority* [1995] Fam 133, CA). However, if a severely handicapped woman becomes pregnant, her pregnancy may have been caused in part by her disorder, but it was accepted in *Re F (Mental Patient: Sterilisation)* [1990] 2 AC 1 that sterilisation was not treatment for her mental disorder. In *GJ v The Foundation Trust and others* [2009] EWHC 2972 Fam, para 54, Charles J concluded that while treatment for mental disorder could include both medical and surgical treatment for the consequences of mental disorder, it could not include treatment for quite unrelated physical conditions where giving that treatment would not impact upon the pre-existing mental disorder. Treatment for an unrelated physical disorder is excluded even if the patient is refusing the treatment because of a mental disorder. In *St George's Healthcare NHS Trust v S* [1999] Fam 26, CA, a pregnant woman with pre-eclampsia refused to go into hospital and was sectioned under section 2. The Court of Appeal held that the criteria for making an application for admission were not made out. Thus, if a schizophrenic refuses to have his appendix out because his thought control forbids this, it is permissible under section 63 to treat the schizophrenia but not the appendix. However, the patient might well lack capacity to make the decision for himself and so could be treated under section 5 of the MCA 2005.

(b) Community patients

There is no equivalent to section 63 for community patients. A community patient may not be given medical treatment for his mental disorder unless: (a) there is authority to give it to him, and (b) if required by the special safeguards for particular treatments (see (c) below), it is certified by a SOAD (s 64B(2), (3)). There is authority to treat a patient aged 16 or more in three circumstances. These reflect the circumstances in which it would be possible to treat him without the CTO, but with some extra procedural safeguards. It remains impossible to force treatment upon a patient who has capacity and refuses his consent.

The first circumstance is where there is a valid consent, given either by the patient who has capacity to give it (s 64C(2)(a)) or by a donee or deputy or the Court of Protection on his behalf (s 64C(2)(b)). The donee or deputy must be authorised to do this (s 64K(3),(4)). It follows that they cannot give consent if the patient has capacity. Treatment with consent may be given by anyone qualified to give it, which could cause problems if, for example, a general practitioner prescribed treatment without reference to the responsible clinician.

The second circumstance is where the patient lacks capacity (within the meaning of the MCA) and it is possible to give him the treatment without using force (for example, by giving him an injection to which he offers no resistance). A person is only authorised to do this if she is an approved clinician in charge of the treatment or the treatment is given under the direction of that clinician (s 64D(1) and (5)). The person giving the treatment must first take reasonable steps to establish whether the patient lacks capacity (s 64D(2)). She must then form the reasonable belief that the patient does lack capacity (s 64D(3)). She must also have no reason to believe that the patient objects to being given the treatment or, if she does have reason to believe that the patient objects, it must not be necessary to use force to give the patient the treatment in question (s 64D(4)). In considering whether there is reason to believe that the patient objects, she must consider all the circumstances so far as they are reasonably ascertainable, including the patient's behaviour, wishes, feelings, views, beliefs and values, but need only consider circumstances from the past if it is still appropriate to do so (s 64J). In addition, the treatment must not conflict with an advance decision made by the patient which the clinician is satisfied is valid and applicable or with a decision made by a donee or deputy or the Court of Protection (s 64D(6) and (7)). So an advance decision is effective in the community when it will not be effective in hospital and a donee or deputy can veto treatment in the community which they could not veto in hospital.

The third circumstance is where emergency treatment is necessary for a patient who lacks capacity. The person giving the treatment (who need not be an approved clinician) must reasonably believe that the patient does not have the capacity to consent (s 64G(2)). The treatment must be immediately necessary (s 64G(3)). This means necessary: (a) to save the patient's life, (b) to prevent a serious deterioration in the patient's condition (and which is not irreversible), (c) to alleviate serious suffering by the patient (and is irreversible or hazardous), or (d) to prevent the patient behaving violently or being a danger to himself or others (and is not irreversible or hazardous); in case (d) the treatment must be the minimum interference necessary to prevent this (s 64G(5)). In these circumstances, force may be used if necessary in order to give treatment which is needed to prevent harm to the patient, but the use of force must be a proportionate response to the likelihood and seriousness of the harm (s 64G(4)). This is puzzling: although an emergency may arise because the patient presents a danger to others (case (d) above), force may only be used to administer the treatment in order to prevent harm to the patient. There are, however, other justifications for using force to prevent a patient causing harm to other people (see section 3 below).

Separate provisions deal with the treatment of community patients under the age of 16 (ss 64E, 64F and 64G). However, the basic rules are the same as for adult community patients but with the difference that the Act uses the term "competence" rather than "capacity". This suggests that there is a difference between the test for capacity under the MCA 2005 (see p 63, earlier) and the test of "Gillick competence" for children under 16 (see p 92, earlier). Perhaps it is thought that a degree of wisdom, maturity or deeper understanding may be required before a child is considered competent, whereas an adult has only to have a basic grasp of the relevant information and be able to use it to make a choice.

Nothing in the Act authorises treatment to be given to a community patient who has the capacity to consent to it and does not give that consent, even in an emergency. If such a patient fails to comply with the conditions of his order, it may be possible to recall him to hospital where he can immediately be treated under section 63 (see p 196, above), but that is not a foregone conclusion.

(c) Special safeguards for particular treatments

There are special safeguards for three different kinds of treatment if given to patients who are liable to be detained or to community patients (and in two cases also to informal patients). This means that patients on leave of absence and community patients are protected by these safeguards, but conditionally discharged restricted patients generally are not. It is important to remember that there must still be a justification for the treatment, whether in section 63, or in consent, or in the power to treat patients without capacity in their own best interests. These safeguards are extra.

(i) Section 58-type treatments

The safeguards in section 58 apply to the administration of medicine by any means at any time during a period for which the patient is liable to be detained (or would be were he not a community patient), once three months or more have elapsed since the first time *in that period* when the patient was given medicine *for his mental disorder* (s 58(1)(b); s 64C(3)). They also apply to any other treatment specified in regulations (s 58(1)(a)), but nothing is currently specified.

Section 58 treatment can only be given in the following circumstances:

(a) Where a patient who is liable to be detained (within the meaning of section 56(3) above) consents, and *either* the approved clinician in charge of the treatment in question *or* an independent doctor appointed by the Care Quality Commission (usually referred to as a "second opinion appointed doctor" or SOAD) certifies (on Form T2) not only that the patient has consented but also that he is capable of understanding the nature, purpose and likely effects of the treatment (s 58(3)(a)).

(b) Where a patient is liable to be detained (within the meaning of section 56(3)) and an independent SOAD (not the responsible clinician or approved clinician in change of the treatment) certifies (on Form T3) either that the patient is not so capable or that he is so capable but has not consented, but that it is appropriate for the treatment to be given (s 58(3)(b)). Thus the approved clinician can certify consensual treatment but only a SOAD can certify treatment without consent. Before certifying non-consensual treatment, the SOAD must consult two other people who have been professionally concerned with the patient's medical treatment, one of whom must be a nurse and the other of whom must be neither a nurse nor a doctor, and neither of whom can be the responsible clinician or the clinician in charge of the treatment in question (s 58(4)).

(c) Where the patient is a community patient, the "certificate requirement" must be met (s 64B(2)(b)). The certification requirement is different from that for hospital patients, because even if the patient consents, a SOAD must certify that it is appropriate for the treatment to be given, or to be given subject to specified conditions, and if so that the conditions are met (s 64C(4)). The SOAD must consult two other people who have been professionally concerned with the patient's medical treatment, neither of whom may be the patient's responsible clinician or person in charge of the treatment in question and one of whom must not be a doctor (s 64H(3)). But this certification requirement does not apply for the first month after the community treatment order is made (s 64B(4)); nor does it apply until three months have gone by since the first time, in a period when he was or would have been liable to be detained, that the patient was given medication for his disorder, whether in or out of hospital (s 58(1)(b)), which could be longer than a month.

(d) Where a community patient is recalled to hospital or becomes liable to be detained once more after the CTO is revoked, section 58 applies as if he had been liable to be detained since the making of the CTO (s 62A(1), (2)); but he carries back into hospital a community certificate, if it expressly provides that it is appropriate for the treatment to be given following recall or revocation, or if stopping the treatment would cause serious suffering to the patient, pending compliance with section 58 if the CTO is revoked (s 62A(3),(5)(a), (6), (7)). SOADs giving certificates for community treatment should therefore think about what would be appropriate if the patient were to be recalled to hospital.

200

There are two oddities about these rules. First, while the approved clinician can certify the consensual treatment of a patient detained in hospital without any independent scrutiny, the consensual treatment of a community patient has to be certified by a SOAD. Yet it might be thought that hospital patients required more rather than less protection than those in the community, as there is much more reason to suspect that their consent may not be "real". Another oddity is that the Act does not require the SOAD to certify that there is legal authority to treat a community patient, so on the face of it he is concerned only with whether the treatment is appropriate and not with whether the patient has or has not capacity and, if he has, whether he has consented. Yet it may be hard to disentangle the appropriateness of the treatment from these questions (MHAC, 2009a).

(ii) Section 58A treatments

The safeguards in section 58A apply to ECT and any other form of treatment specified in regulations. Currently only medication associated with giving ECT is specified (Mental Health (Hospital, Guardianship and Treatment) Regulations 2008, SI 2008/1184, (MHHGT Regs), reg 27(3)(a); for Wales see Mental Health (Hospital, Guardianship, Community Treatment and Consent to Treatment) (Wales) Regulations 2008/2439). This treatment can only be given in the following circumstances:

(a) A patient aged 18 or more who is liable to be detained (within the meaning of section 56(3) above) can be given it with his consent if either the approved clinician in charge or a SOAD has certified in writing (on Form T4) that he is capable of understanding its nature, purpose and likely effects and has consented (s 58A(3)).

(b) A patient under 18 who is liable to be detained (as above) can be given it with his consent if a SOAD (not the approved clinician in charge) certifies that he is capable of understanding the nature, purpose and likely effects of the treatment and has consented to it, *and* that it is appropriate for the treatment to be given (s 58A(4)).

(c) A patient of any age who is liable to be detained can be given it if a SOAD (not the responsible clinician or clinician in charge) certifies (on Form T6) that he is not capable of understanding the nature, purpose and likely effects of the treatment, but that it is appropriate for the treatment to be given. However, the SOAD must also certify that this would not conflict with an advance decision which the SOAD is satisfied is valid and applicable, or with a decision made by a donee or deputy or the Court of Protection (s 58A(5)). Before certifying, the SOAD must consult other professionals in the same way as is required under section 58 (s 58A(6)).

(d) As with section 58-type treatment, section 58A-type treatment can only be given to a community patient if the certificate requirement is met. This is the same as the certificate required for section 58 treatments (ss 64B(2), 64C(4)). But the one-month period of grace does not apply (cf s 64B(4)).

(e) As with section 58-type treatment, a community certificate follows a community patient back into hospital when he is recalled or his CTO is revoked, if it expressly provides for this or stopping the treatment would cause serious suffering to the patient, pending compliance with section 58A (s 62A(1), (4), (5)(a), (6)).

(f) A patient under 18 who is not liable to be detained (within the meaning of section 56(3)) and is not a community patient is also protected by section 58A (s 56(5)). This means that he can only be given ECT and associated medication in the same circumstances as if he were detained: that is, if (b) or (c) above applies. However, the source of the power to impose such treatment on a patient who is not capable of consenting to it is the MCA: the exclusion of regulated treatments from the MCA does not apply to section 58A treatment of informal patients under the age of 18 (MCA s 28(1A)).

ECT is therefore an exception to the general rule that compulsory admission can override an advance refusal of treatment by a patient who has lost capacity and that donees and deputies cannot veto the hospital treatment of detained patients. It is also no longer possible to impose ECT upon a patient of any age who has the capacity to decide for himself and refuses his consent.

(iii) Section 57 treatments

Section 57 lays down even more stringent safeguards for any surgical operation for destroying brain tissue or destroying the functioning of brain tissue, or any other treatment specified in regulations. Currently these cover the surgical implantation of hormones for the purpose of reducing male sexual drive (MHHGT Regs, reg 27(1)(a)). But this does not include the subcutaneous injection of a depot of Goserelin, a "hormone analogue" which reduces testosterone to castrate levels (*R v Mental Health Act Commission, ex p X* (1988) 9 BMLR 77). This section applies to *any* patient, detained, community or informal, in or out of hospital (s 56(1)).

These treatments may only be given if *both* of two conditions are fulfilled:

(a) a SOAD and two other people who are not doctors must certify (on Form T1) that the patient is capable of understanding the nature, purpose and likely effects of the treatment and has consented to it; it was said in *ex p X* that the section only requires the capacity to understand rather than actual understanding, but actual understanding would be required for actual consent and the Mental Health Act Commission (1991, para 6.12) advised to that effect; *and*

(b) that SOAD (after the same consultation as is required under section 58) must certify (also on Form T1) that the treatment should be given, having regard to the likelihood of its alleviating or preventing a deterioration of the patient's condition.

Thus patients who lack capacity cannot be given section 57 treatments at all, either under the MHA or under the MCA (see MCA, s 28). Capable informal and compulsory patients can only be given them with consent, a multi-disciplinary assessment of their capacity to understand the treatment, and an independent assessment of whether it should be done. Some might prefer that psycho-surgery be banned altogether (Gostin, 1982) but in the tiny number of cases where it is authorised each year, it appears to have done some good (MHAC, 2009a).

Even informed consent is not always enough. A patient who runs the risk of a long period of confinement in prison or a high security hospital if he cannot be cured may be ready to agree to anything which holds out the prospect of a cure. In *R v Mental Health Act Commission, ex p X*, above, an informal outpatient with a long record of paedophile offences was so anxious to have the Goserelin treatment that he challenged the SOAD's refusal to certify that he could have it. Had section 57 applied, the judge would have quashed the refusal because the Commissioner had applied too high a test of capacity, had no good reason for holding the patient capable on one visit and incapable on the next, and had not applied his mind to the beneficial effects of the treatment before concentrating on the alternatives which might be available or preferable. The judge was obviously reluctant to deprive an intelligent and consenting patient of treatment which he and his doctor thought was doing good, just because the Commissioner thought that his case might be handled differently. But maybe the section did not apply at all, because the young man was not a "patient" being treated for "mental disorder" but a sexual deviant being treated for his deviancy (Fennell, 1988).

(iv) Emergencies and other provisions ancillary to sections 57, 58 and 58A

Any consent or certificate given may relate to a "plan of treatment" under which the patient is to be given one or more of the forms of treatment to which the section applies, and the plan need not have a defined time limit (ss 59, 64H(1)).

A patient covered by section 56 who has given consent to a regulated treatment may withdraw his consent to further treatment (s 60(1)). A patient who has given consent but becomes incapable before the treatment is completed is treated as having withdrawn his consent (s 60(1A) and (1B)). A patient who was certified as lacking capacity may recover capacity (s 60(1C)). In each case, the remainder of the treatment must be treated as a separate form of treatment (s 60(1), (1B), (1D)) and certified again if need be. But this does not prevent treatment continuing if the approved clinician thinks that stopping it would cause serious suffering to the patient (s 62(2)).

Where treatment is given to any patient under section 57, or to a patient who falls within section 56 without consent under sections 58 or 58A, or with the consent of an under-18-year-old under section 58A, or to a recalled community patient under a community certificate, the approved clinician in charge of the treatment must report to the Care Quality Commission (CQC) when the detention comes up for renewal (s 61(1)(a)) or, for restricted patients, after the first six months of the order or direction and thereafter when he reports to the Justice Secretary (s 61(2)). The CQC can also require a report at any other time (s 61(1)(b)). The CQC can cancel the certificate at any time (s 61(3)). Where treatment is given to a community patient under a community certificate, the person in charge must report to the CQC if required to do so (s 64H(4)). The CQC can then cancel the certificate (s 64H(5)). Cancelling any certificate does not prevent treatment continuing if the person in charge thinks that stopping it would cause serious suffering to the patient (ss 62(2), 64H(8)).

Section 62(1) provides that, for patients covered by section 56:

"Sections 57 and 58 above shall not apply to any treatment—(a) which is immediately necessary to save the patient's life; or (b) which (not being irreversible) is immediately necessary to prevent a serious deterioration of his condition; or (c) which (not being irreversible or hazardous) is immediately necessary to alleviate serious suffering by the patient; or (d) which (not being

203

irreversible or hazardous) is immediately necessary and represents the minimum interference necessary to prevent the patient from behaving violently or being a danger to himself or others."

Section 58A does not apply to ECT (and associated medication) if (a) or (b) above applies (s 62(1A); reg 27(4)). Treatment is "irreversible" if it has unfavourable irreversible physical or psychological consequences and "hazardous" if it entails significant physical hazard (s 62(3)). It is hard to see, therefore, how (b), (c) or (d) could apply to psycho-surgery. Section 62 is *not* a blanket permission to impose treatment upon any patient in those four circumstances. The effect is simply to *exempt* those listed emergency situations from the need to comply with the extra safeguards laid down in sections 57, 58 and 58A.

The position is essentially the same for community patients. If there is a valid consent by or on behalf of the patient, the treatment may be given without certification if it is immediately necessary (s 64B(3)(b)). Treatment given to community patients without capacity which is immediately necessary can also be given without certification (s 64(3)(a)). Section 58 treatment is immediately necessary in the four situations listed in section 64G(5), which are the same as those in listed section 62(1)(a) to (d) above; but ECT (and associated medication) is only immediately necessary if it falls within (a) or (b) (s 64G(6)). This also applies if a community patient is recalled to hospital or his CTO is revoked (s 62A(1), (3)(b)).

(v) The safeguards in operation

In the first four years after these safeguards were introduced by the 1983 Act, there was an average of 183 requests for second opinions a month. In February 2009, there were 1,383 requests (MHAC, 2009a). Most of these relate to long term medication. The MHAC was in two minds. The requirement to certify even the consensual long term medication of community patients was quite a burden, especially as these patients can be harder to track down than patients detained in hospital; but the Commission was worried that detained patients might be certified by the approved clinician as consenting when in fact they either lacked the capacity to consent or their consent was not real. It was curious that the proportion of patients admitted from the criminal justice system who consented to their treatment was much higher than the proportion of civil patients who did so (Healthcare Commission, 2008). Offenders may feel much more pressure from their situation than do civil patients. Clinicians were warned not to confuse compliance with consent.

Not surprisingly, there has been a marked fall in certification requests for ECT after November 2008, when this could no longer be given to patients with capacity without their consent. But the proportion of those deemed incapable of consenting also rose from 60 per cent to 75 per cent in the period between the passing of the 2007 amendments and their coming into force. The MHAC has been troubled about capacity-based thresholds for intervention (MHAC, 2005; 2008; 2009a). They could in practice lead to more stringent tests of capacity being applied, no doubt unconsciously, in order to legitimate the treatment which the clinicians thought best. It is also troubling that ECT was used on an emergency basis before nearly a quarter of requests for SOAD certification (and that an unknown number of emergency uses did the trick without the need for further certification). It may seem surprising that ECT can sometimes save the life of an elderly, profoundly depressed patient who has lost the will to live and simply stopped eating and drinking.

There has also been a marked rise in the proportion of second opinions which lead to some change in the patient's treatment. In 1990–1991 Fennell (1996) found that only one per cent led to significant changes and six per cent to slight changes. By 1997, the rate of change had risen to 15 per cent and in 2008 it was 27 per cent. This may depend in part upon how the SOADs see their role: is it simply to check that the clinician's decision is one which a reasonable clinician might make? Or is it to decide what the SOAD would do herself if she were in charge?

3. MANAGEMENT AND CONTROL

Under the old lunacy legislation, there was some regulation of what went on in licensed houses, hospitals and asylums, under the overall supervision of the Board of Control. The law was also specific about what should be done when "individual mechanical restraint" was imposed. There is, or should be, a distinction between providing a patient with the medical treatment which he either wants or needs and controlling his disruptive or violent behaviour, whether for his own good or that of others. The MHA Code, for example, points out that hospital guidelines should distinguish between psychological behaviour therapy interventions (such as "time out") and seclusion to control severely disturbed behaviour which is likely to cause harm to others (para 15.47). Euphemisms, such as "therapeutic isolation", "single-person wards" or "enforced segregation" should not be used to disguise this (para 15.44). The common law does provide justifications for controlling any patient's behaviour, principally through the power to prevent him doing harm to other people or to himself or to property, and a combination of the MHA and the common law may justify further measures of confinement or control over detained patients. We shall look at each of these before examining their limits and practical application in the treatment and care of mental patients.

(a) Preventing harm and self harm

The ordinary law allows one person to prevent another from doing harm to himself or others in several circumstances. First, any person "may use such force as is reasonable in the prevention of crime" (Criminal Law Act 1967, s 3(1)) The crime must actually be in progress or about to be committed. This cannot apply where there is no crime because the patient is insane within the M'Naghten Rules (see chapter 5). Secondly, any person,

> "in whose presence a breach of the peace is being, or reasonably appears to be about to be, committed has the right to take reasonable steps to make the person who is breaking or threatening to break the peace refrain from doing so; and those reasonable steps in appropriate cases will include detaining him against his will" (*Albert v Lavin* [1982] AC 546, at p 565).

A breach of the peace normally takes place in public, but can occur on private property (see *McConnell v Chief Constable of Greater Manchester Police* [1990] 1 WLR 364). A breach of the peace takes place when:

> "harm is actually done or is likely to be done to a person or in his presence to his property or a person is in fear of being so harmed through an assault, an affray, an unlawful assembly or other disturbance" (*R v Howell* [1982] QB 416, at p 427).

Thirdly, a person may use reasonable force in self defence or to defend other persons or property. This will almost invariably also involve the prevention of crime. But the object is not to assist in preserving law and order, rather, it is to enable individuals to escape being harmed by aggressors, and this includes aggressors who are mentally ill.

All three powers can be summed up by the proposition that there is a right to restrain a patient who is doing, or is about to do, physical harm to another person or to property. But all are subject to the requirement of "reasonableness" (see Harlow, 1974; *R v Shannon* (1980) 71 Cr App R 192). "Reasonableness" has two separate components. The first is that the force used must be no more than is in fact necessary to accomplish the object for which it is allowed. Exact calculation is not expected of people responding to an emergency, but neither is gross over-reaction to the danger, or the continuation of force once the need for it is over. None of these powers permit anything in the nature of retaliation, revenge or punishment for what has happened. The second is that the reaction must be in proportion to the harm threatened. The police cannot shoot to kill in order to prevent someone from using a mobile phone while driving even if it is the only way to stop him. These principles apply to any patient, whether or not he lacks capacity.

But what about a patient who is doing physical harm to himself? We have already seen (p 111, earlier) that the common law allowed anyone to "confine a person disordered in his mind who seems disposed to do mischief to himself or any other person". This may have been limited to people who were actually insane or of unsound mind, rather than reasonably believed to be so (*Fletcher v Fletcher* (1859) 1 El & El 420). It is not clear whether the patient had actually to be dangerous, or whether a reasonable belief in the danger was enough (see Lanham, 1974). However, the point is probably academic now, as the MCA 2005 deals specifically with this sort of case.

We have already seen (above) that section 5 of the MCA 2005 allows staff to take steps in the care and treatment of a person if they reasonably believe that he lacks the capacity to decide upon the matter for himself and that it will be in his best interests for it to be done (s 5(1)(b)). However, restraint is only possible under the MCA if the person imposing it reasonably believes it necessary to prevent harm to the person concerned and it is "proportionate" to the likelihood and seriousness of that harm (s 6(3)). Restraint for this purpose means using or threatening to use force to secure the doing of an act which the person concerned resists, or restricting the person's liberty of movement, whether or not he resists (s 6(4)).

But what can be done when a patient who does have capacity is about to do harm to himself? It is probably always lawful to prevent someone committing suicide, although it is also lawful to allow a hunger-striking prisoner deliberately to starve himself to death (*Home Office v Robb* [1995] 1 FLR 412). Following the Human Rights Act, there is a positive duty, stemming from the right to life protected by article 2 of the ECHR, to take reasonable steps to protect the life of a prisoner or detained patient where there is a real and immediate risk to life about which the authorities knew or ought to have known at the time: see *Savage v South Essex Partnership NHS Foundation Trust* [2008] UKHL 74, [2009] 1 AC 681. But there was already a duty of care at common law. The police and prison authorities have a duty to take care to prevent their prisoners committing suicide. The fact that the injury is self-inflicted does not break the chain of causation, although it may amount to contributory negligence: *Reeves v Metropolitan Police Commissioner* [2000] 1 AC 360. In *Kirkham v Chief Constable of Greater*

Manchester [1990] 2 QB 283, CA, the police were held liable for the suicide of a man detained in a remand centre because they failed to pass on the information about his suicidal tendencies. The same obviously applies to a detained patient. But hospitals have also been held liable for serious failure to supervise a suicidal informal patient: see *Selfe v Ilford and District Hospital Management Committee* (1970) 114 SJ 935. And in *Thorne v Northern Group Hospital Management Committee* (1964) 108 Sol Jo 484, Edmund Davies J said that:

> "As a matter of general principle a hospital is under a duty to take precautions to avoid the possibility of injury, whether self-inflicted or otherwise, occurring to patients whom it knows, or ought to know, have a history of mental illness".

Obviously, there are limits to what can be done to control a patient who is not liable to be detained under the Act and anything done would have to be proportionate to the likelihood and severity of the possible harm. If there is any doubt, it is safer to section the patient under the MHA.

(b) "Detention" and discipline

In *Pountney v Griffiths* [1976] AC 314, where a Broadmoor patient sued a member of staff for allegedly assaulting him to get him to go back to the ward after visiting time, all parties accepted that mental hospitals have powers of control and discipline over their patients. Some control, over and above that necessary to prevent harm, is implicit in the hospital's power to detain compulsory patients. However, the only clear power which is given in the MHA is to detain the patient *in the hospital* (see ss 5(4), 6(2), 40(1) and (2)). Thus there is obviously power to keep the patient within the named hospital or secure unit. But does this give the hospital *carte blanche* to detain the patient in whatever conditions it wishes, subject only to its criminal or civil liability for ill-treatment or neglect?

Some control may also be incidental to the patient's medical treatment. In *Pountney v Griffiths* itself, visiting time was regarded as an aspect of the patient's treatment, and thus the act of inducing him to return to the ward when visiting time was over was incidental to it. In a hospital such as Broadmoor, where the secure and highly disciplined environment is itself regarded as a therapy for the patients, the dividing line between what is permitted in the name of treatment and what can only be justified in the name of detention is particularly difficult to draw. But neither concept should be used to justify any and every regime, however harsh, arbitrary or oppressive.

Finally, some control may be necessary to enable the institution to function as a hospital at all. Glanville Williams (1983, p 484) suggested that the authorities of a psychiatric hospital possess common law powers of discipline similar to those enjoyed by the master of a ship, which involve "no more than restraining passengers or crew who are endangering the vessel or those aboard, or who are seriously disrupting life aboard".

If an informal patient withdraws his consent to abide by the hospital's rules, the proper course is not to impose discipline as such, but either to ask him to leave or (where the criteria exist) to impose compulsory powers. Thus the MHA Code advises that if it becomes necessary to restrain or seclude an informal patient, or to restrain a patient detained in hospital under the MCA DoLS, consideration should be given to whether he should be detained under the MHA instead (paras 15.34, 15.35, 15.46). The need for restraint may show that he objects to some aspect of his treatment, in which case he becomes ineligible for the DoLS.

Compulsory patients cannot so readily be asked to leave and so cannot be permitted to cause serious disruption to hospital life. Once again, however, this should be governed by the concepts of reasonableness: in other words, that any force used is necessary for the purpose permitted and proportionate to the harm presented. The nurse in *Pountney v Griffiths* (above) was entitled to take hold of the patient to escort him back to the ward but would not have been entitled to beat him unconscious.

(c) Restraint, sedation and seclusion

As the MHA Code points out, patients in need of care and treatment for mental disorder may present particular risks to themselves or others which other patients do not. These include hyperactivity, self-harming, aggressive or threatening behaviour towards others, physical violence, substance abuse and leaving without permission (para 15.4). On the other hand, such patients are also particularly vulnerable to over-reaction from often hard-pressed staff. And the techniques used to control them include "physical intervention, rapid tranquillisation and seclusion", where there is always a risk of disproportionate response to the threatened harm. This may violate, not only the common law principles discussed above, but also the rights protected by articles 3 and 8 of the ECHR. The Code of Practice is there, at least in part, to try and prevent this happening.

Hence the Code requires all hospitals to have a policy, the primary focus of which should be on early recognition, prevention and "de-escalation" of potential aggression. Physical restraint, rapid tranquillisation and seclusion should be used only when de-escalation is not enough. They should never be used as punishment or in a punitive manner (paras 15.6 to 15.8). Patients should be encouraged to express their own views about what they would and would not like to be done if their behaviour becomes disturbed or violent (para 15.11). This should be part of their individual care plan. But the general atmosphere and running of the ward can also help to minimise the problems—through such things as patient participation, ensuring an appropriate mix of patients and of patients and staff, giving patients their own space, access to the outside, and enough to do, organising the ward into quiet rooms, recreation rooms, single sex rooms, and encouraging patients to recognise their own trigger factors and how to respond to early warning signs (para 15.16).

Using medication as an unplanned response to disturbed behaviour (presumably this is what is meant by "rapid tranquillisation") should be exceptional (para 15.15). Using physical restraint to manage aggressive behaviour should be a last resort (para 15.23). Any physical restraint used should be reasonable, justifiable and proportionate to the risk posed, used only for as long as absolutely necessary, "involve a recognised technique that does not depend on the deliberate application of pain (the application of pain should be used only for the immediate relief or rescue of staff where nothing else will suffice)", and be carried out by trained staff (para 15.22). Staff should be alert to the risk of respiratory or cardiac distress (para 15.27). The use of "mechanical restraint" should be exceptional. Tying the patient to the building or its fixtures should never be done (para 15.31). But restraint may have to be used to administer medicine (or other treatment) to an unwilling patient when there is power to treat without consent, especially if not administering the treatment would

208

increase the risk of an emergency (paras 15.32, 15.33). Patients should never be deprived of day-time clothing as a means of restricting movement or of other aids necessary for their daily living (para 15.67). It is obviously important that staff should be properly trained in the use of restraining techniques, for this is a major cause of untoward deaths among mental hospital patients (MHAC, 2009a).

Seclusion is "the supervised confinement of a patient in a room, which may be locked. Its sole aim is to contain severely disturbed behaviour which is likely to cause harm to others" (para 15.43). It should be used only as a last resort and for the shortest possible time, never as a punishment or threat, or because of shortage of staff. It should not form part of a treatment programme. It is to protect *others* from harm, not the patient (para 15.45). There should be clear procedures laid down for secluding patients, with an initial multi-disciplinary review as soon as practicable after it begins. Unless that review concludes otherwise, the need for seclusion should be reviewed every two hours by two nurses (or other suitable professionals) and every four hours by a doctor (or suitable approved clinician). A multidisciplinary review should take place if a patient is secluded for more than 8 hours consecutively or 12 hours in a period of 48 hours (paras 15.50, 15.51, 15.54). There should be a suitably qualified professional within sight and sound of the seclusion room at all times, in order to monitor the condition and behaviour of the patient, and identify when seclusion should be ended, reporting at least every 15 minutes (paras 15.55, 15.56).

Seclusion of this sort is obviously a very short term "cooling off period". But the 2008 MHA Code of Practice also identifies a "very small number" of patients who could be described as "long term dangerous". They present a constant risk to others which cannot be reduced by short term seclusion coupled with other treatment. If they are allowed to mix freely in the ward "other patients or staff would continuously be open to the potential of serious injury or harm" (para 15.63). The Code accepts that these patients may have to be segregated from the others, and accompanied whenever they are not locked in their own rooms (para 15.64). Although the use of longer term seclusion of this sort should be periodically reviewed by a senior clinician who is not involved with the case (para 15.66), the Code is not more prescriptive about how these cases should be handled. It accepts that a thorough multi-disciplinary risk assessment will be necessary before such patients can be returned to the "general community" (para 15.65).

Thus the Code appears to contemplate that some patients may be kept in a "prison within a prison". This is a retreat from the position taken in the previous Code, no doubt in response to the case of *R (on the application of Munjaz) v Mersey Care NHS Trust* [2005] UKHL 58, [2006] 2 AC 148. The patient challenged the seclusion policy in Ashworth Hospital because, among other things, it allowed for patients to be kept in seclusion for long periods without the frequent reviews then required by the then Code. The Court of Appeal, [2003] EWCA Civ 1036, [2004] QB 395, held that the policy was unlawful, because the Code should be observed in all hospitals unless there was a good reason to depart from it in a particular case. Otherwise the hospital might be failing in its obligations under article 3 or 8 of the ECHR. The House of Lords disagreed. Four out of the five Law Lords decided that the Ashworth policy, if properly operated, would be sufficient to prevent any possible breach of article 3. Three out of the five decided that it did not involve an interference with private life under article 8 or, if it did, that this was justified. Lord Steyn, who dissented on both articles, observed that:

"given the manifest dangers inherent in seclusion, and the extreme vulnerability of the patients, . . . a dilution of minimum centrally imposed safeguards by pragmatic policy decisions from hospital to hospital is not appropriate" (para 46).

Lord Brown, who dissented on article 8, considered that seclusion did constitute an interference with private life and hospital policy was not enough to make this "in accordance with the law" for the purpose of article 8(2).

Lord Steyn would, however, have gone further than the Court of Appeal and held that article 5 was also engaged. The general principle in English law is that, if imprisonment is lawful, it is not made unlawful by the conditions in the prison in which the prisoner is held: *Hague v Deputy Governor of Parkhurst Prison, Weldon v Home Office* [1992] 1 AC 58. The general principle under the ECHR is that, as long as a person is detained in an institution which is appropriate to the justification for the detention (an offender in a prison, a psychiatric patient in a psychiatric hospital, a child in an educational establishment, and so on), article 5 is not concerned with the conditions of detention: *Ashingdane v UK* (1985) 7 EHRR 528. But the Strasbourg Court has not ruled out that in exceptional circumstances, measures adopted within a prison might disclose interferences with the right to liberty: *Bollan v UK, App no 42117/98*, 4 May 2000. Generally, however, the issues arise under article 3 or article 8 rather than article 5.

Although times have changed a good deal since five weeks' of solitary confinement were imposed upon a patient suspected of causing a fire (see *A v United Kingdom*, App no 6840/74), it is perhaps unfortunate that the Code has responded by leaving so much to the discretion of individual hospitals. But even if its policy complies with the Code, a hospital will be liable under the Human Rights Act if it does in fact breach the human rights of any of its patients.

4. PATIENTS' RIGHTS TO INFORMATION AND CONTACT

(a) Explanations

Article 5(2) of the European Convention on Human Rights requires that "everyone who is arrested shall be informed promptly, in a language which he understands, of the reasons for his arrest and of any charge against him". In *X v United Kingdom* (1982) 4 EHRR 188, the European Court of Human Rights found it unnecessary to decide whether this also applied to detained mental patients. Judge Evrigenis dissented. The right to an explanation:

"constitutes a safeguard of personal liberty whose importance in any democratic system founded on the rule of law cannot be underestimated. Quite apart from enabling the person detained to make proper preparations for bringing legal proceedings (under Article 5(4)), it is the embodiment of a kind of legitimate confidence or expectation . . . in the relations between the individual and the public powers" (p 213).

No doubt for that reason, the MHA 1983 requires that whenever any patient is detained, the hospital managers must do their best to ensure that he understands his legal position (s 132(1)). Steps have to be taken "as soon as practicable" after the detention has begun, and again if the section under which the patient is detained changes, for example from a section 2 admission for assessment to a section 3 admission for treatment. The steps required are such "as are practicable to ensure that the patient understands" and they must include giving the required information both orally and in writing (s 132(3)). If it is impossible to explain matters to the patient when he is admitted, the managers should continue their efforts until it does become possible. Similar steps have to be taken to explain the legal position to community patients as soon as practicable after the CTO is made (s 132A(1), (2)).

The information required is considerable. A hospital patient must understand under which section he is detained, the effect of that section, and his right to apply to a tribunal (s 132(1)). The hospital must also explain who has the power to discharge him, including the possible bar on a discharge by his nearest relative and the relative's right to challenge this before a tribunal; the hospital's powers to censor his correspondence; the Act's provisions relating to the treatment of detained patients and the extra safeguards where certain treatments are proposed; and the protective powers of the Care Quality Commission (the Welsh Ministers in Wales) and the effect of the Code of Practice (s 132(2)). A community patient must be told of the effect of the provisions of the Act applying to him and of his rights to apply to a tribunal (s 132A(1)). Unless the patient asks otherwise, the hospital must also "take such steps as are practicable" to supply his nearest relative (if any) with a copy of this information, either at the same time as it is given to the patient or within a reasonable time afterwards (ss 132(4), 132A(3)). A guardianship patient and the person appearing to be his nearest relative must be told of their rights to apply to a tribunal and of the relative's power of discharge (MHHGT Regs, reg 26(3), (4)).

There is also a statutory duty to inform the patient when his detention, guardianship or CTO is renewed, including retrospective renewals after having gone absent without leave (ss 20(3), 20(6), 20A(5), reg 26(1)(d), (g), (n)) and when his nearest relative is prevented from discharging him from hospital (s 25(2)). The nearest relative obviously must be informed of the latter and, unless the patient requests otherwise, of all transfers, renewals or extensions of compulsory powers; for hospital and community patients, this is the responsibility of the hospital managers; for guardianship patients, it is the responsibility of the local social services authority (reg 26(1)). Unless the patient or the relative has asked that this should not be done, the hospital "must take such steps as are practicable" to warn the nearest relative of the patient's impending discharge from detention or on a community treatment order, if possible at least seven days beforehand (s 133).

The MHA Code emphasises that "effective communication is essential in ensuring appropriate care and respect for patients' rights" (para 2.1). The purpose is to ensure that patients understand, not only their legal position, but also why they are in hospital and are engaged in the process of making decisions about themselves while they are there. So they should be given a copy of the formal documentation unless this might have adverse consequences to them or others (para 2.14). They should be told when their compulsion comes to an end and what happens next (para 2.26).

Although there is no legal obligation to do so, the Code insists that informal patients be made aware of their rights and given a clear explanation of the hospital's policy about moving around the hospital and grounds (para 2.45). Otherwise there is a risk of unlawful deprivation of liberty.

This emphasis on informing and engaging the patient and other people whom he would like to be involved (MHA Code, paras 2.34–2.38) is a far cry from the secrecy of the not-so-distant past. Then it was assumed that the professionals knew best and that it might be harmful to the patients' welfare for them to know their rights. Curiously, however, neither the main MCA Code nor the DoLS Code place any emphasis on helping a person who lacks capacity to understand his rights, other than through an independent mental capacity advocate, if there is one (see section 5, below).

(b) Mail, email and telephone calls

Contact with the outside world is a particularly important safeguard for people in any sort of institution, the more closed the institution the more important the contact. The forcibly treated patient in *Herzegfalvy v Austria* (1993) 15 EHRR 437 lost his claim under article 3 but won his claim under article 8 because the hospital had been tampering with his mail without justification.

The 1983 Act greatly reduced the scope for censoring detained patients' mail. Nevertheless, the hospital managers, acting through a member of staff as authorised censor (s 134(7)), may open and inspect any postal packet addressed to or by a detained patient in order to discover whether it qualifies for censorship (s 134(4)). In practice, however, this is unlikely to happen outside the high security hospitals. In any other type of hospital, the only interference allowed is to withhold from a postal operator any outgoing mail addressed by a detained patient to a person who has asked that communications to him from the patient should be withheld (s 134(1)(a)). Such a request must be made in writing, either to the hospital managers, or to the responsible clinician or to the Secretary of State.

In high security hospitals or units, staff may also withhold outgoing mail if the censor considers that it is likely to cause danger to anyone (including someone on the hospital staff), or to cause distress to anyone (other than someone on the hospital staff) (s 134(1)(b)). Incoming mail may be withheld if this is thought necessary in the interests of the safety of the patient (not just his health or well-being) or for the protection of other people (s 134(2)). However, neither of these wider powers applies to mail to or from any of the following: any Minister of the Crown or the Scottish Ministers or Member of either House of Parliament or the Scottish Parliament, their Welsh equivalents, a judge or officer of the Court of Protection or Court of Protection Visitor or anyone asked to compile a report for that Court, any of the public sector ombudsmen for England, Wales or Scotland, the Care Quality Commission (or Welsh Ministers), the tribunal, an NHS body, local social services authority, Community Health Council, local probation board or provider of probation services, an NHS provider of a patient advocacy and liaison service at that hospital, a provider of independent mental health or independent mental capacity advocacy services for the patient (see below), the managers of the hospital where the patient is detained, any *legally qualified* person instructed by the patient to act as his legal adviser, or the European Court of Human Rights (s 134(3), (3A), reg 31). However, there is nothing to stop any individual named on this list putting in a request under section 134(1)(a) that mail from a particular patient be withheld.

If mail is opened but nothing is withheld, the hospital censor must nevertheless enclose a note, giving his name and that of the hospital and explaining what has happened, before resealing the packet (MHHGT Regs, reg 29(1)). If anything is withheld, he must record in a special register the fact that it has been withheld, the date when this was done, the grounds for doing so, a description of the contents of the package or any item withheld, and his name (s 134(5); reg 29(2)(a)). He must also enclose a note that the packet has been opened, that an item or items have been withheld, a description of them, his name and the name of the hospital, and in either of the two high security hospital cases, an explanation of the Care Quality Commission's (or Welsh Ministers') powers of review (reg 29(2)(b)).

This last regulation is because the Act requires such notice to be given within seven days to the patient and also to the person (if known) by whom an incoming packet was sent (s 134(6); and reg 29(3)(a)). The note which must be enclosed in the packet can be sufficient notice to the addressee for this purpose (reg 29(3)(b)). The sender will require a separate notice.

If asked to do so (in any way they think sufficient, not necessarily in writing; reg 30(1)), either by the patient or by the sender of incoming mail, the CQC must review the hospital's decision (s 134A(1)). The application must be made within six months of getting the notice that the mail was withheld and should include that notice (s 134A(2); reg 30(2)). The CQC can direct the production of any documents, information or evidence that they reasonably require (reg 30(3)), including, of course, the offending letter itself. They have complete discretion to overrule the hospital's decision, for whatever reason they think fit (s 134A(3)).

This was, as the MHAC (2009a) pointed out, the only provision in the Act where the hospital had to comply with its direction. But there have never been many appeals. Over the 26 year life-time of the MHAC, there were around 150 (data for 1991–1993 are missing) and roughly one third of these were wholly or partly successful. A letter from a patient who had been moved from one high security hospital to another to a patient at his first hospital, discussing the staff there, was released: staff distress was not a good enough reason to withhold. But unsolicited fan-mail to a notorious offender patient was withheld to protect the authors from risk.

The MHA says nothing about telephone calls, email and the internet, but article 8 will apply to them as it does to ordinary mail. According to the Code, the principle should be that, as detained patients are not free to leave the premises, their individual freedom to communicate with family and friends should be maintained as far as possible (para 16.4). Restrictions should be kept to a minimum, but of course the use of mobile phones (especially those with cameras) can interfere with the peace and privacy of other patients, staff and visitors and have an anti-therapeutic effect or constitute a security risk. So it may be necessary to restrict the areas or the times when mobile phones can be used (para 16.6). But it would be more worrying still if patients were denied access to a phone at all, or only allowed to use one within hearing of staff, unless there were a very good reason for this. The same principles should apply to people who are subject to the DoLS, but there is nothing in the MCA or the Code about this.

(c) Visitors

The MHA also says nothing about other means of keeping in touch with the outside world, but article 8 also protects the right to respect for private and family life, so any interference with such contacts would have to be necessary and proportionate to a legitimate aim. The MHA Code takes the view that "maintaining links with family and community is a key element in a patient's care and treatment" (para 19.2). This includes visits by children, as long as this is consistent with their best interests and safety (para 19.18). Prohibiting a visit by anyone a patient has asked or agreed to see should be regarded as a serious interference with his rights (para 19.11). It might be justified on clinical grounds if the responsible clinician, after assessment and discussion with the multi-disciplinary team, deems it detrimental to the safety or wellbeing of the patient, the visitor, other patients or staff on the ward (para 19.12). It may be justified on security grounds if the behaviour of the visitor is or has been so disruptive as to make this necessary, for example by smuggling illicit substances into the hospital, incitement to abscond, or "attempts by the media to gain unauthorised access" (para 19.13). Denying visitors to an informal patient might, of course, be an indication that he is deprived of his liberty (see chapter 1). All refusals should be properly explained, documented and monitored. Once again, the same principles ought to apply to people who are subject to the DoLS, who are just as entitled to the benefit of article 8 as anyone else, but of course may be deprived of particular contacts if this is in their best interests.

Some people have a statutory right to visit a particular patient or resident. These include SOADs, independent doctors or clinicians appointed to examine a patient detained under the MHA for the purpose of a tribunal hearing or to advise the nearest relative or an NHS body on their powers of discharge (MHA, ss 76, 24), appropriate tribunal members (Tribunal Procedure (First-Tier Tribunal) (Health, Education and Social Care Chamber) Rules 2008, SI 2008/2699, r 34), people visiting patients detained under the MHA or the MCA DoLS on behalf of the Care Quality Commission (or Welsh Ministers) (MHA, s 120; Mental Capacity (Deprivation of Liberty: Monitoring and Reporting; and Assessments—Amendment) Regulations 2009, reg 4); independent mental health or mental capacity advocates (MHA, s 130B; MCA, s 35); officers of the Public Guardian (MCA, s 58); and Court of Protection Visitors (MCA, s 61).

5. ADVOCACY

Both the MHA and MCA have introduced requirements to appoint independent advocates to help and support mentally disordered or incapacitated people in a range of situations where they may have no-one to do this apart from the professionals who are looking after them.

(a) Independent mental health advocates (IMHAs)

Mental health patients qualify for an advocate if they are:

- Liable to be detained under any provision of the MHA apart from sections 4, 5, 135 or 136 (s 130C(2)(a)); this includes patients on leave of absence and conditionally discharged restricted patients, but not community patients unless they have been recalled.
- Subject to MHA guardianship (s 130C(2)(b)).
- A community patient (s 130C(2)(c)).
- Discussing with a doctor or approved clinician the possibility of having, and having, treatment regulated under section 57 (s 130C(3)(a), (4)).
- Under 18 and discussing with a doctor or approved clinician the possibility of having, and having, treatment regulated under section 58A (s 130C(3)(a), (4)).

Whatever steps are practicable must be taken, and as soon as practicable, to ensure that the patient understands that such help is available to him and how to obtain it (s 130D(1), (3)). The information should be given both orally and in writing and, in the case of patients subject to civil compulsory powers (but not those liable to be detained under Part 3) copied to the nearest relative unless the patient asks otherwise (s 130D(4), (5)). This should be done by the managers of the hospital where the patient is liable to be detained or which is responsible for a community patient, the local social services authority responsible for a guardianship patient, the clinician responsible (RC) for a conditionally discharged restricted patient, or the doctor or approved clinician with whom the patient first discusses having the treatment in question (s 130D(2)).

The patient does not have to take up the offer: nothing in the MHA prevents him from declining to be provided with the help of an advocate (s 130B(6)).

In principle (but only in principle), advocates should, so far as practicable, be independent of anyone who is professionally concerned with the patient's medical treatment (s 130A(4)). This does not disqualify advocates and others who act as representatives for patients and people who lack capacity (s 130A(5); Mental Health Act 1983 (Independent Mental Health Advocates) (England) Regulations 2008, SI 2008/3166, (the IMHA Regs) reg 7; for Wales, see Mental Health (Independent Mental Health Advocates) (Wales) Regulations 2008, SI 2008/2437). They must have appropriate experience and/or training, be of integrity and good character and have an enhanced criminal records bureau certificate which includes information on their suitability to work with children (if the patient is under 18) or vulnerable adults (if he is over 18). They must also be able to act independently, not only of anyone who is professionally concerned in the patient's medical treatment but also of anyone who asks them to visit or interview the patient (IMHA Regs, reg 6).

Their role is, broadly, to help the patient obtain information about and understand his legal position under the Act, the medical treatment he is being given or is being proposed or discussed, the legal position in relation to that, his rights and any help in exercising those rights (s 130B(1), (2)). They have the right to visit and interview the patient in private and to visit and interview anyone who is professionally concerned with his medical treatment (s 130B(3)(a), (b)). They also have the right to inspect any records relating to his detention or treatment or his after-care or held by the LSSA about him (s 130B(3)(c),(d)). But if the patient has the capacity to consent, his consent to inspecting the records is necessary. If he does not have that capacity the inspection must not conflict with a decision made by a donee or deputy or the Court of Protection and the person holding the records must think that they may be relevant and that inspecting them is appropriate (s 130B(4)).

IMHAs are obliged to comply with any reasonable request to visit and interview the patient made to them by the person appearing to be the patient's nearest relative, the patient's responsible clinician or an AMHP (s 130B(5)).

(b) Independent mental capacity advocates: non DoLS situations

An independent mental capacity advocate (IMCA) must be instructed for a person who lacks capacity in relation to a number of important decisions, usually if he has no-one apart from professional or paid carers to look after his interests. So an IMCA does not have to be appointed if the person who lacks capacity has nominated someone to be consulted about the matter in question; or where he has a donee of a lasting power of attorney or a deputy who is authorised to make the decision for him (MCA, s 40(1)). An IMCA must be instructed in the following situations:

(i) Serious medical treatment

An NHS body must instruct an IMCA if they propose to provide serious medical treatment for a patient without the capacity to agree to it, either themselves or by arrangement with another provider. This must be done before the treatment is provided (s 37(1)(a), (3)). But if the treatment has to be provided urgently, they may go ahead even if they have not been able to instruct an IMCA beforehand (s 37(4)). The implication is that they should try to do so if they can.

"Serious medical treatment" is treatment which has serious consequences or for which the pros and cons are finely balanced. It involves providing, withholding or withdrawing treatment in three circumstances:

(a) where only one type of treatment is proposed, there is a fine balance between its benefits to the patient and the burdens and risks it is likely to entail for him;
(b) where the choice between different treatments being considered is finely balanced; or
(c) where what is proposed would be likely to involve serious consequences for the patient,

(s 37(6); Mental Capacity Act 2005 (Independent Mental Capacity Advocates) (General) Regulations 2006, SI 2006/1832 (the IMCA General Regs), reg 4; for Wales see Mental Capacity Act 2005 (Independent Mental Capacity Advocates) (Wales) Regulations 2007, SI 2007/852). The MCA Code suggests that serious consequences may include serious and prolonged pain, distress or side effects; potentially major consequences for the patient; or a serious impact on the patient's future life chances (para 10.44). Examples might be: chemotherapy and surgery for cancer; ECT; therapeutic sterilisation; major surgery or amputations; treatments resulting in permanent loss of hearing or sight; withholding or denying artificial nutrition and hydration; and abortion (para 10.45). Some of these decisions are so serious that only the court may make them (see above). But an IMCA should still be instructed. However, the requirement does not apply to treatment which is regulated under Parts 4 and 4A of the MHA (MCA, s 37 (2)).

Nor does it arise unless there is no-one, apart from a professional or paid carer, whom it would be appropriate to consult when deciding what will be in the patient's best interests (s 37(1)(b)). The patient may have no friends or family, or they may be unable or unwilling to act for some reason. The fact that they may disagree with what is proposed does not mean that it is inappropriate to consult them (Code, para 10.79).

(ii) Arranging or changing long term hospital or care home accommodation

An NHS body must instruct an IMCA if they propose to arrange accommodation for a person without capacity in a hospital or care home or to move him to another hospital or care home (s 38(1), (3)). This does not apply if the hospital stay is likely to last less than 28 days or the care home stay is likely to last less than 8 weeks or if either has to be arranged urgently; but if it then turns out that the person is likely to stay longer, an IMCA must be instructed (s 38(3),(9),(4)).

Similarly, a local authority must instruct an IMCA if they propose to arrange or change accommodation for a person who lacks capacity. This applies to all accommodation arranged under sections 21 or 29 of the National Assistance Act 1948 or section 117 of the MHA as a result of an assessment under section 47 of the National Health Service and Community Care Act 1990 (s 39(1), (2)), so it can include accommodation in places other than registered care homes (see chapter 9). Once again, this does not apply if the stay is likely to last for less than eight weeks or has to be arranged urgently; but if it later turns out that it is likely to last longer, an IMCA must be instructed (s 39(4), (5)).

Neither of these applies unless the NHS body or local authority are satisfied that there is no-one, apart from a professional or paid carer, whom it would be appropriate to consult when deciding what will be best for the proposed patient or resident (ss 38(1), 39(1)). Nor do they apply if the person is to be admitted to a place covered by a DoLS authorisation and an IMCA has to be appointed under section 39A or section 39C (see (c), below) (ss 38(2A), 39(3A)); or if the patient or resident has to be accommodated there under the compulsory powers in the MHA (ss 38(2), 39(3)). Examples are where he has been compulsorily admitted to hospital, or is required by an MHA guardian to live in a particular place, or living there is a condition of his leave of absence, of a community treatment order or of a conditional discharge. In all of these situations, he will normally be entitled to an IMHA (see (a), above).

(iii) Reviewing long term accommodation

Where (i) or (ii) above do not apply, there is a power—but not a duty—to instruct an IMCA when an NHS body or a local authority are reviewing or propose to review the accommodation of someone whom they have been accommodating for 12 weeks or more. They may instruct an IMCA if this would be "of particular benefit" to the person concerned (s 41; Mental Capacity Act 2005 (Independent Mental Capacity Advocates) (Expansion of Role) Regulations 2006, SI 2006/2883, regs 3 and 5). Curiously, this does not apply where there is a donee of a lasting power of attorney or of an enduring power of attorney or a court-appointed deputy, irrespective of whether they are authorised to make decisions about accommodation (reg 3(1)(d)). This must be a mistake.

(iv) Protecting against abuse

Again where (i) or (ii) do not apply, there is power to instruct an IMCA if it would be "of particular benefit" to a person without capacity when there has been an allegation that he is being or has been abused or neglected by another person, or that he is abusing or neglecting another person, and an NHS body or local authority propose to take or have taken protective measures under the *No Secrets* guidance (see p 303, later) (Expansion of Role Regulations, reg 4). The usual requirement that there must be no-one else whom it is appropriate to consult does not apply, for the obvious reason that this may be the very person who present a risk to the person concerned.

(c) Independent mental capacity advocates under the DoLS

There are three different kinds of independent mental capacity advocates appointed under the MCA deprivation of liberty scheme: a section 39A IMCA, a section 39C IMCA, and a section 39D IMCA. A advocate is one or the other, because they cannot co-exist (MCA, Sch A1, para 158). The object is to ensure that the person who may be deprived of his liberty has an independent person to protect his interest, when otherwise there is no-one to consult about him. Once made subject to the DoLS, the person concerned must have a representative (see p 133, earlier). The IMCA is there to fill in the gaps: before a representative is appointed; between representatives; and where an unpaid representative may not be sufficient to protect the person concerned.

(i) A section 39A IMCA

The supervisory body must instruct a section 39A IMCA when a person first becomes the subject of the procedure leading to the authorisation of deprivation of liberty (s 39A(1)(a)). That is:

- where an urgent authorisation is given, or
- where a request for a standard authorisation is made, apart from one which is to follow on immediately after a current authorisation expires (for then the person concerned will already have a representative), or
- where there is an independent investigation into whether or not a person is being detained (s 39B).

These only apply if the managing authority of the hospital or care home involved are satisfied that there is no-one, apart from a professional or paid carer for the person concerned, whom it would be appropriate to consult when deciding upon his best interests (s 39A(1)(b)). The managing authority has to notify the supervisory body if the section applies (s 39A(2)). This leaves a good deal to the judgment of the managing authority—how remote and uninterested does a relative or friend have to be before it becomes inappropriate to consult them? What if the relative is very interested and concerned but at loggerheads with the hospital or home? As we have seen, the fact that they disagree does not mean that it is not appropriate to consult them.

A representative must be appointed as soon as practicable *after* a standard authorisation is given (MCA, Sch A1, Pt 10). Such a representative is not a "paid or professional" carer for the purpose of section 39A (s 39A(6)), so could be a person whom it is appropriate to consult. And if there is a representative appointed (whether or not she is currently the representative of the person concerned), the IMCA has no powers or duties, apart from the power to apply to the Court to challenge the giving of a standard authorisation; nor does anyone else have any powers or duties towards the IMCA apart from that (Sch A1, para 161). So if the person concerned has previously been the subject of a standard authorisation, it should only be necessary to appoint a section 39A IMCA if for some reason it is not appropriate to consult the person who is or has been his representative. And even if a section 39A IMCA is appointed for a person who has a representative, there is not much she can do. However, if this is the first time the DoLS have been used, then an IMCA has an important role in looking after the interests of the person concerned during the assessment process.

(ii) A section 39C IMCA

If a person is subject to a standard authorisation, and his representative's appointment comes to an end for some reason, the supervisory body must appoint a section 39C IMCA to fill the gap until the appointment of a new representative (s 39C(1)(a), (b), (5)). Once again, this only applies if the managing authority think that there is no-one apart from a professional or paid carer whom it would be appropriate to consult (s 39C(1)(c)) and it is up to them to notify the supervisory body that this section applies (s 39C(2)). The IMCA then assumes the role of the representative for the time being (but not if the representative's functions have been suspended) (Sch A1, paras 159 and 160).

(iii) A section 39D IMCA

There are three circumstances in which the supervisory body must appoint a section 39D IMCA for a person who is currently subject to a DoLS authorisation, even though he already has a representative. They only arise if the representative is not being paid for acting. These are:

- where either the person concerned or his representative asks for an IMCA to be appointed; or
- where the supervisory body have reason to believe that between them they would be unable to exercise the right to apply to the Court of Protection or for a review; or
- where the supervisory body have reason to believe that they are unlikely, or have failed, to exercise those rights when it would have been reasonable for them to do so (s 39D).

There is no need to instruct a second advocate at the request of the person concerned, if a section 39D IMCA has already been instructed for the other reasons: that is, because the representative has asked for one or the supervisory body thinks there is a problem (s 39E).

This is the one situation in which an IMCA has to be appointed even though the person concerned does have someone apart from a professional or paid carer who can be consulted about his best interests. The person may be deprived of his liberty, and either he or his unpaid representative feels that he needs more help and support; or the supervisory body feels that they need help in exercising their rights to challenge the authorisation. The particular role of a section 39D IMCA is, first, to help them both to understand the effect, purpose and duration of the DoLS authorisation, any conditions to which it is subject, the reasons why the assessors thought that the person concerned met the criteria, and the right to go to court or to a review and how to exercise these; and secondly, to help them do this (s 39(7), (8)).

(d) Independent mental capacity advocates: qualifications and role

LSSAs are responsible for delivering the IMCA service, which they commission from independent organisations. No-one can be appointed an IMCA unless she has appropriate experience and/or training, and is a person of good character and integrity; this includes having an enhanced criminal record bureau certificate which clears her to work with vulnerable adults. She must also be able to act independently of the body instructing her. IMCAs have to be individually approved by a local authority or belong to a "class of persons" approved because everyone in it satisfies these requirements (IMCA General Regs, reg 5).

The principle is that, in all these situations, which may have serious and long-lasting effects for a person who does not have the capacity to make his own decisions, he should be represented and supported by someone independent of the people who will be responsible for carrying out the decision in question (s 35(4)). Deprivation of liberty is, of course, subject to independent assessment and scrutiny but is such a serious step that the person concerned should have someone who is there to speak up for him alone. Decisions about serious medical treatment or moving into or between hospitals and care homes are not necessarily subject to any independent assessment or scrutiny at all, unless there is a dispute or they have to be referred to the Court of Protection. No-one will be very anxious to do this, because of the cost and delay involved. And an independent advocate on the spot may be more effective than any court in negotiating the best solution for the person concerned. If need be she can invoke the formal complaints procedures rather than resorting to the Court. But as a last resort she can ask the Official Solicitor to apply to the Court as litigation friend for the client or ask for the Court's permission to make the application herself (see p 279, later).

The IMCA General Regulations require an IMCA instructed in a non-DoLS case to check the validity of her instructions and then think how best to represent and support her client. So far as practicable and appropriate, she should interview the client and examine his records. She has the right to interview the client in private and to examine and take copies of any health record, social services record, or record kept by a person registered under the Care Standards Act 2000 which the holder of the record thinks may be relevant (MCA, s 35(6)). So far as practicable and appropriate, she should consult professional and paid carers and anyone else who may be able to comment on the client's wishes, feelings, beliefs and values, and take all practicable steps to obtain the information she thinks necessary about the client and what is proposed. The object is to find out how much support has been given to the client to help him take part in the decision, what his wishes and feelings, beliefs and values, would be if he had capacity, what alternatives are available, and, in a serious medical treatment case, whether he would be likely to benefit from a further medical opinion about the proposed treatment. She has to prepare a report for the person who instructed her and she can include "submissions" about the client and what is proposed (s 36; IMCA General Regs, reg 6). The body which instructed her has to take into account any information given or submissions made by the IMCA when making the decision in question (ss 37(5), 38(5), 39(6), IMCA General Regs, reg 5(2)). Once a decision is made, the IMCA has the same rights to challenge it as a carer or person interested in the client's welfare (reg 7).

An IMCA instructed in a DoLS case also has the right to interview the client in private and inspect relevant records, including assessments and authorisations (s 35(6), (7)). The bodies who instruct her have to take seriously what she says. The IMCA General Regulations have not been expressly amended so as to include DoLS IMCAs, apparently because the Department of Health think that they already do. The reality is that their role is the same (subject to the express limitations above) and IMCAs themselves are unlikely to be deterred by any gap in the Regulations from doing what they think right for their clients.

6. RESEARCH

It is all too tempting to use populations of people who may lack the capacity to give a proper consent as "guinea pigs" for medical or scientific research. There have been some horrific examples of this in the not too distant past. Yet at the same time it is important that research into the causes, diagnosis, treatment and care of conditions which cause people to lack or to lose capacity can be carried out. But it is not always in the best interests of the individual participant in this research for him to take part. So how are the interests of the individual and of science and society to be reconciled? The Law Commission (1995) found a "striking degree of consensus over the factors which make non-therapeutic research ethical" (1995, para 6.31) and these are largely reflected in the MCA scheme.

(a) The research

The MCA makes special rules for "intrusive research". This is research which would be unlawful if carried out without the consent of a person who had the capacity to consent (s 30(2)). Research may be unlawful for several different reasons, not only because it involves what would otherwise be an assault: for example, where use of the data or samples collected would breach confidentiality or data protection laws or the Human Tissue Act 2004.

Clinical trials which are regulated under the Medicines for Human Use (Clinical Trials) Regulations 2004, SI 2004/1031, are excluded (s 30(5)). These trials have to be conducted in accordance with the "conditions and principles of good clinical practice in relation to the use of incapacitated subjects" (reg 28 and Sch 1, Pt 5). These are very similar, although not identical, to the rules laid down by the MCA.

Under the MCA intrusive research in relation to a person who lacks capacity to consent to it is unlawful unless it is part of an approved research project and various other safeguards are complied with (s 30(1)). These relate both to the characteristics of the research itself and to the participation of individuals in it.

(b) Approving the research

The project must be approved by an "appropriate body". This means a research ethics committee established for approving this sort of research and recognised by the Secretary of State (Mental Capacity Act 2005 (Appropriate Body) (England) Regulations 2006, SI 2006/2810; for Wales, see Mental Capacity Act (Appropriate Body) (Wales) Regulations 2007, SI 2007/833).

The committee may not approve a project unless it is connected with an "impairing condition" or its treatment (s 31(2)). An impairing condition is one which is, or may be, either the cause or the effect of an impairment or disturbance in the functioning of the mind or brain or contribute to it (s 31(3)). This condition has to affect the people taking part in the research—so they cannot be made guinea pigs for research into conditions which they do not have. There must also be reasonable grounds for believing that the project will not be as effective if it is confined to people who can consent (s 31(4)).

As far as the impact upon the individuals taking part is concerned, the project must either have the potential to benefit them personally without imposing a disproportionate burden upon them or it must be intended to provide general knowledge of the causes or treatment or care of people affected by the same or a similar condition. Examples of possible benefits to participants include developing more effective ways of treating them or managing their condition, improving the quality of their care, discovering the cause if this would be helpful to them, and reducing the risk of harm or disadvantage (MCA Code, para 11.14). Examples of useful general knowledge might be to see whether a particular way of helping people with congenital learning disabilities might also help people with disabilities caused by head injuries (para 11.17). But if there is no potential for personal benefit, just for an increase in the sum total of useful general knowledge, any risk to the people taking part must be negligible, and what is done must not interfere with their freedom of action or their privacy in a significant way or be unduly invasive or restrictive (s 31(5),(6)). So, it appears, a rather greater level of risk or inconvenience is thought justified if participants stand to benefit personally from the research.

To be approved, a project must also have arrangements in place for complying with the requirements below relating to the individual participants (s 31(7)).

(c) Protecting individual participants

Once the project is approved, there are various steps which must be taken to protect the interests of potential or actual participants. The first is to consult. The researcher must try to identify someone to consult who is caring for the participant or interested in his welfare but not a paid or professional carer (s 32(2)). This could be a donee or deputy (s 32(7)). If the researcher cannot find someone, he must nominate an independent consultee (s 32(3)). He must ask the consultee's advice about whether an individual should take part in the project and what that individual's wishes and feelings about it would be likely to be if he had the capacity to consent (s 32(4)).

If at any time the consultee advises that the individual would be likely to refuse to take part if he could, then he must not take part or continue to take part (s 32(5)). But the researcher need not stop treatment which a person is already having as part of the research project, if the researcher reasonably believes that stopping it would be a significant risk to the participant's health (s 32(6)).

Consultation need not take place if the participant is or is about to be receiving urgent treatment and it is urgently necessary also to do something for the purposes of the research; instead, the researcher must have the agreement of a doctor who is not involved in the research or, if this is not practicable, comply with some other procedure laid down by the ethics committee when the project was approved (s 32(8), (9)). Once the urgency had gone, the researcher must not continue on this basis (s 32(10)).

There are also limits to what may be done during the research. Nothing can be done to or about the person taking part to which he appears to object, unless it is to protect him from harm or to reduce his pain or discomfort (s 33(2)(a)). Nor can anything be done which is contrary to an advance decision or any other form of statement by the participant of which the researcher is aware (s 33(2)(b)). The person taking part must be withdrawn without delay if he indicates in any way that he wants to withdraw, or if the project no longer meets the relevance, benefit and risk requirements in section 31 (s 33(4), (5)). Once again, treatment need not be discontinued if there would be a significant risk to the participant's health (s 33(6)).

Throughout his participation, the interests of the person taking part must be assumed to outweigh the interests of science and society (s 33(3)).

There are transitional provisions to cater for people who had agreed before 31 March 2008 to take part in a research project which was begun before 1 October 2007 when the MCA came into force and who lose capacity during the project. Essentially, only information or material obtained before a participant lost capacity can be used and even then much the same safeguards about consultation, the participant's wishes and feelings, and lack of objection apply (MCA, s 34; Mental Capacity Act 2005 (Loss of Capacity during Research Project) (England) Regulations 2007, SI 2007/679; for Wales, see Mental

Capacity Act 2005 (Loss of Capacity during Research Project) (Wales) Regulations 2007, SI 2007/837).

7. THE CARE QUALITY COMMISSION

The old Board of Control combined the roles of overseeing the management and general standards of mental hospitals and protecting the interests of individual patients. In 1959, it was assumed that both could safely be left to the internal machinery of the NHS. However, a succession of allegations of neglect and misconduct in mental hospitals (see particularly Robb, 1967, and Morris, 1969), and inquiries such as those into the Ely, Farleigh and Whittingham hospitals, revealed that some special oversight of standards in hospitals catering for the most vulnerable patients was still needed. Meanwhile, patients in Scotland had the benefit of the Mental Welfare Commission, first established under the Mental Health (Scotland) Act 1960, to protect anyone who might because of mental disorder be unable adequately to protect themselves or their own interests The Commission championed many causes on behalf of patients and anyone reading its publications would find it hard to understand why the Scots were thought to need such an informed and caring body while the English and Welsh were not. The Scottish Commission still has a much wider remit than its English equivalent. This includes, for example, investigating whether a patient is being unlawfully detained in hospital or may be ill-treated or neglected or subject to some other deficiency in his care or treatment (Mental Health (Care and Treatment) (Scotland) Act 2003, s 11(2)(a), (d)). The patients protected include, not only those subject to compulsory powers under the 2003 Act, but also anyone with mental disorder who is covered by the Adults with Incapacity (Scotland) Act 2000 (see s 9).

The main advocates for a Commission south of the border were the Royal College of Psychiatrists (1981). They undoubtedly hoped that the medical members might provide an informal means of reviewing questions of clinical judgment, by supplying general guidance and second opinions when asked. This might have avoided the need for the more specific restrictions and controls over their clinical judgment which were then being proposed by other bodies, such as MIND and the Butler Committee on Mentally Abnormal Offenders. In the event, they got both, although the SOAD system stopped short of the full multi-disciplinary assessment which others had wanted. The 1983 Act established the Mental Health Act Commission for England and Wales (MHAC) to deal with both general issues and individual complaints, but (with minor exceptions) only in relation to detained patients.

In 2009, the Mental Health Act Commission was wound up and its functions transferred to the Care Quality Commission (CQC) in England and the Welsh Ministers in Wales, where they are exercised by Health Inspectorate Wales (Health and Social Care Act 2008, s 52 and Sch 3). The CQC and Health Inspectorate Wales have also been given similar functions in relation to the operation of the DoLS (MCA 2005, Sch A1, paras 162, 164; Mental Capacity (Deprivation of Liberty: Monitoring and Reporting; and Assessments— Amendment) Regulations 2009, SI 2009/827, (the DoLS Monitoring Regs)). The MHAC (2008) was understandably concerned that the amalgamation might lead to a dilution of specialist skills and a reduction in the already stretched resources available at a time when its role was expanding rather than contracting. The alternative view is that the quality of patient and resident care should be

223

improved by combining the specific duties to protect individual detained and compulsory patients with strong powers to enforce better standards across the whole field of health and social care.

In addition to its role in reviewing decisions to withhold mail (see section 4, above) and in making proposals about what should go into the Code of Practice (see chapter 1), the CQC's specific functions under the MHA and the MCA are as follows.

(a) Reviewing regulated treatments

The CQC appoints the SOADs and other people to give certificates for the treatments covered by sections 57, 58 and 58A of the MHA (ss 57(2)(a), 58(3)(a)). Allied to this is the function of receiving reports from the clinician in charge about all section 57 treatment and about SOAD certificated section 58 and 58A treatment of detained hospital patients, including recalled community patients (ss 61(1)). There is no obligation to report on the certificated treatment of community patients unless the CQC asks (s 64H(4)). The CQC can cancel the certificates authorising these treatments, by notifying the clinician in charge (ss 61(3), 64H(5)). This will stop the treatment until a fresh certificate is issued, unless stopping it will cause serious suffering to the patient.

(b) Reviewing the operation of the MHA

The CQC has a general protective function over all compulsory patients. It must:

> "keep under review, and where appropriate investigate, the exercise of the powers and the discharge of the duties conferred or imposed by this Act so far as relating to the detention of patients or their reception into guardianship or to relevant patients" (s 120(1)).

"Relevant patients" are those who are liable to be detained, community patients and patients subject to guardianship (s 120(2)). This power covers the admission and detention process, so the CQC can scrutinise admission documents and consider whether it is happy with the way in which, for example, medical recommendations are being completed. But it also covers practice in relation to renewal of detention, leave of absence and discharge. The CQC has no power to discharge individual patients. It can consider how detained patients are treated in hospital, and the MHAC took a close interest in such issues as seclusion and the management of particularly difficult patients. It can also look at other issues relating to the treatment of detained patients, provided that some power or duty contained in the Act is involved. Examples over the years have included transfer delays, patients' money and benefits, equality issues, women detained in hospital (see MHAC 2009b) and deaths in hospital. A broad approach to the terms of reference enabled the MHAC also to look at "de facto" detention, compulsory care and after-care in the community, and the treatment of people who lacked capacity. It was at the forefront of the calls for a review of the 1983 Act (eg MHAC, 1993).

(c) Visiting compulsory patients

The CQC must make arrangements to visit and interview "relevant patients" in private; if the patient is detained, in the place where he is detained; if he is not detained, in a hospital or registered establishment or, if access is granted, other places (s 120(3)). "Registered establishment" for the purpose of these powers includes not only private hospitals but all registered premises where activities regulated under the 2008 Act are carried out (s 120(9)).

It is left to the CQC to decide its policy on how often to visit and how many patients to see. This is governed as much by the available resources as by the perceived need. The MHAC gave priority to the high security hospitals, which in its early days were still run much like prisons and where there was a great deal of work to be done. Visitors dealt with both individual patients and general points and some visits were "out of hours" or unannounced. The MHAC considered that regular and frequent visits were the only way to ensure that patients' rights were protected, the potential for abuse minimised and appropriate care provided at all times. Experience had shown that the quality of care could deteriorate very quickly if both regular and unannounced visits did not take place (MHAC, 2008, p 263).

(d) Investigating complaints

The CQC must make arrangements to investigate any complaint "as to the exercise of the powers or the discharge of the duties conferred or imposed by this Act in respect of a patient who is or has been detained or who is or has been a relevant patient" (s 120(4)). The arrangements made can exclude specified matters from investigation and the investigator does not have to pursue an investigation which he does not consider "appropriate" (s 120(5)). Complaints may be made by the patient or by anyone else, for example the patient's Member of Parliament.

(e) Ancillary powers

The 2008 Act has expanded the CQC's ancillary powers to help it to carry out its review and investigative functions. These are a considerable improvement on the powers of the MHAC. At all reasonable times, the investigator may visit and interview in private any patient in a hospital or registered establishment (whether detained or not). If the investigator is a doctor or approved clinician, she may examine the patient in private there. And the investigator may require the production of and inspect any records relating to the detention or treatment of anyone who is or has been detained under the Act or who is or has been a community patient or a patient subject to guardianship (s 120(7)).

On top of this, hospital managers, local social services authorities, and other people prescribed by the regulations, must provide the CQC with "such information as [it] may reasonably request for or in connection with the exercise of its functions under section 120"; the same applies to a person authorised by the CQC to carry out those functions. Information includes documents and records (s 120C).

The CQC may publish a report of a review or investigation carried out under (b) above. Regulations may provide for people to be able to make representations to the CQC before such a report is published (s 120A): this is to afford a right of reply to people who may be criticised in the report. The CQC may also direct the hospital managers, a local social services authority, or other people prescribed by the regulations, to publish an "action statement", saying what they propose to do about a review or investigation which the CQC has carried out (s 120B).

(f) Annual reports

The MHAC was required to publish a report on its activities every second year, which had to be laid before Parliament. The CQC is now required to publish annual reports on the exercise of its functions under the MHA (s 120D). The reports of the MHAC contain many helpful comments on the Act and its operation, speak with pride of the invaluable work of the Commission in reducing the sum total of human misery, and document considerable progress over its 26 years of existence. Even so, the MHAC was not always able to produce results. Rather ruefully, it commented (1989, para 11.9) on the "dramatic activity" at Broadmoor, and the other special hospitals, prompted by a Report from the Health Advisory Service and the Social Services Inspectorate (1988). The Commission was not able to achieve improvements at Broadmoor until others stepped in, nor did they detect the seriousness of the problems revealed by the Ashworth inquiry (Blom-Cooper, 1992). Combining the MHAC's protective functions towards individual patients with the powers of the CQC to regulate hospitals of all kinds may prove a way to combat this problem. The CQC has more than its powers under the MHA to help it to promote best practice and protect the safety, health and welfare of the most vulnerable patients for whom the NHS is responsible.

(g) Monitoring the DoLS

Under the MHA 1983, the Secretary of State had power to extend the remit of the MHAC to the care and treatment of informal hospital patients (s 124(4) and (5), now repealed). The MHAC repeatedly pressed for its jurisdiction to be extended to cover patients who did not need to be sectioned but were *de facto* detained in hospital because of their mental condition. Now that the DoLS have been introduced to protect these patients, and residents similarly detained in care homes, the CQC has been given the task of monitoring their operation (DoLS Monitoring Regs 2009, reg 2). It is only required to report on their operation to the Secretary of State when he asks (reg 3). However, it also has power at any time to give him advice or information about this, and must give him any specific advice or information for which he asks (reg 5).

For the purpose of monitoring and reporting, the CQC has the power, but not the duty, to visit hospitals and care homes, to interview people accommodated there (the regulations do not specify that this may be in private), and to inspect the records of people accommodated there who are or have been subject to a DoLS authorisation or whom the CQC has reason to believe should have been assessed for authorisation (DoLS Monitoring Regs 2009, reg 4).

(h) Early days?

The abolition of the MHAC is "not a re-run of 1959" but "rather more metamorphosis than annihilation" (MHACa, 2009, pp 227–228). The CQC has declared that it will continue the dedicated and expert work of the MHAC. It will "retain a strong focus on the need for mental health services to provide in-patient care in a safe environment that places the least restriction possible on people's autonomy and choice" (CQC, 2009, p 8). Among the key areas for improvement which the CQC has identified in response to the final report from the MHAC (2009) are: informing and involving service users, safeguarding women and children, improving outcomes for people from black and minority ethnic groups, the safety and quality of in-patient care, and the use of community treatment orders. The Commission emphasises that it does have "strong new powers" to enforce improvements where necessary, but it is also establishing a Mental Health Improvement Board which will be particularly concerned with the statutory functions under the MHA and MCA. No doubt the Board's efforts will be carefully watched. In the words of an epitaph for the MHAC as well as for one of its founding members,

"the Commission throughout its life has represented the very best of what might be termed enlightened concern about and recognition of one of the most serious acts that the state can ever undertake: the deprivation of an individual's liberty on account of their mental disorder" (Blom-Cooper and others, 2009).

The CQC has a hard act to follow.

7 MOVING OUT AND MOVING ON

It has long been the policy that mental patients, and in particular civil compulsory patients, should spend as little time in hospital as possible. Patients who have committed serious crimes or are otherwise considered dangerous to the public, on the other hand, may have to spend a great deal of time there. But moving to progressively less secure conditions is usually regarded as a necessary precondition of eventually moving out of hospital. One problem facing patients and their doctors in the high security hospitals may be persuading others, not only the Justice Secretary but also the NHS authorities who would have to provide or to fund a less secure placement, that this is appropriate. The responsible clinician (RC) cannot dictate to others what they should do: see *R (K) v West London Mental Health NHS Trust* [2006] EWCA Civ 118, [2006] 1 WLR 1865.

This chapter deals with the ways in which a compulsory hospital patient may move out of the hospital where he is currently detained, either into another hospital or into the community. There are several legal routes along which a patient may do this and the choice between them is not always obvious. Apart from a transfer between hospitals, these include a straightforward discharge, leave of absence, transfer into guardianship, a community treatment order (CTO) for unrestricted patients and a conditional discharge for restricted patients. The resources available within the hospital, as well as what will be on offer in the community (see chapter 9), are a crucial component in making these decisions. There is also the unlikely question of legal liability to the patient or to third parties if the hospital gets it wrong (see p 243, below).

1. PLANNING AND AFTER-CARE

From 1991, the Department of Health required both health and social services to operate the care programme approach (CPA) for all mentally ill patients and others insofar as it was relevant (Circular HC(90)23; LASSL (90)11). The key features were a systematic assessment of the patient's health and social care needs, an agreed care plan, a key-worker (now called a care co-ordinator) to monitor its delivery, and regular reviews of the patient's progress. These continue to be good practice for all service users. But not everyone requires the complicated bureaucratic procedures involved, so the CPA has been "refocused" to concentrate only on those higher risk patients with complex needs requiring services from a variety of different agencies (Department of Health, 2008b). All service users on CTOs or subject to guardianship should qualify. The new guidance stresses that the CPA is simply an approach to delivering services, not a test of eligibility for them. These will continue to be governed by the statutory criteria and individual need (see chapter 9). The High Court has also held that a CPA assessment is no substitute for the full community care assessment to which a user may be entitled (*R (HP) v Islington LBC* [2004] EWHC 7 (Admin), [2005] 82 BMLR 113).

There is a specific statutory duty to provide after-care for some detained patients. Section 117 of the Mental Health Act 1983 (MHA) requires both the

Primary Care Trust (PCT) or Local Health Board and the local social services authority (LSSA) to provide, in co-operation with relevant voluntary agencies, after-care services (s 117(2)) for former compulsory in-patients who are resident in or sent to their area on discharge (s 117(3)). This applies to any patient detained under an admission for treatment, a hospital order, hospital direction or transfer direction, who ceases to be detained and (whether or not immediately afterwards) leaves hospital (s 117(1)). This includes patients on leave of absence, patients subject to CTOs, and conditionally discharged restricted patients. The duty continues until the PCT and LSSA think that the patient no longer needs their services; but they are not allowed to think this of patients who are still on CTOs (s 117(2)).

This is a free-standing duty, not simply a duty to arrange services under the authorities' other powers (*R v Manchester City Council, ex p Stennett* [2002] UKHL 34, [2002] 2 AC 1127). The services which may be provided are not defined. It has been said that they would normally include "social work, support in helping the ex-patient with problems of employment, accommodation or family relationships, the provision of domiciliary services and the use of day centre and residential facilities" (*Clunis v Camden and Islington Health Authority* [1998] QB 978, CA, at 992, approved in *Stennett*). As well as health and community care services provided by the statutory bodies, they might include co-ordination with services provided by voluntary organisations or even by other statutory bodies, but those bodies are not under the section 117 duty to provide them.

This is a mandatory duty owed to the individual patient. In *R v Ealing District Health Authority, ex p Fox* [1993] 1 WLR 373 a tribunal had granted a restricted patient a conditional discharge, deferred until the conditions were met, but the local psychiatrists were not prepared to act, so the health authority refused to provide supervision in the community. This decision was quashed and a declaration granted that the authority had acted unlawfully in failing to make practical arrangements for the patient's after-care. However, the judge refused to grant an order compelling them to do so, because the effect would have been to force a doctor to act against his clinical judgment; but there were other steps they could take to resolve matters. In effect, however, it is a duty to use their best endeavours to provide the services required: see *R (H) v Secretary of State for the Home Department* [2003] UKHL 59, [2004] 2 AC 253.

Some might think that a patient who no longer requires to be treated in hospital can no longer be compulsorily detained there. But the grounds for compulsory detention are so broadly stated that they might well cover a patient who only requires to be in hospital because there are no suitable facilities for him in the community. Nor is article 5 of the ECHR much help. All the European Court of Human Rights requires is that the patient's "mental disorder be of a kind or degree warranting compulsory confinement": *Winterwerp v The Netherlands* (1979) 2 EHRR 327, p 98, earlier. In *R (H) v Secretary of State for the Home Department*, above, the House of Lords held that there was no violation of article 5, even though a tribunal had granted a conditional discharge, when the community agencies would not make the arrangements necessary to meet the conditions. So is this a licence to keep patients indefinitely in hospital when they do not need to be there?

The MHA Code advises that planning for after-care should begin as soon as a patient is compulsorily admitted to hospital (para 27.8). It should be planned within the framework of the CPA (para 27.11). As well as the patient, all the relevant professionals in and out of hospital should be involved, along with representatives of relevant voluntary organisations, housing and employment (if these are an issue), an advocate, attorney or deputy (if the patient has one) and any other representative nominated by the patient (para 27.12). The issues to be considered may include: his mental and physical healthcare; activities or employment; accommodation; risks and safety issues; specific needs resulting from physical disability or substance abuse; parenting or caring needs; social, cultural or spiritual needs; counselling and personal support; help with benefits and finances; and contingency plans should the patient's health deteriorate (para 27.13). For restricted patients, the probation service should also be involved and the conditions likely to be imposed by the Justice Secretary or tribunal (see p 245, below) considered. If a tribunal has provisionally decided upon a conditional discharge, the Code states firmly that "the PCT and LSSA must do their best to put after-care in place which would allow that discharge to take place" (para 27.9).

2. LEAVE OF ABSENCE

Generally speaking, compulsory patients cannot leave the hospital where they are detained, even for a short time, unless they are given leave of absence under the MHA. The Responsible Clinician (RC) can grant leave of absence to any compulsory patient (s 17(1)), apart from one remanded to hospital or made subject to an interim hospital order by a criminal court (cf s 40(4)); but if the patient is restricted, the permission of the Justice Secretary must also be obtained (s 41(3)(c)(i); see Sch 1, Pt 2, para 3(a); for his policy on leave for restricted patients, see Ministry of Justice, 2008b). The exclusion of remand and interim hospital order patients is understandable, because they remain subject to the jurisdiction of the court; but it could be anti-therapeutic, especially for patients remanded for treatment or on interim hospital orders. Consistently with this exclusion, the Justice Secretary does not normally agree to leave for transferred remand prisoners (Ministry of Justice, 2008b).

Leave can be given for a special occasion (such as a wedding), or for a definite period (such as a weekend), or indefinitely. It can be extended without bringing the patient back to hospital (s 17(2)). In practice, leave may be authorised in broad terms by the RC, while the nurses decide whether it is appropriate to allow the patient to leave the ward on any particular occasion. This can cause problems if resources or other considerations mean that a patient does not get the leave which he expected (MHAC, 2009a). Hospital managers cannot overrule the RC's decision to grant leave, but of course he cannot oblige either them or anyone else to fund the necessary arrangements (MHA Code, para 21.12).

Leave can be subject to whatever conditions the RC thinks necessary in the patient's own interests or to protect other people (s 17(1)). These can include staying in another hospital, living with a particular person, attending a clinic for treatment, or coming back to the hospital for tests or medication. The patient is still liable to detention and can be obliged to accept medical treatment, subject to the usual safeguards; but the Code now advises that if it becomes necessary to administer treatment without consent, "consideration should be given to whether it would be more appropriate to recall the patient to hospital" (para 21.24). If necessary for the patient's own health or safety or the protection of others, the RC can also direct that while on leave the patient remains in the custody of a member of the hospital staff (or the staff of the hospital where he has been given leave to go) or of some other person authorised in writing (s 17(3)). The effect of this is that the patient is in "legal custody" and can be recaptured the moment he escapes, rather than if and when he fails to return to hospital when he should do (see p 248, later).

The MHA Code (paras 28.7 and 28.8) points out that leave can be combined with the "deprivation of liberty" procedures (the DoLS) for patients who lack capacity and may need to be detained *in a care home* for treatment for mental or physical disorder, or in a hospital for treatment for physical disorder, provided that there is no conflict with the conditions of their leave. However, patients on leave who lack capacity and need treatment in hospital for their mental disorder are not eligible for the DoLS (see p 19, earlier) and should be recalled under the MHA (para 28.9).

Leave of absence can be revoked at any time and the patient recalled to hospital if the RC thinks this necessary in the interests of the patient's own health or safety or for the protection of other people (s 17(4)). The Code advises that refusing to take medication would not "on its own" be a reason to revoke leave, but it would almost always be a reason to consider doing so (para 21.31). Notice of revocation and recall must be in writing and addressed either to the patient or to the person in charge of him (s 17(4)). The Justice Secretary can himself recall a restricted patient from leave (Sch 1, Pt 2, para 3(b)).

Unrestricted patients cannot be recalled once the power to detain them has lapsed (s 17(5)). In *R v Hallstrom, ex p W* [1986] QB 1090, it was held that the authority to detain could not be renewed while a patient was on leave; and that the patient could not be recalled to hospital simply in order to renew his detention, if it was not in fact appropriate for him to be detained in hospital for treatment at the time. However, in *B v Barking, Havering and Brentwood Community Healthcare NHS Trust* [1999] 1 FLR 106, the Court of Appeal held that detention could be renewed while the patient was "liable to be detained" even if he was not actually there; and, more importantly, that treatment in hospital was "appropriate" if it contained some element of in-patient care, even though the patient was on leave for most of the time. This was taken further in *R (DR) v Merseycare NHS Trust* [2002] MHLR 386, where Wilson J found the distinction between treatment *at* hospital and treatment *in* hospital "too subtle for me". So detention could be renewed when the patient was attending the hospital two days a week, for occupational therapy and the ward round. And in *R (CS) v MHRT* [2002] MHLR 355, a decision not to discharge the patient was upheld even though she was only attending every four weeks for the ward round and her injections.

Thus indefinite leave of absence can be within the law, even for unrestricted patients, provided that some element of hospital treatment is appropriate (the former limit of six months was abolished by the Mental Health (Patients in the Community) Act 1995). Restricted patients can be recalled by the Justice Secretary at any time, but not after 12 months by the RC (Sch 1, Pt 2, para 3(c)). Patients who are on leave can apply to a tribunal just as if they were still in hospital. Tribunals also have power to recommend that unrestricted patients be given leave, although they cannot order it (see chapter 8).

Things can go badly wrong whatever the legal label attached to the patient (for the risk of legal liability, see p 243, below). In 1979, for example, Ronald Sailes committed a particularly brutal murder while on leave from Broadmoor, where he had spent 15 years as a restricted patient and remained for another year as an unrestricted patient. The MHA Code points out that leave can be an important part of the care plan but it can also be a time of risk. The RC should balance the benefits to the patient against the risks that it may pose to other people (in general or in particular); be aware of any child welfare or protection issues or issues relating to the victims of offender patients; take account of the views of the patient, carers, friends, and anyone else involved in the arrangements; and consider the conditions, support and community services which will be needed, including contingency plans for early return to hospital (para 21.8).

In considering requests to grant leave to restricted patients, the Ministry of Justice "recognises that well thought out leave, which serves a definable purpose and is carefully and sensitively executed, has an important part to play in treating and rehabilitating restricted patients" (Ministry of Justice, 2009b, para 1). But it also,

"expects leave programmes to be designed and conducted in such a way as to preserve public safety, sustain public confidence in the arrangements as a whole, and respect the feeling and possible fears of victims and others who may have been affected by the offences" (para 5).

And transferred prisoners should generally not be allowed privileges in hospital which they would not have been allowed in prison (Annex B). If a patient is allowed on an escorted trip to Scotland, he can be kept in the charge of his escort and recaptured there if they escape (Mental Health (Cross-border Visits) (Scotland) Regulations 2008, SSI 2008/181, reg 2(1)(a) and (b)).

Now that there is a choice between prolonged leave of absence and a CTO for unrestricted patients, the RC cannot grant "longer term leave" without first considering whether a CTO would be more appropriate (s 17(2A)). Longer term for this purpose means indefinitely or for longer than seven consecutive days (including a later extension which will take the total period of leave granted to over seven days) (s 17(2B)). This does not apply to restricted patients, for whom CTOs are not available.

The MHA Code lists the following (apparently alternative) factors as suggesting that longer term leave is more appropriate: the "discharge" (sic) is for a specific purpose or period; or deliberately on a trial basis to see how the patient can manage; or the patient is likely to need further in-patient treatment without consent or compliance; or there is a serious risk of the arrangements in the community breaking down or proving unsatisfactory. A CTO is more likely if the patient is ready for discharge on an indefinite basis; there are good reasons to believe that he will not need to be detained for the necessary treatment to be given; and the patient appears prepared to consent or comply with the necessary treatment; but the risk of the arrangements breaking down is enough to justify a CTO, "but not to the extent that it is very likely to happen" (para 28.6).

3. COMMUNITY TREATMENT ORDERS

Over the years psychiatrists in particular (RCPsych, 1987, 1993) have pressed for some other way of trying to ensure that detained patients keep up with their medication and do not get lost after leaving hospital, while others have resisted any power to impose treatment outside hospital where it is much harder to regulate and police. The Mental Health (Patients in the Community) Act 1995 introduced a form of supervised discharge which was legally very like guardianship, but was operated by the health rather than the social services. However, there was no power to impose treatment without consent nor was there any automatic power of recall to hospital. The 2007 amendments have now replaced it with a Community Treatment Order. This is confusingly referred to as supervised community treatment, or SCT, in the Code of Practice and other Departmental Guidance, although this term is nowhere to be found in the MHA. The principal aim is to prevent the "revolving door" scenario, where the patient is successfully treated in hospital, discharged, fails to keep up with his medication, relapses and has to be readmitted. However, as we have already seen (p 198, earlier), a community patient can only be given treatment if there is a valid consent or, if he lacks the capacity to consent, he does not actively object (or there is an emergency). There is no power to impose treatment upon an unwilling patient, whether or not he has the capacity to refuse it. The additional safeguards, requiring second opinions for certain types of treatment, also apply.

(a) The criteria

A CTO is made by the patient's RC (s 17A(1),(3)). The only eligible patients are those admitted under section 3 for treatment or under ordinary hospital orders (s 17A(2), Sch 1, Pt 1, para 1). The criteria, laid down in section 17A(5), are that:

- the patient is suffering from mental disorder of a nature or degree which makes it appropriate for him to receive medical treatment;
- it is necessary for his health or safety or for the protection of other persons that he should receive such treatment;
- it can be provided without his continuing to be detained in a hospital, subject to his being liable to recall;
- it is necessary that the RC should be able to recall him to hospital; and
- "appropriate medical treatment is available for him".

The key is therefore whether the power of recall is necessary in order to ensure that the patient will in fact receive the treatment he needs. In deciding whether the power to recall is necessary, the RC must consider, having regard to the patient's history of mental disorder and any other relevant factors, what risk there would be of deterioration if he were not detained in hospital, for example because of his refusing or neglecting to receive the necessary medical treatment (s 17A(6)).

As we have seen above, the Code takes the view that leave of absence is more appropriate where there is a serious risk of arrangements in the community breaking down, while a CTO is indicated if the risk is serious enough to justify making the order at all, "but not to the extent that it is very likely to happen" (para 28.6). A history of repeated admissions, or a tendency to fail to follow a treatment plan or to discontinue medication, may suggest this; other relevant factors would include the patient's current mental state, his insight and attitude to treatment, and the circumstances into which he would be discharged (paras 28.7–28.11). The risk of relapse is significant, but not enough: the RC should be satisfied that the risk of harm from relapse is sufficiently serious to justify the power of recall (para 28.13). Good care planning will also be important (para 25.16). A care co-ordinator should be appointed and it may be that a different responsible clinician will take over. Community patients are entitled to section 117 after-care services for as long as the CTO is in force (s 117(2)).

(b) The process

The RC can only make a CTO if an approved mental health professional (AMHP) agrees that the criteria are met and that it is appropriate to make the order (s 17A(3)). The Act does not say who this AMHP should be. It could be someone on the staff of the hospital where the patient is detained (which would not be much of a safeguard). It could be a health professional from the community team (perhaps the community psychiatric nurse who would be the patient's care co-ordinator). Or it could be a local authority social worker. Any AMHP has, of course, to act on behalf of an LSSA (see p 76, earlier). The Code advises that if no other LSSA is willing, responsibility for ensuring that an AMHP considers the case should lie with the LSSA which would become responsible for the section 117 after-care services (para 25.26). The AMHP is, of course, entitled to take a different view from the RC, but should explain why. The RC should not then go on the hunt for an AMHP who will agree (para 25.27).

If the patient is subject to a hospital order or transfer direction, the hospital will need to know whether he is covered by Chapter 2 of Part 3 to the Domestic Violence, Crimes and Victims Act 2004 (the DVCVA). This depends upon whether the crime for which the sentence was imposed was one of the violent or sexual offences listed in Schedule 15 to the Criminal Justice Act 2003. Victims of these offences have the right to ask to make representations about the conditions to be imposed if a CTO is made and to be informed if the order is made and of any conditions which relate to contact with them or their families. So before making a CTO, the RC will have to tell the managers that she is considering this, so that the hospital can invite representations from the victim. The RC has to take these into account before making the CTO (or changing any conditions) and the AMHP has to take them into account before agreeing. However, the Ministerial Guidance states that once an RC has decided that the patient should be discharged, she should not delay just so that the victim can make representations (Department of Health and Ministry of Justice, 2008, para 3.2). Hospitals also have a discretion to give the victim further information which they think appropriate, but this is not intended to breach patient confidentiality, so the victim cannot be told where and why the patient is to be discharged unless he agrees. The Mental Health Act Commission (MHAC) has commented that:

"it is not hard to envisage that it could be profoundly unsettling to a victim who has requested to be given information to be told only that there is a likelihood that they might come into contact with the patient, without more specific details" (2009b, para 2.49).

The CTO is made by the RC and AMHP completing Form CTO1, prescribed by the Mental Health (Hospital, Guardianship and Treatment Regulations) 2008, SI 2008/1184, reg 6 (the MHHGT Regs); for Wales, see Mental Health (Hospital, Guardianship, Community Treatment and Consent to Treatment) (Wales) Regulations 2008, SI 2008/2439. The RC has to explain in Part 1 why she thinks that the criteria are made out and confirm that, in deciding on the need for a power of recall, she has considered the risk of deterioration. The AMHP is required only to agree in Part 2. The RC then makes the order in Part 3, stating the time and date at which the CTO is to be effective. There is no time limit between the AMHP's agreement and the making of the order, but it would not be wise to rely on a stale agreement. The form has then to be furnished to the managers of the hospital where the patient was detained before it was made.

The RC must also state the conditions to which the patient is subject under the CTO (s 17B(1)). The RC and AMHP must think these necessary or appropriate for ensuring that the patient receives medical treatment, for preventing the risk of harm to the patient's heath or safety, and/or for protecting other people (s 17B(2)). Two conditions are mandatory. One is that the patient make himself available for examination for the purpose of deciding whether the CTO is to be extended under section 20A (s 17B(3)(a)). The other is that he make himself available to a second opinion appointed doctor (SOAD) if it is proposed to give a certificate authorising treatment which requires a second opinion under Part 4A of the Act (s 17B(3)(b)).

But the RC can impose other conditions as well. The Code suggests that these might cover things like where and when the patient is to receive treatment in the community; where he is to live; and avoiding known risk factors or high risk situations which are relevant to his mental disorder (para 25.34). Conditions should be kept to a minimum and restrict the patient's liberty as little as possible. They should have a clear rationale, linked to the permissible purposes, which can be properly explained to the patient (paras 25.33, 25.35). This does not have to be explained on Form CTO1 but ought to be on the patient's record. For example, if an offender patient is covered by "Chapter 2" of the DVCVA (see above), the victim may have asked for a condition that he stay away from an area, place or person.

Oddly, although the AMHP must agree to the initial conditions, the RC can vary or suspend these at any time (s 17B(4), (5); and subject, in the case of "Chapter 2 patients", to the victim's rights). The variation (but not the suspension) has to be done on the prescribed form, Form CTO2. This does not require the agreement of an AMHP to the variation, although the Code says that it would not be good practice to vary conditions which had been recently agreed with an AMHP without first discussing this with that AMHP (para 25.41).

It is obviously important that the patient and everyone else involved knows exactly where they stand, not least because failure to comply with the conditions can be taken into account in deciding whether to recall the patient to hospital (s 17B(6)). The hospital managers have the duty "to take such steps as are practicable" to see that the community patient understands the effect of the CTO and his rights to apply to a tribunal (s 132A(1)). This has to be done orally and in writing (s 132A(2)). Unless the patient requests otherwise, the nearest relative should also be given copies (s 132A(3)).

(c) **The effect**

A CTO does not bring a hospital order or admission for treatment to an end (s 17D(1)). It merely suspends the hospital's power to detain the patient for as long as the CTO is in force (s 17D(2)(a)). It also means that references in the Act to a patient who is detained or *liable* to be detained do not for the time being include him (s 17D(2)(b)). The provisions relating to the duration and extension of the hospital order or admission for treatment do not apply while the CTO is in force (s 17D(3), (4)), so the admission or order does not expire and does not have to be renewed, but remains there in the background. The hospital managers can transfer responsibility for a patient under a CTO to a different hospital using Form CTO10 (s 19A; MHHGT Regs 2008, reg 17).

The Code stresses the importance of maintaining close contact with a community patient and monitoring his mental health and wellbeing (para 25.38). Particular attention should be paid to the concerns of carers and relatives, who are "typically in much more frequent contact with the patient than professionals, even under well-run care plans" (para 25.46). Action will have to be taken if he becomes unwell, engages in high risk behaviour or refuses treatment (para 25.39). This could mean adjusting the treatment plan, but it could also mean recall to hospital.

The rules about the duration and renewal of a CTO mirror the rules about the duration and renewal of an admission for treatment (see p 125, earlier). A CTO lasts initially for up to six months beginning on the day when it was made (s 20A(1)). This can be extended for a further period of six months, and then for periods of one year at a time (s 20A(3)). Within the two months before the CTO would expire, the RC must examine the patient and decide whether the criteria for renewal exist (s 20A(4)). These criteria are the same as those for making the order in the first place (s 20A(6), (7)). The RC has to consult with one or more other people who have been professionally concerned with the patient's medical treatment (s 20A(9)). If an AMHP agrees that the criteria exist and it is appropriate to extend the CTO, the RC must report to the managers of the responsible hospital on Form CTO7. This again follows the tripartite structure of the initial CTO, with a Part 4 on which the managers record receipt. The CTO is then extended unless the managers decide instead to discharge the patient (s 20A(10), (5)).

A community patient can be discharged at any time in all the same ways that a patient admitted for treatment or under an ordinary hospital order or direction can be discharged: that is, by the RC, the managers of the responsible hospital, an NHS body which is maintaining the patient in an independent hospital, or (unless he is under a hospital order or direction) his nearest relative (s 23(1A), (2), (3), (3A), Sch 1, Pt 1, para 8). If an offender patient is covered by "Chapter 2", a victim who has asked for this must be informed. The effect of the discharge is not only that he is no longer subject to the CTO, but also that he is no longer subject to recall to hospital, or to the underlying admission, order or direction (s 23(1A)).

This much is clear. The effect of simply letting the CTO lapse on expiry without renewal is less clear. The CTO is no longer in force (s 17C(a)) but the patient has not been discharged from the underlying hospital admission and this is no longer suspended (s 17D(2)). The Code blandly remarks that a patient's CTO should not simply be allowed to lapse (para 25.77) but does not explain what it thinks the effect of this will be.

(d) Recall

The RC can recall a community patient to hospital at any time if, in her opinion, the patient requires medical treatment in hospital for his mental disorder and there would be a risk of harm to the health or safety of the patient or to other persons if the patient were not recalled for that purpose (s 17E(1)). The RC can also recall the patient for breach of either of the two mandatory conditions in section 17B(3) (s 17E(2)). Breach of the other conditions is not automatically a ground for recall but may be taken into account in deciding whether the grounds exist (s 17B(6)). Out of an abundance of caution the MHA explains that a patient can be "recalled" even though he is already in the hospital on some other basis—no doubt the draftsman did not want clever lawyers arguing that "recall" was inconsistent with being there already (s 17E(4)).

Recall is always discretionary—the RC does not have to do it even if the grounds are met. She should, for example, consider whether there is a valid excuse for failing to comply with the conditions or whether there are other ways of handling the situation (Code, paras 25.49–25.51). Recall is done by notice on

Form CTO3 (MHHGT Regs, reg 6(3)(a)). If done on the general grounds in section 17E(1), the RC must explain why the criteria are met. The notice has to be served on the patient (s 17E(5)), preferably in person. Otherwise, it can be sent by first class post (it is deemed to arrive the second working day after posting) or by hand delivery to his last known address (it is deemed to arrive the day after it is delivered) (reg 6(5)). Once the notice has been served, the patient can be treated as absent without leave, recaptured and returned to hospital (see p 249, later) unless he returns voluntarily. A copy has to be forwarded to the managers of the hospital to which the patient is to be recalled as soon as reasonably practicable (reg 6(3)(b)). The patient may be recalled to a different hospital from the one from which he was discharged on the CTO (s 17E(3)), in which case the RC should tell the managers of the new hospital the name and address of the old (reg 6(3)(c)).

On recall, the patient may be detained in the hospital to which he has been recalled (s 17E(6)). It follows that he may also be forced to have treatment to which he objects. The hospital must record the date and time when his detention began on Form CTO4 (reg 6(3)(d)). He may also be transferred to another hospital in the usual way (see below) (s 17F(2)). Either way, the RC has to make up her mind what to do within 72 hours of the patient's detention in the hospital to which he was initially recalled (s 17F(6), (2)). She has two choices. She can release the patient from being recalled, in which case the patient remains subject to the CTO (s 17F(5), (7)). Or she can revoke the CTO (s 17F(4)). She can only do this if in her opinion the grounds for an admission to hospital for treatment are satisfied and an AMHP agrees with that and that it is appropriate to revoke the CTO (s 17F(4)). This is done on Form CTO5, which follows the same tripartite structure as Form CTO1. The default position, if the RC does nothing, is that the patient is released from the recall (s 17F(6)). But by then it may have achieved its object, if this was to ensure that the patient had his medication.

If the CTO is revoked after the patient has been recalled, it is as if it had never been, except that the rules about the duration and renewal of the authority to detain assume that the patient was first admitted for treatment on the day on which the CTO was revoked (s 17G(1), (2), 5)). In other words, his admission lasts initially for six months, may be renewed for another six months, and then for periods of one year at a time (s 20(1), (2)). If he is now detained in a different hospital, the paperwork is treated as if he had originally been admitted to that hospital (s 17G(4)). The case must also be referred to the tribunal without delay (see chapter 8). Even so, if the RC is not a doctor, the patient may be detained for some time without up to date medical advice: the Department of Health thinks that this complies with article 5; some commentators have their doubts.

4. TRANSFERS BETWEEN HOSPITALS AND INTO GUARDIANSHIP

(a) Into guardianship

Any unrestricted patient can be transferred into the guardianship of the LSSA or a private individual approved by them (s 19(1)(a) and MHHGT Regs 2008, reg 7(4)). The procedure is much simpler than a fresh application for guardianship, and does not require the consent of the patient's nearest relative, but it must be done before the compulsory admission runs out. The transfer is authorised by the hospital managers or by an NHS body which is maintaining the patient in an independent hospital using part 1 of Form G6 (reg 7(5)(b)). They must record that the LSSA have agreed to the transfer and the date specified by the LSSA for it to take place. The agreement of a private guardian named to act must be recorded in part 2 of the form (reg 7(4)).

Guardianship (see chapter 9) was meant to be an alternative to hospital for patients who did not need in-patient treatment but did need a structure to their lives in the community. However, it has not been widely used as a form of statutory after-care, perhaps because it is a social services rather than a health service function and the guardian's limited powers no longer include a power to insist upon treatment. In future, CTOs may be more popular with both health and social services. The Code lists the following (apparently cumulative) factors as suggesting a transfer to guardianship rather than a CTO: a focus on the patient's general welfare rather than medical treatment; little risk of the patient needing to be admitted compulsorily and quickly to hospital; but a need for an enforceable power to require the patient to live in a particular place. A CTO is suggested where the focus is on ensuring that the patient receives the necessary medical treatment for his mental disorder without having to be detained again, but a speedy compulsory recall may be necessary (para 28.6).

(b) To other hospitals in England or Wales

A patient detained in an NHS or independent hospital can be transferred at any time without formality to another hospital, or accommodation used as such, under the same management (s 19(3); MHHGT Regs 2008, reg 7(5)(a)); if the patient is restricted, the Justice Secretary must consent (s 41(3)(c)(ii)). A patient detained in a high security hospital (unless sent there by a court on remand or an interim hospital order) can also be transferred to another high security hospital at any time by direction of the Justice Secretary (s 123(1)).

A patient detained in any kind of hospital can be transferred into another hospital under different management, with only a little more formality (s 19(1)(a) and reg 7(2)). Part 1 of Form H4 must be signed by the authorised officer of the managers of the first hospital, who must be satisfied that the patient can be admitted to the new hospital within the 28 days beginning on the date when the transfer is authorised. The form allows the patient to be taken there within that time, by an officer of the managers of either hospital, or by someone else authorised by the receiving hospital (reg 11(1)(a)). Restricted patients can be transferred in just the same way as unrestricted, provided that the Justice Secretary agrees (s 43(3)(c)(ii) and Sch 1, Pt 2, para 5(a)). Patients maintained in independent hospitals by an NHS body can alternatively be transferred by that body (reg 7(5)(b)).

This procedure can also be used to transfer patients into and out of the high security hospitals. Any compulsory patient originally admitted to an ordinary hospital can be transferred into a high security hospital if he meets the criteria and a bed is available. Once there, it can be difficult to obtain a transfer back into an ordinary hospital. Transfer to a less secure environment is usually an important step towards obtaining discharge or even leave of absence. But it is not a breach of the patient's rights under article 5 of the ECHR to detain him in a high security hospital for longer than he needs to be there, provided that the criteria for detaining him as a "person of unsound mind" still apply: *Ashingdane v United Kingdom* 19850 7 EHRR 528. The Secretary of State also has power to direct a transfer out of a special hospital (s 123(2)), but apparently this is never used. The same regulations as to transport apply (reg 11(2)(b)).

After a patient has been transferred, the authority to detain him is simply amended as if he had been admitted to the new hospital on the date of his original admission (s 19(2)(a)).

Recalled community patients can be transferred to another hospital in the same way, using Form CTO6, but have to be taken to the new hospital within 72 hours of their detention in the first (regs 9, 12).

(c) To other parts of the United Kingdom and islands

Ministers have power to transfer most compulsory hospital patients, patients on CTOs and conditionally discharged restricted patients from England or Wales to Scotland (ss 80, 80ZA, 80A) or Northern Ireland (ss 81, 81ZA, 81A), provided that this is in their interests and the necessary arrangements have been made. Once again, this does not apply to patients remanded to hospital by a court or on an interim hospital order. Guardianship patients can be transferred to Northern Ireland but references to guardianship have been removed from the section dealing with transfers to Scotland (cf ss 80(1) and 81(1)). The transfer of unrestricted patients is authorised by the Secretary of State for Health and of restricted patients by the Justice Secretary. Regulations under the Mental Health (Care and Treatment) (Scotland) Act 2003, ss 289, 290 provide for the transfer of compulsory patients from Scotland to any other country: see Mental Health (Cross border transfer: patients subject to detention requirement or otherwise in hospital) (Scotland) Regulations 2005, SSI 2005/467; Mental Health (England and Wales Cross-border transfer: patients subject to requirements other than detention) (Scotland) Regulations 2008, SSI 2008/356. The Department of Health and Social Services for Northern Ireland can transfer unrestricted patients, and the Secretary of State for Northern Ireland can transfer restricted patients (MHA 1983, s 82). Similar powers exist between England or Wales and the Channel Islands or Isle of Man (MHA 1983, ss 83–85A and local legislation).

The general effect of a transfer is that the patient is treated as if he had been newly admitted under the equivalent law in the receiving country on the date when he arrives there (see, eg, MHA, ss 80B(1), 80C, for detained and community patients moved from Scotland to England). This is bound to alter the period for which he is liable to be detained. But a patient who was admitted for assessment here is treated as a short term admission in the receiving country and vice versa. Similarly, a restriction order or direction must end whenever it would have ended if he had remained in the original country. When the patient is admitted to hospital here or arrives where he is to reside under guardianship or a CTO, the hospital, guardian or responsible hospital must record the date on Form M1 and must tell the nearest relative as soon as possible (MHHGT Regs 2008, regs 15 and 16). If a patient is transferred out of England or Wales, the old application, order or direction ceases to have effect when he reaches the new place (s 91(1), (2A)).

(d) Abroad

There is power to remove foreign patients from the country, although this is very rarely done. The patient must be neither a British citizen nor a Commonwealth citizen with a right of abode under section 2(1)(b) of the Immigration Act 1971; he must be receiving hospital in-patient treatment for mental disorder in England, Wales or Northern Ireland; and he must be compulsory detained for treatment under either civil or criminal powers (s 86(1)). Community and guardianship patients and patients detained only for assessment, or remanded to hospital by a court or under an interim hospital order, cannot be removed under this section.

It must appear that proper arrangements have been made, not only for the transfer, but also for the patient's treatment and care in the country where he is going, and that it is in the patient's own interests for him to go (s 86(2)). In theory, the patient could be sent to any country outside the United Kingdom or islands, but only his own country is likely to accept him. The Secretary of State for Health authorises the transfer of civil patients by warrant. He may also direct how the patient is to travel to his destination. This can be under escort or in some other form of custody, but obviously the Secretary of State can only insist on this until arrival in the receiving country. The Justice Secretary authorises the transfer of offender patients, both restricted and unrestricted. But if the patient is detained under a restriction order when he is transferred under section 86, it remains in force so as to apply if he ever comes back (s 91(2)).

These transfers must also be approved by a tribunal (s 86(3)). This safeguard was introduced at the suggestion of the old Race Relations Board. The dangers of misinterpretation are particularly great where there are cultural differences and some independent protection is certainly desirable. The Government (DHSS et al, 1978) expected that the tribunal would "form an opinion on the adequacy of information as to facilities in the receiving country", but that the Secretary of State would still have to make sure that the arrangements had been made.

However, the Government may have other powers to remove the patient, for example under the Immigration Act 1971 or the Repatriation of Prisoners Act 1984, where there is no safeguard for the patient's care. These may be used instead (*R v Secretary of State for Home Department, ex p Alghali* [1986] Imm AR 376), unless the patient is so severely ill that it would be inhumane to do so (*R v Secretary of State for the Home Department, ex p Talmasani* [1987] Imm AR 32, CA). It is a breach of the patent's rights under article 3 of the ECHR for this country to export him to a place where there is a real risk that he will be subjected to torture or inhuman or degrading treatment or punishment: see *D v United Kingdom* (1997) 24 EHRR 423. The Ministry of Justice (2009a) suggests that an RC who is responsible for a restricted patient who might be liable to deportation may wish to consider whether it would be better to repatriate him voluntarily or under section 86. This would be done by conditional discharge.

5. DISCHARGE

Patients may be discharged from compulsion by their RC, the hospital, or a tribunal. Civil patients may also be discharged by their nearest relative. Restricted patients may also be discharged by the Justice Secretary, whose consent is required to a discharge by the hospital or RC. Patients for whom an independent hospital is responsible may also be discharged by the registration authority or an NHS body which is maintaining them in the hospital. If an offender patient is covered by Chapter 2 of Part 3 of the DVCVA 2004 (see p 235, above), the responsible hospital managers will have to inform any victim, who has asked to be kept informed, that the patient has been discharged.

(a) By the patient's nearest relative

The nearest relative can discharge any hospital, community or guardianship patient who is subject to civil powers (s 23(2)). Understandably, he cannot discharge a hospital, community or guardianship patient who is subject to any kind of court order (Sch 1, Pt 1, para 8(b); Pt 2, para 7(b)). It is one thing for the court to abandon control to the medical authorities, another for the nearest relative to be able to override the order of a criminal court. The nearest relative is entitled to instruct an independent doctor or approved clinician to visit the patient at any reasonable time, to examine him in private and to inspect the records relating to his detention and treatment, in order to advise on a possible discharge (s 24(1), (2)). This could be wise, because the nearest relative must always give the hospital at least 72 hours' prior notice of his intention to discharge a hospital or community patient (s 25(1), (1A)). During this time, the RC can report to the managers on Form M2 (MHHGT Regs 2008, reg 25(1)) that the patient, if discharged, "would be likely to act in a manner dangerous to other persons or to himself". This prevents the nearest relative from discharging the patient, not only at once, but for the next six months (s 25(1), (1A)).

The relative must be told that his discharge has been barred. He can then apply to a tribunal within 28 days (s 66(1)(g)). The tribunal have power to discharge the patient in any event and must discharge a section 3 or community patient if they are not satisfied that, if discharged, he would be likely to act in a manner dangerous to himself or others (s 72(1)(b)(iii), (c)(v)). It is a curious thought that a community patient might be dangerous if discharged, but perhaps he might become so if this inducement to continue taking his medication were removed. The RC has no power to prevent the nearest relative from exercising his power to discharge a patient under guardianship. As we have seen in chapter 3, however, the nearest relative can be replaced by the county court if he has exercised, or proposes to exercise, his power of discharge without due regard for the patient's welfare or the interests of the public (s 29(3)(d)). An interim order enables the position to be preserved in the mean time.

(b) By the hospital, responsible clinician, Secretary of State or NHS bodies

The RC or the hospital managers can discharge a hospital, community or guardianship patient at any time (s 23(2)). This includes an ordinary hospital order patient (Sch 1), but not one remanded to hospital or under an interim hospital order. A restricted patient can only be discharged with the consent of the Justice Secretary (s 41(3)(c)(iii)). The managers cannot prevent the RC from discharging the patient and neither can the RC prevent the managers from discharging him. Technically, a discharge is by order in writing (s 23(1)), but there is no form laid down in the English regulations (unlike the Welsh).

However difficult it may be for the hospital managers to act contrary to their consultant's advice, and however difficult it is to distinguish their role from that of a tribunal, their independent power of discharge is seen as an important extra safeguard for patients. The Code advises that they may undertake a review at any time, should consider doing so if asked by the patient or if the RC makes a report barring the nearest relative from discharging. They must do so if the RC makes a report renewing the authority to detain or a CTO (para 31.11). They can either do this themselves or set up a managers' panel of at least three people, but none of the people on the panel can be employees of the management body, apart from the chairman of an NHS body (s 23(4), (5), (6)).

It is up to them how to conduct the review, balancing informality "against the rigour determined by the importance of the task" (MHA Code, para 31.32). However, the Code expects them to behave very much like a tribunal. They should inform themselves with written reports in advance and show these to the patient unless this is likely to cause serious harm to the physical or mental health of the patient or any other person (paras 31.25, 31.26). They should also involve the nearest relative and other relatives or carers. If the patient objects to this, the Code advises that "a suitable member of the professional care team should be asked to include the person's views in their report" (para 31.29). This is the worst of both worlds—the views are there but cannot effectively be challenged by or on behalf of the patient. The patient should be given a full opportunity to explain why he should no longer be detained or on a CTO; he should be allowed a representative of his choosing and also a relative, friend or advocate to accompany him; and the RC and other professionals should be allowed to state their views (para 31.32).

There is much to be said for emphasising the hospital's independent role in deciding whether it should still be detaining or responsible for a patient. But it is not so clear why this should be turned into something which is like, but not quite like, a tribunal. The hospital, being the detaining body, can never amount to an "independent and impartial tribunal" within the meaning of article 6(1) of the ECHR. In the days when rights to apply to a tribunal were more limited, it was understandable that the hospital managers' independent powers should have been emphasised. These days, it may be worth asking what they can add to the powers of the professionals and the tribunal without unnecessary and costly duplication of effort. But they undoubtedly add an extra layer of protection for the patient, especially when his detention or community treatment is renewed. This may be especially helpful for community patients, whose orders might otherwise continue indefinitely, because they are not occupying a precious hospital bed.

Patients liable to be detained in independent hospitals, and community patients for whom an independent hospital is responsible, may additionally be discharged by the Secretary of State, or by any NHS body which is maintaining them there (s 23(3), (3A)). An officer of these authorities may visit a patient at all reasonable times, interview him in private and inspect the documents authorising his detention. A doctor instructed by any of these authorities may do all those things and also examine the patient and his medical records (s 24(3) and (4)).

The Act does not expressly state the circumstances in which a patient must or may be set free. There is nothing to prevent a discharge even though the statutory grounds for detention still exist. Equally, the Act does not insist on discharge the moment that they do not. The Code advises that "the essential yardstick" is whether the grounds for continued detention or a CTO are satisfied (para 31.14) although there is a residual discretion to discharge even if they are (para 31.22). It would raise a question under article 5 of the ECHR as to whether the patient could continue to be lawfully detained if the statutory criteria no longer applied to him: the *Winterwerp* criteria may be less demanding (see p 98, earlier) but would the detention be "lawful"?

The RC and hospital managers may still wonder where they stand if they release a patient whom they could lawfully continue to detain, particularly if he promptly does harm to himself or others. They cannot, of course, be liable to anyone if they have without negligence decided that the criteria for detention no longer exist. They could only be liable if they had been negligent in reaching that decision or if they had a discretion whether or not to release (whether on leave of absence or a CTO or by discharge). In that event, they will owe their usual duty of care towards the patient himself (see p 206, earlier). But it is unlikely that their liability to him could include the adverse consequences *to him* of the damage he does to others. In *Clunis v Camden and Islington Health Authority* [1998] QB 978, CA, Christopher Clunis tried unsuccessfully to sue for the harm he had suffered from having unlawfully killed Jonathan Zito.

But what about their liability to the people harmed? In *Holgate v Lancashire Mental Hospitals Board* [1937] 4 All ER 294, the hospital authorities and doctors were found to have failed in their duty of care towards people whom they could foresee would be injured when they allowed a dangerous patient out on licence without adequate supervision. However, in *Palmer v Tees Health Authority* [1999] EWCA Civ 1533, [2000] PIQR P1, the Court of Appeal held that *Holgate* could not be reconciled with later House of Lords' decisions on the question of proximity to the victim. They had mainly in mind the comments of Lord Keith of Kinkel, in *Hill v Chief Constable of West Yorkshire* [1989] 1 AC 53, on the decision in *Dorset Yacht Co v Home Office* [1970] AC 1004: it is one thing to hold that prison officers were liable to owners whose yachts were damaged when they carelessly allowed borstal boys to escape from a camping outing and steal a yacht to get away; it is another to hold the West Yorkshire police liable to another victim of the Yorkshire ripper killed after, it was alleged, they should have caught him. The hospital does not owe a duty to the whole wide world to protect everyone from the harm that a released patient may do. There must be a close relationship between the defendant and the claimant if a duty of care to protect the claimant from the criminal acts of the patient is to be imposed. That might arise if the hospital knew or ought to have known of a specific threat to a particular individual (for example, his wife or child) if the patient were released; but not because of a foreseeable risk to numberless unknown individuals. However, if the hospital know or ought to know that a particular person's life is at immediate risk if the patient is allowed to leave (including the life of the patient), they might be liable both in the common law of negligence and under article 2 of the ECHR: see *Savage v South East Essex Partnership NHS Foundation Trust* [2008] UKHL 74, [2009] 1 AC 681.

(c) By the Justice Secretary

The Justice Secretary's consent is needed before the hospital or RC can discharge a restricted patient (s 41(3)9c)(iii)). But the Justice Secretary also has his own power to release a restricted patient (s 42(2)). This is more frequently used, because he can choose between an absolute and a conditional discharge. These decisions are taken extremely seriously and a high proportion are considered personally by a Minister.

There used to be a clear division of responsibility between the hospital and the Justice Secretary. The RC would decide whether, on medical grounds, the patient was fit to leave. The Justice Secretary would then decide whether it was safe to let him go. This would only be allowed when it was clear that no undue risk was involved, having regard to all the circumstances, including the patient's response to treatment, the prognosis, and the "safeguards which the arrangements proposed offer against recurrence of anti-social behaviour" (Aarvold Report, 1972). Fear of public opinion, as well as fear for the public themselves, led to a very cautious policy. The system was generally very effective in protecting the public (see Walker and McCabe, 1973). But no system can guarantee complete success unless people are locked up forever, and there has always been much public concern about patients who commit murder following their discharge. Graham Young, for example, committed murder and other offences by poisoning shortly after he had been released from Broadmoor, where he had been sent because of very similar offences committed when a boy. As a result, an independent multi-disciplinary Advisory Board on Restricted Patients (the "Aarvold Board") was set up to consider cases which were thought to require "special care in assessment". But this no longer met after 2001 and ceased to function in 2003.

A transferred prisoner or a patient subject to a hospital and limitation direction (a "hybrid order") can be returned to prison if his mental condition no longer warrants treatment in hospital. But a restriction order patient cannot be detained as a "person of unsound mind" under article 5(1)(e) of the ECHR unless he has a true and persisting mental disorder of a kind or degree which warrants his compulsory confinement (the *Winterwerp* criteria). If he has not, he can no longer be detained in a hospital, no matter how likely he is to misbehave again if set at large. The MHA does not require the Justice Secretary to consider whether the statutory criteria for detention still exist. Nevertheless, it is clear that he should do so, at least whenever he receives the annual report or a specific proposal for discharge from the RC.

Restricted patients may also be discharged by a tribunal (see chapter 8) and more of them are now discharged by a tribunal than by the Justice Secretary. Why then does a Government Minister retain the power of discharge? After all, his powers to determine how long prisoners serving life sentences shall stay in prison once they have served the punitive element of their sentence have been progressively taken away in the light of decisions from the European Court of Human Rights, culminating in *Stafford v United Kingdom* (2002) 35 EHRR 32. However, his powers are wider than the tribunal's. First, a patient may become fit for discharge some time before his next right to apply to a tribunal comes round. Secondly, the tribunal can only discharge him if they are not satisfied that the criteria for detention exist, whereas the Justice Secretary has power to grant a discharge even if they do. In practice, he may also find it easier than a tribunal to make the necessary arrangements for a conditional discharge.

A conditional discharge is the equivalent of a CTO for restricted patients but the statutory provisions are much simpler. The Justice Secretary will usually impose conditions of residence at a stated address and for both clinical and social supervision. One purpose is to help the patient's reintegration in the community after what may have been a long time in hospital. Another is to keep an eye on what is going on. The clinical supervisor is responsible for the regular assessment of the patient's mental health and monitoring his medication. There is no power to impose treatment upon the patient unless he consents or the MCA principles apply. However, it is usually a condition that the patient "shall comply with treatment as directed by the clinical supervisor". In *R (H) v Mental Health Review Tribunal* [2007] EWHC 884 (Admin) the judge rejected the suggestion that this interfered with his common law freedom of choice as well as his right to respect for his private life under article 8 of the ECHR. He still had the right to refuse and refusal would not, by itself, lead to his recall to hospital. He might still feel a sense of grievance that (curiously) the MHA safeguards for particular forms of treatment do not apply to him, although they do apply to community patients.

The social supervisor is there to provide practical support for the patient in everyday life, liaising with providers of accommodation, employment, day care and other services. Section 117 applies to conditionally discharged patients in the same way that it applies to other hospital order patients. Meetings with the patient should be at least once a week for the first month, then once a fortnight, and then once a month. But the Ministry of Justice expects a report from each supervisor one month after discharge and then every three months as well as an annual review by them both. The Ministry Guidance (2009e) stresses that supervisors should never overlook problems for fear of jeopardising patients' progress: reluctance to show their clients in an unfavourable light was a "repeated theme" in reports into homicides committed by discharged restricted patients.

Could the conditions require the patient to live in a hospital? In *Secretary of State for the Home Department v Mental Health Review Tribunal for Mersey Regional Health Authority* [1986] 1 WLR 1170, it was held that discharge must mean release from hospital, or at least from having to stay there. More recent case law distinguishes between discharge from one state of detention to another, which is unlawful, and discharge to conditions which restrict but do not amount to a deprivation of liberty, which is not: see *R (Secretary of State for the Home Department) v Mental Health Rerview Tribunal and PH* [2002] EWCA Civ 1868, [2003] MHLR 202; *T v Secretary of State for Justice* [2008] EWHC 1707 (Admin), [2008] MHLR 290.

The Justice Secretary can vary the conditions at any time, whether these were imposed by a tribunal or by himself (s 73(4) and (5); the power to vary his own conditions is implicit rather than explicit). If the tribunal does not impose his usual conditions, he will do so himself. In due course, he may grant an absolute discharge. This requires a positive act: simply allowing all the conditions apart from the power of recall to lapse is not enough (*R v Secretary of State for the Home Department, ex p Didlick* [1993] COD 412, DC). The patient may also apply to a tribunal for the conditions to be varied or the restrictions lifted altogether. But unless the tribunal grants an absolute discharge, the Justice Secretary will still be in effective control of the conditions and how they operate. The real dilemma is that the criteria for detaining the patient may still exist unless appropriate facilities for him can be found in the community and the tribunal has no power to order that they are. This is a "Catch 22" situation to which the courts have not yet found a solution.

Until the restrictions end or the patient is granted an absolute discharge, he remains liable to be recalled to hospital (s 42(3)). The Justice Secretary issues a warrant and the patient can then be taken into custody and back to hospital as if he had gone absent without leave on the warrant date (s 42(4)). He can be recalled to a different hospital from the one in which he was originally detained, but not to some other kind of establishment. The Butler Committee (1975) were concerned about conditionally discharged restriction order patients whose conduct was worrying, but whose medical condition was not suitable for hospital, but agreed that it would be a grave impairment of liberty to provide for recall to prison on mere suspicion.

The Act lays down no criteria for recall, nor does it state that the Justice Secretary must obtain medical evidence beforehand. However, in *Kay v United Kingdom* (1998) 40 BMLR 20, the patient committed further offences soon after his conditional discharge and was sent to prison. The Home Secretary issued a warrant for him to be recalled to hospital the moment he was released from prison, even though a tribunal had found that he was not mentally disordered. The European Commission on Human Rights held that it was a breach of article 5(1) of the ECHR to recall him without up to date medical evidence that he was suffering from a mental disorder. Since then, the Justice Secretary has accepted that, except in an emergency, there must be up to date medical evidence showing that the *Winterwerp* criteria are met. In fact, the courts expect him to have evidence from which he can reasonably conclude that the rather more stringent MHA criteria are met: that the patient is suffering from mental disorder of a nature or degree making it appropriate for him to be detained in hospital for treatment and that it is necessary in the interests of his own health or safety or for the protection of others that he should receive it: see *R (M) v Secretary of State for the Home Department* [2007] EWCA Civ 687, (2007) 98 BMLR 130. But this is still not very demanding. Hospital treatment may be appropriate even if the patient has not yet deteriorated into a florid state if there is a risk that he will do so. A disorder may be of a nature which justifies detention even if it is not yet of a degree which would do so.

Provided that there are grounds to believe that the criteria are met, the Ministry of Justice will put public safety before therapeutic considerations. The decision will largely turn on the gravity and imminence of the risk. But recall will not be used to deal with anti-social or offending behaviour which is unconnected with the patient's mental disorder. In theory, recall should not be used as a sanction for breach of the conditions if there is no reason to believe that the criteria for detention apply. In practice, failing to keep in touch with the supervisor or to comply with medication will trigger consideration of whether the patient should be recalled (Ministry of Justice, 2009e). However, it is also possible for a conditionally discharged patient to be admitted to hospital informally or under civil powers (*R v North West London Mental Health NHS Trust, ex p Stewart* [1997] 4 All ER 871). The Justice Secretary welcomes this for a short period, but if the use of civil powers remains necessary "immediate recall will almost invariably be appropriate" (Ministry of Justice 2009e, para 60). The MHAC (2009a) questions whether this follows—the civil criteria do not necessarily connote the degree of danger which would normally lead to recall.

If the patient is recalled, he is entitled to an explanation, but health service guidance was to give this in stages because he might be "in an excitable and nervous state" (HSG(93)20; LAC (93)9). He is also entitled to ask for a speedy judicial review of the merits of his recall, under article 5(4) of the ECHR. The MHA requires that every recall be referred to a tribunal within one month of the day on which patient arrives back in hospital (s 75(1)(a)). In *R (Rayner) v Secretary of State for Justice* [2008] EWCA Civ 176, [2008] 1 MHLR 115, the referral was more than two months after the patient got back to hospital and he complained that he did not have the right to bring proceedings himself. The Court of Appeal held that his right to bring judicial review to compel the Justice Secretary to refer the case was enough. But a reference is one thing and a hearing another. The two years it took for the patient's case to reach a tribunal in *Kay v United Kingdom*, above, was a breach of article 5(4).

(d) By courts or tribunals

The age-old remedy for challenging unlawful detention in English law was the writ of *habeas corpus*, but the European Court of Human Rights found this inadequate to challenge the factual as opposed to the legal case for a patient's detention: see *X v United Kingdom* (1981) 4 EHRR 188. The same applies to the more commonly used modern remedy of judicial review. Ever since the 1959 Act, the principal way of challenging the factual case for a patient's detention under the MHA has been an application or reference to a tribunal with the power to direct the discharge of detained, community and guardianship patients. In England, this jurisdiction is now exercised by the Health, Education and Social Care chapter of the First-tier Tribunal, but in Wales it remains with the Mental Health Review Tribunal. Deprivations of liberty authorised under the MCA

DoLS can be challenged in the new Court of Protection. But if a person is deprived of his liberty without authorisation it would still be possible to challenge this by way of habeas corpus or judicial review. All these are discussed in chapter 8.

6. ABSCONDERS AND ESCAPERS

Theoretically, there is no difference between the escape of a dangerous psychopath from Broadmoor and the failure of a harmless schizophrenic to return from a shopping expedition, although the response in practice will be quite different. It is a crime punishable with up to two years' imprisonment to "induce or knowingly assist" any compulsory hospital, guardianship or community patient to absent himself without leave (s 128(1)) or to induce or knowingly assist a person to escape from legal custody under the MHA (s 128(2)), or knowingly to harbour a patient who is AWOL or at large and liable to be retaken, or to give him help in order to prevent or hinder his recapture (s 128(3)). It has also been held to be a conspiracy to commit a common law public nuisance to bring in such things as rope, a hacksaw, glass cutters and other tools in order to help a "homicidal lunatic" escape from Broadmoor (*R v Soul* (1980) 70 CrAppR 295); but Lord Bingham has found this "hard to explain" because there was no proof of actual danger to the public (*R v Rimmington* [2005] UKHL 63, [2006] 1 AC 459, para 20).

The MHA makes elaborate provision for the recapture of compulsory patients. If necessary, a warrant to gain entry to premises to recapture the absconder can be obtained under section 135(2) (p 117, earlier); sometimes there may also be a common law or other power of entry (pp 114, 115, earlier). The distinction drawn in the MHA between absconding and escaping is apparently not the same as the distinction drawn by the Government for statistical purposes (MHAC, 2009a). For the Government, absconding is where a patient who is already outside the hospital perimeter fails to return when he should; escaping is where he gets out of the secure perimeter. For the MHA, the distinction is between those who escape from "legal custody" and those who simply go absent without leave.

(a) Escaping from legal custody

A person who is required or authorised by or under the Act to be conveyed to any place, or to be kept in custody, or to be detained in a place of safety, is in legal custody while being so conveyed, kept or detained (s 137(1)). This usually applies to people on the move to or between hospitals or places where they are required under the Act to be. It does not apply to a compulsory patient who is simply absent without leave: *D'Souza v DPP* [1992] 1 WLR 1073, HL (p 114, earlier). Those who have power to take or detain people in legal custody have all the "powers, authorities, protection and privileges" of a constable for the purpose (s 137(2)). This does not mean that they can do what they like. Even constables can only use such force as is reasonably necessary to achieve their lawful object.

A person who escapes from legal custody can be retaken by the person from whom he escaped, or by any police officer, or by any AMHP. If he has already been compulsorily admitted to a hospital (and escapes, for example, when being escorted back from leave of absence), he can also be retaken by someone on the staff of, or authorised by, that hospital (s 138(1)). If he is being taken to or from a hospital under any of the Act's transfer powers or under any of the powers relating to people concerned in criminal proceedings or transferred from prison, or if he is being taken to or detained in a place of safety pending admission to hospital under those latter powers, he can also be retaken by someone on the staff of, or authorised by, the hospital to which he is eventually going as well as from the one from which he may be coming (s 138(4)). (This does not apply to transfers to and from the islands, or to patients remanded to hospital by a court, or those under interim hospital orders, or civil and Immigration Act detainees being returned to prison.)

There are important time limits to some of these powers. A patient who escapes from or on the way to a "place of safety" under sections 135 or 136 can only be retaken within 72 hours of his escape or his arrival at the place of safety, whichever expires earlier (s 138(3)). A patient escaping on the way to hospital under a civil application for admission can only be retaken if he can be got back to the hospital within the 14 days which begin on the date of the second medical examination. If it is only an emergency application, he must arrive within 24 hours of the medical examination or the time when the application was signed, whichever is the earlier (s 6(1)). A patient who escapes before getting to hospital under criminal powers can be retaken at any time (s 138(5)). A patient who has already been admitted to a hospital or guardianship, or recalled from a CTO, can be retaken within the same time as one who goes absent without leave (s 138(2)).

(b) Going absent without leave

A patient is absent without leave if he absconds from a hospital to which he has been compulsorily admitted; or if he fails to return at the expiry of or when recalled from leave of absence; or if he breaks a residence condition in his leave of absence (s 18(1)); or if he fails to attend or absconds from hospital after being recalled from a CTO (s 18(2A)); or if he fails to return to hospital when recalled by the Justice Secretary from conditional discharge. He may be taken into custody and returned to hospital by any police officer, any AMHP or by anyone on the staff of or authorised by, that hospital (s 18(1)). If he is living in another hospital as a condition of leave of absence, he can also be retaken by someone on the staff of, or authorised by, that hospital (s 18(2)). Recalled CTO patients may also be returned by anyone authorised by the RC (s 18(2A)).

It is one thing to have power to retake and return an absconding patient. It is another to make the necessary arrangements, especially if the patient absconds from a hospital in Wales and makes his way to London (see MHAC, 2009a). Ideally, the local mental health services in the place where he is found should help out, but this does not always happen. The MHA Code requires hospitals to have a clear policy on what to do if a patient is AWOL, including the circumstances in which other agencies such as the LSSA, other people such as the nearest relative, and the police, should be informed (para 22.11). The police should only be asked to help if this is necessary. If the patient's whereabouts are known, their role should if possible only be to help a suitably qualified mental health professional get the patient back to hospital (para 22.13). However, the police should always be informed immediately that a restricted patient goes missing, or if the patient is thought dangerous or particularly vulnerable (para 22.14). If they have been informed that a patient is missing they should of course be told if he turns up again (para 22.16).

Once again, there are time limits. An in-patient detained for six or 72 hours under section 5, or a patient admitted for assessment for 72 hours or 28 days under sections 4 or 2, can never be retaken once that time has gone by (s 18(5)). Patients admitted for treatment or recalled from a CTO can be recaptured within the six months which began on the first day of absence without leave or the end of the current period of detention or the CTO, whichever is the longer (s 18(4)). Detention cannot be renewed while a patient is absent without leave; but if he is absent when or during the week before his detention expires, and is either recaptured or returns voluntarily within the time limit, he remains liable to detention for a further week beginning with the day of his return (s 21). This is to enable the renewal formalities to be completed. Renewal reports completed before the patient went AWOL do not count unless the renewal period started before the patient absented himself (s 18(4A)).

If a patient is recaptured or returns within 28 days of going absent without leave, the hospital can complete the renewal formalities if required; otherwise the detention will continue as if he had never been away (s 21A). But if he has been at large for more than 28 days, then the RC has to review the case, in consultation with an AMHP and one or more other professionals involved with the patient's treatment, and decide whether the renewal criteria exist (s 21B(1),(2),(3)); if the RC does not report that they do within a week of return, the patient is no longer liable to be detained even if he otherwise would have been (s 21B(4)); if the RC does so report, the patient's detention is renewed from the time it would otherwise have expired (s 21B(5)); if the detention still had some time to run but the report is within the last two months, it will operate like the usual renewal report (s 21B(7)). The patient can apply to a tribunal if his detention is renewed under this procedure (s 66(1)(fa) and (fb)). None of this, of course, applies to restricted patients, whose detention does not have to be renewed and who can be recaptured at any time.

These provisions were introduced in 1995 to replace the old rule that any unrestricted patient could achieve his "discharge by operation of law" simply by remaining absent without leave for 28 days. In the days of tight security in psychiatric hospitals, the patient's ability to survive in the community for such a long time was considered proof that he was not ill at all. This makes no sense these days, and caused particular concern with hospital order patients, as many as nine per cent of whom used to achieve their discharge in this way (Walker and McCabe, 1973). So the rule was abolished but replaced with a requirement positively to consider whether the patient ought still to be detained.

The equivalent of these renewal and re-examination provisions now also apply to recalled CTO patients who return after having been absent without leave. This means that if they come back before their CTO expires, but only within the last week, there is an additional week within which to complete the formalities (s 21). It also means that if they have been away for more than 28 days, they must be examined and reported on within a week, otherwise their CTO will end automatically (s 21B). The Code says that it is always good practice to re-examine a detained or CTO patient who returns after a substantial period of absence without leave to see whether the criteria for detention or a CTO still apply (para 22.19).

(c) Remands to hospital and interim hospital orders

Patients remanded to hospital or on interim hospital orders, who abscond from the hospital or on the way to or from it, may be arrested without warrant by any police officer and must then be brought before the court which made the remand or order as soon as possible (ss 35(10), 36(8) and 38(7)). The court can then end the remand or order and deal with the patient in another way. There is no time limit on these recaptures. Other people can presumably act under the usual procedures, where these apply.

(d) Escaping from England or Wales

A patient who would be subject to recapture under sections 138 or 18 if he were still in England or Wales can be retaken and returned from Northern Ireland, the Channel Islands or Isle of Man. Those who can do this include the national equivalents of an English constable and an AMHP (s 88). Regulations under the Mental Health (Care and Treatment) (Scotland) Act 2003, s 309, provide for the return of patients who have absconded to Scotland (Mental Health (Absconding Patients from Other Jurisdictions) (Scotland) Regulations 2008, SSI 2008/333). There are also powers to recapture in England or Wales patients escaping from Northern Ireland (MHA, s 87), the islands (MHA, s 89), or Scotland (Mental Health (Care and Treatment) (Scotland) Act 2003 (Consequential Provisions) Order 2005, SI 2005/2078). Offender patients who escape to countries outside the United Kingdom and Islands may be extradited if this is provided for by treaty between that country and the United Kingdom and vice versa.

7. SUBSEQUENT CRIMINAL COURT ORDERS

A short period of imprisonment (or the equivalent) under the sentence or order of a United Kingdom court (including a committal or remand) has no effect upon a pre-existing admission to hospital for treatment, CTO or guardianship. If the compulsory measure would normally have expired while the patient was in custody, it does not do so until the day of his discharge from custody (s 22(5)). He is then treated as if he had gone absent without leave on that day (s 22(6)). He can be taken back to hospital within 28 days (s 22(7)). The hospital then has the usual week in which to complete the formalities for renewal (s 21(1) and (2)). The same would apply if he returned to hospital of his own accord. A community patient who had not been recalled to hospital is treated as if he had absented himself without leave on the day on which he was released from custody and had returned himself to hospital on the 28th day after his release (s 22(8)). This is an elaborate way of saying that the order can be renewed during the following week.

But if the patient is imprisoned for more than six months (or for successive periods totalling more than six months) these compulsory measures automatically cease to have effect (s 22(1) and (2)). A restriction order, however, carries on regardless (see, eg, *R v Secretary of State for the Home Department, ex p K* [1991] QB 270). A fresh hospital or guardianship order cancels any previous hospital admission or guardianship (s 40(5)), except a restriction order (s 41(4)). Section 22 applies, however, if that second order is quashed on appeal.

8. COMMENTARY

The drastic reduction in the number of hospital beds for patients with mental disorders, coupled with the changes in the way in which treatment for mental disorder is provided, led many to think that there should be some way of imposing treatment upon people who were not in-patients in hospital. The Richardson Committee (1999) proposed that all long term treatment plans should be authorised by a mental health tribunal, which could approve treatment either in hospital or in the community. The Mental Health (Care and

Treatment) (Scotland) Act 2003 has set up a similar scheme in Scotland which has been widely admired, but is struggling to keep up with the demand (McManus, 2009). In England and Wales, we have not been so bold. But the MHA has been made much longer and more complicated by the introduction of Community Treatment Orders.

Were they necessary? Once the courts had increased the flexibility of long term leave of absence, where was the need to introduce another power to achieve something not quite as effective? Was it "a complete red herring" simply "shuffling around the deck of powers rather than creating new ones" (Gledhill, 2007)? Does it in fact provide better patient protection? What is the difference in practice between requiring a patient on long term leave to attend a clinic for assessment, tests and medication and requiring a community patient to do so? The penalty for disobedience is swifter and surer in the former but is that a good thing or a bad thing? And if we had to have a new power to require co-operation in the community, why not simply extend the concept of conditional discharge to unrestricted patients? This would have made the law a great deal simpler. At the same time, why did we not extend the safeguards attached to ECT and long term medication to conditionally discharged restricted patients?

But the MHAC's fear was that, now that we have this "half way house" between long term hospital admission and getting lost in the community, it will become routine to use it, rather in the same way that the Ministry of Justice expects restricted patients to progress down through the levels of security before being released from their control. Once made, a CTO can be renewed indefinitely. But civil patients have not been convicted of any crime and should not be kept on a string in the same way as those who have. Early indications are that CTOs are being used much more often than the Government thought that they would be. The situation needs to be watched.

8 TRIBUNALS AND COURTS

Under article 5(4) of the European Convention on Human Rights, everyone deprived of his liberty by arrest or detention is entitled to take proceedings "by which the lawfulness of his detention shall be decided speedily by a court and his release ordered if the detention is not lawful". In *X v United Kingdom* (1982) 4 EHRR 188, the European Court of Human Rights decided that, because mental disorder is a fluctuating condition, all people who were detained because they were "of unsound mind", even those who were admitted by order of a criminal court, were entitled to a periodic judicial consideration of the merits of their continued detention. *Habeas corpus* proceedings were not enough because they could not provide a full assessment of the merits. Where the initial admission is from a court, the review obviously need not be immediate. But where the initial admission is not from a court, as when the patient is "sectioned" under the Mental Health Act 1983 (MHA) or detained under the Mental Capacity Act 2005 (MCA) deprivation of liberty safeguards (the DoLS), article 5(4) applies straightaway, although the European Court thought that *habeas corpus* might be a sufficient safeguard for a brief period of detention in an emergency.

Mental health review tribunals were first established under the MHA 1959 to review a patient's detention under a civil admission for treatment or an ordinary hospital order. They could not review admissions for assessment and could only make recommendations to the Home Secretary about restricted patients. The Percy Commission (1957) took the view that a specialist tribunal using informal inquisitorial procedures would be a much more effective safeguard for patients than the single magistrate who used to put a judicial rubber-stamp on the hospital's decisions. Following the decision in *X v United Kingdom*, the right to apply to a tribunal was extended to cover almost all patients detained under the MHA 1983.

In November 2008, the mental health review tribunals for England (but not for Wales) were absorbed into the new tribunal structure set up under the Tribunals, Courts and Enforcement Act 2007 (see Transfer of Tribunal Functions Order 2008, SI 2008/2833, art 3 and Sch 1). The first tier of that structure is organised into "chambers", where jurisdictions which are thought to deal with similar subject-matter are grouped together. Mental health has been placed in the Health, Education and Social Care Chamber, along with determining special educational needs and regulating the standards of health and social care providers. An appeal on a point of law lies from the first tier tribunal to the Upper Tribunal and from there to the Court of Appeal. However, the Ministry of Justice (2008a) confidently stated that the transition "should have few implications for patients or for hospitals or local social services authorities. The Tribunals Service will continue to provide the secretariat, and hearings will remain largely as they are now".

A tribunal hearing is the way to challenge the merits of the use compulsory powers under the MHA. However, patients who consider that their detention is unlawful (rather than simply unwarranted on the facts) have always been able to challenge this in the High Court, either by way of *habeas corpus* or by judicial review. The legality of tribunal decisions could also be challenged by way of judicial review but this role has now been taken over by the Upper Tribunal.

Article 5(4) also applies to people who are deprived of their liberty under the MCA DoLS but, like all other disputes under that Act, these cases go to the Court of Protection. This too is a specialist court, with procedures designed specially for the purpose. But it is part of the ordinary court structure and its rules are modelled more closely on those of the civil courts. Both the Court of Protection and the Family Division of the High Court may authorise the detention of incapacitated people. Some fear that the difference between courts and tribunals is being steadily eroded, with tribunals becoming more and more like courts, while the courts have not yet evolved into places where the voice of mentally disordered and disabled people can effectively be heard.

1. THE TRIBUNAL

It is unusual for a tribunal to be deciding questions of personal liberty. The Leggatt Report (2001) suggested three tests of whether a case should go to a tribunal rather than a court: first, whether users should be able to prepare and present their own cases effectively rather than rely upon others to do so; second, the need for expertise in the area of law involved so that users should not have to explain to the tribunal what the law is, as they so often have to do in court; and third, the need for special expertise in the subject matter of the dispute. In mental health, tribunals have all these advantages. Their membership can be tailored to the particular problem and their more flexible and informal procedures to the peculiarities of the subject-matter and people involved. They are not stuck in the adversarial model of British court procedure and can adopt elements of a more inquisitorial approach. They should not be too overawed by the hospital evidence and should be able to minimise any adverse effect which the proceedings may have on the patient's health and treatment. But these admirable objectives have to be reconciled with the rules of natural justice: that a person should know the case against him and have an opportunity of challenging the evidence upon which it is based and that the tribunal should listen impartially to both sides of the dispute.

(a) Membership and composition

There is now a single tribunal for England and a single mental health review tribunal for Wales (MHA, s 65(1), (2) and Sch 2). Each has three types of member, appointed by the Lord Chancellor but chosen for him by the Judicial Appointments Commission set up under the Constitutional Reform Act 2005:

   (i) legal members, who have such legal experience as he considers suitable; they are expected to have a professional qualification giving them at least rights of audience in the county and magistrates' courts, but both practitioners and academics have been appointed;
  (ii) medical members, chosen after consultation with the Department of Health; these are expected to be Members or Fellows of the Royal College of Psychiatrists and have held an appointment as a consultant psychiatrist for at least three years; and
 (iii) other members, also chosen after consultation with the Department of Health, who have "such experience in administration, such knowledge of social services or such other qualifications or experience as the Lord Chancellor considers suitable" (Sch 2, para 1); they are expected to have a "well-founded and practical experience of working in the health and

welfare fields in either the statutory, voluntary or private sector" (see the tribunal website). It is wrong, therefore, to think of them as "lay" members.

All tribunal members must retire at the age of 70, but the Lord Chief Justice can authorise individuals to continue up to the age of 75 (Sch 2, para 2A).

There is a President for England and a President for Wales, appointed from among the legal members of each tribunal (Sch 2, para 3). There are nearly 1,000 tribunal members in England and 90 in Wales. The Council on Tribunals (2000) was particularly keen on the Presidential model of tribunal organisation, thinking that it would provide a greater degree of independence and separation from the sponsoring Government department. Under the new tribunal structure in England, the staff are members of the Tribunals Service, which comes under the aegis of the Ministry of Justice, and not from the Department of Health. Thus the clerks dealing with any particular case are now independent both of the Department and of the hospital where the patient is detained. It may be doubted whether patients will notice or appreciate the difference (tribunal clerks in Wales are independent of the hospital but not of the Government). There are more important things to worry about. Under the old system, the Council on Tribunals and the Mental Health Act Commission (MHAC) often voiced their concerns about the ever-increasing workload of the tribunals, the lengthening delays, the high incidence of unclerked hearings, and the general shortage of resources (Council on Tribunals, 2000; MHAC, 2005, 2008, 2009a). Whether the transfer to the new system will result in significant improvements remains to be seen.

While the clerks are managed by the Tribunals Service, the President is responsible for advising on the recruitment and deployment of tribunal members, monitoring the performance of tribunals, promoting communication between them and fostering a "team spirit", acting as spokesman and negotiator for the tribunal with the Government, and giving guidance to tribunals on issues of practice and procedure. The President is also responsible for training. Before 1983, this was a much neglected area. The only training provided might be a few sittings-in on tribunal hearings. Members did not sit frequently outside the high security hospitals and hardly ever met other members from their own areas let alone from elsewhere. This was a recipe for wide divergences in practice, which in turn made it difficult to secure consensus on the correct approach. Training and interchange between members improved after the 1983 changes, but some felt that it was still inadequate (eg Council on Tribunals, 2000) and research suggested that there were still differences in both process and outcome for apparently similar patients (Peay, 1989). However, such findings are not unique to these tribunals, which have now received a great deal more attention from lawyers and the higher courts than they did before *X v United Kingdom* and the 1983 reforms.

As the name implies, the tribunal for an individual case is made up of at least three members, one from each of the three groups. It is chaired by the legal member (Sch 2, paras 4 and 6), who is now known in England as a tribunal judge. The tribunal judges may also be called upon to give directions and make procedural decisions before the hearing. But there are no decisions which, under the rules, are reserved for them. In practice, Fennell (1979) found that the lawyer was usually the most powerful member of the tribunal, but the doctor's opinions and character were crucial because of her peculiar role (see below). The legal member may be particularly powerful in cases concerning restricted patients. When tribunals were given power to discharge restricted patients under the 1983 Act, experienced criminal judges were imported to hear these cases (s 78(4), which provides that the rules may restrict the people qualified to chair such tribunals, now only applies in Wales). The fear was that, without this, neither the sentencing courts nor the general public would have confidence that enough weight would be given to questions of public safety, and even that the doctors might have to modify their treatment plans to ensure that patients were not discharged prematurely. In practice, many applications by restricted patients were supported by their doctors, who had been unable to persuade the Home Secretary to agree to a transfer or discharge. Most restricted patients are now discharged by tribunals rather than by the Justice Secretary (who has taken over the Home Secretary's role). Introducing experienced criminal judges may have led the tribunals to take a greater interest in the index offence and the patient's previous criminal record, but not to greater consistency in either procedure or substance (Peay, 1989).

It is an essential feature of a "court" for the purpose of article 5(4) that it is independent and impartial. This means that it must not only be institutionally separate from the detaining authorities, but also that the individual members must be, and must be seen to be, impartial. This can be difficult in any tribunal which includes specialist medical expertise as this is often in short supply (see *Gillies v Secretary of State for Work and Pensions* [2006] UKHL 2, [2006] 1 WLR 781). In *R (PD) v West Midlands and North West Mental Health Review Tribunal* [2004] EWCA Civ 311, [2004] MHLR 174, the medical member was employed at a different hospital from the one where the patient was detained but by the same NHS Trust which managed them both. The Court of Appeal decided that he was nevertheless impartial. The "fair minded and informed observer" would understand that the Trust had no interest in the outcome of the case, that it was not in a position to benefit or disadvantage the doctor if he made a decision of which they did or did not approve, and that there was nothing to suggest that he had worked with the clinicians who were responsible for the patient. However, psychiatry is quite a small profession. The responsible clinician and the medical member will often know one another, sometimes quite well. If so, it is particularly important to conduct the hearing in a way which avoids any impression of cosy complicity between the tribunal and the authorities.

(b) Applications and references

(i) Rights to apply

Patients admitted for assessment can apply to the tribunal within the 14 days beginning on the day of their admission (MHA, s 66(1)(a) and (2)(a)). Emergency admissions are not excluded, but there will be no need to proceed if the admission is not converted into a full admission for assessment within the first 72 hours.

Patients (of any age) admitted for treatment, received into guardianship, made subject to a CTO, recalled to hospital from community treatment and the CTO revoked, or transferred from guardianship to hospital can apply during the first six months of that taking place (s 66(1)(b), (c), (ca), (cb), (e), and (2)(b), (c), (ca), (cb) (e)).

Patients placed under guardianship by a court can also apply during the first six months (s 69(1)(b)(i)), but patients placed under hospital or restriction orders cannot do so: the decision of the court is sufficient judicial authority for their detention until there is a realistic possibility of change.

However, patients found unfit to plead or not guilty by reason of insanity and admitted under section 5(1) of the Criminal Procedure (Insanity) Act 1964 can apply in their first six months, and so can patients transferred from prison (with or without restrictions) by the Justice Secretary, patients transferred from other parts of the United Kingdom, and patients who become ordinary hospital order patients when their restriction orders come to an end (s 69(2)).

All long term unrestricted patients can apply once within each period for which their detention, community treatment or guardianship is renewed (s 66(1)(f), (fza), (faa) and (2)(f),(fza)). This means once during their second six months and once in every year after that. Patients transferred from prison without restrictions are in just the same position as ordinary hospital order patients.

The detention of restricted patients does not have to be formally renewed, but they too have the right to apply within the second six months of their detention and in every year after that (ss 70 and 79(1)). Conditionally discharged restricted patients, who have not been recalled to hospital, may apply within the second 12 months after their discharge, and in every two year period after that (s 75(2)). Where a tribunal has ordered conditional discharge subject to specified conditions being met (p 273, later), the discharge dates from the patient's release from hospital after the tribunal has confirmed that the conditions have been fulfilled, and not from the original order (*R v Canons Park Mental Health Review Tribunal, ex p Martins* [1996] COD 41). If a conditionally discharged patient is recalled, he is treated as if a new order or transfer had been made on that date, and so can apply during the second six months and in every year after that. But there is also an automatic review after each recall (see p 274, later).

The patient's nearest relative can apply within 28 days of the responsible clinician (RC) blocking his attempt to discharge a patient admitted for treatment or a community patient on the ground that the patient would be likely to act "in a manner dangerous to other persons or to himself" (s 66(1)(g) and (2)(d)). The relative does not have the right to apply to a tribunal if he is prevented from discharging a patient admitted for assessment, presumably because the admission will have lapsed before a hearing can be arranged.

The nearest relative can also apply in the other cases where he cannot discharge the patient, but the test is then the same as that in an application by the patient himself. If the patient is detained under a hospital or restriction order, or is a community patient who was previously detained under a hospital or restriction order, the nearest relative may apply during the second six months and in every year after that (s 69(1)(a)). After a guardianship order, he may apply at any time during the first 12 months and in every year after that (s 69(1)(b)(ii)). Lastly, if an order has been made replacing him as nearest relative, he may apply during the first 12 months and in every year after that (s 66(1)(h) and (2)(g)).

(ii) Duties and powers to refer

Article 5(4) only requires that a person deprived of his liberty by arrest or detention be entitled to "take proceedings". But many patients never apply, sometimes because they lack the mental capacity to do so, sometimes because they have forgotten their rights, and sometimes even because they are reluctant to upset themselves or the hospital staff. Hence the MHA 1983 introduced automatic periodic reviews for long term compulsory patients.

Under the 2007 amendments, the hospital managers must refer to a tribunal any patient admitted for assessment, or for treatment, or subject to a CTO, or recalled from community treatment or transferred from guardianship to hospital (s 68(1)). They must do this the moment the six months has passed since the "applicable day" (s 68(2)). This means the day on which the patient was first admitted to hospital, so that if a patient admitted for treatment was previously admitted for assessment, it means six months from the date on which he was first admitted for assessment (s 68(5)). The managers do not have to do this if during that six months there has been an application to a tribunal by or in respect of a patient, other than an application by a patient detained for assessment (s 68(3)(a)). So, if a patient was admitted for assessment and made an unsuccessful application then, but did not make an application after he was admitted for treatment, the case must be referred once he has been detained in hospital for six months. So must the case of a patient whose detention for assessment has been extended pending an application to replace his nearest relative (see below). The managers must also refer a community patient as soon as possible after he is recalled to hospital and the CTO revoked (s 68(7)).

Apart from these initial references, the hospital must refer a patient aged 18 or more if it is more than three years since his case was last considered by a tribunal for any reason; if the patient is under 18, his case must be referred if more than one year has gone by (s 68(6)). (There is power for the Secretary of State to reduce the periods of six months, three years and one year by statutory order, but this has not been done; s 68A.)

The Secretary of State for Health can refer the case of any patient detained or subject to guardianship under Part 2 of the Act, or any community patient, to a tribunal at any time (s 67(1)). This must include ordinary hospital order patients, to whom most of the provisions of Part 2 apply without modification and who are certainly detained under those provisions rather than the court order once the first renewal has taken place.

The equivalent provision in the 1959 Act was not thought to apply to restricted patients, whose detention does not have to be renewed at all. However, the Justice Secretary has power to refer the case of any restricted patient to a tribunal at any time (s 71(1)). This includes a restricted patient who has been conditionally discharged from hospital. The Justice Secretary must also refer any restricted patient whose case has not been considered for three years (s 71(2)). If a conditionally discharged restricted patient is recalled to hospital, the Justice Secretary must refer his case to a tribunal within one month of the day on which he arrives back (s 75(1)(a)). This was the response to the precise problem raised by the case of *X v United Kingdom* (1981) 4 EHRR 181. However, such is the delay in obtaining a hearing that there may still not be the "speedy" review required by the Convention (a delay of five months was unacceptable to the Court in *Van der Leer v The Netherlands* (1990) 12 EHRR 567).

A request for a reference may be useful if the patient's own rights have been lost on a technicality or if the situation has changed and the next right to apply is some time away. The power to refer the case to a tribunal proved vital in *R (H) v Secretary of State for Health* [2005] UKHL 60, [2006] 1 AC 441. A severely mentally disabled young woman was admitted for assessment and that admission was extended under section 29(4) (p 89, earlier) while proceedings to replace her mother as nearest relative dragged on for more than two years. There was no right to apply to a tribunal during that time and so the Court of Appeal declared that section 29(4) was incompatible with article 5(4) of the Convention. The House of Lords held that the section was not incompatible because there were ways of bringing the case to court: a Secretary of State's reference to a tribunal was the most satisfactory because the tribunal is much better suited to determining the merits of the case than the administrative court. That was in fact what had happened, but only because in the meantime the patient had been transferred into guardianship. Hence the 2007 amendments extended the reference duty to patients admitted for assessment who are detained for more than six months.

The patient in *H* was too disabled to make an application for herself and the Court of Appeal also held that section 2 was incompatible with article 5(4) because her detention might not be speedily reviewed. Once again the House of Lords disagreed, because article 5(4) guarantees the right to "take proceedings", rather than the right to have the case considered. In practice, however, every effort should be made to enable even the most disabled patient to make an application to the tribunal, which ought to be both accessible and user-friendly for all patients.

(c) Information, advice and representation

It is obviously important that patients and their relatives should be aware of their rights to apply. Hospital managers have a statutory duty to do their best to ensure that the patient understands these (s 132(1)(b)). This includes giving him the information both orally and in writing and (unless the patient asks them not to) sending a copy to his nearest relative (s 132(3) and (4)). The Department of Health produces standard leaflets for hospitals to use, but the MHAC (2009a) still found instances where patients seemed unaware of their rights. In the past, hospitals varied a good deal in their attitudes towards tribunals. Some enthusiastic doctors saw an application as a helpful step in encouraging the patient to take responsibility for himself. Some saw it as a way of sharing or even relieving themselves of their own responsibility. Others feared that knowing his rights would unsettle the patient and interfere with his treatment. Some might see the tribunal as a threat to their professional judgment, although the tribunal have no jurisdiction over treatment decisions. Rather more feared that the hearing would drive a wedge between them and their patient. The MHA Code reminds managers of their duty to advise patients of their rights, and also of the right to free legal advice and representation. This should be done when the patient is first detained, when his status changes, or when his detention or CTO is renewed (para 32.5). The Code also requires hospitals to inform patients of their right to present their own case to the tribunal as well as their right to be represented by someone else. Staff should be available to help patients make an application (para 32.25). The tribunal also provide some helpful information and guidance for patients and family, legal representatives, and health and social care professionals.

Patients are entitled to independent medical advice (if it can be funded). A doctor or approved clinician instructed by or on behalf of any patient or applicant may visit him at any reasonable time, examine him in private, and inspect any records relating to his detention and treatment in this or any other hospital, in order to advise on whether to make an application or to provide evidence for it (s 76). They can do this whether or not the patient consents (MHA Code, para 32.8). The same applies if there is a reference by the hospital (s 68(8)) or the Secretary of State for Health (s 67(2)). There is no equivalent provision for references by the Justice Secretary (cf s 71), but it is inconceivable that the hospital would deny access in such cases. Payment for this advice can now usually be obtained through the patient's legal representation (see below).

Although the object is to provide confidential advice to the patient and he should obviously feel free to unburden himself completely, the doctor can disclose information to the authorities if she fears that "decisions may be made on the basis of inadequate information and with a real risk of danger to the public". A psychiatrist who learned, on examining a paranoid schizophrenic patient who had been convicted of manslaughter by shooting 10 years earlier, that the patient was still interested in guns, was not liable in damages for sending a copy of his report to the Home Office (*W v Edgell* [1990] 1 WLR 471).

Patients are entitled to have anyone to represent them at the tribunal, as long as this is not another compulsory patient (detained, subject to a CTO or under guardianship) or even an informal patient at the same hospital (Tribunal Procedure (First-tier Tribunal) (Health, Education and Social Care Chamber) Rules 2008, SI 2008/2699 (the Tribunal Rules), r 11(1), (8); for Wales, see Mental Health Review Tribunal for Wales Rules 2008, SI 2008/2705). The patient (or a legal representative) must notify the tribunal and other parties of the name and address of the representative (r 11(2)). The representative can then do anything which the patient could do under the rules, except sign the application or a witness statement (r 11(3)). He will then be sent all the documents and notices which would normally go to the patient (r 11(4)). But the patient can take someone else along to the hearing, in addition to or instead of any representative, and the tribunal may allow that person to represent him or otherwise help him in the hearing (r 11(5)). If the patient has not appointed a representative, the tribunal may appoint a legal representative for him, if he has said that he does not want to conduct his own case or that he wishes to be represented, of if he lacks the capacity to appoint a representative and the tribunal believes that representation would be in his best interests (r 11(7)). This should prove particularly helpful in references concerning severely disabled patients who are unable to do anything for themselves. Most compulsory patients, however, are quite capable of instructing someone to represent them. The rules about representation apply equally to any other "party" to the proceedings.

The tribunal can pay travelling, subsistence and loss of earnings allowances to anyone who attends as a witness or representative of the applicant (apart from a barrister or solicitor). This also applies to the applicant and to the patient if he is not the applicant, although a detained patient will rarely have far to come as hearings are normally held in the hospital (s 78(7)). But these expenses do not cover any fee for the representative or for an expert witness, or any expenditure on preparatory work before coming to the hearing. This is still the position if the patient or applicant is represented by someone other than a practising lawyer.

Originally, there was no public funding for representation in tribunals, although some lawyers would help patients under the "green form" scheme, which provided means-tested legal help short of full representation. In 1982, following pressure from lawyers and from bodies such as the Council on Tribunals, and with the requirements of the European Convention on Human Rights in mind, mental health review tribunals became the first, and so far the only, tribunal in which free legal representation is available. Representation before the tribunal is now "controlled representation" under the Community Legal Service. There is no means test if a tribunal application or reference is involved (other kinds of help and advice for mental patients are means-tested) but there is a merits test: funded representation may be refused if it is not reasonable to provide it. Peay (1989) cites a case where representation was denied to a patient who had spent two years in a special hospital, on the ground that he stood no chance of success. However, the MHA Code takes an optimistic view of patients' entitlement to free legal advice and representation (para 32.5). It also advises that managers and professionals should enable patients to be visited by their legal representatives at any reasonable time (para 32.7). They should be given prompt access to the patient's records, provided that the patient consents (para 32.8).

Legal representation has become very common, although it is not universal and there are regional variations. There are disadvantages. Speed is obviously important where a client is deprived of both his liberty and his right to object to many kinds of treatment. Any delay should be caused by his needs and not those of his representative. Unfortunately, representative-induced delays are common in many courts and tribunals. This is partly because of the time needed to prepare cases properly: a lawyer is likely to seek an independent psychiatric report and these have a significant influence on delay (Blumenthal and Wessely, 1994). But there can also be a professional "culture of delay" in which the convenience of tribunals and representatives is given higher priority than the clients' interests. However, mental health work is now mainly conducted by specialist firms who are familiar with its peculiar demands and used to working under considerable time pressures.

A courtroom style of advocacy is often unsuitable for these hearings, which depend so much upon an understanding of the personalities involved. If not only the patient, but also the hospital and on occasions the Ministry of Justice, feel the need to employ an advocate, a major advantage of tribunals over the ordinary courts may be lost. It was for these reasons that Bell (1969; 1970) advocated a skilled non-legal representation service for some tribunals. Even now, a non-lawyer may be just as helpful, but there remains the problem of finance. The great advantage of any representative is that he can be shown all the relevant materials, can seek alternative evidence and solutions and articulate these along with the patient's point of view at the hearing. It is scarcely surprising, therefore, that representation in tribunals generally is associated not only with greater delay but also with greater success (Genn and Genn, 1989). Somewhat surprisingly, Peay (1989) concluded that it was difficult to assess how many benefits representation in mental health review tribunals brought. The MHAC (2008) was understandably concerned that introducing fixed fees for this work would cause many specialist firms to leave the field; it would certainly make it harder for them to tailor their efforts to the needs of the particular case.

(d) Procedure before the hearing

(i) The parties

The parties to the proceedings are the patient; the "responsible authority" (that is, the hospital managers or the local social services authority responsible for a patient under guardianship); the Justice Secretary if the patient is a restricted patient or if he is seeking approval to remove a foreigner under section 86 (see p 240, earlier); and any other person who starts the proceedings by making an application (Tribunal Rules, r 1(3)). Does this include the Secretary of State for Health who makes a reference under section 67? Perhaps so, as an "applicant" means any person who starts tribunal proceedings in any way (r 1(3)). Be that as it may, the tribunal can add anyone else as a respondent (r 9(2)). So important is it thought that the Justice Secretary should be able to represent the public interest in cases about restricted patients that failure to notify him has been held to invalidate the whole proceedings (*R v Oxford Regional Mental Health Review Tribunal, ex p Secretary of State for the Home Department* [1988] AC 120).

(ii) Withdrawing the case

The general rule is that any party can withdraw his case by notice in writing at any time before the final hearing or orally at a hearing (r 17(1)), but the tribunal must consent, except when the Secretary of State for Health wishes to withdraw a reference under section 67 or the Justice Secretary a reference under section 71(1) (r 17(2)). Those references are discretionary. Mandatory references by the hospital managers under section 68, or by the Justice Secretary under sections 71(2) or 75(1) cannot be withdrawn at all (r 17(3)). A party who has withdrawn his case may apply for it to be reinstated within 28 days of the tribunal learning of the withdrawal (r 17(4), (5)). Normally, as we have seen, only one application is allowed during each period of compulsion, but if an application is withdrawn in accordance with the Tribunal Rules the applicant can apply again (s 77(2)). One reason to withdraw might be that there has recently been a hearing, on a reference or some other application, about the same patient.

(iii) The documentation

All applications and references must be made in writing, signed and arrive at the tribunal within the time specified in the MHA (see above). An application may be signed either by the applicant or by any person authorised by the applicant to do so (r 32(1)). If the patient is able to understand what an application is for, it does not matter that he cannot read or write. There is no statutorily prescribed form. An application must, if possible, include the name and address of the patient, the name and address of the responsible authority, the provision under which the patient is detained or subject to a CTO or guardianship, whether the applicant intends to appoint a representative and if so his name and address, and if the nearest relative is applying, his name, address and relationship to the patient (r 32(2)).

The information which must be supplied to the Tribunal by the responsible authority and the Justice Secretary is now covered by a Practice Direction rather than by the Rules, no doubt so that it can more easily be updated (*Tribunals Judiciary, Practice Direction, Health, Education and Social Care Chapter, Mental Health Cases*). In assessment cases, where time is tight, the hospital must send to the tribunal, as soon as it receives either the application or a request from the tribunal: the application for admission, the medical recommendations, and as much of the information and documentation required by the Practice Direction as can reasonably be provided within the time available (r 32(5)). In most other cases, the information required must be provided at the latest within three weeks of receiving a copy of the application or reference (r 32(6)). In the case of conditionally discharged restricted patients, the Justice Secretary must get the required information and documentation to the tribunal within six weeks (r 32(4)).

The *hospital's statement* about a patient currently liable to detention must provide full factual details about the patient and his admission to hospital, including the name of his responsible clinician, care co-ordinator (if any), nearest relative, and any person who plays a significant part in his care but is not professionally concerned with it (para 11); the documentation which constitutes the original authority for the patient's detention; a copy of every tribunal decision since the admission under review; and in section 3 cases, a copy of any section 2 application in force immediately before it (para 12). The hospital's statement must also include up to date clinical and social circumstances reports and, for in-patients, a nursing report.

The *clinical report*, unless this is not practicable, should come from the patient's RC, and cover the patient's medical history, full details of his mental state, behaviour and treatment, whether (if known) he has ever neglected or harmed himself or harmed or threatened others while mentally disordered, an assessment of the extent to which he or others would be likely to be at risk if he were discharged and how such risks might be managed, and (if appropriate) why he might be treated in the community but should remain subject to recall (para 15).

The *social circumstances report* should cover his home and family circumstances, the views of the nearest relative (unless having consulted the patient it would be inappropriate to consult the nearest relative), the views of any non-professional carer (as above), the views of the patient, his "concerns, hopes and beliefs" about the tribunal proceedings, the employment and housing opportunities and any community support available, his financial circumstances, an assessment of his strengths and any other positive factors of which the tribunal should be aware, and an assessment of risk and how it could be managed (paras 16, 17).

For in-patients, a *nursing report* relating to his current in-patient episode (with current nursing plan attached) should cover the patient's understanding of and willingness to accept the current treatment for mental disorder provided or offered, the level of observation to which he is subject, any occasions of seclusion or restraint and the reasons for these, any occasions of absence without leave, including failure to return from leave of absence, and any incidents where he has harmed himself or others or threatened others with violence (para 18).

For all restricted patients, the Justice Secretary must send in any comments he wishes to make on the hospital's statement and any further relevant information, as well as a summary of the "index" offence which resulted in the detention, the patient's criminal record, and full details of his liability to detention under the MHA since the restrictions were imposed (paras 9, 20, 21).

For a conditionally discharged restricted patient, the Justice Secretary has to send in a statement to the tribunal, as soon as possible and in any event within six weeks of receiving a copy of the application or a request from the tribunal (para 4); this should, where possible, include the clinician's, social circumstances and for an in-patient, the nursing reports listed above (para 6).

For a community patient, the Practice Direction appears to require only an up to date clinical report and a social circumstances report (paras 25, 26); but for a patient who is or will be "subject to aftercare under supervision" (a legal concept which has been repealed), it requires all the usual factual information, documents, clinical and social circumstances reports, as well as information about the aftercare services being or to be provided under section 117, requirements to be imposed under (the now repealed) section 25D, and a supervisor's report (Annexe). No doubt the tribunal also want this information for community patients.

Thus it appears that the tribunal regard the clinicians as responsible for information about the patient's mental state; the social workers or community psychiatric nurses who write the social circumstances reports as responsible for information, not only about the home circumstances but also about the patient's own views about the proceedings; and the nurses as responsible for information about his tractability and willingness to accept treatment. All three are to some extent responsible for assessing the risks which a change in his legal status might involve.

(iv) Disclosure and non-disclosure

All the documents received by the tribunal must be copied by the tribunal to every other party, unless disclosure is prohibited under rule 14 (r 32(3)). This rule gives the tribunal power to make a direction prohibiting disclosure of a document or information to a person if satisfied:

(a) that disclosure would cause that person or some other person *serious* harm, and
(b) that, having regard to the public interest, it is "proportionate" to give such a direction (r 14(2)).

Thus it is not enough that the clinical team believe that disclosure will harm their relationship with the patient. In practice, the fear that disclosure of the family's views may harm their relationship with the patient is a more serious problem, but is it "serious harm"?

If any party wants information to be withheld, he must put that information in a separate document and also give reasons for excluding it, so that the tribunal can decide what to do (r 14(3)). If the party (usually but not invariably the patient) from whom information is to be withheld has a representative, the tribunal has power to direct that the information be disclosed to the representative, if this would be in the interests of the person from whom the information is withheld (as it usually will be) and the tribunal can trust the representative not to pass it on without their consent (r 14(5), (6)).

One of the advantages of having a representative is that he can be shown all the evidence and information, even if there are grounds for withholding some of this from the patient. He can remain throughout the hearing, even if the patient (or anyone else) is excluded. Professionally, this is ethical because the rules provide for it, but any representative must beware of colluding too closely with the tribunal to achieve a result which may be in the client's best interests but contrary to his instructions. It is for the doctors, social workers and other professionals to devote themselves to the patient's best interests. A representative must advise his client where he thinks the client's best interests lie, but in the end he must do as the client instructs him.

Clearly the starting point is that there should be full disclosure of all relevant material (*R (Roberts) v Home Secretary* [2005] UKHL 45, [2005] 2 AC 738). This is where the English common law starts, as do the principles of a fair hearing under article 6 of the European Convention on Human Rights. The rule allowing non-disclosure is now much more restrictive than it used to be, being limited to cases where disclosure is likely to cause serious harm and even then only if it is "proportionate". But proportionate to what: the risk of harm or the detriment to a fair trial or both? The rule does not explain. It may mean that infringing the ordinary right to full disclosure is a proportionate means of achieving the legitimate aim of protecting the patient or others from serious harm. If so, there may be instances where non-disclosure would be so detrimental to a fair hearing that it should not be allowed no matter how serious the risk of harm.

The Upper Tribunal have taken the view that information may be withheld under other procedures than rule 14 (*Dorset Healthcare NHS Foundation Trust v MH* [2009] UKUT 4 (AAC)). They have in mind that some information in the patient's records may be covered by duties of confidence to third parties. In such a case there could be a conflict between the privacy rights of the third parties, whether under common law or article 8 of the Convention, and the fair trial rights of the patient. In most cases, they believe that this can be resolved by disclosure to the patient's representative, so that each side can take a view upon whether the patient's or the third party's rights should override the other's. This may be so, but there are both procedural and substantive difficulties with this approach. The European Court of Human Rights has insisted that the system of special advocates, who may test the closed evidence against suspected terrorists but not disclose it to (or even talk with) their clients after they have seen it, is not always sufficient to secure a fair trial, if the person concerned is unable to effectively challenge the decisive evidence against him (*A v United Kingdom* (2009) 49 EHRR 29). In striking the balance between article 6 and article 8, it would appear that, at least where liberty is at stake, there is an irreducible minimum of disclosure required by article 6 whatever the justifications for protecting privacy under article 8 may be. We may not have heard the last of this question.

(v) Notifying others

Once the tribunal have received the required information, they must also give notice of the proceedings to any private guardian, the Court of Protection if there is an extant order of the Court, the person exercising the functions of the nearest relative (unless a patient with capacity requests otherwise), an NHS health authority or trust which has power to discharge the patient, and any other person who, in the tribunal's opinion, should have an opportunity of being heard (r 33).

(e) The hearing

The tribunal cannot dispose of the proceedings without a hearing (Tribunal Rules, r 35(1)). Although the Rules do not say so, in practice this takes place at the hospital where the patient is detained or which is responsible for a CTO patient. Reasonable notice of the time and place of the hearing has to be given to each party and to any interested person notified under rule 33 (above): at least three working days for assessment cases and 14 working days for others, unless the parties consent to shorter notice or there are urgent or exceptional circumstances (r 37(3), (4), (5)).

(i) Timing

The hearing of an application made by a patient detained for assessment must begin within seven days after the date when the tribunal receive the application (r 37(1)). This was achieved in 91 per cent of cases in 2008–2009 (Tribunals Service, 2009). The hearing of a reference relating to a recalled conditionally discharged patient must begin at least five weeks but no more than eight weeks after the date on which the tribunal received the reference (s 37(2)). Otherwise there are no statutory deadlines for beginning the hearing but the tribunal aim to fix hearings between six and eight weeks from receiving the application for non-restricted patients and from 14 to 16 weeks for restricted patients. In the past, especially for restricted patients and patients in the high security hospitals, targets have been hard to achieve and there have been unacceptable delays (Blumenthal and Wessely, 1994); but the implementation of the Human Rights Act, with its requirement for a "speedy" determination, may have improved things.

(ii) Examining the patient

Before the hearing takes place (usually but not always on the same day), an "appropriate" member of the tribunal *must*, so far as practicable, examine the patient and take such other steps as she considers necessary to form a view of the patient's mental condition (r 34(1)). The rules no longer require the "appropriate" member to be a doctor but a Practice Direction from the Senior President of Tribunals does. She may examine the patient in private, examine the records relating to his detention or treatment and any after-care services, and take notes or copies for use in the proceedings (r 34(2)). The original purpose was to give the tribunal their own objective medical opinion, so that an independent report on behalf of the patient would rarely be needed. But there are at least two problems with this. First, a doctor who is to play a part in deciding whether the patient is fit for release obviously approaches his examination in a different way from a doctor whose responsibility is to the patient himself. Some medical members might enter into dialogue with the hospital consultant in the hope of finding a constructive way forward. This may benefit the patient but is not always conducive to the objective examination of the issues before the tribunal.

More importantly, is the role of the medical (or now other "appropriate") member compatible with the article 6 right to a fair hearing before an "independent and impartial" tribunal? Traditionally, the medical member's opinion was given in confidence and there was no formal opportunity to learn what it was or to challenge it. Tribunals differed in whether they asked for it before the hearing began, so that any differences of view between the medical member and the hospital consultant might be explored, or after the hearing had concluded, so as to avoid any appearance of pre-judging the case. Even before the Human Rights Act, it was said that it would be contrary to the principles of natural justice for a tribunal to decide on a basis known only to themselves. They should therefore ensure that the parties were aware of any new facts or arguments adduced by their medical member and had an opportunity of dealing with them (*R v Mental Health Review Tribunal, ex p Clatworthy* [1985] 3 All ER 699). Tribunal members were advised that the medical member should report to the others before the hearing, explain any technicalities and help to identify the likely issues, but without giving her opinion at that stage.

In *R (S) v Mental Health Review Tribunal* [2002] EWHC 2522 (Admin), [2003] MHLR 118, the patient went further, relying principally on *DN v Switzerland* (2003) 37 EHRR 21 where a medical juge-rapporteur performing a similar function was found not to have the necessary appearance of impartiality. He argued that the requirement in the Rules that he be examined by a tribunal member was incompatible with article 6. The member was both a witness who could not be cross-examined and a decision-maker who could not be seen as impartial. Stanley Burnton J concluded that the rule was not incompatible in itself but that care was needed in its operation. The medical member should not form a preconceived concluded opinion on the merits of the patient's case, and should not express herself during the hearing in such a way as to give the

266

impression that she had. But there was nothing wrong in her forming a provisional view as long as she kept, and was seen to keep, an open mind (para 32). Any views which differed from those of the hospital consultant (and no doubt also of the patient's independent medical adviser) should be disclosed at the outset of the hearing. Also, if there was a conflict of evidence between the patient and the medical member about what was said during the private interview, and this might matter to the decision, the tribunal would have to consider whether they could properly continue to hear the case (para 34). But one should not to get too worried about all this. In *R (RD) v Mental Health Review Tribunal* [2007] EWHC 781 (Admin), Munby J pointed out that the medical member, like other members of the tribunal, was clearly entitled to discuss all aspects of the case with her colleagues before the hearing and to express preliminary views about them to the other members and to the parties at the hearing.

(iii) Attendance, privacy and publicity

The tribunal must sit in private, unless they consider that it is in the interests of justice to sit in public, although they may then direct that part of the hearing should be in private (r 38(1), (2)). If it is held in private, the tribunal decide who may attend all or part of the proceedings (r 38(3)). Normally, of course, each party is entitled to attend the hearing (r 36(1)). But whether the hearing is in public or in private, the tribunal have power to exclude any person, including a party:

(a) whose conduct the tribunal considers is disrupting or likely to disrupt the hearing, or

(b) whose presence is likely to prevent another person from giving evidence or making submissions freely, or

(c) who should be excluded because of a direction allowing harmful information to be withheld, or

(d) where the purpose of the hearing would be defeated if that person were to attend it (r 38(4)).

These very wide powers must obviously be used with considerable care if the patient, in particular, is to have a proper opportunity of knowing and challenging the case against him. Tribunals cannot revert to the old practice of informal hearings, in which the patient, the hospital consultant, the family, and any other witnesses were heard sequentially in private without the others knowing, let alone hearing, what had been said. The tribunal may also exclude a witness (but not a party) until he has given evidence (r 38(5)). This is the usual practice in criminal trials but not in civil or family cases.

The tribunal may proceed with the hearing if a party fails to attend, so long as the party has been notified or reasonable steps have been taken to do so and it is in the interests of justice. But they may not proceed in the absence of the patient unless the required medical examination has taken place and the tribunal are satisfied that the patient has decided not to attend or is unable to do so because of ill health (r 39(1), (2)). The absence of one of the parties is among the reasons why the tribunal may set aside their decision and make a fresh one if they think this just (r 45(1), (2)(c)). The other reasons are that a document was not sent to or received in time by a party or representative, or not sent to the tribunal in time, or a party's representative was not present, or there has been some other procedural irregularity (r 45(2)). Applications to set aside a decision must be received not more than 28 days after the tribunal sent it out (r 45(3)).

Tribunals are courts, so that publishing information about proceedings in private is a contempt of court unless the tribunal give leave (Administration of Justice Act 1960, s 12(1)(b)). It can also be contempt to publish prejudicial comments before the hearing, but only in the (perhaps unlikely) event that the tribunal are likely to be prejudiced by them. It is not easy to achieve a proper balance between the patient's right to privacy and the public's interest in the prospect of certain notorious patients, especially if restricted, being released.

(iv) The hearing

The "overriding objective" is to deal with the case "fairly and justly" (r 2(1)). This includes "avoiding unnecessary formality and seeking flexibility in the proceedings"; ensuring, so far as practicable, that the parties are able to participate fully; using any special expertise of the tribunal effectively; avoiding delay and dealing with the case in ways which are proportionate to their importance (r 2(2)). The tribunal aim to put everyone, but particularly the patient, at their ease. It is good practice to begin by introducing the members and the other people present, explaining their functions, and stressing that the tribunal are independent of the hospital and (for restricted patients) the Ministry of Justice. The presider should also explain how the tribunal intend to conduct the hearing. Informality can be a great benefit in all kinds of tribunal, but particularly here where there are advantages in questioning people directly, rather than listening to the advocates doing so. The patient may well be addressed by whatever name he feels most comfortable with (and in the past smoking was not uncommon). The Rules do not require the tribunal to hear the parties in any particular order. Some tribunals like the hospital to begin, partly because that is now where the burden of proof lies, and partly so that the patient will know the case he has to meet. Others believe that the patient wants his "day in court" and will not understand the proper method of proceeding by examination and cross-examination if he is not allowed to go first. This is less of a problem when he has legal representation.

The tribunal can admit evidence which would not be admissible in ordinary civil proceedings and exclude evidence which would otherwise be admissible if it was not provided in time or in accordance with the rules or it would otherwise be unfair to admit it (r 15(2)). These days there is very little evidence which is inadmissible in a civil court, the rule against hearsay having been abolished in civil proceedings. But there are obvious dangers in relying too heavily on the accuracy of accounts, for example of violent incidents or outbursts, given in hospital and other records. These are often copied uncritically from one document to another long after the original source has disappeared. The tribunal may take evidence on oath but do not have to do so (r 15(3)). They may summon witnesses to attend the hearing (giving 14 days' notice and paying their expenses if they are not a party) or require any person to answer questions or produce documents they have relating to an issue in the proceedings (r 16(1), (2)). No-one may be compelled to give evidence or produce a document which they could not be compelled to give or produce in ordinary civil proceedings (r 16(3)); thus, for example, they cannot be obliged to answer questions which might incriminate them.

Among the tribunal's extensive case management powers is the power to adjourn or postpone the proceedings, for example to obtain further information or until something else has happened (see r 5).

(f) The tribunal's powers and duties

The tribunal are not concerned with whether the admission procedures were properly carried out: the legality of the patient's detention must be challenged by *habeas corpus* or judicial review (*ex p Waldron* [1986] QB 824). Nor are they directly concerned with how the patient is being treated in hospital. Their task is to decide whether the grounds for his continued liability to detention, community treatment or guardianship are made out. The burden of proving this (except in guardianship cases) now lies squarely on the hospital or other party wishing to continue the compulsion. The patient no longer has to prove that he is either sane or safe.

The standard of proof, where facts are disputed, is the ordinary civil standard of proof "on the balance of probabilities". There is no different or higher standard just because the allegations or the consequences are serious, as they often will be in cases about mental patients. But if something is inherently improbable, then it may need stronger or more compelling evidence to prove that it did happen (*R (N) v Mental Health Review Tribunal (Northern Region)* [2005] EWCA Civ 1605, [2006] QB 468). However, the Law Lords have emphasised that there is no necessary link between seriousness and improbability: some very serious allegations are all too likely to have taken place (*Re B (Children) (Sexual Abuse: Standard of Proof)* [2008] UKHL 35, [2009] 1 AC 11).

(i) Unrestricted patients: the tribunal's powers and duties

(a) If the *patient is detained for assessment*, the tribunal must direct his discharge if they are not satisfied:

- that he suffers from mental disorder, or
- that the mental disorder from which he suffers is of a nature or degree which warrants his detention in hospital for assessment (or for assessment followed by medical treatment) for at least a limited period, or
- that his detention is justified in the interests of his own health or safety or with a view to the protection of other persons (s 72(1)(a)).

At this stage, the incident or behaviour which led to the admission should be fresh in everyone's minds and the issue will not be unduly clouded by what has since happened in hospital. Misinterpretation of events by family, neighbours, social workers, doctors and other hospital staff is not unknown. There is an opportunity to clarify matters before the patient embarks upon his "career".

(b) If the *patient is detained for treatment, under section 3 or an ordinary hospital order*, the tribunal must direct his discharge if they are not satisfied:

- that he is suffering from mental disorder, or
- that the mental disorder from which he suffers is of a nature or degree which makes it appropriate for him to be liable to be detained in hospital for medical treatment, or
- that it is necessary for his health or safety or for the protection of other persons that he should receive such treatment, or

- that the appropriate medical treatment is available for him (s 72(1)(b)).

(c) A *community patient* must be discharged if the tribunal are not satisfied:

- that he is suffering from mental disorder, or
- that the mental disorder from which he suffers is of a nature or degree which makes it appropriate for him to receive medical treatment, or
- that it is necessary for his health or safety or the protection of other persons that he should receive it, or
- that it is necessary for the responsible clinician to be able to recall him to hospital, or
- that appropriate medical treatment is available for him (s 72(1)(c)).

The recall criterion is the only one which focuses on the need for compulsion rather than the need for treatment: the other criteria could be satisfied even if the patient could perfectly well be treated in the community without the use of compulsory powers. Curiously, the Act provides that in determining whether this criterion is met, the *responsible clinician* must consider, having regard to the patient's history of mental disorder and any other relevant factors, what risk there would be of a deterioration of his condition if he were to continue not to be detained in a hospital (as a result, for example, of his refusing or neglecting to receive the medical treatment he requires for his mental disorder) (s 72(1A)). This looks more like a criterion for recall than a criterion for discharging him from the possibility of recall. Another curiosity is that, unlike their powers in relation to conditionally discharged restricted patients, the tribunal have no power to alter the conditions to which a community patient is subject.

(d) If the *nearest relative has been barred* from discharging a patient detained under section 3, or a community patient, the tribunal must also discharge unless satisfied that, if released, the patient would be likely to act in a manner dangerous to other persons or to himself (s 72(1)(b)(iii), (c)(v)). The test of whether someone is *dangerous* is obviously meant to be narrower than the test of whether he should be in hospital or under a CTO for his own sake or that of others.

(e) The tribunal also have *a complete discretion to discharge any* unrestricted patient, short term or long term, even if they are satisfied that the criteria for his continued detention or community treatment exist (s 72(1)).

(f) Even if they do not discharge a patient from hospital straightaway, the tribunal have some *additional powers* to influence the rehabilitative effort:

- They may direct the patient's discharge on a future specified date, rather than straightaway (s 72(3)). This applies to any discharge under section 72(1), presumably whether it is mandatory or discretionary. Logically, however, the tribunal should not delay a discharge to which the patient is immediately entitled. But he might only be entitled to it once the necessary arrangements have been made, and a short delay could be proper to enable this to be done. In discretionary cases, a longer period might be appropriate.
- If the tribunal do not discharge the patient under section 72(1), they may recommend that he be granted leave of absence, or transferred to another hospital, or into guardianship, with a view to facilitating his discharge on a future date (s 72(3)(a)). They may also recommend that the responsible clinician consider whether to make a CTO (s 72(3A)). In both these

situations, they may "further consider the case" in the event that the recommendation is not complied with or the CTO is not made (s 72(3)(b), (3A)(b)).

It is curious that, just as they have no power to vary the conditions in a CTO, the tribunal have no power to make a CTO over an unrestricted patient, while they do have the equivalent of both powers over a restricted patient. One (unconvincing) explanation may be that the circumstances in which they have to power discharge a restricted patient are more limited (see below).

(ii) The real issues

In practice, the issue does not usually turn on whether the patient is indeed suffering from a mental disorder. This is such a broad term that any recognised diagnosis will probably do. Several of the reported cases do, however, reveal disagreements about whether a patient who was originally diagnosed as suffering from psychopathic disorder is still suffering from any disorder within the meaning of the Act (eg *R v Secretary of State for the Home Department, ex p K* [1991] QB 270, CA). If the patient is not now suffering from any mental disorder, he must be discharged, no matter how badly he may have behaved in the past, or how much of a nuisance or even a danger he may be in the future. This may be a "well-known lacuna" in the Act (Peay, 1989), but it is the inevitable concomitant of detaining someone to treat his mental disorder rather than to punish him for a crime.

The patient must also be discharged, even if he is still disordered, if his disorder is no longer a type or severity to warrant (or make appropriate) his treatment in hospital. The disorder may be such that everyone would much prefer it if he could be kept out of harm's way. But that is not the same as to "make it appropriate that he should be detained in hospital for medical treatment". Nor can it be appropriate to keep him in hospital for treatment if he is not receiving any treatment there, still less if he is out on leave and not receiving treatment in the hospital or in the community. It is no longer possible to keep a patient under compulsion if there is no medical treatment appropriate to his case available for him. We have already seen that medical treatment "includes nursing, psychological intervention and specialist mental health habilitation, rehabilitation and care" (s 145(1)) and that its purpose must be "to alleviate or prevent a worsening of the disorder or one or more of its symptoms or manifestations" (s 145(4)). This is wide, but not, it might be thought, so wide as to cover simply accommodating people for whom no specialist care is either appropriate or available. The fact that the patient is unwilling to co-operate with the only available treatment which is likely to do him any good probably does not make it inappropriate to detain him for the purpose. This should not depend upon the patient's recalcitrance or reluctance rather than on the clinicians' judgment (*R v Canons Park Mental Health Review Tribunal, ex p A* [1994] 2 All ER 659, CA). Even if treatment is "appropriate" and "available", the patient must be discharged if it is not "necessary" for his own health or safety or for the protection of other persons for him to receive it.

Nevertheless, tribunals are often concerned with what medical treatment the patient needs and how it might be delivered. There will be discussion about his medication. The non-medical members can ask the doctors to justify their opinions and to explain the advantages and disadvantages of the various drugs involved. Even if medication is clearly needed, it is often possible for the patient to receive depot injections in an out-patient clinic or from a community nurse. It may be possible for the patient to go on being treated in hospital, but on an informal rather than compulsory basis. The question then changes to whether the patient will be prepared to co-operate with these plans. Tribunals have been known to grant a patient's discharge after accepting his assurances of co-operation, but with the clear threat that compulsion will be reimposed if he actually tries to assert the rights which his discharge theoretically gives. The practice may be difficult to justify, but it can benefit the patient's morale and does improve his legal status.

The other issue which often arises is how the patient is going to cope in the outside world, if he intends to leave the hospital rather than to remain as an informal patient. Strictly speaking, this is irrelevant if his condition is not bad enough to make hospital treatment appropriate. But patients who are still disordered will need some sort of care, although not always under medical supervision. The question of whether hospital treatment is appropriate and necessary will often depend upon the alternatives. The tribunal will be keenly interested in where the patient might live, whether he could get a job, how else he might occupy his time, and what support would be available from social services, family and community.

Tribunals may find it easier to hold that hospital treatment is both appropriate and "necessary for the protection of other persons" if the patient was originally detained because of his behaviour towards other people. This question may depend upon his ability to resist the influences which triggered his earlier antisocial conduct. Unfortunately, hospital treatment, particularly in a secure unit, makes this difficult to assess. The tribunal have no control over the social skills training and general rehabilitative effort made in hospital. All they can do is to subject its predictions of future behaviour to critical scrutiny and bear in mind that this is an area in which the inter-relationship of mental condition and social situation is particularly important.

Thus, the tribunal may be faced with the problem that the patient cannot be discharged unless the hospital has at least been trying to prepare him for it. The worse the hospital, or the facilities available in the community, the worse the patient's chances before the tribunal are likely to be. In unrestricted cases, tribunals have some influence over rehabilitation through their powers to delay discharge and recommend a transfer or a CTO. Valuable though these powers may be, there is no direct obligation on the medical or social services to comply (although there is a duty to provide after-care under section 117). The fact that a patient would not have to be detained if there were suitable facilities for him in the community does not necessarily mean that his continued detention is unlawful under the MHA or in breach of his rights under the ECHR (*R (H) v Secretary of State for the Home Department* [2003] UKHL 59, [2004] 2 AC 253).

But even if the tribunal have no formal power effectively to move things on, they may still be able to engage in constructive dialogue with the clinicians. Some medical members may take the options up during their discussions with the hospital representatives. There is nothing to stop the tribunal making their views clear, both during the hearing and when they come to give written reasons for whatever they decide to do.

(iii) Restricted patients: the tribunal's powers and duties

(a) A *restriction order patient* must be discharged if the tribunal are not satisfied:

- that he is suffering from mental disorder, or
- that the disorder from which he is suffering is not of a nature or degree which makes it appropriate for him to be liable to be detained in a hospital for medical treatment, or
- that it is necessary for his own health or safety or for the protection of other persons that he should receive such treatment, or
- that appropriate medical treatment is available for him (s 73(1)(a)).

These are exactly the same as the criteria for the mandatory discharge of unrestricted patients and raise exactly the same issues (see above). But tribunals (and indeed hospitals) may be a little sceptical if someone who has recently been sent to hospital as a psychopath after committing a very serious offence claims (or is thought) to have no disorder at all or nothing for which any suitable treatment is available. However, the gulf between purely preventive detention and some sort of medical care and treatment may be very narrow, but it is nonetheless deep. If detention in hospital for medical treatment is not appropriate, the patient must be discharged, no matter how dangerous he may be. On the other hand, if this is still appropriate, the tribunal are not concerned with whether it is necessary to protect the public from *serious* harm. Unlike the Justice Secretary, they have no power to lift the restrictions while leaving the patient to be detained as an ordinary hospital order patient.

If any of the criteria for continued detention is not met, the tribunal must choose between an *absolute* and a *conditional discharge.* They must grant an absolute discharge if they are satisfied that it is not appropriate for the patient to remain liable to recall to hospital for further treatment (s 73(1)(b)). The effect is that the patient ceases to be liable to be detained by virtue of the hospital order and the restriction order automatically comes to an end (s 73(3)).

However, if the tribunal are not satisfied that it is not appropriate for the patient to be liable to recall—that is, if they think it may be—they must direct his *conditional discharge* (s 73(2)). This is the one element in the criteria where the patient must establish a negative: if he cannot do so, the default position is that he remains on a string. However, he could not be recalled to hospital unless the criteria for detention were met. The tribunal can decide what the conditions should be. The Act gives no guidance, but the obvious candidates are the conditions which the Justice Secretary would impose if he were granting a conditional discharge—residence, clinical and social supervision and compliance with medical treatment (see p 245, earlier). If they do not, he will. Like the Justice Secretary, the tribunal cannot impose conditions which amount to detention in hospital (*Secretary of State for the Home Department v Mental Health Review Tribunal for the Mersey Regional Health Authority* [1986] 1 WLR 1170) but continued informal residence without any condition would be permissible, as would conditions which restricted rather than deprived the patient of his liberty. The tribunal might insist that he attend elsewhere or as an outpatient for treatment, although the treatment cannot be forced upon him should he refuse it (s 56(3)(c)). The safeguards governing certain types of treatment do not apply to conditionally discharged restricted patients (cf Pt 4A, p 199, earlier). The tribunal may also decide on what the patient can or cannot do, in the way of going to public houses or other provoking places. The discharge may be deferred until the necessary arrangements have been made (s 73(7)). This power to defer a conditional discharge does *not* give the tribunal power to defer deciding the case or to reconsider its decision in the light of later developments

(*R v Oxford Regional Mental Health Review Tribunal, ex p Secretary of State for the Home Department* [1988] AC 120).

A conditional discharge by a tribunal has the same effect as a conditional discharge by the Justice Secretary (s 73(4)). He can recall the patient at any time, in theory immediately after an unwelcome decision by a tribunal. But in *R (Von Brandenburg) (aka Hanley) v East London and the City Mental Health NHS Trust* [2003] UKHL 58, [2004] 2 AC 280 (p 121, earlier), Lord Bingham held that it would not be lawful for an AMHP to make an application for the admission of a recently discharged patient:

> "unless [the AMHP] has formed the reasonable and bona fide opinion that he has information not known to the tribunal which puts a significantly different complexion on the case compared with that which was before the tribunal" (para 10).

The same should in principle apply to the recall of a conditionally discharged restricted patient. In any event, unless the criteria for detention can be shown to exist, the patient would have to be released when his case is referred to a tribunal within a month of recall. More curiously, the Justice Secretary can also vary the tribunal's conditions at any time (s 73(5)). Recall apart, however, there is no sanction for breach. If, for example, an alcoholic is discharged on condition that he does not drink (not perhaps the wisest thing to do), the mere fact that he has a lapse will not invariably justify a recall.

When a conditionally discharged patient who has not been recalled to hospital applies to the tribunal, the tribunal may vary the conditions or even impose new ones (s 75(3)(a)). Alternatively, they can lift the restrictions altogether (s 75(3)(b)). This has the same effect as an absolute discharge. Both mean that the patient is no longer subject to any form of compulsion (s 73(3)).

If a restriction order patient does not qualify for mandatory discharge, the tribunal have no residual discretion to release him. Tribunals may find it easier to decide that the patient no longer needs to be in hospital, because of their power to impose conditions and ensure that he is liable to instant recall. Nevertheless, the lack of discretion is surprising, given the usually strengthened membership of tribunals in these cases. Nor does the formal power to recommend leave of absence or transfer to another hospital apply to restricted patients (*Grant v Mental Health Review Tribunal, ex p O'Hara, The Times*, 28 April 1986). Before tribunals acquired the power to discharge restricted patients, they used to give detailed advice to the Home Secretary. Apparently he found this most valuable in building up a picture of how the patient was progressing. Although it was confidential, it could also help the patient to make progress through the hospital system (Wood, 1993). These days the tribunal can make their views clear when giving reasons for their decision, which must generally be disclosed to all parties (see below).

(b) If a *restricted patient* is subject to a *hospital and limitation direction* (a "hybrid order") or has been transferred from prison with *restrictions*, the task of the tribunal is not to discharge the patient, but to decide whether or not the criteria for keeping him in hospital are met. The tribunal must notify the Justice Secretary whether the patient would be entitled to an absolute or conditional discharge if he were a restriction order patient (s 74(1)(a)). If he would be entitled to a conditional discharge, they may recommend that he should stay in hospital if he is not released, rather than be returned to prison (s 74(1)(b)). The

274

task of the Justice Secretary is then to decide whether to transfer him back to prison, or in some cases to leave him in hospital, or in others to release him into the community.

If a remand, civil or Immigration Act prisoner transferred under section 48 becomes entitled to an absolute or conditional discharge, the Justice Secretary must transfer him back to prison, unless he is only entitled to a conditional discharge and the tribunal have recommended that he should be allowed to stay in hospital, in which case the Justice Secretary can leave him there (s 74(4)). As there is no possibility of such a patient receiving the treatment he needs in the community, it is lawful not to discharge him from hospital if he will not receive the treatment he needs in prison (*R (Abu-Rideh) v Mental Health Review Tribunal* [2004] EWHC 1999 (Admin), [2004] MHLR 308). If the patient was transferred after sentence or is subject to a hybrid order, the Justice Secretary can instead decide to allow his discharge. The tribunal will do this in the usual way, if they are notified by the Ministry of Justice within 90 days of giving their views (s 74(2)). If nothing is heard from the Ministry of Justice within that time, the hospital must transfer the patient back to prison, unless the tribunal have recommended that he is entitled to a conditional discharge but should be allowed to stay in hospital instead (s 74(3)). If the patient is sent back to prison, the hospital and limitation directions or transfer and restriction directions cease to have effect and he becomes a prisoner once more (s 74(5)).

However, even if the patient would not be entitled to either an absolute or a conditional discharge, the tribunal can notify the Justice Secretary that he no longer requires treatment in hospital for mental disorder or that no effective treatment can be given for his disorder in the hospital where he is. The Justice Secretary may then decide to transfer the patient back to prison. Alternatively, if the patient was under sentence, he can exercise any power of releasing on licence or under supervision which would have applied from prison (ss 50(1), 51(3), and 53(2)). There is no power to do this if the patient was originally remanded by a magistrates' court (cf s 52). But even if there is no effective treatment for these patients, the Justice Secretary could decide to leave them in hospital for the time being.

If the tribunal make a recommendation that a prisoner patient who is entitled to a conditional discharge should be allowed to remain in hospital (s 74(1)(b)) the fact that the restriction or limitation direction remains in force does not prevent an application or reference to the Parole Board. If the Parole Board decide that he would be entitled to release from prison, whether unconditionally or on licence, were he not in hospital, then the restriction or limitation direction will cease to have effect when he would have become entitled to his release from prison (s 74(5A)). This is to meet the possibility that his detention may no longer be justified either under article 5(1)(a) of the ECHR, as a convicted offender, or under article 5(1)(e), as a person of unsound mind (and thus to respond to the declaration of incompatibility made in *R (D) v Secretary of State for the Home Department* [2002] EWHC 2805 (Admin), [2003] 1 WLR 1315).

(iv) Guardianship patients

If the patient is subject to *guardianship*, whether under a court order or civil powers, the tribunal always have power to discharge him. But they must do so if satisfied:

- that he is not then suffering from mental disorder; *or*

275

- that it is not necessary in the interests of the welfare of the patient, or for the protection of other persons, that he should remain under such guardianship (s 72(4)).

Thus guardianship patients remain under the burden of proving that they do not need to be subject to the regime, whereas for hospital and community patients the burden has shifted to the other side. This anomaly came about because the law had to be changed for hospital patients when it was found incompatible with article 5 of the ECHR (*R (H) v Mental Health Review Tribunal for North and East Region* [2001] EWCA Civ 415, [2002] QB 1, CA); but it did not have to be changed for guardianship patients because for most of the time they are not deprived of their liberty and so are not covered by article 5. However, they can be taken into custody for the purpose of getting them to or back to the place where they are required to live, so it seems particularly unfair that they should be in a worse position than hospital and community patients. However, it may not matter much, as the tribunal also have a discretionary power to discharge even if the criteria for discharge are not met (s 72(4)).

(g) The decision and after

The tribunal may give their decision orally at the hearing (Tribunal Rules, r 41(1)). It is suggested that wherever possible the patient should be told the result orally when the hearing is over. But in any event, after making a final decision (which for this purpose includes a decision with recommendations or a deferred conditional discharge), the tribunal must provide all parties with a decision notice, written reasons for the decision, and information about any right of appeal. This must be done as soon as reasonably practicable, either at the hearing, or within three working days after the hearing of an assessment case and seven days after the hearing of other cases (r 41(2), (3)). Giving reasons for a decision is not the same as stating the legal ground upon which it was made. Several High Court cases have emphasised the need to explain fully why the patient has not succeeded (*Bone v Mental Health Review Tribunal* [1985] 3 All ER 330; *R v Mental Health Review Tribunal, ex p Clatworthy* [1985] 3 All ER 699; and *R v Mental Health Review Tribunal, ex p Pickering* [1986] 1 All ER 99). The reasons may, however, accommodate the non-disclosure of information which has been withheld under rule 14 (see p 264, above).

It used to be possible to challenge the decision of a mental health review tribunal either by way of judicial review in the Administrative Court or by asking the tribunal to state a special case for the determination by the High Court of any point of law arising before them (MHA s 78(8), now repealed). Judicial review was seen as preferable and so the case stated procedure fell into disuse. It has now been abolished (Transfer of Tribunals Functions Order 2008, SI 2008/2833, Sch 3). An appeal on a point of law now lies, with permission, from both the first-tier tribunal in England and the mental health review tribunal in Wales to the Upper Tribunal.

An application for permission to appeal must be received by the first-tier tribunal no later than 28 days after the tribunal sent out the reasons for their decision (although time can be extended). It must explain why the applicant argues that the decision is wrong in law and what the applicant wants instead (r 46). The tribunal must then consider whether to review the decision, which they can only do if satisfied that there has been an error of law (rr 47(1) and 49(1)(a)). If they decide not to review the decision or take no action following a review, they must decide whether or not to grant permission to appeal (r 47(2)). If the first-tier tribunal refuse permission, the Upper Tribunal may nevertheless grant it (Tribunal Procedure (Upper Tribunal) Rules 2008, SI 2008/2833, rr 21(1) and 22(2)).

Now that there is a straightforward appeal on a point of law, there should be little scope of judicial review of tribunal decisions. In practice, there is not much difference between judicial review and an appeal on a point of law. However, in judicial review, the court quashes the decision and sends the case back to the tribunal to be decided properly, whereas on an appeal, the Upper Tribunal may substitute their own decision for that of the first-tier tribunal. On the other hand, the decisions of the Administrative Court are more readily accessible to lawyers and the wider public, so that it was easier to discover what the law was. Some may think this transparency an advantage.

2. THE COURT OF PROTECTION

The court has a long history as it stems from the power (and duty) of the monarch to look after the property of lunatics and idiots, which was recognised even before the Statute *De Praerogativa Regis* of Edward II (usually cited as 17 Edward II, c 9, which would date it at 1324). The King delegated this function to the Lord Chancellor, and later to other judges. Patients had to be found of unsound mind by inquisition, and then their property and affairs would be managed by a "committee". It was also possible to appoint a committee of the person, but this was rarely done. Legislation modified both the inquisition procedure and the powers of the court, but the basis of the jurisdiction remained the royal prerogative, delegated by warrant under the sign manual of the Monarch, until the Mental Health Act 1959. This put the Court of Protection on a fully statutory basis, but only as an office of the Supreme Court, and dealing only with the "property and affairs" of a patient. The royal warrant was revoked and no one was quite sure whether it could ever be reissued and if so how (see Hoggett, 1988). The Court established under the Mental Health Acts 1959 and 1983 has now been replaced by the new Court of Protection established under section 45 of the Mental Capacity Act 2005.

No longer simply an "office" of the Supreme Court, the new Court of Protection is a superior court of record with the same powers, rights, privileges and authority as the High Court (MCA, s 47). It can deal with matters of health care and personal welfare, previously dealt with under the jurisdiction of the High Court to make binding declarations of right, as well as financial and property matters, previously dealt with by the old Court of Protection. It is solely concerned with people who do, or may, lack capacity and not with other mental patients.

(a) The new court

The President of the Court of Protection is nominated by the Lord Chief Justice and is currently the President of the Family Division of the High Court. The Vice-President is currently the Vice-Chancellor (who heads the Chancery Division of the High Court). Its judicial functions are carried out by judges nominated by the Lord Chief Justice or, on his delegation, by the President of the Court of Protection or some other judicial office holder (s 46(1)). These are the judges of the Family and Chancery Divisions of the High Court and some specialist circuit and district judges, who do the great majority of the work.

Either a circuit or a district judge is nominated by the Lord Chief Justice to be the Senior Judge of the Court of Protection with the attendant administrative responsibilities (s 46(4)).

Appeals from a district or circuit judge lie to a higher judge of the Court and thence to the Court of Appeal. Appeals from a High Court judge go direct to the Court of Appeal (s 53(2); see Court of Protection Rules 2007, SI 2007/1744, Pt 20).

The Court has jurisdiction to make declarations as to whether a person has the capacity to make a particular decision or to make decisions on any particular matter (s 15(1)(a), (b)); or whether a particular act, omission or course of conduct done or to be done in relation to such a person is or will be lawful (s 15(1)(c), (2)). If a person does lack capacity in relation to a particular decision or matter, the Court may either make the decision on his behalf or appoint a deputy to make decisions on that matter for him (s 16(1), (2)). The Court also registers enduring and lasting powers of attorney and has various powers in relation to their validity and operation (MCA, ss 22, 23). All of these are discussed in chapter 10. The focus of this chapter is upon the deprivation of liberty.

(b) The Court's jurisdiction over deprivation of liberty

As we have seen in chapter 1, section 4A(1) of the MCA makes it clear that the Act does not authorise anyone to deprive another person of his liberty within the meaning of article 5(1) of the European Convention on Human Rights. There are three exceptions.

(i) Court orders

The Court may make an order under section 16(2)(a), in the exercise of its jurisdiction over the personal welfare of a person who lacks capacity, authorising others to deprive him of his liberty (s 4A(3), (4)). It seems clear from section 4A(1) that the Court cannot give a deputy power to decide whether or not a person should be deprived of his liberty. The authorisation must come direct from the Court or through the MCA DoLS. Nor can the Court authorise a person to be deprived of his liberty if he is "ineligible" within the meaning of Schedule 1A, either because he is already subject to compulsion under the MHA or because he should be (s 16A). Subject to this, however, the Court could authorise a plan of action which involved the deprivation of liberty in circumstances where the DoLS do not apply, for example where a person is to live somewhere other than a hospital or care home.

(ii) Challenging the DoLS

Deprivation of liberty may be authorised under the MCA DoLS scheme (see chapter 1). Challenges to the "lawfulness" of these authorisations go to the Court of Protection rather than to a tribunal. In relation to a standard authorisation, the Court can decide disputes about whether the person "qualifies" to be deprived of his liberty (an odd way of putting it, but meaning whether he satisfies the age, mental disorder, mental capacity, best interests, eligibility and no refusals criteria laid down by the Act); or about how long the authorisation is to be in force; or about the purpose for which the authorisation is given; or about the conditions to which it is subject (s 21A(2)). The Court may then make an order ending or varying the authorisation or directing the supervising body to do so (s 21A(3)).

In relation to an urgent authorisation, the Court may decide disputes about whether the urgent authorisation should have been given, the period for which it is to be in force, and the purpose for which it is given (s 21A(4)). It may then make an order ending or varying the authorisation or directing the managing authority of the hospital or care home to do so (s 21A(5)).

The Court may also make an order about any person's liability for what happened before the variation or termination and this may include excluding a person from liability (s 21A(6), (7)). It is not entirely clear whether this includes exempting anyone from what would otherwise be their clear liability for false imprisonment or breach of the Convention rights or whether it simply means deciding whether or not this has happened.

Thus the Court can resolve disputes, not only about whether the criteria for an authorisation were made out, but also about the details of the authorisation itself—its duration, terms and conditions. This might be thought curious, bearing in mind the much more limited powers of a tribunal under the MHA. It might be thought that the Court is in general rather less suited to micro-managing a person's care and treatment than is the specialist tribunal.

(iii) Pending a Court decision

It is also lawful to deprive a person of his liberty where this is necessary in order to provide life-sustaining treatment or to prevent a serious deterioration in his condition while a decision is sought from the Court (s 4B).

(c) Procedure in deprivation of liberty cases

There has to be an application to the Court. In DoLS cases, the person concerned, his deputy, or his representative can apply without permission (s 50(1)(a), (d), (1A)). Anyone else needs the permission of the Court. Because these cases are so urgent, special procedures apply (Court of Protection Rules 2007, r 82A and *Practice Direction: Deprivation of Liberty Applications*, 2009). There is a dedicated team in the Court office who can be contacted before an application is made. There are also special forms for the application, any request for urgent consideration, any application for permission to apply and certificates about and acknowledging service, so that these cases can easily be recognised by the staff. The application will be placed before a judge as soon as possible, who will direct how the case is to proceed, and may make orders, even before the application is issued. The Court will aim to have the first hearing (which could also be the last) before a judge within five working days of the application, but the applicant can ask for an earlier one. If it is extremely urgent, the team can organise a telephone application to the judge. The team is only available between 10:00 and 16:00 on working days, but applications can be made to the out of hours applications judge of the Family Division of the High Court (through the duty officer at the Royal Courts of Justice).

The usual Court of Protection Rules (see p 336, later) will apply only so far as they are consistent with the judge's directions in the individual case. He may very well have to limit the people who should be notified or the time for notifying them or the evidence which should be obtained. He will have to decide whether the detained person should be a party and represented by the Official Solicitor. It is standard practice to notify the person alleged to lack capacity and give him an opportunity to be heard, even if he is not made a party to the proceedings.

Other issues, for example about medical treatment, may arise in connection with a section 21A application and these can be indicated on the special application form. But deprivation of liberty issues may also arise in other applications, for example about where someone is to live. Here the special forms should not be used but the proposed applicant should contact the deprivation of liberty team to discuss handling at the earliest possible stage before issuing the application.

In urgent cases the Court may not have time to commission independent reports of its own, but there is power to do so from a local authority or NHS body, the Public Guardian or a Court of Protection Visitor (see p 338, later).

(d) Issues

The Court is governed by the general principles in section 1 of the MCA (see p 5, earlier), by the definition of capacity in sections 2 and 3 (see p 63, earlier) and by the best interests approach in section 4 (see p 65, earlier). The MCA does not explicitly say this in relation to its scrutiny of authorisations under the DoLS (cf s 16(3)), but it must follow. The criteria for depriving a person of liberty encompass the general principles but also impose extra requirements, of mental disorder and eligibility, which the Court may have to consider. It also seems clear from the breadth of its powers under section 21A that the Court is not merely exercising a supervisory jurisdiction and may substitute its own decision for that of the supervisory body or managing authority.

Thus far, the Court has been concerned with the boundary line between the DoLS and the MHA and whether the patient is "ineligible" for the DoLS or a Court of Protection order because he could be sectioned under the MHA. Difficult issues may also arise about the boundary line between deprivation and restriction of liberty (see chapter 1).

3. THE FAMILY DIVISION OF THE HIGH COURT

The MCA does not abolish the inherent jurisdiction of the High Court to make declarations as to what will, or will not, be lawful in the best interests of a person who lacks the capacity to decide the matter for himself. It seems that these can continue to co-exist alongside the powers of the Court of Protection and the DoLS. Indeed, in theory the Family Division might declare it lawful to deprive a patient of his liberty even though he would be "ineligible" within the meaning of Schedule 1A to the MCA (and so could not be made subject to the DoLS or to a Court of Protection order under section 16(2)(a)). But the Family Division would be just as mindful of the requirements of article 5, including the necessity for regular reviews, and in practice may model its orders on the requirements of the DoLS: see *Re BJ (Incapacitated Adult)* [2009] EWHC 3310 (Fam). There are also practical advantages in transferring cases from the Family Division to the Court of Protection, where they can be heard locally by specialist judges. But of course this would not work if the Family Division had authorised action which the Court of Protection could not.

4. THE ADMINISTRATIVE COURT

The tribunal and the Court of Protection are there to consider the merits of the decisions which the professionals have made, although the Court of Protection can also decide that depriving a person of his liberty was unlawful on technical grounds, for example because there had not been all the required assessments, or they had been conducted by the wrong people, or were otherwise technically deficient.

An important constitutional remedy for anyone who considers himself illegally detained is the ancient writ of *habeas corpus*. Application is made to the Administrative Court (part of the Queen's Bench Division of the High Court), or, if it is not sitting, to any High Court judge, at his home if necessary. This should be done by or with the consent of the detained person, but if he is incapable, a relative or friend can proceed on his behalf. If the evidence shows a prima facie case of illegal detention, the court will issue the writ. This requires the detainer to produce the body or show lawful justification for holding him. The court is concerned with whether there is legal power to detain the person concerned. There are limits to how far the court can go in investigating the truth of the facts alleged by the gaoler or the merits of his case.

At the lowest level, the hospital's power to detain a person suffering from mental disorder patient depends upon the existence of orders from a court, warrants or directions from the Justice Secretary, applications, recommendations and renewal reports from those authorised to make them under Part 2 of the MHA or authorisations under Schedule A1 of the MCA. If no such document exists or if the document itself were bad on its face, then the court would have to order the patient's release.

The next level is where the document is apparently valid but has been completed in breach of the procedures laid down in the Act. The consequence of breach will depend upon what Parliament is taken to have intended. Some provisions simply say, for example, that the doctors must examine the patient either together or with no more than five days between the days on which their examinations took place (MHA, s 12(1)) or that an AMHP must interview the patient (s 13(2)). Others say that the application shall not be made, for example, if the applicant has not seen the patient within the prescribed time (s 11(5)), or the AMHP has not consulted the nearest relative (s 11(4)(b)) or has a potential conflict of interest (s 11(1A)). Parliament may well have intended that it would be unlawful to detain a person if these requirements have not been strictly followed. If so, *habeas corpus* should be granted.

In *Re S-C (Mental Patient: Habeas Corpus)* [1996] QB 599, CA, a social worker made a section 3 application knowing that the nearest relative actively objected (contrary to s 11(4)(a)). The Court of Appeal held that *habeas corpus* is "*an* appropriate, possibly even *the* appropriate remedy" in such cases. Section 6(3), which allows the hospital managers to act upon an application form which appears to be "duly completed", might protect the hospital from liability for damages for false imprisonment, but it could not turn an unlawful detention into a lawful one. Otherwise, in the view of Sir Thomas Bingham MR, the implications would be "horrifying"—the forms might appear to be in order even if the social worker or the doctors were entirely bogus. In such cases, as Neill LJ pointed out, the challenge goes to the validity of the application and the existence of the power to detain.

This may also happen at the third level, where it is sought to challenge the decision that the grounds for detention exist. In the famous case of *R v Board of Control, ex p Rutty* [1956] 2 QB 109 (see also *R v Rampton Institution Board of Control, ex p Barker* [1957] Crim LR 402; *Re Sage* [1958] Crim LR 258), the applicant was a borderline "feeble-minded" patient who had been compulsorily admitted to an institution on the ground that she had been "found neglected".

This was curious, because at the time she was living and working in a hospital under the care of the county council. The court held that there was no evidence that she was "neglected" and ordered her release. As a result, it seems that over 3,000 other patients in mental deficiency institutions had to be released. However, it is clear that if there had been *some* evidence upon which the authorities could reasonably have concluded that she was neglected the court would not have interfered.

If the formalities necessary for a valid detention have been complied with, and a decision reached within the scope of the powers entrusted by Parliament to the body in question, the Administrative Court will not intervene simply because it would have made a different decision. The decision has to be illegal, procedurally unfair, or irrational (outside the bounds of what a reasonable decision-maker could have decided). This includes a decision which is perverse, or cannot be supported on the evidence, as in the *Rutty* case. Occasionally, Parliament has only left the decision to the administrative body if certain facts exist. These are known as "precedent" or "jurisdictional facts", without which the body would not have had the power to act. This is another way to explain the *Rutty* case. The best known modern example is *R v Secretary of State for the Home Department, ex p Khawaja* [1984] AC 74, where the power to detain depended upon whether the person concerned was an "illegal entrant". This issue has tended not to arise since the 1959 Act, because the tribunal have power to decide whether or not a person is mentally disordered and whether the grounds for detention exist (and now the Court of Protection has power to decide whether or not a person lacks the capacity to make the decision for himself).

The alternative to *habeas corpus* is to apply for judicial review of the decision to detain. There were important procedural differences between *habeas corpus* and judicial review. Judicial review applications require the Court's permission, affidavit evidence can be filed, and a wide range of remedies are available, but all are discretionary. If it is necessary to do so, disputed questions of fact can be determined with oral evidence: see *R (Wilkinson) v Broadmoor Special Hospital Authority* [2001] EWCA Civ 1545, [2002] 1 WLR 419. In practice, however, as Lord Woolf explained in *B v Barking, Havering and Brentwood Community Healthcare NHS Trust* [1999] 1 FLR 106, 115, the differences between *habeas corpus* and judicial review are of less significance than they may seem. He disagreed with Sir Thomas Bingham that *habeas corpus* was "the" remedy. He would discourage it unless it was clear that nothing other than an order for release would be required. Where the issue was the propriety, rather than the obvious illegality, of the detention, it may be that judicial review is the only appropriate remedy.

The main thing, of course, is that a patient whose detention is unlawful should be able to secure his immediate release, without delay and without any question of needing the Court's permission to apply or of a discretion to refuse. That is what the "liberty of the subject" has always meant.

5. COMMENTARY

Who would you rather have to decide your fate? A court or a tribunal? The great criticism levelled at tribunals in the past was that they tended to operate more like a case conference or "patient's welfare assessment panel" (Fennell, 1977) than like a court. Indeed, this is how they saw themselves (Peay, 1981 and 1982). They were usually dealing with patients who had been in hospital for some time and to whom the various labels were firmly attached. Their procedures were not well suited to examining the evidence upon which earlier judgments had been made. The issue was whether the patient was yet ready for a change and if so how to find the best placement for him. The tribunal were interested in getting some "feel" for his present mental state and assessing his needs along with the risks to his family and the public.

The normal model of adjudication, based upon the application of fixed rules to proven facts about the past, does not fit well with these cases. They are more like child welfare decisions than running-down actions. They will always centre round what sort of person the patient is and how he can be expected to behave in the future. But the best guide to future behaviour is usually how someone has behaved in the past. So it can be important that the evidence for this is properly scrutinised and evaluated. It is also important that the legal criteria are properly applied. The involvement of lawyers as advocates for patients should focus minds on the proper legal issues; lead to a more careful scrutiny of assumptions about the future made on the basis of past events; and enable an independent psychiatric investigation. All of this may take time, especially in the inevitably more difficult and complex cases involving special hospital and restricted patients. The MHAC (2008, 2009a) was therefore concerned that changes in the fee structure for this work might result in some specialist lawyers leaving the field.

There is also concern about delays in fixing a hearing and adjournments caused by inadequate information. The tribunal handles a considerable volume of work—around 23,000 cases in 2008–2009. But by and large the patients' experience of tribunal hearings was positive—and this despite their low success rate in achieving discharge, which was only 13 per cent in 2008. However, many more patients were discharged between the application and the hearing, perhaps because it was expected that their application would succeed (surely not because the hospital did not want the bother of preparing for and appearing at the tribunal hearing). Many other applications were withdrawn—over 10,000 in 2008–2009—perhaps suggesting that it was expected that they would fail.

It is interesting to compare the powers and procedures of the tribunal with those of the Court of Protection. The tribunal might be thought well designed for reviewing the professionals' decisions over a much wider range of issues than whether the patient should remain subject to compulsory powers: indeed, the same Chamber has power to decide exactly what education should be provided for a child with special educational needs. The composition and procedures of the Court of Protection are much closer to those of an ordinary court of law deciding upon the legal consequences of what has happened in the past. Yet the Court has power to determine the details of what should happen to a person without capacity in a way which the tribunal does not. Why should this be?

On the other hand, the patient appearing before a tribunal is assumed to have the capacity to conduct his own case and to instruct his own lawyer if he has one. Yet, despite the presumption of capacity in the MCA, the Court of Protection Rules assume that the person involved lacks capacity, should not necessarily be made a party, and should act through a litigation friend if he does become a party (see r 141(1)). And the reported cases to date suggest that contested proceedings in the Court of Protection take longer than tribunal cases do.

Are these differences simply an accident of history or are there sound reasons for them? Only time will tell.

9 COMMUNITY CARE

"Community care means providing the right level of intervention and support to enable people to achieve maximum independence and control over their own lives" (DH et al, 1989). For most disabled and elderly people, this means keeping them out of institutions for as long as possible. For people with mental disorders and disabilities, however, it initially meant closing down the old mental hospitals and discharging as many patients as possible into the community. The process began with the Percy Commission, which recommended that:

"no-one should be excluded from benefiting from any of the general social services simply because his need arises from mental disorder rather than from some other cause" (1957, para 592).

The Mental Health Act 1959 therefore extended the powers of local authorities to provide services for adults in need of care to people with mental disorders. Progress was slow at first, as it always is when switching resources from one part of the public sector to another, but gathered real momentum during the 1970s (DHSS, 1971 and 1975).

This normalisation policy was relatively uncontroversial for people with learning disabilities. Their principal need is for social care, education and occupation, rather than for specialist health care, unless they also have serious physical disabilities. The debate was about what sort of residential settings would suit them best (see Emerson and Hatton, 1994). For people with mental illnesses, however, it was more controversial. The dividing line between the health care responsibilities of the NHS and the social care responsibilities of local authorities is harder to draw. There was concern, not only about the arrangements which ought to be made for patients who once upon a time would have been looked after in hospital, but also that abandoning the old asylum role could lead to more and more people being out of touch with the system altogether, thus increasing the numbers of homeless "crazies" on city streets and disturbed or inadequate petty offenders in prison because there was nowhere else for them to go.

More positively, community care should mean a flexible range of health and social services to meet the needs, and enhance the quality of life, of the people who need them, both as an end in itself and so that they are less likely to have to go into institutional care. The Government has recently announced that its "vision is for a system that is fair, simple and affordable for everyone. It must be underpinned by national rights and entitlements, but personalised to people's individual needs" (Department of Health, *Shaping the Future of Care Together*, 2009, p 25). This can scarcely be said of the present system of adult social care, which is complex and based, not on individual entitlements, but on a patchwork of local authority duties. The Law Commission is currently reviewing the law relating to adult social care, which it has described as "inadequate, often incomprehensible and outdated" (2008b).

The shift to community care has been informed by human rights values, both nationally and internationally. The UN Convention on the Rights of People with

Disabilities (2006), ratified by the United Kingdom in 2009, contains a number of socio-economic rights as well as the more familiar civil and political rights. The emphasis is not only on equal access to the same health, educational and other services as are available for other people, but also on providing "an inclusive education system at all levels", with "reasonable accommodation of the individual's requirements" and "effective individualised support" (art 24); "health services needed by people with disabilities precisely because of their disabilities" (art 25(b)); comprehensive habilitation and rehabilitation services to enable people with disabilities to attain and maintain maximum independence (art 26(1)); ensuring that "reasonable accommodation is provided to people with disabilities in the workplace" (art 27(1)(i)); and perhaps above all, in article 19:

> "States parties . . . recognise the equal right of all persons with disabilities to live in the community, with choices equal to others and shall take effective and appropriate measures to facilitate full enjoyment by persons with disabilities of this right and their full inclusion and participation in the community".

This involves ensuring that they have the opportunity to choose where to live and are not obliged to live in a particular living arrangement, and that they have

> "access to a range of in-home, residential and other community support services, including personal assistance necessary to support living and inclusion in the community, and to prevent isolation and segregation from the community".

Here at home, individuals can bring actions against public authorities who act in breach of the rights defined in the European Convention on Human Rights. The most relevant in this context are the right not to be subjected to inhuman or degrading treatment or punishment under article 3 and the right to respect for private and family life, home and correspondence protected by article 8. It is unlawful for a public authority to act incompatibly with these rights (Human Rights Act 1988, s 6(1)). Under section 6(3)(b), a public authority includes "any person certain of whose functions are functions of a public nature"; but section 6(5) then says that "in relation to a particular act, a person is not a public authority by virtue only of subsection (3)(b) if the nature of the act is private". One of the most contentious issues to emerge under the 1998 Act is whether private and voluntary organisations which provide services by arrangement with or under contract to local authorities or the NHS are "public authorities" for this purpose. As we shall see below, this has caused problems for people placed by local authorities in private care homes.

This chapter concentrates upon the legal position of individuals: what community services may be available to people with mental disorders and disabilities and how they can gain access to these; how they may be protected against ill treatment, neglect and exploitation; and the impact of the Mental Health Act 1983 (MHA) and the Mental Capacity Act 2005 (MCA) upon people living in the community. This all affects vastly more people with mental disorders and disabilities than does the law relating to hospital admission but it was a comparatively unexplored area of the law until the 1990s. The subject has now taken off (see Clements and Thompson, 2007) and there is only space to skim the surface here.

1. COMMUNITY CARE SERVICES

Legal responsibility for providing community services rests with local social services authorities (LSSAs), local children's services authorities and the National Health Service. The dividing line between health and social care for people with mental disorders and disabilities is not easy to draw and has shifted over the years. When the welfare state was established after the Second World War, the NHS was largely responsible for looking after both mentally ill and mentally disabled people. Nowadays, the principal responsibility for providing or arranging social care lies with local social services authorities, while the health service remains responsible for health care both in and out of hospital.

The present legal framework for adult social care is mainly contained in the National Health Service and Community Care Act 1990 (NHSCCA) but this merely built upon earlier legislation and has itself been built upon since. The NHSCCA followed reports from the Audit Commission (1986) and Sir Roy Griffiths (1988) and a white paper, *Caring for People* (1989). Fewer and fewer people were living in long-stay hospitals but more and more public money was being spent on paying the fees of old and other vulnerable people living in private or voluntary nursing or care homes without any assessment of their individual needs. This simply switched money from one sort of institutional care to another without considering whether there might be better ways of meeting a person's needs. Instead, therefore, the budget was to be given to LSSAs, along with the task of "ensuring that the needs of individuals within the specified groups are identified, packages of care are devised and services co-ordinated" (Griffiths, 1988, para 24). The idea was that local authorities should draw up plans to develop a "mixed economy of care", making use of not for profit and private providers wherever this was most cost-effective. They should move away from the post-war vision of the welfare state as the exclusive provider of social services and into the role of service arranger and procurer.

Section 46(3) of the NHSCCA defines "community care services" as those which an LSSA may provide under the following statutory provisions:

- Part 3 of the National Assistance Act 1948 (NAA); this includes both residential accommodation for people in need of care and attention under section 21 and welfare services for disabled people under section 29; the courts have held that services for disabled people under section 2 of the Chronically Sick and Disabled Persons Act 1970 (CSDPA) are also included, as these are an extension of section 29 (*R v Kirklees MBC, ex p Daykin* (1997–98) 1 CCLR 512);
- section 45 of the Health Services and Public Health Act 1968 (HSPHA);
- section 254 and Schedule 20 to the National Health Service Act 2006 (NHSA) and their Welsh equivalents in section 192 and Schedule 15 to the National Health Service (Wales) Act 2006; and
- section 117 of the Mental Health Act 1983 (MHA 1983).

Residential care can now be provided only under section 21 of the NAA (apart from some limited powers to provide hostel accommodation in connection with other services). A wide range of non-residential and ancillary services, such as training, occupation and leisure activities, as well as help with daily living and obtaining access to other services, can be provided for disabled people under section 29 of the NAA and section 2 of the CSDPA, for old people under section 45 of the HSPHA and for sick people under Schedule 20 to the NHSA. There is considerable overlap between these powers as they apply to mentally disordered, disabled or elderly people. All of them (apart from s 2 of the CSDPA) begin by saying that a local social services authority "may with the approval of the Secretary of State and to such extent that he may direct shall" provide the services described to the particular client group. Thus the precise extent of their powers and duties is defined in departmental circulars: Department of Health Circular No LAC(93)10, for all but section 45 of the HSPHA, and DHSS Circular 19/71 for section 45. All kinds of service can be provided directly or by arrangement with the voluntary or private sectors (NAA 1948, ss 26, 30; HSPHA, s 45(3); Circular LAC(93)10).

(a) Residential accommodation under section 21 of the NAA 1948

Under section 21(1)(a) of the NAA, LSSAs have a duty to make arrangements to provide residential accommodation for people who because of "age, illness, disability or any other circumstances are in need of care and attention which is not otherwise available to them". Authorities are specifically directed to make arrangements to provide accommodation for people who are or have been suffering from mental disorder or for the purpose of preventing their mental disorder and who are ordinarily resident in their area or who have no settled residence and are present there (DH Circular LAC(93)10, App 1, para 2(3)). There is also power to accommodate people who ordinarily live elsewhere but come to live in the area after discharge from hospital (para 2(4)).

This includes arranging "board and other services, amenities and requisites provided in connection with the accommodation" (s 21(5)) and transport to and from, and "other services" on, the premises (s 21(7)(b)). Local authorities cannot, however, make any provision under section 21 which is *authorised or required* to be made under some other legislation (such as the Housing Act 1996) or under the National Health Service Acts (s 21(8)). This means, in effect, that if the Government has decided that something can or should be done by the NHS, then a local authority cannot provide it. But if it is merely incidental or ancillary to providing accommodation and does not go beyond what a social services authority could be expected to provide, then the authority may still provide it (*R v North and East Devon Health Authority, ex p Coughlan* [2001] QB 213, CA).

Accommodation may be provided in the authority's own care homes. But LSSAs do not have to have their own homes as long as suitable accommodation is available elsewhere (*R v Wandsworth LBC, ex p Beckwith* [1996] 1 WLR 60, HL). Many have now closed their homes or transferred them to the voluntary or private sectors. Section 21(1)(a) arrangements can be made in homes managed by other local authorities (s 21(4)) or by voluntary organisations or others who provide such accommodation for reward (s 26(1)). The National Assistance Act 1948 (Choice of Accommodation) Directions 1992 (see LAC(2004)20) allow an eligible client to choose which care home is provided, as long as it is suitable to his assessed needs, is available on the local authority's usual terms, and will not cost more than the authority would usually expect to pay for someone with the client's needs.

If accommodation is provided in a care home, the home must be registered under the Care Standards Act 2000 (CSA). A care home is defined in the CSA (s 3) as one which provides "accommodation, together with nursing or personal care" for people (a) who are or have been ill, (b) who have or have had a mental disorder, (c) who are disabled or infirm, or (d) who are or have been dependent on alcohol or drugs. Hospitals and children's homes are excluded because they are covered by other legislation. All care homes, whether in the private, public or voluntary ("third") sector, must now be registered under the CSA. So for the first time homes provided by public authorities became subject to the same requirements and supervision as homes provided in the private and third sectors; no longer is it assumed that public sector establishments are so well run that independent regulation is not required.

But it may be possible to meet the client's needs in accommodation which is not a registered care home. The key to entitlement under section 21(1)(a) is the person's need for "care and attention" which is not otherwise available to him. This does not have to be as much as "nursing or personal care" and so accommodation may be arranged in ordinary dwellings as well as in registered care homes (*R v Newham LBC, ex p Medical Foundation for the Victims of Torture* (1997–98) 1 CCLR 227; *R v Bristol City Council, ex p Penfold* (1997–98) 1 CCLR 315; *R (Batantu) v Islington LBC* (2000) 4 CCLR 445). But the people accommodated must need some form of looking after—doing something for them which they cannot or should not be expected to do for themselves, such as household tasks which they cannot do or do only with great difficulty, protection from risks which a mentally disabled person cannot perceive, or personal care (see *R (M) v Slough LBC* [2008] UKHL 52, [2008] 1 WLR 1808; also *R (Wahid) v Tower Hamlets LBC* [2002] EWCA Civ 287, [2002] LGR 545). The duty may be owed to the wealthy as well as the poor (*R (Westminster City Council) v National Asylum Support Service* [2002] UKHL 38, [2002] 1 WLR 2956, para 32), but the wealthy will be expected to bear the full cost whereas others will not. And if they can arrange and fund appropriate accommodation for themselves, this will be "otherwise available to them" so that the duty does not arise.

The quality of life for residents in all types of home, whether public or private, is crucially affected by how far the home is prepared to go in respecting their dignity and autonomy, allowing them to live their own lives and take their own decisions. The home's own rules may restrict the residents' rights to choose how and where they spend their time. In principle, homes are entitled to offer their accommodation on these terms, take it or leave it, but LSSAs can now dictate the terms for the residents whom they place. Homes are also only too conscious of their common law duty to take reasonable care of their residents. Rules may be devised in order to avoid a claim for personal injuries brought, for example, by an elderly resident who falls downstairs because there was no one to accompany him. However, homes have nothing to fear if they have taken reasonable precautions, or if a resident has chosen to take a risk of which he is perfectly well aware.

A more serious problem may be the seemingly petty indignities which are not the result of defensive caution, or of cruelty or deliberate neglect, but of a lack of respect for individual human dignity: giving residents their breakfast while sitting on a commode, performing intimate care tasks in full view of passers-by and the like (see Joint Committee on Human Rights, 2006–2007). If serious enough, these might reach the threshold of "inhuman or degrading treatment" under article 3 of the ECHR; more probably, they could be a lack of respect for private life under article 8. It is usually a term of the home's contract with the LSSA that it respect the residents' human rights, but could the resident sue the home if it does not? In *YL v Birmingham City Council* [2007] UKHL 27, [2008] 1 AC 95, the House of Lords held, by a majority of three to two, that it was not a "function of a public nature" for a private or voluntary organisation to provide accommodation, even though it was arranged and paid for by a local authority under section 21. Fortunately, section 145 of the Health and Social Care Act 2008 reverses this decision; but it only applies to providers of accommodation, together with nursing or personal care, in a care home under arrangements made under sections 21(1)(a) and 26 of the NAA. The position of providers of other kinds of service pursuant to statutory arrangements will have to be considered on a case by case basis.

Another problem is that staff may be tempted to take decisions for their residents but are unsure about whether the law gives them power to do so. Residents who have the capacity to do so are entitled to make their own choices about such things as medical and dental treatment and how to spend their own money. The mere fact that a person lives in a care home, even a home for mentally disabled or elderly mentally infirm residents, does not remove his right to self-determination in such matters. However, section 5 of the MCA makes it clear that a carer can take steps in connection with the care and treatment of a resident or patient, if he reasonably believes that the resident or patient lacks the capacity to decide the matter for himself and that what the carer is doing is in that person's best interests: all of this is fully explained at pp 61–68 and 191–193, earlier. The MCA also provides a mechanism for resolving disputes about such matters as where a person without capacity should live (see chapter 10) and for independent advocates to represent them when decisions are taken to place them in hospital or care homes or to move them between placements (see chapter 6).

(b) Services for disabled people under section 29 of the NAA 1948 and section 2 of the CSDPA 1970

Under section 29 of the NAA, arrangements can be made for promoting the welfare of disabled people. These are defined to include people who suffer from mental disorder of any description. There is a duty to provide a social work service, advice and support, facilities for social rehabilitation and adjustment to disability, at centres or elsewhere, and for occupational, social, cultural and recreational activities, for people who are ordinarily resident in the area (Circular LAC(93)10, App 2, para 2(1)). There is power to do this for anyone who qualifies, wherever they live, and there is also power to provide holiday homes, free or subsidised travel, help in finding accommodation to enable people to participate in these facilities, to contribute towards the cost of employing a warden on warden assisted housing schemes, and to provide warden services for occupiers of private housing (para 2(1) and 2(2)).

The circular also approves making arrangements, for anyone eligible, to tell them what services are available, give them instruction in methods of overcoming their disabilities, provide workshops and hostels for people working there (or in workshops provided for disabled people under other legislation), provide work at home or elsewhere, and help them to sell what they produce (s 29(4) and LAC(93)10, App 2, para 2(3)).

LSSAs also have a duty to compile and maintain a register of disabled people who are ordinarily resident in their area (s 29(4)(g); LAC(93)10, App 2, para 2(2)). The details are spelt out in Appendix 4 to Circular LAC(93)10.

However, section 29 does not authorise the provision of any accommodation or services which are *required* to be provided under the NHS Acts (s 29(6)(b)). This is not as restrictive as section 21(8) (see p 288, above) but may preclude local authorities from providing services for mentally disordered people under section 29 which they are required to provide under the NHS Acts (see p 291, below). This probably does not make much difference in practice to the services provided.

Section 2 of the CSDPA was designed to strengthen these powers by imposing a specific duty upon an LSSA to arrange certain things for an individual disabled person who is ordinarily resident in their area, if satisfied that it is necessary to do so in order to meet his needs. These things are: practical assistance in his own home; providing or helping with wireless, television, library and similar recreational facilities; lectures, games, outings and other recreational facilities outside the home or help in accessing educational facilities; travel to and from his home to section 29 or similar services; home adaptation or additional facilities "to secure his greater safety, comfort or convenience"; facilitating holidays; providing meals at home or elsewhere; and providing or helping to obtain a telephone and any special equipment needed to enable him to use it. Like most recent legislation about people with disabilities, this was a private members' bill and driven by a "welfare rights" ethos rather than by the "welfare for all" philosophy of the post-war welfare state.

(c) Welfare services for old people under section 45 of the HSPHA 1968

Part 3 of the NAA concentrated on residential accommodation for people needing "care and attention" and non-residential services for disabled people. With the shift away from institutional care, the range of people for whom non-residential services could be provided was tentatively widened to include old people, whether or not they were mentally disordered or disabled. Under section 45 of the 1968 Act, LSSAs can make arrangements for promoting the welfare of old people, but these are not a duty. The arrangements may involve meals and recreation in the home and elsewhere, help with travel to participate in services, help with finding boarding accommodation, practical help in the home, including adaptations and additional facilities to "secure greater safety, comfort and convenience", help towards employing a warden in warden assisted housing schemes and warden services for occupiers of private housing, as well as visiting and advisory services and social work support and information about the services available (DHSS Circular 19/71). District councils also have power to provide meals and recreation for old people under Part 2 of Schedule 9 to the Health and Social Services and Social Security Adjudications Act 1983 (the HASSASSA Act).

(d) Prevention, care and after-care services under the NHS Acts

Under paragraph 2 of Schedule 20 to the NHSA 2006, LSSAs may make arrangements for the prevention of illness, the care of people suffering from illness, and the after-care of people who have been so suffering. "Illness" includes any form of mental disorder within the meaning of the MHA 1983. The NHS authorities have a parallel responsibility to provide facilities for the prevention, care and after-care of "illness", if these are considered appropriate as part of the health service (under s 3(1)(e) of NHSA 2006). This dual responsibility dates back to the first National Health Service Act of 1946. Department of Health Guidance on Adult Social Care (2010, para 66) stresses that people who use specialist health services, such as mental health service users or people with learning disabilities, should be supported by both health and social care teams, so that all their needs are appropriately addressed.

Under Circular LAC(93)10, the NHS Act appears to be the principal source of LSSAs' responsibilities to provide non-residential services for mentally disordered people. LSSAs are directed to make arrangements for the purposes of preventing mental disorder, or in relation to people who are or have been suffering from mental disorder, for providing centres (including training centres and day centres) or other facilities (including domiciliary facilities) for their training or occupation; and they may pay people for work done there (Circular LAC(93)10, App 3, paras 3(2), 3(3)(b)). Once the Local Education Authority's (LEA) responsibilities towards children and young people are over, therefore, social services should assume responsibility for the occupation and training of mentally disordered people, particularly those with learning disabilities.

LSSAs are also directed to arrange for enough approved mental health professionals (AMHPs), for the exercise of their guardianship functions (see below), and for:

> "social work and related services to help in the identification, diagnosis, assessment and social treatment of mental disorder and to provide social work support and other domiciliary and care services to people living in their homes and elsewhere" (para 3(2)).

Curiously, the circular does not limit their duties to persons ordinarily resident in their area, although this must be what was intended, in parallel with sections 21 and 29 of the NAA.

There is also a power, but not the duty, to arrange for meals to be served in these centres and other facilities, for meals on wheels (not otherwise provided for under (c) above), night-sitter services, recuperative holidays, social and recreational facilities and services for alcoholics and drug addicts, and social services for:

> "preventing the impairment of physical or mental health of adults in families where such impairment is likely and for the purposes of preventing the break-up of such families or for assisting in their rehabilitation" (Circular LAC(93)10, App 3, para 3(3)).

They must arrange a home help service and may arrange a laundry service for a household which needs this because it contains someone who is suffering from illness, is aged, or handicapped as a result of having suffered from illness or by congenital deformity (NHSA, Sch 20, para 3).

(e) After-care for detained patients under section 117 of the MHA 1983

As we have seen in chapter 7, LSSAs share with the NHS a duty to provide after-care services for patients who have been detained for treatment under the MHA when they are discharged from hospital. This is a free-standing duty, not simply a duty to arrange services under the authorities' other powers (*R v Manchester City Council, ex p Stennett* [2002] UKHL 34, [2002] 2 AC 1127). But the services which may be provided are not defined. It has been said that they would normally include:

> "social work, support in helping the ex-patient with problems of employment, accommodation or family relationships, the provision of domiciliary services and the use of day centre and residential facilities" (*Clunis v Camden and Islington Health Authority* [1998] QB 978, CA, at 992, approved in *Stennett*).

(f) Services for carers

Many of the above services for mentally disordered people (or the household where they live) will also help their carers. But under the Carers and Disabled Children Act 2000, local authorities must consider the carer's needs in relation to the care which she gives or intends to give, whether those needs could be satisfied by services which the local authority may provide, and if so, whether to provide them (s 2(1)). The services involved are not listed or defined: they are any which the authority see fit to provide and which will, in the authority's opinion, help the carer to care, and can take the form of physical help or other forms of support (s 2(2)). The authority may also supply vouchers to enable the carer to obtain replacement care while she takes a short break (s 3; for regulations see SI 2001/441 and WSI 2001/2186).

A carer for this purpose is someone aged 16 or over who provides or intends to provide "a substantial amount of care on a regular basis" to someone of 18 or over, for whom the LSSA may provide or arrange community care services; but excluding people doing so under a contract or as a volunteer for a voluntary organisation (s 1(1), (3)). This also excludes child carers under 16, although there are many children who look after their mentally disordered parents, siblings or other relatives. Perhaps it was thought that these children are by definition "in need" within the meaning of the Children Act 1989 (CA), because their development must be affected by their caring responsibilities (see p 301, below).

(g) Direct payments

If an LSSA decide to provide a community care service for a client, they can instead, with his consent, make direct payments to him from which he can buy the service for himself (Health and Social Care Act 2001, s 57; Community Care, Services for Carers and Children's Services (Direct Payments) (England) Regulations 2009, SI 2009/1887). It must appear to the local authority that the client is capable of managing a direct payment and they must also be satisfied that his need for the service can be met through a direct payment. Currently, clients subject to compulsory powers under the MHA are excluded. But in 2008 section 57 was amended so that a suitable person could consent to and receive direct payments on behalf of someone who lacks the capacity to manage them for himself. A suitable person is a deputy appointed by the Court of Protection, the donee of a lasting power of attorney or (if there is neither) any person whom the authority consider suitable (s 57(1C)) (the Welsh Regulations have not yet provided for this: cf WSI 2004/1748).

The idea is to give clients control over their own lives, but these payments cannot be used to buy long term residential care (more than four continuous weeks in any 12 months or 120 days in one year) or to buy local authority or NHS services. Direct payments only amounted to two per cent of total social care expenditure in 2006–2007. There were great variations between different areas, perhaps because the idea is not popular with some local politicians and officials. Some may think them more suitable for younger physically disabled clients than for the mentally ill, disabled or elderly clients with whom this book is concerned (Commission for Social Care Inspection 2004; Haslar and Stewart 2004). The Guidance on Adult Social Care (Department of Health, 2010, para 127) envisages that everyone eligible should have the option of a "personal budget", either as a direct payment or as a notional budget to be held on their behalf by the LSSA or a third party.

293

(h) Charging and paying for community care services

Unlike the National Health Service, Part 3 accommodation has never been free. Local authorities are required to charge up to the full cost (NAA, s 22). It was a point of pride in 1948 that people who went into local authority old people's homes were not going into the poor house. They were expected to pay what they could. The amount actually paid is determined by a means test (under the HSSASSA Act 1983, Pt 7). Essentially the same system applies to residential care "bought in" from the voluntary and private sectors (NAA, s 26(2), (3), (3A)). If hostel accommodation is provided under section 29 of the NAA (see above), it also comes within this system (NHSCCA, s 44(7)) rather than the discretionary charges which apply to other social care services.

Under section 17 of the HASSASSA Act, there is power to make whatever charges the authority think reasonable for their non-residential services. But they do not have to do so and cannot charge more than it is reasonably practicable for the client to pay. This allows the authority to charge for such things as home help, home care, meals on wheels and day care. The Government accepts that it would not be appropriate to charge for social work support, advice and assessment of client needs (Department of Health, *Fairer Charging Policies*, 2003; see also *Fairer Contributions Guidance*, 2009). Under Part 2 of the Community Care (Delayed Discharges etc) Act 2003, regulations may require that any "qualifying service" be provided free of charge. These are the provision of residential accommodation under Part 3 of the NAA and of any other services covered by the charging powers in section 17 of HASSASSA Act, but at present accommodation or personal care can only qualify for up to six weeks (2003 Act, s 15(3), (4)). Also, the current regulations only cover "intermediate care" (defined as a structured programme of care for no more than six weeks to help a client maintain or regain the ability to live in his own home) and "community equipment" (defined as an aid or minor adaptation to property to help with either nursing at home or to aid daily living) (Community Care (Delayed Discharges etc) Act (Qualifying Services) (England) Regulations 2003, SI 2003/1196; there are no Welsh regulations).

If the Personal Care at Home Bill 2009–2010 becomes law, however, it will remove the six week limit and there are plans to widen the scope of the services which LSSAs will have to provide free of charge. But the proposed focus is on clients with the highest personal care needs (needs which are assessed as "critical" and involving help with four or more of the activities of daily living). There is understandable concern that this is aimed at elderly people who will soon have to go into residential care in any event, rather than at people with mental health problems who need different sorts of help but have a better chance of staying out of hospital or residential care if they are given it.

The courts have held that after-care services provided under section 117 of the MHA are not covered by the charging powers in section 17 of HASSASSA Act, so patients who had been admitted to hospital under section 3 of the MHA could not be charged for the residential accommodation with which they were provided on discharge (*R v Manchester City Council, ex p Stennett* [2002] UKHL 34, [2002] 2 AC 1127).

2. ASSESSMENT AND ENTITLEMENT

However, it is one thing for local authorities to have all these wonderful powers and duties. It is quite another thing for individuals to gain access to them.

(a) Assessment

The first step is to assess their needs. The primary duty to assess is in section 47 of the NHSCCA. An LSSA *must* carry out an assessment (in accordance with any directions given by the Secretary of State) if it appears to them that any person for whom they have power to provide or arrange community care services may be in need of them (s 47(1)(a)). This includes someone who is about to be in need, for example when his discharge from hospital is imminent (*R (B) v Camden LBC* [2005] EWHC 1366 (Admin), [2005] 1 MHLR 258, para 66). This duty arises whether or not the client or anyone else requests it (*R v Gloucestershire CC, ex p RADAR* (1997–98) 1 CCLR 476). Nor does it matter that there may be little prospect of the client qualifying for local authority services (*R v Bristol City Council, ex p Penfold* (1997–98) 1 CCLR 315). The NHS Primary Care Trust and local housing authority should be brought into the assessment when necessary (s 47(3)). Having made the assessment, the authority must then decide "whether his needs call for the provision by them of any such services" (s 47(1)(b)). Services can be provided on a temporary basis without an assessment if they are urgently needed (s 47(5)). The Guidance on Adult Social Care (2010, para 71) points out that the client's ability to pay only comes into the picture after his needs have been assessed and decisions taken about what services should be provided. It cannot be used as a reason for not providing services, except where the client needs residential accommodation which he is able both to arrange and to finance for himself (for then it is "otherwise available to him" and he does not qualify under section 21).

Section 47 was super-imposed upon the existing duty to assess the needs of disabled (but not other) clients. Such a duty seemed implicit in the local authority's duty to arrange services under section 2 of the CSDPA ("Alf Morris' Act") if "satisfied" that the client needed them. It was put beyond doubt by section 4 of the Disabled Persons (Services, Consultation and Representation) Act 1986 ("Tom Clarke's Act"). This required local authorities to consider and decide upon a disabled person's need for services under the CSDPA or the Disabled Persons (Employment) Act 1958, if asked to do so either by the client or by a carer: that is, someone who is providing him with "a substantial amount of care on a regular basis" but not employed to do so by a statutory agency. The carer's ability to go on doing this has to be taken into account in the assessment (1986 Act, s 8(1)). Under the NHSCCA, the LSSA have to conduct this assessment along with the section 47 assessment, if the client appears to be disabled, even if they have not been asked to do so (s 47(2)).

The Secretary of State's directions under section 47 (2004) require assessors to consult the client and, where appropriate, his carers; to take all reasonable steps to reach agreement with them on the services the authority are considering providing; and to inform them about what these will cost the client. The emphasis now is upon working with clients and their carers to identify the outcomes which they would like to be able to achieve, rather than focussing on their eligibility for particular services (Guidance on Adult Social Care, 2010, para 59). There should also be regular reviews (para 141). People who lack capacity are likely to need these more often than others, because they may be less able to communicate their needs and wishes and there may be issues about fluctuating capacity (para 146). For mental health service users, LSSAs should consider synchronising reviews for social care with the Care Programme Approach framework (para 149). A Care Programme Approach assessment of the healthcare needs of a client with mental health problems is not the same as a full community care assessment: a person may have needs which could be met by arranging community care services even if he does not meet the criteria for continuing specialist mental health care (*R (HP) v Islington LBC* [2004] EWHC 7 (Admin), (2005) 82 BMLR 113).

On top of the duty to assess the needs of clients, there is also a duty to assess the situation of a carer. The Carers (Recognition and Services) Act 1995 ("Malcolm Wicks' Act") requires that when conducting a section 47 assessment, if asked to do so by a carer who provides or intends to provide a substantial amount of care on a regular basis for the client, the authority must assess the carer's ability to do this, and take that into account when deciding what to do for the client. But a carer may need help even if the client has refused a section 47 assessment, so the Carers and Disabled Children Act 2000 gives a carer aged 16 or over a free-standing right to request an assessment of his ability to provide or continue to provide care for someone for whom the local authority may provide or arrange community care services. Under the Carers (Equal Opportunities) Act 2004 ("Hywel Francis' Act") the local authority have a duty to inform carers of the right to request assessment under either the 1995 or 2000 Acts if the authority believe that they may have a right to it. The 2004 Act also amended the 1995 and 2000 Acts to require the assessment to take into account the carer's own desire to work, undertake education or training, or for leisure activities. Carers, too, are entitled to a life of their own. Oddly, while the private members' Acts apply to carers of any age, the one piece of Government legislation in this list, the 2000 Act, only applies to carers aged 16 or more. Yet it is known that many children under 16 play a large part in looking after their ill or disabled parents, including those who are mentally ill.

Clearly, there is a need for all these assessment duties to be clarified and rationalised (Law Commission, 2008a, 2010).

(b) Eligibility and entitlement

It is for each local authority to devise the eligibility criteria for their community care services in the light of the Guidance on Adult Social Care given by the Secretary of State. *Fair Access to Care Services, Guidance on Eligibility Criteria for Adult Social Care* (2003; Welsh equivalent NAFWC 09A/2002), known as FACS, has been superseded in England by new Guidance on Adult Social Care, *Prioritising need in the context of Putting People First: A whole system approach to eligibility for social care* (Department of Health, 2010). LSSAs should use its eligibility framework when setting their eligibility criteria, taking account of their own resources, local expectations and local costs (para 44). A client's "presenting needs" are not the same as his "eligible needs" (para 47). LSSAs should identify the client's eligible needs according to the risks to independence and well-being both in the immediate and longer-term (para 52). The eligibility framework is graded into four bands which define the seriousness of the risks to independence and well-being: critical, substantial, moderate and low (para 54). All local authorities must follow this framework, but it is for each of them to decide which level of risk to include in their own criteria. They can take their own resources into account, although this cannot be the only factor they consider: *R v Gloucestershire CC, ex p Barry* [1997] AC 584.

This approach led to wide variations in practice across the country and a tendency to restrict rather than to expand eligibility. In 2006–2007, four per cent of councils restricted services to clients whose needs were critical; a further 58 per cent also included substantial; a further 32 per cent also included moderate;

and only six per cent included all four bands. But more were intending to restrict eligibility to critical or substantial need in the following year (Commission for Social Care Inspection, 2008). Examples of the differences are: that "serious abuse or neglect has occurred or will occur" is "critical", while that "abuse or neglect has occurred or will occur" is "substantial"; or that "an inability to carry out vital personal care or domestic routines" is "critical", while an inability to carry out the majority of such routines is "substantial", an inability to carry out "several" such routines is "moderate", and an inability to carry out "one or two" such routines is a "low" risk factor. Not surprisingly, given how narrow it is, the court has taken a dim view of the advice that local authorities are entitled to limit services to the "critical" band: see *R (Bernard) v Enfield LBC* [2002] EWHC 2282 (Admin), (2002) 5 CCLR 577, para 88. The 2010 Guidance advises LSSAs to avoid using eligibility criteria to restrict support to those with the very highest needs. This could lead to a short term dip followed by a longer term rise. Instead they should invest in prevention and early intervention (para 35).

Eligible needs must be met, but the authority are entitled to take their resources into account in deciding how to meet them (*R v Kirklees MBC, ex p Daykin* (1997–98) 1 CCLR 512). A sad illustration is a former principal ballerina with the Royal Ballet, who had mobility problems following a stroke and suffered a series of falls. She was assessed as having a substantial need for help to use the commode at night and was thus eligible for services under her council's criteria. But instead of providing her with help to use the commode, the authority decided to supply her with incontinence pads. It was held that they could do this, and there was no breach of her right to respect for her private life (*R (McDonald) v Kensington and Chelsea LBC* [2009] EWHC 1582 (Admin)). It was not suggested that this was inhuman or degrading treatment, but it certainly showed a lack of respect for basic human dignity.

So what are the remedies if the client or a carer is dissatisfied with the local authority's decisions? The answers arrived at by the courts in recent years have been rather different from those in relation to claims upon the National Health Service.

Parliament sometimes intends that people who suffer harm because of a failure to comply with a public duty of this sort can sue for *damages*. But Parliament rarely says so expressly and the courts are extremely reluctant to imply a right to sue for breach of statutory duty. The leading case is *Cocks v Thanet DC* [1983] AC 286, confirmed in *O'Rourke v Camden LBC* [1998] AC 188. Both of these concerned the duty to house the homeless. But Christopher Clunis was not allowed to sue for damages when he claimed that he would not have attacked and killed a complete stranger, Jonathan Zito, at Finsbury Park tube station had he been given the appropriate after-care services under section 117 of the MHA 1983: *Clunis v Camden and Islington Health Authority* [1998] QB 978. However, even if there is no liability for breach of statutory duty, the relationship between the client and the service-provider may sometimes give rise to a duty of care: *K v Central and North West London Mental Health NHS Trust* [2008] EWHC 1217 (QB), [2008] MHLR 168.

On the other hand, *judicial review* has proved a fruitful means of challenging the authorities' decision-making processes. The court may require an authority to think again if they have withheld services because of an error of law or because they have acted irrationally or unreasonably in considering the client's case and what to do for him, for example by taking irrelevant considerations into account or by failing to take relevant considerations, such as the statutory

Guidance, into account. Much will depend upon the terms of the particular statutory provision relied upon.

As we have already seen, the courts have decided that section 117 of the MHA gives the client a right to after-care services, so that a failure to use their best endeavours to provide these may be unlawful: *R v Ealing District Health Authority, ex p Fox* [1993] 1 WLR 373. The courts have also decided that section 21 of the NAA gives a right to accommodation once the authority have concluded that the client is in need of care and attention which is not otherwise available to him: *R v Sefton MBC, ex p Help the Aged* [1997] 4 All ER 532. This may be surprising, given that the NAA 1948 was part of the package setting up the welfare state, long before anyone thought in terms of specific duties towards individuals as opposed to "target duties" towards groups. (It may be explained by the courts' even more surprising decision that LSSAs could be obliged to accommodate destitute asylum seekers under section 21: for the history, see *R (M) v Slough LBC* [2008] UKHL 52, [2008] 1 WLR 1808.) Logically, the same approach should apply to the authority's duties towards disabled people under section 29 of the NAA, which are in the same terms as their duties under section 21: *R (Hughes) v Liverpool City Council* [2005] EWHC 428 (Admin), [2005] LGR 531, para 26. But there is a decision dating from before the *Sefton* case, describing section 29 simply as a "set of target duties", failure to meet which is not, in itself, a breach of duty: *R v Islington LBC, ex p Rixon* [1997] 32 BMLR 136, 139. Section 2 of the CSDPA was undoubtedly intended to strengthen what was seen at the time as a weak duty in section 29, so that once the authority are satisfied that arrangements under section 2 are necessary to meet the client's needs, those arrangements must be made: see, eg, *R v Gloucestershire CC, ex p Barry*, above. The duties towards mentally disordered people under Schedule 20 to the NHSA have not, it appears, been the subject of judicial decision, but they are also in the same terms as section 21 of the NAA and logically therefore should give eligible individuals a right to services. Section 45 of the HSPHA 1968, on the other hand, gives rise only to powers, so that failure to exercise them is not, of itself a breach, although an unreasonable or irrational failure may be.

There is a view that complaints procedures, including resort to the local government or health service ombudsmen, are a fairer and more appropriate remedy than legal action (Hoffmann, 2009). The Secretary of State may make regulations about how complaints about both NHS and social services are to be handled (Health and Social Care (Community Health and Standards) Act 2003, ss 113 and 114). Under the Local Authority Social Services and NHS Services Complaints (England) Regulations 2009, SI 2009/309 (for genesis, see Department of Health, *Making Experiences Count*, 2007, 2008c), the two separate schemes have been replaced by a single scheme for both health and social care complaints. This consists of local resolution by the relevant responsible authority and independent investigation by the Health Services Ombudsman or Local Government Ombudsman as the case may be. Complaints may be made by anyone who receives or has received services from a responsible body, or who is affected or likely to be affected by the act, omission or decision of a responsible body (reg 5(1)). A representative can complain on behalf of a child or person who lacks the capacity to complain, but the responsible body must discontinue consideration of the complaint if satisfied that the representative is not conducting the complaint in the best interests of the person on whose behalf the complaint is made (reg 5(2), (4), (5)).

Finally, the Secretary of State has power to declare a local authority in default if they fail to comply with any of their social services duties, to direct them to comply, and to enforce that direction by an order for mandamus from the High Court (Local Authority Social Services Act 1970, s 7D).

Judicial review has undoubtedly helped some individuals or groups who have been lucky enough to gain access to the High Court and brought about significant developments in the law. In practice, however, neither judicial review nor the complaints and default procedures are any substitute for a proper appeal process, in which the merits as well as the legality of the authorities' decisions can be challenged. The courts may not be qualified or equipped to do this, but why, asked the Law Commission (2008a), should adults who need social care not have the same right to go to a tribunal to obtain the services they need as have the parents of children who are disabled or have special educational needs? The Commission have provisionally proposed a single eligibility framework for all social care needs, coupled with a strong and enforceable duty to meet eligible needs (Law Commission, 2010).

If the right to social care were a "civil right" within the meaning of article 6(1) of the ECHR, everyone would be entitled to have his rights determined by an independent and impartial tribunal established by law. But the Supreme Court has recently decided that claims to public services of this sort (unlike claims to cash benefits) are not a "civil right": *Tomlinson v Birmingham City Council* [2010] UKSC 8. Although the context was housing the homeless, it is unlikely that claims to community care services would be any different: see *R (A) v Croydon LBC* [2009] UKSC 8, [2009] 1 WLR 2557 which was about looking after children.

3. CHILDREN'S SERVICES

(a) Education

Since 1971, it has been impossible to declare any child ineducable. LEAs are responsible for securing that all children in their area, no matter how severe their learning difficulties or disabilities, receive an appropriate education. LEAs have a duty, which may be shared with the funding authority, to ensure that there are sufficient schools suitable for all the pupils of compulsory school age in their area (Education Act 1996, s 13). They have power to provide for the education of people up to the age of 19 (s 15A(1)). This is particularly important for young people with learning disabilities, who are often just beginning to make real progress around the age of 16. LEAs also have the power, but not the duty, to provide schools for children below compulsory school age, which is again particularly valuable for those with disabilities (s 17).

In performing this duty, LEAs must have regard to the need for securing that special educational provision is made for pupils who have special educational needs (s 14(6)(b)). Generally, children with special needs should be educated in mainstream schools (s 316(1)), but only if this is compatible with giving a particular child the special education he needs, with the efficient education of his school mates, and with the efficient use of resources (s 316(3)). Otherwise, he will usually be educated in a special school, including a non-mainstream independent school (s 316A). But if the LEA are satisfied that this would be "inappropriate", they may, after consultation with his parents, arrange for some or all of his education to be provided in another way (s 319).

The procedures for identifying children with special educational needs, and deciding how best to provide for these, are laid down in Part 4 of the Education Act 1996 (see Warnock, 1978; DES, 1980; Audit Commission and HMI, 1992; see also DfES, 2004, DCSF, 2009). These cover all children below compulsory school age and those up to 19 who are still at school (1996 Act, s 312(5)). Special educational needs means one of three things: (a) that the child has significantly greater difficulty in learning than the majority of children of his age; this concept of learning difficulty is much wider than the concept of learning disability or mental handicap; or (b) that he has a disability which prevents or hinders him from using the educational facilities generally provided for children of his age in the local schools; or (c) that he is under the age of five and likely to fall within either of these categories, or to do so unless special provision is made for him now (s 312(2)).

LEAs are obliged to identify all the children for whom they are responsible who have special educational needs and for whom it is necessary to decide what special educational provision is called for (s 317(1)). They are responsible for all the children in their area who are being educated at public expense (s 321(3)(a), (b)), or who are at school or aged at least two and under compulsory school age and are drawn to their attention as having, or probably having, special educational needs (s 321(3)(c), (d)). If the LEA think a determination is or is probably necessary they must carry out an assessment (s 323). Parents can ask the LEA to assess any child for whom the LEA are responsible (s 329). The LEA can also assess a child under the age of two if the parents consent (s 331). Early identification is most important and will usually take place during the developmental assessments provided by the health service. If an NHS body think that a child under compulsory school age probably has special needs, they must tell the parents about this, and also about any voluntary organisation which may be able to help. After giving the parents an opportunity of discussing things, they must notify the LEA (s 332).

Parents must be involved in the assessment, but they also have a duty to co-operate with any medical, psychological, educational or other examination required (s 323 and Sch 26). If the result of the assessment and any representations made by the parents is that it is necessary for the LEA to determine the special educational provision called for, the LEA must make a "statement" of the child's needs and the provision to be made for them (s 324 and Sch 27). The parents can also ask for the reassessment of a "statemented" child who has not been assessed for the last six months (s 328(2)). The statement itself must always be reviewed if there is a reassessment and within 12 months of its making or last review (s 328(5)). While a statement exists for a child for whom the LEA is responsible, the LEA *must* provide the education specified in it, unless the parents have made suitable arrangements for themselves (s 324(5)).

The parents can appeal to a tribunal against the LEA's decision not to make an assessment for which they have asked (s 329(2)); or not to review the assessment of a statemented child (s 328); the tribunal can then order the LEA to carry out an assessment. The parents may also appeal against the decision not to make a statement for any child who has been assessed (s 325); the tribunal can then order the LEA to make a statement or ask them to think again. Finally, the parents may appeal against the contents of a statement (s 326); the tribunal can amend or end the statement. The LEA is then obliged to do what the statement says. Thus, in special education cases, the tribunal can order the authorities to do what the tribunal think necessary, whereas in mental health cases, the tribunal cannot dictate what services are to be provided. This especially ironic, now that both are assigned to the same chapter of the First-tier tribunal. An attempt to claim damages under the Human Rights Act for a child who was denied the education to which he was entitled under his statement has so far proved unsuccessful: see *A v Essex CC* [2008] EWCA Civ 364, [2009] LGR 812.

Parents have a duty to ensure that children of compulsory school age receive efficient full-time education suitable to their age, ability, aptitude and any special educational needs they may have (1996 Act, s 7). If parents do not send such a child to school or make proper alternative provision, the usual enforcement procedures can be invoked (1996 Act, Pt 6). The LEA can make a school attendance order requiring the parent to register the child at the school named in the statement (ss 437, 441). Failure to comply is an offence (s 443), as is failure to send a registered pupil to school without a good excuse (s 444). Alternatively, the LEA may seek an education supervision order under section 36 of the Children Act 1989, requiring the parents and the child to comply with the supervisor's directions about his education. As a last resort, it may be necessary to bring care proceedings on the basis that the child is suffering significant harm because his educational development is being impaired.

(b) Social services

It has been official policy since 1981 that no child should grow up in a mental handicap hospital. The Children Act 1989 brought together the social services designed for handicapped or disabled children with those designed for children whose families were for some other reason unable to look after them properly. It tried to combine the best features of each system, so that all children being looked after by social services would have the same protection, and wherever possible services would be provided in partnership, rather than in conflict, with the parents. There are still some, however, who may regret including disabled children with committed and caring parents within the same framework as abandoned, neglected or abused children, whose parenting leaves something to be desired.

The authority's general duty is to safeguard and promote the welfare of "children in need" and, if consistent with that, to promote their upbringing by their own families (s 17(1)). "Children in need" include all disabled children, as well as others who are unlikely to attain a reasonable standard of health or development, or whose health or development is likely to be significantly impaired, without social services (s 17(10)). Each authority must keep a register of disabled children in their area (Sch 2, para 2). If assessing needs under other legislation, such as the CSDPA, they may also assess needs under the Children Act itself (para 3). Parent carers of disabled children are also covered by the Carers (Representation and Services) Act 1995 and the Carers and Disabled Children Act 2000 (see p 296, above).

There is a particular duty to provide services designed to minimise the effect of disability and to give disabled children the opportunity of leading lives which are as normal as possible. This includes giving their carers breaks from caring (CA 1989, Sch 2, para 6). There must be appropriate provision to make available advice, guidance and counselling, occupational, social, cultural or recreational facilities, home help (including laundry), travel to and from these or similar services, and holidays, to children living with their families (para 8). There are also duties to provide family centres (para 9); to promote contact between children living away from home, for example in hospital, and their families (para 10); to prevent ill-treatment and neglect (para 4); to seek to avoid legal proceedings of any sort concerning a child and his future (para 7); to provide appropriate day care for pre-school children and care and supervised activities for older children outside school hours and in holidays (s 18).

These duties simply require the authority to make appropriate provision for the disabled children in their area. It has been held that the duties towards "children in need" under section 17 and Schedule 2 to the CA 1989 are merely "target duties", subject to the usual requirements to act rationally and fairly, but not broken simply because the children's needs have not been met: *R (G) v Barnet LBC* [2003] UKHL 57, [2004] 2 AC 208. In practice, it is unlikely that disabled children are any less well catered for under the CA 1989 than they would be under the community care legislation.

Under section 20 of the CA, however, there is a duty to provide accommodation for any individual child "in need" in the area who requires this because there is no-one with "parental responsibility" for him, or he is lost or abandoned, or "the person who has been caring for him [is] prevented (whether or not permanently, and for whatever reason) from providing him with suitable accommodation and care" (s 20(1)). This duty is owed to the individual child. It is intended to cover families who need respite or long term care for their learning disabled or mentally disordered children; but there is also a power to accommodate *any* child (even if his parents are able to do so) if this would safeguard or promote his welfare (s 20(4)). This service is entirely voluntary and the parents may remove the child at any time (s 20(8)). The authority must safeguard and promote the welfare of any child being accommodated under this or any social services powers; this includes promoting his educational achievement (s 22(3)). They must consult both the child and his parents before making any decision (s 22(4)). They may arrange any type of accommodation, including their own or private or voluntary children's homes, or fostering (s 23(2)); but this should be near his home if practicable (s 23(7)), and for a disabled child "not unsuitable" to his particular needs (s 23(8)). Most placements are governed by detailed regulations (eg on fostering). The authority must promote contact with the child's parents, relatives and friends; they must, usually, tell his parents where he is; similarly the parents must keep the authority informed of their address (Sch 2, para 15).

A common system of charging applies to all accommodation provided by the authority. It is discretionary, in that contributions may only be sought if the authority consider it reasonable to do so (Sch 2, para 21(2)). There is a ceiling of the authority's normal fostering rate for such a child, irrespective of the actual cost which is likely to be much higher (para 22(5)(a)). Parental means must be taken into account (paras 22(5)(b) and 23(3)(b)) and disputes about what should be paid can be taken to court (para 23). Charging anything at all to the parents of a severely handicapped child may seem like adding insult to injury, particularly as they would not be charged if the child were in hospital; but it seemed equally questionable that the poor and disadvantaged parents whose children have to be looked after by others, sometimes against their will, might be charged for it, while the better off parents of a handicapped child were not.

4. PROTECTION FROM ABUSE AND EXPLOITATION

There is a well-developed system of powers, duties and procedures to protect children from harm (outlined in chapter 3). There is also a growing recognition of the problems of elder abuse (O'Keefe et al, 2007; Mowlam et al, 2007) and of sexual and institutional abuse of adults with learning disabilities (Brown and Craft, 1989; Turk and Brown, 1993; Commission for Social Care Inspection and Health Care Commission, 2004; Healthcare Commission, 2007). But there is not such a well-developed system of law and practice to combat it. It has recently been held that the LSSA did not owe a duty of care at common law to protect a couple with learning disabilities from the risk of being harmed by other people (*X and Y v Hounslow LBC* [2009] EWCA Civ 286, (2009) 12 CCLR 254). As we have seen in chapter 4, under sections 115 and 135 of the MHA 1983, an approved mental health professional (AMHP) may enter private premises and may apply for a warrant to gain entry and remove a mentally disordered person to a place of safety; alternatively, any social worker may seek the help of the community physician to invoke the powers under section 47 of the National Assistance Act 1948 (but this does not apply to people who are subject to orders of the Court of Protection or are or should be subject to the deprivation of liberty safeguards under the MCA). Together, these scarcely add up to a clear and comprehensive framework for protecting adults who are at risk of abuse and neglect in their own homes, while preserving their right to take their own decisions when they can.

In 1995, the Law Commission (1993c, 1995) proposed a new scheme for protecting vulnerable people from harm. A "vulnerable" person was defined as someone aged 16 or over, who may be in need of community care services because of mental disorder or disability, age or illness, and is or may be unable to take care of himself or to protect himself against significant harm or serious exploitation. There would be a new duty to investigate if a vulnerable person was thought to be at risk. The existing powers would be replaced with new powers to enter premises and to see the vulnerable person in private; to obtain a warrant if entry were denied; to obtain an order authorising them to carry out an assessment; and as a last resort to remove the person for a short time to protective accommodation. None of these powers could be exercised if the vulnerable person objected unless he was or might be suffering from mental disorder or disability: even then, only a short period of assessment or protection would be allowed.

Although the Law Commission's other proposals on mental incapacity were implemented in the MCA, these proposals were not. But the Scottish Parliament has provided for very similar powers to protect "adults at risk" under the Adult Support and Protection (Scotland) Act 2007. Instead, the Government issued statutory guidance in 2000: *No Secrets* for England, *In Safe Hands*, for Wales. This recommended the development of inter-agency policies and strategies for protecting adults from abuse, including setting up adult safeguarding committees along similar lines to child protection committees; nevertheless adult protection remains the "poor relation" (Cornwall Adult Protection Committee, 2007).

The Law Commission (2010) has now provisionally proposed a new duty to make enquiries and take appropriate action to protect "adults at risk" and to establish an Adult Safeguarding Board. But they are also proposing the repeal of section 47 of the NAA without any new powers of entry or rescue, which they regard as matters of policy for the Government. There is not much point in having a duty to take appropriate action without having any appropriate action to take.

5. MENTAL HEALTH ACT COMMUNITY POWERS

(a) Powers on leaving hospital

There are three ways in which patients who are liable to be detained for treatment under the MHA may be allowed to leave hospital but are still subject to some form of compulsion: they may be given leave of absence, or, if not subject to restrictions, placed on a community treatment order (also known as supervised community treatment), or, if subject to restrictions, discharged conditionally. All of these have been discussed in chapter 7. The Royal College of Psychiatrists (see 1987) have long wanted some form of community treatment order in preference to guardianship under the MHA. The important difference is that one is operated by the health services and the other by the social services.

(b) Guardianship

Guardianship was originally intended as the community equivalent of compulsory admission for treatment in hospital. The grounds and procedures are still remarkably similar and in theory patients can readily be transferred from hospital to guardianship and vice versa. In practice, even under the 1959 Act, it was hardly ever used and predominantly for mentally disabled people rather than the mentally ill. The 1959 Act gave the guardian the powers of a parent over a child under the age of 14. No-one in practice was very clear what this meant but it must have included the power to consent to medical treatment. Even then, guardianship was not thought necessary unless the patient seemed reluctant to accept the authority of those who were looking after him.

Before the 1983 Act, the professionals all thought that more use should be made of guardianship but disagreed about what it should be used for (see Butler Report, 1975; BASW, 1977; Gostin, 1977). Organisations concerned with elderly and mentally disabled people, on the other hand, were generally opposed to a concept which they thought authoritarian, stigmatising and unnecessary. No one seems to have considered whether it might actually be illegal to exercise control over the life and affairs of a mentally disabled adult without obtaining some statutory power to do so. As it turned out in *Re F (Mental Patient: Sterilisation)* [1990] 2 AC 1, they were right not to worry. In 1978, the Government were sympathetic to the argument that compulsion outside hospital should be kept to a minimum. They were clearly suspicious of the ability of social workers to handle it properly and of the lack of any effective sanctions for patients who refused to co-operate. Hence, they opted for limiting guardianship to the "essential powers" thought necessary to secure the patient's co-operation with his community care and for excluding the great majority of mentally disabled people.

(i) The grounds

In both civil and criminal cases, the patient must be at least 16 years old (MHA, ss 7(1) and 37(2)(a)(ii)). He must be suffering from mental disorder of a nature or degree which warrants his reception into guardianship under the Act (ss 7(2)(a) and 37(2)(a)). But, as we have seen in chapter 2, people with learning disabilities are excluded unless their impaired intelligence and social functioning is also associated with abnormally aggressive or seriously irresponsible conduct (s 1(2)). This limits the ability to protect people with multiple handicaps such as Beverley Lewis, a rubella victim who died of neglect while living with her mother, who was herself a schizophrenic who resisted all attempts to help them. Beverley may have been "seriously irresponsible" in the sense that she was unable to take any responsibility for herself at all, but whether this amounted to "conduct" is doubtful.

The second criterion in a civil case is that "it is necessary in the interests of the welfare of the patient or for the protection of other persons that the patient should be so received" (s 7(2)(b)). "Welfare" is wider than "health or safety" and indicates that guardianship is meant to help the patient and improve his general quality of life. The alternative of protecting other people is unlikely to arise very often, because the guardian's powers are not exactly designed to do this. For a court order, there is no reference to the patient's welfare or the protection of other people, but the court must consider it the most suitable method of dealing with the case in all the circumstances (s 37(2)(b)). As hospitals have become more reluctant to accept offenders with learning disabilities, guardianship might well provide a suitable alternative if only courts and social services authorities could be persuaded to adopt it. But there is no power to make an interim guardianship order to test this out.

Guardianship is apparently used mainly for people with mental illnesses, two thirds of them over 65, who fall into two groups: the elderly mentally infirm, to back up care in their own homes or care homes, and younger people with psychotic illnesses, to ensure support and follow-up in the community (DH, 1994; Cox, 1994). There are between 900 and 1,000 people under guardianship at any one time; 375 new guardianship cases were opened in 2008–2009, compared with 561 in 2001–2002. This is a drop in the ocean compared with the half million people whom the Department of Health thinks are living in he community without the capacity to make decisions for themselves.

(ii) The procedures

In civil cases, the application for reception may be made either by an AMHP (on Form G2) or by the patient's nearest relative (on Form G1) (s 11(1)). The AMHP must if possible consult the nearest relative and cannot apply if the relative objects (s 11(4)). But she could then ask the county court to replace the nearest relative on the ground that the objection was unreasonable (s 29(3)(c)). There is nothing to prevent the applicant proposing herself as guardian, but neither the nearest relative nor an AMHP is at all likely to do so. It is obviously not contemplated that the nearest relative might become guardian, so as to provide a limited form of "extended minority" for someone with a severe learning disability.

The application must be founded on the recommendations of two doctors (on Form G3 or G4) (s 7(3)). They must give a clinical description of the patient's mental condition and explain why he cannot appropriately be cared for without powers of guardianship. The implication is that guardianship is to be avoided unless the patient will not accept care without it. The rules about the medical examinations, the doctors' qualifications and about conflicts of interest are the same as those for compulsory admission to hospital (see chapter 3).

The application is addressed to "the local social services authority". This must mean either the local social services authority which is to become the patient's guardian (not necessarily the authority for the area where the patient currently lives) or the local social services authority for the area where a proposed private guardian lives. The application must reach the authority within 14 days of the second medical examination (s 8(2)). If the proposed guardian is a private individual, the application must state that she is willing to act, and is ineffective unless accepted on her behalf by the LSSA for the area where she, not the patient, lives (s 7(5)). If the proposed guardian is an LSSA, the application has no effect unless accepted by that authority (s 8(1)). Section 8 does not expressly state that the application must be accepted within the 14 days (unlike an admission to hospital). Authorities are unlikely to accept responsibility for patients to whom they owe no legal duty to provide care. Even where they do owe a duty, they may not approve of providing it compulsorily, or welcome the extra responsibility entailed.

Courts can make guardianship orders for the same offences and with the same sort of medical evidence as is required for an ordinary hospital order. They cannot make a guardianship order unless satisfied that the proposed guardian is willing to act (s 37(6)). If she is a private individual, she must be approved by an LSSA (s 37(1)). Guardianship is effective the moment the order is made or the application accepted.

(iii) The effect

According to the MHA Code of Practice, guardianship "provides an authoritative framework for working with a patient, with a minimum of constraint, to achieve as independent a life as possible within the community" (para 26.4). Applications should be "accompanied by a comprehensive care plan, established on the basis of multi-disciplinary discussions" (para 26.19). The care plan should indicate which of the guardian's powers are necessary to achieve the plan. If none are required, guardianship should not be used (para 26.20).

The guardian has three powers over the patient, to the exclusion of any other person who might have them: (a) to require the patient to reside at a place specified by the guardian or by the LSSA; (b) to require the patient to attend at places and times similarly specified for the purpose of medical treatment, occupation, education or training; and (c) to require access to the patient to be given, at any place where the patient is residing, to any doctor, AMHP or other person similarly specified (ss 8(2) and 40(2)).

The guardian can therefore insist that the patient attends a clinic for treatment, or receives a visit from a doctor or a nurse. But should the patient refuse the treatment, the MHA gives no power to force it on him or to consent on his behalf. And while the guardian can insist upon the patient's seeing certain people, he cannot insist upon the patient's *not* seeing certain people, however undesirable. Although there is no precise equivalent to the power in section 6(1) to convey a patient to hospital, a patient who has "yet to comply" with a requirement to be in a particular place (s 18(7)), or who "absents himself without permission" (s 18(1)(c)) from the place where his guardian requires him to live, can be taken into custody in the same way as a hospital patient who goes absent without leave (see chapter 7). Curiously, therefore, there is power to force a guardianship patient to go or return to a particular place, but no power to detain him while he is there.

As an imposition of authority, therefore, guardianship has few teeth. There is no sanction (other than recapture) for disobeying any of the guardian's instructions. So the Code of Practice advises that for guardianship to work the patient will have to recognise the guardian's authority and be willing to work with him (para 26.8). If so, one wonders how it can be "necessary" in achieving the plan. Some people, however, may respond to apparent authority however toothless in fact it may be.

The Code does suggest that the guardian should be willing to act as the patient's "advocate" in securing the services needed to carry out the care plan (para 26.22). Her more limited legal duties are laid down in the Mental Health (Hospital, Guardianship and Treatment) (England) Regulations 2008. A private guardian is under the supervision of the responsible LSSA, for she must comply with their directions when exercising her powers and duties. She must appoint a doctor as the patient's "nominated medical attendant" and notify the name and address to the authority. She must notify her own and the patient's address to the authority straight away, and any permanent change in either address beforehand or within seven days. If she moves into a different local authority area, she must give all these particulars to the new authority and also tell the old one what has happened. She must also furnish the responsible authority with whatever reports or other information about the patient they require, and tell them as soon as possible if the guardianship comes to an end (reg 22). Whether the guardian is a private individual or the LSSA, the responsible LSSA must arrange for the patient to be visited at regular intervals. This must be at least every three months, and at least one visit annually must be by an approved doctor (reg 23).

The role of a private guardian is not unlike that of a foster parent, which reflects its origins in the long-standing Scottish system of boarding-out mentally handicapped people on remote crofts and farms. It is inappropriate for care within the patient's own family and is even more rarely used than local authority guardianship: of the 901 guardianship cases open at the end of the year 2008–2009, 99.4 per cent were local authority guardians, leaving only a handful of private guardians. The Law Commission (1995) recommended that private guardianship be abolished.

(iv) Relationship with the MCA and the DoLS

In reality, if the patient lacks the capacity to make decisions for himself, about where he should live and what medical or other treatment he should have, the MCA framework may be more appropriate than the MHA. The MHA Code advises that guardianship is unlikely to be necessary where the move can be carried out under the general authority in section 5 of the MCA or of the decision of an attorney or deputy (para 26.11) or indeed of the Court of Protection. It may still be appropriate where there are other reasons—unconnected with the move to residential care—to think that the patient might benefit from the attention and authority of a guardian; or there may be a particular need for statutory power to bring him back if he goes missing; or where it is important to identify who is in charge of decisions about where the patient is to live, for example where there have been long-running disputes about this (para 26.12). On the other hand, it may be a good idea to submit these to the determination of the Court of Protection (para 26.13).

If it is thought necessary to deprive the patient of his liberty, the Deprivation of Liberty Safeguards (DoLS) in the MCA apply to patients under guardianship in the same way as they apply to informal patients and other people who are not subject to the other compulsory powers under the MHA. This means that a guardianship patient can be deprived of his liberty under the MCA safeguards, as long as this is not for the purpose of making him a "mental health patient"—ie someone who is to receive medical treatment in hospital for mental disorder—if he objects to this (MCA, Sch A1, paras 2 and 5). In those circumstances, he is ineligible for the MCA DoLS and should be "sectioned" under the MHA. But if the object is to keep him in a care home for the same purpose, or in a care home or hospital for any other purpose, then he is eligible for the DoLS, unless what is proposed is incompatible with the requirements imposed by his guardian (MCA, Sch A1, paras 2 and 3). Thus the MHA, where appropriate, takes precedence over the MCA.

One is left wondering whether the elaborate DoLS machinery would have been needed at all, if guardianship had been adapted to include a power to detain the patient in the place where the guardian required him to live. The MHA would have had to be used more often for compliant patients both in and out of hospital, but would that have been such a bad thing?

(v) Duration, termination and variation

Like hospital admission for treatment, guardianship lasts initially for six months, but may be renewed for a further six months and then for a year at a time (s 20(1)). The responsible clinician or nominated medical attendant must examine the patient within the last two months of the period, and report to the guardian and to the responsible LSSA on Form G8 if the grounds for guardianship still exist. This automatically renews it, unless the LSSA decide to discharge the patient (s 20(6), (7) and (8)). The patient can be discharged at any time by the RC, by the responsible LSSA, or in civil cases but not in court orders (section 40(4) and Sch 1, Pt I) by his nearest relative (who may use Form M2 and must serve the order on the LSSA) (s 23(2)(b)). The RC cannot prevent the nearest relative from discharging the patient, but an application could be made to a county court to replace the relative on the ground that he was proposing to discharge, or had discharged, the patient without due regard to the patient's welfare or the interests of the public. Interestingly, however, neither a private guardian nor the nominated medical attendant of a patient with a private guardian can discharge the patient. He may of course also be discharged by a tribunal (see chapter 8) or transferred into hospital (see chapter 4).

If a private guardian dies or resigns (by written notice to the authority) the LSSA automatically take over for the time being, but could transfer the patient into the guardianship of another individual (s 10(1)). The authority, or someone authorised by them, may also exercise the functions of a private guardian while she is incapacitated in some way (s 10(2)). A private guardian may also be replaced by order of a county court, on the application of an AMHP, if she has performed her functions negligently or in a manner contrary to the patient's interests (s 10(3)). The guardian can authorise the transfer of the patient into the guardianship of another individual or LSSA (using Form G7), provided that this is confirmed by the incoming responsible LSSA, which must specify a date, and agreed to by any proposed new private guardian (reg 8(1)).

6. THE MENTAL CAPACITY ACT IN THE COMMUNITY

The reality is that people looking after people with mental disorders and disabilities in the community are much more likely to have to know about the MCA than the MHA. The general principle is that people who lack the capacity to make a decision for themselves may be looked after without formality but within limits. The limits are concerned with the use or threat of force to make someone do what he does not want to do and with depriving a person of his liberty in his own best interests. These are all discussed in chapter 1 and chapter 6. The machinery for resolving disputes about where someone is to live or whom he should be allowed to see is discussed in chapter 10. But some decisions are so important that the person concerned (if he has no-one else looking after his interests) should have an advocate to represent him even if there is no dispute. These include moves into longer-term residential care and between homes. They may also include reviews of residential care and protection from abuse or neglect. This is discussed in chapter 6. The tests of incapacity and how to decide upon the best interests of a person without capacity are discussed in chapter 2.

7. COMMENTARY

English law still cuts a pretty poor figure on the issues of entitlement and non-discrimination outlined at the beginning of this chapter. In theory, the welfare state has accepted the "ideology of entitlement" (Gostin, 1983a). Significantly, the most progress has been made in education. Here the law is much more explicit and is allied to a century-long tradition of universal provision. There is not, and never has been, any such tradition in the social services. In relying on social services to allocate resources for community care packages, the element of universal, albeit means-tested, provision involved in income support for people in nursing and residential homes was lost. Since 1996, however, the courts have played a significant part in expanding the ideology of entitlement into adult social care. But the most important decisions, on eligibility and on the efficient and proportionate use of resources, are still left to the politicians and their officials. This is understandable: courts cannot raise money or balance competing claims across the whole client population. But in 2009 the Government consulted on a new system for adult social care, proposing to have a National Care Service alongside the National Health Service, albeit not free to all at the point of need (*Shaping the Future of Care Together*, 2009). As always, there are fears that the ageing and physically disabled population have a higher profile and will therefore receive a higher priority than people with mental illness or disability (MIND, 2009). The Law Commission (2010) has provisionally proposed a single assessment duty, coupled with a common eligibility framework and an enforceable duty to meet the eligible needs assessed. A simplified and rationalised structure would undoubtedly be an improvement (as it was when a similar exercise was undertaken for children's services in the Children Act 1989). But as always the crunch comes with the eligibility criteria. What is the point of a duty to provide when the provider can decide the circumstances in which it will be provided?

We are, on the other hand, getting better at respecting the dignity and autonomy of people in residential care. People are much more conscious of the status of residents in homes and of the need to enhance their independence as well as the quality of their care. In theory, the "essential powers" approach to guardianship also has advantages, in providing a framework for both advocacy and protection with the loss of very little legal status for the patient. In practice, however, it is seen as cumbersome, stigmatising, toothless and unnecessary. It is not designed to provide a substitute decision-maker for an adult who is unable to take decisions for himself. That task has now been provided for under the Mental Capacity Act's scheme for substitute decision-making by carers, attorneys, deputies or the Court of Protection. This is underpinned by a set of principles but whether it will be successful in ensuring that decisions are indeed taken in the best interests of people who are unable to take them for themselves remains to be seen.

Our law still falls far short of a comprehensive scheme for protecting adults who are at risk of abuse, neglect or exploitation while living in the community. Serious thought needs to be given to the range of powers and duties which the health and social services need in order to do this properly. Leaving things as they are is not an option.

10 LEGAL CAPACITY AND LEGAL RIGHTS

The exercise of a great many everyday legal rights can be affected by a person's mental disorder or disability. In most cases, the legal position turns on the individual's capacity to perform the particular function in question. It does not depend upon whether or not he is in a hospital or a care home, or whether he is an informal or a compulsory patient or resident. Nor does it turn on his capacity to perform the function well or wisely. It turns on whether he can understand what he is doing and the effects of doing it and use that understanding to arrive at a decision. If he cannot do so, others may sometimes have the power to take the decision for him.

Until the Mental Capacity Act 2005 (MCA), English law did not have a comprehensive scheme for empowering others to take decisions on behalf of adults who lacked the capacity to take the decision for themselves (Law Society, 1989; Law Commission, 1991). The MCA, introduced in response to the Law Commission's Report on Mental Incapacity (1995), replaced the jurisdiction developed by the Family Division of the High Court relating to personal welfare and healthcare decisions and the statutory jurisdiction of the Court of Protection relating to decisions about a person's property and financial affairs. In *Re P* [2009] EWHC 163 (Ch), [2009] 2 WLR 253, para 36, Lewison J commented that the MCA "marks a radical change in the treatment of persons lacking capacity". In particular, it adopts a common "best interests" principle guiding the decisions made by courts, deputies, attorneys, doctors, carers and anyone else taking a decision on behalf of a person who cannot take it for himself. This is closer to the previous approach of the Family Division than to the approach of the Court of Protection.

Hopefully, the scheme also conforms to the principles laid down in the United Nations Convention on the Rights of Persons with Disabilities 2006 (the UNCRPD), defined in article 1 to:

"include those who have long term physical, mental, intellectual or sensory impairments which in interaction with various barriers may hinder their full and effective participation in society on an equal basis with others".

Article 12.4 deals with the exercise of legal capacity:

"States Parties shall ensure that all measures that relate to the exercise of legal capacity provide appropriate and effective safeguards to prevent abuse in accordance with international human rights law. Such safeguards shall ensure that measures relating to the exercise of legal capacity respect the rights, will and preferences of the person, are free of conflict of interest and undue influence, are proportional and tailored to the person's circumstances, apply for the shortest time possible and are subject to regular review by a competent, independent and impartial authority or judicial body. The safeguards shall be proportionate to the degree to which such measures affect the person's rights and interests."

Of course, there are some decisions, principally in relation to sexual relationships and family life, but also in relation to citizenship rights such as voting, which no-one can take on another person's behalf (see MCA, ss 27 and 29).

1. RIGHTS OF CITIZENSHIP

(a) Standing and voting in elections

At common law, "persons of unsound mind" and "idiots" can neither vote nor stand in elections. But these terms probably depend upon the common law test of legal capacity: at the time of voting, can the individual understand in broad terms what he is doing and the effects of doing it? If the person is on the register and turns up to vote, the question is one of fact for the officer presiding at the polling station. People are in practice asked only their name and address and whether they have already voted in the election. If they can answer, they are allowed to vote and the result is unlikely to be challenged.

However, in order to vote, a person must first be registered, and to be registered he must normally be resident in the Parliamentary constituency or local government ward on the qualifying date. A hospital patient may still be resident in his home constituency. This depends on factors such as the length of absence, his intention to return, and any legal restraint on his return home. But there used to be considerable resistance to allowing mental hospital patients who had no other place of residence to register as resident in the hospital. In the days of large mental handicap institutions in the countryside it was feared that the results of local if not national elections would be affected (why not, one might ask?). Article 3 of Protocol No 1 to the European Convention on Human Rights binds the contracting parties to "hold free elections at reasonable intervals by secret ballot, under conditions which will ensure the free expression of the opinion of the people in the choice of the legislature". Although certain people may be disqualified, the restrictions should not be arbitrary or disproportionate (*Mathieu-Mohin and Clerfayt v Belgium* (1987) 10 EHRR 1). A disqualification which depends upon a person's address, rather than on his actual capacity to vote or some other disqualifying factor, is clearly arbitrary.

The Representation of the People Act 1983 (the RPA) was amended in 2000 to draw a distinction between offenders who are detained under the Mental Health Act and other detained or informal patients. A person who is detained anywhere under a hospital order or direction made under the powers in the MHA relating to criminal offenders (ss 37, 38, 44, 45A, 47, or 51(5)); or an order under the Criminal Procedure (Insanity) Act 1964; or the equivalent orders made by the Court of Appeal (Criminal Division); or who would be so detained if he were not unlawfully at large, is "legally incapable of voting at any parliamentary or local government election" (RPA, s 3A(1), (2)). This is logical, in that it treats detained offender patients in the same way as other convicted prisoners (see RPA, s 3); but in *Hirst v United Kingdom* (2006) 42 EHRR 41, the Grand Chamber of the European Court of Human Rights held that the automatic disqualification of all convicted prisoners was disproportionate. The Government is still pondering what, if anything, to do about this.

Patients remanded to hospital (under section 35 or 36) or remand prisoners transferred to hospital (under section 48) can still vote. They are regarded as resident in the hospital where they are detained if the length of time they are likely to stay there is enough for them to be regarded as resident there for electoral purposes (RPA, s 7A(2), (6)(b) and (c)). Exactly the same rule applies to informal and non-offender compulsory patients in mental hospitals (RPA, s 7(1), (2)). A "mental hospital" for this purpose is any establishment, or part of an establishment, maintained wholly or mainly for the reception and treatment of people suffering from any form of mental disorder (s 7(6)). But this does not prevent their being registered somewhere else if they are either resident there or have made a "declaration of local connection" (ss 7(5), 7A(5)).

These declarations are a special privilege given to non-offender mental patients who have no residence outside the hospital (and also to homeless persons who have no residence anywhere) (RPA, s 7B(2)). A patient must give the name of the institution where he is currently living and also either an address in the United Kingdom where he would be living if he were not in hospital (or on remand), or if he cannot give such an address, any United Kingdom address where he has resided (s 7B(3) and (4)). The patient is then entitled to be registered as resident at that address on the date of the declaration (s 7C(1)). He can, however, cancel the declaration at any time (s 7B(9)). If he gives more than one address, or makes more than one declaration on the same date, the declaration is void (s 7B(8)). The declaration is effective for both national and local elections, but it cannot be made specially for the purpose of local elections unless the patient is a Member of the House of Lords (who is only entitled to vote in local elections) (s 7B(7)).

Getting to the polling station is much less of a problem than it used to be, as anyone, including hospital patients and care home residents, may vote by post or by proxy if registered to do so (see Representation of the People Act 2000, s 12, Sch 4). The MCA Code of Practice points out that no-one may vote on behalf of a person who lacks the capacity to do so (see MCA, s 29); but it would also be helpful if staff in hospitals and care homes were encouraged to help patients and residents who do have that capacity to exercise their democratic rights, by explaining the registration processes and getting the proper forms for them. It is good practice to help and encourage people to continue and develop outside interests and activities. A healthy interest in politics and how we are governed is surely part of this.

It is to be hoped that no legally incapable candidate would ever be elected, but a sitting member might later become so. There is a statutory procedure for vacating the seat of any Member of Parliament who has been compulsorily detained because of mental illness for more than six months (MHA 1983, s 141). The Royal College of Psychiatrists believes that this discriminates against mental disorder and should be repealed.

(b) Serving on juries

Apart from standing and voting in elections, the main badge of citizenship is the right and duty to serve on a jury. But a large number of people with mental disorders are ineligible to do so. These are anyone who suffers or has suffered from mental disorder within the meaning of the MHA and because of that is either resident in a hospital or similar institution or regularly attends for treatment by a medical practitioner (Juries Act 1974, s 1 and Sch 1, Pt 1, para 1). Also ineligible are people subject to MHA guardianship or community treatment orders (para 2) and people who lack the capacity, within the meaning of the MCA 2005, to serve as a juror (para 3). It would be consistent with the principles of the MCA if only the people without that capacity were unable to serve (and of course no-one can serve on their behalf). Yet strictly speaking, an anxious or depressed person who regularly takes medication prescribed by a doctor is ineligible, while a psychopath who has been discharged from Broadmoor and is at present receiving no medical treatment is eligible, unless disqualified for other reasons. Rethink, supported by the Criminal Bar Association, is campaigning to limit disqualification to people who lack the capacity to serve on a jury but the Government seems unconvinced.

(c) Disqualifications from other activities

An applicant for or holder of a driving licence must disclose any prescribed disability (Road Traffic Act 1988, s 92). These include "severe mental disorder", which still means mental illness, arrested or incomplete development of the mind, psychopathic disorder or severe impairment of intelligence or social functioning. They also include epilepsy, unless the patient has been free from attacks for one year or has had attacks only while asleep for the past three years, complies with his doctor's directions as to treatment and regular check-ups, and the Secretary of State is satisfied that his driving is not likely to be a source of danger to the public (Motor Vehicle (Driving Licences) Regulations 1999, SI 1999/2864, regs 71(1)(a), (b), (4)(a), 72(2)). If the person has a prescribed disability, a licence must be refused or revoked.

Not surprisingly, persons of unsound mind used to be singled out as a class of people to whom the police had to refuse a firearms (but not a shotgun) certificate. Now, there are general fitness criteria for the grant of a certificate but a specific power to revoke one if the police have reason to believe the holder to be "of unsound mind" (Firearms Act 1968, ss 27 and 30A).

2. FAMILY LIFE

Article 8 of the European Convention on Human Rights reads:

"(1) Everyone has the right to respect for his private and family life, his home and his correspondence.
(2) There shall be no interference by a public authority with the exercise of this right except such as is in accordance with the law and is necessary in a democratic society in the interests of national security, public safety or the economic well-being of the country, for the prevention of disorder or crime, for the protection of health or morals, or for the protection of the rights and freedoms of others."

The UNCRPD, article 23.1, obliges States parties to "take effective and appropriate measures to eliminate discrimination against persons with disabilities in all matters relating to marriage, family, parenthood and relationships ... ". Once again, these are decisions which have to be made by the people involved and cannot be made on their behalf. There are obvious risks of degradation and exploitation, against which some people may need protection. But that need not be given at the cost of denying to people with mental disabilities the opportunity to form warm and satisfying relationships. There are some delicate dilemmas involved here. Providing advice, contraception, abortion or sterilisation to an individual may be either a recipe for exploitation or a means of protecting the right to make a free and informed choice.

Other aspects of everyday life, such as where to live and whom to see, can be decided by carers, proxies, deputies or the Court on behalf of people who lack the capacity to decide for themselves. These will be dealt with in the following sections of this chapter.

(a) Having sexual relationships

All the usual offences which punish sexual aggression or the exploitation of youth may protect mentally disordered people. It is rape if A penetrates B without B's consent and without a reasonable belief in B's consent (Sexual Offences Act 2003 (SOA), s 1(1)). Whether a belief is reasonable depends upon all the circumstances, including any steps A has taken to discover whether B does consent (s 1(2)). If B is incapable of understanding the situation and exercising choice in the matter, she does not consent (*R v Howard* [1966] 1 WLR 13; see also *R v Barratt* (1873) LR 2 CCR 81). However, there are also several specific offences aimed at protecting mentally disordered people whose capacity to consent is impaired.

These include any sexual touching of B if A knows or ought to know that B is unable to refuse because of or for a reason related to mental disorder (SOA, s 30(1)). B is "unable to refuse" if she lacks the capacity to choose whether to agree to the touching (whether because she lacks sufficient understanding of the nature or reasonably foreseeable consequences of what is being done, or for any other reason) or she is unable to communicate her choice to A (s 30(2)). This offence is clearly intended to protect a person who because of her mental disorder either cannot make or cannot communicate a genuine choice about whether or not to agree to this particular sexual touching. Unlike the previous law, which banned all sexual contact with mental "defectives", it does not assume that she is at all times and in all circumstances either capable or incapable of agreeing to sexual activity. That would be quite contrary to the principles underlying the MCA upon which the SOA was also based (Home Office, 2000). The choice to engage in sexual activity is, as the House of Lords held in *R v C* [2009] UKHL 42, [2009] 1 WLR 1786, person-specific and situation-specific (casting some doubt, in this respect, on the observations in *Local Authority X v M* [2007] EWHC 2003 (Fam), [2009] 1 FLR 443, and *X City Council v MB* [2006] EWHC 168 (Fam), [2006] 2 FLR 968, pp 316, 318, below, under the inherent jurisdiction). One may be able to decide to have sex with a particular person at a particular time and not able to do so if the circumstances are different.

Another offence covers sexual touching to which A has obtained B's agreement by inducement, threat or deception and A knows or ought to know that B has a mental disorder (SOA, s 34(1)). It may be difficult to know in advance whether the evidence in court will eventually support a charge based on lack of consent, or an inability to refuse, or an agreement procured by inducement, threat or intimidation. In this case it may be sensible to charge all three offences in the alternative. The object is not to prohibit all sexual activity with people who have mental disorders or disabilities, but to respect their genuine choices and protect them from those which are not.

The only complete prohibition, irrespective of whether there is a real, unforced agreement, is of sexual activity by a care worker with a mentally disordered person in whose care the accused in involved (SOA, s 38). This covers a very wide range of people whose work brings them into regular face to face contact with B: either because B is looked after in a care home, community home, voluntary home or children's home; or because B is a patient for whom services are provided by an NHS body, independent medical agency, in an

315

independent clinic or hospital; or simply because A, whether or not in the course of employment, provides care, assistance or services in connection with B's mental disorder (s 42(2), (3), (4)).

For all three of these offences there are related offences of causing or inciting B to engage in sexual activity; of engaging in sexual activity in B's presence; and of causing B to watch sexual activity in each of the prohibited sets of circumstances (SOA, ss 31, 32, 33; 35, 36, 37; 39, 40, 41).

But is prosecution the answer? Convictions are notoriously difficult to secure in all sex offences, but particularly where the victim's evidence may present problems (see p 340, below). Under the MCA 2005, the Court of Protection has power to decide what, if any, contact an incapacitated person is to have with specified people and to make an order prohibiting contact with a specified person (s 17(1)(b), (c); see p 334, below). The inherent jurisdiction of the High Court has been used by local authorities to prohibit sexual relationships which they think harmful (see *Local Authority X v M* [2007] EWHC 2003 (Fam), [2009] 1 FLR 443). Given, however, that capacity is fluctuating and may be specific to the situation as well as to the person, it may not be easy for the Court to decide whether the person concerned will always be incapable of agreeing to sexual activity with a particular person.

(b) Marriage and civil partnership

Article 12 of the European Convention on Human Rights guarantees that "men and women of marriageable age have the right to marry and found a family, according to the national laws governing the exercise of this right". The UNCRPD, article 231(a), echoing article 12, emphasises the right of disabled persons of marriageable age to marry and found a family "on the basis of free and full consent of the intending spouses". The law has for some time gone out of its way to help patients who are detained under any of the long term powers in the MHA to marry, by allowing them to be married at the hospital (Marriage Act 1983, s 1 and Sch 1). Neither Convention has yet been expanded to include same sex relationships, but the Civil Partnership Act 2004 (CPA 2004) now provides for civil partnerships which are in almost all respects the same as marriage.

But marriage in English law is a "voluntary union" (*Hyde v Hyde* (1866) LR 1 P & D 130, 133). There are two grounds on which the marriage (or civil partnership) of a mentally disordered person may be annulled, although it is valid until that happens. The first is that he did not give a valid consent to it, because of "unsoundness of mind" (Matrimonial Causes Act 1973, s 12(c); CPA, s 50(1)(a)). This only applies if at the time of the ceremony the bride or groom could not understand the nature of the contract being entered and appreciate its basic responsibilities. As marriage is said to be a relatively simple concept, few people who can actually get through the ceremony are likely to be held incapable under this test. An elderly and confused person might be able to get married but unable to make a new will on the same day (*In the Estate of Park; Park v Park* [1954] P 112).

The second ground is that, although able to give a valid consent, the bride or groom was suffering (whether continuously or intermittently) from mental disorder within the meaning of the Mental Health Act, but this must be "of such a kind or to such an extent as to be unfitted for marriage" (1973 Act, s 12(d); CPA, s 50(1)(b)). In *Bennett v Bennett* [1969] 1 WLR 430, Ormrod J decided that it was not enough that the wife was difficult to live with because of her disorder and should probably not have got married. She had to be incapable of living in the married state and carrying out the ordinary duties and obligations of marriage, and this she was not.

In *Bennett*, it was the mentally disordered person's spouse who wished to have the marriage annulled. But the mentally disordered person might well wish to do so, particularly if he has been tricked or exploited in some way. However, although either party may apply to the court, these grounds render the marriage voidable, rather than void. They simply allow the court to annul it, if asked to do so by either party while they are both still alive. Even after a decree, it is treated as if it had existed up until that time (1973 Act, s 16). A previous will is automatically revoked by marriage, unless that will provides that this is not to happen when the testator marries a particular person (Wills Act 1837, s 18). Even if the testator was so disordered as to be incapable of consenting to the marriage, therefore, his surviving spouse will have a claim to his estate under the rules of intestacy (*Re Roberts, Roberts v Roberts* [1978] 1 WLR 653).

There must be a danger that "old and lonely people not fully in control of all their mental faculties are particularly susceptible to the attentions of fortune hunters" (Law Commission, 1982). There are two possible solutions. If the person is unable to make a new will for himself, the Court of Protection may make one for him (see p 322, below; and *Re Davey (Deceased)* [1980] 1 WLR 164). The alternative is to petition for nullity. This will not revive an earlier will, but it will remove the automatic right of the spouse to a share in the intestacy or to benefit under any will which was made after the marriage (Wills Act 1837, s 18A). If the mentally disordered person is unable to petition for himself, the Court of Protection may do it for him (see p 335, below). The normal time limit of three years from the marriage may be extended in such cases if the family court thinks it just (1973 Act, s 13(4) and (5)).

None of this solves the problem of the person who dies before anything is done. Some might think it better to prevent a voidable marriage taking place at all. Anyone can enter a *caveat* with a superintendent registrar against the issue of a certificate or licence for the marriage of a named person (Marriage Act 1949, s 29). The registrar cannot then issue the certificate or licence until he has looked into the matter and satisfied himself that the *caveat* ought not to obstruct it. If in doubt, he can refer it to the Registrar-General, or if he refuses the certificate or licence, the person named can appeal to the Registrar-General. A frivolous *caveat* can result in costs, and damages for the named person. If the Registrar-General refuses the certificate or licence, the matter could be taken to the High Court by way of judicial review.

The purpose of the *caveat* procedure must be to prevent marriages which would otherwise be void. It cannot be intended to obstruct the freedom of adults to marry whom they wish. But marriages which might be voidable on either of the mental health grounds fall between these two extremes. The general reason for making a marriage voidable rather than void is to allow the parties themselves to decide whether they wish to continue it or not. If they are happy, the State does not interfere. Logically, therefore, the registrar should not deny a certificate for the marriage of a mentally disordered person any more than he should deny one to a person who cannot consummate the marriage. He certainly should not deny one simply because some doctor believes that his patient ought not to get married. But this logic rather breaks down at the point where the person is actually incapable of consenting to the marriage, for to carry out such a ceremony knowing this fact would be contrary to the long-standing tradition of the "voluntary union".

In *Sheffield City Council v E* [2004] EWHC 2808 (Fam), [2005] Fam 326, a local authority invoked the inherent jurisdiction of the High Court to try to prevent a vulnerable young woman with spina bifida from marrying a 37-year-old sex offender. The preliminary issue was whether the consultant psychiatrist should be asked to assess her capacity to consent to marriage in general or her capacity to consent to this particular marriage. Munby J held that it should be the former: could she understand the nature and implications of marriage in general rather than the nature and implications of marriage to this particular man? (A similar approach was adopted in *X City Council v MB* [2006] EWHC 168, [2006] 2 FLR 968, where it was conceded that a mentally disabled Pakistani young man lacked the capacity to marry.) Under the MCA 2005, however, the test is not only the ability to understand the relevant information but also the ability to use that information to make a real choice. It might be thought that, as in the case of sexual activity, the capacity to marry is person-specific and situation-specific (see *R v C*, above). With respect, marriage is not the same for everybody.

(c) Divorce and dissolution

An existing marriage or civil partnership may well break down because of one party's mental disorder. The fact that he is not to blame is no longer an obstacle to divorce or other forms of relief. The sole ground for divorce (or dissolution of a civil partnership) is that the relationship has irretrievably broken down. There are five ways of proving this for a marriage and four for a civil partnership (Matrimonial Causes Act 1973, s 1(1), (2); CPA, s 44(3),(5)). One is that they have lived apart for five years (out of the previous five and a half), unless the divorce or dissolution would cause the respondent grave financial or other hardship and it would be wrong to grant it (1973 Act, ss 1(2)(e) and 5; CPA, ss 44(5)(c) and 47). People living in hospital or long term care are unlikely to suffer grave hardship simply because they are no longer married. A divorce can also be granted after only two years' separation (out of the previous two and a half), provided that the respondent consents (1973 Act, s 1(2)(d); CPA, s 44(5)(b)). In *Mason v Mason* [1972] Fam 302, Sir George Baker P decided that the test of capacity to agree to a divorce was the same as that to agree to a marriage. A person might be able to do this even if he was not otherwise capable of managing his property and affairs. But if he could not, no-one could consent on his behalf. The MCA 2005, s 27(1)(c), (d), confirms this for both marriage and civil partnership.

An immediate divorce may be obtained for adultery (but this concept does not apply to civil partnerships) (1983 Act, s 1(2)(a)) or if the respondent has behaved in such a way that the petitioner cannot reasonably be expected to live with him (1983 Act, s 1(2)(b); CPA, s 44(5)(a)). The test is whether a:

"right-thinking person would come to the conclusion that *this* husband has behaved in such a way that *this* wife cannot reasonably be expected to live with him, taking into account the whole of the circumstances and the characters and personalities of the parties" (*Livingstone-Stallard v Livingstone-Stallard* [1974] Fam 47; approved in *O'Neill v O'Neill* [1975] 1 WLR 1118, CA),

not whether the behaviour itself is unreasonable or blameworthy. A spouse may reasonably be expected to be more tolerant of behaviour which is the result of illness than of the deliberate, malicious or merely thoughtless behaviour of a normal person (*Richards v Richards* [1972] 1 WLR 1073). But conduct which has a serious effect upon the petitioner will certainly be enough (*Williams v Williams* [1964] AC 698; *Katz v Katz* [1972] 1 WLR 955). It may even be both completely blameless and largely negative in character. In *Thurlow v Thurlow* [1976] Fam 32, the wife suffered from a severe neurological disorder leading to a gradual mental and physical deterioration at an early age. She had displayed some temper, thrown things at her mother-in-law, burned things, and had a tendency to wander. She eventually became bedridden, unable to walk or stand unaided, or to feed and dress herself. Her husband coped with her at home for as long as he could, until his own health was affected and she had to go into hospital, where she would require indefinite care. The husband was granted his decree. Rees J expressly disagreed with the result in *Smith v Smith* (1973) 118 SJ 184, where the husband failed to get a decree after caring for his wife for many years while she degenerated into a "cabbage-like" existence as a result of pre-senile dementia. Ironically, he would have been able to do so had he put her into hospital or care home five years earlier instead of looking after her at home for as long as possible.

Finally, a divorce or dissolution may be granted after two years' desertion (1983 Act, s 1(2)(a); CPA, s 44(5)(d)), which normally requires an intention to desert. But if a person who has deserted his spouse later becomes incapable of retaining the necessary intent, he remains in desertion for this purpose provided that the court thinks that he would have done so had he been capable (1983 Act, s 2(4); CPA, s 45(5)). In practice, desertion is rarely alleged in divorce cases. Indeed, defended divorces are almost unknown. Most people find ways of establishing that the marriage has broken down and then concentrate on sorting out appropriate arrangements for the couple's finances, property and children, where questions of fault are largely irrelevant. The welfare of the children, and the couple's actual and foreseeable resources and needs, are usually the predominant factors, but any physical or mental disability has also to be taken into account (1973 Act, s 25(2)(e); CPA, Sch 5, para 21(2)(e)).

(d) Having children

The UNCRDP insists on the rights of people with disabilities to retain their fertility and to "decide freely and responsibly on the number and spacing of their children" (art 23.1(b), (c)) and that children are not to be separated from their parents on the basis of a disability (art 23.4). But it is the relationships of mentally disordered people with their children that are the most vulnerable to outside intervention by the agencies of the State. This is because the welfare of the child has to be the paramount consideration (Children Act 1989, s 1(1)). If parents split up, it is often (but not always) better for the children to stay with their primary carer, more often the mother, especially if they are young. But should mental disorder seriously affect her capacity to love and care for them properly, she may lose them to the father, to other members of the family or to the local children's services authority. A high proportion of parents whose children are looked after by local authorities have mental health problems (Quinton and Rutter, 1984; Isaac, Minty and Morrison, 1986; Howard, 2000). Local authorities can provide accommodation for a child in need if the person caring for him is prevented for any reason from providing him with suitable accommodation or care (CA 1989, s 20(1)(a)). This is a voluntary service, so a parent can remove the child at any time; but formal parental agreement is not necessary. Where a parent lacks the capacity to decide, it may be lawful to

319

accommodate her child without legal proceedings, controversial though this may be.

Generally, however, and whenever the parent objects, the local authority will seek to acquire parental responsibility for the child by obtaining a care order. The court must first be satisfied of the "threshold criteria": that the child is suffering or likely to suffer significant harm which is attributable to a lack or likely lack of reasonable parental care or to being beyond control (CA 1989, s 31(2)). The care expected is that of a reasonable parent, not this particular parent. A parent with a learning disability, or problems with drugs and alcohol, may well be doing her very best, but it may not be "good enough" to protect her children from significant harm to their health or development. The court must then decide what to do about it. The child's welfare is the paramount consideration (s 1(1)), taking into account a "checklist" of factors relevant to his needs, wishes and feelings and the capacity of others to meet those needs, as well as the alternative orders available (s 1(3), (4)); these include a supervision order or an order that the child live with someone else, usually another member of the family (see s 8). The court can only make an order if to do so would be better for the child than doing nothing (s 1(5)).

If a permanent substitute home is needed for the child, his existing foster parents may apply for a residence or special guardianship order or to adopt him. Alternatively, the local authority may seek the authority of the parents or of the court to place him with another family for adoption (Adoption and Children Act 2002, ss 19, 21). Unless the child is already subject to a care order, the "threshold criteria" must be satisfied and parental consent is required unless it can be dispensed with. The MCA 2005 is clear that no-one can consent to placement or to an adoption order on behalf of a parent who lacks the capacity to do so (s 27(1)(e),(f)). However, consent can be dispensed with if the parent cannot be found or lacks the capacity (within the meaning of the MCA 2005) to give it or if the welfare of the child requires that consent be dispensed with (2002 Act, s 52(1)). So the outcome is the same but the decision is made by the family court rather than the Court of Protection.

Many local authorities try long and hard to help parents with mental illnesses or learning disabilities to bring up their children; but in the end they have to put the children's welfare and safety before the parents' mental health, let alone their wishes and feelings. These cases are always difficult, for they are quite different from those in which the parents callously or selfishly ill-treat or neglect their children. For once, the media may be on the side of the parents rather than the authorities.

If a woman is severely disabled, some might think abortion or sterilisation preferable in her own best interests. But the dangers of allowing involuntary removal of, or even interference with, fertility are obvious. This can be authorised under the MCA, but the best interests test rules out interference for the sake of eugenics and the convenience of carers. It is still all too tempting to conclude that the traumas of childbirth and the almost inevitable loss of the child will be worse for the mother than the loss of her reproductive capacity. It is also tempting to apply the concept of mental or intellectual age to equate her with a child, when by definition it is not childhood capacities and activities we are considering. But if she is thought incapable of making her own decisions about the effects of intercourse, should she also be thought incapable of giving consent to the intercourse itself? And which should she be protected from? These difficult questions require sensitive, individualised attention. At least under the MCA, the guiding principles in sections 1 and 4 (see pp 5–6 and pp 65–68, earlier) encourage her participation, are sensitive to her wishes and feelings and the views of others who know her, avoid discrimination, consider whether she might regain capacity, and attempt the least restriction on her freedom of action and decision.

The Law Commission (1995) proposed that any procedure intended or likely to render a person permanently infertile should require court authorisation unless it was to treat a disease of the reproductive organs or relieve the existing detrimental effects of menstruation. But sterilisations for "menstrual management" should require an independent second medical opinion, as should abortions. These proposals have not been carried through into the MCA, which relies on the earlier more limited decisions of the High Court about what should be referred for court approval (see p 191, earlier; MCA Code, para 6.18). However, this will usually amount to "serious medical treatment" so that it will be necessary to instruct an independent mental capacity advocate for a patient who has no-one to be consulted about her interests (see p 217, earlier). The problem is that there often is a parent to be consulted who is more anxious than anyone else for the procedure to be performed.

3. WILLS AND OTHER GIFTS

(a) Wills

Unlike other transactions, a person's capacity to make a will depends upon his passing, not only a test of his understanding, but also a test of his memory. According to the classic statement,

> "He ought to be capable of making his will with an understanding of the nature of the business in which he is engaged, a recollection of the property he means to dispose of, of the persons who are the objects of his bounty, and the manner in which it is to be distributed between them . . .",

but only in simple terms—he does not have to be a lawyer (*Banks v Goodfellow* (1870) LR 5 QB 549). Provided that he has this capacity, the testator does not have to weigh these various factors wisely. He can make whatever dispositions he chooses, however foolish, cruel or improvident (although if he fails to make reasonable financial provision for certain members of his family and dependants, they may apply for the court to order such provision from the estate, under the Inheritance (Provision for Family and Dependants) Act 1975). Despite this, it is often the eccentricity of the will itself which prompts the dispute.

Testators rarely fall into the easy category of being permanently, totally and completely incapable. Even if they do, it may be possible, although very difficult, to prove that the will was made in a "lucid interval". If the testator has recovered enough, and for long enough, to have the required capacity, he need not have recovered completely and may relapse again quite quickly (*ex p Holyland* (1805) 11 Ves Jun 10; *Cartwright v Cartwright* (1793) 1 Phill Ecc 90; *Banks v Goodfellow*, above). Alternatively, a testator may have delusions about some things, but not about others. Thus,

> "a degree or form of unsoundness which neither disturbs the exercise of the faculties necessary for such an act, nor is capable of influencing the result ought not to take away the power of making a will . . . " (*Banks v Goodfellow*, above).

321

If so, it will all depend on whether his particular delusional system has influenced the provisions in the will. So, for example, in *Kostic v Chaplin* [2007] EWHC 2298 (Ch), the testator left the whole of his considerable fortune to the Conservative Party Association in the hope that they would found a cultural institution to maintain Christian Democratic values. He suffered from a delusional disorder in which he believed that there was an international conspiracy of dark forces against him in which his son was implicated. He would not have made such a will had it not been for the delusions, and so it was set aside. Mere eccentricity, whether in previous lifestyle or in the contents of the will, is not the same as incapacity; but capricious, harsh and unreasonable views could amount to delusions (*Boughton v Knight* (1873) LR 3 P & D 64). Similarly, confusion and forgetfulness are not enough, if the testator was able to concentrate at the time when he made the will; but of course they could be if they induced him to make it (*Benyon v Benyon* (1844) 2 LT 477; *Singh v Armirchand* [1948] AC 161).

If the testator does have capacity to make a will, he can do so even if he is otherwise incapable of managing his property and affairs. However, since 1969, the Court of Protection has been able to make a statutory will where it has reason to believe that a person is incapable of making a valid will for himself (now under the MCA, s 18(1)(i) and Sch 2). This must be done by the Court itself and cannot be entrusted to a deputy (s 20(3)(b)). The will can do anything that the person concerned could have done if he had had the capacity to do so (Sch 2, para 2). It will then have the same effect (at least for property which is governed by the law in England and Wales) as if the patient had made it and was capable of doing so.

The first case to deal with the new statutory will provisions under the MCA was *Re P* [2009] EWHC 163 (Ch), [2010] Ch 33. Lewison J found that the "best interests" approach required by the MCA was different from the old approach under the MHA 1983; this had required the "counter-factual" assumption that the testator was not incapacitated (see, eg, *Re D (J)* [1982] Ch 237; *Re C (A Patient)* [1991] 3 All ER 866; *G v Official Solicitor* [2006] EWCA Civ 816). The "best interests" approach requires the Court to take the testator as he is, and to consider his wishes and feelings, beliefs and values. These were not lightly to be set aside, but the ultimate test was his best interests, not substituted judgment. Although the fact that a person makes an unwise decision does not mean that he lacks capacity (MCA, s 1(4)), once the decision-making shifts to a third party, the carer, deputy or court should not consciously make an unwise decision because the person concerned would have done so. The Court was also entitled to take into account how the person would be remembered after his death.

An example of making a statutory will in an emergency is *Re Davey (Deceased)* [1981] 1 WLR 164. An elderly spinster with quite a large estate moved into a nursing home in June. In July, she made a will dividing her property between her relations. In September she was married to a middle-aged employee at the nursing home. This automatically revoked the July will. The marriage came to light in December during the process of placing her affairs under the control of the Court of Protection. Her receiver immediately applied for a statutory will in the same terms as the one which she herself had made in July. The Court granted this without giving notice to her husband or to the proposed beneficiaries. She died six days after it was executed. The husband's appeal was dismissed. In all the circumstances, this had been the best possible way of providing for a full investigation and a just result in the end, because the husband could always apply for reasonable provision under the Inheritance

(Provision for Family and Dependants) Act 1975 while the other beneficiaries could not.

(b) Gifts

Giving away property while alive seems to cause far fewer disputes than do wills, perhaps because the Court of Protection can intervene before it is too late. The first modern case was *Re Beaney* [1978] 1 WLR 770, where it was held that the degree of understanding required to make a gift depends on the importance of the transaction: so if the gift is trivial in relation to the donor's other assets a low degree of understanding is enough; but if he gives away his only asset of value, effectively disinheriting his heirs, then the degree of understanding required will be as high as that for a will. The same test was applied to gifts made by an eminent forensic scientist after he had developed a brain tumour in *Simpson v Simpson* [1992] 1 FLR 601; and to giving away a half share in a house in *Williams v Williams* [2003] EWHC 742 (Ch), where the importance of a proper explanation was stressed, and *Wainwright v Wilson* [2006] All ER (D) 180 (Nov), where it was held that the donor had to understand the difference between a joint tenancy and a tenancy in common. The donee can be obliged to return an invalid gift, but an innocent third party may be in the same position as someone who has made a contract with an incapacitated person (see below).

4. CONTRACTS WITH SUPPLIERS, EMPLOYERS AND OTHERS

(a) Validity of contracts

A person's capacity to make contracts (see *Boughton v Knight* (1873) LR 3 P & D 64) also depends upon whether he is capable of understanding the nature of the contract involved. Some contracts are obviously more complicated than others. Even a person who usually lacks capacity may have contracted in a lucid interval, or the particular transaction may be one which he is quite capable of understanding, or his particular delusional system may have nothing to do with the transaction in question. Hence, the incapacity may affect all transactions at all times, or only some transactions or at some times (Law Commission, 1976). Once again, the test is understanding, not wisdom.

However, the law has to balance conflicting policy considerations. One is the need to protect people who lack the capacity to protect themselves. But another is that the other party to the contract should not be prejudiced by an incapacity which he had no reason to suspect. The general rule is that a mentally incapable person is bound by a contract he has made, unless he can prove that the other person knew of his incapacity (*Imperial Loan Co v Stone* [1892] 1 QB 599). However, the circumstances may be such that any reasonable man would have realised that the patient was incapable (*York Glass Co v Jubb* (1925) 134 LT 36). This may apply particularly to people with severe mental disabilities. But apart from very obvious cases, the other person does not seem to have any duty to make inquiries.

The only exception to this general rule relates to "necessaries". Section 7(1) of the MCA 2005 (replacing section 3(2) of the Sale of Goods Act 1979 and reflecting the common law rule relating to services) provides that:

> "If necessary goods or services are supplied to a person who lacks the capacity to contract for the supply, he must pay a reasonable price for them".

By section 7(2), " 'Necessary' means suitable to a person's condition in life and to his actual requirements at the time when the goods or services are supplied". The object of the rule is that tradesmen are not deterred from supplying the needs of mentally incapable people by fear of not being paid (Law Commission, 1976). But it also protects the incapacitated person, who need only pay a reasonable price, rather than the inflated one which may have been agreed.

(b) Disability discrimination

These rules assume that the other person is only too happy to deal with the mentally disordered person. But even if there is no risk of incapacity, suppliers may be reluctant to provide goods and services, accommodation or finance to people suffering from mental disorder; and employers may be reluctant to employ them. The general rule is that suppliers and employers are free to choose the people with whom they will do business or to whom they will provide employment, whether they are doing so for a good reason or out of pure prejudice. However, there is now quite a long list of prohibited grounds of discrimination. The existing patchwork is due to be replaced, clarified and strengthened by the Equality Bill 2009–2010 but the basic concepts will remain much the same.

The Disability Discrimination Act 1995 (DDA) prohibits discrimination against a person who has or has had "a physical or mental impairment which has a substantial and long term adverse effect upon his ability to carry out normal day-to-day activities" (s 1(1)). "Mental impairment" only includes an impairment resulting from mental illness "if it is a clinically well-recognised illness" (Sch 1, para 1(1)). Generally the person must be, have been or expect to be impaired for 12 months (para 2). But if the disabling effects of a long term illness such as schizophrenia are controlled by medication, the person is still to be treated as disabled (para 6). The definition of disability in the Bill is very similar (see cl 6 and Sch 1).

It is unlawful for employers (DDA, Pt 2), providers of goods, facilities and services or premises, or public authorities performing their functions (Pt 3), to discriminate against people with such disabilities. But the meaning of discrimination in the DDA has led to difficulties (see *Malcolm v Lewisham LBC* [2008] UKHL 43, [2008] 1 AC 1399). The Equality Bill will prohibit direct discrimination, treating someone less favourably because of a disability (cl 13; more favourably is permitted); indirect discrimination, applying a criterion which it is more difficult for a disabled person to fulfil unless this is a proportionate means of achieving a legitimate aim (cl 19); failing to make reasonable adjustments to cater for disability when required by the Bill to do so (cl 21); and generally treating someone less favourably "because of something arising in consequence of B's disability" unless A can show that the treatment was a proportionate means of achieving a legitimate aim" (cl 15). It is then made unlawful to discriminate in various ways relating to the provision of services and public functions (Pt 3), premises (Pt 4), work (Pt 5), education (Pt 6) and associations (Pt 7).

So what about an employee who is able to do the job but fails to disclose a history of mental illness for fear of not being appointed? In *Cheltenham BC v Laird* [2009] EWHC 1253, [2009] IRLR 621, the Council sued their former managing director for damages for failing to disclose her history of depression. The Court held that a deliberately false reply to a request for medical information could lead to liability in damages although it did not do so in that case because the questions were vague and the answers had not been misleading. But what if her depression had amounted to a disability within the meaning of the DDA and the Council would have been guilty of discrimination if they had failed to employ her as a result? The relationship between the employee's contractual obligations and the employer's obligations under the DDA is unresolved.

Ironically, the more disabling a person's mental disorder, the better protected he is from discrimination as a result of it. Unjustified discrimination may in fact be more of a problem for people whose mental disorders are not sufficiently severe for them to qualify for DDA protection.

5. PROXY DECISION-MAKERS

(a) Without formalities

As we have seen in chapter 1, one object of the MCA was to place on a statutory footing the principle of necessity recognised in *Re F (Mental Patient: Sterilisation)* [1990] 2 AC 1. Section 5 provides that there is no liability for doing an act "in connection with the care or treatment of another person", provided that: (a) before doing the act, the person doing it has taken reasonable steps to establish whether the other person lacks capacity in relation to the matter in question, and (b) when doing it, he reasonably believes that the person lacks capacity and that it will be in his best interests for it to be done. There are, as we have also seen, restrictions on the power to restrain or deprive the person of his liberty (see p 16 and pp 191–193, earlier).

Looking after a person who lacks the capacity to look after himself may well involve spending money upon him. (We have already seen that he is liable to pay a reasonable price for necessary goods and services supplied to him.) Section 8(1) of the MCA provides that if an act which is lawful under section 5 involves expenditure, the person doing it may pledge the credit of, or use money in the possession of, the person concerned in order to meet that expenditure. Alternatively, section 8(2) provides that the person who does the act can spend his own money and reimburse himself out of money in the possession of the person concerned or otherwise be indemnified by that person (this reflects the common law rule in *Re Beavan* (1912) 1 Ch 196). Of course, he will only be protected if he reasonably believes in the person's lack of capacity and that what he is doing is in that person's best interests. Otherwise he will be at risk of liability for conversion, theft or fraud.

But section 5 does not give a carer any power to receive or look after the property or financial affairs of a person without capacity. Statute allows for some types of payment to be made to someone other than the person who is entitled to it, if that person is incapable of managing his property and affairs. We have already seen the example of direct payments with which to obtain community care services for oneself (see chapter 9). The most important, however, is social security and other cash welfare benefits. If the claimant or recipient is "unable to act", and no deputy has been appointed by the Court of Protection to claim or receive the money on his behalf, the paying agency or authority can appoint someone to do so (eg Social Security (Claims and Payments) Regulations 1987, SI 1987/1968, reg 33).

Mentally disordered people are now entitled to the same benefits as anyone else in their situation: though prisoners transferred to hospital are treated like prisoners rather than like other hospital patients, a discriminatory state of affairs deplored by the Mental Health Act Commission (2008) but held to be justifiable in *R (RD and PM) v Secretary of State for Work and Pensions* [2010] EWCA Civ 18. Section 122 of the MHA 1983 is also still in force. This gives hospital managers power to pay pocket money to in-patients in hospitals which are wholly or mainly used for the treatment of people suffering from mental disorder, if they would otherwise be without resources for personal expenses. In practice the hospitals only take responsibility for a few remaining patients who were admitted before 17 November 1975. The amount should be the same, but benefits are a right whereas hospital pocket money is not.

However, a person in a hospital or care home is entitled to have and to spend his own money unless he is incapable of doing so. That right can only be taken away if he cannot manage his own money and his personal allowance is usually all that he has. Many severely disabled patients should be able, with a little help, to decide whether to spend this on sweets, cigarettes or other transient comforts, or to save for new clothes, a radio, iPod or the like. If he really is incapable, the money must still be spent for his personal benefit. Hence there are practical problems about pooling some of it to buy such things as mini-buses for excursions, because of the difficulty of proving individual benefit in proportion to contributions and of reimbursement should the patient be discharged. Nor should the money be spent on general improvements and amenities inside a hospital or home which it is clearly the responsibility of the management to provide.

Hence there is at least a potential conflict of interest where hospital or care home managers are appointed to receive their patients' or residents' benefits. The paying authorities do look for an alternative "appointed person" whenever possible. But there are few formal safeguards over appointed persons, other than the ordinary laws against theft and fraud. The Law Commission (1993a, 1995) canvassed various possible safeguards but concluded that these were for departmental regulations rather than Parliamentary legislation.

There are some other statutory provisions allowing for money due to a person without capacity to be paid to some suitable person (eg Industrial and Provident Societies Act 1965, s 26; National Savings Bank Regulations 1972, reg 7(4)). Some building societies have rules which allow for payments to be made to some other suitable person if the account holder becomes unable to deal with them. There is nothing to stop such clauses being included in pension schemes and contracts between insurance companies, banks and similar institutions and their customers, but this is far from universal. The Law Commission (1995) recommended that certain institutions should be protected from liability if they release funds to a person who provides a certificate that the customer lacks capacity and a formal acknowledgement that the money must be applied in the best interests of the customer, that there may be civil and criminal liability if it is not, and that no-one else is entitled to receive it on the customer's behalf but that was not included in the MCA.

(b) Powers of attorney

But what if a person would like to appoint his own agent to manage his personal or financial affairs if and when he becomes incapable of doing so for himself? Many people would like to put their affairs in the hands of a trusted friend or adviser before their faculties fail. They would prefer this to having their health and welfare taken over by anonymous professional carers or their finances taken over by the Court. Before the MCA, if a person was found incapable of managing his property and affairs, these were taken out of his hands entirely and placed under the control of the Court of Protection. This led to procedures which were, "it is said, inevitably cumbersome, time-consuming and expensive" (Law Commission, 1976). There was therefore a great temptation to ignore them which left the person concerned without any protection at all.

Any ordinary agency, even if given by deed in a power of attorney, is automatically revoked if the person giving it becomes incapable of making contracts. It is not always easy to know when this has happened, because capacity can vary from time to time and from transaction to transaction. For as long as the agent remains in ignorance of the incapacity, he is safe if he acts under a power of attorney (Powers of Attorney Act 1971, s 5(1)). The transaction itself will be valid if the third party who deals with an agent who has power of attorney does not know of the incapacity (s 5(2)). This also applies to any contract which is within the scope of the agent's apparent authority (*Drew v Nunn* (1879) 4 QBD 661). Other transactions, however, may be invalid even if the third party did not know of the incapacity. In that case, the agent will be liable to the third party for breach of warranty of authority (*Yonge v Toynbee* [1910] 1 KB 215). This is so even if the agent did not know about the incapacity, although in that case he should be able to claim reimbursement from his principal. The moment that the agent knows of the incapacity, however, he acts at his peril, unless what he does is covered by sections 7 or 8 of the MCA (see pp 323, 325, above).

(i) Enduring and lasting powers of attorney

The Enduring Powers of Attorney Act 1985 (see Law Commission, 1983) introduced a new type of power of attorney, which could continue in force after the donor became incapable, but was limited to making decisions about his property and affairs. It was for the donor to decide on the scope of his attorney's powers. An enduring power of attorney (EPA) operates like an ordinary power of attorney until the donor becomes incapable but only continues thereafter if it is registered with the Court of Protection. It is for the attorney to apply to register the power when the donor is or is becoming incapable (see Farrand, 1989; Cretney et al, 1991; Law Commission, 1993a, 1995). Many EPAs were executed, often as a precaution long before there was any question of incapacity, but never registered (Cretney et al, 1991). By the time an EPA came to be registered, it might be too late to object to its validity.

The MCA 2005 has introduced an entirely new scheme for lasting powers of attorney (LPAs). This replaces the scheme under the 1985 Act, which is repealed, but the legal effect of existing EPAs is preserved and so the two will co-exist for a long time to come (see s 66(3) and Sch 4). Some features of the LPA scheme are borrowed from the EPA scheme but many are different.

(ii) Scope of LPAs

The first difference is that an LPA can cover decisions about the donor's "personal welfare or specified matters concerning [his] personal welfare" and/ or decisions about the donor's "property and affairs or specified matters concerning [his] property and affairs" but it must include express authority to make decisions in circumstances where the donor no longer has capacity (s 9(1)). The Lasting Powers of Attorney, Enduring Powers of Attorney and Public Guardian Regulations 2007, SI 2007/1253 (the LPA etc Regs), reg 5 and Sch 1, provide two separate forms for these, but no doubt they could be combined in a single document.

(iii) Donees of an LPA

A donee must be an individual, ie a human being, aged at least 18 or, if the LPA relates only to the donor's property and affairs, it could be a trust corporation instead (s 10(1)). A bankrupt cannot be appointed to look after a donor's property and affairs but could be appointed to look after his personal welfare (s 10(2)). In practice, it is often difficult to disentangle the two. The donor may appoint only one person to act as his attorney; or more than one to act jointly (ie all must agree in the decision in question); or more than one to act jointly and severally (ie any one of them can act alone); or more than one to act jointly on some matters and jointly and severally on others (s 10(4)); the default position, if the LPA is silent, is that they act jointly (s 10(5)). An LPA cannot give the donee(s) power to appoint a substitute or successor; but it can appoint a person to replace a donee whose appointment is automatically revoked (s 10(8); see p 330, below).

(iv) Formalities for making an LPA

The second difference is that an LPA is not effective at all unless the instrument creating it is both made in accordance with the formalities prescribed by Part 1 of Schedule 1 to the MCA and registered with the Office of the Public Guardian in accordance with Part 2 (s 9(2)). Unlike an EPA, therefore, it cannot be used until it is registered but it can be registered at any time after it is executed: either by the donor while he is still capable of doing so or by the donee(s) irrespective of the donor's capacity (MCA Code, para 7.14). An EPA, on the other hand, can be used before it is registered but should be registered when the donor is or is becoming incapable.

The formalities for making LPAs prescribed by and under Part 1 of Schedule 1 (and the LPA etc Regs) are also a considerable improvement upon the old scheme. The prescribed form must not only explain the purpose and effect of the instrument but also contain statements by both the donor and the donee(s). The donor must state that he has read or had read to him the prescribed explanation and intends the instrument to include authority to take decisions on his behalf when he no longer has capacity. He may also name no more than five persons whom he wishes to be notified of an application to register the instrument (reg 6). So the donor can choose who, if anyone, should be told about it.

Each donee must state that he has read or had read to him the required explanation and, most importantly, that he understands the duties imposed upon him by sections 1 and 4 of the MCA—that is, the general principles (see p 5, earlier) and the best interests requirements (see p 65, earlier). This was notably lacking from the EPA form, which did not give clear guidance to the attorney about the way in which he should exercise his powers, or emphasise that they were given for the sake of the donor and not for the sake of the donee. The signatures of both donor and donee(s) must be witnessed (for the required sequence of events, see reg 9).

The form must also contain a certificate that, in the opinion of the person giving the certificate, the donor when he executes the instrument understands the purpose of the instrument and the scope of the authority conferred under it, that no fraud or undue pressure is being used to induce the donor to create it, and that there is nothing else which would prevent an LPA being created by the instrument (Sch 1, para 2(1)). The donor can choose who will give such a certificate. It must be either someone who has known him personally for at least two years or a person who, because of his professional skills and expertise, considers himself reasonably competent to make the judgments required. Examples of the latter are health care professionals, lawyers, social workers and independent mental capacity advocates. But the donee(s), family members, business partners or employees of the donor or donee(s), owners, directors, managers or employees of any care home (but not hospital) in which the donor is living and their family members are disqualified (reg 8). If the donor does not name anyone (under reg 6 above) to be told of an application to register, there must be two of these certificates (reg 7). Such a safeguard was also notably lacking from the EPA form, although prudent solicitors would no doubt advise that there be contemporaneous medical evidence of the donor's capacity at the time the EPA was executed. Immaterial differences from the prescribed form do not invalidate the instrument and even if there are material differences the Court of Protection may treat it as an LPA if satisfied that that was what the donor intended (Sch 1, para 3).

(v) Registering an LPA

A third difference is that the registration procedure is simple and largely automatic. Applications may be made either by the donor (presumably while he still has the capacity to do so) or by a sole donee, all the joint donees or one of the donees appointed to act jointly and severally (Sch 1, para 4). The applicant must notify any persons named by the donor (under reg 6 above) that he is about to apply (Sch 1, para 6). The Public Guardian must notify the donee(s) of an application by the donor and the donor of an application by the donee(s) and both the donor and other donees of an application by one of joint donees (Sch 1, paras 7, 8). If there is no objection, registration automatically follows six weeks later (reg 12). Objections must be made within five weeks of the notice (regs 14, 14A). If the donor objects, the Public Guardian cannot register the LPA unless the Court is satisfied that the donor lacks the capacity to object and directs him to register (Sch 1, para 14). A donee or notified person can only object on very limited grounds—that the LPA has been automatically revoked (see (vii) below) (there is power to prescribe further grounds but this has not been done). Then the Public Guardian cannot register unless the Court directs him to do so (Sch 1, para 13).

If the Public Guardian thinks that the instrument has not been made in accordance with the prescribed formalities, he cannot register unless the Court directs him to do so (Sch 1, para 11(1)). If he thinks that the instrument contains a provision which would be ineffective as part of an LPA or would prevent its operating as a valid LPA, he must refer it to the Court, which can then decide whether or not to cut out the offending provision and let the instrument be registered with a note to that effect (Sch 1, para 11(2) to (6)). If the Court has already appointed a Deputy for the donor whose powers would conflict with the donee(s)'s powers, the Public Guardian must not register the LPA unless the Court directs him to do so (para 12). Subject to these exceptions, the Public Guardian must register the instrument as an LPA (Sch 1, para 5). The scope for objection and dispute is therefore very limited indeed.

(vi) Using an LPA

Another difference is that an LPA cannot be used until it is registered, but after registration the donee(s) can use its powers in relation to the donor's property and affairs at any time, irrespective of whether the donor does or does not have capacity. If the donor does have capacity in relation to his property and affairs (or the particular matter in question), he can of course continue to act for himself as well. As with an EPA, this can cause some confusions, but it is no different from any other power of attorney.

However, an LPA does not generally authorise the donee(s) to make gifts (s 12(2)); the exceptions are Christmas, anniversary or other customary gifts to relatives or friends and gifts to charities to whom the donor made or might have been expected to make gifts, if the value of each such gift is not unreasonable in all the circumstances (including how well off the donor is) (s 12(3), (4)). The MCA does not allow the donor expressly to authorise the donee(s) to be more generous than this, although it does allow him to impose conditions or restrictions (s 12(4)). This is an unusual example of paternalism in the MCA.

However, any powers in a registered LPA relating to the donor's personal welfare can only be exercised when the donor lacks (or the donee(s) reasonably believe that he lacks) the capacity to make such a decision for himself (MCA, s 11(7)(a)). There are some other restrictions on the personal welfare powers conferred by an LPA; these are about life-sustaining treatment and physical restraint. The powers do generally extend to giving or refusing consent to the carrying out or continuing of treatment by a person providing health care for the donor (s 11(7)(c)), subject to any conditions or restrictions in the LPA itself. They do not, however, include the giving or refusing of consent to carrying out or continuing "life-sustaining" treatment unless the LPA contains an express provision to that effect (s 11(8)). Thus the donor must have faced up to this possibility at the time the LPA was made. The donee(s)' powers will also be subject to any later advance refusal of a particular treatment which is valid and applicable in the circumstances (s 11(7)(b)); on the other hand, an advance refusal is not valid if it is inconsistent with a later LPA giving the donee(s) power to give or refuse consent to the treatment in question (s 25(2)(b); see further p 194, earlier for advance refusals in general). In other words, a later LPA or advance refusal prevails over an earlier advance refusal or LPA.

A personal welfare LPA does not authorise the donee(s) to restrain the donor unless the attorney reasonably believes, first, that the donor lacks capacity in relation to the matter in question and, second, that the restraint is necessary to prevent harm to the donor, and the restraint is a proportionate response to the likelihood and seriousness of the harm in question (s 11(1), (2), (3), (4)). Proportionality, it will be noted, is not a matter of what the donee(s) reasonably believe but what is, in fact, proportionate. Restraint for this purpose means using or threatening force to secure the doing of an act which the donor resists or restricting his liberty of movement whether or not he resists (s 11(5)). But an LPA cannot authorise a donee to deprive the donor of his liberty (within the meaning of article 5(1) of the European Convention on Human Rights) because nothing in the MCA authorises this to be done except with the authority of the Court of Protection or under the Deprivation of Liberty Safeguards (the DoLS) in Schedule A1 (s 4A; the provisions of Sch A1 are discussed in chapter 1 and the Court's powers in chapter 8).

(vii) Revocation

The donor can revoke the LPA at any time when he has the capacity to do so, irrespective of whether or not it has been registered (s 13(2)), but not, of course, when he does not have capacity to do so. The donor's bankruptcy automatically revokes an LPA in so far as it relates to his property and affairs (and an interim bankruptcy order suspends it) (s 13(3), (4)). This is because the bankruptcy jurisdiction takes over the control of his estate (but not his person). A donee's appointment is automatically terminated if he disclaims it, dies, goes bankrupt (but only in relation to property and affairs, not to the donor's personal welfare), is wound up or dissolved (being a trust corporation), is divorced from the donor (unless the LPA provided that it was not to do so), or loses capacity (s 13(5)(a), (6) and (8), (9), (11)). These events will normally also revoke the LPA, unless the instrument itself names a person to take over from the donee in that event or he has been appointed to act jointly and severally and there is at least one other donee left to act (s 13(5)(b), (7)). The Public Guardian must cancel the registration if the LPA has been revoked (Sch 1, Pt 3).

(viii) The Court of Protection

The Court of Protection has power to decide upon the validity of any instrument executed or purported to be executed with a view to creating an LPA or registered as an LPA. It may determine whether the requirements for the creation of an LPA have been met, or the power has been revoked or otherwise come to an end (s 2(2)). The Court may also decide upon the meaning and effect of an LPA or instrument purporting to create one (s 23(1)); this includes the power to sever any provision which is ineffective or prevents the instrument operating as a valid LPA, in which case the Court must notify the Public Guardian who must attach a note to that effect (Sch 1, paras 19 and 24).

The Court may give directions about decisions which the donee has power to make and the donor does not have capacity to make (s 23(2)(a)). This is intended to give effect to the power itself, not to tell the donee how to exercise it. Under the equivalent provision in the old law the Court had no power to direct the attorney how to dispose of the donor's property, for example by requiring him to make a gift in recognition of the donor's moral obligations to a housekeeper-companion (Re R (Enduring Power of Attorney) [1990] Ch 647). The Court may also give any consent which the donee would have to obtain from the donor if the donor had the capacity to give it (s 23(2)(b)). If the donor lacks capacity, the Court may give directions to the donee(s) to render reports and accounts, produce records, supply information or produce documents or things in his possession, or about his remuneration or expenses, and relieve him wholly or partly from liability in respect of a breach of his duties as a donee (s 23(3)). Whether or not the donor has capacity, the Court can authorise the giving of gifts which are not covered by the general permissions in section 12(2) (p 330, above) (s 23(4)). Thus in this case, the Court can do something which the donor cannot.

The Court may also prohibit the registration of or (if the donor lacks the capacity to do so) revoke an instrument if fraud or undue pressure was used to induce the donor to execute it or if a donee has behaved, is behaving, or proposes to behave in a way which contravenes his authority or is not in the donor's best interests (s 22(3), (4)). If the Public Guardian has reason to believe that a donee has, is or is proposing to behave in such a way, or has failed to comply with the orders or directions of the Court, he may require specified information and documents from the donee (reg 46).

(ix) Donee and third party protection

Bona fide donees and third parties who act on the basis of registered LPAs which turn out not to be valid are protected from liability towards the donor or anyone else unless they know when the donee acts that a valid LPA was not created or of circumstances which, if it had been a valid LPA, would have ended his authority to act (s 14(1), (2)). Any transaction with a third party is valid unless the third party had the same knowledge (s 14(3)). If the interest of a purchaser depends upon whether such a transaction between the donee and a third party was valid, there is a conclusive presumption in favour of the purchaser that it was valid if it was completed within 12 months of the date or registration or the third party makes a statutory declaration within three months of the transaction that he had no reason to doubt the donee's authority at the time (s 14(4)). As an LPA is simply a particular type of power of attorney, the protection given to attorneys and third parties by the Powers of Attorney Act 1971 (see p 327, above) also applies.

6. THE COURT OF PROTECTION

The new Court of Protection (described in chapter 8) has three types of jurisdiction. It hears challenges to the formal authorisation of deprivation of liberty under Schedule A1 to the MCA (see pp 277–280, earlier). It decides questions about the validity, registration, operation and revocation of enduring and lasting powers of attorney (see above). And it makes decisions about the personal care and welfare or property and financial affairs of people who are unable to take such decisions for themselves. It has therefore taken over from the jurisdiction of the High Court (exercised by the Family Division) to make declarations as to the legality of proposed actions relating to the health or personal care of an incapacitated person (recognised in *Re F (Mental Patient: Sterilisation)* [1990] 2 AC 1) and from the jurisdiction of the old Court of Protection in relation to the property and affairs of a person who was incapable of managing them for himself.

(a) Declarations, decisions and deputies

The Court may declare whether a person has the capacity to make a particular decision or to make decisions on any particular matter (s 15(1)(a), (b)). It may also declare whether a particular act, omission or course of conduct done or to be done in relation to such a person is or will be lawful (s 15(1)(c), (2)). If a person does lack capacity in relation to a particular decision or matter, the Court may either make the decision on his behalf or appoint a deputy to make decisions on that matter for him (s 16(1), (2)). A decision by the Court is to be preferred to appointing a deputy and the deputy's powers should be as limited in scope and direction as is reasonably practicable (s 16(4)). This is to cater for the possibility of fluctuating capacity and to interfere as little as possible with the personal autonomy of the person concerned.

A deputy must consent to act (s 19(3)). He must usually be an individual, ie a human being, aged at least 18; however in relation to a person's property and affairs, but not to his personal welfare, the Court may appoint a trust corporation instead (s 19(1)). An individual can be identified not by name but as the holder for the time being of a specified office or position (s 19(2)). Examples might be the Director of Social Services for the LSSA or the manager of a particular hospital or care home. Like the donor of an LPA, the Court can appoint two or more deputies to act either jointly (when all must agree in a decision) or jointly and severally (when only one need agree) or jointly in some matters and severally in others (s 19(4)). The Court may also limit the duration of an appointment or name a successor to take over in specified circumstances or for a specified period (s 19(5)). The Court also has power to make any further orders or directions, or to confer any powers and duties upon a deputy, as it thinks "necessary or expedient" for giving effect to its order or appointment (s 16(5)). A deputy is entitled to be reimbursed his reasonable expenses in discharging his functions and, if the Court so directs when appointing him, to be remunerated for his services out of the estate of the person concerned (s 19(7)).

Unlike an attorney, who may make decisions about the donor's property and affairs even if the donor is capable of making them for himself, a deputy cannot take any decision on behalf of the person concerned if he knows or has reasonable grounds for believing that the person concerned has the capacity to make that decision for himself (s 20(1)). Furthermore, an attorney appointed by the donor takes precedence over a deputy appointed by the Court: a deputy cannot be given power to make a decision which is inconsistent with a decision made within the scope of his authority and in accordance with the MCA by the donee of an LPA granted by the person concerned (s 20(4)).

There are specific limitations upon what deputies may be empowered to do, dealt with in sections (b) and (c) below. Deputies, like everyone else, must act in accordance with the general and best interests principles in sections 1 and 4 of the Act (s 20(6)).

Like a family court, the Court of Protection is not limited to making the orders for which one or other of the parties has asked. It may make whatever order, appointment or directions it considers to be in the best interests of the person concerned, even if there is no application before the Court for an order in those terms (s 16(6)). It may vary or discharge its orders at any time (s 16(7)). This of course includes revoking or varying the appointment of a deputy; but the MCA also spells out that this may be done if the Court is satisfied that the deputy has behaved, is behaving or proposes to behave in a way which is not authorised by the terms of his appointment or is not in the best interests of the person concerned (s 16(8)).

(b) Personal welfare decisions

The recognition that there ought to be some judicial mechanism for resolving doubts or disputes about the personal welfare of people who lacked the capacity to decide for themselves began with the vexed question of sterilisation (*Re F (Mental Patient: Sterilisation)* [1990] 2 AC 1) and other major health care decisions including the withdrawal of artificial nutrition and hydration (*Airedale NHS Trust v Bland* [1993] AC 789). After this, the jurisdiction of the High Court to make declarations as to what would be lawful in the person's best interests evolved into a general protective jurisdiction in many respects indistinguishable from its inherent jurisdiction over children. It was successfully invoked to resolve a dispute between an elderly stroke victim's family and his mistress over where he should live (*Re S (Hospital Patient: Court's Jurisdiction)* [1996] Fam 1, CA). After that, it was invoked by social services authorities to protect mentally disabled young adults from harm and to resolve disputes with their families about where they should live and how much contact they should have with family members and others (see *Re F (Adult: Court's Jurisdiction)* [2001] Fam 38, CA; *Re S (Adult Patient) (Inherent Jurisdiction: Family Life)* [2002] EWHC 2278 (Fam), [2003] 1 FLR 292; *A Local Authority v BS* [2003] EWHC 1909 (Fam), [2003] 2 FLR 1235). The Court adopted a "balance sheet approach" to deciding what was lawful in the person's best interests, weighing up the pros and cons of the proposed course of action (see *Re A (Mental Patient: Sterilisation)* [2000] 1 FLR 549, CA). In *Re F* [2001], above, the Court of Appeal stressed that despite these developments there was still a need for the comprehensive new jurisdiction proposed by the Law Commission which has now been enacted in the MCA 2005.

The sorts of matters which may be covered by an order about the person's personal welfare include: (a) deciding where he is to live, (b) deciding what contact, if any, he is to have with particular people, (c) prohibiting a named person from having contact with him, (d) giving or refusing consent to the carrying out or continuing of a treatment by a health care provider, and (e) directing the person responsible for his health care to hand over responsibility to another person (see MCA, s 17(1)).

This is not an exhaustive list but it is likely that these new statutory powers will be used for much the same purposes as the old declaratory jurisdiction. In particular, a Court of Protection Practice Direction (PD9E) makes special provision for "serious medical treatment" (see further p 338, below). This preserves the expectation of the Family Division that certain particularly grave decisions should be brought before the Court even though there is no dispute about them. These are: withholding or withdrawing artificial nutrition and hydration from a person in a permanent vegetative state or a minimally conscious state; organ or bone marrow donation; and non-therapeutic sterilisation (PD9E, para 5). Also included might be some abortions, other donations, procedures which require a degree of force to restrain the patient, experimental or innovative treatments, and cases involving an ethical dilemma in an untested area (PD9E, para 6). Cases involving withholding or withdrawing artificial nutrition or hydration or an ethical dilemma in an untested area will be allocated to the President of the Court or someone nominated by him (PD9E, para 11). Other cases about serious medical treatment will be allocated to a High Court judge (PD9E, para 12).

An order about a person's personal welfare could authorise that he be deprived of his liberty in order to give effect to the decision (see s 4A(3), (4)). It might, for example, be necessary to order that he be kept in hospital for the purpose of receiving treatment for a physical illness or injury: an example is the diabetic in *GJ v Foundation Trust, CT, SS for Health* [2009] EWHC 2972, p 20, earlier. Like all decisions of the Court, this is governed by the usual criteria for judging his capacity and best interests. But in addition the Court cannot authorise deprivation of liberty if the person is ineligible for the MCA scheme because he is or could be covered by the compulsory admission procedures in the MHA (s 16A(1) and Sch 1A; see p 18, earlier). If a patient becomes ineligible that part of any order is ineffective for as long as he is ineligible (s 16A(2)).

However, a deputy may not be given power to prohibit a named person having contact with the person concerned or to require a handover of health care responsibility (s 20(2)). Nor may a deputy refuse consent to life-sustaining treatment (s 20(5)): that can only be done by the donee of an LPA with the express power to do so (see above) or by the Court. A deputy cannot do an act intended to restrain the person concerned unless the following conditions apply: he must be acting upon the express authority of the Court; must reasonably believe that the person lacks capacity in the matter and that it is necessary to do the act to prevent harm to the person concerned; and the act must be proportionate to the likelihood and the seriousness of the harm to be prevented (s 20(7), (8), (9), (10), (11); cf the conditions under which LPA donees may use restraint, p 330, above). Restraint means the use or threat of force to secure the doing of an act which the person concerned resists or restricting his freedom of movement whether or not he resists (s 20(11)). A deputy cannot be given power to decide whether or not the person concerned should be deprived of his liberty because this can only be done to give effect to a court order or under the authorisation procedures set out in Schedule 1A to the MCA (see s 4A).

(c) Property and affairs

The sorts of decision which can be made about a person's property and affairs include: (a) the control and management of his property, (b) the sale, exchange, charging, gift or other disposition of his property, (c) the acquisition of property in his name or on his behalf, (d) the carrying on, on his behalf, of any profession, trade or business, (e) taking a decision which will dissolve a partnership of which he is a member, (f) carrying out any contract into which he has entered, (g) discharging his debts and obligations, whether or not legally enforceable (paying his gambling debts may well be in his best interests), (h) settling his property, whether for his own benefit or for the benefit of others (making proper provision for his dependants may again be in his own best interests), (i) executing a will for him, (j) exercising any power vested in him either beneficially or as a trustee, and (k) conducting legal proceedings in his name or on his behalf (s 18).

These all look very much like the powers of the old Court of Protection, but it is hoped that they will be operated in a very different way (Law Commission, 1995). The old Court used to take control of all the assets and property of a patient who became subject to its powers. The capital would be invested and administered by the Public Trust Office (PTO), which also supervised and advised the patient's receiver. A receiver would usually be appointed to enable the income to be spent for the patient's benefit and otherwise to carry out the Court's instructions. In the past, it was felt that the PTO was not always very efficient either in managing the patient's capital or in controlling the actions of the receiver. And it all cost a great deal of money in fees, which had to be paid out of the estate. There is still media concern about this. But the original intention was that the Court would exercise its powers in a much more flexible way: perhaps by appointing trustees and making a settlement if the estate is large, perhaps by appointing a deputy with much wider powers to administer the capital as well as apply the income, or by making the large decisions as they arise and entrusting a deputy with the smaller ones.

The Court is expressly empowered to give a deputy power to take possession or control of all or any specified part of the person's property and to exercise all or any specified powers in relation to it, including such powers of investment as the Court may determine (s 19(8)). The Court may also require a deputy to provide security to the Public Guardian for the due performance of his functions (s 19(9)(a)). This is normally done through an insurance company's fidelity guarantee bond, the premium being allowable out of the person's estate. The deputy may also be required to submit periodic reports to the Public Guardian (s 19(9)(b)). Annual reports and accounts used to be the norm.

A deputy may not be authorised to make a settlement of the property of the person concerned, or to make a will for him, or to exercise a power vested in him (s 20(3)). These are things that only the Court can do. In relation to anything done within the scope of his appointment and in accordance with the MCA, however, a deputy is to be treated as if he were the agent of the person concerned (s 19(6)).

(d) Principles

The structured approach for deciding whether a person lacks capacity for the purposes of the MCA is set out in sections 2 and 3, explained in chapter 2.

The Court, like everyone else making decisions under the MCA is governed by the general principles set out in section 1 of the Act and the best interests test as defined in section 4, also explained in chapter 2.

(e) Procedure

The Court's procedures are governed by the Court of Protection Rules 2007, SI 2007/1744 (CPR 2007) (made under MCA 2005, s 51) and their accompanying Practice Directions (MCA, s 52). These combine features from the Rules of the old Court of Protection and features from the Civil Procedure Rules 1998 (CPR 1998) which govern civil cases in the ordinary courts. Some may think these unduly cumbersome, particularly when compared with the tribunal rules (see chapter 8). Only a few features need be mentioned here.

Cases are begun by an application. The Act provides that the following people can apply without permission: the person who lacks, or is alleged to lack, capacity; anyone with parental responsibility for such a person who has not yet reached the age of 18; the representative of a person to whom a DoLS application under section 21A relates; a deputy appointed by the Court for a person to whom the application relates; a person named in an existing order of the Court to which the application relates; and the donee of an LPA to which the application relates (s 50(1), (1A)). The Rules also provide that permission is not required for applications by the Official Solicitor or Public Guardian, for applications relating to an LPA or EPA, for most applications relating to a person's property and affairs, or for applications made in the course of existing proceedings (CPR 2007, rr 51, 52). Otherwise, permission is needed (s 50(2)). In deciding whether to grant it the Court must have regard to the applicant's connection with the person to whom the application relates, the reasons for the application, the benefit of the proposed order or directions to the person to whom the application relates and whether that benefit can be achieved in any other way (s 50(3)). The Court can deal with permission applications without a hearing (r 55). If it decides to hold a hearing it also decides who should be notified (r 56). However, the general view appears to be that many personal welfare applications are unnecessary because the matter can be resolved informally.

The general rule is that the proceedings begin when the Court "issues" an application form at the applicant's request (r 62). There are prescribed forms for particular types of application. The form must state what the applicant wants the Court to decide and what order he wants the Court to make. It must name the applicant, the person (P) who is alleged to lack capacity, any other person whom the applicant reasonably believes to have an interest which means that he ought to be heard, and any other person whom he intends to notify (r 63). The people who should be notified (see r 70) are described in a Practice Direction (PD 9B). They will vary according to the nature of the application, but the Court expects an applicant to try to identify at least three people who are likely to have an interest in knowing of the application. It should be presumed that a spouse or civil partner, any other partner, parents and children are likely to have an interest, unless there are circumstances suggesting that they should not be notified but someone else should. The presumed order of closeness is spouse or civil partner, someone living with P as such, parents or guardians, children, brothers and sisters, grandparents and grandchildren, aunts and uncles, nieces and nephews, step-parents, half brothers and half sisters. Everyone in the particular category should be notified if one of them is, unless there are good reasons not to do so. In addition to close relatives, any person who is likely to be affected by the outcome should be notified, such as an NHS or other body responsible for P's accommodation or treatment; as should a deputy, attorney or donee of an LPA who has power to make decisions about the matter in question, any person with parental responsibility for P if he is under 18, and anyone else who has an interest in being notified, such as a close friend who provides informal care.

As a rule, P is not to be named as a respondent unless the Court so directs (r 73(4)). But unless the Court directs otherwise he must be notified that an application has been made or withdrawn and the date of any hearing to dispose of the matter (r 42(1); see PD 7A). He must be told who has applied, that the application raises the question of his capacity to take a decision and what that means, what will happen if the Court makes an order, who any proposed deputy is, and that he may seek advice and assistance about it all (r 42(2), (4)). He must also be told about any final order, its effect must be explained, and that he may seek advice and assistance about it (r 44). He must also be told about any appeal (r 43) and any other matter which the Court directs (r 45). These explanations must be given to P personally and "in a way which is appropriate to P's circumstances (for example, using simple language, visual aids or any other appropriate means)" (r 46). P (and anyone else who has been notified but not made a party) will be bound by the order even though he is not a party to the proceedings (r 74).

If P is a party to the proceedings, and although these may be all about whether he has the capacity to make the decision in question, the Rules assume that he lacks the capacity to conduct the proceedings for himself. This runs counter to the general principle in section 1(2) of the MCA, that a person must be assumed to have capacity unless it is established that he lacks it. It also adds to the length and complexity of the proceedings. The Rules say that he must have a litigation friend (r 141(1)) who must be appointed by the Court (rr 142(1)(a), 143). Such an appointment continues until brought to an end by the Court, even if P "ceases" to lack the capacity to conduct the proceedings (rr 147, 148). However, the Court has a general power to dispense with the requirements of any Rule (r 26) so it must have some discretion in the matter.

The application form (COP1) usually has to be accompanied by any evidence on which the applicant intends to rely, the prescribed information in support of a personal welfare (COP1B) or property and affairs application (COP1A) as the case may be, and an "assessment of capacity form" (r 64; PD 9A; not required if there has already been one or in cases about lasting or enduring powers of attorney). The assessment of capacity in the old Court of Protection was always a cause of some concern: a simple certificate from a GP that the patient was incapable of managing his property and affairs was all that was required. The assessment of capacity form (COP3) is now much more detailed and requires the practitioner giving it to go through the structured process for determining capacity laid down in sections 2 and 3 of the Act (see p 63, earlier). Unlike the application form, however, it does not have to be verified by a "statement of truth" with the attendant penalties (r 14). The certificate may be completed by any doctor, psychologist or psychiatrist who has examined and assessed the capacity of the person to whom the application relates, or even by some other professional such as a speech or occupational therapist (the qualifications and examination expected are stated only in the form and not laid down in any statute, rule or even practice direction). This is somewhat less stringent than the requirements for a capacity assessment for the purpose of authorising the deprivation of liberty (see p 130, earlier) yet the consequences may often be just as serious.

However, much more detailed expert evidence is likely to be required in some cases. Like the family courts, the Court also has power to make its own inquiries. It may require reports about any matter relating to a person who is the subject of proceedings before the Court (s 49). These may be required from the Public Guardian, a Court of Protection Visitor, or a local authority or NHS body (who may arrange for an officer, employee or other appropriate person to make it). Court of Protection Visitors are appointed by the Lord Chancellor to one of two panels: the special and the general (s 61(1)). Special Visitors must be doctors or have other suitable professional qualifications and "have special knowledge of an experience in cases of impairment of or disturbance in the functioning of the mind or brain" (s 61(2)). General Visitors need not have a medical qualification (s 61(3)). Both officers of the Public Guardian and Court of Protection Visitors have power to examine and take copies of any health or social services record or record by any person registered under the Care Standards Act 2000 in relation to the person concerned (ss 58(5), 61(5)). They also have power to interview the person in private (ss 58(6), 61(6)).

The hearing will normally be in private (r 90), in which case it will be contempt of court (see Administration of Justice Act 1960, s 12(1)) to publish any information about it unless the Court gives leave (r 91(1)). But the Court may authorise anyone to attend a private hearing (r 90(3)(a)). It may also exclude anyone from attending either a private or a public hearing (rr 90(3)(b) and 92(1)(c)) and impose reporting restrictions about either a private or a public hearing (rr 91(3) and 92(2)). But hearings may be in public or reported if there is "good reason" to do so. The Court can tailor the order, so as to allow some things to be reported and others not: see *Independent News and Media Ltd v A* [2009] EWHC 2858 (Fam). Proceedings about "serious medical treatment" will normally be heard in public, though subject to reporting restrictions (PD9E).

"Serious medical treatment" means treatment where there is a fine balance between the pros and cons for the patient; or where the choice between different treatments is finely balanced; or where the proposed treatment, procedure or investigation would be likely to involve serious consequences for the patient. Serious consequences mean those which could have a serious impact upon the patient, such as causing serious and prolonged pain, distress or side effects, having potentially major consequences for him, or seriously affecting his life chances. This definition is far wider than the list of cases which must be brought to court (see p 334, above) but mirrors the definition of serious medical treatment for which an independent mental capacity advocate must be instructed (see p 215, earlier). The Official Solicitor may be asked to advise and the Court will consider making P a party to the proceedings.

The Court charges a hefty fee for its services (unless the applicant is exempt). In cases concerning a person's property and affairs, the parties' legal costs will normally be paid out of his estate. In cases concerning his personal welfare, the parties will normally be expected to bear their own legal costs (rr 156, 157).

(f) The Public Guardian

The Public Guardian has taken over from the Public Trust Office as the administrative arm of the Court of Protection. His office is now part of the Courts Service. His functions are listed in section 58 of the MCA and the Lasting Powers of Attorney, Enduring Powers of Attorney and Public Guardian Regulations 2007, SI 2007/1253. He maintains the registers of Enduring Powers of Attorney, Lasting Powers of Attorney, and Court orders appointing deputies, which the public may search on application (regs 30, 31, 32). He takes and enforces any security which the Court has ordered should be provided, for example by a deputy appointed to make decisions about property and affairs (regs 33, 34, 35, 36). He receives any reports and accounts which the Court has ordered a deputy to provide (regs 38, 39). He may require a final report from a deputy whose appointment comes to an end (reg 40). He may require a deputy to provide him with information if he receives representations or complaints about the way in which the deputy is exercising his powers, or his failure to exercise them, or where there are concerns about the deputy's performance, or some other good reason to require the information (reg 41). He also receives reports and deals with any complaints relating to a person, who though not appointed as a deputy, has been authorised by the Court to carry out a particular transaction for person who lacks capacity (reg 45). A deputy has the right to require the Guardian to review any decision he has made about the deputy (reg 42). He may require the donee of an LPA to provide him with information if there are concerns about the donee contravening his authority or acting otherwise than in the best interests of the donor or failing to comply with an order or directions of the Court (reg 46). He may also require information from attorneys under an EPA (reg 47). He can direct a Court of Protection Visitor to visit a donee of an LPA, a deputy appointed by the Court, and the donor or person for whom the deputy is appointed (MCA 2005, s 58(d), reg 44). He may apply to the Court in connection with his functions if he thinks it necessary or appropriate (reg 43) and must refer to the Court questions about the validity and registration of lasting and enduring powers of attorney (see p 329, earlier).

7. CRIMINAL AND CIVIL PROCEEDINGS

(a) Criminal offences protecting people with mental disorders

All the ordinary offences against the person can be charged against people who attack mentally disordered or disabled people. But there are also some special offences protecting them against sexual exploitation (see p 315, above), and ill-treatment and neglect.

It is an offence under section 127 of the MHA for anyone who is an officer on the staff of, or otherwise employed in, or one of the managers of an NHS hospital, an independent hospital, or a care home to ill-treat or wilfully neglect a patient who is receiving treatment for mental disorder as an in-patient there (presumably wherever the ill-treatment or neglect takes place) or to ill-treat or wilfully neglect a patient who is receiving out-patient treatment (but only while on the premises of which the hospital or home forms part) (s 127(1)). It is also an offence to ill-treat or wilfully neglect a patient in his guardianship under the Act or "otherwise in his custody or care (whether by virtue of any legal or moral obligation or otherwise)" (s 127(2)). The maximum penalty is imprisonment for five years, or an unlimited fine, or both (s 127(3)). Prosecution for these offences requires the consent of the Director of Public Prosecutions (s 127(4)). This is usually an indication that an offence can cover a very wide range of behaviour, some of it very serious but some scarcely meriting a prosecution at all. In *R v Newington* (1990) 91 Cr App R 247, the Court of Appeal decided that ill-treatment and wilful neglect are two separate offences. Ill-treatment is any deliberate conduct "which could properly be described" as such, whether or not it had caused or was likely to cause harm. The defendant must either realise that he is inexcusably ill-treating the patient or be reckless as to whether he is doing so.

It is also an offence under section 44 of the MCA for anyone who has the care of a person who lacks, or whom he reasonably believes to lack, capacity, or any donee of an LPA or EPA, or any deputy appointed by the Court, to ill-treat or wilfully neglect the person without capacity: the Act does not explain what he must lack the capacity to decide. The maximum penalty is the same as those under the MHA but the consent of the DPP is not required.

Other offences relate to falsifying MHA documentation. It is an offence to wilfully make a false entry or statement in any document required or authorised to be made for the purposes of the Act, or to use such an entry or statement with intent to deceive knowing it to be false (s 126(4)). It is also an offence to have any such document in your custody or control without lawful authority or excuse, knowing or believing it to be false (s 126(1)), or without lawful authority or excuse to make or have in your custody or control any document which so closely resembles one made under the Act as to be calculated to deceive (s 126(2)). The maximum penalties are two years imprisonment or an unlimited fine or both (s 126(5)). There are no equivalents in the MCA.

Local social services authorities can prosecute for offences under the MHA, sections 126 and 127 (s 130), as well as for the offences of helping compulsory patients to escape (s 128; p 248, earlier), and of obstructing inspection, visiting, interviewing, examining, or any other function authorised under the Act (s 129). But they need the consent of the DPP to prosecute for ill-treatment or neglect under section 127. They do not have power to prosecute for the offence under section 44 of the MCA. These provisions are a recipe for confusion between the police and the LSSA as to who should take responsibility in these cases.

(b) Mentally disordered witnesses

Obtaining sufficient reliable evidence can be a major difficulty in prosecuting offences against mentally disordered people, but recent reforms have been designed to try and make it easier for mentally disordered and disabled people to give evidence in criminal trials.

The law now allows either sworn or unsworn evidence from adult witnesses. Any witness, whatever his age, is able to give unsworn evidence if he meets the lower test of competence for that purpose even if he does not meet the higher test of competence to give evidence on oath. All witnesses of any age are competent to give evidence in criminal proceedings (Youth Justice and Criminal Evidence Act 1999 (YJCEA), s 53(1)) unless it appears to the court that a witness is not able to understand questions put to him as a witness and give answers to them which can be understood (s 53(3)). If the issue is raised, it is for the party wanting to call the witness to establish his competence on the balance of probabilities (s 54(2)). Expert evidence may be given on this question (s 54(5); but not on whether a witness is telling the truth: *R v Turner* [1975] QB 834). The court must also assume that the witness will be given whatever special help the court can direct (see further below) (s 54(3)). Perhaps the court should also assume that the questions to be asked are asked in plain terms and simple language rather than in the deliberately obfuscatory style adopted by many advocates? The special help available does include help with understanding the questions and the answers. There is a penalty for wilfully giving false unsworn evidence but this is not as serious as giving perjured evidence on oath (s 57).

To be competent to give evidence on oath in a criminal trial the witness must additionally have reached the age of 14 and have "a sufficient appreciation of the solemnity of the occasion and of the particular responsibility to tell the truth which is involved in taking an oath" (s 55(2)). This is assumed if the witness is able to give intelligible testimony unless evidence is given to the contrary (s 55(3)). If such evidence is given, once again it is for the party wishing to have the witness sworn to satisfy the court on the balance of probabilities of his competence to be sworn and expert evidence is admissible (s 55(4), (5)).

The law has struggled with two competing views of the evidence of people with mental disorders. One is the traditional belief that their evidence is likely to be unreliable. In several prosecutions of Rampton staff for abusing patients, culminating in the House of Lords ruling in *R v Spencer* [1987] AC 128, it was held that juries must be warned in clear terms of the dangers of convicting on the unsupported evidence of special hospital patients, who were of bad character, mentally unstable, and might have a common grudge against the staff. Is this—or was it then—true of all special hospital patients or a case of old stereotypes dying hard? (See the careful discussion of these issues in the Ashworth Inquiry Report: Blom-Cooper, 1992, Ch III).

Competing with this is the understanding that people with mental disorders and disabilities are often especially vulnerable to exploitation and abuse, perhaps particularly if they are detained in closed institutions, but may lack the courage and skills to give a good account of themselves in the witness box. Under article 8 of the European Convention on Human Rights, the State has a positive obligation to protect them from interference with their right to respect for their private lives, which is undoubtedly engaged by unwanted sexual attentions (*X and Y v The Netherlands* (1985) 8 EHRR 235). A witness who suffers from mental disorder within the meaning of the MHA 1983 or otherwise has a significant impairment of intelligence and social functioning is eligible for assistance in giving his evidence if the court considers that the quality of his evidence is likely to be diminished as a result of his impairment (YJCEA, s 16(1), (2)). The "special measures" available are screening the witness from seeing the accused (s 23); giving evidence by live television link from another room (s 24); excluding certain people from the courtroom (but not the accused, the lawyers, any interpreter, and a media representative) in cases involving sexual offences or where there is a reasonable fear of intimidation (s 25); removing wigs and gowns (s 26); video-recording the witness's evidence in chief (s 27), as happened in *R v C*, p 315, above; video-recording cross examination and re-examination (s 28) but this is not to be brought into force; providing "aids to communication", that is, devices which will enable the questions and answers to be communicated to and by the witness despite any disability, disorder or impairment from which he may suffer (s 30); and examining the witness through an interpreter or other approved intermediary. The intermediary's function is not only to communicate the questions to the witness and the answers to the questioner but also "to explain such questions or answers so far as necessary to enable them to be understood by the witness or [questioner]" (s 29). This is no easy task in our adversarial trial system but early experience was encouraging (Plotnikoff and Woolfson, 2007). However, the judge still has to give the jury such warning (if any) as he considers necessary to ensure that the special measures do not prejudice the accused (s 32).

(c) Protection for people operating the MHA and the DoLS

All the usual torts may be committed against people with mental disorders and disabilities. It is the tort of false imprisonment to detain a person without proper legal authority. This is normally a tort of strict liability. The prisoner governor who wrongly calculated a prisoner's release date relying on the accepted interpretation of the legislation was liable in damages when the House of Lords decided that the accepted interpretation was wrong (*R v Governor of Brockhill Prison, ex p Evans (No 2)* [2001] 2 AC 19). However, doctors, hospitals, AMHPs and others operating the MHA procedures are given special protection from actions brought by their patients. Section 139(1) of the MHA 1983 provides that:

> "No person shall be liable, whether on the ground of want of jurisdiction or on any other ground, to any civil or criminal proceedings to which he would have been liable apart from this section in respect of any act purporting to be done in pursuance of this Act or any regulations or rules made under this Act, unless the act was done in bad faith or without reasonable care."

Thus a recommending doctor or applicant approved mental health professional (AMHP) will not be liable if they make an innocent mistake and the patient's detention turns out to be unlawful. The same is true of detaining people under the MCA DoLS (Sch A1, para 3). But neither will excuse the professional who fails to take the care that a reasonable professional would take in the circumstances (*Harnett v Fisher* [1927] AC 573; MCA, Sch A1, para 4). For example, in *Winch v Jones* [1986] QB 296, a patient was given leave to sue the recommending doctors and the responsible medical officer for negligence (and the claim was later settled for £27,500). In *Buxton v Jayne* [1960] 1 WLR 783, leave was given to sue the applicant social worker (but the eventual action was unsuccessful). But section 139(1) does give protection to people who have made an honest and reasonable mistake, including a mistake about the extent of their powers. If the Act is so clear that even a layman could not have misconstrued it, then the defendant will still be liable, but if it could reasonably be thought to mean what she thought it did, then she will be protected (see *Richardson v LCC* [1957] 1 WLR 751).

This could be particularly useful for staff in their day-to-day dealings with detained patients, where the precise extent of their powers of control and discipline can be difficult to determine. The House of Lords held in *Pountney v Griffiths* [1976] AC 314 that the actions of a Broadmoor nurse which he claimed were done to control a detained patient were acts "purporting to be done in pursuance of the Act" even though there was no specific provision in the Act to which this related. But how far might the section apply to patients who are not detained? Clearly a person may purport to act in pursuance of the Act when she thinks that that is what she is doing even if in fact she is not (the example given by the Government during the passage of the 1982 amendments was an ambulance man who has been told that he is taking a detained patient to hospital). In *R v Moonsami Runighian* [1977] Crim LR 361, a Crown Court judge held that the section did not cover an alleged assault by a nurse upon an informal patient. But in *Lebrooy v Hammersmith and Fulham LBC* [2006] EWHC 1976 (QB), Cox J held that it did cover the passing on of information between professionals which was part of assessments and inquiries carried out to determine whether a mentally disordered claimant should be admitted under the MHA or what other medical or social care was appropriate for him. Insofar as this might cover anything said or done in relation to a person who might at some time need to be admitted under the Act, this may go too far. But Jones (2010, para 1–1224) helpfully suggests that the section "does apply if the individual undertaking the act genuinely believes at the relevant time that he or she is acting under a provision of this Act".

More important in practice than the substantive defence is the procedural requirement in section 139(2) of the MHA. In order to sue in respect of acts covered by section 139(1) the patient must first have the leave of a High Court judge, even though the case is one which would normally be heard in a county court; and any prosecution for such an act must have the consent of the Director of Public Prosecutions. The High Court judge no longer has to be satisfied (as he did under the 1959 Act) that there is "substantial ground" for the contention of bad faith or lack of reasonable care. The object of the section is to prevent harassment by "clearly hopeless actions", so leave should be granted if the case deserves fuller investigation, even if it is unlikely to succeed on the law or the merits (*Winch v Jones* [1986] QB 296). But leave may be refused, even if there is a conflict of evidence, if it is "virtually unarguable" that there has been a lack of reasonable care, for example by a social worker or doctor making decisions in an obvious emergency (eg *James v London Borough of Havering* (1992) 15 BMLR 1). In *Lebrooy*'s case (above) a variety of claims for defamation were struck out because the exchanges were clearly covered by qualified privilege and the claimant had no reasonable prospect of proving malice.

In *Pountney v Griffiths* (above) it was assumed and conceded that any proceedings begun without the required leave or consent would be void. In *Seal v Chief Constable of South Wales* [2007] UKHL 31, [2007] 1 WLR 1910, the House of Lords confirmed by a majority of three to two that this was so. The result was that the claimant, who had begun the case without leave just before the limitation period ran out, was unable to seek leave for what, on the face of it, looked like a very sound claim.

It was held in *ex p Waldron* [1986] QB 824 that section 139 does not cover applications for judicial review to quash allegedly illegal admissions. This must be right, for judicial review itself requires leave, and the release of unlawfully detained patients should not be effectively discretionary. Nor does it now cover actions against the Secretary of State or an NHS authority, board or trust (s 139(4)), although it does still cover actions against a local social services authority. The section does not apply to the offences of ill-treatment or neglect under section 127 (s 139(3)).

This still means that mental patients suing in respect of acts covered by section 139(1) are at a disadvantage compared with other litigants. They have to go first to a High Court judge even if the claim is within the jurisdiction of the county courts (now very wide). They have to persuade the judge that they have a case which should be tried, whereas with other litigants the burden is on the defendant to show that it should not be tried. In any event, there is no objective justification for the section even in its now attenuated form. Only a minority of patients, even of those compulsorily detained, are suffering from disorders which make it at all likely that they will harass other people with groundless accusations. Rather more of them are suffering from disorders which make it likely that they will not complain at all, even if they have every reason to do so. There are other means of protecting defendants against hopeless, abusive or vexatious claims. Litigants who repeatedly bring unmeritorious civil claims can be restrained from bringing any or a particular sort of proceedings by a "civil restraint order" (CPR 1998, r 3.11) or in extreme cases declared a vexatious litigant (Supreme Court Act 1981, s 42). But there is no necessary connection between vexatiousness and the use of compulsion under the MHA. There is no evidence that the floodgates would open if section 139 were entirely repealed.

No equivalent protection is given in the MCA to those who operate the DoLS, although there is an enigmatic provision giving the Court of Protection power when varying or ending an authorisation, to "make an order about a person's liability for any act done in connection with" the authorisation before it was varied or ended (MCA, s 21A(6)). Two of the Law Lords in *Seal v Chief Constable of South Wales*, above, thought the absolute bar on proceedings without leave, which could result in the total denial of the claim, was a disproportionate interference with the right of access to a court under article 6(1) of the European Convention on Human Rights, but the majority did not.

(d) Conducting litigation

There is another way in which people who lack capacity may be denied the usual access to the courts, although this is meant for their benefit rather than their detriment. Actions cannot be brought or defended in the civil and family courts by a "protected party" unless they are represented by a "litigation friend" (CPR 1998, Pt 21; Family Proceedings Rules 1991, Pt 11). A "protected party" is someone who lacks the capacity, within the meaning of the MCA, to conduct the proceedings (CPR 1998, r 21.1). A deputy appointed by the Court of Protection with power to conduct proceedings on behalf of the protected party is entitled to act as his litigation friend (CPR 1998, r 21.4). Otherwise, any person who can fairly and competently conduct the proceedings on his behalf, has no adverse interest, and is prepared to undertake to pay any costs ordered against a protected party who is a claimant, can become a litigation friend simply by filing a certificate to that effect (CPR 1998, rr 21.4(3), 21.5(3)). The court in which the litigation is taking place can prevent a person acting as litigation friend and can appoint a suitable person for a protected party who has none (CPR 1998, rr 21.6, 21.7). The Official Solicitor often acts for people who have no-one else. He may also be asked by the court to inquire into whether a person ought to have a litigation friend (this is named after the case of *Harbin v Masterman* [1896] 1 Ch 351, in which the appeal was so clearly not in the best interests of the appellant that the Court of Appeal asked the Official Solicitor to make inquiries as to her mental state, revealing that the appellant's solicitor was to blame).

A litigation friend has to conduct the action in the interests of the protected party, but he cannot settle the case without the approval of the court (CPR 1998, r 21.10). However wise his decisions, the protected party is denied the right to conduct the action in the way that he would like. And even if he regains the capacity to act, the appointment continues until it is ended by the court (CPR 1998, r 21.9(2)). If money is recovered on behalf of a protected party, the court will decide how it is to be dealt with (CPR 1998, r 21.11). This could be by paying it into court or passing the matter over to the Court of Protection. So the court must consider whether the protected party is also a "protected beneficiary": that is, someone who lacks the capacity to manage and control any money recovered (CPR 1998, r 21.1(2)). Of course, it is possible that someone will have the capacity to conduct the litigation but not the capacity to look after the proceeds. In that case, the Court of Protection should be asked to take over.

In other respects, however, the law is kind. There may be no point in making an injunction against a mentally disordered person, for example to protect an elderly wife against the obsessive and violent jealousy of her demented husband, if he cannot understand the nature and requirements of the order; it will have no deterrent effect and he would have a good defence to any enforcement proceedings (*Wookey v Wookey* [1991] Fam 131, CA). The Divisional Court has also recently held that an anti-social behaviour order should not be made against a person whose mental impairment meant that he was truly incapable of understanding or complying with it; but this was different from having a personality disorder which made him prone to disobey an order which he could understand (*R (Cooke) v DPP* [2008] EWHC 2703 (Admin), [2008] MHLR 348).

People under a disability are also exempt from the normal rules requiring that actions be brought within a certain time of the cause of action arising. In general, time only begins to run from when the patient ceases to be under a disability (Limitation Act 1980, s 28). People under disability include not only those who are incapable of managing their property and affairs, but also those subject to detention or guardianship under the MHA 1983, and even those informal in-patients whose treatment immediately follows a period of detention (s 38(2) to (4)). This tenderness towards them in ordinary litigation contrasts oddly with the barriers placed in their way by section 139 of the MHA.

8. COMMENTARY

The world is now very different from the world in which this book was first written, only 15 years after the Mental Health Act 1959 came into force. Until that Act, many, perhaps most, people with serious mental disorders and disabilities had lived in institutions. Many, perhaps most, had been detained. And all detained patients were presumed to lack the ability to make any kind of decision for themselves.

Nowadays, very few people with serious mental disorders and disabilities live in hospital. Very few are formally detained. And no-one is assumed to lack the capacity to make a decision simply because of where he lives or what his legal status may be. Every legal distinction between people with mental disorders and disabilities and people with physical disorders and disabilities (and indeed everyone else) has to be justified, at least in the public mind if not under article 14 of the European Convention on Human Rights, and very few can be. Why are Members of Parliament with mental disorders automatically disqualified after six months' detention in hospital when those with physical disorders are not? Why are people who have been taking tranquillisers for years disqualified from jury service when regular petty offenders are not? Why are mentally ill prisoners who have been transferred to hospital treated like prisoners rather than patients by the benefits system? Why do people detained under the Mental Health Act still have to get permission to bring proceedings for false imprisonment when people detained under the Mental Capacity Act do not? These are just a few of the discriminatory provisions which still trouble the law.

It is a tribute to our society that the people who look after the mentally disordered and disabled members of our society also care deeply about these issues. The law too has come a long way from when this book was first written 15 years ago. But it may have some way further yet to go.

BIBLIOGRAPHY OF REFERENCES AND FURTHER READING

Aarvold, Sir C (1972), *Report on the Review of Procedures for the Discharge and Supervision of Psychiatric Patients subject to Special Restrictions*, Cmnd 5191 (London: HMSO).

American Psychiatric Association (1994), *Diagnostic and Statistical Manual of Mental Disorders (DSM-IV)* (Washington DC: American Psychiatric Association).

American Psychiatric Association (2000), *Diagnostic and Statistical Manual of Mental Disorders (DSM-IV-TR)* 4th edn (Washington DC: American Psychiatric Association).

Anderson, EW (1962), "The Official Concept of Psychopathic Personality in England" in Krauze, H (ed), *Psychopathalogie Heute* (Stuttgart: Georg Thieme Verlag).

Appleby, L (National Director for Mental Health) (2004), *The National Service Framework for Mental Health—Five Years On* (London: Department of Health).

Ashworth (2010), *Sentencing and Criminal Justice*, 5th edn (Cambridge: Cambridge University Press).

Ashton, G, Letts, P, Oates, L, and Terrell, M (2006), *Mental Capacity: The New Law* (Bristol: Jordans).

Audini, B and Lelliott, P, "Age, gender and ethnicity of those detained under Part II of the Mental Health Act 1983" (2002) *British Journal of Psychiatry 180*, 222.

Audit Commission (1986), *Making a Reality of Community Care* (London: HMSO).

Audit Commission (1994), *Finding a Place: A Review of Mental Health Services for Adults* (London: HMSO).

Audit Commission and HMI (1992), *Getting in on the Act. Provision for Pupils with Special Educational Needs: the National Picture* (London: HMSO).

Auld, Lord Justice (2001), *Review of the Criminal Courts of England and Wales* (London: TSO).

Bacon, M (1846) *A New Abridgement of the Law, Volume IX* (Philadelphia: Thomas Davis).

Baker, E, "Dangerousness. The neglected gaoler: disorder and risk under the Mental Health Act 1983" (1992) 3 *J Forensic Psych* 31.

Bamford, D (2007), *The Bamford Review of Mental Health and Learning Disability (Northern Ireland): A Comprehensive Legislative Framework*.

Barnes, M, Bowl, R and Fisher, M (1990), *Sectioned: Social Services and the 1983 Mental Health Act* (London: Routledge).

Barlett, P (2005), *Blackstone's Guide to the Mental Capacity Act 2005* (Oxford: Oxford University Press).

Bartlett, P and Sandland, R (2007), *Mental Health Law: Policy and Practice*, 3rd edn (Oxford: Oxford University Press).

BASW: see British Association of Social Workers.

Bather, P (2006), *Review of Section 136 Mental Health Act* (London: London Development Centre).

Bean, P (1980), *Compulsory Admissions to Mental Hospitals* (Chichester: Wiley).

Bean, P (ed) (1983), *Mental Illness: Changes and Trends* (Chichester: Wiley).

Bean, P (ed) (1986), *Mental Disorder and Legal Control* (Cambridge: Cambridge University Press).

Bean, P *et al* (1991), *Out of Harm's Way* (London: MIND).

Beebe, M, Ellis, D and Evans, R, "Research Report on Statutory Work under the Mental Health Act 1959: Experience in the London Borough of Camden" (1973) 5 *The Human Context* 377.

Bell, K (1969), *Tribunals in the Social Services* (London: Routledge and Kegan Paul).

Bell, K, "Mental Health Review Tribunals: A Question of Balance" (1970) 16 *Case Conference* 385.

Bernos, G and Freeman, H (eds) (1991), *150 Years of British Psychiatry 1941–1991* (London: Gaskell). See also Freeman, H and Bernos, G.

Bloch, S, Chodoff, P and Green, SA (eds) (1999), *Psychiatric Ethics*, (3rd edn, Oxford: Oxford University Press).

Blom-Cooper, Sir L (1992), *Report of the Committee of Inquiry into Complaints about Ashworth Hospital*, Cm 2028 (London: HMSO).

Blom-Cooper, Sir L, Hally, H and Murphy, E (1995), *The Falling Shadow: One patient's mental health care 1978–1993* (London: Duckworth).

Blom-Cooper, Sir L, Murphy, Baroness E, Napier QC, M and Bingley, W, "Appendix A" in Mental Health Act Commission (2009), *op cit*.

Bluglass, R and Bowden, P (eds) (1990), *Principles and Practice of Forensic Psychiatry* (London: Churchill Livingstone).

Bluglass, R, "The special hospitals should be closed" (1992) *British Medical Journal 305,* 323.

Blumenthal, S and Wessely, S (1994), *The Pattern of Delays in Mental Health Review Tribunals* (London: HMSO).

Bowen, P (2007), *Blackstone's Guide to the Mental Health Act 2007* (Oxford: Oxford University Press).

Boynton, Sir J (1980), *Report of the Review of Rampton Hospital*, Cmnd 8073 (London: HMSO).

Bradley, Lord (2009), *The Bradley Report, Lord Bradley's review of people with mental health problems or learning disabilities in the criminal justice system* (London: COI for the Department of Health).

British Association of Social Workers (1977), *Mental Health Crisis Services: A New Philosophy* (Birmingham: British Association of Social Workers).

British Medical Association (2007), *Advance decisions and proxy decision-making in medical treatment and research* (London: British Medical Association).

British Medical Association and The Law Society (2010), *Assessment of Mental Capacity: a practical guide for doctors and lawyers* (London: British Medical Association).

Brown, H and Craft, A (1989), *Thinking the Unthinkable: Papers on Sexual Abuse and People with Learning Difficulties* (London: FPA Education Unit).

Buchanan, AE and Brooks, DW (1990), *Deciding for Others: the Ethics of Surrogate Decision-Making* (Cambridge: Cambridge University Press).

Butler, Lord (1974), *Interim Report of the Committee on Mentally Abnormal Offenders*, Cmnd 5698 (London: HMSO).

Butler, Lord (1975), *Report of the Committee on Mentally Abnormal Offenders*, Cmnd 6244 (London: HMSO).

Campbell, T and Heginbotham, C (1991), *Mental Illness: Prejudice, Discrimination and the Law* (Aldershot: Dartmouth).

Care Quality Commission (2009), *Briefing: The Mental Health Act Commission's biennial report 2007–2009. Key Lessons and the Care Quality Commission's Response* (London: Care Quality Commission).

Carson, D (1982a), "Detention of the Mentally Disordered" (1982) 146 *Loc Gov Rev* 887.

Carson, D (1989a), "The Meeting of Legal Rights and Therapeutic Discretion" (1989) 2 *Current Opinion in Psychiatry* 737.

Carson, D (1989b), "Prosecuting People with Mental Handicap" [1989] *Crim LR* 87.

Carson, D (1989c), "The Sexuality of People with Learning Difficulties" [1989] *JSWL* 355.

Carson, D (ed) (1990), *Risk Taking in Mental Disorder* (Chichester: SLE Publications).

Carson, D, "Holding the patient to account at the gatekeeping stage" (1992) 2 *Criminal Behaviour and Mental Health* 224.

Carson, D, "Disabling Progress: the Law Commission's proposals on mentally incapacitated adults' decision-making" [1993] *JSWFL* 304.

Carson, D and Bain, AJ (2007), *Professional Risk and Working with People: Decision-making in Health, Social Care and Criminal Justice* (London: Jessica Kingsley).

Cavadino, M (1988), *Mental Health Law in Context: Doctor's Orders?* (Aldershot: Gower).

Cavadino, M (1991a), "Mental Illness and Neo-Polonianism" (1991) 2 *J Forensic Psych* 294.

Cavadino, M (1991b), "Community Control?" [1991] *JSWFL* 259.

Cavadino, M, "Commissions and Codes: A Case Study in Law and Public Administration" [1993] *Public Law* 333.

Chief Inspector of Prisons (2007), *The Mental Health of Prisoners, A thematic review of the care and support or prisoners with mental health needs* (London: HM Inspectorate of Prisons).

Children's Commissioner for England (2007), *Pushed into the Shadows: Young people's experience of adult mental health facilities* (London: Office of the Children's Commissioner).

Children's Commissioner for England (2008), *Out of the Shadows. A review of the responses to recommendations made in* Pushed into the Shadows: young people's experience of adult mental health facilities (London: 11 Million, Children's Commissioner).

Churchill, R *et al* (1999), *A systematic review of research relating to the Mental Health Act (1983)* (London: Department of Health).

Clare, AW (1980), *Psychiatry in Dissent: Controversial Issues in Thought and Practice*, 2nd edn (London: Tavistock).

Clements, L (2009), "The discreet harm of the *Bournewood* reforms", paper presented at *Taking Stock* conference, Manchester, October 2009.

Clements, L (2009), *Carers and their rights—the law relating to carers*, 3rd edn (London: Carers UK).

Clements, L and Thompson, P (2007), *Community Care and the Law* (London: Legal Action Group).

Clerk, JF and Lindsell, WHB (2009), *Torts*, 19th edn and supplement (Dugdale, A, Jones, M and Simpson, M, eds) (London: Sweet and Maxwell).

Cocozza, JJ and Steadman, HL, "The Failure of Psychiatric Predictions of Dangerousness: Clear and Convincing Evidence" (1976) 29 *Rutgers LR* 1084.

Cohen, D (1981), *Broadmoor* (London: Psychology News Press).

Commission for Social Care Inspection (2008), *Raising Voices: Views on Safeguarding Adults.*

Commission for Social Care Inspection and Health Care Commission (2004), *Joint Investigation into the Services for People with Learning Disabilities at Cornwall Partnership NHS Trust.*

Cooper, DG (1967), *Psychiatry and Anti-Psychiatry* (London: Tavistock).

Cope, R, "A survey of forensic psychiatrists' views on psychopathic disorder" (1993) 4 *J Forensic Psych* 215.

Cornwall Adult Protection Committee (2007), *Annual Report April 2006–2007; The Murder of Steven Hoskin: A Serious Case Review.*

Council on Tribunals (2000), *Mental Health Review Tribunals, Special Report* (London: Council on Tribunals).

Cox, B (1994), *Research on Guardianship for Mentally Ill People* (London: Social Services Inspectorate).

Cretney *et al* (1991), *Enduring Powers of Attorney: A Report to the Lord Chancellor* (London: Lord Chancellor's Department).

Cretney, SM and Lush, D (2008), *Enduring Powers of Attorney*, 6th edn (by Lush, D) (Bristol: Jordan).

Crichton, J, "Supervised Discharge" (1994) 34 *Med Sci and Law* 319.

Crichton, J, "Psychiatric In-Patient Violence: Issues in English Law and Discipline" (1995) 35 *Med Sci and Law* 53.

Crichton, J (ed) (1997), *Psychiatric Patient Violence: Risk and Response* (London: Duckworth).

Criminal Law Revision Committee (1980), 14th Report, *Offences against the Person*, Cmnd 7844 (London: HMSO).

Crown Prosecution Service (2010a), *The Code for Crown Prosecutors* (London: Crown Prosecution Service).

Crown Prosecution Service (2010b), *Legal Guidance: Mentally Disordered Offenders* (London: Crown Prosecution Service).

Dell, S, "The Transfer of Special Hospital Patients to the NHS" (1980) 136 *Brit J Psych* 222.

Dell, S, "Diminished Responsibility Reconsidered" [1982] *Crim LR* 809.

Dell, S, and Robertson, G (1988), *Sentenced to Hospital: Offenders in Broadmoor* (Oxford; Oxford University Press).

Dell, S and Smith, A, "Changes in the Sentencing of Diminished Responsibility Homicides" (1983) 142 *Br J Psych* 20.

Department for Children, Schools and Families (2009), *Achievement for All: Local Authority Prospectus (A Commitment from the Children's Plan)*, (DCSF-00633-2009) (Nottingham: DCSF Publications).

Department of Education and Science (1980), *Special Needs in Education*, Cmnd 7996 (London: HMSO).

Department of Education and Science (1992), *Choice and Diversity. A New Framework for Schools*, Cm 2021 (London: HMSO).

Department for Education and Skills (2004), *Removing Barriers to Achievement: the Government's Strategy for Special Education Needs*, (DfES/0117/2004) (Nottingham: Department for Education and Skills).

Department of Health, Joint Health/Social Services Circular No HC (90)23, LASSL(90)11, *The Care Programme approach for People with a Mental Illness referred to the Specialist Psychiatric Services.*

Department of Health (1992), *The Health of the Nation* (London: HMSO).

Department of Health (1993), *Legal Powers on the Care of Mentally Ill People in the Community, Report of the Internal Review* (London: Department of Health).

Department of Health, Circular No LAC(93)10, *Approvals and Directions for Arrangements From 1 April 1993 Made Under Schedule 8 of the National Health Service Act 1977 and Sections 21 and 29 of the National Assistance Act 1948.*

Department of Health, NHS Management Executive, Health Service Guidelines HSG(93)20, *Recall of Mentally Disordered Patients subject to Home Office Restrictions on Discharge.*

Department of Health, NHS Executive, Health Service Guidelines HSG (94)27, LASSL(94)4, *Guidance on the discharge of mentally disordered people and their continuing care in the community.*

Department of Health (1994), *Mental Health Act Guardianship: A Discussion Paper* (London: Department of Health).

Department of Health (1995), *Building Bridges: A guide to arrangements for inter-agency working for the care and protection of severely mentally ill people* (enclosed with HSG(95)56 and LASSL(95)12) (London: Department of Health).

Department of Health (1999), *National Service Framework for Mental Health: Modern Standards and Service Models* (London: Department of Health).

Department of Health (1999), *Reform of the Mental Health Act 1983 proposals for consultation,* Cm 4480 (London: TSO).

Department of Health (2001), *The Mental Health Act 1983, Guidance for General Practitioners: Medical Examinations and Medical Recommendations under the Act* (London: Department of Health).

Department of Health (2002) *Draft Mental Health Bill,* Cm 3558 (London: TSO).

Department of Health (2003), *Fairer Charging Policies for Home Care and other Non-Residential Social Services. Guidance for Councils with Social Services Responsibilities.*

Department of Health (2004a), *Draft Mental Health Bill 2004,* Cm 6305 (London: TSO).

Department of Health (2004), *LAC (2004)20: Guidance on National Assistance Act 1948 (Choice of Accommodation) Directions 1992 and National Assistance (Residential Accommodation) (Additional Payment and Assessment of Resources) (Amendment) (England) Regulations 2001.*

Department of Health (2007), *Arrangements for approving doctors under section 12(2) of the Mental Health Act (1983)—post 1 April 2002,* revised 8 February 2007.

Department of Health (2007), *Making Experiences Count. A new approach to responding to complaints. A document for information and comment.*

Department of Health (2008a), *Code of Practice: Mental Health Act 1983* (London: TSO).

Department of Health (2008b), *Refocusing the Care Programme Approach: Policy and Practice Guidance* (London: COI for the Department of Health).

Department of Health (2008c), *Making Experiences Count. The proposed new arrangements for handling health and social care complaints. Response to consultation* (London: COI for the Department of Health).

Department of Health (2009), *Shaping the Future of Care Together,* Cm 7673 (London: TSO).

Department of Health (2009b), *New Horizons, A shared vision for mental health* (London: COI for the Department of Health).

Department of Health (2009), *Fairer Contributions Guidance. Calculating an Individual's Contribution to their Personal Budget* (London: www.dh.gov.uk/publications).

351

Department of Health (2010), *Prioritising need in the context of* Putting People First: A whole system approach to eligibility for social care. *Guidance on Eligibility Criteria for Adult Social Care, England 2010.*

Department of Health *et al* (1989), *Caring for People: Community Care in the Next Decade and Beyond*, Cm 89 (London: HMSO).

Department of Health and Home Office (2000), *No Secrets: Guidance on developing and implementing multi-agency policies and procedures to protect vulnerable adults from abuse* (London: Department of Health).

Department of Health and Home Office (2000), *Reforming the Mental Health Act*, Cm 5016 (London: TSO).

DHSS, Circular 19/71, *Welfare of the Elderly: Implementation of Section 45 of the Health Services and Public Health Act 1968.*

DHSS (1971), *Better Services for the Mentally Handicapped*, Cmnd 4683 (London: HMSO).

DHSS (1975), *Better Services for the Mentally Ill*, Cmnd 6233 (London: HMSO).

DHSS (1976), *A Review of the Mental Health Act 1959* (London: HMSO).

DHSS (1981), *Patients' Money: Accumulation of Balances in Long Stay Hospitals.*

DHSS, Circular No HC(84)12, LAC(84)9, Marriage Act 1983, Marriage of Housebound Persons and of Patients Detained under the Mental Health Act 1983.

DHSS *et al* (1978), *Review of the Mental Health Act 1959*, Cmnd 7320 (London: HMSO).

DHSS *et al* (1981), *Reform of Mental Health Legislation*, Cmnd 8405 (London: HMSO).

DHSS and Home Office (1986), *Consultation Document: Offenders suffering from Psychopathic Disorder* (London: DHSS).

Dolan, B and Coid, J (1993), *Psychopathic and Antisocial Personality Disorders: Treatment and Research Issues* (London: Gaskell).

Dolan, M *et al*, "An audit of recalls to a Special Hospital" (1993) 4 *J Forensic Psych* 249.

Dunn, J, "Community Treatment Orders: do we need them?" (1991) 2 *J Forensic Psych* 153.

Dunn, J and Fahy, TA, "Police admissions to a psychiatric hospital. Demographic and clinical differences between ethnic groups" (1990) *156 British Journal of Psychiatry* 373.

Eastman, N, "Hybrid orders: an analysis of their likely effect on sentencing practice and on professional psychiatric practice on services" (1996) 7 *J Forensic Psych* 481.

Eastman, N and Peay, J, "Sentencing psychopaths: Is the 'Hospital and Limitation Direction' an ill-considered hybrid?" (1998) *Crim LR* 93.

Eastman, N and Peay, J, "Bournewood: an indefensible gap in Mental Health Law" (1998) 317 BMJ 94.

Eekelaar, J and Pearl, D (eds) (1989), *An Aging World: Dilemmas and Challenges in Law and Social Policy* (Oxford: Clarendon).

Emerson, E, and Hatton, C (1994), *Moving Out: The Impact of Relocation from Hospital to Community on the Quality of Life of People with Learning Disabilities* (London: HMSO).

Emery, D (1961), *Report of the Working Party on the Special Hospitals* (London: HMSO).

Ennis, BJ (1972), *Prisoners of Psychiatry: Mental Patients, Psychiatry and the Law* (New York, Harcourt, Brace, Jovanovich).

Ennis, BJ and Litwack, TR, "Psychiatry and the Presumption of Expertise: Flipping Coins in the Courtroom" (1974) 62 *Calif LR* 693.

Fallon, P (1999), *Report of the Committee of Inquiry into the Personality Disorder Unit, Ashworth Special Hospital,* Cm 4194 (London: TSO).

Fahy, TA, "The Police as a Referral Agency for Psychiatric Emergencies—A Review" (1989) 20 *Med Sci and Law* 315.

Farrand, JT, "Enduring Powers of Attorney" in Eekelaar and Pearl (eds) (1989), *op cit.*

Fennell, P, "The Mental Health Review Tribunal: A Question of Imbalance" (1977) 4 *Brit J Law and Soc.* 186.

Fennell, P (1979), *Justice, Discretion and the Therapeutic State,* M Phil Thesis, University of Kent.

Fennell, P, "Detention and Control of Informal Mentally Disordered Patients" [1984] *JSWL* 345.

Fennell, P, "Sexual Suppressants and the Mental Health Act" [1988] *Crim LR* 660.

Fennell, P, "The Beverley Lewis Case: was the law to blame?" (1989) 139 *New LJ* 559.

Fennell, P, "Inscribing Paternalism in the Law: Consent to Treatment and Mental Disorder" (1990) 17 *J Law and Soc* 29.

Fennell, P, "The Mental Health Act Code of Practice" (1990) 53 *Modern LR* 499.

Fennell, P, (1991a), "Diversion of Mentally Disordered Offenders from Custody" [1991] *Crim LR* 333.

Fennell, P, (1991b), "Double Detention under the Mental Health Act 1983: A Case of Extra-Parliamentary Legislation?" [1991] *J Soc Welfare and Fam L* 194.

Fennell, P, "Balancing Care and Control: Guardianship, Community Treatment Orders and Patient Safeguards" (1992) 15 *Int J Law and Psych* 1.

Fennell, P, "The Criminal Procedure (Insanity and Unfitness to Plead) Act 1991" (1992) 55 *Modern LR* 547.

Fennell, P, "Informal Compulsion—The Psychiatric Treatment of Juveniles under Common Law" [1992] *JSWFL* 311.

Fennell, P (1996), *Treatment without Consent: Law, psychiatry and the treatment of mentally disordered people since 1845* (London: Routledge).

Fennell, P, "Joined Up Compulsion: the White Paper on Reform of the Mental Health Act 1983" (2001) 3 *J Mental Health L* 5.

Fennell, P, "Informed Consent and Clinical Research in Psychiatry" in Doyal, L and Tobias, G (eds) (2001), *Informed Consent in Clinical Research* (London: BMJ Books).

Fennell, P, "Radical Risk Management, Mental Health and Criminal Justice", in Gray, N, Laing, J and Noakes, L (2002), *Criminal Justice, Mental Health and the Politics of Risk* (London: Cavendish).

Fennell. P ,"Convention Compliance, Public Safety and the Social Inclusion of Mentally Disordered People" (2005) 32 J Law and Soc 90.

Fennell, P (2008), *Mental Heath: The New Law* (Bristol: Jordans).

Fennell, P and Gostin, L, "Health: the Healthcare System, Therapeutic Relationships and Public Health", in Cane, P and Tushnet, M (eds) (2003) *Oxford Handbook of Legal Studies* (Oxford: Oxford University Press).

Fennell, P, and Yeates, V, "To Serve which Master? Criminal Justice Policy", in Buchanan, A (ed) (2002), *Community Care and the Mentally Disordered Offender* (Oxford: Oxford University Press).

Fisher, Sir HAP (1977), *Report of an Inquiry into the circumstances leading to the trial of three persons on charges arising out of the death of Maxwell Confait and the fire at 27 Doggett Road, London SE6,* Session 1977–78, HC 90 (London: HMSO.

Flew, *AGN*(1973), *Crime or Disease?* (London: Macmillan).

Floud, J and Young, W (1981), *Dangerousness and Criminal Justice* (London: Heinemann).

Forrester, A, Ozdural, S, Muthukumaraswamy, A and Carroll, A, "The evolution of mental disorder as a legal category in England and Wales" (2008) 19 *J Forensic Psych and Psychol* 543.

Foucault, M(1967), *Madness and Civilisation: A History of Insanity in the Age of Reason,* trs Howard, R (London: Tavistock).

Freeman, MDA, "The Rights of Children in the International Year of the Child" (1980) 33 *Current Legal Problems* 1.

Freeman, MDA (ed), (1988) *Medicine, Ethics and the Law* (London: Stevens).

Freeman, H and Bernos, G (1996) *150 Years of British Psychiatry, vol II: The Aftermath* (London: Athlone).

Gelder *et al* (2009), *New Oxford Textbook of Psychiatry* , 2nd edn (Oxford: Oxford University Press).

General Social Care Council (2007), *Approved Mental Health Professional Training Requirements: Revised PQ Specialist Mental Health Requirements and Standards* (London: General Social Care Council).

Genn, H and Genn, Y (1989), *The Effectiveness of Representation at Tribunals,* Report to the Lord Chancellor's Department.

Genn, H *et al* (2006), *Tribunals for Diverse Users,* DCA Research Series 1/06 (London: Department for Constitutional Affairs).

Glancy, J (1974), *Revised Report of the Working Party on Security in NHS Psychiatric Hospitals* (London: DHSS).

Gledhill, K, "Community Treatment Orders" (2007) *J Mental Health L* 149.

Glover-Thomas, N (2002), *Reconstructing Mental Health Law and Policy* (London: Butterworths LexisNexis).

Goffman, E (1961), *Asylums: Essays on the Social Situation of Mental Patients and other Inmates* (New York: Doubleday).

Goldstein, J, "For Harold Laswell: Some Reflections on Human Dignity, Entrapment, Informed Consent and the Plea Bargain" (1975) 84 *Yale LJ* 683.

Gostin, L (1975), *A Human Condition: The Mental Health Act from 1959 to 1975: Observations, analysis and proposals for reform,* Vol 1 (London: MIND).

Gostin, L (1977), *A Human Condition: The law relating to mentally abnormal offenders: Observations, Analysis and proposals for reform,* Vol 2 (London: MIND).

Gostin, L, "The Merger of Incompetency and Certification: The Illustration of Unauthorised Medical Contact in the Psychiatric Context" (1979) 2 *Int J Law and Psych* 127.

Gostin, L, "Psychosurgery: A Hazardous and Unestablished Treatment? The Case for the Importation of American Legal Safeguards to Great Britain" [1982] *JSWL* 83.

Gostin, L (1983a), "The Ideology of Entitlement: The Application of Contemporary Legal Approaches to Psychiatry" in Bean (ed) (1986), *op cit.*

Gostin, L (1983b), *The Court of Protection—a legal and policy analysis of the guardianship of the estate* (London: MIND).

Gostin, L (ed) (1985), *Secure Provision: A review of special services for the mentally ill and mentally handicapped in England and Wales* (London: Tavistock).

Gostin, L (1986), *Institutions Observed: towards a new concept of secure provision* (London: King's Fund).

Grey, M, "Forcing Old People to Leave Their Homes: The Principle", *Community Care*, March 8 1979, p 19.

Griffiths, Sir R (1988), *Community Care: Agenda for Action: A Report to the Secretary of State for Social Services* (London: HMSO).

Grounds, A, "Transfers of Sentenced Prisoners to Hospital" [1990] *Crim LR* 544.

Grubb, A (ed) (1994), *Decision-Making and the Problems of Incompetence* (Chichester: Wiley).

Grubin, DH, "Unfit to Plead in England and Wales, 1976–88: A Survey" (1991) 158 *Brit J Psych* 540.

Grubin, D, "What Constitutes Fitness to Plead?" [1993] *Crim LR* 748.

Gunn, J, "The Law and the Mentally Abnormal Offender in England and Wales" (1979) 2 *Int J Law and Psych* 199.

Gunn, J, Maden, T and Swinton, M (1991), *Mentally Disordered Prisoners* (London: Home Office).

Gunn, J, Maden, T and Swinton, M, "How many prisoners should be in hospital?" (1991) 31 *Home Office Research Bulletin* 9.

Gunn, J and Joseph, P, "Remands to hospital for psychiatric reports: a study of psychiatrists' attitudes to section 35 of the Mental Health Act 1983" (1993) 17 *Psych Bull* 197.

Gunn, M, "The Meaning of Incapacity" (1994) 2 *Med LR* 8.

Gunn, MJ and Wheat, K "General principles of the law relating to people with mental disorder", in Gelder *et al* (2009), *op cit.*

Hale, B, "Mentally Incapacitated Adults and Decision Making: The English Perspective" (1997) 20 *Int J Law and Psych* 59.

Hale, B, "What can the Human Rights Act do for my mental health?" (May 2005) *J Mental Health L* 7.

Hale, B, "Justice and Equality in Mental Health Law: the European Experience" (2007) 30 *Int J Law and Psych* 18.

Hale, B, "The Human Rights Act and Mental Health Law: Has it Helped?" (May 2007) *J Mental Health L* 7.

Hale, B and Fortin, J, "Legal Issues in the Care and Treatment of Children with Mental Health Problems", in Rutter (2008), *op cit.*

Hamilton, JR, "The Special Hospitals", in Gostin, L (ed) (1985), *op cit.*

Harlow, C, "Self Defence: Public Right or Private Privilege" [1974] *Crim LR* 528.

Harvey, C, "Forcing Old People to Leave Their Homes: The Practice", *Community Care*, 8 March 1979, p 20.

Haslar, F and Stewart, A (2004), *Making Direct Payments Work: Identifying and Overcoming Barriers to Implementation*

Health Advisory Service and Social Services Inspectorate (1988), *Report on the Services provided by Broadmoor Hospital.*

Health and Social Care Information Centre (2008a), *In-patients formerly detained in hospitals under the Mental Health Act 1983 and other legislation, England: 1997–98 to 2007–08* (UK: Health and Social Care Information Centre).

Health and Social Care Information Centre (2008b), *Mental Health Bulletin. First Report and experimental statistics from the Mental Health Minimum Dataset (MHMDS) annual returns, 2003–2007* (UK: Health and Social Care Information Centre).

Healthcare Commission (2007), *Count me in 2007. Results of the 2007 national census of inpatients in mental health and learning disability services in England and Wales* (UK: Commission for Healthcare, Audit and Inspection).

Healthcare Commission (2008), *Count Me In 2008. Results of the 2008 national census of inpatients in mental health and learning disability services in England and Wales* (UK: Commission for Healthcare, Audit and Inspection).

Hepworth, D, "The Influence of the Concept of 'Danger' on the Assessment of 'Danger to Self or Others'" (1982) 22 *Med Sci and L* 245.

Herbst, K and Gunn, J (eds) (1991), *The Mentally Disordered Offender* (London: Butterworth-Heinemann).

Heywood, NA and Massey, A, *Court of Protection Practice*, 13th (looseleaf) edn, Lush, D and Rees, R (eds) (London: Stevens).

Hodgins, S (ed) (1993), *Mental Disorder and Crime* (London: Sage).

Hodgins, S, "The Criminality of Mentally Disordered Persons", in Hodgins S (ed) (1993), *op cit*.

Hoffmann, Bar Society Annual Law Reform Lecture, 17 November 2009.

Hoggett, B, "Legal Aspects of Secure Provision", in Gostin (ed) (1985), *op cit*.

Hoggett, B, "The Royal Prerogative in Relation to the Mentally Disordered: Resurrection, Resuscitation or Rejection?" in Freeman (ed) (1988), *op cit*.

Hoggett, B (1996), *Mental Health Law*, 4th edn (London: Sweet & Maxwell).

Home Office Circular 66/90, *Provision for Mentally Disordered Offenders* (London: Home Office).

Home Office (1995), *Circular No 12/95, Mentally Disordered Offenders: Inter-agency working* (London: Home Office).

Home Office (1996), *Protecting the Public: the Government's strategy on crime in England and Wales,* Cmnd 3190 (London: Home Office).

Home Office (2005), *Memorandum submitted to the Select Committee on Home Affairs,* HC 656-I. (London: TSO).

Home Office (2008), *Police and Criminal Evidence 1984 (PACE) Code C. Code of Practice for the Detention, Treatment and Questioning of Persons by Police Officers.*

Home Office and DHSS (1987), *Report of the Interdepartmental Working Group of Home Office and DHSS Officials on Mentally Disturbed Offenders in the Prison System in England and Wales* (London: Home Office).

Home Office and Department of Health (2005), *Offender Health Care Strategies, Improving health services for offenders in the community.*

House of Commons Health Committee (1993), *Community Supervision Orders, Fifth Report,* Session 1992–93, HC 667 (London: HMSO).

House of Commons Health Committee (1994), *Better off in the Community? The Care of People who are seriously mentally ill, First Report,* Session 1993–94, HC 102 (London: HMSO).

House of Commons Social Services Committee (1985), *Community Care, with special reference to adult mentally ill and mentally handicapped people, Second Report,* Session 1985–86, HC 13 (London: HMSO).

House of Lords (1989), *Report of the Select Committee on Murder and Life Imprisonment,* Session 1988–89, HL 78 (London: HMSO).

House of Lords (1994), *Report of the Select Committee on Medical Ethics,* Session 1993–94, HL 21 (London: HMSO).

Howard, LM, "Psychotic disorders and parenting—the relevance of patients' children for general adult psychiatric services" (2000) 24 *Psychiatric Bulletin* 324.

Ingleby, D (ed) (1981), *Critical Psychiatry: the Politics of Mental Health* (Harmondsworth: Penguin).

Huxtable, R, "Re M (Medical Treatment: Consent): time to remove the flak jacket?" (2000) 12 *Child and Family L Q* 83.

Independent Police Complaints Commission (2008), *Police Custody as a "Place of Safety", Examining the Use of Section 136 of the Mental Health Act 1983 (IPCC Research and Statistics Series: Paper 11)* (London: IPCC).

Isaac, BC, Minty, EB and Morrison, RM, "Children in Care—the Association with Mental Disorder in the Parents" (1986) 16 *Brit J Social Work* 325.

Jacob, J, "The Right of the Mental Patient to his Psychosis" (1976) 39 *Modern LR* 17.

Joint Committee on the Draft Mental Health Bill (2004), *Draft Mental Health Bill. Session 2004–05, HL 79, HC 95*.

Joint Committee on the Draft Mental Incapacity Bill (2003), Session 2002–03, HL 189, HC 1083.

Joint Committee on Human Rights (2007), *The Human Rights of Older People in Healthcare, Eighteenth Report*, Session 2006–2007, HL 156-I, HC 378-I (London: TSO).

Jones, K, "The Limitations of the Legal Approach to Mental Health" (1980) 3 *Int J Law and Psych* 1.

Jones, K, "Scull's Dilemma" (1982) 141 *Brit J Psych* 221.

Jones, K (1993), *Asylums and After. A Revised History of the Mental Health Services from the early 18th Century to the 1990s* (London: Athlone).

Jones, RM (1996), *Mental Health Act Manual*, 5th edn (London: Sweet & Maxwell).

Jones, RM (2009), *Mental Health Act Manual*, 12th edn (London: Sweet & Maxwell).

Jones, RM (2009), *Mental Capacity Act Manual*, 3rd edn (London: Sweet & Maxwell).

Kenny, A, "The Expert in Court" (1983) *99 Law QR* 197.

King, M, "Welfare and Justice" in King, M (ed) (1981), *Childhood, Welfare and Justice* (London: Batsford).

Kittrie, NN (1971), *The Right to be Different* (Baltimore: Johns Hopkins Press).

Laing, RD (1959), *The Divided Self* (London: Tavistock).

Laing, RD and Esterson, A (1971), *Sanity, Madness and the Family*, 2nd edn (London: Tavistock).

Lanham, D, "Arresting the Insane" [1974] *Crim LR* 515.

Law Commission (1976), *The Incapacitated Principal*, Working Paper No 69 (London: HMSO).

Law Commission (1982) *Time Restrictions on the Presentation of Divorce and Nullity Petitions*, Law Com No 116 (London: HMSO).

Law Commission (1983), *The Incapacitated Principal*, Law Com No 122, Cmnd 8977 (London: HMSO).

Law Commission (1989), *A Criminal Code for England and Wales*, Law Com No 177 (London: HMSO).

Law Commission (1991), *Mentally Incapacitated Adults and Decision-Making: An Overview*, Consultation Paper No 119 (London: HMSO).

Law Commission (1993a), *Mentally Incapacitated Adults and Decision-Making: A New Jurisdiction*, Consultation Paper No 128 (London: HMSO).

Law Commission (1993b), *Mentally Incapacitated Adults and Decision-Making: Medical Treatment and Research*, Consultation Paper No 129 (London: HMSO).

Law Commission (1993c), *Mentally Incapacitated and Other Vulnerable Adults: Public Law Protection*, Consultation Paper No 130 (London: HMSO).

Law Commission (1995), *Mental Incapacity*, Law Com No 231 (London: HMSO).

Law Commission (2004), *Partial Defences to Murder*, Cm 6301 (London: TSO).

Law Commission (2005), *A New Homicide Act for England and Wales?* LCCP 177 (London: TSO).

Law Commission (2006), *Murder, Manslaughter and Infanticide*, Law Com No 304 (London: TSO).

Law Commission (2008a), *Adult Social Care: Scoping Report* (London: TSO).

Law Commission (2008b), *Tenth Programme of Law Reform*, Law Com No 311 (HC 605) (London: TSO).

Law Commission (2010), *Adult Social Care: Consultation Paper*, LCCP 192 (London: TSO).

Law Society, Mental Health Sub-Committee (1989), *Decision-Making and Mental Incapacity: A Discussion Document* (London: The Law Society).

Lawson, A (1966), *The Recognition of Mental Illness in London: A Study of the Social Processes determining Compulsory Admission to an Observation Unit in a London Hospital* (London: Oxford University Press).

LCD: see Lord Chancellor's Department.

Le Mesurier, A A, "The Duly Authorised Officer" (1949) 1 *Brit J Psych Soc Work* 45.

Lee, R and Morgan, D, "Sterilisation and Mental Handicap: Sapping the Strength of the State?" (1988) 15 *J Law and Soc* 229.

Leggatt, Sir A (2001), *Tribunals for Users, One System, One Service. Report of the Review of Tribunals by Sir Andrew Leggatt* (London: TSO).

Lewis, P (1980), *Psychiatric Probation Orders: Roles and Expectations of Probation Officers and Psychiatrists* (Cambridge: Institute of Criminology).

Littlewood, R and Lipsedge, M (1997), *Aliens and Alienists: Ethnic Minorities and Psychiatry*, 3rd edn (London: Routledge).

Longford, Lord (1992), *Prisoner or Patient* (London: Chapmans).

Lord Chancellor's Department (1997), *Who Decides? Making Decisions on behalf of Mentally Incapacitated Adults*, Cm 3803 (London: HMSO).

Lord Chancellor's Department (1999), *Making Decisions: The Government's proposals for making decisions on behalf of mentally incapacitated adults*, Cm 4465 (London: TSO).

McCreadie, C (1991), *Elder Abuse: An Exploratory Study* (London: Age Concern Institute of Gerontology).

MacDermott, J (1981) *Report of the Northern Ireland Review Committee on Mental Health Legislation* (Belfast: HMSO).

Mackay, R D, "Fact and Fiction about the Insanity Defence" [1990] *Crim LR* 247.

Mackay, R D, "Dangerous Patients, Third Party Safety and Psychiatrist's Duties —Walking the Tarasoff Tightrope" (1990) 30 *Med Sci and Law* 52.

Mackay, R D, "Appendix B, The Diminished Responsibility Plea in Operation—An Empirical Study" in Law Commission (2004), *op cit*.

Mackay, R D, Mitchell, B J and Howe, L, "Yet more facts about the insanity defence" (2006) *Crim LR* 399.

Mackay, R D, "Appendix D: Infanticide and Related Diminished Responsibility Manslaughters—an Empirical Study" in Law Commission (2006) *op cit*.

McManus, J (2009), *Limited review of the Mental Health (Care and Treatment)*

(Scotland) Act 2003: Report as presented to the Scottish Ministers, March 2009 (Edinburgh: Scottish Government)

MacMillan, HP (1926), *Report of the Royal Commission on Lunacy and Mental Disorders 1924–1926*, Cmd 2700 (London: HMSO).

MENCAP (1989), *Competency and Consent to Medical Treatment, Report of the Working Party on the Legal, Medical and Ethical Issues of Mental Handicap* (London: MENCAP).

Mental Health Act Commission (1985, 1987, 1989, 1991, 1993, 1995, 1997, 1999, 2001), *First, Second, Third, Fourth, Fifth, Sixth, Seventh, Eighth and Ninth Biennial Reports* (London: HMSO).

Mental Health Act Commission (2004), *Placed amongst strangers*, Tenth Biennial Report 2001–2003 (London: TSO).

Mental Health Act Commission (2005), *In place of fear?* Eleventh Biennial Report 2003–2005 (London: TSO).

Mental Health Act Commission (2008), *Risks, Rights, Recovery*, Twelfth Biennial Report 2005–2007 (London: TSO).

Mental Health Act Commission (2009a), *Coercion and Consent*, Thirteenth Biennial Report 2007–2009 (London: TSO).

Mental Health Act Commission (2009b), *Women detained in Hospital: A Report by the Mental Health Act Commission* (Nottingham: MHAC).

Mental Health Foundation (1994), *Creating Community Care Report of the Mental Health Foundation Inquiry into Community Care for People with Severe Mental Illness* (London: Mental Health Foundation).

Merrison, Sir A (1979), *Report of the Royal Commission on the National Health Service*, Cmnd 7615 (London: HMSO).

Mill, JS (1859), *On Liberty* (reprinted as Three Essays: *On Liberty, Representative Government, The Subjection of Women*) (London: Oxford University Press).

Miller, DW, "The Mentally Disordered Patient in Hospital" (1975) 125 *New LJ* 884.

MIND (1978), *The Great Debate: MIND's comments on the White Paper on the review of the Mental Health Act* 1959 (London: MIND).

MIND (2009), *Shaping the Future of Care Together: the Government's Green Paper on social care, Response from Mind* (London: MIND).

Ministry of Justice (2008a), *Changes to the Mental Health Review Tribunal from November 2008* (London: Ministry of Justice).

Ministry of Justice (2008b), *Leave of absence for patients subject to restrictions. Guidance for Responsible Clinicians* (London: Ministry of Justice).

Ministry of Justice (2008c), *Mental Health Act 2007: Guidance for the courts on remand and sentencing powers for mentally disordered offenders* (London: Ministry of Justice).

Ministry of Justice (2009a), *Foreign National Restricted Patients—Guidance on repatriation* (London: Ministry of Justice).

Ministry of Justice (2009b), *Guidance for clinical supervisors* (London: Ministry of Justice).

Ministry of Justice (2009c), *Guidance for social supervisors* (London: Ministry of Justice).

Ministry of Justice (2009d), *Mental Health Unit Bulletin*, February 2009.

Ministry of Justice (2009e), *The recall of conditionally discharged restricted patients* (London: Ministry of Justice).

Ministry of Justice and Public Guardian (2008), *Mental Capacity Act 2005 Code of Practice on the Deprivation of Liberty Safeguards, Code of Practice to Supplement the Main Mental Capacity Act 2005 Code of Practice* (London: TSO).

Mittler, P (1979), *People not Patients: Problems and Policies in Mental Handicap* (London: Methuen).

Mokhtar, A E, and Hogbin, P, "Police May Underuse Section 136" (1993) 33 *Med Sci and Law* 188.

Monahan, J, "John Stuart Mill and the Liberty of the Mentally Ill: A Historical Note" (1977) 134 *American J of Psych* 1428.

Morris, GH (1978), *The Insanity Defense: A Blueprint for Legislative Reform* (Farnborough: Lexington).

Morris, P (1969), *Put Away: a Sociological Study of Institutions for the Mentally Retarded* (London: Routledge and Kegan Paul).

Mowlam, A, Tennant, R, Dixon, J and McCreadie, C (2007), *UK Study of Abuse and Neglect of Older People: Qualitative Findings* (Prepared by the National Centre for Social Research and King's College London for Comic Relief and the Department of Health).

National Assembly for Wales and Home Office (2000), *Implementing Adult Protection Procedures in Wales* (Cardiff: National Assembly for Wales and Home Office).

National Audit Office (1994), *Report by the Comptroller and Auditor General, Looking After the Financial Affairs of People with Mental Incapacity*, Session 1993–94, H C 258 (London: HMSO).

National Institute of Mental Health in England (NIMHE) (2003), *Personality Disorder; No longer a diagnosis of exclusion* (Leeds: Department of Health).

National Institute for Mental Health in England (2005), *Guiding Statement on Recovery* (Leeds: Department of Health).

National Institute for Mental Health in England (2008), *Mental Health Act 2007: New Roles. Guidance for approving authorities and employers on Approved Mental Health Professionals and Approved Clinicians* (Leeds: Department of Health).

NCCL (1973), *The Rights of the Mentally Abnormal Offender: The National Council for Civil Liberties' Evidence to the Butler Committee* (London: National Council for Civil Liberties, now Liberty).

NIMHE: see National Institute for Mental Health in England.

Norman, A (1980), *Rights and Risk: A Discussion Document on Civil Liberty in Old Age* (London: National Corporation for the Care of Old People, now Centre for Policy on Ageing).

North, C, Ritchie, J and Ward, K (1993), *Factors Influencing the Implementation of the Care Programme Approach* (London: HMSO).

Northern Ireland Executive (2009), *Delivering the Bamford Vision: The response of the Northern Ireland Executive to the Bamford Review of Mental Health and Learning Disability. Action Plan 2009–2011* (Belfast: Department of Health, Social Services and Public Safety).

O'Keefe, *et al* (2007), *UK Study of Abuse and Neglect of Older People Prevalence Survey Report* P2512 (London: National Centre for Social Research prepared for Comic Relief and the Department of Health).

Parker, E and Tennent G, "The 1959 Mental Health Act and Mentally Abnormal Offenders: A Comparative Study" (1979) 19 *Med Sci and Law* 29.

Peay, J, "Mental Health Review Tribunals: just or efficacious safeguards?" (1981) 5 *Law and Human Behaviour* 161.

Peay, J, "Mental Health Review Tribunals and the Mental Health (Amendment) Act" [1982] *Crim LR* 794.

Peay, J, "Offenders suffering from Psychopathic Disorder: The Rise and Demise of a Consultation Document" (1988) 23 *Brit J Criminol* 67.

Peay, J (1989), *Tribunals on Trial: A Study of Decision-Making under the Mental Health Act 1983* (Oxford: Clarendon Press).

Peay, J (1998), *Criminal Justice and the Mentally Disordered* (Dartmouth: Ashgate).

Peay, J (2003), *Decisions and Dilemmas. Working with Mental Health Law* (London: Hart Publishing).

Peay, J (2005), *Seminal Issues in Mental Health Law* (Aldershot: Ashgate).

Peay, J and Eastman, N (eds) (1999), *Law without enforcement: integrating mental health and justice* (Oxford: Hart Publishing).

Peay, J, Roberts, C and Eastman, N, "Legal knowledge of mental health professionals: report of a national survey" [2001] *J Mental Health L* 44

Percy, Lord (1957), *Report of the Royal Commission on the Law relating to Mental Illness and Mental Deficiency 1954–1957*, Cmd 169 (London: HMSO).

Pipe, R, Bhat, A, Matthews, B and Hampstead, J "Section 136 and African/Afro-Caribbean Minorities" (1991) 37 *Int J Psych* 14.

Plotnikoff, J and Woolfson, R (2007), *The 'Go-Between': evaluation of intermediary pathfinder projects'* (UK: Lexicon Limited).

Porter, R (1987), *Mind-Forg'd Manacles: A History of Madness in England from the Restoration to the Regency* (London: Athlone).

Prichard, JC (1835), *Treatise on Insanity and other Disorders affecting the Mind* (London: Sherwood, Gilbert and Piper).

Prison Reform Trust (1993), *Report of the Committee on the Penalty for Homicide* (London: Prison Reform Trust).

Prison Reform Trust (Edgar, K and Rickford, D) (2009), *Too Little Too Late: an independent review of unmet mental health needs in prison* (London: Prison Reform Trust).

Prins, H, "A Danger to Themselves and Others (Social Workers and Potentially Dangerous Clients)" (1975) 5 *Brit J Social Work* 297.

Prins, H (1986), *Dangerous Behaviour: The Law and Mental Disorder* (London: Tavistock).

Prins, H (1993), *Report of the Committee of Inquiry into the Death in Broadmoor Hospital of Orville Blackwood and a Review of the Deaths of Two Other Afro-Caribbean Patients. "Big, Black and Dangerous?"* (London: Special Hospitals Service Authority).

Prins, H (2005), *Offenders, Deviants or Patients? An Introduction to the Study of Socio-Forensic Problems*, 3rd edn (London: Routledge).

Prior, P M, "The Approved Social Worker—Reflections on Origins" (1992) 22 *Brit J Social Work* 105.

Quinton, D and Rutter, M, "Parents with children in care. 1. Current circumstances and parenting" (1984) 25 *Psychology and Psychiatry* 211.

Radnor, Lord (1908), *Report of the Royal Commission on the Care and Control of the Feeble-Minded 1904–1908*, Cd 4202 (London: HMSO).

Reed, J (1992), *Review of Health and Social Services for Mentally Disordered Offenders and others requiring similar services: Final Summary Report*, Cm 2088 (London: HMSO).

Reed, J (1994a), *Report of the Working Group on High Security and Related Psychiatric Provision* (London: Department of Health).

Reed, J (1994b), *Report of the Department of Health and Home Office Working Group on Psychopathic Disorder* (London: Department of Health and Home Office).

Richardson, G (1993), *Law, Process and Custody: Prisoners and Patients* (London: Weidenfeld and Nicholson).

Richardson, G (1999), *Report of the Expert Committee: Review of the Mental Health Act 1983* (London: Department of Health).

Richardson, G, "Reforming Mental Health Laws: Principle or Pragmatism" (2002) 54 *Current Legal Problems 2001* 415.

Richardson, G, "The European Convention and Mental Health Law in England and Wales: Moving Beyond Process" (2005) 28 *Int J Law and Psych* 127.

Richardson, G, "Balancing autonomy and risk: A failure of nerve in England and Wales?" (2007) 30 *Int J Law and Psych* 71.

Richardson, G and Genn, H, "Tribunals in Transition: Resolution or Adjudication?" [2007] *Public Law* 116.

Ritchie, JH *et al* (1994), *Report of the Inquiry into the Care and treatment of Christopher Clunis* (London: HMSO).

Robb, E (1967), *Sans Everything: A Case to Answer* (presented on behalf of AEGIS) (London: Nelson).

Rogers, A and Faulkner, A (1987), *A Place of Safety: MIND's research into police referrals to the psychiatric services* (London: MIND).

Rollin, HR (1969), *The Mentally Abnormal Offender and the Law* (Oxford: Pergamon).

Rosenhan, DC, "On Being Sane in Insane Places" (1973) 179 *Science* 250.

Roth, M and Bluglass, R (eds) (1985), *Psychiatry, Human Rights and the Law* (Cambridge: Cambridge University Press).

Royal College of Psychiatrists (1981), *Mental Health Commissions: The Recommendations of the Royal College of Psychiatrists* (Approved by Council, June 16).

Royal College of Psychiatrists (1987), *Community Treatment Orders—A Discussion Document* (London: Royal College of Psychiatrists).

Royal College of Psychiatrists (1993), *Community Supervision Orders* (London: Royal College of Psychiatrists).

Royal College of Psychiatrists (2007), *Prison Psychiatry: Adult Prisons in England and Wales* (College Report CR 141) (London: Royal College of Psychiatrists).

Royal College of Psychiatrists (2008), *Court Work* (College Report CR 147) (London: Royal College of Psychiatrists).

Royal College of Psychiatrists (2008), *Standards on the Use of Section 136 of the Mental Health Act 1983 (2007)* (College Report CR 149) (London: Royal College of Psychiatrists).

Royal College of Psychiatrists (2008), *Rethinking Risk to Others in Mental Health Services* (College Report CR 150) (London: Royal College of Psychiatrists).

Royal College of Psychiatrists (2009), *Good Psychiatric Practice (3rd edn)* (College Report 154) (London: Royal College of Psychiatrists).

Rutter *et al* (eds) (2008), *Rutter's Child and Adolescent Psychiatry*, 5th edn (Oxford: Blackwell Publishing).

Ryan, J, with Thomas, F (1998), *The Politics of Mental Handicap*, revised edn (London: Free Association Books).

Scottish Law Commission (1991), *Mentally Disabled Adults: Legal Arrangements for Managing their Welfare and Finances*, Discussion Paper No 94 (Edinburgh: Scottish Law Commission).

Scottish Law Commission (1993), *Mentally Disordered and Vulnerable Adults: Public Authority Powers*, Discussion Paper No 96 (Edinburgh: Scottish Law Commission).

Scottish Law Commission (1995), *Report on Incapable Adults*, Scot Law Com No 151, Cm 2962 (Edinburgh: HMSO).

Scott-Moncrieff, L and Vassall-Adam, G, "Yawning Gap" (2006) *Counsel*, October 14.

Seymour, L and Rutherford, M (2008), *The Community Order and the Mental Health Treatment Requirement* (London: The Sainsbury Centre for Mental Health).

Scull, AT (1979), *Museums of Madness: The Social Organisation of Insanity in Nineteenth Century England* (London: Allen Lane).

Scull, AT (ed) (1981), *Madhouses, Mad-doctors and Madmen: The Social History of Psychiatry in the Victorian Era* (London: Athlone Press).

Sedgwick, P (1982), *Psychopolitics* (London: Pluto Press).

Seebohm, F (1968), *Report of the Committee on the Local Authority and Allied Personal Social Services*, Cmnd 3703 (London: HMSO).

Sensky, T *et al*, "Compulsory Treatment in the Community. I. A Controlled study of compulsory community treatment with extended leave under the Mental Health Act: special characteristics of patients treated and impact of treatment. II. A controlled study of patients whom psychiatrists would recommend for compulsory treatment in the community." (1991) 158 *Brit J Psych* 792.

Sheppard, D (1995), *Learning the Lessons. Mental Health Inquiry Reports published in England and Wales between 1969–1994 and their recommendations for improving practice* (London: The Zito Trust).

Showalter, E (1987), *The Female Malady: Women, Madness and English Culture 1830–1980* (London: Virago).

Simmons, P and Hoar, A, "Section 136 Use in the London Borough of Haringey" (2001) 41 *Med Sci and Law* 342.

Skegg, PDG, "A Justification for Medical Procedures Performed without Consent" (1974) 90 *LQR* 512.

Smith *et al*, "Transfers from Prison for Urgent Psychiatric Treatment: a study of section 48 admission" (1992) 304 *BMJ* 967.

Social Services Inspectorate (1992), *Confronting Elder Abuse* (London: HMSO).

Social Services Inspectorate (1993), *No Longer Afraid: The Safeguard of older people in domestic settings* (London: HMSO).

Social Services Inspectorate (1995), *Social Services Departments and the Care Programme Approach: An Inspection* (London: Department of Health).

Special Hospitals Service Authority (1993), *The Use of Seclusion and the Alternative Management of Disturbed Behaviour within the Special Hospitals* (London: Special Hospitals Service Authority).

Spokes, J (1988), *Report of the Committee of Inquiry into the Care and After-care of Miss Sharon Campbell*, Cm 440 (London: HMSO).

Steadman, HJ, "Attempting to Protect Patients' Rights under a Medical Model" (1979) 2 *Int J Law and Psych* 185.

Sugarman, P and Collins, P, "Informal admission to secure units: a paradoxical situation" (1992) 3 *J Forensic Psych* 477.

Szasz, TS (1961), *The Myth of Mental Illness: Foundations of a Theory of Personal Conduct* (New York: Harper and Row).

Szasz, TS (1963), *Law, Liberty and Psychiatry* (New York: Macmillan).

Szasz, TS (1970), *Ideology and Insanity: Essays on the Psychiatric Dehumanisation of Man* (New York: Doubleday).

Terrell, M (2009), *A Practitioners' Guide to the Court of Protection*, 3rd edn (London: The Law Society).

Tomlin, S (1989), *Abuse of Elderly People: an unnecessary and preventable problem* (London: British Geriatrics Society).

TNS UK for the Care Services Improvement Partnership, Department of Health (2009), *Attitudes to Mental Illness 2009, Research Report*, JN189997 (London: Department of Health).

Tribunals Service, *Practice Direction, Health, Education and Social Care Chapter, Mental Health Cases*.

Tribunals Service (2009), *Annual Report and Accounts 2008–09* (London: TSO).

Turk, V and Brown, H, "The Sexual Abuse of Adults with Learning Disabilities: Results of a Two Year Incidence Survey" (1993) 6 *Mental Handicap Research* 193.

Turner, T, Ness, MN and Imison, CT, "Mentally disordered persons found in public places" (1992) 22 *Psychological Medicine* 765.

United Nations (1971), *Declaration on the Rights of Mentally Retarded Persons*, General Assembly Resolution 2856 (XXVI), 20 December 1971 (New York: United Nations).

United Nations (1975), *Declaration on the Rights of Disabled Persons*, General Assembly Resolution 3447 (XXX), 9 December 1975 (New York: United Nations).

United Nations (1991) *Principles for the Protection of Persons with Mental Illness and for the Improvement of Health*, General Assembly Resolution 46/119, 17 December 1991.

United Nations (1994), *The Standard Rules on the Equalization of Opportunities for Persons with Disabilities*, General Assembly Resolution 48/96, 20 December 1993 (New York: United Nations).

United Nations (2006), *United Nations Convention on the Rights of People with Disabilities & Optional Protocol*, 13 December 2006 (New York: United Nations).

Unsworth, C (1987), *The Politics of Mental Health Legislation* (Oxford: Clarendon Press).

Unsworth, C "Law and Lunacy in Psychiatry's 'Golden Age'" (1993) 13 *Oxford J Legal Studies* 479.

Walker, ND (1973), *Crime and Insanity in England. Vol 1: The Historical Perspective* (Edinburgh: Edinburgh University Press).

Walker, ND, "Butler v the CLRC and Others" [1981] *Crim LR* 596.

Walker, ND and McCabe, S (1973), *Crime and Insanity in England. Vol 2: New Solutions and New Problems* (Edinburgh: Edinburgh University Press).

Warnock, M (1978), *Report of the Committee of Enquiry into the Education of Handicapped Children and Young People*, Cmnd 7212 (London: HMSO).

Webb, D, "Wise after the Event: Some Comments on 'A Danger to Themselves and Others' [Prins, 1975]" (1976) 6 *Brit J Social Work* 91.

Welsh Assembly Government (2008), Mental Health Act (1983), A Code of Practice for Wales (Cardiff Welsh Assembly Government).

Welsh Office (2000), *In Safe Hands* (Cardiff: Social Services Inspectorate).

West, DJ and Walk, A (1977) *Daniel McNaughten: His Trial and the Aftermath* (London: Gaskell).

Wexler, DB (1990), *Therapeutic Jurisprudence: The Law as a Therapeutic Agent* (Durham, NC: Carolina Academic Press).

White, S, "Insanity Defences and Magistrates' Courts" [1991] *Crim LR* 501.

White, S, "The Criminal Procedure (Insanity and Unfitness to Plead) Act 1991" [1992] *Crim LR* 4.

Whitehead, JA and Ahmed, M, "Chance, Mental Illness and Crime" [1970] 1 *Lancet* 137.

Williams, GL (1983), *Textbook of Criminal Law*, 2nd edn (London: Stevens).

Wilson, M (1993), *Mental Health and Britain's Black Communities* (London: King's Fund Centre).

Wing, JK (1978), *Reasoning about Madness* (Oxford: Oxford University Press).

Wood, Sir J, "Reform of the Mental Health Act 1983: An Effective Tribunal System" (1993) 162 *Brit J Psych* 14.

Wootton, B (assisted by Seal, VG and Chambers, R) (1959), *Social Science and Social Pathology* (London: Allen and Unwin).

Wootton, B, "Diminished Responsibility—A Layman's view" (1960) 76 *Law Quarterly R* 224.

Wootton, B, "Psychiatry, Ethics and the Criminal Law" (1980) 136 *Brit J Psych* 525.

World Health Organisation (1977), *International Classification of Diseases (ICD–9)* (Geneva: World Health Organisation).

World Health Organisation (1990), *International Classification of impairments, disabilities and handicaps* (Geneva: World Health Organisation).

World Health Organisation (1992), *The ICD–10 Classification of Mental and Behavioural Disorders: Clinical descriptions and diagnostic guidelines* (Geneva: World Health Organisation).

Younghusband, EL (1959), *Report of the Working Party on Social Workers in the Local Authority Health and Welfare Services* (London: HMSO).

INDEX

This index has been prepared using Sweet & Maxwell's Legal Taxonomy. Main index entries conform to keywords provided by the Legal Taxonomy except where references to specific documents or non-standard terms (denoted by quotation marks) have been included. These keywords provide a means of identifying similar concepts in other Sweet & Maxwell publications and online services to which keywords from the Legal Taxonomy have been applied. Readers may find some minor differences between terms used in the text and those which appear in the index. Suggestions to *sweet&maxwell.taxonomy@thomson.com*.

368

378

384

386